Finland

Jennifer Brewer
Markus Lehtipuu

LONELY PLANET PUBLICATIONS
Melbourne • Oakland • London • Paris

FINLAND

INARI
A centre of Sami culture – take a morning trek to the Wilderness Church, an afternoon cruise on lake Inarinjärvi, and then visit Saamelaismuseo in the evening

NAPAPIIRI (THE ARCTIC CIRCLE)
The official Arctic Circle marker is here, and so is the 'official' Santa Claus Village and Santapark

ROVANIEMI
Home to the The Arktikum Museum and a great base for exploring Lapland

OULANKA NATIONAL PARK
Excellent fell walking, well-maintained free wilderness huts and the best scenery in Finland

YLLÄS
One of Finland's most popular skiing centres, with a music festival in July, and mountain biking in summer

KEMI
Cruise the Gulf of Bothnia on the *Sampo*, an authentic Arctic icebreaker

OULU
A lively, fast-growing university town with an extraordinary number of outdoor bars, lots of festivals, and in June and July it never gets dark at night

Elevation
1000m
500m
200m
100m
0

0   75   150 km

ARCTIC OCEAN

Barents Sea

White Sea

RUSSIA

NORWAY

SWEDEN

Kirkenes
Nikel'
Murmansk
Nuorgam
Utsjoki
Kandalaksha
Karigasniemi
Kovdor
Alakurtti
Laiselv
Kaamanen
Inari
Ivalo
Saariselkä
Tankavaara
Tulppio
Savukoski
Pelkosenniemi
Tanhua
SODANKYLÄ
Kuusamo
Posio
KEMIJÄRVI
Rauna
Pudasjärvi
Unari
ROVANIEMI
Napapiiri
Sinettä
Ounasjoki
Pallas-Ounastunturi National Park
Köngäs
Ylläs
Unari
Kolari
Lappea
Pello
TORNIO
KEMI
Pajala
Övertorneå
Arctic Circle
Överkalix
OULU
Kaaresuvanto
Kilpisjärvi
Kiruna
Boden
LULEÅ
Hailuoto
Luleå

Inarijärvi
Lokan tekojärvi
Porttipahdan tekojärvi
Oulanka National Park
Yli-Kitka

SWEDEN

SWEDEN

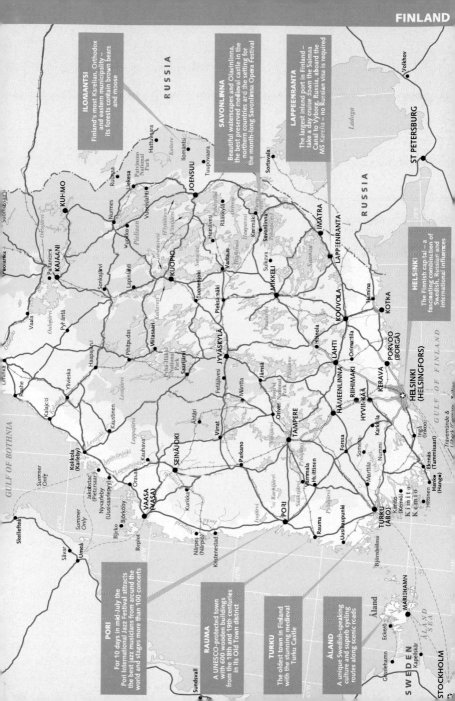

FINLAND

ILOMANTSI
Finland's most Karelian, Orthodox and eastern municipality – its forests contain brown bears and moose

SAVONLINNA
Beautiful waterscapes and Olavinlinna, the best preserved medieval castle in the northern countries and the setting for the month-long Savonlinna Opera Festival

LAPPEENRANTA
The largest inland port in Finland – take a day cruise down the Saimaa Canal to Vyborg, Russia, aboard the MS Karelia – no Russian visa is required

HELSINKI
The Finnish capital – a fascinating combination of Swedish, Russian and international influences

PORI
For 10 days in mid-July, the Pori International Jazz Festival attracts the best jazz musicians from around the world and stages more than 100 concerts

RAUMA
A UNESCO-protected town with 600 wooden buildings from the 18th and 19th centuries in its Old Town district

TURKU
The oldest town in Finland with the stunning medieval Turku Castle

ÅLAND
A unique Swedish-speaking culture and superb cycling routes along scenic roads

Finland
3rd edition – April 1999
First published – January 1993

Published by
Lonely Planet Publications Pty Ltd A.C.N. 005 607 983
192 Burwood Rd, Hawthorn, Victoria 3122, Australia

Lonely Planet Offices
Australia PO Box 617, Hawthorn, Victoria 3122
USA 150 Linden St, Oakland, CA 94607
UK 10a Spring Place, London NW5 3BH
France 1 rue du Dahomey, 75011 Paris

Photographs
Many of the images in this guide are available for licensing from
Lonely Planet Images.
email: lpi@lonelyplanet.com.au

Front cover photograph
Boathouse, Åland (Jennifer Brewer)

ISBN 0 86442 649 6

Printed by The Bookmaker Pty Ltd
Printed in China

Although the authors and Lonely Planet try to make the information as accurate as possible, we accept no responsibility for any loss, injury or inconvenience sustained by anyone using this book.

Contents – Text

Contents – Maps

MAP INDEX

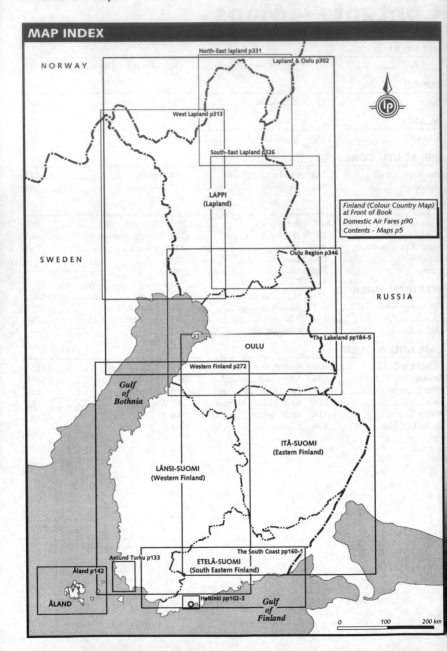

NORWAY

North-East lapland p331

Lapland & Oulu p302

West Lapland p313

South-East Lapland p326

LAPPI
(Lapland)

*Finland (Colour Country Map)
at Front of Book
Domestic Air Fares p90
Contents - Maps p5*

SWEDEN

Oulu Region p346

RUSSIA

The Lakeland pp184-5

OULU

Western Finland p272

*Gulf
of
Bothnia*

ITÄ-SUOMI
(Eastern Finland)

LÄNSI-SUOMI
(Western Finland)

The South Coast pp160-1

Around Turku p133

ETELÄ-SUOMI
(South Eastern Finland)

Åland p142

Helsinki pp102-3

*Gulf
of
Finland*

ÅLAND

0   100   200 km

The Authors

Jennifer Brewer
Jennifer is a native Californian and an honours graduate of the University of California at Berkeley. She worked for several years at a New York City-based fashion magazine before becoming a freelance travel journalist. Since then, she has covered the California desert, New York City, Belize, London and Hungary for Berkeley Guides, and has contributed articles on travel to various magazines. A year-long trip from London to Lhasa via the Middle East in 1996 led her to become involved in the Committee of 100 for Tibet organisation, for which she has served on the Board of Directors. Jennifer is currently earning herself a graduate writing degree from the School of Film and Television at the University of California at Los Angeles – but she still travels as often as possible. Home is in the Los Feliz neighbourhood of Los Angeles, California.

Markus Lehtipuu
Markus is a native of Finland and has travelled to over 60 countries since 1982, including working spells in Sweden, Norway and Canada, and seven months in India. He contributed to Lonely Planet's *Scandinavian Europe phrasebook* and *Scandinavian & Baltic Europe*, and authored the first two editions of *Finland*. He has also produced several guidebooks in Finnish, including guides to Finland, Morocco, Thailand, Malaysia and Singapore.

FROM THE AUTHOR
Jennifer Brewer Researching and writing this book was no small feat – I logged close to 16,000km of driving in the process, and met many wonderful, helpful people along the way. To all of you who contributed suggestions, corrections, or even just a smile – thank you! A few individuals deserve special praise for assistance to a travel writer above and beyond normal call of duty. So, deepest thanks go to Saskya, Andy & Mieke for their hospitality in Helsinki and Åland; to Sanna of the Finnish Tourist Board; to Erik & Annikki of Björnträ Hostel in Kaskinen; to Lars V of Kuopio for returning a lost wallet; to Seppo Nykänen of Haukivuori for lessons in ice-fishing; to Matti K and Janne K of Joensuu University for a terrific *vapunpäivä*; and to Chirstopher W and Krista for rescuing me and the Fiat Brava from an unusually fierce spring snowstorm in Helsinki. Thanks also to Riina at Eurohostel; David Henschel; Victor & Jodi; Connie & Alex; Laura & Steve; Vikram & Victoria; Scott McNeely; the entire BG gang (you know who you are); Reno Down; Christina Knight; Gina Hyams & family; Sam Lu;

8 The Authors

Scott Moyers; Richard & Lulie H; Carla & Joel G; Darren & Susan B; Brendan, Susie & Liam H; Patty & Andrew Y; Frank & Linda D; and to all of the other friendly Finns and travellers who I met along the way, and to friends at home for email support. For encouragement during the final marathon writing days, thanks to new friends at UCLA – Pentti Halonen, Kellen Hertz, Eric Wald, Lisa Dalesandro, Susan Chapman, Tyler Kelly, Lisa Chang, Rita Augustine, Hal Ackerman, Richard Walter & everyone else! To Mom, Dad, Papa, Kim and Linda, much love and thanks.

This Book

The 1st edition of *Finland* was the result of research by Virpi Mäkelä and Markus Lehtipuu. Markus updated the 2nd edition and this 3rd edition was thoroughly revised and updated by Jennifer Brewer.

From the Publisher

This book was edited by Ron Gallagher and Shelley Muir, and proofed by Janet Austin, Carolyn Bain, Ada Cheung, Anne Mulvaney, and Chris Wyness. Paul Dawson coordinated the mapping and laid out the book. Jamieson Gross designed the cover and Clint Curé penned the cartoons. Thanks also to Piotr Czajkowski, Liz Filleul, Marcel Gaston, Annette Högnäs, Russell Kerr, Matt King, Adrian Persoglia, Gerald Porter, Tim Uden and all on the A-team for help and advice.

THANKS
Many thanks to the travellers who used the last edition and wrote to us with helpful hints, advice and interesting anecdotes. Your names appear in the back of this book.

Foreword

ABOUT LONELY PLANET GUIDEBOOKS

The story begins with a classic travel adventure: Tony and Maureen Wheeler's 1972 journey across Europe and Asia to Australia. Useful information about the overland trail did not exist at that time, so Tony and Maureen published the first Lonely Planet guidebook to meet a growing need.

From a kitchen table, then from a tiny office in Melbourne (Australia), Lonely Planet has become the largest independent travel publisher in the world, an international company with offices in Melbourne, Oakland (USA), London (UK) and Paris (France).

Today Lonely Planet guidebooks cover the globe. There is an ever-growing list of books and there's information in a variety of forms and media. Some things haven't changed. The main aim is still to help make it possible for adventurous travellers to get out there – to explore and better understand the world.

At Lonely Planet we believe travellers can make a positive contribution to the countries they visit – if they respect their host communities and spend their money wisely. Since 1986 a percentage of the income from each book has been donated to aid projects and human rights campaigns.

Updates Lonely Planet thoroughly updates each guidebook as often as possible. This usually means there are around two years between editions, although for more unusual or more stable destinations the gap can be longer. Check the imprint page (following the colour map at the beginning of the book) for publication dates.

Between editions up-to-date information is available in two free newsletters – the paper *Planet Talk* and email *Comet* (to subscribe, contact any Lonely Planet office) – and on our Web site at www.lonelyplanet.com. The *Upgrades* section of the Web site covers a number of important and volatile destinations and is regularly updated by Lonely Planet authors. *Scoop* covers news and current affairs relevant to travellers. And, lastly, the *Thorn Tree* bulletin board and *Postcards* section of the site carry unverified, but fascinating, reports from travellers.

Correspondence The process of creating new editions begins with the letters, postcards and emails received from travellers. This correspondence often includes suggestions, criticisms and comments about the current editions. Interesting excerpts are immediately passed on via newsletters and the Web site, and everything goes to our authors to be verified when they're researching on the road. We're keen to get more feedback from organisations or individuals who represent communities visited by travellers.

Lonely Planet gathers information for everyone who's curious about the planet – and especially for those who explore it first-hand. Through guidebooks, phrasebooks, activity guides, maps, literature, newsletters, image library, TV series and Web site we act as an information exchange for a worldwide community of travellers.

10

Research Authors aim to gather sufficient practical information to enable travellers to make informed choices and to make the mechanics of a journey run smoothly. They also research historical and cultural background to help enrich the travel experience and allow travellers to understand and respond appropriately to cultural and environmental issues.

Authors don't stay in every hotel because that would mean spending a couple of months in each medium-sized city and, no, they don't eat at every restaurant because that would mean stretching belts beyond capacity. They do visit hotels and restaurants to check standards and prices, but feedback based on readers' direct experiences can be very helpful.

Many of our authors work undercover, others aren't so secretive. None of them accept freebies in exchange for positive write-ups. And none of our guidebooks contain any advertising.

Production Authors submit their raw manuscripts and maps to offices in Australia, USA, UK or France. Editors and cartographers – all experienced travellers themselves – then begin the process of assembling the pieces. When the book finally hits the shops, some things are already out of date, we start getting feedback from readers and the process begins again ...

WARNING & REQUEST

Things change – prices go up, schedules change, good places go bad and bad places go bankrupt nothing stays the same. So, if you find things better or worse, recently opened or long since closed, please tell us and help make the next edition even more accurate and useful. We genuinely value all the feedback we receive. Julie Young coordinates a well travelled team that reads and acknowledges every letter, postcard and email and ensures that every morsel of information finds its way to the appropriate authors, editors and cartographers for verification.

Everyone who writes to us will find their name in the next edition of the appropriate guidebook. They will also receive the latest issue of *Planet Talk*, our quarterly printed newsletter, or *Comet*, our monthly email newsletter. Subscriptions to both newsletters are free. The very best contributions will be rewarded with a free guidebook.

Excerpts from your correspondence may appear in new editions of Lonely Planet guidebooks, the Lonely Planet Web site, *Planet Talk* or *Comet*, so please let us know if you *don't* want your letter published or your name acknowledged.

Send all correspondence to the Lonely Planet office closest to you:

Australia: PO Box 617, Hawthorn, Victoria 3122
USA: 150 Linden St, Oakland, CA 94607
UK: 10A Spring Place, London NW5 3BH
France: 1 rue du Dahomey, 75011 Paris

Or email us at: talk2us@lonelyplanet.com.au

For news, views and updates see our Web site: www.lonelyplanet.com

HOW TO USE A LONELY PLANET GUIDEBOOK

The best way to use a Lonely Planet guidebook is any way you choose. At Lonely Planet we believe the most memorable travel experiences are often those that are unexpected, and the finest discoveries are those you make yourself. Guidebooks are not intended to be used as if they provide a detailed set of infallible instructions!

Contents All Lonely Planet guidebooks follow the same format. The Facts about the Country chapters or sections give background information ranging from history to weather. Facts for the Visitor gives practical information on issues like visas and health. Getting There & Away gives a brief starting point for researching travel to and from the destination. Getting Around gives an overview of the transport options when you arrive.

The peculiar demands of each destination determine how subsequent chapters are broken up, but some things remain constant. We always start with background, then proceed to sights, places to stay, places to eat, entertainment, getting there and away, and getting around information – in that order.

Heading Hierarchy Lonely Planet headings are used in a strict hierarchical structure that can be visualised as a set of Russian dolls. Each heading (and its following text) is encompassed by any preceding heading that is higher on the hierarchical ladder.

Entry Points We do not assume guidebooks will be read from beginning to end, but that people will dip into them. The traditional entry points are the list of contents and the index. In addition, however, there is a complete list of maps and an index map illustrating map coverage.

There's also a colour map that shows highlights. These highlights are dealt with in greater detail in the Facts for the Visitor chapter, along with planning questions and suggested itineraries. Each chapter covering a geographical region begins with a locator map and another list of highlights. Once you find something of interest in a list of highlights, turn to the index.

Maps Maps play a crucial role in Lonely Planet guidebooks and include a huge amount of information. A legend is printed on the back page. We seek to have complete consistency between maps and text, and to have every important place in the text captured on a map. Map key numbers usually start in the top left corner.

Although inclusion in a guidebook usually implies a recommendation we cannot list every good place. Exclusion does not necessarily imply criticism. In fact there are a number of reasons why we might exclude a place – sometimes it is simply inappropriate to encourage an influx of travellers.

Introduction

Finland was the world's most expensive country back in 1990, but it is now much, much more affordable, especially compared with its Scandinavian neighbours. Despite its size – at 338,000 square kilometres this is Europe's seventh largest country – Finland has less than five and a half million inhabitants. Even Helsinki, the capital, is called home by a mere one million souls. So you won't see skyscrapers in any Finnish cities! This is instead a land of considerable wilderness, of 187,888 lakes, 5100 rapids and 179,584 islands.

The Lakeland offers endless activities: fishing, swimming, rafting, canoeing. But for real beauty trek to the far north, to Lapland – where you'll see more moose and reindeer than human beings as you hike through vast pine forests, and where the eerie beauty of the midnight sun in summer is matched by the strange fire of the aurora borealis, or northern lights, in autumn and winter.

Despite Finland's physical beauty, it's the people that make Finland such an unforgettable place to visit. Although 93% of the population speaks Finnish, a sizeable minority speaks Swedish. The Russian influence is strong too, particularly in Helsinki and the south-east. Finally, Lapland is home to 6500 Sami, who have their own language and customs and who identify readily with the Sami of Norway and Sweden.

Wherever you go, whoever you meet, you might find Finns a bit aloof or hesitant at first – but never, ever does that last.

FINLAND

Facts about Finland

HISTORY

Finnish history is the story of how a group of people emigrated from central Russia and strove for centuries to emancipate themselves from Swedish and Russian rule. The unfortunate thing about this history is that the earliest chronicles were written by Swedes, and much of ethnic Finnish culture and events before and well after the Swedish crusades has escaped written record altogether.

Prehistory

Little is known of human settlement in Finland before or during the Stone Age. However, the region was clearly inhabited at that time, as more than 60 Stone Age paintings have been discovered in Finland, predominantly around Lake Saimaa in the east. Sami emigrants arrived from the east approximately 6000 years ago. It's less clear when the Finns arrived in Finland, and there are a number of competing theories.

By language, Finno-Ugrians are a unique group, with more links to Asia than Europe. Most theories about the settlement of Finland by Finns hold that the Finns are descendants of nomadic tribes that arrived – some time after the Sami – from the land bordering Europe and Asia, near the Ural Mountains and the Volga River. It is likely that after migrating through North Russia, Finns, Estonians and Karelians (as they are known today) arrived during a relatively short period of time and settled along the Baltic coast and Karelia. It is believed that Estonia was inhabited first, and migration farther north took place thereafter.

The population of present-day southwest Finland became known as people of Fennia (or Finns) and the inhabitants of the interior became known as Häme people, from an old Baltic word meaning 'an inhabitant of the interior', which is also the original word for Sami (or Sábme as Lapps call themselves). During their migration, Hämenites and Karelians displaced the Sami tribes, who migrated farther north to Lapland.

Why Finland?

The Finns call their country *Suomi* (pronounced 'SWAM-ee'), so why is it generally known as Finland?

French may provide a clue. *Fin* means 'end', and *fin de lande* could easily be, if not 'the end of the world', the northern end of the European land mass.

The early Romans called this land *Fennia*. In English the word *fen* describes a swampy land, and is mostly used to refer to the watery land in eastern England. But Romans went to England too, and Finland is exactly such a swampy land, and swamp in Finnish is *suo*. A Finn in Finnish is *suomalainen*, whereas *suomaalainen* (with double a) means an inhabitant of a swampy land.

The resemblance of the word suo to Suomi is too close to be ignored, but the derivation of the name of the long-time inhabitants of Lapland, the Sami, offers another explanation. Finland is called *Somija* in Latvian, *Suomija* in Lithuanian and *Soome* in Estonian. The Lapps call themselves *Sábme*. The original word for Sami is *Häme*, which means 'an inhabitant of the interior'. The Häme are a ancient tribe that have given their name to part of the interior of South Finland.

Unimpressed by all these references to inferior interior swampy wetlands, many Finns would like their country to be called *Finlandia* or *Fennica* (in Latin) because that sounds more respectable.

Of course, Swedish-speaking Finns have always called Finland Finland.

Early Finnish Society

Approximately 2000 years ago south Finland was sparsely inhabited by ethnic Finns and an untold number of other European peoples. The two Finnish tribes, Hämenites (Swedish: Tavastians) and Karelians, lived separately, in the west and the east respectively, but were constantly at war with each other.

There were trading contacts with Estonians and Swedish Vikings. The lands around the Kokemäki River and its tributary Vanajavesi in Häme (Swedish: Tavastland) were the most densely populated areas, with a chain of hill fortresses providing defence. In the east, there was a similar chain of defence fortresses in Savo, and along the shores of Lake Ladoga in Karelia (now an autonomous republic within Russia).

Furs were the main export item, and there were trading posts in present-day Hämeenlinna, Turku and Halikko. Many burial grounds and hill defences remain. It is probable that there was friendly contact between fortresses, despite each having its own social system. A common law and judicial system existed in each region.

The Åland Islands and coastal regions south-east of Turku were frequented by Viking sailors. One theory placed Birka, the main Viking centre during the 10th century, on Åland, although with the help of more elaborate scientific methods it has since been established that Birka was on Björkö Island in a lake to the west of Stockholm. Six hill fortresses on Åland date back to the Viking era and indicate the former importance of these islands.

Swedish Rule

To Swedes, Finland was a natural direction of expansion, on a promising eastern route towards Russia and the Black Sea. The Swedish chapter of Finland's history starts in 1155, when Bishop Henry arrived in Kalanti on a mission for the Catholic Church. The Swedish crusaders manned Finnish fortresses to ward off Russian attacks and protect its Christianisation efforts from Russian influence. As the

Finland's Foreign Rulers

Up until 1919, when Kaarlo J Stahlberg became the first president, Finland had had at least 20 royal rulers – and not a single one of these was Finnish! The kings and two queens (listed below) came from the royal families of Sweden, Germany and Russia.

Viking Era	(to 1060)
Stenkil Family	(1060-1130)
Sverker and Erik Families	(1130-1250)
Folkung Family	(1250-1389)
Union Era	(1389-1521)

Vasa Family	(1521-1654)
Gustav I Vasa	(1521-62)
Erik XIV	(1562-68)
Johan III	(1568-93)
Sigismund	(1593-99)
Karl IX	(1599-1611)
Gustav II Adolf	(1611-32)
Kristina (regency 1632-44; 1644-54)	

Pfalz Family	(1654-1751)
Karl X Gustav	(1654-60)
Karl XI	(1660-97)
Karl XII	(1697-1718)
Ulrika Eleonora	(1718-20)
Fredrik I av Hessen	(1720-51)

Holstein-Gottorp Family	(1751-1809)
Adolf Fredrik	(1751-71)
Gustav III	(1771-92)
Gustav IV Adolf	(regency 1792-1796; 1796-1809)

Romanov Family	(1809-1917)
Alexander I	(1809-25)
Nicholas I	(1825-55)
Alexander II	(1855-81)
Alexander III	(1881-94)
Nicholas II	(1894-1917)

Church became established, its headquarters moved to Nousiainen, and in 1229, by the order of Pope Gregorius, to today's

Turku. Swedish settlement began in earnest in 1249 when Birger Jarl established fortifications in Tavastia and along the northern coast of the Gulf of Finland.

The upper layer of society in Finland was made up of newly arrived Catholic bishops and Swedish nobility, sent to govern the eastern province of the Catholic kingdom of Sweden. The Swedish nobility dates back to the 14th century cavalry, consisting of the *frälset*, who enjoyed tax-free status.

It took more than 200 years to define the border between Sweden and Russia (Novgorod). In 1323, the first such border was drawn in a conference at Nöteborg (Finnish: Pähkinäsaari) on Lake Ladoga. Sweden gained control of south-west Finland, much of the north-west coast and, in the east, the strategic town of Vyborg (Finnish: Viipuri), with its magnificent castle. A suzerainty was established over Karelia by Novgorod and was controlled from a castle at Käkisalmi (Russian: Priodzorsk) that was founded in the 13th century. Novgorod spread the Russian Orthodox faith in the Karelia region, which became influenced by eastern Byzantine culture.

To attract Swedish settlers to the unknown land, a number of incentives were created, such as large estates of land and tax concessions. These privileges were granted to many soldiers of the Royal Swedish Army.

In 1527, King Gustav Vasa of Sweden adopted the Lutheran faith and confiscated much of the property of the Catholic Church. Finland had its own supporters of the Reformation: Mikael Agricola, born in Pernå (Finnish: Pernaja) in 1510, studied literature and religion with Martin Luther in Germany for three years, and returned to Finland in 1539 to translate parts of the Bible into Finnish. More importantly, he was the first to properly record the traditions and animist religious rites of ethnic Finns. Agricola's work changed the religious tradition. Most of the colourful frescoes in medieval grey-stone churches, for example, were whitewashed with lime

(only to be rediscovered some 400 years later in relatively good condition).

Sweden was not satisfied with its share of power in the east. In 1546 King Gustav Vasa founded Ekenäs (Tammisaari) and in 1550, Helsinki. Using his Finnish subjects as agents of expansion, the Swedish king told Finns to 'sweat and suffer' as pioneers in Savo and Kainuu, well beyond the legitimate territory set down in treaties with the Russians. Russians grew alarmed and attempted to throw the intruders out. The bloody Kainuu War raged on and off between 1574 and 1584, with most new settlements destroyed by fire.

Golden Age of Sweden

The 17th century was the golden age of Sweden. During this period it controlled Finland, Estonia and parts of today's Latvia, Denmark, Germany and Russia.

After 65 years of Lutheranism, the Catholic Sigismund (grandson of Gustav Vasa) assumed the Swedish throne. Karl IX, Gustav Vasa's youngest son and Sigismund's uncle, was given control over Finland. Karl IX didn't give a hoot for the family business, however: he encouraged peasants in western Finland to mutiny in 1596, attacked the Turku Castle in 1597, and defeated his nephew Sigismund in 1598 to bring all of Finland under his reign.

While Gustav II Adolf (son of Karl IX and king from 1611 to 1632) was busily involved in the Thirty Years War in Europe, political power in Finland was exercised by the General Governor, who resided at the Castle of Turku, capital of Finland. Count Per Brahe, a legendary figure of the local Swedish administration, travelled around the country at this time and founded many towns. You will see his statue in places like Turku, Raahe, Kajaani and Lieksa.

After Gustav II Adolf, Sweden was ruled from 1644 to 1654 by the eccentric Queen Kristina, namesake for such Finnish towns as Kristinestad and Ristiina. The queen's conversion to Catholicism and move to Rome marked the end of the Swedish Vasa dynasty.

Sweden's Count Per Brahe
founded many towns in Finland

The German royal family of Pfalz-Zweibrücken ruled Sweden (including Finland) after the Vasa family folded. Throughout this period, Finland was considered an integral part of Sweden. The official language was Swedish, Stockholm was the de facto capital, and Finns were considered loyal subjects of the Swedish king (or queen).

By Swedish decree, Finland grew. A chain of castle defences was built to protect against Russian attack and new factory areas were founded. The *bruk* was often a self-contained society, which harnessed the power of water, built ironworks and transport systems for firewood. Social institutions such as schools and churches were also established.

Ethnic Finns didn't fare particularly well during this time. The burgher class was dominated by Swedish settlers, as very few Finns engaged in industrial enterprises. Some of the successful industrialists were central Europeans who settled in Finland via Sweden. Furthermore, the Swedish 'caste system', the House of Four Estates, was firmly established in Finland. The Swedish and Finnish nobility maintained their status in the Swedish Riksdagen until

1866 and in the Finnish parliament until 1906. (The Finnish nobility still exists through a registered organisation.)

Although Finland never experienced feudal serfdom to the extent seen in Russia, ethnic Finns were largely peasant farmers who were forced to lease land from Swedish landlords. The last Finnish manor to release its serfs did so in 1858.

In 1697 Karl XII ascended the throne. Within three years he was drawn into the Great Northern War (1700-21), which marked the beginning of the end of the Swedish Empire.

The Turbulent 1700s

While the Swedish King Karl XII was busy fighting for his empire elsewhere, the Russians under Peter the Great seized the moment. The Great Northern War saw Vyborg defeated (in 1710) and much of Finland conquered, including the Swedish-dominated west coast.

From 1714 to 1721 Russia occupied Finland, a bitter time still referred to as the Great Wrath. Russians destroyed practically everything they had access to, particularly in Åland and western Finland. The 1721 Treaty of Uusikaupunki (Swedish: Nystad) brought temporary peace at a cost – Sweden lost south Karelia, including Vyborg, to Russia. To regain its lost territories, Sweden attacked Russia in 1741-43, but with little success. Russia again occupied Finland, for a period called the Lesser Wrath, and the border was pushed farther west. The Treaty of Turku in 1743 ended the conflict by ceding parts of Savo to Russia.

Only after the 1740s did the Swedish government try to improve Finland's socio-economic situation. Defences were strengthened by the building of fortresses off the coast of Helsinki (Sveaborg, now Suomenlinna) and Loviisa, and new towns were founded. Sweden and Russia were to clash once again, in the sea battles of Ruotsinsalmi off Kotka in 1788-89. This time it was King Gustav III who led the Swedish fight, which involved up to 500 vessels. Sweden won, but to no territorial advantage. The 'Gustavian Wars' continued along the eastern border of Finland until the king was murdered by a conspiracy of aristocrats in 1792. Gustav IV Adolf, who reigned from 1796, was drawn into the disastrous Napoleonic Wars and lost his crown in 1809.

Russian Rule

After the Treaty of Tilsit was signed by Russian tsar Alexander I and Napoleon, Russia attacked Finland in 1808. Following a bloody war, Sweden ceded Finland to Russia in 1809 as an autonomous grand duchy, with its own senate and the Diet of the Four Estates, but all major decisions had to be approved by the tsar. At first, Finland benefited from the annexation and was loyal to the tsar, who encouraged Finns to develop the country in many ways. The Finnish capital was transferred to Helsinki in 1812, as Russians felt that the former capital, Turku, was too close to Sweden.

The early 19th century saw the first stirring of indigenous Finnish nationalism. One of the first to encourage independence during the 1820s was AI Arwidsson, who uttered the much-quoted sentence: 'Swedes we are not, Russians we will not become, so let us be Finns'. His views were not widely supported and he was advised to move to Sweden in 1823.

As a Russian annexation, Finland was involved in the Crimean War (1853-56), where Russia fought Turkey and its allies, including Britain and France. British troops attacked Finland in many locations, and destroyed fortifications at Loviisa, Helsinki and Bomarsund. Following the Crimean War, the Finnish independence movement picked up credibility. While still a part of Russia, Finland issued its first postal stamps in 1856 and gained its own currency, the markka, in 1860.

In 1905, a new unicameral parliament, the Eduskunta, was introduced in Finland with universal and equal suffrage (Finland was the first country in Europe to grant women full political rights). Despite these many advances, life under Russian rule

continued to be harsh. Many artists, notably Jean Sibelius, were inspired by this oppression, which made Finns emotionally ripe for independence.

Independence

The Communist revolution of October 1917 caused the downfall of the Tsar of Russia and enabled the Finnish senate to declare independence on 6 December 1917. Independent Finland was first recognised by the Soviet Union one month later, and a crafty Vladimir Lenin, looking for support for Russian troops devastated by WWI, followed by offering 10,000 guns to the Finnish Red cadres. Russian troops and the newly armed Finnish Reds attacked the Finnish civil guards in Vyborg during the following year. This sparked the Finnish Civil War.

On 28 January 1918, the Civil War flared in two separate locations. The Reds attempted to foment revolution in Helsinki. The Whites (as the government troops were now called), lead by CGE Mannerheim, clashed with Russian troops near Vaasa. During 108 days of fighting in two locations, approximately 30,000 Finns were killed by their fellow citizens. The Reds, comprising the rising working class, aspired to Russian-style socialist revolution while retaining independence. The nationalist Whites dreamed of monarchy and sought to emulate Germany.

The Whites eventually gained victory under Mannerheim, with help from Germany. The bloody and devastating war ended in May 1918. The Prince of Hessen, Friedrich Karl, was elected king of Finland by the Eduskunta on 9 October 1918 – but the German monarchy collapsed just one month later, following Germany's defeat in WWI. Finland now faced a dilemma: the Russian presence was a clear security risk, but Germany was a discredited political model because of its war loss.

Building a Nation

The defeat of imperial Germany made Finland choose a republican state model and the first president was KJ Ståhlberg. Relations with the Soviet Union were normalised by the Treaty of Tartu in 1920, which saw Finnish territory grow to its largest ever, including the 'left arm', the Petsamo region in the far north-east. But more trouble awaited the new nation.

Following WWI, bitter language wars between Finnish and Swedish speakers shook the administration, universities and cultural circles. Civil War skirmishes continued, mostly with illegal massacres of Reds by Whites. Indeed, the right wing became increasingly outspoken in Finland (as well as elsewhere in Europe). In 1930, 12,000 right-wing farmers marched from Lapua to demand laws banning communism. A mutiny in Mäntsälä in 1932 tried to prevent socialists from meeting and to make Marxism illegal in Finland.

Despite its internal troubles, Finland at this time gained fame internationally as a brave new nation, as the only country to pay its debts to the USA, and as a sporting nation. Paavo Nurmi, the most distinguished of Finnish long-distance runners, won seven gold medals in three Olympic Games and became an enduring national hero (see Flying Finns boxed text in the Turku chapter). With continuing Finnish success in athletics, Helsinki was chosen to host the 1940 Olympic Games (these were postponed until 1952 due to WWII).

WWII

During the 1930s, Finland developed close ties with Nazi Germany, partly in response to the security threat posed by the USSR. On 23 August 1939, the Soviet and German foreign ministers, Molotov and Ribbentrop, stunned the world by signing a nonaggression pact. A secret protocol stated that any future rearrangement would divide Poland between them; Germany would have a free hand in Lithuania, the Soviet Union in Finland, Estonia, Latvia and Bessarabia. The Red Army was moving toward the earmarked territories less than three weeks later.

The Soviet Union pressed more territorial claims, arguing its security required a slice of south-eastern Karelia. JK Paasikivi (later to become Finland's seventh president) visited Moscow for negotiations on the ceding of the Karelian Isthmus to the Soviet Union. The negotiations failed. On 30 November 1939, the 'Winter War' between Finland and the Soviet Union began.

This was an especially harsh winter, with temperatures reaching -40°C, and soldiers died in their thousands. After a full 100 days of courageous fighting Finnish forces were defeated. In the Treaty of Moscow, signed in March 1940, Finland ceded part of Karelia and some nearby islands. About half a million Karelian refugees flooded over the new border.

In the months that followed the Soviet Union pressured Finland for more territory. Isolated from western allies Finland turned to Germany for help, and although no formal agreement was signed, Finland allowed the transit of German troops. When hostilities broke out between Germany and the Soviets in June 1941, German troops were already on Finnish soil and the 'Continuation War' between Finland and the Red Army began. In the fighting that followed the Finns slowly began to resettle Karelia, including some areas that had been in Russian possession since the 18th century. When Soviet forces staged a huge comeback in the summer of 1944, President Risto Ryti resigned and Marshal Mannerheim took his place. Mannerheim negotiated an armistice with the Russians and ordered the evacuation of German troops. Finland pursued a bitter war to oust German forces from Lapland until the general peace in the spring of 1945. Finland remained independent, but at a price: it was forced to cede territory and pay heavy war reparations to the Soviet Union. The Porkkala Peninsula west of Helsinki was a Soviet military base and off-limits to Finns until 1956.

The Cold War

Finland's reparations to the Soviet were chiefly paid in machinery and ships. Thus reparations played a central role in laying the foundations of the heavy engineering industry that stabilised the Finnish economy following WWII. Finland had suffered greatly in the late 1940s, with almost everything rationed and poverty widespread. The vast majority of the population was still engaged in agriculture at that time.

Things changed quickly in the following decades, with domestic migration to southern Finland especially strong in the 1960s and 70s. New suburbs appeared almost overnight in and around Helsinki. Large areas in the north and the east lost most of their young people, often almost half their population.

Finland maintained an uneasy truce – bordering on friendship – with the Soviet Union throughout the Cold War. The Treaty of Paris in 1947 dictated that the Karelian Isthmus be ceded to the Soviet Union, as well as the eastern Salla and Kuusamo regions and the 'left arm' of Finland in the Kola Peninsula. Many Finns remain bitter about the loss of these territories to the present day.

The Treaty of Friendship, Cooperation & Mutual Assistance (Finnish: YYA) with the Soviet Union was signed in 1948. This agreement bound the two countries into an awkward semimilitary relationship, in spite of Finland's claim to neutrality. The agreement remained valid until 1992, when it was replaced by a loose agreement with Russia without reference to military co-operation.

Urho K Kekkonen, the Finnish President from 1956 to 1981, a master of diplomacy and one of the great leaders of his age, was largely responsible for steering Finland through the Cold War and its difficult relationship with the Soviet Union. Often this meant bowing to the wishes of the Soviet Union. On 30 October 1961 the Soviet Union exploded a 58 megatonne nuclear bomb on Novaja Zemlja Island, not far from Finland. What shook Finland even more was a short message from Moscow: the Communist Party wanted changes in Finland's domestic politics. It got what it

wanted. The Berlin Wall had just been erected and the Cold War was at its height.

Kekkonen gained fame abroad as an eccentric and witty president, and was also known for his role as host of the initial Conference on Security & Cooperation in Europe (CSCE) meeting, in Helsinki in 1975. However free-wheeling the Finnish president seemed to those abroad, at home he brought democracy to an all-time low in 1974, when a vast majority of delegates from all major parties decided to extend his term by four years. Political nominations were submitted to Moscow for approval within the framework of 'friendly coexistence'.

As recently as the late 1980s, the Soviet Communist Party exercised Cold War tactics by infiltrating Finnish politics, with the aim of reducing US influence in Finland and preventing Finnish membership of the European Community (today's European Union). Although continuous concerns about the Soviet Union overshadowed most of Finland's foreign policy decisions, relations with Scandinavia were also extremely important in the decades following WWII. Finland was a founding member of the Nordic Council (along with the Scandinavian countries), pursuing a similar social welfare program to Scandinavia and enjoying the benefits of free movement of labour, passport-free travel, and even common research and educational programs with its western neighbours.

Modern Finland

In the 1990s Finland's overheated economy, like many in the western world, went through a cooling off period. The bubble economy of the 1980s had burst, the Soviet Union disappeared with debts unpaid, the markka was devalued, unemployment jumped from 3% to 20% and the tax burden grew alarmingly.

Things began to change for the better after a national referendum on 16 October 1994, when 57% of voters gave the go-ahead to join the EU. Since January 1995, food has become cheaper and strict alcohol laws have been relaxed. In the ensuing years Finland has also received considerable assistance from the EU – assistance with rural development, tourism, infrastructure and agricultural diversification. Finland was one of 11 countries that qualified to begin using the new euro currency in 1999.

By all accounts, Finland seems poised for prosperity as it enters the new millennium. Unemployment is now at around 9% and inflation is between 1% and 2% annually. Indeed, in a 1998 survey by the United Nations, Finland was rated fifth in the world in terms of quality of life (the survey measured health, education, life expectancy and income). The top four countries were Canada, France, the USA and Iceland.

GEOGRAPHY

Finland, with an area of 338,000 sq km, is the seventh largest country in Europe – right behind Russia, Ukraine, France, Spain, Sweden and Germany.

The southernmost point, the town of Hanko, lies at the same latitude as Oslo in Norway, Anchorage in Alaska, and the southernmost tip of Greenland. The shape of Finland has been compared to that of a female, holding up her right arm (the 'left arm' was lost to the former Soviet Union after WWII).

Finland shares a 1269km border with Russia in the east; a 727km border with Norway in the far north; and a 586km border with Sweden in the west. The Gulf of Finland separates south Finland from Estonia.

Approximately 70% of Finland is covered by forest – the highest proportion in the world. There are no real mountains; rather, sandy ridges and wooded hills dominate. The highest hills, or *tunturi*, are in Lapland, which borders the mountainous areas of northern Norway and Sweden. Finland's highest point, the Halti in the north-west corner of the country, rises only 1328m above sea level.

Much of the country is lakeland – there are 187,888 lakes in Finland. Together with marshes and bogs, inland water covers about 10% of the country. Finland is shaped by water: lakes and ponds, rivers and creeks, rapids and small waterfalls, islands and islets, bays, capes and straits, and the large archipelagos of Turku, Åland, Helsinki and Vaasa.

GEOLOGY

Most of present-day Finland was under water until very recently. About 10,000 years ago, when vast expanses of ice were melting away, the powerful moving ice and water masses produced the characteristic Finnish geography: sandy ridges, solid rock layers, deep stone-drilled wells and thousands of lakes, often flowing from north-west to south-east. Vegetation slowly covered the barren landscape, with many (now rare) deciduous trees finding root: since then, trees have dropped their leaves every autumn, almost 10,000 times, thus accumulating a fertile black soil. After the thick ice layer had disappeared, lifting a huge weight off the bedrock, the Finnish land mass started to rise – this is happening even today, at the rate of 0.6cm per year.

CLIMATE

Finland enjoys four distinct seasons: from continuing darkness in Arctic winter to a two-month-long 'day' in northern Lapland's summer. Thanks to factors such as the Baltic

Midnight Sun & Winter Gloom

From mid-May to late July the town of Utsjoki, in the far north of Finland, experiences continuous daylight – this is the land of the midnight sun. Farther south, Rovaniemi, on the Arctic Circle, enjoys the midnight sun from roughly 20 May to 20 July. In central and southern Finland, it isn't possible to see the midnight sun, but it never really grows dark during the summer months. Night is replaced by a kind of dusk in which it is possible to hike, cycle and play outdoor games at midnight.

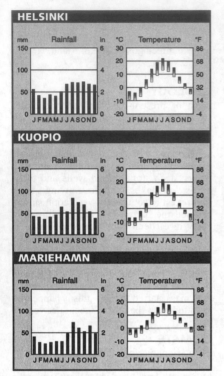

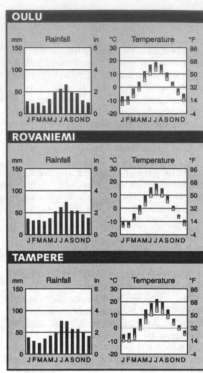

Sea and the mild winds from the Gulf Stream along the Norwegian coast, Finland's climate is, on average, much warmer than in other places of similar latitude, such as Siberia, Greenland and Alaska.

Summer sees hot spells and weeks of little rain, although temperatures can be as low as 10°C at any time in summer. That said, every now and then in summer, Finland is the warmest country in Europe! It is not unusual to have temperatures rise to 5°C in January or to get showered by a freak snowstorm in June, but yearly averages follow a logical curve: the shorter the nights, the warmer the days, and vice versa.

Of course, winters *are* cold, but the cold is dry. In most parts of the country snow first falls in October and vanishes by the end of March, but in Lapland snow can fall as early as September and linger until late May. In northernmost Lapland you might even find snow as late as June.

ECOLOGY & ENVIRONMENT

In Finland, forestry products are the main source of income and employment, the main cause of pollution and the main topic of environmental debate. Paper and pulp industries provide work for thousands but also cause environmental hazards, which are easily seen in areas surrounding factories. To put it bluntly, pulp factories stink, literally and figuratively.

Finland is the second largest exporter of paper products in the world and is dependent on paper manufacturing. Around 70% of the country is forest land – the highest percentage in the world – and most of this land is managed forest that is harvested for cutting. If you look closely, you'll see that many thousands of acres of Finnish forest have only one, or at best two, species of tree – which creates a serious disturbance in the local ecosystem. Furthermore, pulp factories – and other heavy industries long a staple of the Finnish economy – contribute to massive domestic water pollution.

Finland, the land of lake, river and ocean, may look idyllic and pristine – but in fact it isn't, or at least not very. A 1997 survey ranked Finland's lake and ocean waters as some of the most polluted in the EU, failing to meet even minimum EU standards of cleanliness. Sweden was also at the bottom in terms of water quality.

Domestic conservation efforts are spearheaded by the Finnish Forest and Park Service, which oversees 120,000 sq km of publicly owned lands. This organisation also works to protect endangered species and promote biodiversity on forest lands that are used for commercial purposes. For more information about the National Park Service and protected wilderness areas, see the National Parks section that follows.

FLORA & FAUNA

Finnish flora is at its best during the dynamic period between late May and September. The three main types of forest are pine, spruce and birch. Pine grows generally on dry ground and sand ridges, conditions which don't foster undergrowth. Spruce forests are dark and dense, while birch is the typical tree found in deciduous forests.

There are quite a few mammals in Finnish forests. The largest (and one of the rarest) is the brown bear, which was once so feared that even mentioning its name *(karhu)* was taboo. Other mammals include moose, fox, lynx, wolf and wolverine, and there are plenty of small animals such as lemming, hedgehog, muskrat, marten, beaver, otter and hare. Moose *(hirvi)* are solitary, shy animals – to see one is a real treat. Reindeer *(poro)*, on the other hand, abound in north Finland, with some 230,000 animals. These are all in semi-domesticated herds owned by the Sami; truly wild reindeer are rare. The lynx *(ilves)* used to be very rare but numbers are increasing. There are practically no home-grown wolves left in Finland, but plenty cross the border regularly from Russia. Hatred for, and fear of, the wolf *(susi)* is deep-rooted in eastern Finland, where they are hunted and killed.

There are over 300 bird species in Finland (see also the Bird-watching section of the Activities chapter). Large species include black grouse, capercaillie, whooper swan and birds of prey, such as the osprey. Chaffinches and willow warblers are the two most common forest species; sparrows are common in inhabited areas. Crested-tits, black woodpeckers, black-throated divers, ravens and many owls are common throughout the country. The Siberian jay is a common sight in Lapland because it

Brown bear

Crested-tit

follows people. Finns who watch migratory birds arrive from the south have a saying for how to determine when summer will come: it is one month from sighting a skylark, half a month from a chaffinch, just a little from a white wagtail and not a single day from a swift.

Less popular creatures include the viper, which is the most common poisonous snake. Antivenins are readily available in pharmacies. June and July are the most active months for mosquitoes and other pesky insects, particularly in Lapland.

National Parks

Much of Finland's 70% forest covering is private, managed forest cultivated by forest-products companies. However, to keep everyone else happy, Metsähallitus, the Finnish Forest and Park Service, manages magnificent trekking and fishing areas totalling 120,000 sq km, with well-maintained hiking trails and a wide range of accommodation options available to all. Additionally, the independent Finnish Forest Research Institute manages a handful of superb nature preserves, including Koli and Pallas-Ounastunturi. All together, national parks account for 7300 sq km of all publicly owned lands.

The Forest and Park Service publishes *Finland's National Parks*, a comprehensive booklet listing all of the national parks, with information on trails and accommodation as well as notes on flora and fauna. The cost of the booklet is 20 mk. This is an extremely helpful resource if you are planning to visit several parks or are particularly interested in the Finnish wilderness. Alternatively, check out www.metsa.fi/ where national parks are described in detail in English. Pamphlets describing individual parks are available at the national park tourist information offices in Helsinki and Rovaniemi, and are usually available at local tourist offices.

The largest and most pristine national parks are in northern Finland, particularly Lapland; see also the Lapland & Oulu chapter later in the book for detailed descriptions of each park. Liminganlahti Bird Sanctuary, near Oulu in northern Finland, is arguably the best place in the country for bird-watching.

Linnansaari National Park, near Savonlinna, is probably the best park in the Lakeland and is also home to the extremely endangered Saimaa ringed seal. To see larger mammals – such as the shy and elusive moose – it's best to visit one of the national parks in the north-east, such as Oulanka National Park, or farther north in Lapland, such as Lemmenjoki, Pallas-Ounastunturi and Urho Kekkonen national parks. These parks are vast, and services and facilities are few; to make the most of a visit you should be prepared to spend several days trekking and camping. See the Activities chapter for trail recommendations and more information about trekking.

GOVERNMENT & POLITICS

Finland is a presidential republic. The president, in council with the prime minister and cabinet, forms the executive government. The president is elected to a six-year term by the people. The voting age is 18. Presidential duties include overseeing foreign policy and acting as the commander in chief of the Finnish army. The president has the right to veto a bill. The president's home page at www.tpk.fi/ has further information. Martti Ahtisaari was elected in 1994. He's a keen traveller who did a stint with the UN as a specialist in Namibia.

The prime minister is elected every four years by the 200-member Eduskunta (parliament). Eduskunta members all serve four-year terms. The prime minister until 1999 is Paavo Lipponen.

Seven of the 18 portfolios are currently held by women. Members of parliament are elected from 14 national districts. There are six provinces (*lääni*): Lapland, Oulu, Western Finland, Eastern Finland, Åland and Southern Finland, and 452 municipalities (*kunta*). Åland has a small local parliament with a high degree of autonomy.and sends one member of parliament to Helsinki.

Major political parties (*puolue*) in Finland include the Social Democratic

Party (which received 28% of the vote in the 1995 election), the agrarian Centre Party (20%), the conservative National Coalition Party (18%), the left-wing Alliance (11%), the Greens (7%), the Swedish People's Party (5%) and the Christian Union (3%). Left-wing parties have increased their share of the vote in the 1990s. Martti Ahtisaari, the current president, is a Social Democrat. The previous Finnish presidents are listed below.

Kaarlo J Ståhlberg	1919-25
Lauri K Relander	1925-31
Per E Svinhufvud	1931-37
Kyösti Kallio	1937-40
Risto Ryti	1940-44
C G E Mannerheim	1944-46
Juho K Paasikivi	1946-56
Urho K Kekkonen	1956-81
Mauno Koivisto	1982-94
Martti O K Ahtisaari	1994-

ECONOMY

The recent economic history of Finland is not very different from that of many other western countries, but it may be more extreme. The transformation from a rural society to an urban industrialised country was a quick one. Economic growth was impressive. Post-WWII rationing was soon replaced by supermarkets with a wide variety of imported goods. When the regulated financial market was liberated in the mid-1980s, the result was an overheated economy, a well-known phenomenon in most western economics at that time.

When the bubble inevitably burst, Finland went through one of the worst recessions any western country experienced in the 1990s. For a time, Finland had been the most expensive country in the world; soon it was one of the cheapest in Western Europe. From almost full employment, 500,000 jobs disappeared in two years, saddling Finland with an embarrassing and costly 20% unemployment rate, the second highest in Europe. In order to reduce its budget deficit the government slashed spending by 20%. Two areas were spared these cuts: education was one,

and grants for private research and development were actually increased. The gamble paid off – in 1995 Finland was a net exporter of know-how and high-tech products.

The whole export sector boomed in the 1990s, and exports now account for about 40% of the GDP. The reason for the success of exports is the abandoning of the 'strong markka doctrine' in 1991. Timber products, pulp and paper as well as metal products and mobile phones were shipped from Finland at a pace never seen before. The highly automated export industries, however, didn't much improve the unemployment situation.

Finland is the world's second largest exporter of paper and paperboard (Canada is the largest). Metal mining, technology and engineering contribute almost as large a share of export income; Finland's Nokia company is the world's second largest manufacturer of mobile phones. That said, services and construction are increasingly important to the Finnish economy. The construction boom in the Helsinki area has locals joking that it is now the 'Berlin of the North'.

Finland has made a remarkable recovery since the early 1990s. At press time, unemployment was about 9% (a good average in Europe) and inflation hovered between 1% and 2%. Less than 10% of the population earned a living from agriculture, 32% from industry and 58% from services. The GDP per capita in 1996 was 112,174 mk.

Domestic tourism has been booming for some time, much of it centred around amusement and theme parks that appeal to Finnish families. Trade unions are a powerful force in the Finnish economy. They have a virtual monopoly on the workforce, with over two million members (or 83% of the working population). Wages are centrally determined, and there are strict rules governing working hours and holidays.

POPULATION & PEOPLE

The earliest Finno-Ugrians were nomadic tribespeople who inhabited much of North Russia, and there are still small Finnic groups living in the Ural Mountains.

Karelians, Estonians and Hungarians are some other close relatives of the Finns. Over the centuries, however, a substantial Indo-European influence has affected the population of Finland, to the extent that many Finns now look very Scandinavian.

Finland's population is currently 5,132,000, with an annual growth rate of 0.4%. Over half the population lives in the three south-western provinces (around Helsinki, Turku and Tampere), which have 15% of the total land area.

The Greater Helsinki area, including Espoo, Vantaa and several municipalities, houses one million people, or 20% of the national total. The next biggest towns, in order of size, are Tampere, Turku, Oulu, Lahti and Kuopio.

The main minority groups in Finland are the 300,000 Swedish-speaking Finns (*Finlandssvensk*, or 'Finland's Swede') and the 4000 Sami people of Lapland. Only 2% of all Finnish residents are foreigners, the lowest percentage of any country in Europe. However, large numbers of Finns have emigrated to other countries: some 250,000 to Sweden, 280,000 to the USA, 20,000 to Canada and 10,000 to Australia. The average household size in Finland is currently 2.4 people, although 10 children in a family was not uncommon just 50 years ago. About 19% of the population is under 15 years.

EDUCATION

The literacy rate in Finland hovers around 99% and the number of newspapers and books printed per capita is one of the highest in the world. Indeed, Finland's investment in education is higher than any other industrialised country: just over 7% of its GNP.

The nine-year comprehensive school *(perus-koulu)* is one of the most equitable systems in the world – tuition, books, meals and commuting to and from school are free. All Finns learn English and Swedish in school and many also study German or French. Secondary school *(lukio)* is three years in length and serves as a stepping stone

to universities in Helsinki, Turku, Tampere, Oulu, Jyväskylä, Joensuu, Kuopio, Rovaniemi and Vaasa. Approximately 18,000 new university students start every year.

The first university in Finland was founded in Turku in 1640 and transferred in 1828 to Helsinki, where it now has some 26,000 students. These and other universities are state-owned and there are practically no fees. State grants, state-guaranteed low-interest loans, subsidised health care, meals and student hostels are available to most students. With these benefits, Finnish students stay an average of seven to eight years at university. In addition to higher education, Finns can choose from other kinds of educational institutes, from vocational schools to those specialising in an individual subject or just in 'how to live a happy life'. With so much education, no wonder Finns borrow books from their libraries at the highest rate in the world, 19.7 books or recordings per person per year.

ARTS

Finland boasts the world's highest per capita rate of public funding for the arts, spending about 540 mk per person annually on museums and arts programs.

Architecture

The high standard of modern Finnish architecture was established by the works of Alvar Aalto and Eliel Saarinen. People interested in architecture make pilgrimages to Finland to see superb examples of modern building. Unfortunately, much great Finnish architecture is overshadowed by supermarkets and other concrete blocks that dominate towns and villages.

The oldest architectural monuments include medieval castles and 75 stone churches, scattered around villages in South Finland. In these Catholic churches, Gothic ideals were emulated but with little success, and as a result, an original Finnish style emerged. Wood has long been the dominant building material in Finland. Some of the best early examples of wooden architecture include churches on Finland's west coast.

Eastern influences date back to 1809, when Finland became an autonomous grand duchy under Russian rule, and to 1812 when Helsinki was made the new capital. The magnificent city centre was created by CL Engel, a German-born architect, who combined neoclassical and St Petersburg features in designing the cathedral, the university and other buildings around Senate Square. Engel also designed a large number of churches in Finland. All the largest churches in Finland were built during Russian rule. After the 1850s, National Romanticism emerged in response to pressure from the Russians.

The Art Nouveau period, which reached its climax at the turn of the 20th century, combined Karelian ideals with rich ornamentation. Materials were wood and grey granite. The best examples of this style are the National Museum (Eliel Saarinen) and the Cathedral of Tampere (Lars Sonck). After independence was achieved in 1917, rationalism and functionalism emerged, as exemplified by some of Alvar Aalto's work. The following list contains some of the most famous names in Finnish architecture.

Alvar Aalto (1898-1976) is the most famous Finnish architect. His earliest works can be seen at Alajärvi, and there is a museum dedicated to Aalto in Jyväskylä. There are individual churches in Lahti and Imatra, and public buildings in Rovaniemi. Several buildings can be seen in Helsinki, and at Otaniemi in Espoo, near Helsinki.

Juha Leiviskä was awarded the international Carlsberg prize in 1995 for his works in Helsinki (Vallila Library and much more), Vantaa (Myyrmäki Church) and Kuopio (Männistö Church).

Raili and Reima Pietilä, a married couple, worked together and designed churches and other buildings in Tampere (Kaleva, Hervanta and the library in town centre) and Lieksa (the church).

Eliel Saarinen (1873-1950) designed a great number of attractive town houses in Helsinki, as well as working with two other architects, Herman Gesellius and Armas Lindgren, on projects like the National Museum and the

Hvitträsk House, north-west of Helsinki. Town halls in Lahti and Joensuu are his own works, as well as the railway station in Helsinki. Eliel's son Eero Saarinen worked primarily in the USA until he died in 1961.

Lars Sonck (1870-1956) designed some notable stone edifices in National Romantic style, including Kultaranta in Naantali and churches in Tampere, Mariehamn and Helsinki (Kallio).

Josef Stenbäck (1854-1929) designed over 30 churches, most of them Art Nouveau.

Among the most famous postwar architects are Viljo Revell, Aarno Ervi, Heikki Siren, Toivo Korhonen, Timo Penttilä, Aarno Ruusuvuori, Erkki Kairamo and Kristian Gullichsen and Timo and Tuomo Suomalainen (Rock Church in Helsinki).

Emerging regional schools of architecture include the Oulu School, featuring small towers, porticoes and combinations of various elements, most evident in the region around Oulu. Erkki Helasvuo, who died in 1995, did plenty of work in North Karelia, providing the province with several public buildings which hint at modern Karelianism.

Design

Finns have created their own design style through their craft tradition, the use of natural materials (wood, glass, ceramics, fabric and metal) and simple but pure forms. Stylistically they combined colourful, geometric, ornamental Karelian (originally Byzantine) design with a more Western European style.

Traditional textile art, such as *ryijy* (woven rugs) and *raanus* (national costumes) as well as wooden furniture and everyday utensils and implements, can be seen in various museums. This heritage is also clearly visible in the works of modern designers.

The products of some early designers, such as Louis Sparre, Gallen-Kallela and Eliel Saarinen, reflected the ideas of Karelianism, National Romanticism and Art Nouveau. In the 1930s architect Alvar Aalto invented wooden furniture made of bent and laminated plywood, as well as his famous Savoy vases. Aalto won a prize for his furniture in the Milan Triennale of 1933.

A Guide to Finnish Churches

The casual traveller will probably be happy to look at just two or three Finnish churches (which even at their best don't come close to Chartres), but any serious student of architecture will want to track them *all* down. Some of the churches mentioned below are described in more detail later in this book; for others, contact the local or regional tourist office, or simply jump aboard a bus with camera and sketchbook in hand. The following is a guide to the various styles common throughout Finland.

Medieval (1200s to 1520s)
Era: Swedish Catholic
Style: Gothic
Material: Stone, sometimes red brick in the façade
There are 70 medieval churches in Finland. The oldest ones are on Åland, in Hammarland, Finström, Lemland, Sund, Saltvik and Kumlinge. There are almost 30 medieval churches in the Turku area, including Nousiainen, Turku, Mynämäki, Korppoo, Parainen, Taivassalo, Rymättylä, Kalanti, Laitila, Sastamala and Rauma. Churches like those in Pyhtää, Hattula, Hollola and Isokyrö were once the religious headquarters for entire regions, and remain historically significant and worth visiting.

In addition to paintings and sculpture, note the unique façade and the shape of the ceiling in medieval churches.

Wooden (1600s to 1700s)
Era: Swedish Lutheran
Style: Varies locally
Material: Logs of locally obtained wood, painted red
Remote areas of Finland never enjoyed the privilege of having an imposing stone church. Instead, wood was used, as this was one material that was cheap and plentiful. Some of the oldest such churches were continuously renovated over the centuries and the original simplicity has been replaced by 19th century style.

The best example of a Finnish wooden church is certainly the Petäjävesi Church in Central Finland. Others include the churches of Irjanne, Keuruu, Maakalla, Paltaniemi, Pihlajavesi, Pyhämaa, Sodankylä, Tervola and Tornio. There are also some colourful churches in Swedish-speaking western Finland, such as Vörå and Nykarleby.

In addition to fine paintings in many of the old wooden churches, look for detailed woodcarving.

Empire & European Gothic (1800s)
Era: Russian, Lutheran
Style: Imitations of central European styles, especially neoclassical and neogothic
Material: Wood, painted various colours
The 20 largest churches in Finland were all built during the Russian era, between 1815 and 1907. They include imitations of central European Gothic cathedrals. Johannes Church in Helsinki and churches in Pori, Kotka, Forssa and Nurmes are the most notable examples. Communities in the Lakeland and Western Finland are especially famous for their large wooden churches. Kerimäki Church in Savo is the largest wooden church in the world, dwarfing even the enormous churches of Mäntyharju, Merikarvia, Mikkeli and Heinävesi.

A Guide to Finnish Churches

Many of these churches were built according to a style called Empire, which was influenced by Roman and French architecture. Carl Ludwig Engel, a German architect, was the leading designer of Finnish churches during this era.

National Romantic (late 1800s to early 1900s)
Era: Russian, Lutheran
Style: Art Nouveau, Karelian
Material: Cut granite, oak and other heavy wood, seldom painted
During the tsarist era, Josef Stenbäck designed the greatest number of granite churches, 30 in all, but others, such as Tampere Cathedral, by Lars Sonck, are more famous. The rich ornamentation, often a reflection of Karelian heritage, is the main feature of these churches.

Orthodox (1700s to 1900s)
Era: Russian, Independence
Style: Byzantine, Karelian
Material: Red brick for the old ones; round logs for the more recent *tsasounas* (chapels)
Most Orthodox churches in Finland date from the Russian era, or time of independence. The style is Byzantine, with Russian flourishes, such as onion domes. Although there are fine examples of Orthodox architecture in eastern Finland, in towns such as Ilomantsi, Joensuu, Polvijärvi and Kotka, there are also chapels further west, most notably in Tampere and Helsinki.

The main feature of Orthodox churches, however, is the wall of icons, rather than the architecture. There is a fine collection of Orthodox art at the Orthodox Church Museum in Kuopio.

Sankta Catharina Church of Hammarland in Åland is an example of Medievial church design in Finland

Modern (1900s)
Era: Independence, Lutheran
Style: Art Deco, modern
Materials: Various, but especially concrete painted white and light wood as interior decoration and/or furniture
The most famous modern churches in Finland are Alvar Aalto's churches in Seinäjoki, Lahti and Imatra, as well as more recent ones in Tampere (Kaleva Church by Pietilä), Myyrmäki (by Leiviskä) and Helsinki's Temppeliaukio Church (by Suomalainen). Some of these churches do not look like churches at all, but more like a successful architectural adventure.

After WWII the 'Golden Age of Applied Art' began, and in Milan in 1951 Finland received 25 prizes for various designer products. Tapio Wirkkala, Kaj Franck, Timo Sarpaneva, Eero Aarnio and Yrjö Kukkapuro were the most notable designers of the time. Iittala, Nuutajärvi and Arabia are some of the best brands of Finnish glassware and porcelain, and Pentik is a more recent brand. Aarikka is famous for wooden products, Kalevala Koru for silver designs.

The *enfant terrible* of the current Finnish design scene is Stefan Lindfors, whose reptile and insect-inspired work has been described as a warped updating of Aalto's own influence from nature.

Painting

Of the many prehistoric rock paintings across Finland, those at Hossa and Ristiina are the most famous. Medieval churches in Åland and in South Finland have frescoes, while interesting paintings by Mikael Toppelius and others feature in several 18th century wooden churches, most notably in the village of Haukipudas, near Oulu. Modern art is alive and well in Finland; each large town exhibits paintings that provoke anything from astonishment to despair.

Golden Age Although contemporary art enjoys a high profile in Finland, it is works by National Romantic painters that have been bestowed with Golden Age status. The main features of these artworks are virgin forests and pastoral landscapes. The following list includes museums that exhibit the best works. The most comprehensive collections are displayed by the Ateneum and National Museum in Helsinki, and the Turku Art Museum.

Brothers von Wright – Magnus (1805-68), Wilhelm (1810-87) and Ferdinand (1822-1902). The brothers von Wright are considered the first Finnish painters of the Golden Age, most famous for their paintings of birds. They worked in their home near Kuopio and in Porvoo. The Ateneum in Helsinki has devoted a room to their work.

Robert Wilhelm Ekman (1808-73), one of the founders of the Finnish school of art, worked in Turku and painted mostly altars for churches. See the Cygnaeus Gallery (Helsinki), National Museum and Ateneum.

Werner Holmberg (1839-60). The *Ideal Landscape* is one of the classic paintings of this early Finnish artist. See Ateneum.

Hjalmar Munsterhjelm (1840-1905), one of the most notable landscape painters in Finland, studied in Germany. There are paintings at Ateneum, Turku Art Museum and Turku Ett Hem.

Berndt Lindholm (1841-1914) is mostly known for his paintings of waves hitting a rocky shore. He has also painted Finnish landscapes and rural life but unfortunately many of his works are in private collections. Some examples can be seen at Ateneum, Turku Art Museum and Turku Ett Hem.

Fanny Churberg (1845-92), one of the most famous female painters in Finland, created landscapes, self-portraits and still lifes. See Ateneum.

Albert Edelfelt (1854-1905), one of the most appreciated of Finnish artists, was educated in Paris, and a number of his paintings date from this period. Many paintings are photo-like depictions of rural life. Most Edelfelt paintings are to be found at Ateneum, but there are also a few at Joensuu Art Museum and Turku Ett Hem.

Victor Westerholm (1860-1919), most famous for his large Åland landscapes, had his summer studio in Önningeby (see Åland for details) but there are landscapes from other locations too. Ateneum, Turku Art Museum, Hämeenlinna Art Museum and Turku Ett Hem display some of his best works.

Helene Schjerfbeck (1862-1946), probably the most famous female painter of her age, is known for her self-portraits, which reflect the situation of Finnish women 100 years ago; Helene didn't live a happy life. Go to Ateneum, Turku Art Museum and Turku Ett Hem.

Eero Järnefelt (1863-1937) was a keen visitor to Koli, where he created over 50 paintings of the 'national landscape'. His sister married Jean Sibelius, the composer. See his work at Ateneum, as well as Mikkeli, Hämeenlinna, Turku and Kuopio art museums.

Akseli Gallen-Kallela (1865-1931), probably the most famous Finnish painter, had a distinguished career as creator of *Kalevala*-inspired paintings. His masterworks can be seen as frescoes in the National Museum in Helsinki,

Ateneum, Turku Art Museum, Turku Ett Hem and at the Jusélius Mausoleum in Pori.

Magnus Enckell (1870-1925) is known for his paintings in Tampere Cathedral. His work can also be seen at Ateneum, Joensuu Art Museum and Jyväskylä Alvar Aalto Museum.

Ellen Thesleff (1869-1954) used strong colours in her landscape paintings. Visit Ateneum.

Hugo Simberg (1873-1917) is famous for his series of watercolours drawing on folk tales and employing a kind of rustic symbolism. His work can be seen at Ateneum and Turku Art Museum.

Juho Rissanen (1873-1950) depicted life among ordinary Finns, and his much-loved paintings are displayed at Ateneum and Turku Art Museum.

Pekka Halonen (1865-1933) was a popular artist of the National Romantic era. His work, mostly devoted to typical winter scenery, is largely privately owned. Some of the best works are displayed in the Ateneum and Turku Art Museum.

Dance

Dance is nurtured in Finland. The Finnish National Opera has its own ballet school, and there are a handful of small dance groups in Helsinki and other large towns. Attend the annual Kuopio Dance & Music Festival to catch the latest trends.

Few traditional folk dances *(kansan-tanssit)* remain, but they can be seen on ceremonial occasions. In summer you may come across a noisy dance stage in the middle of nowhere. Get ready to experience *lavatanssit*, where local singers and their bands play pop music, and people dance. If the participants are older, the music is *humppa* or *tango*, and instruments include accordion and violin. Younger people demand a contemporary band, so the *lava* (stage) is almost like a disco. You may be interested in a *naistentanssi*, or 'women's dance', where women propose a dance. This arrangement is generally held once a week in many local dance restaurants.

Literature

Written Finnish was created by Mikael Agricola (1510-57), who wrote the first Finnish alphabet and covered traditional Finnish culture and religion in his writings.

Because Finnish remained a spoken more than written language (although it was emerging in schools), the earliest fiction was written in Swedish.

The most famous of all 19th century writers was Elias Lönnrot, who collected poems, oral runes, folk legends and stories to pen the *Kalevala*, the national epic of Finland, which became the foundation of Finnish culture, literature and history (see boxed text). Other notable 19th century writers include JL Runeberg *(Tales of the Ensign Ståhl)*, fairy-tale writer Zacharias Topelius, and Aleksis Kivi, who founded modern Finnish literature with *Seven Brothers*, a story of brothers who try to escape education and civilisation in favour of the forest.

In the 20th century, Mika Waltari gained fame through *The Egyptian*, and FE Sillanpää received the Nobel Prize for literature in 1939. The national best seller in the postwar period was *The Unknown Soldier* by Väinö Linna. The seemingly endless series of autobiographical novels by Kalle Päätalo and the witty short stories by Veikko Huovinen are also very popular in Finland. Another internationally famous author is Tove Jansson, whose children's books on the Moomin family have much to offer adult readers too. Tove Jansson's books are available in English translations, although most other works by Finnish authors are not.

Music

The work of the composer Jean Sibelius (see boxed text in Lakeland chapter) dominates the musical identity of Finland. Born on 8 December 1865 in Hämeenlinna, Sibelius wrote music for the glorification of his own people and in defiance of the oppressor, Russia. His most famous composition, *Finlandia*, became a strong expression of Finnish patriotism and pride. Sibelius can be said to have composed the music for the *Kalevala* saga, while Gallen-Kallela painted it.

Sibelius' musical heritage can be seen, and heard, in the work of a new generation

The Kalevala

Elias Lönnrot was an adventuresome country doctor who trekked in eastern Finland on a scholarship during the first half of the 19th century in order to collect traditional poems, oral runes, folk stories and legends. Altogether, Lönnrot undertook 11 long tours, by foot or on reindeer, to complete his research. The results, together with some of his own writing, he put together to form the *Kalevala*, which came to be regarded as the national epic of Finland.

Equally important was Lönnrot's work in creating a standard Finnish grammar and vocabulary by adopting words and expressions from various dialects. Finnish has remained very much the same ever since, at least in written form.

The first version of the *Kalevala* appeared in 1833, another version in 1835 and yet another, the final version, *Uusi-Kalevala* (New Kalevala), in 1849. Since then, the *Kalevala* has been translated into almost 40 languages.

Kalevala is an epic mythology which includes stories of creation and tales of the fight between good and evil. Although there are heroes and villains, there are also more nuanced characters who are not so simply described. The main story line concentrates on the events in two imaginary countries, Kalevala (characterised as 'our country') and Pohjola ('the other place'). Some of the characters are:

Väinämöinen – The main protagonist, a god-like, omnipotent figure. He was a bard and probably a shaman, a Santa Claus-type old man and a strong personality.
Aino – The bride of Väinämöinen and sister of Joukahainen.
Antero Vipunen – A shaman. In one story, Väinämöinen is looking for the Right Words (which give omnipotence to the user) and ends up in Antero's belly. Eventually, Antero Vipunen has to let him go and give him the Words.
Ilmarinen – One of the main characters, and the husband of the princess of Pohjola. He is a smith who makes the Sampo (a mysterious and powerful machine).
Joukahainen – A youngster who is threatened with drowning in a swamp to the singing of the powerful Väinämöinen. In a vain attempt to be saved, he promises his sister Aino to Väinämöinen.
Kalervo – The father of Kullervo.
Kullervo – The main character of the Kullervo series of poems; he suffers under a terrible curse.
Lemminkäinen – A hero whose character was created by Lönnrot based on oral tradition.
Louhi – The matron of Pohjola, also called Pohjan Akka or Pohjolan emäntä, the leader of Pohjola.

Places associated with Lönnrot and the *Kalevala* include Sammatti, Ilomantsi, Kuhmo and Kajaani. There is a *Kalevala* theme park in Kuhmo and a *Kalevala* exhibition in Parppeinvaara, Ilomantsi. The most notable *Kalevala*-inspired paintings are to be found in the Ateneum Art Museum and in the National Museum, both in Helsinki.

Elias Lönnrot – father of modern Finnish literature

of young composers, conductors and musicians currently emerging from Finland onto the international stage. Many of these conductors were pupils of the legendary Jorma Panula, professor of conducting at the Sibelius Academy in Helsinki until 1994. Esa-Pekka Salonen, 39, is currently the musical director of the Los Angeles Philharmonic. Osmo Vänskä, 44, has reversed the fortunes of the troubled BBC Scottish Symphony Orchestra with a series of Beethoven and Sibelius cycles. Jukka-Pekka Saraste, 40, is in charge of the Toronto Symphony Orchestra, and Sakari Oramo, 32, has succeeded Simon Rattle as the head of the Birmingham Symphony Orchestra.

Another graduate of Helsinki's Sibelius Academy is composer Magnus Lindberg. At 39 he already has a reputation for writing difficult pieces. His 1997 work *Related Rocks* reputedly took the musicians of the LA Philharmonic 50 hours of rehearsal to master. Other works such as *Coyote Blues* are easier to play.

The national anthem of Finland, *Maamme* (Our Land; *Nårt Land* in Swedish), was composed by Fredrik Pacius. Karelian-type folk music is a popular alternative to the usual rock and pop, most notably performed by a group called Värttinä, which has released several CDs.

Finland has a lively jazz and rock scene. During the summer there are numerous open-air concerts in parks, featuring the best and the worst of Finnish rock. International jazz acts are attracted to Finland during the summer months for events such as the Pori, Tampere and Espoo jazz festivals. Helsinki also has a lively year-round jazz and rock scene.

Cinema

About a dozen movies are produced in Finland annually, and many of these films are sold to Norwegian state television. Mika and Aki Kaurismäki are currently the best known directors. Their success in *film noir* is based on their education in Leningrad (during the USSR era). Aki is probably best known for his 1989 road film *Leningrad Cowboys Go to America*, and more recently for the downbeat 'grotty realism' of *Drifting Clouds* (1997).

The American director Jim Jarmush is a personal friend of the Kaurismäki brothers, and has also presented his view of Finnish culture in some of his works. Another talented director, Markku Pölönen, has produced some very fine movies on Finnish rural life.

The most successful Finn in Hollywood, Renny Harlin (also known as the husband of actor Geena Davis), directed the strongly anti-communist action movie *Born American* in the 1980s, portraying an imaginary Soviet prison camp. When the film was banned in Finland and Harlin accused of presenting a 'foreign nation in a hostile manner', the young director found himself directing box-office hits for Hollywood, including *Die Hard II* and *Cliffhanger*.

There are several annual film festivals in Finland, the Midnight Sun festival in Sodankylä being one of the most interesting.

SOCIETY & CONDUCT
Traditional Culture

Finns do not consider themselves Scandinavian, nor do they see themselves as part of Russia, nevertheless Finnish tradition owes something to both cultures. For centuries Finns maintained a pragmatic indepenence from their eastern and western neighbours, preserved their own language (the language of the *Kalevala*) and developed their own distinctive culture.

The Finns' long struggle for emancipation, together with their ongoing struggle to survive in a harsh environment, has engendered an ordered society which solves its own problems in its own way. It has also engendered the Finnish trait of *sisu*, often translated as 'guts', or the resilience to survive prolonged hardship. Even if all looks lost, until the final defeat, a Finn with sisu will fight – or swim, or run, or work – valiantly.

The Rules about Finnish Rules

Finns are either the world's worst bureaucrats or the world's most obedient people, judging by the plethora of rigorously enforced rules and regulations that govern Finnish life.

Road laws in particular are strictly enforced. The government collects hundreds of millions of markkaa annually as income from traffic tickets alone. Wearing a seat belt is compulsory for all occupants of a car. It is compulsory to turn on your headlights on rural roads (or outside urban areas). If you fail to comply, you pay.

A businessperson recently started a small guesthouse offering catering services. If only it was so simple ... no less than 15 different authorities inspected the building, checking everything from hygiene to plumbing, making sure all rules and every word of the law was obeyed. 'In Italy only 50% of EU rules are honoured', remarked the owner of the establishment. 'Finland [at that time not an EU member] already obeys 120% of all EU rules!'

Perhaps the new millennium will bring change now that Finns are showing signs of obedience fatigue. On the other hand, they've always excelled at endurance sports.

Despite increased urbanisation, Finns remain a forest people at heart. The forests are crisscrossed with skiing tracks, some leading to the summer cottages (see Summer Cottages boxed text in the Facts for the Visitor chapter) where Finns get away from it all when life in the city gets too hectic.

Other Cultures

The very few Jews in Finland have kept a low profile because of the Nazis, the pro-Arab sentiments of Finnish leftists, and anti-Semitic voices from the Soviet Union and Russia. Some talented Jews have enriched Finnish cultural life, and there's a very beautiful synagogue and a small kosher shop in Helsinki.

Russians have also kept an extremely low profile, perhaps because in the past the Finnish authorities were notorious for expelling Russian defectors back to the Soviet Union. There is in Finland an ethnic Russian Orthodox Church different from the national Orthodox Church. Russian restaurants in Finland, particularly in Helsinki, are said to serve better Russian cuisine than those in Russia.

Vietnamese refugees have established a few restaurants and shops, but Somalian refugees, still banned from taking jobs, are yet to create a subculture. A few mosques in Finland attract Mediterranean Arabs and a small number of Tatars who have lived in Finland for more than a century.

Sami Culture The unique Sami culture is almost exclusive to Lapland. See the Lapland & Oulu chapter for coverage.

Swedish Culture The Swedish-speaking minority in Finland is neither Swedish nor Finnish. Centuries of history divide them from the people of Sweden, and by their own definition they are ethnically distinct from the Finns.

Some Swedish-speaking people are children of ethnic German, Russian or Jewish families who adopted the Swedish language before learning enough Finnish to deal with daily life. Swedish-speakers are well represented in most cultural, economic and public fields. Although they are usually considered representatives of the 'old money' in Finland, the Swedish minority also has some well-known leftists, greens and other influential members in various 'alternative' groups.

Swedish speakers are found mostly in coastal towns and communities, maintaining Swedish literature, newspapers, TV programs, and a number of cultural traditions different from Finns and even from Sweden. Their small towns and gardens are among the most attractive and well-kept in Finland. Sagalund on the island of Kimito, and Stundars near Vaasa are two museums with plenty of cultural interest, and Åland province is culturally exclusively Swedish.

With a constant presence in the national government, the Swedish party makes sure that everything is fine with the 'most protected minority in the world', as some jealously put it.

Romany Culture The Finnish Romany (Gipsies) number about 4000. They are descendants of people who emigrated from India from around 500 AD and travelled throughout Europe. Romany people have their own language (with elements of Indian languages) and distinctive dress. After 1584 when the first Romany people arrived in Finland, a law was passed in which it was illegal *not* to kill a Gipsy. Today the term Romaani is preferred over the old racist term Mustalainet ('black people').

Dos & Don'ts
The Finns are naturally a reserved people, particularly towards foreigners. At first meeting they are likely to be quite formal – a handshake is appropriate, a hug is not. Likewise, extreme chattiness is viewed by many Finns with surprise or even suspicion – remember that silence is a virtue here – see the Silence boxed text following).

The rules when visiting a Finnish family are quite simple: always remove your shoes when entering a home, and never, ever refuse the offer of a sauna or cup of coffee.

You will come across many Swedish-speaking Finns along the west and south coasts of Finland (see Language section). Don't mistake these people for Swedes, or assume that they are Swedophiles – that would be a faux pas not dissimilar to mistaking a Canadian for an American, or a New Zealander for an Australian.

A final tip: Finns, ever the stoic individuals, rarely drink in rounds. You always pay for your own beer, even when drinking with friends. Writes a traveller from the UK:

Don't get caught as happened to me by spending all of your money on shouting drinks for the whole company, and then having to go thirsty as no-one feels the compulsion to return the compliment.

RELIGION
About 86% of Finns are Evangelical Lutherans, 1.1% are Orthodox and the remainder are unaffiliated. Minority churches, including the Roman Catholic Church, make up only a few per cent.

Early Beliefs
In the past, Finns lived in close harmony with nature and made a simple living by fishing, hunting and cultivating land. There were few gods; Finns generally preferred spirits that inhabited both forests *(haltija)* and back yards *(tonttu)*. These spirits were offered gifts to keep them happy. Finns also believed that the dead wandered around, especially during festival seasons, and should be treated with great respect. The *kalmisto* (graveyard) was the place for offerings.

With the arrival of Catholicism, the animist religion was soon influenced by 'new gods' (Catholic saints), which were incorporated into the polytheistic society, although a handful of old shamans kept the old traditions alive for decades. The Church confiscated all traditional sacrifice sites around the 1230s but perpetuated their religious significance: churches were erected on traditional sacrifice sites or burial grounds.

Today's Finland still bears witness to the distant past. The Midsummer is a pagan holiday that is celebrated with bonfires, although it also commemorates St John the Baptist. Easter is a Finnish version of Halloween, with trick-or-treat-style traditions among kids, who dress up for the holiday season as witches and trolls. Some of the old Finnish gods are: *Ahti* (god of waters and fish), *Ilmarinen* (god of winds and storms), *Tapio* (god of forests) and *Ukko* (god of growth, rain and thunderstorms).

Christianity

The Christian faith was brought to Finland by the Roman Catholic Bishop Henry from England, who arrived in mainland Finland from Sweden in about 1155. There were even earlier crusades to Åland, where the oldest churches in Finland are to be found. The Catholic Church was gradually displaced by the Reformation of Martin Luther, which reflected the rugged individualism typical of Finns.

Finland's own reformer was Mikael Agricola, who also created the written Finnish language in the early 16th century. The first complete Bible in Finnish appeared in 1642. The Eastern (Greek or Russian) Orthodox Church is prominent in eastern Finland, but there are also small chapels (*tsasouna* in Finnish) in many western towns, as many refugees from Soviet-annexed Karelia settled in these places after WWII. The Evangelical-Lutheran Church of Finland and the Orthodox Church are the 'official' churches and still collect taxes and register births, but about 10% of the population belong to the civil register. Some of these people were opposed to paying the church taxes, and many women left the Church in protest when the battle over women's priesthood was at its fiercest. However, there are now female priests in the Lutheran Church.

LANGUAGE

Finland is officially a bilingual country, with 6% of the population speaking Swedish as their first and primary language. Even more have at least some Swedish proficiency, as all students learn Swedish at school, and university students must pass a language test in order to graduate. In some areas of south-west Finland, as well as on Åland, up to 90% of the local population may be primarily Swedish-speaking. Some local dialects are very difficult to understand, but usually your Swedish lessons will bear fruit.

Municipalities where speakers of either Finnish or Swedish form a minority of over 8%, or where the minority is over 3000, are officially bilingual. Street signs and official notices will be in both Finnish and Swedish.

Some helpful Swedish words and phrases can be found in the Language chapter at the end of this book.

Lappish is spoken by the small Sami population of Lapland. For helpful words and phrases see the chapter on Lapland & Oulu.

Place Names

For the purposes of this book, if more than 85% of the local population speaks Swedish, the coverage will use Swedish names for places, hotels, restaurants and things to see. The Finnish name of the town or village is always included, except for Åland province, where there is no Finnish version. Note that even with predominantly Swedish-speaking towns, you might see the Finnish name on all signs outside the town. On maps, bilingual towns are usually labelled with the majority language first and then the minority language. In general, the majority language always appears first on street signs (See also Appendix – Alternative Place Names.)

Silence

Finns don't go around babbling like noisy southern Europeans. No, they appreciate a cool, sophisticated atmosphere, where each individual is accorded space and privacy. Sounds great? Well, an Australian traveller who spent half a year living in a student apartment in Helsinki gave this comment:

In six months my mate hardly spoke to me more than 10 times. Probably the loudest form of communication I've ever experienced was when, after several weeks of silence, he one morning said abruptly: 'It is your turn to buy toilet paper'.

Finns don't feel uncomfortable with silence, they have no need to fill in the gaps in a conversation with small-talk.

With a little help from intoxicating liquids, a Finn can be most talkative during a long evening in a pub. But the next day, your loquacious friend may not even nod to say hello and you may wonder whether you've been recognised at all.

Winter is the most hopeless time, when many people are depressed, and at minus 15°C are disinclined to stop and chat on the street. There are ways to cope with the Finnish tendency to stoicism and quietness. One is to accept it as a local custom and just read or meditate more in Finland. Or you can plan your trip to coincide with the summer months, when Finns break out in a frenzy of dancing, singing, and all-around merry-making.

Facts for the Visitor

HIGHLIGHTS

Finland, the land of lakes, is an ideal country to visit if you enjoy the great outdoors. There's plenty to see and do, whether you're travelling under the midnight sun or by the eerie glow of the aurora borealis. See the Highlights section at the beginning of each regional chapter for specific recommendations, and the Activities chapter for details on outdoor pursuits.

Museums & Galleries

Kiasma in Helsinki is the daring new national museum of contemporary art – the bulk of the national art collection is at Ateneum. Retretti at Punkaharju is also a noteworthy art venue. Helsinki's Mannerheim Museum, preserving the home of Finland's great independence-era leader CGE Mannerheim, is intimate and intriguing. Seurasaari, near Helsinki, and Luostarinmäki, in Turku, are two of the best open-air history museums in the country. For experiencing the northern culture, Arktikum, in Rovaniemi, and Saamelaismuseo, in Inari, are top class.

Castles & Manor Houses

Olavinlinna, at Savonlinna, is the mightiest and best preserved of the northern medieval castles and is superbly set between two lakes. It's home to a world-class opera festival in summer. Less imposing are the castles of Turku and Hämeenlinna, each with extensive museums. Åland has the smaller Kastelholm castle. There are many manor houses in Finland, and Louhisaari in Askainen is one of the most stunning.

Historic Towns

Quite a number of towns in Finland qualify as 'medieval' – though due to the ravages of war and fire few actually *look* their age. Turku, founded around 1200, is the oldest city in Finland but its oldest buildings date from the 18th century. Porvoo, Rauma, Hamina and Naantali have picturesque old town quarters, and Hanko is a place to see late 19th century Russian villas.

Churches

Finland boasts the largest wooden church in the world, in Kerimäki. The Tampere cathedral is the most noteworthy example of national romantic edifices. The medieval churches of Åland are particularly attractive and easy to visit, as they are along popular bicycle routes.

Winter Activities

Finland may not have the rugged mountains of Norway, but it does have some fine ski centres, particularly in Lapland. Better yet, these centres offer hundreds of kilometres of cross-country skiing trails, and some are illuminated for winter cruising. Other winter activities unique to Finland include ice-fishing, dog sledding, reindeer sleigh safaris, snowmobile touring and snowshoeing.

Summer Activities

In summer, there's superb trekking in northern Finland, and many of the wilderness huts along trails are well maintained and free of charge. The Lakeland is the place to take an idyllic cruise on an old steamer ferry, or rent canoes and kayaks and explore the riverways on your own. Cycling is best in Åland, where distances are short and the scenery very pretty.

SUGGESTED ITINERARIES

Depending on the length of your stay you might like to see and do the following things:

Two days
   Helsinki: Kiasma Museum of Contemporary Art or Mannerheim Museum, plus a stroll down Pohjoisesplanadi to the market square, and a boat trip to Suomenlinna; second day take a trip to Porvoo (by historic ferry in summer).
One week
   After a day or two in Helsinki, you can do a

loop to Lapland or explore the Lakeland – Savonlinna, Lappeenranta and Kuopio.

Two weeks
A triangle from Helsinki to Turku to Tampere and back to Helsinki, the Lapland route and several days in the Lakeland or Åland.

One month
You can cover practically all major regions, and include a bicycle tour in Åland, or a trek in Lapland or North Karelia.

PLANNING
When to Go
The tourist season in southern Finland and the Lakeland is from early June to the end of August, when all attractions, hostels and camping grounds are open, steamboats ply the lakes and rivers, and festivals are in full swing. This is the time of the midnight sun, when Finland doesn't sleep! During the rest of the year, Finland – or at least its tourist infrastructure – hibernates.

The tourist season in northern Finland, including Lapland, is quite different. There, mosquitoes are unbearably annoying in July, but September is delightful with its autumn *(ruska)* colours. October and February/March are good times to visit Lapland to view the northern lights *(aurora borealis)* and enjoy winter activities. The Christmas holiday period is also delightful in Lapland – after all, this is the 'official' home of Santa Claus!

Helsinki also has a unique tourist season in July local folk desert the city for their summer cottages, and many offices are closed for the duration. However, it's a grand time to visit as a foreign tourist – the weather is pleasant, the markets bustling, and cafés and bars set up their outdoor tables.

See the section on Climate in the Facts about Finland chapter for further information on when and when not to go.

Maps
Almost all local tourist offices offer superb city and regional maps, free of charge. Trekking, canoeing and road maps are available from Karttakeskus (☎ 0204 45 5911, fax 0204 45 5929), Unionkatu 32, 00100 Helsinki. This company produces and sells the largest variety of Finnish maps, and will also ship maps abroad. You can also study trekking maps at local libraries – these are usually stored in special drawers, so ask if you don't see them.

Karttakeskus' 1:800,000 AT road map *(Autoilijan Tiekartta)* of the entire country is sufficient for most basic road travel. The cost is 55 mk. Additionally, there is a series of 19

Interpreting Maps

Here is a list of common Finnish words, some of which will appear as word endings on maps.

Finnish	English
asema	station
järvi, selkä	lake
joki	river
katu	street
kirkko	church
koski	rapids
kylä	village
lahti	bay
linna	castle
lääni	province
kauppahalli	indoor market
kauppatori	market square
maa	land, area
museo	museum
mäki	hill
niemi	cape
pankki	bank
puisto	park
ranta	shore
saari, salo	island
salmi	strait
suo	swamp, marshland
taival	rail, track
talo	house
tie	road
tori	market or square
tunturi	fell
vuori	mountain
yliopisto	university

GT road maps at a scale of 1:200,000. These maps are very clear and show practically all the places that you might be interested in, including hostels and wilderness huts. The GT series road maps are also 55 mk each.

Karttakeskus has produced approximately 40 titles for trekking areas, including walking-track presentations of town areas (in 1:25,000 to 1:50,000 scale) and national park maps (1:50,000 to 1:100,000). For the highest level of detail and accuracy, there are 1:20,000 maps available as well. Prices are 55 to 85 mk per map.

Maps for lakes and waterways are approximately 65 mk each.

What to Bring

You can buy almost anything that you need in Finland, but bring what you can from home to avoid the high retail prices of Finnish shops.

Sheets (or a sleeping sheet) and a pillowcase are essential if you plan to stay in hostels or cabins. Budget travellers should consider a sleeping bag, a tent and the regular trekking kit.

Finns are very casual about clothing, although some of the best restaurants require a tie for men. Even in summer you should have warm clothes and a waterproof and windproof jacket, particularly if visiting Lapland. Layers of clothing work best.

If you travel in winter (which can last through April), you'll need all of the above plus lined boots and mittens, a woollen cap and either an overcoat, quilted jacket, thermal suit or parka.

TOURIST OFFICES
Local Tourist Offices

All major Finnish towns have a tourist office with a helpful, English-speaking staff, English-language brochures and excellent free maps. Usually these offices are able to provide information on the city itself as well as the surrounding region. Additionally, many offices stockpile brochures, maps and advice for every single other town and region in Finland.

The national tourist information organisation is the Finnish Tourist Board, or Matkailun Edistämiskeskus (MEK). The main office is in Helsinki:

Finnish Tourist Board
(☎ 09-4176 9300, fax 09-4176 9301, mek@ mek.fi), PO Box 249, 00131 Helsinki

Tourist Offices Abroad

The Finnish Tourist Board has offices in the following countries:

Australia
    Finnish Tourist Board (☎ 02-9290 1950, fax 02-9290 1981), Level 4, 81 York Street, Sydney, NSW 2000
Canada
    Finnish Tourist Board (☎ 800-346 4636), PO Box 246, Station Q, Toronto M4T 2M1
Denmark
    Finlands Turistbureau (☎ 3313 1362, fax 3332 0501), Nyhavn 43A, 1051 Copenhagen K
Estonia
    Soome Turismiarendamise (☎ 6-997 010, fax 6-997 011), Uus 31, EE-0001 Tallinn
France
    Office National du Tourisme de Finlande (☎ 01 42 66 40 13, fax 01 47 42 87 22), 13 rue Auber, 75009 Paris
Germany
    Finnische Zentrale für Tourismus (☎ 069-719 1980, fax 069-724 1725), Lessingstrasse 5, 60325 Frankfurt
Italy
    Ente Naxionale Finlandese per il Turismo (☎ 02-8646 4914, fax 02-7202 2590), Via Arco 4, 20121 Milan
Japan
    Finnish Tourist Board (☎ 03-3501 5207, fax 03-3580 9205), Imperial Hotel, Room 505, 1-1-1 Uchisaiwai-cho, Chiyoda-ku, Tokyo 100-0011
Netherlands
    Fins Nationaal Verkeersbureau voor de Benelux (☎ 020-671 9876, fax 020-675 0359), Johannes Vermeerplein 5, 1071 DV Amsterdam
Norway
    Finlands Turistkontor (☎ 2310 0800, fax 2310 0808, mek.oslo@mek.fi), Lille Grensen 7, 0159 Oslo
Russia
    Tsentr po razvitiju turizma Finljandii (☎ 812-279 3081, fax 812-279 3084), Europa House, 1 Artillerijskaya str, 191104 St Petersburg

Spain

(☎ 91 319 7440, fax 91 319 6948), Fernando el Santo, 27-5A, 28010 Madrid

Sweden

Finska Turistbyrån (☎ 08-5451 2430, fax 08-5451 2431, mek.sto@mek.fi), Snickarbacken 2-4, 11139 Stockholm

Switzerland

Finnische Zentrale für Tourismus (☎ 01-389 1989, fax 01-389 1980), Apollostrasse 5, 8032 Zürich

UK

Finnish Tourist Board (☎ 0171-930 5871, after April 2000 ☎ 020-7930 5871, fax 0171-321 0696, after April 2000, 020-7321 0696, mek.lon@mek.fi), 30-35 Pall Mall, 3rd Floor, London SW1Y 5LP

USA

Finnish Tourist Board (☎ 212-885 9700, fax 212-885 9710), PO Box 4649, Grand Central Station, New York, NY 10163-4649

VISAS & DOCUMENTS
Passport

For most foreign visitors, a valid passport is required to enter Finland. Citizens of the EU countries (except Greece), and of Liechtenstein, San Marino and Switzerland may use either a national identity card or a passport. Citizens of Denmark, Iceland, Sweden and Norway do not need a passport to visit Finland.

Your passport is your most important travel document, and should remain valid until well after your trip. If it's just about to expire, renew it before you go; having this done while travelling can be inconvenient and time-consuming. You may also expect questions from immigration officials if your passport is due to expire in a short time.

If you don't have a passport, you'll have to apply for one, which can take anything from an hour to several months. Things happen much faster if you do everything in person at the actual passport-issuing office rather than relying on the mail or agents. Check in advance what you'll need to bring with you, such as birth certificate etc.

Australian citizens can apply at a post office or the passport office in their state capital; Britons can get application forms from major post offices, and the passport is issued by the regional passport office; Canadians can apply at regional passport offices; New Zealanders can apply at any district office of the Department of Internal Affairs; US citizens must apply in person (but usually may renew by mail) at a US Passport Agency office or some courthouses and post offices.

Once you start travelling, carry your passport at all times and guard it carefully (see Photocopies later for extra security procedures).

Visas & Residence Permits

Most western nationals don't need a tourist visa for stays of less than three months. However, all foreigners (except citizens of Denmark, Iceland, Norway and Sweden) need a residence permit if they wish to stay in Finland for three months or longer. Unless you are a citizen of the EU or EEA you will need to apply for a residence permit *before* arriving in Finland, through the Finnish embassy or consulate in your home country. You will also need to apply for a residence permit if you plan to work in Finland, even if the term of employment is less than three months. Typically, residence permits are valid for one year and allow multiple entries into Finland, and cost US$75. Renewals are possible. For more information contact the nearest Finnish embassy or consulate, or the Finnish Directorate of Immigration (☎/fax 09-4765 5857), Siltasaarenkatu 12A, 00530 Helsinki.

Russian Visas Travel into Russia from Finland requires a visa, for all foreigners. Russian visas take about eight working days to process in Helsinki so you may want to get one before leaving home.

Travel Insurance

A travel insurance policy to cover theft, loss and medical problems is a good idea. The policies handled by STA Travel and other student travel organisations are usually good value. Some policies offer lower and higher medical-expense options; the higher ones are chiefly for countries such as the

USA which have extremely high medical costs. There is a wide variety of policies available so check the small print. Some policies specifically exclude 'dangerous activities', which can include scuba diving, motorcycling, even trekking. A locally acquired motorcycle licence is not valid under some policies. You may prefer a policy which pays doctors or hospitals directly rather than you having to pay on the spot and claim later. If you have to claim later make sure you keep all documentation. Some policies ask you to call back (reverse charges) to a centre in your home country where an immediate assessment of your problem is made. Check that the policy covers ambulances or an emergency flight home.

Driving Licence & Permits

An international licence is not required to drive in Finland. However, you'll need the driving licence from your home country to bring a car into Finland, or if you plan to rent a car – your passport alone won't do. A green card (insurance card) is recommended but not required for visitors from most countries that subscribe to this plan. Those who are from countries who do belong to the green-card plan will need to arrange for insurance on arrival.

For more information see the Car & Motorcycle section in the Getting Around chapter. The Finnish national motoring organisation, Autoliitto (☎ 09-774 761), Hämeentie 105A, 00550 Helsinki, can also answer questions.

Camping Card International

Check with your local automobile association to see if they issue the Camping Card International, which is basically a camping ground ID. These cards are also available from your local camping federation and incorporate third-party insurance for damage you may cause. Many camping grounds offer a small discount if you sign in with one.

In Finland, a camping card good for one year is available on the spot at most camping grounds; the cost is 20 mk.

Hostelling Card

A hostelling card is useful for those staying at hostels. It may not be mandatory in Finland, but the Hostelling International (HI) card will mean a 15 mk discount every time you check in at an HI-affiliated hostel. (Prices quoted in this book are without the 15 mk HI membership discount.)

In Finland, hostelling cards may also bring discounts on some ferry transportation, rental cars, museum admissions and train tickets. There are also 'Hostelling by Bike' and 'Hostelling by Rent-A-Car' discount packages.

Ideally, you should purchase your HI card in your home country, but some hostels will issue one on the spot. You can also purchase one at the main office of the Finnish Youth Hostel Association, Suomen Retkeilymajajärejesö (SRM; ☎ 09-694 0377 or 09-693 1347, fax 09-693 1349, info@srm.inet.fi or srm@srmnet.org), Yrjönkatu 38B, 00100 Helsinki. The cost is 100 mk and the card is good for one year.

See Hostels in the later Accommodation section for more details. The Web sites for the SRM are www.srmnet.org/ and www.iyhf.org/.

Student & Youth Cards

The most useful of these is the International Student Identity Card (ISIC), a plastic ID-style card with your photograph, which provides discounts on many forms of transport (including airlines, ferries and local public transport), reduced or free admission to museums and sights, and cheap meals in student cafeterias – a worthwhile way of cutting costs in expensive Finland.

If you're aged under 26 but not a student, you can apply for a GO25 card issued by the Federation of International Youth Travel Organisations (FIYTO), or the Euro26 card, which goes under various names in different countries. All of these cards are available through student unions, hostelling organisations or youth-oriented travel agencies. They don't automatically entitle you to discounts, and some companies and institutions refuse to recognise them altogether, but you won't find out until you flash the card.

Seniors Cards

For a small fee, European nationals aged over 60 can get a Rail Europe Senior Card as an add-on to their national rail senior pass. It entitles the holder to reduced fares in some European countries, and percentage savings vary according to the route. There are also rail passes available for travel within Scandinavia for nationals of any country who are aged over 55; inquire at your local travel agency for information.

International Health Certificate

You'll need this yellow booklet only if you're coming to Scandinavia from certain parts of Asia, Africa and South America, where outbreaks of such diseases as yellow fever have been reported. See the Health section for more information.

Photocopies

All important documents (passport data page and visa page, credit cards, travel insurance policy, air/bus/train tickets, driving licence etc) should be photocopied before you leave home. Leave one copy with someone at home and keep another with you, separate from the originals.

EMBASSIES & CONSULATES
Finnish Embassies & Consulates

Visas and information can be obtained at Finnish diplomatic missions, including:

Australia
 (☎ 06-273 3800), 10 Darwin Avenue, Yarralumla, 2600 ACT
Austria
 (☎ 1-531 590), Gonzagagasse 16, 1010 Vienna
Belgium
 (☎ 02-287 1212), Avenue des Arts 58, 1000 Brussels
Canada
 (☎ 613-236 2389), 55 Metcalfe St, Suite 850, Ottawa, Ontario K1P 6L5
China
 (☎ 10-6532 1817), Tayuan Diplomatic Office, Building 1-10-1, Beijing 100600

Denmark
 (☎ 3313 4214), Sankt Annae Plads 24, 1250 Copenhagen K
Estonia
 (☎ 6-103 200), Kohtu 4, 0100 Tallinn
France
 (☎ 01 44 18 19 20), 1 place de Finlande, 75007 Paris
Germany
 (☎ 0228-382 980), Friesdorferstrasse 1, 53173 Bonn
Ireland
 (☎ 01-478 1344), Russell House, St Stephen's Green, Dublin 2
Italy
 (☎ 06-852 231), Via Lisbona 3, 00198 Rome
Japan
 (☎ 03-3442 2231), 3-5-39 Minami-Azabu, Minato-ku, Tokyo 106
Netherlands
 (☎ 070-346 9754), Groot Hertoginnelaan 16, 2517 EG The Hague
Norway
 (☎ 2243 0400), Thomas Heftyesgate 1, 0244 Oslo
Russia
 (☎ 095-246 4027), Kropotkinskij Pereulok 15/17, 119034 Moscow G-34
Sweden
 (☎ 08-676 6700), Jakobsgatan 6, 6tr, 111 52 Stockholm
UK
 (☎ 0171 235 9531, after April 2000 ☎ 020-7235 9531), 38 Chesham Place, London SW1X 8HW
USA
 (☎ 202-298 5800), 3301 Massachusetts Ave NW, Washington DC 20008

Embassies & Consulates in Finland

The following is a list of foreign government representatives in Helsinki. Use the Helsinki area telephone code (☎ 09) if calling from elsewhere.

Austria
 (☎ 171 322), Keskuskatu 1A
Australia
 (☎ 447 233), Museokatu 25B
Belgium
 (☎ 170 412), Kalliolinnantie 5
Canada
 (☎ 171 141), Pohjoisesplanadi 25B
China
 (☎ 2289 0110), Vanha Kelkkamäki 9-11

Denmark
(☎ 171 511), Keskuskatu 1A
Estonia
(☎ 622 0260), Itäinen Puistotie 10
France
(☎ 171 521), Itäinen Puistotie 13
Germany
(☎ 458 580), Krogiuksentie 4
Ireland
(☎ 646 006), Erottajankatu 7A
Italy
(☎ 175 144), Itäinen Puistotie 4
Japan
(☎ 633 011), Eteläranta 8
Latvia
(☎ 476 4720), Armfeltintie 10
Lithuania
(☎ 608 210), Rauhankatu 13A
Netherlands
(☎ 661 737), Raatimiehenkatu 2A 7
Norway
(☎ 171 234), Rehbinderintie 17
Poland
(☎ 684 8077), Armas Lindgrenintie 21
Russia
(☎ 661 876), Tehtaankatu 1B
Spain
(☎ 170 505), Kalliolinnantie 6
Sweden
(☎ 651 255), Pohjoisesplanadi 7B
Switzerland
(☎ 649 422), Uudenmaankatu 16A
UK
(☎ 2286 5100), Itäinen Puistotie 17
Ukraine
(☎ 228 9000), Vähäniityntie 9
USA
(☎ 171 931), Itäinen Puistotie 14A

Your Own Embassy

It's important to realise what the embassy of the country of which you are a citizen can and can't do to help you if you get into trouble.

Generally speaking, it won't be much help in emergencies if the trouble you're in is remotely your own fault. Remember that you are bound by the laws of the country you are in. Your embassy will not be sympathetic if you end up in jail after committing a crime locally, even if such actions are legal in your own country.

In genuine emergencies you might get some assistance, but only if other channels have been exhausted. For example, if you need to get home urgently, a free ticket home is exceedingly unlikely – the embassy would expect you to have insurance. If you have all your money and documents stolen, it might assist with getting a new passport, but a loan for onward travel is out of the question.

Some embassies used to keep letters for travellers or have a small reading room with home newspapers, but these days the mail holding service has usually been stopped and even newspapers tend to be out of date.

CUSTOMS

Travellers should encounter few problems with Finnish customs. Travellers arriving from outside the EU can bring currency and gifts up to the value of 1100 mk into Finland without declaration, as well as 15L of beer, 2L of wine and 1L of strong alcohol. Travellers arriving from another EU country may bring up to 350 mk worth of duty-free goods, plus 15L of beer, five litres of wine and 1L of strong alcohol. Check current rules at the border post or on an international ferry.

MONEY
Currency

The Finnish unit of currency is the *markka* (plural markkaa), abbreviated as mk. Notes come in 20, 50, 100, 500 and 1000 mk denominations and coins in one, five and 10 markkaa and 10 and 50 *penniä*. One markka is equal to 100 penniä. Five markka is often called *vitonen*, 10 mk *kymppi* and 100 mk *satanen*.

All banknotes issued before 1980 (and one, five and 20 penniä coins) are now annulled, and can be changed only at Suomen Pankki (Finland's Bank) offices until 31 December 2003.

The Swedish krona (including coins) is accepted on Åland and in western Lapland, and the Norwegian krona can be used in areas near the Norwegian border in northern Lapland.

Exchange Rates

The markka may be pegged to the main EU currencies by the time you reach Finland.

country	unit		markka
Australia	A$1	=	3.15 mk
Canada	C$1	=	3.32 mk
Estonia	1 Ekr	=	0.38 mk
euro	€1	=	5.97 mk
France	1FF	=	0.90 mk
Germany	DM1	=	3.04 mk
Ireland	IR£1	=	7.40 mk
Japan	¥100	=	4.51 mk
Netherlands	f1	=	2.64 mk
New Zealand	NZ$1	=	2.66 mk
Norway	1 Nkr	=	0.68 mk
Sweden	1 Skr	=	0.63 mk
UK	UK£1	=	8.45 mk
USA	US$1	=	5.10 mk

Exchanging Money

In Finland, ATMs are the best way to obtain local currency. Or you can go the traditional route, with travellers cheques and cash. Finland has three national banks with similar rates and charges. In the big cities independent exchange facilities such as Forex usually offer better rates and charge smaller fees or commissions than banks. They usually also keep better hours than the banks, and some are open daily during summer. All Finnish post offices provide banking services too; they tend to keep longer hours than banks, particularly in remote villages. The exchange rate on international ferries tends to be lousy – you're better off waiting until you get into port.

Cash Nothing beats cash for convenience – or risk. If you lose it, it's gone forever and very few travel insurers will come to your rescue. Those that will, limit the amount paid out to about US$300.

It's still a good idea, though, to carry some local currency in cash, if only to tide you over until you get to the next exchange facility or find an automatic teller machine (ATM). The equivalent of, say, US$100 should usually be enough. Some extra cash in an easily exchanged currency (eg US dollars or Deutschmarks) is also a good idea. Remember that banks will always accept paper money but very rarely coins in foreign currencies, so you might want to spend (or donate) your local coins before you cross a border. International ferries are another good place to use up the last of your markkaa, as these generally accept the currency of both port cities.

Travellers Cheques The exchange rate for travellers cheques is slightly better than the exchange rate for cash, and travellers cheques offer greater protection from theft. American Express, Visa and Thomas Cook cheques are widely accepted and have efficient replacement policies for stolen and lost cheques.

Keeping a record of the cheque numbers and those you have used is vital when it comes to replacing lost travellers cheques. You should keep this separate from the cheques themselves.

Cheques denominated in US dollars and Deutschmarks are the easiest to cash. Don't just look at the exchange rate; ask about fees and commissions as well. Banks in Finland charge as much as 40 mk per transaction to exchange travellers cheques, while independent facilities such as Forex may have a fee of 10 mk per cheque. Either way, your costs can mount quickly without careful planning.

ATMs & Credit Cards Travellers cheques are losing their popularity as more travellers – including those on tight budgets – deposit their money in their bank at home and withdraw it as they go along through ATMs. Indeed, this is probably the best way to go in Finland. Finns conduct most of their banking transactions using an ATM, and ATMs can be found on every corner in central Helsinki, and even in the smallest villages.

Finnish ATMs accept foreign bank cards with Cirrus, EC, Eurocard, Visa and Plus symbols. Withdrawals using a foreign ATM may incur a small transaction fee – contact your home bank for details. On the plus side, the exchange rate is usually

Europe's New Currency

Don't be surprised if you come across two sets of prices for goods and services in some European countries. From 1 January 1999 Europe's new currency – the euro – is legal tender here along with the local monetary unit.

It's all part of the harmonisation of the EU. Along with national borders, venerable currencies like the franc and escudo are being phased out. Not all EU members have agreed to adopt the euro, but Finland's markka will be among the first of 11 currencies to go the way of the dodo.

No actual coins or banknotes will be issued until 1 January 2002; until then, the euro will in effect be 'paperless'. Prices can be quoted in euros, but there won't actually be any euros in circulation. Companies will use the new European currency for their accounting, banks can offer euro accounts and credit card companies can bill in euros. Essentially, the euro can be used anytime it is not necessary to hand over hard cash.

This can lead to confusion, and travellers should be forewarned that the scheme is open to abuse. For instance, a restaurant might list prices in both markkaa and euros. Check your bill carefully – your total might have the amount in markkaa, but a credit card may bill you in the euro equivalent.

Things will probably get worse during the first half of 2002. There is a six-month period when countries can use both their old currencies and the newly issued euro notes and coins.

Coins and notes have already been designed. The banknotes come in denominations ranging from €5 to €500. All bills feature a generic 'European' bridge on one side and a vaguely familiar but unidentifiable 'European' arch on the reverse. Each country will be permitted to design coins with one side bearing a national emblem (the other side will be standard for all euro coins).

Euro Exchange Rates

Australia	A$1	=	€0.52	Japan	¥100	=	€0.71
Canada	C$1	=	€0.55	Netherlands	f1	=	€0.45
Denmark	1Dkr	=	€0.13	New Zealand	NZ$1	=	€0.43
Estonia	1Ekr	=	€0.06	Norway	1Nkr	=	€0.11
Finland	1Fmk	=	€0.16	Russia	R1	=	€0.04
France	1FF	=	€0.15	Sweden	1Skr	=	€0.10
Germany	DM1	=	€0.51	UK	UK£1	=	€1.41
Ireland	IR£1	=	€1.27	USA	US$1	=	€0.85

better than that offered for travellers cheques or cash exchanges.

Credit cards are widely accepted in Finland at hotels, fine restaurants, larger shops and department stores.

Remember that ATMs aren't completely fail-safe. If an ATM swallows your card abroad it can be a major headache.

International Transfers If you run out of money, or your card gets swallowed by the ATM, you can instruct your bank back home to send you a draft. Make sure you specify the city, the bank and the branch to which you want your money directed, or ask your home bank to tell you where a suitable one is, and ensure you get the details correct.

The whole procedure will be easier if you've authorised someone back home to access your account. Also, a transfer to a bank in a remote village in Lapland is obviously going to be more difficult than to the head office in Helsinki. If you have the choice, find a large bank and ask for the international division.

Money sent by telegraphic transfer (there will be costs involved, typically from US$40) should reach you within a week; by mail, allow at least two weeks.

You can also transfer money quickly through Western Union, Moneygram (formerly American Express) or Thomas Cook.

Costs

Finland is cheaper than the other Scandinavian countries but certainly not a bargain. Your costs will depend on how you travel, and where to – if you stick to the big cities like Helsinki and Tampere your costs will soar much higher than if you concentrate on small towns and the countryside. In terms of basic expenses, if you camp or stay in hostel dormitories and prepare your own meals you might get by on less than 175 mk a day. If you stay in guesthouses (or private rooms in hostels) and eat at inexpensive restaurants, expect to pay about 300 mk a day if you're travelling alone or 250 mk a day if you have a travel partner.

To this you need to factor in museum admission fees, entertainment, transportation and incidentals. Trains are cheaper than buses (unlike in Sweden). Petrol is expensive but there are no extra charges such as road tolls or ferry charges for car travel. A single night on the town can really wreck your budget, thanks to the high 'sin tax' on alcohol.

Students with valid ID and seniors can receive substantial discounts on museum admission prices quoted in this book, as well as on transportation (including ferries) – if you fit the description, always ask.

Tipping & Bargaining

Tipping is not necessary and Finns generally don't do it. You will pay service charges in restaurants as percentages; these are generally included in the quoted menu price. You might ask the taxi driver to keep the change (pidä loput). Doormen at fancy clubs and restaurants may also expect a small tip.

Bargaining is not common in Finland, except at markets or when purchasing second-hand goods.

Taxes & Refunds

The value-added tax (VAT) of 22% is included in marked prices but may be deducted if you post goods from the point of sale. Alternatively, at stores showing the 'Tax Free for Tourists' sign foreign visitors who are not EU citizens can get a 12% to 16% refund on items priced over 250 mk. Present the tax-refund 'cheque' to the refund window at your departure point from the EU (eg airport transit halls, aboard international ferries, overland border crossings). For more information on VAT refunds contact Europe Tax-Free Shopping Finland Oy (☎ 09-6132 9600, fax 09-6132 9675), PO Box 460, 00101 Helsinki.

The 22% tax also applies to alcohol, whether it is bought at a pub or in a store.

POST & COMMUNICATIONS
Post

Stamps can be bought at bus or train stations and R-kioski newsstands as well as at the post office (called *posti* in Finnish). Post offices sell packing material of various sizes.

Postcards and letters weighing up to 20g cost 3.20 mk to EU countries, 2.70 mk to other countries in Europe, and 3.40 mk elsewhere (air-mail or *lentoposti*). Within Finland anything under 50g costs 2.80 mk.

Letters posted before 5 pm Monday to Friday will reach their destination in Finland the next working day. Letters to Scandinavia take a few days, to Australia less than a week, to North America almost two weeks.

There is poste restante at the main post offices in cities. Address mail to: name, poste restante, postcode and town. Postcodes in Finland are five-digit numbers that follow this logic: the first two numbers indicate towns and areas, the next two identify the post office in the town or area, and the last number is always 0, except when you are sending mail to a post office box or poste restante, in which case the last number is 1. The main post office is always '10' in all large towns, so the postcode for the main post office in Helsinki is 00101, for Turku 20101, for Tampere 33101, for Savonlinna 57101, for Vaasa 65101 and for Rovaniemi 96101.

Telephone

Finnish pay phones often have an option that lets you see the instructions in English, which can be quite handy. The vast majority accept plastic phonecards but a few older public phones accept coins. Phonecards come in denominations costing 30, 50 or 100 mk and can be purchased at post offices, shops and R-kioski newsstands.There are several different pay telephone networks in Finland, which can cause some headaches. In a few cities – such as Turku – some of the public telephones may only accept a local phonecards that is completely useless elsewhere in Finland. Watch out for these! The Tele company has the widest network of card phones.

A short call to a local number will cost at least 2 mk. A three minute call placed during peak time to another European country costs about 18 mk, to the USA 23 mk, to Australia 26 mk and to other countries 48 to 84 mk. Calls placed weekdays between 10 pm and 8 am and all day Saturday and Sunday are cheaper. For national directory assistance dial ☎ 020 202, international ☎ 020 208.

Finland has 13 area codes, each starting with a zero (these were adopted in 1996). Include the zero when dialling from one area code to another in Finland, but omit it if you are calling from abroad. The country code for calling Finland from abroad is ☎ 358.

To make international calls from Finland you first need to dial an international access code (☎ 999, 990, 994 or 00), then the country code for the country you're

calling followed by the telephone number. Access code ☎ 994 usually offers the lowest rates.

With a Country Direct telephone number, you can place a call which is paid for by the receiver or billed to your credit card (this may be more expensive than if you pay in Finland). Country Direct telephone numbers for use in Finland are as follows:

Australia	– Optus	☎ 0800 11 0611
	– Telstra	☎ 0800 11 0610
Canada		☎ 0800 11 0011
Germany		☎ 0800 11 0490
Ireland		☎ 0800 11 0353
New Zealand		☎ 0800 11 0640
Norway		☎ 0800 11 0470
Sweden	– Telia	☎ 0800 11 0460
	– TELE 2	☎ 0800 11 0461
UK	– BT	☎ 0800 11 0440
	– MCL	☎ 0800 11 0289
USA	– AT&T	☎ 0800 11 0010
	– MCI	☎ 0800 11 0280
	– US Sprint	☎ 0800 11 0284
	– Worldcom	☎ 0800 11 0282

Fax

Faxes can be sent from local telephone offices (usually adjacent to the post office in big cities). The going rate tends to be 10 mk for the first page and 5 mk for each additional page for domestic faxes, and 25/15 mk for international faxes. Tourist offices, hotels and some hostels will also send and receive faxes for a fee.

Email & Internet Access

You can use public access points such as cybercafés, post offices, libraries, hostels, hotels and universities to stay connected to the Internet during your travels. Cybercafés are common in most of Europe (see www.netcafeguide.com for a list) but are rare in Finland, perhaps because it's possible to use Internet terminals free of charge in almost all public libraries. Most town libraries have at least one terminal, and bigger ones have three or more. The busiest ones require that you book a day or more in advance, and usually impose a strict 30 minute time limit.

If you have one of the free, Web-based email accounts such as those offered by Hotmail (www.hotmail.com) or Yahoo! Mail (mail.yahoo.com) you will be able to send and receive email on the road without trouble. The Internet terminals at Finnish libraries usually don't have an Outgoing Mail (SMTP) Server, so other types of email accounts generally aren't valid.

Portable Computers Travelling with a portable computer is a great way to stay in touch with life back home, but unless you know what you're doing it's fraught with potential problems. If you plan to carry your notebook or palmtop computer with you, remember that the power supply voltage in the countries you visit may vary from that at home, risking damage to your equipment. The best investment is a universal AC adaptor for your appliance, which will enable you to plug it in anywhere without frying the innards. You'll also need a plug adapter for each country you visit – often it's easiest to buy these before you leave home.

Also, your PC-card modem may or may not work once you leave your home country – and you won't know for sure until you try. The safest option is to buy a reputable 'global' modem before you leave home, or buy a local PC-card modem if you're spending an extended time in any one country. Keep in mind that the telephone socket in each country you visit will probably be different from that at home, so ensure that you have at least a US RJ-11 telephone adapter that works with your modem. You can almost always find an adapter that will convert from RJ-11 to the local variety.

Once you've dealt with the hardware, you'll need to worry about local dial-up numbers. Major Internet service providers such as AOL (www.aol.com), CompuServe (www.compuserve.com) and IBM Net (www.ibm.net) have dial-in nodes throughout Europe; it's best to download a list of the dial-in numbers before you leave home.

For more information on travelling with a portable computer, see www.teleadapt.com or www.warrior.com.

INTERNET RESOURCES
The World Wide Web is a rich resource for travellers. You can research your trip, hunt down bargain air fares, book hotels, check on weather conditions or chat with locals and other travellers about the best places to visit (or avoid!).

There's no better place to start your Web explorations than the Lonely Planet Web site (www.lonelyplanet.com). Here you'll find succinct summaries on travelling to most places on earth, postcards from other travellers and the Thorn Tree bulletin board, where you can ask questions before you go or dispense advice when you get back. You can also find travel news and updates to many of our most popular guidebooks, and the subWWWay section links you to the most useful travel resources elsewhere on the Web.

As you'll soon come to realise, Finland has more Web sites per capita than any other country – virtually all of the city tourist offices have them, and so, it seems, does every other person, place and thing in Finland.

A few good Web sites to start with might be those of the Finnish Tourist Board (MEK; www.mek.fi), the Finnish Youth Hostel Association (SRM; www.srmnet.org), the Forest and Park Service (Metsähallitus; www.metsa.fi) and the Helsinki city tourist office (www.hel.fi). Virtual Finland (virtual .finland.fi/) is an excellent site maintained by the Finnish Ministry of Foreign Affairs.

Finnish Web sites usually offer an English-language translation page or pages.

BOOKS
Most books are published in different editions by different publishers in different countries. As a result, a book might be a hardcover rarity in one country while it's readily available in paperback in another. Fortunately, bookshops and libraries search by title or author, so your local bookshop or

library is best placed to advise you on the availability of the following recommendations.

Guidebooks

For a detailed treatment of languages in the region, see Lonely Planet's *Scandinavian Europe phrasebook*.

Facts about Finland (Otava, Helsinki) contains plenty of background information on the history, economy and society of Finland, written by Finns. This book is sold in Helsinki in several languages and costs around 120 mk.

History & Politics

Finnish history is constantly unfolding, especially with the opening of former president UK Kekkonen's archives, and of Russian archives from the Soviet Union era.

For a very readable history, see the paperback *A Short History of Finland* (Cambridge University Press, 1998) by Fred Singleton.

Finland in the New Europe (Praeger Publishers, 1998) is by Max Jakobson, a leading scholar of European history, a diplomat and a Finn. *Finland at Peace and War* by HM Tillotson and *Let Us Be Finns: Essays on History* by Matti Klinge are also of note.

Finland: Myth and Reality by Max Jakobson deals with postwar history. *Blood, Sweat and Bears* (1990) by Lasse Lehtinen is a parody of a war novel and deals with Soviet relations.

General

The Kalevala – Poems of the Kaleva District compiled by Elias Lönnrot (Harvard University Press, 1997) is the national folk epic and provides insight into the country and its people.

English-language translations of the works of notable Finnish authors – such as *The Egyptian* and *The Dark Angel* by Mika Waltari, and *The Unknown Soldier* by Väinö Linna – are produced by the WSOY publishing company and are available within Finland.

NEWSPAPERS & MAGAZINES

The *Helsingin Sanomat*, the largest daily in Finland, doesn't have a word in English. Some local papers regularly publish an English-language summary of international and local news, but it may take a while to find these columns inside the paper.

English-language newspapers and magazines such as the *International Herald Tribune*, the *European* and *The Economist* are available at R-kioski newsstands and at train stations in big cities and major tourist hubs (eg Helsinki, Turku, Tampere, Savonlinna, Oulu, Rovaniemi). The libraries and newspaper reading rooms in these cities may also keep some copies.

The weeklies *Keltainen pörssi* and *Palsta* are the best sources for ads for used cars and bicycles.

RADIO & TV

There are four national (non commercial) radio stations. A summary of world news is broadcast in English daily at 10.55 pm on the national radio stations YLE 3 and YLE 4. In Helsinki, Capital FM (FM 103.7Mhz) broadcasts English programs such as BBC World News, Voice of America and Radio Australia. Radio Mafia, the popular youth channel, plays pop music and a wide variety of 'world music'. For more information on Finnish radio stations offering programming in English visit www.yle.fi/rfinland/.

The two national television networks, TV1 and TV2, broadcast British and US programs in English with Finnish and Swedish subtitles. Hotels usually offer cable satellite channels such as the NBC Super Channel, MTV and EuroSport.

VIDEO SYSTEMS

Finland uses the VHS – PAL 525 system. V-8 videos are not commonly available in Finland.

PHOTOGRAPHY & VIDEO
Photography

Finland's seasonal extremes – snow and very little sunlight in winter, followed by almost continuous daylight in summer –

can pose some challenges for the inexperienced photographer. In particular, the risk of underexposure is great when photographing snowy landscapes – you should know how your camera works, and whether you'll need to correct for this.

Print and slide film is readily available in Finnish cities, and film processing is speedy, fairly cheap and of high quality. A roll of standard 36 exposure print film costs 35 mk and 36 exposure slide film costs 55 mk. Anttila department stores generally offer good prices on film.

Kuva-Ahti at Mikonkatu 8 in Helsinki is a reliable camera shop with good prices on second-hand gear.

Video

Properly used, a video camera can give a fascinating record of your holiday. As well as videoing the obvious things – sunsets, spectacular views – remember to record some of the ordinary everyday details of life in the country. Often the most interesting things occur when you're actually intent on filming something else. Remember too that, unlike still photography, video 'flows' – so, for example, you can shoot scenes of countryside rolling past the train window, to give an overall impression that isn't possible with ordinary photos.

Video cameras these days have amazingly sensitive microphones, and you might be surprised how much sound will be picked up. This can also be a problem if there is a lot of ambient noise – filming by the side of a busy road might seem OK when you do it, but viewing it back home might simply give you a deafening cacophony of traffic noise.

One good rule to follow for beginners is to try to film in long takes, and don't move the camera around too much. Otherwise, your video could well make your viewers seasick! If your camera has a stabiliser, you can use it to obtain good footage while travelling on various means of transport, even on bumpy roads. And remember, you're on holiday – don't let the video take

over your life and turn your trip into a Cecil B de Mille production.

Make sure you keep the batteries charged and have the necessary charger, plugs and transformer for the country you are visiting. In most countries, it is possible to obtain video cartridges easily in large towns and cities, but make sure you buy the correct format. It is usually worth buying at least a few cartridges duty-free to start off your trip.

Finally, remember to follow the same rules regarding people's sensitivities as for still photography – having a video camera shoved in their face is probably even more annoying and offensive for locals than a still camera. Always ask permission first.

TIME

Finnish time is two hours ahead of GMT/UTC in winter. Daylight Saving Time applies from late March or early April to the end of October, when Finnish time is three hours ahead of GMT. Noon in Finland is 2 am in Los Angeles, 5 am in New York, 10 am in London and 8 pm in Sydney.

ELECTRICITY

The electric current is 220V AC, 50Hz, and plugs are of the standard European type with two round pins which require no switch.

WEIGHTS & MEASURES

Finland uses the metric system (see the conversion table at the back of this book). Decimals are indicated by commas.

LAUNDRY

Laundrettes are thin on the ground in Finland. Check the local telephone book – they are listed as *Pesuloita*. *Itsepalvelupesula* denotes self-service laundrettes.

The best options for travellers are the self-service laundry facilities at hostels and camping grounds. You might want to bring a universal sink plug, a length of clothesline and some soap powder so you can do your washing manually, in a pinch.

Fine hotels typically offer laundry and dry-cleaning services.

TOILETS

Finnish bus and train stations charge 5 to 10 mk for the privilege of using their potties. Other public facilities – such as the 'French toilet' kiosks in city centres – also charge 5 mk or more. The good news is, they're very clean.

By law, all restaurants and cafés must have a public toilet and it must be accessible to a person using a wheelchair. There are also free toilets in public libraries, department stores and hotels.

HEALTH

Health-wise, there's very little to worry about while travelling in Finland, unless you engage in endurance tests in the wilderness. Your main risks are likely to be viral infections in winter, sunburn and mosquito bites in summer, plus typical traveller's complaints like foot blisters and upset stomach at any time.

A healthy trip depends on your predeparture preparations and fitness, your day-to-day health care while travelling, and how you handle any medical problem or emergency that does develop. Although it's rather large to lug around, *Travellers' Health* by Dr Richard Dawood (Oxford University Press) is comprehensive, easy to read, authoritative and highly recommended as a guide to staying healthy on the road.

Predeparture Planning

If you're reasonably fit, the only things you should organise before departure are a visit to your dentist to get your teeth in order, and travel insurance with good medical cover (see the Visas & Documents section).

No special immunisations are required for entry into Finland. However, to put your mind at ease you might also ensure that your normal childhood vaccines (against measles, mumps, rubella, diptheria, tetanus and polio) are up to date and/or you are still showing immunity, particularly if you're planning a lengthy trip.

If you wear glasses bring your prescription and a spare pair – new spectacles are not cheap in Finland.

Antibiotics are quite expensive in Finland and available only with a doctor's prescription. If you require a particular medication take an adequate supply as it may not be available locally. Bring the part of the packaging that shows the generic name, rather than the brand, as this will make getting replacements easier. To avoid any problems, carry a legible prescription or letter from your doctor to show that you legally use the medication.

Health Insurance Make sure that you have adequate health insurance. See Travel Insurance under Visas & Documents earlier in this chapter.

Basic Rules

Water You can drink the tap water in all Finnish towns and villages, although it is not always good-tasting.

Always be wary of drinking natural water; a recent survey ranked Finland's lakes and rivers among the most polluted in Europe. A burbling stream may look crystal clear and very inviting, but there may be people, sheep and pulp factories lurking upstream.

If you are planning extended hikes where you have to rely on natural water it may be useful to know about water purification. The simplest way to do this is to boil water thoroughly. Technically this means boiling for 10 minutes, something which happens very rarely. You can also use a water filter, or treat the water chemically. Flavoured powder will disguise the taste of treated water and is a good idea if you are travelling with children.

Many trekkers in the wilderness of Eastern Lapland claim that springs there are safe to drink from without purifying – use your own best judgement as to whether you'd care to follow suit.

Food If a place looks clean and well run, then the food is probably safe. In general, places that are packed with locals or travellers will be fine. Be careful with food that has been cooked and left to go cold – as is the case with some Finnish buffets.

Mushroom and berry-picking is a favourite pastime in this part of the world, but make sure you don't eat any that haven't been positively identified as safe.

Nutrition If your food is poor or limited in availability, if you're travelling hard and fast and therefore missing meals or if you simply lose your appetite, you can soon start to lose weight and place your health at risk. Make sure your diet is well balanced – and consider taking vitamin and iron pills if it isn't.

During treks and hot spells make sure you drink enough – don't rely on thirst to indicate when you should drink. Not needing to urinate or very dark yellow urine are danger signs. Always carry a water bottle with you on long treks.

Everyday Health Normal body temperature is up to 37°C (98.6°F); more than 2°C (4°F) higher indicates a high fever. The normal adult pulse rate is 60 to 100 per minute (children 80 to 100, babies 100 to 140). As a general rule the pulse rate increases about 20 beats per minute for each 1°C (2°F) rise in fever.

Respiration (breathing) rate is also an indicator of illness. Count the number of breaths per minute: between 12 and 20 is normal for adults and older children (up to 30 for younger children, 40 for babies). People with a high fever or serious respiratory illness breathe more quickly than normal. More than 40 shallow breaths a minute may indicate pneumonia.

Medical Problems & Treatment

From anywhere in Finland dial ☎ 112 for emergency ambulance service and ☎ 10023 for 24 hour emergency medical advice.

Local pharmacies – of which there are many in Finland – and neighbourhood health care centres are good places to visit if you have a minor medical problem and can explain what it is. (Pharmacy is *apteekki* in Finnish.) Hospital casualty wards will help if it's more serious, and will tell you if it's not. Hospitals, health care centres and pharmacies are indicated on the maps in this book and/or are mentioned in the text. Tourist offices and hotels can put you onto a doctor or dentist; your embassy will probably know one who speaks your language.

Visitors whose home countries have reciprocal medical-care agreements with Finland and who can produce a passport (or sickness insurance card or form E111 for those from EU countries) are charged the same rates as Finns – 50 mk for a visit to a doctor and 125 mk per day for hospitalisation. Those from other countries are charged the full cost of treatment.

Environmental Hazards

Jet Lag Jet lag is experienced when a person travels by air across more than three time zones (each time zone usually represents a one hour time difference). It occurs because many of the functions of the human body (such as temperature, pulse rate and emptying of the bladder and bowels) are regulated by internal 24 hour cycles. When we travel long distances rapidly, our bodies take time to adjust to the 'new time' of our destination, and we may experience fatigue, disorientation, insomnia, anxiety, impaired concentration and loss of appetite. These effects will usually be gone within three days of arrival, but to minimise the impact of jet lag:

- Rest for a couple of days prior to departure.
- Try to select flight schedules that minimise sleep deprivation; arriving late in the day means you can go to sleep soon after you arrive. For very long flights, try to organise a stopover.
- Avoid excessive eating (which bloats the stomach) and alcohol (which causes dehydration) during the flight. Instead, drink plenty of noncarbonated, nonalcoholic drinks such as fruit juice or water.
- Avoid smoking.
- Make yourself comfortable by wearing loose-fitting clothes and perhaps bringing an eye mask and earplugs to help you sleep.
- Try to sleep at the appropriate time for the time zone you are going to.

Motion Sickness Eating lightly before and during a trip will reduce the chances of motion sickness. If you are prone to motion sickness try to find a place that minimises movement – near the wing on aircraft, close to midships on boats, near the centre on buses. Fresh air usually helps; reading and cigarette smoke don't. Commercial motion-sickness preparations, which can cause drowsiness, have to be taken before the trip commences. Ginger (available in capsule form) and peppermint (including mint-flavoured sweets) are natural preventatives.

Hypothermia If you are trekking in Lapland or simply staying outdoors for long periods, particularly in winter, be prepared for the cold. In fact, if you are out walking or hitching, be prepared for cold, wet or windy conditions even in summer.

Hypothermia occurs when the body loses heat faster than it can produce it and the core temperature of the body falls. It is surprisingly easy to progress from very cold to dangerously cold due to a combination of wind, wet clothing, fatigue and hunger, even if the air temperature is above freezing. It is best to dress in layers; silk, wool and some of the new artificial fibres are all good insulating materials. A hat is important, as a lot of heat is lost through the head. A strong, waterproof outer layer (and a 'space' blanket for emergencies) is essential. Carry basic supplies, including food containing simple sugars to generate heat quickly and fluid to drink.

Symptoms of hypothermia are exhaustion, numb skin (particularly toes and fingers), shivering, slurred speech, irrational or violent behaviour, lethargy, stumbling, dizzy spells, muscle cramps and violent bursts of energy. Irrationality may take the form of sufferers claiming they are warm and trying to take off their clothes.

To treat mild hypothermia, first get the person out of the wind and/or rain, remove their clothing if it's wet and replace it with dry, warm clothing. Give them hot liquids – not alcohol – and some high-kilojoule, easily digestible food. Do not rub victims, but instead allow them to slowly warm themselves. This should be enough to treat the early stages of hypothermia. The early recognition and treatment of mild hypothermia is the only way to prevent severe hypothermia, which is a critical condition.

Sunburn You can get sunburnt surprisingly quickly, even through cloud. Use a sunscreen, hat, and barrier cream for your nose and lips. Calamine lotion or Stingose are good for mild sunburn. Protect your eyes with good-quality sunglasses, particularly if you are going near water, sand or snow.

Fungal Infections Hot weather fungal infections are most likely to occur on the scalp, between the toes or fingers (athlete's foot), in the groin (jock itch or crotch rot) and on the body (ringworm). You get ringworm (which is a fungal infection, not a worm) from infected animals or by walking in damp areas, like the shower floors in Finnish saunas.

To prevent fungal infections wear loose, comfortable clothes, avoid synthetic fibres, wash frequently and dry carefully. If you do get an infection, wash the infected area daily with a disinfectant or medicated soap and water, and rinse and dry well. Apply an antifungal powder like the widely available Tinaderm. Try to expose the infected area to air or sunlight as much as possible and wash all towels and underwear in hot water as well as changing them often.

Infectious Diseases

Diarrhoea Simple things like a change of water, food or climate can all cause a mild bout of diarrhoea, but a few rushed toilet trips with no other symptoms is not indicative of a major problem.

Dehydration is the main danger with any diarrhoea, particularly in children or the elderly as dehydration can occur quite quickly. Under all circumstances *fluid replacement* (at least equal to the volume being lost) is the most important thing to remember.

Weak black tea with a little sugar, soda water, or soft drinks allowed to go flat and diluted 50% with clean water are all good.

Sexually Transmitted Diseases Gonorrhoea, herpes and syphilis are among these diseases; sores, blisters or rashes around the genitals, discharges or pain when urinating are common symptoms. In some STDs, such as wart virus or chlamydia, symptoms may be less marked or not observed at all, especially in women. Syphilis symptoms eventually disappear completely but the disease continues and can cause severe problems in later years. While abstinence from sexual contact is the only 100% effective prevention, using condoms is also effective. The treatment of gonorrhoea and syphilis is with antibiotics. The different STD's each require specific antibiotics. There is no cure for herpes or AIDS.

HIV & AIDS HIV, the Human Immunodeficiency Virus, develops into AIDS, Acquired Immune Deficiency Syndrome, which is a fatal disease. HIV is a major problem in many countries. Any exposure to blood, blood products or body fluids may put the individual at risk. The disease is often transmitted through sexual contact or dirty needles – vaccinations, acupuncture, tattooing and body piercing can be potentially as dangerous as intravenous drug use. HIV/AIDS can also be spread through infected blood transfusions; some developing countries cannot afford to screen blood used for transfusions.

If you do need an injection, ask to see the syringe unwrapped in front of you, or take a needle and syringe pack with you. Fear of HIV infection should never preclude treatment for serious medical conditions.

For assistance while in Finland contact the AIDS Information & Support Centre (☎ 09-665 081), Linnankatu 2B, 00160 Helsinki.

Cuts, Bites & Stings

Mosquitoes In Finland, the mosquito breeding season is very short (about six weeks in July/August), but the mosquitoes make good use of the time. They are a major nuisance in most parts of Finland, and those in Lapland are particularly large, fierce and persistent.

The best way to handle the mosquito problem is through prevention. From June to August, travellers are advised to wear light-coloured clothing, particularly long pants and long sleeved shirts, and avoid highly scented perfumes or aftershave. Use *Ohvi* (mosquito repellent) liberally; the 'Off' brand seems to be particularly effective. If you have a mosquito net, use this too. There are net hats available in sports shops; if you don't mind how absurd they look these are useful for treks and outdoor activities.

When all else fails, look for Etono, a concentrated antihystemine salve that is sold in stick form, for relief from mosquito bites. It is available at most pharmacies for about 30 mk.

Insect Bites & Stings Bee and wasp stings are usually painful rather than dangerous. However in people who are allergic to them severe breathing difficulties may occur and require urgent medical care. Calamine lotion or Stingose spray will give relief and ice packs will reduce the pain and swelling.

Cuts & Scratches Wash well and treat any cut with an antiseptic such as povidone-iodine. Where possible avoid bandages and Band-aids, which can keep wounds wet.

Ticks You should always check all over your body if you have been walking through a potentially tick-infested area – this would include rural areas of the Åland islands – as ticks can cause skin infections and other more serious diseases. If a tick is found attached, press down around the tick's head with tweezers, grab the head and gently pull upwards. Avoid pulling the rear of the body as this may squeeze the tick's gut contents through the attached mouth parts into the skin, increasing the risk of infection and disease. Smearing chemicals on the tick will not make it let go and is not recommended.

Snakes To minimise your chances of being bitten always wear boots, socks and long trousers when walking through undergrowth where snakes may be present. Don't put your hands into holes and crevices, and be careful when collecting firewood.

Snake bites do not cause instantaneous death and antivenenes are usually available. Immediately wrap the bitten limb tightly, as you would for a sprained ankle, and then attach a splint to immobilise it. Keep the victim still and seek medical help, if possible with the dead snake for identification. Don't attempt to catch the snake if there is a possibility of being bitten again.

Tourniquets and sucking out the poison are now comprehensively discredited.

Women's Health
Gynaecological Problems Sexually transmitted diseases are a major cause of vaginal problems. Symptoms include a smelly discharge, painful intercourse and sometimes a burning sensation when urinating. Male sexual partners must also be treated. Medical attention should be sought and remember in addition to these diseases HIV or hepatitis B may also be acquired during exposure. Besides abstinence, the best thing is to practise safe sex using condoms.

Antibiotic use, synthetic underwear, sweating and contraceptive pills can lead to fungal vaginal infections when travelling in hot climates. Maintaining good personal hygiene, and wearing loose-fitting clothes and cotton underwear will help to prevent these infections. Fungal infections, characterised by a rash, itch and discharge, can be treated with a vinegar or lemon-juice douche, or with yoghurt. Nystatin, miconazole or clotrimazole pessaries or vaginal cream are the usual treatment.

Pregnancy Most miscarriages occur during the first three months of pregnancy. Miscarriage is not uncommon, and can occasionally lead to severe bleeding. The last three months should also be spent within reasonable distance of good medical care. A baby born as early as 24 weeks stands a chance of survival, but only in a good modern hospital.

Additional care should be taken to prevent illness and particular attention should be paid to diet and nutrition. Alcohol and nicotine, for example, should be avoided.

WOMEN TRAVELLERS
Scandinavia is one of the safest places to travel in all of Europe. Women often travel alone or in pairs around the region, which should pose no problems, but women do tend to attract more unwanted attention than men, and common sense is the best guide to dealing with potentially dangerous situations like hitchhiking, walking alone at night etc.

Solo women are particularly vulnerable to harassment at Finnish pubs – that's a scene you might want to avoid, or at least gear yourself for plenty of unwanted attention.

Unioni Naisasialiitto Suomessa (☎ 09-643 158) at Bulevardi 11A, 00120 Helsinki is the national feminist organisation.

Recommended reading is the *Handbook for Women Travellers* by M & G Moss, published by Piatkus Books (London).

GAY & LESBIAN TRAVELLERS
Though nowhere in Finland will you find the equivalent of Copenhagen's large and active gay community, it is in most respects as tolerant as other Nordic countries. Current information can be obtained from SETA (Seksuaalinen Tasavertaisus; ☎ 09-135 8302, fax 09-135 8306), Postios, PL55, 00531 Helsinki, the Finnish organisation for gay and lesbian equality.

The *Spartacus Inernational Gay Guide*, published by Bruno Gmünder Verlag (Berlin), is an excellent international directory of gay entertainment venues, but it's best used in conjunction with more up-to-date information; as elsewhere, gay venues can change with the speed of summer lightning. *Places for Women* (Ferrari Publications) is the best international guide for lesbians.

DISABLED TRAVELLERS
By law, most public and private institutions must provide ramps, lifts and special toilets for disabled persons, making Finland one of the easiest countries to negotiate. Trains and

city buses are also accessible by wheelchair. Some national parks offer accessible nature trails. Rullaten Ry (☎ 09-694 1155), Malminkatu 38, 00100 Helsinki is the Finnish disabled travellers organisation. It specialises in advice on 'friendly' hotels. A booklet is available.

If you have a physical disability, get in touch with your national support organisation – preferably the 'travel officer' if there is one. These places often have complete libraries devoted to travel, and can put you in touch with travel agents who specialise in tours for the disabled.

The British-based Royal Association for Disability & Rehabilitation (RADAR) publishes a useful guide titled *European Holidays & Travel: A Guide for Disabled People* (UK£5), which gives a good overview of facilities available to disabled travellers in Europe (in even numbered-years) and farther afield (in odd-numbered years). Contact RADAR (☎ 0171-250 3222, after April 2000, ☎ 020-7250 3222) at 12 City Forum, 250 City Rd, London EC1V 8AF.

SENIOR TRAVELLERS

Senior citizens are entitled to many discounts on public transport, museum admission fees etc, provided they can show proof of their age (such as a passport). The minimum qualifying age is generally 60 or 65.

In your home country, a lower age may already entitle you to all sorts of interesting travel packages and discounts (on car hire, for instance) through organisations and travel agents that cater for senior travellers. Start hunting at your local senior citizens advice bureau.

TRAVEL WITH CHILDREN

People with children should definitely visit Finland: it's one of the most child-friendly countries around. Domestic tourism is largely dictated by children's needs: theme parks, water parks and so on, not to mention a real live Santa Claus waiting to greet children in Lapland, at the Arctic Circle! Most Finnish hostels have special 'family' rooms,

supermarkets stock everything your children need and many trains and ferries have special children's play areas. If in doubt, ask around – special needs can usually be met.

Car-rental firms have children's safety seats for hire at a nominal cost, but it is essential that you book them in advance. The same goes for highchairs and cots (cribs); they're standard in many restaurants and hotels, but numbers may be limited.

Successful travel with young children requires planning and effort. Don't try to overdo things; even for adults, packing too much into the time available can cause problems. And make sure the activities include the kids as well – balance a day at museums with a trip to one of Finland's amusement parks. Include your children in the trip planning; if they've helped to work out where you will be going, they will be much more interested when they get there. Lonely Planet's *Travel with Children* by Maureen Wheeler is a good source of information.

USEFUL ORGANISATIONS

The following organisations may assist you with information and support:

Finnish British Society – friendship society for Britons and Finns; (☎ 639 625) Puistokatu 16A, 00140 Helsinki

League of Finnish-American Societies – friendly contacts between Americans and Finns; (☎ 440 711) Mechelininkatu 10A, 00100 Helsinki

League of Finnish-Australian Societies – friendly contacts between Aussies and Finns; (☎ 631 549) Mariankatu 8, 00170 Helsinki

DANGERS & ANNOYANCES

Finland is generally a very safe, nonthreatening country to travel in but there are other potential risks to consider. You can easily get lost in rural Finland, including forests and national parks. There are few people around, and if you injure yourself and can't get away, the cold climate might even kill you.

Weather extremes in Lapland can cause unexpected danger at any time of the year. Extreme cold kills lone trekkers almost every winter in the wilderness, and cold rain can also be a problem in summer.

June and July are the worst months for mosquitoes in Lapland. Insect repellent or hat nets are essential.

In more remote places you may run across eccentric people, who you will have to accept as they are: sometimes extremely frustrated (even aggressive) and suspicious of outsiders. The gloom that winter brings may lead to unpredictable behaviour and alcohol abuse.

In urban areas, violence mostly occurs in association with intoxicated local males. Foreign men of dark complexion run the highest risk of street harassment.

Although theft isn't a major problem in Finland, you should use normal precautions, particularly when in busy markets or at crowded festivals – pickpockets do their work here. Parked cars are prime targets for petty criminals in most cities, and cars with foreign number plates and/or rental agency stickers are particularly targeted. If possible, remove the stickers or cover them with something, leave a local newspaper on the seat and generally try to make it look like a local car. Don't ever leave valuables in the car. Likewise, don't leave valuables unsecured in hostels and hotels.

Whatever you do, don't leave friends and relatives back home worrying about how to get in touch with you in case of an emergency. Work out a list of places where they can contact you, or best of all, phone home now and then.

LEGAL MATTERS
Traffic laws are strict, as are drug laws. However, police usually treat bonafide tourists politely in less serious situations. Fishing without a permit is illegal.

BUSINESS HOURS
Banks are open weekdays from 9.15 am to 4.15 pm. Shops and post offices are generally open from 9 am to 5 pm weekdays, and to 1 pm on Saturday. Alko stores (the state-owned network of liquor stores) are open from 10 am to 5 pm weekdays, and until 2 pm Saturday.

In Helsinki you may find that some places (but not Alko stores) stay open until 8 or 9 pm on weekdays and keep Sunday hours, too.

Town markets run from about 7 am to 2 pm Monday to Saturday. Generally, churches open on Sunday morning after 9 am and close soon after the service, around 11.30 am.

Public holidays are taken seriously – absolutely everything shuts at 6 pm on holiday eve and reopens the morning after the holiday ends.

PUBLIC HOLIDAYS & SPECIAL EVENTS
Finland grinds to a halt twice a year: around Christmas (sometimes including the New Year) and during the Midsummer weekend at the end of June. Plan ahead and avoid travelling during those times.

The foremost special events are the Opera Festival in Savonlinna and Jazz Festival in Pori, as well as Midsummer in any part of Finland – though every town and city in Finland puts on a barrage of festivals between mid-June and mid-August! A few smaller communities arrange some of the weirdest events imaginable (eg the Wife-Carrying World Championships in Iisalmi).

Pick up the 'Finland Festivals' booklet in any tourist office – see www.festivals.fi/ or contact Finland Festivals (☎ 09-621 4224; info@mail.festivals.fi) at Uudenmaankatu 36, 00120 Helsinki.

Public Holidays

New Year's Day	1 January
Epiphany	6 January
Good Friday	March/April
Easter	March/April
May Day Eve	30 April
May Day	1 May
Ascension Day	May
Whit Sunday	Late May or early June
Midsummer's Eve & Day	Third weekend in June
All Saints Day	1 November
Independence Day	6 December
Christmas Eve	24 December
Christmas Day	25 December
Boxing Day	26 December

Special Events

February

Runeberg Day
5 February, nationwide. People eat 'Runeberg cakes', available in all shops, to commemorate the national poet.

Laskiainen
Seven weeks before Easter, nationwide. Festival of downhill skiing and winter sports. People eat *laskiaispulla*, a wheat bun with whipped cream and hot milk.

Jyväskylä Winter Festival
Jyväskylä; concerts, dance.

Northern Lights Festival
Rovaniemi; sports and arts events.

March

Pääsiäinen
Easter. On Sunday people go to church or paint eggs and eat *mämmi* (pudding made of rye and malt).

Tampereen Elokuvajuhlat
Tampere; festival of international short films.

Oulu Music Festival
Oulu; classical and chamber music.

Finnish Ice Fishing Championships
Lohja; Lake Lohanjarvi, ice fishing.

Lahti Ski Games
Lahti; ski jumping.

Tar Skiing Race
Oulu; long-distance cross-country ski race.

Marathon Ice Fishing
Oulu; world's longest nonstop ice fishing contest.

Ounasvaara Winter Games
Rovaniemi; skiing and ski jumping competitions.

Maria's Day Festival
Hetta village, Enontekiö; Sami festival of arts, sports contests.

April

Tampere Biennale
Tampere; new Finnish music. Held in even-numbered years only.

Hetan Musiikkipäivät
Hetta village, Enontekiö; chamber music.

April Jazz Espoo
Espoo; jazz.

Reindeer Champion Race
Inari; reindeer sleigh racing.

May

Vappu
May Day, traditionally a festival of students and workers, also marks the beginning of summer, and is celebrated with plenty of alcohol and merrymaking. People drink *sima* mead and eat *tippaleipä* cookies.

Äitienpäivä
Mothers' Day. Everyone takes their mother out for buffet lunch.

Kemin Sarjakuvapäivät
Kemi; international cartoon festival.

Kainuun Jazzkevät
Kajaani; international jazz, blues, rock acts.

Vaasa Chorus Festival
Vaasa; European choirs.

June

Midsummer's Eve & Day
Juhannus (Midsummer) is the most important annual event for Finns. Celebrated with bonfires and dancing. People leave cities and towns for summer cottages to celebrate the longest day of the year. It is also the day of the Finnish flag, as well as the day of John the Baptist.

Praasniekka
These Orthodox celebrations are day-long religious and folk festivals held in North Karelia and in other eastern provinces between May and September, most notably at the end of June.

Koljonvirta Wood Sculpting Week
Iisalmi and Koljonvirta; wood sculpting done traditionally and with a chainsaw.

Pispala Schottishce
Tampere; international folk dance and music.

Ilmajoen Music Festival
Ilmajoki; classical and folk music, folk operas.

Naantali Music Festival
Naantali; chamber music.

Jutajaiset
Rovaniemi; folk music and dance, Lapp traditions.

Midnight Sun Film Festival
Sodankylä; international films.

Down By The Laituri
Turku; rock music.

Riihimäen kesäkonsertit
Riihimäki; classical music.

Provinssirock
Seinäjoki; rock music.

Nummirock
Kauhajoki; rock music.

Åland Organ Festival
Åland; organ music in medieval churches.

Korsholm Music Festival
Vaasa; chamber music.

Puistoblues
Järvenpää; blues, jazz.

Avanti! Summer Sounds
Porvoo; eclectic music from baroque to rock.

International Kalottjazz and Blues Festival
Tornio (Finland) and Haparanda (Sweden); jazz, blues.

Kuopio Tanssii ja Soi
Kuopio; international dance.

Imatra Big Band Festival
Imatra; big band music.

Ruisrock
Turku; oldest and largest rock music festival.

Mikkeli Music Festival
Mikkeli; classical music.

Sata-Häme Soi
Ikaalinen; accordion music.

Midnight Sun Golf Tournament
Tornio (Finland) and Haparanda (Sweden); golf competition.

Postrodden Mail Boat Race
Eckerö (Åland) and Grisslehamn (Sweden); rowing and sailing race.

Jyväskylän Kesä
Jyväskylä; music, visual arts.

Helsinki Day
Helsinki; celebrating founding of Helsinki on 12 June.

Tar Burning Week
Oulu; Midsummer festival.

July

Rauma Lace Week
Rauma; lacemaking demonstrations, carnival.

Festivo
Rauma; chamber music.

Isosaari Rock
Joensuu; rock music.

Savonlinna Opera Festival
Savonlinna; One of Finland's most notable festivals.

Tangomarkkinat
Seinäjoki; tango music.

International Pori Jazz Festival
Pori; One of Finland's most notable festivals.

Hamina Tatoo
Hamina; military music.

Kaustinen Folk Music Festival
Kaustinen; folk music and dance.

Kuhmon Kamarimusiikki
Kuhmo; chamber music.

Joensuu Gospel Festival
Joensuu; gospel music.

Lieksan Vaskiviikko
Lieksa; brass music.

Elojazz & Blues
Oulu; jazz, blues.

Kymenlaakson Folk Art & Music Festival
Miehikkälä; folk music, traditions.

Työväen Musiikkitapahtuma
Valkeakoski; workers' music.

Joutsa Folk Festival
Joutsa; traditional Finnish summer festival.

Wife-Carrying World Championships
Sonkajärvi; unusual husband-and-wife team competition with international participants and big prizes.

Bomba Festival
Nurmes; Karelian folklore festival.

Evakon Pruasniekka
Iisalmi; traditional festival of the Orthodox church.

Kotka Maritime Festival
Kotka; music, sailing races, cruises.

Sleepyhead Day
On 27 July the laziest person in the town of Naantali is thrown into the sea.

Kihaus Folk Music Festival
Rääkkylä; widely acclaimed festival of modern and experimental Finnish folk music and dancing.

Pirkan Soutu
Tampere; rowing competition.

August

Taiteiden yö
A night of art, held in Helsinki and other towns in late August. Street performances, fringe art, concerts – a good atmosphere and exciting.

Lappeenranta Music Festival
Lappeenranta and Lemi; festival of international music.

Tampere International Theatre Festival
Tampere; international and Finnish theatre.

Gipsy Music Festival
Porvoo; concerts and carnival.

Crusell-Viikko
Uusikaupunki; chamber music, especially clarinet.

Savonlinna Beer Festival
Savonlinna; food and beer festival at Savonlinna castle.

Lahden Urkuviikko
Lahti; organ music.

Turku Music Festival
Turku; classical and contemporary music.

Lahti Jazz Festival
Lahti; jazz.

Helsinki Festival
Helsinki; all-arts festival.

Helsinki City Marathon
Helsinki; foot race.

September

Ruska Swing
Kemijärvi; swing dancing and music.

Savonlinna Theatre Festival
Savonlinna; international theatre festival at Savonlinna castle.

October
Oulaisten Musiikkiviikot
Oulainen; eclectic music.
Tampere Jazz Happening
Tampere; jazz music.
Baltic Herring Market
Helsinki; traditional outdoor herring market.

November
All Souls' Day
The first Saturday of November sees people visit the graves of deceased friends and relatives.
Etnosoi
Helsinki; ethnic music.
Oulu International Children's Film Festival
Oulu; international children's films.

December
Itsenäisyyspäivä
Finland celebrates independence on 6 December with torchlight processions, fireworks and concerts.
Pikkujoulu
'Little Christmas.'
Joulu
Christmas is a family celebration.

LANGUAGE COURSES

The Council for Instruction of Finnish for Foreigners (UKAN) offers accelerated courses in Finnish each summer at the universities in Helsinki, Rauma, Savonlinna, Kuopio and Jyväskylä. Those who wish to participate must submit an application. For more information contact UKAN at the Centre for International Mobility (CIMO; ☎ 09-7747 7067, fax 09-7747 7064), PO Box 343, 00531 Helsinki. The CIMO office is at Hakanimenkatu 2 in Helsinki.

Additionally, the following universities teach basic (or 'survival') courses in Finnish language and culture, with classes typically running a full term and costing about 1000 mk:

University of Helsinki
Language Centre (☎ 09-1912 3234 or 09-1912 3110, fax 09-1912 2551), PO Box 33, 00141 Helsinki

University of Jyväskylä
Language Centre & Department of Finnish (☎ 014-603 761, fax 014-603 751, kalin@tukki.jyu.fi), PO Box 35, 40351 Jyväskylä
University of Oulu
Language Centre (☎ 08-553 3200, fax 08-553 3203), PO Box 111, 90571 Oulu
Unversity of Tampere
Language Centre & Department of Finnish Language and General Linguistics, PO Box 607, 33101 Tampere
University of Turku
Language Centre (☎ 02-333 5975), Horttokuja 2, 20014 Turku

WORK

There is very little work open to foreigners due to high local unemployment. It's possible to get a job teaching English at a Finnish company, but standards are very high so previous experience and good references are essential. Students can apply for limited summer employment, and au pair arrangements are possible for up to 18 months.

Work Permits

For any serious career-oriented work, a work permit is required of all foreigners other than EU and EEA citizens. Employment must be secured before applying for the work permit, and the work permit must be filed in advance of arrival in Finland, together with a letter from the intended employer and other proofs of employment. Work permits can be obtained from the Finnish embassy in your home country. A residence permit may also be required (see the earlier Visas & Documents section). For more information contact the Directorate of Immigration (☎ 09-476 5500, fax 09-4765 5858), PO Box 92, 00531 Helsinki, or see www.uvi.fi/.

Street Performing

Tim Morgan of England has written to us to say that if you have a good voice and/or a musical instrument and are a bit short of cash, you should consider busking in Finland.

The major towns – Rovaniemi, Oulu, Tampere, Turku and Helsinki – are good starting points. Rules about licences generally aren't enforced if you're considerate and only stick around for a day or two. English songs go down very well, especially those of The Beatles. Even a moderate talent can bring in several hundred markkaa a day.

Gather your courage and give it a go!

ACCOMMODATION

Accommodation in Finland doesn't necessarily have to be expensive. Most of the wilderness huts along trekking routes are absolutely free. Hostels are probably a bit cheaper than in the USA or Western Europe on average, and several people can share cottages at camping grounds. Hotels are more expensive but there are discounts in summer. The Finnish Tourist Board publishes an annual budget accommodation guide, available at local tourist offices.

Camping

There are more than 200 official camping grounds in Finland. They tend to cater for caravans rather than those carrying their own tents, but are still fine if you're looking for somewhere to sleep on the cheap. Note that the majority are open only in summer, eg late May to mid or late August at the latest, and some only open during June and July. Tent sites cost from 35 to 80 mk, with discounts given for camping cards (see the Visas & Documents section). Typical camping ground facilities include a kitchen area, laundry, sauna, children's play area, boat and bicycle rentals, and café or grilli – and the majority are near a river, a lake or the sea.

What makes camping grounds in Finland so recommendable is the availability of pleasant cabins and bungalows. If you have a group of two to six, prices are comparable to hostels, typically starting at 100 mk for two-bed cottages and 150 mk for four-bed cottages. Amenities vary, but a kitchen, toilet and shower are not uncommon. Some even have microwave ovens and TV sets.

In Finland the Right of Public Access (*jokamiehenoikeus*) grants you legal permission to temporarily pitch your tent in a wide range of places. See the Trekking section in the Activities chapter for more information.

Hostels

Hostels in Finland offer the best value for money, in most cases. There are close to 150 hostels in Finland, and about half are open all year. You won't find two that are similar – they are at university dorm buildings, in manors or schoolhouses, at the heart of big cities and way, way out in the boonies.

The majority of Finnish hostels are run by the Finnish Youth Hostel Association (SRM) and are affiliated with Hostelling International (HI). The average cost is less than 100 mk per person per night. Most hostels offer private single and double rooms as well, at higher rates (but still much cheaper than hotels). There are often special 'family' rooms, and special discounts for families.

If you have an HI card you'll receive a 15 mk discount on the rates quoted in this book. Of course, you may stay at a hostel even without an HI card, and there are no age restrictions, despite the term 'youth' hostel.

You should also bring your own sheets (or sleeping sheet) and pillowcase, as linen rentals cost 15 to 30 mk extra. Sleeping bags are not considered acceptable substitutes. Breakfast is generally not included in the price, but is available for 25 mk.

Often you may use the kitchen, although youth hostels that are farmhouses or in rural locations may not have a kitchen. In ordinary town hostels (normally student dormitories), the kitchen may not have any utensils. Saunas are common at hostels – although there may be a small surcharge to use them. Laundry facilities also may be used for a small additional fee.

The free publication *Hostellit* gives a full listing of all HI-affiliated Finnish hostels. For more information on hostelling cards and the SRM, see the Visas & Documents section.

Guesthouses

Guesthouses in Finland, called *matkakoti* or *matkustajakoti*, are usually slightly run-down establishments meant for travelling salespeople and other more dubious types.

They're usually in town centres near the train station.

However, there are a few guesthouses out there – usually in smaller villages – that just don't fit the category. These places are exceptionally clean and offer pleasant, homey accommodation in old wooden houses. Ask to see a room before paying – that's the best way to know what you're getting.

Hotels

Most hotels in Finland cater to upscale businesspeople. They are quite luxurious, service tends to be good and the restaurants and nightclubs may be some of the most popular in town. Listed prices are definitely out of reach for most budget travellers, from around 450 mk for a single. There is some good news – hotels offer much lower rates on weekends, usually Friday through Sunday. And after Midsummer, hotel rates drop drastically and remain that way through to the end of summer. At that time, you can get a 600 mk room for as little as 350 mk. A bargain in practically all Finnish hotels is the buffet breakfast. Hotel guests will need no lunch!

Finncheque The Finncheque plan, available in most chain hotels throughout Finland, allows accommodation in 140 designated luxury hotels at the discounted price of 200 mk per person in a double room. Each Finncheque is a 'coupon' good for one night's stay at a participating hotel (you purchase as many as you need), and any supplements are paid directly to the hotel. Finncheques are valid from mid-May to late September. They may be purchased at a participating hotel or through a travel agency in your home country. If you're travelling during July and August, however, when hotels offer discounted summer prices, you may find Finncheques unnecessary.

Wilderness Huts

See the Activities chapter for details on huts, shelters and other options on trekking routes.

Holiday Cabins & Cottages

There are thousands of cabins and cottages for rent around Finland. They can be booked through regional tourist offices, generally for 1200 mk a week or more for four people. Rarely are these available on a nightly basis, although weekend rentals are possible.

Holiday cabins and cottages are terrific if you'd like to settle down to enjoy a particular corner of the Finnish countryside. They are usually fully equipped with cooking utensils, sauna and rowing boat, although the cheapest, most 'rustic' ones may lack electricity and require that you fetch your own water at a well. However, this is considered a true vacation, Finnish-style.

Prices are highest during Midsummer and the skiing holidays, when you'll need to book well in advance. Tax is not necessarily included in quoted prices. The following are a few companies that specialise in cottage rentals:

Ålandsresor
    (☎ 018-28040, fax 018-28380), PO Box 62, 22101 Mariehamn
Järvi-Savo
    (☎ 015-365 399, fax 015-365 080), Hallituskatu 2, 50100 Mikkeli
Lomarengas
    (☎ 09-3516 1321, fax 09-3516 1370), Malminkaari 23C, 00700 Helsinki
Saimaatours
    (☎ 05-411 7722, fax 05-415 6609), Kirkkokatu 10, 53100 Lappeenranta

---

Summer Cottages

A quarter of the population of Finland owns a summer cottage or *kesämökki*, and the majority of Finns at least have access to one. The *mökki* should ideally be located on the shores of a lake and surrounded by forest. A genuine mökki has only basic amenities – some have no electricity or running water – but always come equipped with a sauna and a rowing boat. These days you can rent a mökki with a fridge, a television and even a telephone!

Farmstays

Many farmhouses around Finland offer bed and breakfast accommodation, a unique opportunity to meet local people and experience their way of life. They offer plenty of activities, too, from horseback riding to helping with a harvest. Some farmstays are independent, family-run affairs, while others are loosely gathered under an umbrella organisation. In general, prices are good – from around 150 mk per night, country breakfast included. The drawback is that farms are – by their very nature – off major roadways and bus routes, so you'll need your own transport (or enough money for taxi fare) to reach them. However, a night at a Finnish farm is certainly a worthy addition to any trip. Some farmstays are listed in this book, and others can be arranged through local tourist offices or by contacting one of the organisations listed below.

Lomarengas
(☎ 09-3516 1321, fax 09-3516 1370), Malminkaari 23C, 00700 Helsinki
Suomen 4H-Liitto
(☎ 09-645 133, fax 09-604 612), Bulevardi 28, 00120 Helsinki

Rental Accommodation

Rental apartments start at something like 2000 mk per month, including utilities. Student apartments rent for as low as 500 mk per month, including utilities, for a *solu* room with a shared kitchen and bathroom. You must be enrolled at a Finnish university or some other educational institution to qualify for student housing.

FOOD

Restaurant meals are expensive in Finland, particularly at dinner. Fortunately most restaurants offer lunch specials from about 30 mk, usually served from 11 am to 2 pm weekdays. These include generous helpings of typical Finnish food, plus salad, bread, milk, coffee and dessert. Only large towns have international restaurants, but these may offer lunch specials as well. University eateries are terrific for travellers: you pay 15 to 20 mk for a full meal.

Cafés in Finland serve snacks, light meals and desserts, as well as coffee – and lots of it! Finns drink more coffee per capita than any other people on earth. A *kahvila* is a café, a *kahvio* is a café inside a supermarket or petrol station, and a *baari* serves snacks, beer and soft drinks, and probably also coffee.

Most hostels and hotels offer breakfast from about 25 mk. Although you get plenty of food for your money (cereal, breads, pastries, porridge, eggs, fruit, sausage, cheese, juice and more) it's cheaper to self-cater.

Warning: the Finns eat their largest meal of the day at lunchtime, and many cheaper restaurants close their kitchens (or shut entirely) around 5 pm.

In Finland, service charge and sales tax is included in the advertised price.

Local Food

Finnish food has elements of both Swedish and Russian cuisines. Originally it was designed to nourish a peasant population who did outdoor manual work in cold weather. Consequently, Finnish food was heavy and fatty, made of fish, game, meat, milk and dairy products, oats, barley and dark rye in the form of porridges and bread, with few spices other than salt and pepper. Vegetables were rarely used in everyday meals, except in casseroles. Potato was the staple food, served with various fish or meat sauces.

So what's modern Finnish cuisine like? Well, little has changed. Soups such as pea soup, meat soup, cabbage soup and fish soup are common. Hot and heavy dishes, including liver, Baltic herring, turnip and cabbage, and even carrot casseroles, are served as the main course or as part of it. Fish dishes – prepared from whitefish, Baltic herring and salmon, and trout – are common everywhere.

In restaurants, Finnish food is generally served as 'home-made', and it makes an inexpensive lunch. 'Gourmet' Finnish cuisine is not easy to find – but a 40 to 60 mk *seisova pöytä* (smorgasbord) with soups, salads and fish dishes galore is a grand experience, something you should try at least once during your trip.

Like the *baguette* with camembert cheese and red wine in France, you can find some simple but tasty options in Finland. Take fresh, preferably still warm, brown rye bread, add medium-hard butter and plenty of cheese (say, Edam or Emmental), and enjoy with very cold milk or lager beer. Or try the Finnish version of sushi: salmon or herring slices on small new potatoes (available from July). Such fare is relatively cheap and delicious.

Fast Food

The *grilli* is the venue for an under 20 mk takeaway meal of hamburgers or hot dogs. It's usually little more than a roadside stand, with or without a few seats. Turkish kebab joints offer good value, and pizzerias serving inexpensive pies are ubiquitous.

McDonald's has hit Finland in a big way, but try the local chain, Hesburger – their burgers are priced the same, yet are meatier and better-tasting. A full burger meal is about 35 mk.

Although you wouldn't immediately think to go to a petrol station or bus terminal for dinner, in Finland these are respectable places to get a quick, hot, nutritious, cheap – and surprisingly good-tasting – meal.

Vegetarian

Finnish cuisine isn't overly friendly to vegetarians, so you might find it easier to self-cater, or rely on ethnic restaurants – Chinese, Thai etc – that reliably serve vegetarian meals. Unfortunately, such restaurants are scarce outside of the big cities of southern Finland, although some northern tourist centres such as Rovaniemi and Oulu also offer a good mix of dining options. There are only a handful of true vegetarian restaurants in Finland, and three of them are in Helsinki! Some others are in Turku and Jyväskylä. Whenever we've found them, we've included vegetarian restaurants in the Places to Eat sections of this book.

Another option if you are in a city with a university is to eat at the student cafeteria – these are required to carry at least one vegetarian dish at every meal. Best of all, student cafeterias are open to anyone, and you can eat a very filling meal for under 20 mk.

Self-Catering

Every town has a *kauppatori* (market square) where you can buy smoked fish, fresh produce (in season) pastries and the like. Many larger towns also have a *kauppahalli* (covered market) where stalls sell cheap, hot meals, sandwiches, meats, cheese, produce etc.

The main supermarket chains are K-Kauppa, T-Market and S-Market. Discount stores include Alepa, Eurospar, Rabatti, Säästäri and Siwa.

Relatively cheap food for a simple meal includes fresh potatoes, yoghurt, eggs, fresh or smoked fish and canned pea soup *(hernekeitto)* and, in late summer, any market vegetables. Salmon can be bought at reasonable prices if you shop around. Cheese, salami and meat are more expensive.

Shopping at discount stores, keeping your eyes open for discounts *(tarjous* means special price) and buying imported food, such as canned tuna fish, pineapple slices, sardines and bananas, are options to stretch the budget.

DRINKS

What is served in Finland as *olut* (beer) is generally light-coloured, lager-type beer, although Guinness stout and other dark brews have gained in popularity in recent years. There's also a growing number of microbreweries in Finland, and these make excellent light and dark beers. Particularly worthy of visits are the Tampere and Turku *panimoravintola* (brewery restaurants).

The strongest beer is called IVA, or *nelos olut*, with 5% alcohol. More popular is III Beer (called *keskari* or *kolmonen*) and I Beer (called *mieto olut* or *pilsneri)*, with less than 2% alcohol. Other local specialities include vodka, and cloudberry or cranberry liqueur.

In restaurants and bars, beer is sold by *tuoppi*. Small, or *pieni* tuoppi, is 0.3L, *iso* (big) tuoppi, or the *pitkä* is 0.5L.

Apart from light beer (which is sold in supermarkets), alcohol is retailed exclusively by the state-owned network of Alko liquor stores. Alcohol stronger than one-fifth by volume is not sold to those under 20 years of age. For beer and wine purchases the age limit is 18.

Beer costs about 25 mk a pint in bars, but as little as 5 mk a bottle in supermarkets. Wines cost 30 to 60 mk a bottle.

Soft drinks and bottled water are expensive, around US$3 for 1L of either. Local soft drinks include Jaffa, Aurinko, Frisco and Pommac. International brands are also widely available.

You pay a deposit for all glass bottles of locally bottled soft drink and beer; when you return them to any store, your deposit is refunded.

ENTERTAINMENT
Discos
Large hotels in most Finnish towns run a disco that opens late in the evening and remains open till 4 am or so. There's always an admission fee. Discos charge from 20 mk at the door, nightclubs up to 60 mk. The usual age limit is 18 or 20 years, sometimes 24.

Classical Music, Opera & Theatre
Live music is the best option if you're seeking high culture, and good classical concerts can be heard in many towns, often in churches and often for free. Inquire locally. Classical music festivals – many with outdoor venues – are extremely popular in Finnish cities and towns during summer.

Little Weekend
On Wednesday nights the restaurants are busy, music is playing at all the nightspots, the bars are full – Finns are celebrating *pikku viikonloppu*, or little weekend. Every mid-week this mini-oasis punctuates the working week.

Theatre performances are almost universally in Finnish and Swedish, and opera performances are subtitled in Finnish and Swedish. The exception is at the world-class Savonlinna Opera Festival.

Cinemas
Cinema tickets cost 40 mk. Films classified K are restricted to people over 16 or 18 years of age, films classified S are for general audiences. Foreign films are always in their original language with subtitles in Finnish and Swedish. Of the 180 or so films shown each year, approximately 100 are American movies. France is the second most popular source of imported movies. Britain is third and Sweden fourth. Finnish movies account for 15% to 25% of films shown.

SPECTATOR SPORTS
In winter, ice hockey is the leading magnet for the masses, with two or three matches weekly. Many indoor sports, including basketball and volleyball, also have their season in winter. Skiing events don't offer the same intensity as team sports, but national (and international) competitions provide a thrill worth experiencing.

You can watch flying Finns at the ski-jumping centres in Lahti, Kuopio and Jyväskylä. Jyväskylä is the home town and former training ground of Olympic champion Matti Nykänen. Ski jumping events are usually part of general ski tournaments, bu even practice sessions can be fascinating.

In summer, football (soccer) has a national league, and is followed diligently Outside big cities, Finnish baseball, called *pesäpallo* or simply *pesis*, is the mos popular team sport in summer.

Athletics (track and field) is very popula in Finland, owing to the country's many suc cessful long-distance runners and javelin throwers. The national games are calle Kalevan Kisat.

Car racing is another national craze, al though not many notable races are arrange annually. Jyväskylän Suurajot (the Thou sand Lakes Rally) is the main event, held in central Finland. While visiting some isolated rural areas, you may come to the conclusion that local drivers think they are in a car race.

SHOPPING

On the whole, prices in Finland are lower than in other Scandinavian countries – which isn't to say that there are any real bargains here, particularly on those items which Finland is famous for: glassware, pottery, woollens and various handicrafts made from pine or birch.

If you're heading to the Baltic countries – particularly to Tallin, Estonia, which can be visited on a day trip from Helsinki – you'll find that prices there are cheaper still, and on many of the same types of items, of more or less the same quality.

Lappish, or Sami handicrafts include jewellery, clothing and hunting knives, as well as other items made from locally found wood, reindeer bone and hide, metals and semi-precious stones. *Duodji* are authentic handicrafts produced according to Sami traditions. A genuine item, which can be expensive, will carry a special 'Duodji' token. Sami handicrafts can be found at markets and shops in Helsinki and throughout Lapland, but for the widest selections visit the Sami villages of Inari and Hetta (Enontekiö).

Trekkers will want to purchase a *kuksa* (cup) made in traditional Sami fashion from the burl of a birch tree. These are widely available throughout Finland, at markets and in handicraft or souvenir shops. Quality of workmanship varies, as does price, but the typical kuksa costs about 100 mk.

Local markets are a good place to purchase colourful woollen mittens (*lapaset*), hats (*myssy* or *pipo*) and sweaters (*villa-pusero*), necessary for surviving the cold Finnish winters, as well as woven wall-hangings (*raanu* or *ryijy*). A good hand-knitted sweater sells for about 2000

mk. Local folk – particularly in Åland – will often 'knit to order' taking your measurements and then posting the sweater to you in two or three months, once it's finished! It's possible to find cheaper, machine-knitted wool sweaters in Finnish markets, but check the labels – they probably were made in Norway.

If you don't care for other people's work, contact the nearest *Käsityöasema* (a centre that preserves cottage industries) and create your own handicrafts. There are hundreds of these in Finland, and many are especially geared towards visitors. You pay only for the material, plus a small fee for rental of the equipment.

For decades, Finland has been world-famous for its indigenous glass production. The Savoy vase designed by Alvar Aalto is a good 'souvenir of Finland', although expensive. Department stores and finer shops carry it as well as other stylish vases by Iittala, Nuutajärvi and Humppila. Big roadside discount shops also stock Finnish glassware, plus designer pottery and cooking utensils; most of this is schlock.

You can find quite nice kitchen utensils of carved pine, and attractive woven pine baskets, at local markets. Every Finnish market also seems to have an old man who makes birdhouses – these, too, are uniquely Finnish souvenirs.

Books in English may be scarce, but when you can find them they're seldom pricey, particularly the classics – Tolstoy's *War and Peace*, for example, can be yours for just 12 mk! The two main book-selling chains are Akateeminen and Suomalainen. You're only likely to find English-language books in the big university cities: Turku, Tampere and, of course, Helsinki.

It's possible – but unlikely – to find bargains on trekking goods such as jackets and down sleeping bags. Chains such as Partio-Aitta and Lassen Retkiaitta specialise in outdoor equipment, but many sports shops, such as Intersport or Kesport, also have good selections.

Activities

Finland may be an expensive country to visit, but some of the most popular activities, such as trekking, bicycling and canoeing, are surprisingly cheap. Better yet, these activities open up some of the most beautiful and fascinating corners of this northern country. Often, there is no 'next bus' waiting to take you to isolated national parks or small fishing villages. You will have to drive, pedal, paddle or walk to get there, and that's part of what makes Finland interesting.

Trekking

Trekking, or fell-walking, is one of the most popular summer activities in Finland. National parks offer marked trails, and most wilderness areas are crisscrossed by locally used walking paths. Nights are short or nonexistent in summer, so you can walk for as long as your heart desires (or at least until your feet start to complain). Water is abundant everywhere, and you can camp practically anywhere – although you should always check for restrictions at national parks, where bird nesting sites and other fragile areas are protected.

The trekking season runs from late May to September in most parts of the country. In Lapland and the north the ground is not dry enough for hiking until late June, and mosquitoes are a serious bother through July.

Trekkers are strongly advised not to go hiking alone. For those who still insist on going solo, it is highly recommended that you sign the trekkers' book as you depart. Write your name and next destination in the log at each hut you visit and don't forget to announce the completion of your trek.

RIGHT OF PUBLIC ACCESS

The *jokamiehenoikeus* (Swedish: *allemansrätt*), literally 'everyman's right', is a code that has been in effect in Finland for centuries. Basically, it gives travellers the right to go anywhere in Finland by land or water – as long as that person agrees to behave responsibly. A person may walk, ski or cycle anywhere in forests and other wilderness areas, and may even cross private land as long as he or she does not disturb the owners or destroy planted fields. Canoeing, rowing, and kayaking on lakes and rivers is also unrestricted; travel by motorboat and jet ski, on the other hand, is severely limited. Likewise, restrictions apply to snowmobiles, which are allowed on established routes only.

You can rest and swim anywhere in the Finnish countryside, and pitch a tent for one night *almost* anywhere. To camp on private property you will need the owner's permission. Camping is not permitted in town parks or on beaches.

Fishing is not restricted if you are using only a hook and line, but you will need a permit if you plan to use a reel (see the Fishing section later in this chapter). Hunting is not allowed unless you have a licence.

Watch out for stricter regulations regarding access in nature reserves and national parks. In these places, camping may be forbidden and travel confined to marked paths.

MAKING CAMPFIRES

Under the right of public access, you may not make a campfire on private land unless you have the owner's permission. In national parks, look for designated campfire areas called *nuotiopaikka* in Finnish, and watch for fire warning signs – *metsäpalovaroitus* means the fire risk is very high. When you do light fires, use extreme caution and chose a place near a river or lakefront if possible. Felling trees or cutting brush to make a campfire is forbidden; use downed wood instead.

GATHERING BERRIES & MUSHROOMS

It's permissible to pick berries and mushrooms – but not other kinds of plants – under

68

Finland's right of public access. Blueberries, which bring many walks to a halt, come into season in late July. Red cranberries are common in late summer (and a good source of vitamin C) but are very sour. They taste best after the first night frost and can also be made palatable crushed and mixed with sugar.

Orange cloudberries are so appreciated by Finns that you probably won't have a chance to sample this slightly sour berry in the wild. In some parts of Lapland, cloudberries are protected – hands off!

Edible mushrooms are numerous in Finnish forests, as are poisonous ones. Unless you already know everything there is to know about mushrooms, you should avoid gathering them, or at least buy a *sieniopas* (mushroom guidebook) and learn such words as *myrkyllinen* (poisonous), *keitettävä* (has to be boiled first) and *syötävä* (edible).

WHAT TO BRING

You can purchase trekking equipment in most Finnish cities at sporting goods stores and supermarkets such as Spar or Citymarket, but it won't be cheap. Your best bet is to bring your own. Kuusamo, a town near one of Finland's best trekking areas, has many shops selling trekkers' equipment and supplies, and prices are pretty good.

Food

You will have to carry all food when you walk in wilderness areas. Good packables that are commonly available in Finland includes oats, macaroni, *jälkiuunileipä* (rye bread), raisins, peanuts, chocolate, smoked fish, salami and soft cheese. Look for the Blå Band brand of trekking food packs in sports shops.

If you plan to walk from one wilderness hut to another, you will not need a cooking kit, but for unexpected situations it's good to have something to boil water in.

Fuel for Stoves

The most common fuels in Finland are kerosene (*petroli* or *paloöljy*), methylated

Things to Take

The following items are highly recommended for any sort of trek:

- all-weather trekking gear
- binoculars
- bottle (plastic)
- candle
- compass
- cup
- cutlery
- first aid kit
- knife
- matches/lighter
- mosquito repellent
- mosquito coil
- mosquito net
- net head cover
- plastic bags
- plate
- sleeping bag
- torch (flashlight)
- trekking maps

spirits (*spriitä*) and paraffin (*lamppuöljy*). Camping Gaz and other butane cartridges are not easily obtainable and you cannot refill the large butane cylinders used in caravans. Coleman fuel is also unavailable.

An MSR stove is recommended as these can handle a variety of fuel types, including kerosene and regular gasoline (*bensiini* or *kaasu*). This type of stove can be tricky to use, however, so familiarise yourself with the parts and maintenance *before* hitting the trail. Petrol stations, camping stores and marine chandlers are the places to go to purchase fuel.

Insect Repellent

Mosquitoes are a problem in Finland, particularly in summer, and particularly in Lapland, where they grow to be the size of elephants and are twice as dangerous. Skimp on protection at your own peril.

ACCOMMODATION

The Forest and Park Service maintains most of the country's wilderness huts. Many of these are free – Finland may be the only country in the world to provide such an extensive network of free, well-maintained wilderness huts – and others require advance booking and payment of 50 mk per person per night.

Huts typically have basic bunks, cooking facilities, a pile of dry firewood and even a wilderness telephone. You are required to leave hut as it was – ie, replenish the firewood and carry away your rubbish. The Finns' 'wilderness rule' states that the last one to arrive will be given the best place to sleep.

The largest network of wilderness huts is in Lapland. Outside Lapland, trekking routes generally have no free cabins, but you may find a simple log shelter, called *laavu* in Finnish. You can pitch your tent inside the laavu or just roll out your sleeping bag.

A 1:50,000 trekking map is recommended for finding wilderness huts.

TRANSPORT

Some trekking routes end in the middle of nowhere. Unless you have arranged for someone to meet you on arrival, you will have to walk to the nearest bus stop, which may be another long trek.

If there are private vehicles parked at the end point, you might want to leave a note under the windscreen wiper indicating that you have just finished a trek, and are walking down the road towards the bus stop. If you are lucky, a fellow trekker might offer you a lift. Remember, hitching is never entirely safe under any circumstances. Be sure to exert caution when accepting lifts from strangers, especially if you are travelling alone.

WHERE TO TREK

You can trek anywhere in Finland, but national parks and reserves will have marked routes, designated campfire places, well-

---

Wilderness Huts

Wilderness huts in Finland have different names, according to their various forms and uses. If you find one with a name that isn't on this list, chances are it's private property – which means that it's off-limits unless you first obtain permission from the owner.

Autiotupa – A general word for 'desolate hut', with unlocked doors, meagre facilities and hard bunks. You may cook inside.

Kammi – A traditional Lappish hut (that is, made out of earth, wood and branches), usually in a very remote location. It will provide basic shelter for one or two people.

Kämppä – This means simply 'a hut'. Kämpät are used by Sami reindeer keepers as a shelter, and are always open and uninhabited. They provide shelter for one to six people. In the south, kämpät are often private and locked.

Rajavartioston tupa – A small hut built for border guards. Most of them have unlocked doors, and sheltering overnight is legal. Keep a low profile, however, as the primary users have a serious mission.

Tunturitupa – A 'fell hut'. It has unlocked doors and basic sleeping and cooking facilities.

Varaustupa – 'A hut to be reserved'. This kind of hut always has a locked door, although some may also have an 'open' side. The reserved side has better facilities, including mattresses.

Yksityiskämppä – A private hut. It should not be used for any purpose other than as an emergency shelter when everything else fails.

A typical *autiotupa* hut

maintained wilderness huts and boardwalks over the boggy bits.

Lapland is the main trekking region, with large national parks that have well-equipped wilderness huts and good trekking routes. These include Pallas-Ounastunturi, Lemmenjoki, Pyhä-tunturi and Urho Kekkonen national parks. The Kevo Gorge Nature Reserve in the north-east corner of Lapland is also a good trekking area, although a tent is essential for travel here.

Some recommended treks are described below. Excellent trekking maps are available in Finland for all of these routes.

Karhunkierros (Bear's Ring) This circular trail in northern Finland is the most famous of all Finnish trekking routes. It covers 75km of rugged cliffs, gorges and suspension bridges from Rukatunturi, 25km north of Kuusamo to the Oulanka National Park. Huts provide shelter and free lodging en route, and there are good services and connections at several locations along the route.

Pirkan Taival In the south-western section of the Lakeland there are some 330km of marked walking tracks. Together, the tracks are called Pirkan taival, or 'trail of Pirkka'. Pirkan taival runs between Parkano and Ähtäri, via Seitseminen, Kuru, Ruovesi, Helvetinjärvi and Virrat. The Pirkan taival map, which is sold in the Tampere tourist information office for approximately 25 mk, shows all accommodation options along the tracks.

Susitaival (Wolf's Path) A 100km trail that runs along the border with Russia. The trail runs from the marshlands of Patvinsuo National Park, north of Ilomantsi, to the forests of Petkeljärvi National Park. From there, it continues as the Bear's Path, or Karhunpolku.

Karhunpolku (Bear's Path) A 133km marked hiking trail of medium difficulty leading north from Lieksa through a string of national parks and nature reserves along the Russian border to end in the town of Kuhmo. Some of the Lakeland's most stunning scenery is along this route. At the northern end of the trail there are connections to the UKK Route.

UKK Route This 240km route in northern Finland is the nation's longest and greatest trekking route. It was named after President Urho K Kekkonen, and it's been in development for decades. The trail starts at the Koli Hill, continues along the western side of Lake Pielinen and ends at the Iso-Syöte Hill, traversing via Vuokatti, Hyrynsalmi and the Ukko-Halla Hill. Farther east, there are more sections of the UKK Route, including the Kuhmo to Lake Peurajärvi leg (connections from Nurmes) and the Kuhmo to Iso-Palonen leg.

Cycling

Riding a bicycle in Finland is one of the best ways to see the country – in summer, that is. Finns do ride their bikes right on through the dark, snowy winters, but to do so voluntarily as a tourist you'd have to be truly masochistic.

What sets Finland apart from both Sweden and Norway is the almost total lack of mountains. Main roads are excellent and minor roads have little traffic (other than farmers' tractors). Bicycle tours are further facilitated by the liberal camping regulations and the long hours of daylight in June and July. All petrol stations have free toilets, and their cafés often serve excellent home-cooked lunches until 4 pm.

Here's the drawback: distances in Finland are vast. From Helsinki to Rovaniemi is 837km, and from Turku to Savonlinna is 446km. If you've got three or more months to explore, terrific. Get a bicycle and hit the road. Alternately, you can cover quite a bit of ground by combining shorter bike tours with bus and train trips – Finnish buses and trains are very bike-friendly. But even if your time is limited, don't skip a few quick jaunts in the countryside. There are very good networks of cycle paths in and around most major cities and holiday destinations (the network around Oulu is very good).

A few words of wisdom you might already have received from your mother, lover or best friend: carry water, as summers are hot and there are few places to fill up. Weather can be unpredictable year-round, so pack rain gear. And don't forget to bring along a repair kit.

In most towns bicycles can be hired for around 20 to 50 mk per day, with even better deals on weekly rentals. Another option is to buy a second-hand bicycle for around 400 mk, then sell it once you're done touring. Check local newspapers for listings; *polkupyörä* is Finnish for bicycle.

BRINGING YOUR BICYCLE

Air

Most airlines will carry a bike free of charge, so long as the bike and panniers don't exceed the weight allowance per passenger, usually 20kg (44lb). Hefty excess baggage charges may be incurred if you do, and this applies to both international and internal flights.

Inform the airline that you will be bringing your bike when you book your ticket. Arrive at the airport in good time to remove panniers and pedals, deflate tyres and turn handlebars around – the minimum dismantling usually required by airlines.

Bus

Bikes can be carried on long-distance buses for 10 to 20 mk if there is space available (and there usually is). Just advise the driver prior to departure. One traveller gave this comment:

When our tandem suffered a serious technical failure on our fifth day, our itinerary was salvaged by the fact that, unlike in the UK, it was transported without difficulty not only on trains but also on buses.

Train

Bikes can accompany passengers on most normal train journeys, with a surcharge up to 50 mk. Notable exceptions are Inter-City (IC) and Pendolino trains. Take your bike directly to the Konduktöörivaunu carriage, pay the conductor in cash and take the receipt. You must collect your bike from the cargo carriage when you reach your destination. To transport a bike as cargo costs up to 100 mk.

WHERE TO CYCLE

You are allowed to cycle on all public roads except motorways – these are either four lane roads that carry a green road-and-bridge symbol, or two lane roads marked by a green symbol of a car. The best place to cycle is Åland.

Åland

The Åland islands are the most bicycle-friendly region in Finland, and are (not surprisingly) the most popular region for bicycle tours. Bikes can be rented in Mariehamn and Eckerö, and come with a free island map. From either town there are clearly marked bike routes (with kilometre markers) to every corner of the island group, passing villages, medieval churches and quaint old farms every few kilometres. Bikes are transported free on car ferries between the islands, but three special bicycle-only ferries also operate in summer, charging 30 to 40 mk per person with bicycle See the Getting There & Away and Getting Around section in the Åland chapter for details of these ferries.

The South Coast

South Finland has more traffic than other parts of the country, but with careful planning you can find quiet roads that offer pleasant scenery. King's Road, a historic route between Turku and Vyborg, passes old settlements, churches and manor houses. Even quieter is the Ox Road that runs through rural areas from Turku to Hämeenlinna. There are also some good shorter rides around Turku.

The Lakeland

Two theme routes cover the entire eastern frontier area, from the south all the way to Kuusamo in the north. Runon ja rajan tie ('Road of the poem and frontier') consists of secondary sealed roads which pass several Karelian-theme houses where you can stuff yourself with eastern food. The route ends in northern Lieksa. Some of the smallest, most remote villages along the easternmost roads have been lumped together to create the Korpikylien tie ('Road of Wilderness Villages'). This route starts at the village of Saramo in northern Nurmes and ends at Hossa, in the north-east of Suomussalmi. Some sections are unsealed.

The provincial tourist office has printed a leaflet, *Karjalan kirkkotie*, which guides riders along the 'Karelian church route' from the Heinävesi monasteries to the municipality of Ilomantsi in the far east.

A recommended loop takes you around Lake Pielinen, and may include a ferry trip across the lake (this costs money, though).

Western Finland

This flat region is good for biking, except that distances are long and scenery is almost oppressively dull. Quiet roads along the rivers Kauhajoki, Kyrönjoki, Laihianjoki and Lapuanjoki are nice for touring. Further north, practically all towns and villages lie along rivers that run from south-east to north-west. Bring your bike by train to Seinäjoki or further north, and continue along the narrow roads.

Winter Sports

Skiing is every Finn's favourite activity during winter. A short list of the best resorts – for downhill or cross-country skiing – includes Ylläs, Levi, Pyhä-Luosto and Ruka; although Pallas, Saariselkä, Iso-Syöte, Koli and Ounasvaara are also fairly good.

Finnish ski resorts offer more than just skiing: dog sledding, snowmobile safaris, reindeer sleigh tours and ice fishing are usually also on tap. As you'd expect, ski resorts aren't really geared towards budget travellers.

In the list below, the nearest town is indicated in parentheses.

Ylläs (Kolari) 34 downhill slopes, 17 lifts. Vertical drop 463km, longest run 3km. Cross-country trails 250km.

Levi (Kittilä) 36 downhill slopes, 16 lifts. Vertical drop 325m, longest run 2500m. Cross-country trails 230km.

Pyhä-Luosto (Sodankylä) 17 downhill slopes, 11 lifts. Vertical drop 280m, longest run 2km. Cross-country trails 145km.

Ruka (Kuusamo) 28 downhill slopes, 18 lifts. Vertical drop 201m, longest run 1300m. Cross-country trails 250km.

Pallas (Kittilä) 9 downhill slopes, 2 lifts. Vertical drop 340m, longest run 2400m. Cross-country trails 160km.

Saariselkä (Inari) 12 downhill slopes, 6 lifts. Vertical drop 180m, longest run 1300m. Cross-country trails 250km.

Iso-Syöte (Pudasjärvi) 21 downhill slopes, 11 lifts. Vertical drop 192m, longest run 1200m. Cross-country trails 110km.

Koli (Lieksa) 6 downhill slopes, 3 lifts. Vertical drop 145m, longest run 1050m. Cross-country trails 100km.

Ounasvaara (Roveniemi) 5 downhill slopes, 3 lifts. Vertical drop 140m, longest run 600m. Cross-country trails 123km.

DOWNHILL SKIING & SNOWBOARDING

Finland has more than 120 downhill ski resorts – in fact, there are ski lifts in all major towns with a hill taller than the local apartment buildings. Most Finnish resorts also offer designated runs and halfpipes for snowboarders.

Finnish slopes are generally quite low and are excellent for beginners – and families! The best resorts are in Lapland, where the vertical drop averages 250m over 3km. In central and southern Finland, ski runs are much shorter, averaging about 1km in length. For steeper, longer and more challenging slopes head across the border to Sweden or Norway.

The ski season in Finland runs from late November to early May, and slightly longer in Lapland and the North, where it's possible to ski through Midsummer. Beware of the busy winter and spring holiday periods – especially around Christmas and Easter – that are too crowded to be appreciated.

Accommodation at ski resorts is expensive in luxury cottages, hotels and apartments but there are hostels convenient to some ski areas. Prices rise dramatically during holiday periods and bookings are advised at those times. In summer, ski resorts become ghost towns and accommodation is quite a good value. Some resorts have started to offer programmes of hiking, river rafting and mountain biking to lure summer customers; inquire at a Finnish tourist office for more information on these resort packages.

You can rent all skiing or snowboarding equipment at major ski resorts for about 80 to 100 mk per day. A one-day lift pass is typically an additional 100 mk, although it is often possible to pay separately for each ride.

CROSS-COUNTRY SKIING

Cross-country skiing is one of the simplest and most pleasant things to do in winter in Finland. It's the ideal way to explore the beautiful, silent winter countryside of lakes, fells, fields and forests.

Practically every town and village maintains ski tracks around the urban centre, and these are typically in use from the first snow fall in November through early May – although die-hard skiers will grimly continue to ski across bare rock in spring if they feel that the season hasn't lasted long enough! In many cases, local tracks are illuminated *(valaistu latu)*. Access is always free, and getting lost is impossible on municipal tracks as they are usually loops of only a few kilometres. The one drawback to using local tracks is that you'll need to bring your own equipment (or purchase some in a sports shop), as rentals usually aren't possible.

Cross-country skiing at one of Finland's many ski resorts is another option. Once you venture to ski resorts, the tracks get much longer but also are better maintained. This means that tracks are in excellent condition soon after a snowfall. Ski resorts offer excellent instruction, and rent equipment (skis, boots and poles) for about 80 to 100 mk per day or 200 to 380 mk per week. The best cross-country skiing is in Lapland, where resorts offer hundreds of kilometres of trails (a fraction of these are illuminated for night and winter skiing).

Keep in mind that there's only about five hours of daylight each day in northern Lapland during winter – if you're hoping to do a longer trek you might want to wait until spring. Cross-country skiing is best during January and February in southern Finland, and from December to April in the north.

Water Sports

Finland is best experienced from its bays, lakes, rivers and canals. You'll find it possible to make trips lasting anywhere from an hour or two to several weeks.

RENTALS

For independent travel on waterways, you will need to rent your own rowing boat, canoe or kayak. The typical Finnish rowing boat is available at camping grounds and some tourist offices, usually for less than 100 mk per day, and hourly rentals are possible. Hostels and rental cottages may have rowing boats that you'll be allowed to use for free. In a rowing boat, your back faces the bow of the boat and you'll have to turn your head to see where you're heading. Controlling a rowing boat is not as easy as canoeing; consequently, rowing boats are never used on rivers with rapids. Use rowing boats on lakes, especially for visits to nearby islands.

Canoe and kayaks are suitable for trips that last several days or weeks. For longer trips you'll need a waterproof plastic barrel for your gear, a life-jacket and waterproof route maps. Route maps and guides may be purchased at the local or regional tourist office, at the Karttakeskus Aleksi map shop in Helsinki or through the Karttakeskus mail-order service (☎ 0204-45 5911, fax 0204-45 5929). Waterproof maps usually cost around 25 to 50 mk; occasionally tourist offices and rental outfits will supply route maps at no cost. Canoe and kayak rentals range in price from 100 to 200 mk per day, 400 to 950 mk per week. You'll pay more if you need over-land transportation to the starting or ending point of your trip, if you wish to hire a guide or if you need to rent extra gear such as tents and sleeping bags. Try to locate a rental company at both ends of the route, and compare rates (including transport). It would probably be more convenient to rent from the end point of your trip so that you will first be transported to the starting point, making your journey a bit more flexible. Some companies that handle canoe and kayak rentals are listed below. Contact local tourist offices for the names of other outfitters.

Helsinki & The South Coast
  Helsingin Melontakesku (☎ 09-436 2500, fax 09-436 2455), Rajasaarenpenger 8, 00250 Helsinki
  Prokajak (☎ 05-226 1096 or 0400-703 155), Ahmankatu 8, 48600 Karhula (near Kotka)

The Lakeland
  Saimaatours (☎ 05-411 7722, fax 415 6609), Kirkkokatu 10, 53100 Lappeenranta
  Vesimatkailu Savolax (☎ 017-262 6644 or 049-340 474), Matkustajasatama, Amakasiini, Kuopio

The North & Lapland
  Rukapalvelu Oy (☎ 08-860 8600, fax 860 8601), 93825 Rukatunturi (near Kuusamo)
  Lapin Safarit (☎ 016-331 1200, fax 331 1222), Koskikatu 1, 96200 Rovaniemi

WHERE TO ROW & PADDLE

The routes described below have been meticulously researched, and a route map and guide with detailed information – including the position of any and all rapids – is an absolutely essential for a safe, fun trip. Most route maps and guides are available in English.

Rapids are classified according to a scale from I to VI. I is very simple, II will make your heart beat faster, III is dangerous for your canoe, IV may be fatal for the inexperienced. Rapids classified as VI are just short of Niagra Falls and will probably kill you. Unless you're an experienced paddler you shouldn't negotiate anything above a class I rapid on your own.

Always be prepared to carry your canoe or kayak around an unsafe stretch of river (rapids, waterfalls, broken dams, hydroelectric power stations). This could save your life.

The Lakeland is, naturally, the most popular region for canoe and kayak travel. On established routes there are easy-to-follow route markers and designated camp sites along the way. North Karelia, particularly around Lieksa and Ruunaa, also offers good paddling. Rivers farther north, in the Kuusamo area and in Lapland, are very

steep and fast-flowing, with tricky rapids, making them suitable for experts only!

If you're uncertain of your paddling skills and just want to experience the thrill and beauty of the mighty northern rivers, contact one of the local tourist offices about joining a white-water rafting expedition. In summer, there are many operators who offer such tours.

Aquatic Nature Trail In the heart of the Lakeland, this is a 52km trail from Juva to Sulkava

Hossa Trails There are four trails that start at Hossa in northern Finland, ranging in length from 8½km to 35km. These trails have class I to class II rapids.

Ivalojoki Route The 70km route along the Ivalojoki in north-east Lapland starts at the village of Kuttura and finishes in Ivalo, crossing 30 rapids along the way.

Kyrönjoki Routes The Kyrönjoki in western Finland totals 205km, but you can do short trips down the river from Kauhajoki, Kurikka or Ilmajoki.

Lakeland Trail This 350km trail is routed through the heart of the lake district (Kangaslampi, Enonkoski, Savonranta, Kerimäki, Punkaharju, Savonlinna and Rantasalmi) and takes 14 to 18 days.

Naarajoki Trail This is an easy 100km route in the Mikkeli area, recommended for families.

Parkano Route This southern Finland route starts in Parkano or farther north in Kihniö and ends in Lake Kyösjärvi. It's a mellow route through narrow lakes and with no difficult rapids.

Savonselkä Circuit The circuit, near Lahti, has three trails that are 360km, 220km and 180km in length. There are many sections that can be done as day trips and that are suitable for novice paddlers.

Seal Trail From Kolovesi to Linnansaari, this is a 120km route that takes one to seven days.

Väliväylä Trail This Lakeland trail goes from Kouvola to either Lappeenranta (90km) or Luumäki (60km) and includes some class I to class III rapids.

Other Activities

FISHING

Finnish waters are teeming with fish – and fishers. Finland has at least one million enthusiastic domestic anglers.

Lapland has the greatest number of excellent fishing spots, but the number of designated places in South Finland is also increasing. Most fishing areas are privately owned. The exceptions are designated 'Government Fishing Areas', which are stocked by the Forest and Park Service with tonnes of fish each year. Some popular fishing areas are Hossa, Ruunaa, Peurajärvi and Teno.

Local tourist offices can direct you to the best fishing spots in the area, and usually can provide some sort of regional fishing map. (The Mikkeli tourist office is particularly good.) An annual guide to fishing the entire country is available from the Forest and Park Service at two offices: Tikankontti, Eteläesplanadi 20, 00130 Helsinki (☎ 09-270 5221, fax 09-644 421), and Etiäinen, 96930 Napapiiri, Rovaniemi (☎ 016-362 526, fax 362 528).

Permits

Several permits are required of foreigners who wish to go fishing in Finland, and the system is strictly enforced by permit checkers. First, you will need a national fishing permit, which is available from all post offices and banks. A one week permit is 20 mk, an annual permit 80 mk. Second, fishing with a rod or lure always requires a special permit, also available at banks and post offices. This permit costs 35 mk for one week, 150 mk for the year. You must obtain these permits in advance. Finally, you will need to pick up a local permit which has time and catch limits (say, two salmon per day and an unrestricted amount of other species). The local permit can be purchased for one day, one week or even for just a few hours. Typically these cost around 45 mk per day, 130 mk per week and are available on the spot, from the location where you're planning to fish. Check local restrictions when buying the daily permit.

The waters in Åland are regulated separately and require a separate regional permit.

Equipment rental

Many camping grounds and tourist offices rent fishing gear in summer. To go ice-fishing in winter, however, you'll either need to buy your own gear or join an organised tour – nobody rents outs ice-fishing tackle in Finland because every Finn has this!

BIRD-WATCHING

Bird-watching is extremely popular in Finland, in no small part because many bird species migrate to northern Finland in summer to take advantage of the almost continuous daylight for breeding and rearing their young. Look carefully when in Finnish forests and you'll see that bird-mad locals have filled the trees with birdhouses to encourage visits by their favourite species. The best months for watching birds are May through June or mid-July, and late August to September or early October.

Liminganlahti (Liminka Bay) near Oulu is a wetlands bird sanctuary and probably the best bird-watching spot in Finland. Other good areas include Puurijärvi-Isosuo National Park in western Finland, Oulanka National Park near Kuusamo, the Porvoo area east of Helsinki, the Kemïo Islands, and about a dozen other places. At any of these areas you can usually hire an ornithological guide from 500 mk per day. Otherwise, bring your own binoculars and a good bird book! An excellent guide is *Birds* by Peter Holden (Collins Wild Guide, HarperCollins, London, 1996). The version available within the country is only in Finnish, so you'll need to purchase an English-language version before you go.

GOLF

You need a Green Card to play on most Finnish golf courses, but many courses are open to the general public for 120 to 250 mk per day. At last count, there were approximately 100 golf courses throughout Finland, typically open from late April to mid-October. The most unusual golf course in Finland is the Green Zone golf course in

Tornio (see the Lapland & Oulu chapter). For information on Finnish golf courses, contact Suomen Golfliitto, Radiokatu 20, 00240 Helsinki (☎ 09-3481 2244, fax 147 145).

TRACING YOUR ANCESTORS

Many visitors to Finland have Finnish ancestors. A trip would be a good chance to find out more about their lives, and you may even find relatives you never knew existed. Do some research in your local library before you go – it is likely that your ancestors are already mentioned in at least one published book.

Useful Organisations

The best place to visit first is Suomen Sukututkimusseura (Finnish Genealogical Society) at Liisankatu 16A, 00170 Helsinki (☎ 09-278 1188, fax 278 1199). There's an extensive library of published books of family surveys, and assistance is provided. The Kansallisarkisto (National Archives) at Rauhankatu 17, 00170 Helsinki (☎ 09-228 521, fax 176 302, kansallisarkisto@narc.fi) covers all of Finland. Other good contacts are Siirtolaisinstituutii (The Institute of Migration) at Piisapankatu 3, 20500 Turku

(☎ 02-231 7536, fax 233 3460, maikal@utu.fi), with archives and a library, and Sukuseurojen Keskusliito (Central Association of Geneological Societies) at Työmiehenkatu 2, 00180 Helsinki, (☎ 09-694 9320, fax 694 9320).

Archives

The best information will come directly from archives, but you will have to pay a fee for the service. If you know for sure where your ancestors lived (and that they were members of the Lutheran church, which is very likely), go directly to the local Kirkkoherranvirasto (Parochial Archives), an office usually found near the local Lutheran church. These archives are the best bet for tracing people who lived during the 20th century. The National Archives (see Useful Organisations, above) is best if you are looking for ancestors from the 19th century, or earlier. If you have several ancestors from various places within a region, go to the Maakuntaarkisto (Regional Archives). There are regional archives in Turku, Vaasa, Hämeenlinaa, Joensuu, Mikkeli and Oulu. Contact the tourist offices of these cities for information and assistance.

Getting There & Away

AIR

Finland is not a bad place to start a northern European tour; look for a cheap return flight, from say London or Athens.

Discount flights are available to and from Finland for holders of GO25 or ISIC (International Student Identity Card) cards from student travel agents. In Finland, contact Kilroy Travels, the main student travel agent in Scandinavia. There are Kilroy offices in Helsinki, Turku, Tampere and Oulu.

Airports & Airlines

There are excellent flight connections to Finland from all over the world. Finnair, the Finnish national carrier, and SAS have scheduled flights to Helsinki from most major cities in Europe, as well as from New York, San Francisco, Cairo, Bangkok, Singapore, Beijing, Sydney and Tokyo.

British Airways, Delta, Lufthansa, KLM, and 18 other airlines fly into the Helsinki-Vantaa International Airport, including many flights daily to/from Scandinavian and Baltic capitals. To Turku, there are several nonstop flights daily from Stockholm.

From outside Europe, you will find that prices are similar to flights to any other European city. Within Europe, there is more variety in fares, depending on which city you want to fly from.

Buying Tickets

The plane ticket will probably be the single most expensive item in your budget, and buying it can be an intimidating business. There is likely to be a multitude of airlines and travel agents hoping to separate you from your money, and it is always worth putting aside a few hours to research the current state of the market. Start early: some of the cheapest tickets have to be bought months in advance, and some popular flights sell out early. Talk to other recent travellers – they may be able to stop you making some of the same old mistakes. Look at the ads in newspapers and magazines, consult reference books and watch for special offers. Then phone around to travel agents for bargains. (Airlines can supply information on routes and timetables; however, except at times of inter-airline war they do not supply the cheapest tickets.) Find out the fare, the route, the duration of the journey and any restrictions on the ticket. Then sit back and decide which is best for you.

You may discover that those impossibly cheap flights are 'fully booked, but we have another one that costs a bit more ...' Or the flight is on an airline notorious for its poor safety standards and leaves you in the world's least favourite airport in mid-journey for 14 hours. Or they claim only to have the last two seats available for that country for the whole of July, which they will hold for you for a

---

WARNING

The information in this chapter is particularly vulnerable to change: prices for international travel are volatile, routes are introduced and cancelled, schedules change, special deals come and go, and rules and visa requirements are amended. Airlines and governments seem to take a perverse pleasure in making price structures and regulations as complicated as possible. You should check directly with the airline or a travel agent to make sure you understand how a fare (and the ticket you may buy) works. In addition, the travel industry is highly competitive and there are many lurks and perks.

The upshot of this is that you should get opinions, quotes and advice from as many airlines and travel agents as possible before you part with your hard-earned cash. The details given in this chapter should be regarded as pointers and are not a substitute for your own careful, up-to-date research.

maximum of two hours. Don't panic – keep ringing around.

Use the fares quoted in this book as a guide only. They are approximate and are based on the rates advertised by travel agencies at the time of going to press. Quoted airfares do not necessarily constitute a recommendation for the carrier. If you are travelling from the UK or the USA, you will probably find that the cheapest flights are being advertised by obscure bucket shops whose names haven't yet reached the telephone directory. Many such firms are honest and solvent, but there are a few rogues who will take your money and disappear, to reopen elsewhere a month or two later under a new name. If you feel suspicious about a firm, don't give them all the money at once – leave a deposit of 20% or so and pay the balance when you get the ticket. If they insist on cash in advance, go somewhere else. And once you have the ticket, ring the airline to confirm that you are actually booked on the flight.

You may decide to pay more than the rock-bottom fare by opting for the safety of a better-known travel agent. Firms such as STA Travel, which has offices worldwide, Council Travel in the USA or Travel CUTS in Canada are not going to disappear overnight, leaving you clutching a receipt for a nonexistent ticket, and they do offer good prices to most destinations.

Once you have your ticket, write down the ticket number, together with the flight number and other details, and keep the information somewhere separate. If the ticket is lost or stolen, this will help you get a replacement. It's sensible to buy travel insurance as early as possible. If you buy it the week before you fly, you may find, for example, that you're not covered for delays to your flight caused by strikes or other industrial action.

Round-the-World Tickets

Round-the-world (RTW) tickets are often real bargains. They are usually put together by a combination of two airlines and permit you to fly anywhere you want on their route systems so long as you do not backtrack. There may be restrictions on how many stops you are permitted and usually the tickets are valid for 90 days up to a year. An alternative type of RTW ticket is one put together by a travel agent using a combination of discounted tickets.

Finnair has combination routes with Qantas, Canadian, Cathay Pacific and American. Contact your local travel agent for details.

Nordic Air Pass

If you're in a hurry to see Scandinavia and the Baltic states, the Nordic Air Pass might be right for you. The pass is good for limited travel in Finland, Denmark, Norway, Sweden, Estonia, Latvia and Lithuania from 1 May to 30 September. (Residents of Scandinavia and Baltic countries may only use the Nordic Air Pass between 15 June and 17 August.) You can purchase the pass – in reality a book of coupons, with each coupon valid for one one-way flight segment – from a travel agent in your home country. Or you can wait until you arrive. However, at least one coupon must be used on an international flight. The minimum purchase is four coupons per passenger, the maximum is 10 coupons per passenger. The fare is US$360 for four coupons, US$90 for each additional coupon. Taxes and service charges are not included. It's possible to receive a refund for unused coupons – contact a travel agent for details. Affiliated airlines are Air Lithuania, Braathens SAFE, Estonian Air, Finnair, Lithuanian Airlines, Maersk Air, Skärgårds-flyg and Transwede.

Travellers with Special Needs

If you have special needs of any sort – you've broken a leg or you're vegetarian, travelling in a wheelchair, taking the baby, terrified of flying – you should let the airline know as soon as possible so that they can make arrangements accordingly. You should remind them when you reconfirm your booking (at least 72 hours before departure) and again when you check in at the

Air Travel Glossary

Baggage Allowance This will be written on your ticket and usually includes one 20kg item to go in the hold, plus one item of hand luggage.

Bucket Shops These are unbonded travel agencies specialising in discounted airline tickets.

Bumped Just because you have a confirmed seat doesn't mean you're going to get on the plane (see Overbooking).

Cancellation Penalties If you have to cancel or change a discounted ticket, there are often heavy penalties involved; insurance can sometimes be taken out against these penalties. Some airlines impose penalties on regular tickets as well, particularly against 'no-show' passengers.

Check-In Airlines ask you to check in a certain time ahead of the flight departure (usually one to two hours on international flights). If you fail to check in on time and the flight is overbooked, the airline can cancel your booking and give your seat to somebody else.

Confirmation Having a ticket written out with the flight and date you want doesn't mean you have a seat until the agent has checked with the airline that your status is 'OK' or confirmed. Meanwhile you could just be 'on request'.

Courier Fares Businesses often need to send urgent documents or freight securely and quickly. Courier companies hire people to accompany the package through customs and, in return, offer a discount ticket which is sometimes a phenomenal bargain. In effect, what the companies do is ship their freight as your luggage on regular commercial flights. This is a legitimate operation, but there are two shortcomings – the short turnaround time of the ticket (usually not longer than a month) and the limitation on your luggage allowance. You may have to surrender all your allowance and take only carry-on luggage.

Full Fares Airlines traditionally offer 1st class (coded F), business class (coded J) and economy class (coded Y) tickets. These days there are so many promotional and discounted fares available that few passengers pay full economy fare.

ITX An ITX, or 'independent inclusive tour excursion', is often available on tickets to popular holiday destinations. Officially it's a package deal combined with hotel accommodation, but many agents will sell you one of these for the flight only and give you phoney hotel vouchers in the unlikely event that you're challenged at the airport.

Lost Tickets If you lose your airline ticket an airline will usually treat it like a travellers cheque and, after inquiries, issue you with another one. Legally, however, an airline is entitled to treat it like cash and if you lose it then it's gone forever. Take good care of your tickets.

MCO An MCO, or 'miscellaneous charge order', is a voucher that looks like an airline ticket but carries no destination or date. It can be exchanged through any International Association of Travel Agents (IATA) airline for a ticket on a specific flight. It's a useful alternative to an onward ticket in those countries that demand one, and is more flexible than an ordinary ticket if you're unsure of your route.

No-Shows No-shows are passengers who fail to show up for their flight. Full-fare passengers who fail to turn up are sometimes entitled to travel on a later flight. The rest are penalised (see Cancellation Penalties).

On Request This is an unconfirmed booking for a flight.

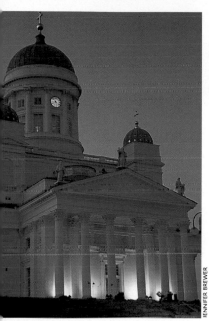

Helsinki Lutheran Cathedral (Tuomiokirrko)

Flowers at Helsinki Market

Ice fishing, Haukivuori

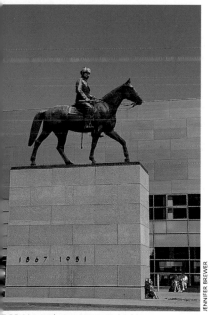

CGE Mannerheim statue, Helsinki

Tourist taxi, Senaatintori, Helsinki

Old Russian villa, Hanko

Pauper statue, Haukipudas Church

Statue at the National Museum, Helsinki

Moomin graffiti, Joensuu

Helsinki kauppatori (market square)

Air Travel Glossary

Onward Tickets An entry requirement for many countries is that you have a ticket out of the country. If you're unsure of your next move, the easiest solution is to buy the cheapest onward ticket to a neighbouring country or a ticket from a reliable airline which can later be refunded if you do not use it.

Open Jaw Tickets These are return tickets where you fly out to one place but return from another. If available, this can save you back-tracking to your arrival point.

Overbooking Airlines hate to fly empty seats and since every flight has some passengers who fail to show up, airlines often book more passengers than they have seats. Usually excess passengers make up for the no-shows, but occasionally somebody gets bumped. Guess who it is most likely to be? The passengers who check in late.

Point-to-Point Tickets These are discount tickets that can be bought on some routes in return for passengers waiving their rights to a stopover.

Promotional Fares These are officially discounted fares, available from travel agencies or direct from the airline.

Reconfirmation At least 72 hours prior to departure time of an onward or return flight, you must contact the airline and 'reconfirm' that you intend to be on the flight. If you don't do this the airline can delete your name from the passenger list and you could lose your seat.

Restrictions Discounted tickets often have various restrictions on them – such as needing to be paid for in advance and incurring a penalty to be altered. Others are restrictions on the minimum and maximum period you must be away, such as a minimum of 14 days or a maximum of one year.

Round-the-World Tickets RTW tickets give you a limited period (usually a year) in which to circumnavigate the globe. You can go anywhere the carrying airlines go, as long as you don't backtrack. The number of stopovers or total number of separate flights is decided before you set off and they usually cost a bit more than a basic return flight.

Stand-by This is a discounted ticket where you only fly if there is a seat free at the last moment. Stand-by fares are usually available only on domestic routes.

Travel Agencies Travel agencies vary widely and you should choose one that suits your needs. Some simply handle tours, while full-services agencies handle everything from tours and tickets to car rental and hotel bookings. If all you want is a ticket at the lowest possible price, then go to an agency specialising in discounted tickets.

Transferred Tickets Airline tickets cannot be transferred from one person to another. Travellers sometimes try to sell the return half of their ticket, but officials can ask you to prove that you are the person named on the ticket. This is less likely to happen on domestic flights, but on an international flight tickets are compared with passports.

Travel Periods Ticket prices vary with the time of year. There is a low (off-peak) season and a high (peak) season, and often a low-shoulder season and a high-shoulder season as well. Usually the fare depends on your outward flight - if you depart in the high season and return in the low season, you pay the high-season fare.

airport. It may also be worth ringing round the airlines before you make your booking to find out how they can handle your particular needs.

Airports and airlines can be surprisingly helpful, but they do need advance warning. Most international airports will provide escorts from check-in desk to plane where needed, and there should be ramps, lifts, accessible toilets and reachable phones. Aircraft toilets, on the other hand, are likely to present a problem; travellers should discuss this with the airline at an early stage and, if necessary, with their doctor.

Guide dogs for the blind will often have to travel in a specially pressurised baggage compartment with other animals, away from their owner; smaller guide dogs may be admitted to the cabin. All guide dogs will be subject to the same quarantine laws (six months in isolation etc.) as any other animal when entering or returning to countries currently free of rabies, such as Australia.

Deaf travellers can ask for airport and inflight announcements to be written down for them.

Children under two travel for 10% of the standard fare (or free, on some airlines), as long as they don't occupy a seat. They don't get a baggage allowance either. 'Skycots' should be provided by the airline if requested in advance; these will take a child weighing up to about 10kg. Children between two and 12 can usually occupy a seat for half to two-thirds of the full fare and do get a baggage allowance. Push chairs can often be taken as hand luggage.

Departure Tax

In Finland, the quoted fares always include VAT and an airport departure tax of 56 mk.

The USA

The *New York Times*, the *LA Times*, the *Chicago Tribune* and the *San Francisco Examiner* all produce weekly travel sections in which you'll find any number of travel agents' ads. Council Travel and STA Travel have offices in major cities nationwide. The magazine Travel Unlimited (PO Box 1058, Allston, MA 02134) publishes details of the cheapest air fares and courier possibilities for destinations all over the world from the USA.

Finnair flies nonstop from Helsinki to New York City daily, to San Francisco twice per week and to Miami once weekly. Delta also flies between New York City and Helsinki, and has a wide range of connecting flights to and from other cities in the USA. Advance purchase return fares from New York City start as low as US\$475.

Another option you might consider is looking for a discounted trans-Atlantic fare to, say, Frankfurt, coupled with a connecting flight to Helsinki, as fares between Helsinki and other major European cities can be quite low.

In Finland, you can fly from Helsinki to New York for as little as 1340 mk one way, and to Los Angeles for 1940 mk one way. Prices are for students and people under 26 years of age, as quoted by Kilroy Travels.

Because of the shape of the globe, Finland is actually closer to the USA and Canada than some destinations in southern Europe, which makes the flying time shorter!

Canada

Finnair flies from Toronto to Helsinki twice weekly, and you will find any number of North American and European airlines with connecting flights all the way to Helsinki. Most airlines fly over Greenland on the way.

Travel CUTS has offices in all major cities. The *Toronto Globe & Mail* and the *Vancouver Sun* carry travel agents' ads. The magazine Great Expeditions (PO Box 8000-411, Abbotsford BC V2S 6H1) is useful.

Australia

Flying from Australia is a two stage journey (at least), with likely stopovers in either Singapore or Bangkok, or cities in Europe. Qantas flies to Frankfurt, and British Airways, KLM, Lufthansa and a few other

European airlines fly to Helsinki from Australia via London, Amsterdam, Frankfurt, or other cities, respectively.

In Australia, STA Travel and Flight Centres International are major dealers in cheap air fares. Check the travel agents' ads in the Yellow Pages and ring around.

New Zealand

Air New Zealand flies to London and Frankfurt. British Airways, Lufthansa and the French airline UTA will fly you to Europe, with frequent connections available to Helsinki. The cheapest way to visit Finland from New Zealand, on the opposite side of the globe, might be an inexpensive RTW ticket which allows you to stop in Helsinki.

As in Australia, STA and Flight Centres International are popular travel agencies.

The UK

Return fares from London to Helsinki start as low as £200, although a fare this cheap carries plenty of restrictions. Student and youth fares from STA Travel London start at £108 one way, £216 return. From Helsinki, Kilroy Travels (the student travel bureau) offers one-way flights to London for 795 mk.

Trailfinders in west London produces a lavishly illustrated brochure which includes air fare details. STA Travel also has branches in the UK. Look in the Sunday papers and Exchange & Mart for ads. Also look out for the free magazines widely available in London – start by looking outside the main railway stations.

Most British travel agents are registered with the Association of British Travel Agents (ABTA). If you have paid for your flight to an ABTA-registered agent which then goes out of business, ABTA will guarantee a refund or an alternative. Unregistered bucket shops are riskier but also sometimes cheaper.

The Globetrotters Club (BCM Roving, London WC1N 3XX) publishes a newsletter called *Globe*, which covers obscure destinations and can help in finding travelling companions.

Continental Europe

Helsinki is well connected to most European capitals and major cities by a number of airlines. Particularly good are the connections with Scandinavian and Baltic state capitals.

Some of the busiest European flight markets include Amsterdam, Athens, Berlin and Paris. In Amsterdam, NBBS is a popular travel agent. In Athens, there are many agents near Syntagma Square. In Berlin, consult the magazines *Zitty* and *TIP* for travel agency ads. In Paris, there are several discount travel agencies on Avenue de l'Opéra, as well as around the Latin Quarter, including the large agency Nouvelles Frontieres.

In other towns, consult local telephone directories: Travel agency is *reisebüro* in German, *agence de voyages* in French, *reisbureau* in Dutch and *rejsebureau* in Danish.

From Helsinki, Kilroy Travels quotes the following one-way fares for students and people under 26 years of age:

Amsterdam	925 mk
Athens	1050 mk
Berlin	855 mk
Copenhagen	675 mk
Frankfurt	925 mk
Moscow	895 mk
Stockholm	495 mk
St Petersburg	955 mk

Asia

Flights from Asia to Europe tend to be cheaper than flights in the other direction, so it's worth purchasing the return flight while in Asia. Most airlines sell a standard European fare, regardless of the distance flown from the first stop.

Hong Kong is the discount-plane-ticket capital of the region. Its bucket shops are at least as unreliable as those of other cities. Ask the advice of other travellers before buying a ticket.

STA Travel, which is reliable, has branches in Hong Kong, Tokyo, Singapore, Bangkok and Kuala Lumpur.

Finnair flies to Helsinki from Osaka, Tokyo, Singapore, Bangkok and Beijing twice weekly.

LAND

Border Crossings

There are six crossings from northern Sweden to northern Finland across the rivers Tornionjoki (Swedish: Torneälv) and Muonionjoki. Some of these crossings are in remote areas, far from towns.

Between Norway and Finland, there are six border crossings along roads plus a few legal crossings along wilderness tracks. The main Nordkapp route goes from Rovaniemi via Inari and Kaamanen to the crossing at Karigasniemi. The western crossing, at Kilpisjärvi, is best if you're heading to the Tromsø or the Lofoten islands.

Along the heavily travelled Helsinki-Vyborg-St Petersburg corridor there are two Finland-Russia road crossings: Nuijamaa (Russian side: Brusnichnoe) and Vaalimaa (Russian side: Torfyanovka).

Farther north, it may be possible to cross into Russia at the Finnish post of Niirala (Russian side: Vyartsilya) and continue 500km to Petrozavodsk.

From Salla, there is a road across the Russia border to Alakurtti, and from Ivalo, a road goes east to Murmansk via the Finnish border post of Raja-Jooseppi. Check current conditions with the Russian embassy in Helsinki.

Swedish and Norwegian border posts are very relaxed, Russian ones are somewhat less so. You must already have a visa to cross into Russia.

Bus

Sweden Buses from Stockholm drive along the Swedish east coast to Haparanda, and further north along the border. Pick a bus stop from where you can walk to Finland. Haparanda, Övertorneå and Karesuando are the most convenient. Swedish trains travel as far north as Boden; from there take buses (train passes are valid) to the Swedish town of Haparanda, from where you can easily walk (or take another bus) to the Finnish town of Tornio. From Tornio, you will have to pay for the bus ride to the nearest railway station, in Kemi. Inter-rail passes cover bus travel all the way from Boden to Kemi.

Norway Finnish buses run frequently between Rovaniemi and the Norwegian border post, and some buses continue on to the first Norwegian town, which is usually along Norwegian bus routes. Free timetables (ask bus drivers or at stations) usually list these connections.

Buses between Hammerfest and Kirkenes are very useful because they will drop you off at Karasjok, Levajok, Skipagurra and Neiden, with further connections to Finland available. There are several daily buses from Kirkenes to Neiden, but you may have to hitchhike on to Näätämö, stay there overnight, and catch the morning post bus to Ivalo via Sevettijärvi. For Nuorgam, you can catch the nightly bus from Skipagurra via Polmak. There are also two daily departures from Polmak for Rovaniemi. From Lakselv, there are buses to Karigasniemi and Ivalo daily from mid-June to mid-August, and several buses from Karasjok to Ivalo, via Karigasniemi. For Kilpisjärvi (the 'arm of Finland'), there are buses from Skibotn daily from mid-June to mid-August, with very early departures on weekdays. You can reach Skibotn daily from Tromsø, on the Norwegian coast. For Kivilompolo and Enontekiö, catch the bus from Kautokeino; there are four buses per week. To get to Kautokeino from Norway, you have a choice of buses from Alta or Karasjok.

Russia There are daily express buses to Vyborg and St Petersburg from Helsinki, Turku, Tampere, Porvoo, Hamina and several other cities in southern Finland, and a visa is required. Check current timetable and book tickets at the city bus station or a travel agency. The one-way fare from Helsinki to Vyborg is 160 mk, to St Petersburg 250 mk.

There are also post buses from Joensuu to Sortavala and Petrozavodsk (Finnish: Petroskoi), and from Rovaniemi and Ivalo to Murmansk. To qualify for travel on a post bus, you need a passport and a visa and you must pay for the journey beforehand at a post office. The receipt of your payment is your ticket. Inquire at the local post office about rates and schedules.

Train

When you leave Finland by train for almost any point in Europe, you can send your luggage at a very low price to the station at your destination. It's worth checking on current rates while in Finland.

There is no train service between Finland and Norway – but there are plenty of buses (see above).

Sweden The typical route to Finland from any point in Europe goes via Denmark to the Swedish town of Helsingborg, from where there are regular trains to Stockholm. There are also direct long-distance trains to Stockholm from various big cities in Europe. Train passes give discounts on most ferry routes across to Finland. If you don't like the idea of a ferry ride, you can continue by train to the Swedish town of Boden in the far north, then transfer to a bus (see the Bus section just above).

Russia Finland uses broad gauges, similar to those in Russia, so there are regular trains to/from Russia. Tickets for these trains are sold at Helsinki railway station at the international ticket counter. The rail crossing is at Vainikkala (Russian side, Luzhayka).

The *Tolstoi* sleeper departs Helsinki daily at 5:32 pm, arrives in Moscow at 8:38 am and costs 1st/2nd class 745/499 mk one way. It departs Moscow daily at 10:15 pm.

The *Sibelius* and *Repin* offer daily service between Helsinki and St Petersburg (7 hrs). The *Sibelius* departs Helsinki at 6:30 am (1st/2nd class 454/286 mk, seats only). The *Repin* departs at 3:35 pm and offers 2nd class seats (286 mk) or 1st class sleeping berths (509 mk). From St Petersburg departures are

at 4:35 pm (*Sibelius*) and 7:15 am (*Repin*). Return fares are twice the one-way fare.

All three trains stop in Lahti and Kouvula in Finland, and Vyborg in Russia. A Russian visa is required.

Asia To/from central and eastern Asia, a train can work out at about the same price as flying, depending on how much time and money you spend along the way, and it can be a lot more fun.

Helsinki is a good place to start your journey across Russia into Asia. Frequent trains run between Helsinki and Moscow (see the previous Russia section), and there are three routes to/from Moscow across Siberia with connections to China, Japan and Korea: the trans-Siberian to/from Vladivostok, and the trans-Mongolian and trans-Manchurian, both to/from Beijing. There's a fourth route south from Moscow and across Kazakstan, following part of the old Silk Road to Beijing. These trips take several days, often involve stopovers, and prices vary according to which direction you are travelling, where you buy your ticket and what is included – the prices quoted here are a rough indication only.

The trans-Siberian takes just under seven days from Moscow via Khabarovsk to Vladivostok, from where there is a boat to Niigata in Japan from May to October. Otherwise you can fly to Niigata as well as to Seattle and Anchorage, Alaska, in the USA. The complete journey from Moscow to Niigata costs from about US$600 per person for a 2nd class sleeper in a four-berth cabin.

The trans-Mongolian travels via Ulaan Baator, in Mongolia, to Beijing and takes about 5½ days. A 2nd class sleeper in a four-berth compartment would cost around US$285 if purchased in Moscow or Beijing. If you want to stop off along the way or spend some time in Moscow, you'll need 'visa support' – a letter from a travel agent confirming that they're making your travel/accommodation bookings as required in Russia or Mongolia. Locally based companies that do all-inclusive packages (with visa support) include the Travellers Guest House (Moscow: ☎ 7095-971 4059, tgh@ glas.apc.org); and Monkey Business (Hong Kong: ☎ 852-2723 1376; fax 852-2723 6653), with an information centre in Beijing (☎ 8610-6329 2244 ext 4406, 100267 .2570@compuserve.com). There are a number of other budget operators.

The trans-Manchurian passes through Harbin, in Manchuria, to Beijing and takes 6½ days, costing about US$325.

Another option transits central Asia and is known as 'Silk Route'. It runs from Moscow to Almaty in Kazakhstan, crosses the border on the new line to Ürümqi (north-western China), and follows part of the old Silk Road to Beijing. At present there is no direct train, and you must change at Almaty. Moscow to Ürümqi in 2nd class costs about US$300 and takes five or more days, depending on connections.

The Trans-Siberian Handbook (Trailblazer) by Bryn Thomas is a comprehensive guide to the route. Lonely Planet's *Russia, Ukraine & Belarus* and *China* guides have detailed information on trans-Siberian travel.

Car & Motorcycle

Drivers of cars and riders of motorbikes will need the vehicle's registration papers, liability insurance and an international drivers' permit in addition to their domestic licence. Beware: there are two kinds of international permits, one of which is needed mostly for former British colonies. You may also need a *Carnet de passage en douane*, which is effectively a passport for the vehicle and acts as a temporary waiver of import duty. The carnet may also need to have listed any expensive spare parts that you're planning to carry with you, such as a gearbox. This is designed to prevent car import rackets. Contact your local automobile association for details about all documentation.

Anyone who is planning to take their own vehicle with them on a long trip needs to check in advance what spare parts and petrol are likely to be available. Unleaded petrol is not on sale worldwide, and neither is every little part for your car. See the Getting Around chapter for information about driving within Finland.

Russia If you plan to drive into Russia, you'll need an international licence and certificate of registration, passport and visa, and insurance. The Ingosstrakh (☎ 09-694 0511, fax 09-693 3560), Salomonkatu 5C, 00100 Helsinki is the only Russian insurer in Helsinki. It will cover you in Russia but not in other republics of the former Soviet Union. Roads on the Russian side are generally horrible, resembling potato fields, so you will want to have a 4WD vehicle or good nerves, preferably both.

Scandinavian rental car companies do not allow their cars to be taken into Russia.

Bicycle

Cycling is a cheap, convenient, healthy, environmentally sound and above all fun way of travelling. One note of caution: before you leave home, go over your bike with a fine-toothed comb and fill your repair kit with every imaginable spare part. As with cars and motorbikes, you won't necessarily be able to buy that crucial gismo for your machine when it breaks down somewhere in Lapland on a beautiful Sunday afternoon. That said, Finns are crazy about bicycles, so you'll probably find a replacement for the broken part eventually – but rest assured that when you do it might cost more than your entire bike!

Bicycles can travel by air. You can take them to pieces and put them in a bike bag or box, but it's much easier simply to wheel your bike to the check-in desk, where it should be treated as a piece of baggage. You may have to remove the pedals and turn the handlebars sideways so that it takes up less space in the aircraft's hold; check all this with the airline well in advance, preferably before you pay for your ticket.

Hitching

Hitching is never entirely safe in any country in the world, and we don't recommend it. Travellers who decide to hitch should understand that they are taking a small but potentially serious risk. People who do choose to hitch will be safer if they travel in pairs and let someone know where they are planning to go.

Hitchhiking between Lapland and Norway is only recommended during June and August (May and September if the weather is fine). Carry waterproof gear and expect long waits. Being positive also helps: getting stranded at an Arctic Sea fjord is a unique experience that you will probably never forget. There's the midnight sun, fresh winds and abundant bird life to enjoy while you wait ... and wait ... and wait ...

SEA

The Baltic ferries are some of the world's most impressive seagoing craft and have been described as floating hotels-cum-shopping plazas. Service is year-round between major cities.

Many ferry lines offer 50% discounts for holders of Eurail, Scanrail and Inter-Rail passes. Some offer discounts for seniors and for ISIC and GO25 card-holders; be sure to inquire when purchasing your ticket.

Make ferry reservations well in advance when travelling in July, especially if you plan to bring a car.

Departure Tax

There are no departure taxes when leaving Finland by sea.

Sweden

Stockholm is the main gateway to Finland, due to the incredibly luxurious passenger ferries that travel regularly between Stockholm and Turku/Helsinki. There are two competing operators, Silja Line (blue-and-white ferries) and Viking Line (red-and-white ferries). Cabins are compulsory on Silja Line but not on Viking Line. However, Silja does give some attractive discounts. To get the best deal, do some comparison shopping before you buy. And be warned – Friday night departures on Viking Line in the low season are considerably more expensive than departures on other days of the week.

The major source of income for these two ferry companies is duty-free shopping. With high sales taxes in both Sweden and Finland, especially for alcohol and cigarettes, Scandinavian ferry operators offer some of the finest (and most enthusiastically patronised) tax-free shopping arcades in the whole world – although prices for alcohol on board are much higher than those in the supermarkets of central Europe. For the average traveller, however, this is all very good news, as it means ferry companies can afford to keep fares unusually low. Whether you choose to blow the rest of your cash on board on a mega-buffet, disco dancing or case of aquavit – well, that's up to you.

Both Silja Line and Viking Line offer Stockholm to Helsinki and Stockholm to Turku services, with year-round daily departures. From Stockholm to Helsinki it's 15 hours, to Turku 11 or 12 hours. In summer, fares from Stockholm to Turku start at 69 mk, and fares to Helsinki start at 205 mk. Add 169 to 189 mk for a car.

Note that 'Åbo' is the Swedish word for Turku; many travellers have left Stockholm for Åbo, only to find out the next morning that they have actually arrived in Turku! It is the same place.

All Viking and Silja ferries travelling between Stockholm and Turku stop at Mariehamn, Åland. Additionally, Birka Cruises travels between Mariehamn and Stockholm, and Viking Line offers service between Mariehamn and Kapellskär, Sweden, a small harbour in the northern part of Stockholm province.

Eckerö Linjen sails from Grisslehamn (another small village in the very north of Stockholm province) to Eckerö in western Åland – at 3 hours and 35 mk (56 mk in summer) this is the quickest and cheapest crossing between Sweden and Finland.

From the main Åland island group it's possible to island-hop across the archipelago to mainland Finland (or vice-versa) aboard free, local ferries. See the Åland chapter for more details.

A final set of options: there are several ferry crossing between Sweden and Western

Finland. Silja Line sails between Vaasa, Finland and Umeå, Sweden (3½ hours, 150 mk) year-round from one to four times daily. In summer Silja sails between the Finnish town of Pietarsaari (Swedish: Jakobstad) and Skellefteå, Sweden (4½ hours, 200 mk) once daily. There are also sailings between Pietarsaari and Umeå once weekly in summer.

Estonia

There are currently a staggering number of ferries, catamarans and hydrofoils plying between Tallinn and Helsinki, just 80km apart. Car ferries cross in 3½ hours, catamarans and hydrofoils in about 1½ hours. Service is heavy year-round, although in winter there are fewer departures, and the traffic is also slower due to the ice. Cancellations occur if the sea is rough.

Ferries are cheapest, with return fares from 125 mk in summer – Tallink, Silja Line and Eckerö Linjen all have daily departures. Catamarans and hydrofoils cost 150 to 270 mk return. Keep in mind that due to special promotions, a return ticket purchased in Helsinki is often cheaper than a one-way ticket purchased in Tallinn! Plan your trip accordingly.

It is advisable to reserve a seat in advance during summer, particularly if you wish to travel on a Saturday or Sunday. You may purchase tickets at the Helsinki city tourist office, at the ferry line's office in central Helsinki or from the ferry terminal itself.

At the time of writing, citizens of Australia, Canada, UK, Japan, Korea, New Zealand, Singapore, USA and many of the countries of Continental Europe need only a passport to visit Tallinn from Helsinki. Other nationals must obtain a visa (80 mk) prior to travel. Situations do change, so it's wise to check current regulations at the Estonian consulate, Helsinki city tourist office or one of the ferry companies' offices before buying your ticket. See the Helsinki chapter for more information.

Germany

Silja Line offers ferry service between Helsinki and Travemünde, connecting with direct buses to Hamburg. The sea passage takes about 23 hours one way. Departures are three times weekly from mid-April to mid-September. Rates are from US$130 to US$660 one way, depending on season and class of service. The one-way rate for car transport starts at US$155.

Beginning in 1999, Finnlines plans to offer year-round service between Helsinki and Travemünde, as well as year-round service between Helsinki and Lübeck. Contact the nearest Finnish Tourist Board office for details.

Russia

At the time of writing there was no ferry service operating between Finland and Russia.

Kristina Cruises (☎ 05-218 1011; info@kristinacruises.com) offers visa-free cruises from Helsinki to St Petersburg and Karelia Lines (☎ 05-453 0380) offers visa-free cruises from Lappeenranta to Vyborg.

ORGANISED TOURS

Finnair offers package tours for those arriving in Finland on Finnair flights, such as fly-and-drive or hotel packages. In conjunction with BirdLife Finland, a local company, Finnair also offers five, eight and 12 day guided bird-watching tours from May to September. Package tours generally cater to a well-heeled clientele rather than the budget traveller, but can be worth looking into. Contact your local travel agent for details.

Getting Around

There is plenty of free travel information available in English, but if you want just one book that contains accurate details of every train, bus, flight and ferry route in Finland, you should outlay 110 mk for *Suomen Kulkuneuvot*, which is published four times a year. The summer edition is generally referred to as *Kesäturisti*. It is in Finnish and Swedish, but there are summaries in English and a few other languages.

AIR
Domestic Air Services
Finnair is the principal domestic carrier, with services between big centres and to Lapland. SAS/Air Bothnia offers a very limited service within Finland; contact a local travel agent for more information about this carrier.

Although air travel within Finland generally isn't economical, Finland can offer some of the cheapest domestic flights in Europe if you are eligible for and take advantage of one of many possible discounts. One of the best deals is the discounted return between Helsinki and Ivalo, which is almost cheaper than taking trains or buses. If you're willing to fly stand-by you can also save a great deal of money.

Call ☎ 9800-3466 toll-free from anywhere in Finland for the Finnair general booking office. Contact information for Finnair offices in some major Finnish cities follows.

Helsinki
(☎ 09-818 800), Telephone Bookings
(☎ 09-818 7750), Asema-aukio 1
(☎ 09-818 7670), Töölönkatu 21
(☎ 09-818 5880), Airport (International)
(☎ 09-818 5980), Airport (Domestic)
Joensuu
(☎ 013-611 7070), Airport
Kajaani
(☎ 08-689 7600), Airport
Kittilä
(☎ 016-642 072), Valtatie 41
Kuopio
(☎ 017-580 7400), Airport

Kuusamo
(☎ 08-852 1395), Kitkantie 15
Mariehamn
(☎ 018-634 502), Airport
Oulu
(☎ 08-880 7950), Airport
Rovaniemi
(☎ 016-363 6700), Airport
Savonlinna
(☎ 015-523 206), Airport
Tampere
(☎ 03-383 5333), Airport
Turku
(☎ 02-415-4909), Airport

Discounts & Passes
One of the best deals in Finland is the stand-by youth fare, available for travellers aged 17 to 24 years old. Under this plan, any one-way, direct flight costs just 249 mk, and unused tickets are fully refundable. The stand-by youth fare must be purchased at an airport ticket office a maximum of one day prior to intended departure. Contact an airport ticket office for more details. On regular return or one-way fares, youths aged 17 to 24 receive 50% discount; for seniors and children aged 2 to 16 the discount is 70%. Advance-purchase return tickets give up to 50% discount, although a number of restrictions apply.

A number of special discounts are offered on selected routes in summer, and 'Snow fares' give discounts of 50 to 70% on selected flights from Helsinki to Lapland during non-holiday periods from January to May.

Packages comprising a domestic flight and three to seven nights in a hotel can be good value; ask for special brochures at any Finnair office around the world. For information on the Nordic Air Pass, a package of discount tickets which must include one international segment, see the Getting There & Away chapter.

Domestic Departure Tax
The VAT and a departure tax of 56 mk are always included in the listed fare.

Domestic Air Fares

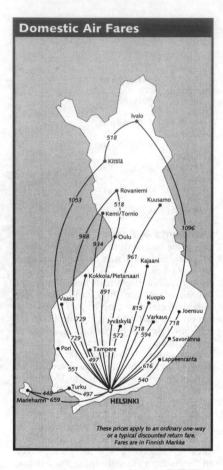

These prices apply to an ordinary one-way
or a typical discounted return fare.
Fares are in Finnish Markka

BUS

Buses in Finland run efficiently and on
schedule. They're comfortable, and service
is extremely comprehensive, covering 90%
of Finland's roads. When compared with
Finnish trains, buses are better for travelling
from village to village, while trains are
more convenient and cheaper for speedy
travel between the big centres. There are
two kinds of intercity service: regular buses
that stop frequently at small towns and villages, and express buses that travel swiftly

between cities. Express buses cover 100km
in under two hours and 400km in about six
hours.

Long-distance and express bus travel is
handled by Oy Matkahuolto Ab (☎ 09-682
701), Lauttasaarentie 8, 00200 Helsinki,
while private companies handle regular bus
services. All share the same ticketing system.

Each town and municipal centre has a
bus terminal (*linja-autoasema*), with local
timetables displayed. National timetables
are available at bus stations and at tourist
offices. Oy Matkahuolto Ab's national
phone number for bus timetables is ☎ 0200-
4000. Further information is available on
the Web at www.matkahuolto.fi/ or www
.expressbus.com/. Bus schedules change
frequently so *always* double-check to avoid
disappointment – particularly in rural areas
where there may be only one bus per week
on some routes.

Most buses run Monday to Friday, hourly
between major towns. Restricted services
operate on Saturday and public holidays.
Very few lines operate on Sunday. Note that
bus stations close at 6 pm Monday to Saturday and at 4 pm on Sunday.

Bus Passes

A Coach Holiday Ticket, valid for two
weeks and up to 1000km, costs 350 mk.
Used wisely it's much cheaper than purchasing individual bus tickets. The Coach
Holiday Ticket is valid on all buses (except
local buses in the Helsinki, Tampere and
Turku regions). There are no refunds. Purchase the Holiday Ticket at most bus
terminals and travel agents in Finland. The
ticket is valid for two weeks from the date
of the first bus trip rather than from the
date of purchase. On some routes, buses
may accept train passes – it never hurts to
ask.

Reservations

Book domestic bus tickets at any bus
station ticket counter or through any travel
agency, regardless of the starting and
ending points. Tickets are valid for one
month from date of purchase. A reserved seat
is optional and carries a 12 mk surcharge.

Reservations are advised on weekends and holidays. One-way bus tickets may be purchased on board the bus at departure if seats are available.

Costs

Ticket prices depend on the number of kilometres travelled; return tickets are usually about 10% cheaper than two one-way fares. There is no difference in price for express and regular buses. Discounts are available for students and seniors, usually only if the ticket is booked in advance and the trip is more than 80km. Children aged 4 to 11 always pay half fare. In summer special discounts are sometimes available on selected routes – ask about these before purchasing your ticket. Bicycles are transported on buses for 10 to 20 mk if there is space available. The surcharge is usually at the discretion of the driver.

Following are some sample fares from Helsinki.

destination	one-way	return
Hämeenlinna	56 mk	112 mk
Inari	647 mk	1165 mk
Joensuu	205 mk	369 mk
Jyväskylä	170 mk	306 mk
Kemi	378 mk	640 mk
Kuopio	226 mk	407 mk
Kuusamo	421 mk	758 mk
Lappeenranta	139 mk	250 mk
Oulu	334 mk	601 mk
Pori	139 mk	250 mk
Rauma	139 mk	250 mk
Rovaniemi	442 mk	796 mk
Savonlinna	181 mk	306 mk
Tampere	94 mk	169 mk
Tornio	401 mk	686 mk
Turku	105 mk	179 mk

TRAIN

Trains of the State Railways of Finland, or Valtion Rautatiet (VR), are clean and usually on schedule. They are fast, efficient and excellent for travelling great distances. On longer routes there are two and three-bed sleepers and special car-carriers.

There are three main rail lines: the Pohjanmaa line runs between Helsinki and Oulu, and continues to Kemijärvi in Lapland; the Karelian route runs from Helsinki to Nurmes via Joensuu; and the Savonian route runs from Kouvola in the south to Iisalmi in the north, continuing to Kajaani.

One of the most popular routes for travellers in a hurry is the triangle between Turku, Helsinki and Tampere. Useful local routes can be found in the Helsinki area. Rovaniemi is the main northern rail terminus.

VR Ltd Finnish Railways (☎ 09-707 3519 in Helsinki) has its own travel bureau at main stations and can advise on all schedules and tickets. Prices, timetables and other information can be found on VR's Web site at www.vr.fi/. Additionally, the Finnish Tourist Board office in Helsinki distributes a free booklet with English and German translations of the national train schedule. It's much easier to understand than the Finnish one (called *Taskuaikataulu*), which costs 5 mk! For individual routes, there are free pocket timetables available at local stations, and every station displays all departures and arrivals.

The dining carriages in Finnish trains serve snacks and meals that are tasty and good value, with a full meal costing around 35 mk.

Train Passes

International rail passes accepted for travel on trains in Finland include the Eurailpass, Eurail Flexipass and InterRail Ticket. See your local travel agent for more information about these rail passes.

ScanRail Pass The ScanRail Pass, for travel within Scandinavia, can be purchased in any of the four Scandinavian countries. The 21 day pass is good for unlimited travel within that period. The flexi pass is good for five days' travel within 15 days, or 10 days' travel within one month. Children travel at half price, and discounts apply for seniors and youths aged 12 to 25. The adult fare for the ScanRail Pass is as follows:

duration	1st class	2nd class
21 days	264 mk	198 mk
5 days/15 days	160 mk	132 mk
10 days/1 month	220 mk	180 mk

Finnrail Pass A national rail pass, the Finnrail Pass, is good for three, five, or 10 days of travel within a one month period. The Finnrail Pass may be purchased from the VR travel agency *Matkapalvelu* at major train stations in Finland, or from your local travel agent before arrival in Finland. Costs for the Finnrail Pass are as follows:

duration	1st class	2nd class
3 days/1 month	860 mk	570 mk
5 days/1 month	1140 mk	770 mk
10 days/1 month	1570 mk	1040 mk

Kesä Rengas Pass The Kesä Rengas Pass is a regional rail pass, valid from 1 June to 31 August for rail travel on one of three routes. Each route forms a circle and stopping en route is possible, although backtracking is not allowed. These passes cost less than 275 mk each. The routes are as follows:

Länsi-Suomen route
Helsinki-Hanko-Turku-Tampere-Hämeenlinna
Keski-Suomen route
Tampere-Helsinki-Lahti-Kouvola-Pieksämäki-Kuopio-Jyväskylä
Itä-Suomen route
Kouvola-Kotka-Lappeenranta-Imatra-Savonlinna-Joensuu-Pieksämäki-Mikkeli

Lomapassi The Lomapassi rail pass is valid for seven days of train travel anywhere within Finland from 1 June to 31 August. The cost for an adult is 690 mk, and for students, seniors and children aged 6 to 16 it's 345 mk.

Classes
VR operates passenger trains in two classes – 1st and 2nd. Most carriages are open 2nd class carriages with soft chairs. Many trains have just one 1st class carriage, containing small compartments, each seating six passengers.

Reservations
Seat reservations are mandatory on Intercity (IC) and the high-speed Pendolino Express trains, and are strongly advised for travel on all trains during summer. The cost of a seat reservation is 25 mk for trips totalling less than 200km, and 30 mk for 200km or more of travel. Reservations on IC and Pendolino trains are an additional 5 mk.

Costs
Train tickets are cheaper in Finland than in Sweden or Norway. A one-way ticket for a 100km train journey costs approximately 50/75 mk in 2nd/1st class. For a journey of 500km, the one-way fare is 224/336 mk. A supplement is charged for travel on IC and Pendolino trains.

Children under 17 pay half fare and children aged under six travel free (but without a seat). There are discounts for families and seniors. Foreign students do not receive discounts on Finnish trains. Check at the train station ticket counter for special summer fares.

If you purchase your ticket from the conductor after boarding from a station where the ticket office was open, a 5 mk 'penalty' is charged (30 mk on Pendolino). Sample one-way and return fares for 2nd class travel from Helsinki are shown below. The 1st class fare is 1½ times the price of a 2nd class ticket. Single tickets are valid for eight days from date of purchase, return tickets for one month.

destination	time	one-way	return
Joensuu	5 hours	226 mk	430 mk
Kuopio	5 hours	206 mk	392 mk
Oulu	6½ hours	276 mk	526 mk
Rovaniemi	9 hours	320 mk	608 mk
Savonlinna	5 hours	196 mk	374 mk
Tampere	2 hours	94 mk	180 mk
Turku	2 hours	94 mk	180 mk

Sleeping Berths Berths are available on overnight trains in one/two/three-bed cabins, at a cost of 250/120/60 mk per person in addition to the cost of an ordinary ticket. During the ski season prices are 350/180/90 mk per person.

Cargo & Bicycles Normal long-distance trains carry cargo; IC and Pendolino trains don't. Large railway stations have a cargo office which takes luggage in advance. Sending a suitcase or backpack anywhere in Finland as cargo costs 25 mk. The cost to transport a canoe is 100 mk.

Transporting a bicycle costs 50 mk if you wish to take the bike with you, or 100 mk if you wish to have it sent as cargo.

Car & Motorcycle Some trains transport cars from the south to Oulu, Rovaniemi and Kittilä – which can come in handy if you've brought your own vehicle and are keen on exploring Lapland. From Helsinki to Rovaniemi the cost is 650 mk for car transport only, 800 mk for a car plus passenger ticket, and 1160 mk for a car and passenger ticket in a sleeping berth that accommodates one to three people. Motorcycles are transported at 50% of the cost for a car. Prices are considerably higher on weekends in winter and spring and on holidays.

CAR & MOTORCYCLE

Driving through Finland is hassle-free, particularly in comparison to other Scandinavian countries where traffic is heavier, routes more complicated and drivers seemingly less polite. Finland's road network is excellent between centres, and very well marked. Only in remote forests and rural areas will you find unsurfaced roads or dirt tracks. There are no road tolls.

Petrol is much more expensive than in the USA and the price is generally above average compared with other European countries. Petrol is cheapest in southern Finland and can be up to 6 mk per litre more expensive in Lapland.

The national motoring organisation is Autoliitto (Automobile and Touring Club

of Finland; ☎ 09-774 761) at Hämeentie 105A, 00550 Helsinki.

Road Rules

Most Finnish roads are only two lanes wide, and traffic keeps to the right. Use extreme caution when passing on these very narrow roads. The speed limit is 50km/h in built-up areas and from 80 to 100km/h on motorways. Accidents must be reported promptly to the Motor Insurers' Bureau (☎ 09-680 401) at Bulevardi 28, 00120 Helsinki. Outside built-up areas all motor vehicles must use headlights at all times, and wearing seat belts is obligatory for all passengers. The blood alcohol limit is 0.05%.

Foreign cars must display their nationality and foreign visitors must be fully insured – bring a Green Card if you have one. Foreign drivers should keep in mind that in Finland, cars entering an intersection from the right *always* have right of way, even when that car is on a minor road. Those who are used to driving in the USA and other countries where stop signs regulate every intersection will find that it takes some time to adjust to this system. When driving in rural areas beware of moose and reindeer, which do not respond to motor horns. In Lapland, reindeer can make motoring somewhat slow and/or hazardous. Expect them to appear at any time. Police must be notified about accidents involving moose and reindeer. Report the accident; if you *don't* might there be legal trouble. To take meat is illegal – moose hunting is possible only if you have a permit, and reindeer in Finland are semi-domesticated and considered private property.

Winter Driving

Snow and ice on Finland's roads from September through April (and as late as June in Lapland) makes driving a very, very hazardous activity without snow tyres. There are two types – regular snow tyres, and the far more serious 'studded' snow tyres which have tiny metal spikes. Studded tyres are allowed on Finnish roads from 1 November to the first Sunday after

Reindeer Roadblocks

The highlight of a visit to Finland is, for many travellers, a glimpse of Finnish wildlife, such as bear or moose. However, those who are yearning to see reindeer should first arm themselves with a few facts.

Reindeer – at least the kind of reindeer commonly found in Finland – are not wild animals. Reindeer herding has been an essential part of the Sami culture for centuries, and reindeer are semi-domesticated but wander freely. Each of the approximately 230,000 reindeer in Lapland is ear-marked and has an owner.

In spring reindeer are rounded up for branding, and in early autumn they are herded together for medical treatment. Animals that are to be used for breeding are turned loose after the medical check, while 130,000 to 150,000 animals are slaughtered each year, yielding 3.5 million kg of valuable meat. (A meal of sauteed reindeer in a nice restaurant costs around 100 mk.)

Reindeer skins, antlers and hooves are used by the Sami to make clothing, household items and furnishings, as well as souvenirs. Reindeer are also used by the Sami as pack animals and to pull sleighs; reindeer racing is a popular sport in winter. Tourists can get a taste of local life on a 'reindeer safari' with reindeer pulling sleighs over the snowy tundra.

The net result of so much reindeer/human interaction is that your average reindeer – none too swift to begin with – is totally blasé about many signs of civilisation – including, sadly, on-coming cars. Some 3000 to 4500 reindeer die annually on Finnish roads, and trains kill an additional 600 every year.

The worst months for reindeer-related accidents are November and December, when hours of daylight are few and road visibility is extremely poor. Also bad are July and August, when the poor animals run amok trying to escape insects. The roads to take extra precautions on are in the far north: Oulu to Kuusamo, Rovaniemi to Kemijarvi and Rovaniemi to Inari, although the problem isn't the quality of the roads – there is a clear relationship between the amount of traffic and the number of accidents. More reindeer-related accidents occur near tourist centres than in uninhabited areas.

The best way to avoid an accident is to slow down immediately when you spot a reindeer, regardless of its location, direction or speed. Reindeer move slowly and do not respond to car horns. Nor do they seem to feel that automobiles deserve right of way. For more information, see the Car & Motorcycle section in this chapter.

Easter and at other times when justified by road conditions. Snow tyres may be hired at Isko Oy (☎ 09-765 566) at Mertakatu 6 in Helsinki from 800 mk for a set of four, installation and storage of your summer tyres included. Cars hired in Finland will be properly equipped with snow tyres when required. It is illegal to drive with tyre chains in Finland. It's also impossible to find them.

Road Distances (km)

	Helsinki	Jyväskylä	Kuopio	Kuusamo	Lappeenranta	Oulu	Rovaniemi	Savonlinna	Tampere	Turku	Vaasa
Helsinki	---										
Jyväskylä	272	---									
Kuopio	383	144	---								
Kuusamo	804	553	419	---							
Lappeenranta	223	219	264	684	---						
Oulu	612	339	286	215	551	---					
Rovaniemi	837	563	511	191	776	224	---				
Savonlinna	338	206	160	579	155	446	671	---			
Tampere	174	148	293	702	275	491	712	355	---		
Turku	166	304	448	848	361	633	858	446	155	---	
Vaasa	419	282	377	533	501	318	543	488	241	348	---

Parking

In central Helsinki, every parking space will cost you money, as much as 10 mk per hour. Some parking spaces in Helsinki and elsewhere require drivers to set a small cardboard parking clock (*pysäköintikiekko*, which means literally 'parking puck') on the dashboard to indicate what time the car arrived. These may be purchased for less than 10 mk at petrol stations and R-kiosks. In other towns, parking is rarely a problem, and much cheaper than in Helsinki. Free parking is possible in small towns. Currently, cars with a foreign licence plate do not receive a ticket for parking violations – although this isn't typical for Scandinavia, and probably won't remain so forever.

Roadside Services

There are petrol stations throughout the country, although in Lapland and in other isolated regions you might want to get in the habit of filling up the tank before it's completely empty. A café or restaurant is very common at Finnish petrol stations, serving hearty meals and snacks at surprisingly low prices and until late hours, especially as shops in Finnish towns close quite early. On Sunday and at night you can fill your tank by using *Automaatti* or *Seteli/kortti* automatic petrol pumps. Bank notes and major credit cards (especially Visa) are always accepted. Some stations have instructions in English and also French. If the instructions are in Finnish and Swedish only, you insert bank notes, press *setelikuittaus* after the last note, choose the right pump, choose the right petrol type, and fill the tank.

Road Numbers

Each major road has a number (often referred to in this book). National highways are numbered with one to two digit numbers. Some of these highways – those between major cities – are also designated European Routes and bear an 'E' prefix (see table on the next page).

Three and four digit numbers are given to less important roads, often gravel ones. There are also plenty of roads with no number at all. The simple road numbering system begins at Helsinki and radiates from west to east as follows:

1	Helsinki-Turku	(E18)
2	Helsinki-Pori	
3	Helsinki-Tampere-Vaasa	(E12)
4	Helsinki-Jyväskylä-Oulu-Rovaniemi-Ivalo-Norway	(E75)
5	Helsinki-Mikkeli-Kuopio-Kuusamo-Kemijärvi-Sodankylä	
6	Helsinki-Lappeenranta-Joensuu-Kajaani	
7	Helsinki-Kotka-Hamina-Russia	(E18)
8	Turku-Pori-Vaasa-Oulu	
9	Turku-Tampere-Jyväskylä-Kuopio	(E63)
10	Turku-Hämeenlinna	
11	Tampere-Pori	
12	Rauma-Tampere-Lahti-Kouvola	
13	Jyväskylä-Mikkeli-Lappeenranta	

Rental

Car rental in Finland is much more expensive than elsewhere in Europe. The smallest, most stripped-down car costs from 170 mk per day and 2 mk per kilometre. Weekly rentals with unlimited mileage are from 2300 mk. Avoid renting at the Helsinki airport, if possible, as pricest are highest there.

Rental car companies with offices in many Finnish cities include Budget (☎ 9800-2535), Hertz (☎ 0800-112 233) and Europcar (☎ 09-7515 5300 in Helsinki). There are also local operators, especially in Helsinki. See the Yellow Pages, under the heading *Autovuokraamoja*, for addresses and telephone numbers.

Purchase

Small 10-year-old sedans and old vans can cost less than 10,000 mk, but those costing less than 5000 mk should have been recently inspected *(katsastettu)*.

BICYCLE

Finland is bicycle friendly, with miles of designated bike roads. Daily hire at about 50 mk is available at tourist offices, train stations, hostels and camping grounds, and there are bargain weekly rates. Additionally, the Finnish hostelling organisation (SRM) offers a cycling and hostel package that takes in the flat south and lake regions.

New bicycles range from 1000 mk, but good second-hand models may cost less than 500 mk. For more information about bicycling in Finland see Cycling in the Activities chapter.

HITCHING

Hitching is never entirely safe in any country, and we don't recommend it. That said, if you're determined to hitch in Finland you'll find that the going is fairly easy, especially if you try it outside the biggest cities and look clean. Relatively few Finns like picking up hitchhikers but the few friendly ones do it with enthusiasm. Drivers will ask *Minne matka?* (Where are you going?), so you just tell them your destination. It is normally not necessary to carry a piece of cardboard with your destination written on it, especially if your route is pretty obvious.

Hitchhiking on motorways (freeways) is forbidden, but there are relatively few motorways in Finland. It is possible to hitch from Helsinki to Turku; more difficult is Helsinki to Tampere or Lahti, where there are longer sections of motorway and continuing a journey after being dropped off may be next to impossible. Some of the best areas to hitch are North Karelia and Lapland, but all regions outside Helsinki and other big cities are fine, although Lapland may sometimes be very frustrating as the interval between passing cars can be quite lengthy. Any secondary road, or a crossing at a middle-sized village, will be easy for hitchhiking. The best time to hitchhike is Monday to Friday, when traffic is heaviest.

BOAT

Before the road network was constructed, lake steamers and 'church longboats' provided the main passenger transport in much of Finland. They disappeared until the 1970s, when quite a few of them were brought back into service. Many of the steamers now in use were built in the early 1900s and have a lot of character.

Lake & River Crossings

Lake and river ferries operate over the summer period. Departures tend to be sporadic from May through mid-June and during August, but are very steady from mid-June to July. These ferries are more than mere transport – a cruise is a bona fide Finnish experience.

Apart from two-hour cruises starting from Jyväskylä, Kuopio, Savonlinna, Tampere, Mikkeli and other towns, you can actually cover half of Finland on scheduled boat routes. The most popular routes are Tampere-Hämeenlinna, Savonlinna-Kuopio and Joensuu-Koli-Lieksa-Nurmes. From Lappeenranta there are visa-free day cruises down the historic Saimaa Canal to Vyborg, Russia (visitors are not allowed to disembark in Vyborg). Most ferries take bicycles.

Sea Ferries

Several kinds of ferries operate between various islands and coastal towns. Most important to travellers on a budget are the free *lossi* ferries, part of the public road system. These run to a schedule or just continuously, connecting important inhabited islands to the mainland. These simple ferries take vehicles, bicycles and pedestrians. Some ferries run between several islands to support the livelihood of small fishing villages, especially near Turku and in the province of Åland. These ferries also may be free to those who stay overnight on one of the islands, making it possible to island-hop from the mainland to Åland free of charge. See the chapters on Åland and Turku for specific information.

Several cruise companies run express boats to interesting islands off the coast. From Helsinki the foremost tour is the short trip to Suomenlinna. Likewise, there are summer cruises aboard historic steamships to mainland towns that may be reached more routinely by car, bus or train. Popular

sea routes are Turku-Naantali and Helsinki-Porvoo.

LOCAL TRANSPORT

The only tram and metro networks are in Helsinki. There is a bus service in all Finnish cities and towns, with departures every 10 to 15 minutes in Helsinki and other large towns, and every half-hour in smaller towns. Fares are under 10 mk per ride. As a rule, train and bus stations are located reasonably close together, usually within walking distance.

Taxi

Hail taxis at bus and train stations or by telephoning; they are listed in the phone book under *Taksi*. Typically the fare is 19 mk plus a per-kilometre charge. The surcharge for night or weekend service is approximately 10 mk. Taxis in small towns are nearly as expensive as in big towns.

There is no shared taxi transport available in Finland, the possible exceptions being airport taxis from Helsinki airport, taxis from Turku train station, and local taxis in some off-the-beaten-track places in Lapland. However, if you have a group of four people and want to cover a lengthy distance 'in the middle of nowhere', you should negotiate with taxi drivers to get a good price.

ORGANISED TOURS

Many Finnish towns offer a great variety of tours – but there are not always enough people to go! Most reliable are those in Helsinki, Turku and Rovaniemi, where weekly tour programs are offered in the summer and winter high seasons. In places like Lieksa and Kuusamo tours can be the cheapest or the only way to visit isolated attractions. It's best to telephone ahead for a confirmation to avoid the disappointment of showing up for a cancelled tour! Also, keep in mind that sometimes only two people are required for a 'group' tour. In addition to regular sightseeing tours, local tour operators take groups into the Finnish wilderness for trekking, white-water rafting, fly-fishing, dog sledding and a range of other activities. Local tourist offices can provide information on how to reach these operators.

Finnair offers package tours for those arriving in Finland on Finnair flights; see the Organised Tours section of the Getting There & Away chapter for more details.

Helsinki

- **pop 532,000**   ☎ 09

Helsinki (Swedish: Helsingfors) is the Finnish capital – but it's the fascinating combination of Swedish, Russian and international influences that makes Helsinki unlike any other Finnish city. Still, compared to the other sprawling Scandinavian capitals, tiny Helsinki feels almost provincial, and its only 'skyscraper' is just 12 storeys high. Its population is predominantly Finnish with relatively few foreign residents.

Helsinki is most pleasant in July and August, with fresh sea winds, nonstop action at the busy fish market, and many open-air cafés. Ferries regularly chug between the city proper and its outlying islands, as well as farther abroad to the Finnish cities of Porvoo, Ekenäs and Turku, and to Tallinn in Estonia and Stockholm.

Helsinki has been chosen to be one of nine 'European Cities of Culture' in 2000, an annually rotating title. New attractions will open for the occasion and others will receive careful makeovers. For updates see www.2000.hel.fi/.

HISTORY

Helsinki was founded in 1550 by King Gustav Vasa and is the sixth oldest town in Finland. The king longed to create a rival to the Hansa trading town of Tallin, the present-day capital of Estonia. An earlier trial at Ekenäs proved unsuccessful, so by royal decree traders from Ekenäs and a few other towns were bundled off to the newly founded Helsingfors.

For more than 200 years Helsinki remained a backwater market town on a windy, rocky peninsula. Then, in 1809, Russia annexed Finland from the decaying Swedish empire. A capital closer to St Petersburg was needed, to keep a better watch on Finland's domestic politics. Helsinki was chosen – in large part because of the

HIGHLIGHTS

- The famous Fish Market, for salmon chowder, cheap souvenirs and lots of local colour
- An afternoon at the new Kiasma Museum of Contemporary Art
- A stroll in Senate Square, designed in the 19th century to look just like St Petersburg
- Views of the city from the observation tower at the 1952 Olympic Stadium
- A ferry ride to Suomenlinna Island or to Helsinki Zoo
- A giant Finnish buffet at Konstan Möljä and real Lappish dishes at Lappi
- Haggling for treasures at Hietalahti flea market
- Rollerblading or bicycling in Kaivopuisto Park
- Gospel and classical concerts at Temppeliaukio Church, an underground church hewn from solid rock
- Cheap, fast ferry service to Tallinn, Estonia, just 90km away

massive sea fortress (now called Suomen-linna) just outside the harbour – and so in 1812 classy Turku lost its long-standing status as Finland's premier town. Its people continue to gripe about this demotion to the present day.

In the 19th and early 20th centuries, Helsinki grew rapidly in all directions. It suffered heavy Russian bombing during WWII, but in the postwar period Helsinki recovered and went on to host the Olympic Games in 1952. It is still the smallest city ever to stage the Summer Games.

In the 1970s and 80s, many new suburbs were built around Helsinki and residents celebrated their 'Helsinki Spirit', a term used for Cold War détente. Since then, Helsinki has served as an international conference point on numerous occasions – for everything from weighty economic summits to the World Dog Show and Sexhibition '98.

ORIENTATION

Helsinki is built on a peninsula and there are links by bridge and ferry with nearby islands. Surrounding towns include Espoo to the west and Vantaa, with the international airport, to the north.

The city centre is built around the main harbour, Eteläsatama. The *kauppatori* (market square) – also known as the fish market – is on the waterfront between the ferry terminals. Farther inland, but still within walking distance, are the bus and train stations. Main streets include Manner-heimintie and the twin shopping avenues of Pohjoisesplanadi and Eteläesplanadi.

The southern suburbs, Eira and Kaivo-puisto, are the 'posh' quarters, with villas and embassies. Katajanokka is an island east of the centre that is connected to the mainland by several bridges. Kallio and Töölö are densely populated residential areas. Meilahti, north-west of the centre, gives you access to the museum island of Seurasaari.

Maps

The city tourist office offers a good free map of Helsinki. There are also excellent maps of the Helsinki region in the local

telephone directory. The *Helsinki Route Map* (free at the city tourist office) is helpful for understanding the public transportation system. *See Helsinki On Foot* is the tourist office's free, step-by-step map and guide to the city centre.

INFORMATION
Tourist Offices

The Helsinki City Tourist Office (☎ 169 3757, tourist.info@hel.fi) at Pohjoises-planadi 19 will give you an updated city map and lists of events, restaurants, nightclubs and much more. Buy your Helsinki Card here (see the Helsinki Card section). You can also book hotel rooms and purchase tickets for rail, bus and ferry travel around Finland and for travel to Tallinn and St Petersburg. The office is open from 9 am to 7 pm Monday to Friday and from 9 am to 3 pm Saturday and Sunday from May to September. Opening hours are 9 am to 5 pm Monday to Friday, 9 am to 3 pm Saturday during the rest of the year.

Just opposite, across Esplanade Park, is another useful office – the Finnish Tourist Board (☎ 4176 9300, mek.espa@mek.fi) at Eteläesplanadi 4. Here you'll find brochures about attractions all over the country. The office is open from 8.30 am to 5 pm Monday to Friday and 10 am to 4 pm Saturday from June to August. It's open weekdays only during the off season.

Tikankontti (☎ 270 5221 or 0203-44 122, tikankontti@metsa.fi) at Eteläesplanadi 20 is the Helsinki office of Metsähallitus, the Finnish Forest and Park Service. It has information and maps for national parks and protected hiking areas, and you can buy maps and fishing licences or rent wilderness cottages around the country. Hours are 10 am to 6 pm Monday to Friday, 10 am to 3 pm Saturday.

The youth information and counselling centre Kompassi (☎ 612 1863), Mikonkatu 8, 2nd floor, offers youth cards, city maps and general information on travelling in Finland. It's open 11 am to 5 pm Monday to Thursday, 11 am to 4 pm Friday in summer (April to August).

Apart from the tourist office publications, free tourist brochures such as *Helsinki This Week* and *The City in English* are available at tourist offices, bookshops and other points around the city.

Money

Forex offers the best rates – with no commission for reconversion – and has an office at the train station open daily from 8 am to 9 pm. The Forex offices at Pohjoisesplanadi 27 and Mannerheimintie 10 keep the same hours during summer but only open from 8 am to 7 pm Monday to Saturday during the rest of the year.

At the airport the exchange counter is open daily from 6.30 am to 11 pm, although a machine operates 24 hours.

The American Express affiliate, Area Travel (☎ 628 788), at Mikonkatu 2D, is open from 9 am to 1 pm and 2.15 to 4.30 pm from Monday to Friday.

Western Union, on the 7th floor of the Stockmann department store at Aleksanterinkatu 52, is open from 9 am to 9 pm Monday to Friday, with shorter hours on weekends.

There are ATMs throughout the city centre, including several on Pohjoisesplanadi. Post offices also have ATMs.

Post & Communications

The main post office (☎ 02045 14400) is in the large building at Mannerheiminaukio 1, between the bus and train stations, and is open from 10 am to 7 pm weekdays, 11 am to 4 pm weekends. In the same building (door F) is the poste restante office (00100 Helsinki) open 8 am to 9 pm Monday to Friday, 9 am to 6 pm Saturday and 11 am to 9 pm Sunday. Mail is held for one month.

The main telephone office, on the 2nd floor in the main post office building, is open 9 am to 5 pm weekdays – you may place calls from here, though it's cheaper to call overseas using a prepaid phonecard at any public telephone. Domestic faxes cost 10/5 mk for the first page/each additional page and international faxes cost 26/13 mk.

The Yellow Pages for the Helsinki region has an index in English.

Internet Resources & Libraries

Helsinki currently lacks an Internet café but Internet access is free at public libraries. Most library Internet terminals must be booked at least a day in advance.

The most central of Helsinki's public libraries is Rikhardinkadun Library at Rikhardinkatu 3, open from 10 am to 8 pm Monday to Friday, 10 am to 4 pm Saturday. It has a good selection of books in English and several Internet terminals – including one that is first come, first served. Kirjakaapeli (the Cable Book Library; ☎ 310 85000, fax 310 85700, kirjakaapeli@ lib.hel.fi), at Lasipalatsi Multimedia Centre at Mannerheimintie 22-24, has at least three terminals that are first come, first served, and the rest may be booked by telephone. It is open from 10 am to midnight Monday to Thursday and midday to 6 pm on weekends.

Useful Web Sites The official Helsinki Web site at www.hel.fi/ has many good links – including one that lists Helsinki public transportation routes and fares. At www.helsinkiexpert.fi/ you can find up-to-date information on the Helsinki Card.

Travel Agencies

Kilroy Travels (☎ 680 7811) at Kaivokatu 10C specialises in student and budget travel.

Area Travel at Mikonkatu 2D is the STA Travel and American Express affiliate (see Money above) and handles general travel.

Tour Expert, in the city tourist office, is an agency handling travel around Finland and to Tallinn and St Petersburg.

From Helsinki you can easily arrange trips to the Baltic States, Russia and beyond. Consult the 'Matkailu' pages of the daily *Helsingin Sanomat* for listings.

Viro is Finnish for Estonia, and *Pietari* is Finnish for St Petersburg.

Bookshops

Akateeminen Kirjakauppa, at Pohjoisesplanadi 39, has books in 40 languages.

HELSINKI

HELSINKI

PLACES TO STAY
3 Hostel Stadion
12 Kallio Youth Hostel
33 Hostel Academica & UniCafé
34 Radisson SAS Royal Hotel
35 Satakuntatalo Hostel
38 Lord Hotel
45 Marttahotelli
47 Hotel Anna
53 Eurohostel
54 Scandic Hotel Grand Marina

PLACES TO EAT
10 Chico's All American Bistro
17 Kolme Kruunua
20 Café Tin Tin Tango
32 Mechelin Restaurant
39 Konstan Möljä
42 Kynsilaukka Garlic
43 Babushka Ira
48 Persepolis
52 Sipuli
58 Kasvisravintola
59 Šašlik
66 Café Ursula
68 Ani

OTHER
1 24-Hour Pharmacy
2 Swimming Stadium
4 Sports Museum of Finland
5 Olympic Stadium &
    Stadium Tower
6 Linnanmäki Amusement Park
7 Museum of Worker Housing
8 Tram Museum
9 Sibelius Monument
11 Opera House
13 Hakaniemi Kauppahalli
14 Helsinki Zoo
15 Maritime Museum of Finland
16 Military Museum
17 Burgher's House
19 Finlandia Hall
21 Töölö Hospital
22 Easywash
23 American Bookshop
24 National Museum
    (Kansallismuseo)
25 Helsinki City Museum
26 Storyville
27 Temppeliaukio Church
28 Parliament House
29 Natural History Museum
30 Groggy
31 Pub Pete
36 Vanha Maestro
37 Orion Theatre
40 Hietalahti Flea Market
41 Sinebrychoff Museum of
    Foreign Art
44 Cable Book Library
    (Kirjakaapeli)
46 Café Soda
49 Museum of Finnish
    Architecture& Museum
    of Art and Design
50 Makasiini Ferry Terminal
51 Uspenski Cathedral
55 Katajanokka Ferry Terminal
56 Olympia Ferry Terminal
57 Russian Consulate
60 K2 Skate Rental
61 Cygnaeus Gallery
62 Mannerheim Museum
63 Estonian Consulate
64 American Embassy
65 British High Commission
67 Temporary Exhibits
    (Kansallismuseo)
69 West Ferry Terminal
    (Länsiterminaali)
70 Finnish Museum of
    Photography & Kaapelitehdas

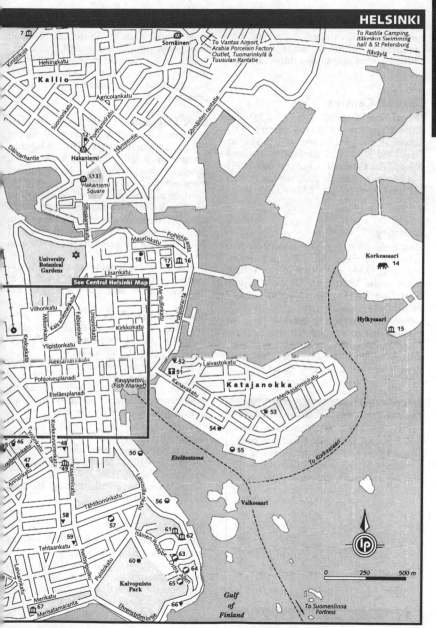

HELSINKI

The American Bookshop at Museokatu 3 has nonfiction books in English, including guidebooks. Karttakeskus Aleksi, at Unioninkatu 32, sells maps for all of Finland – road maps, topographical maps and more.

Cultural Centres

The British Council (☎ 701 8731) at Hakaniemenkatu 2 has a library. The American Center Library (☎ 175 587) at Vuorikatu 20 has magazines, books and videos. The Goethe Institute (☎ 680 3550) is at Mannerheimintie 20A, and the French Cultural Centre (☎ 622 0330) is at Keskuskatu 3.

Laundry

Most Helsinki hotels offer laundry service, and some of the hostels offer self-service facilities. Otherwise, look in the Yellow Pages under 'Pesuloita' for laundry services. *Isepalvelupesula* denotes self-service laundrettes.

Easywash is a self-service place at Runeberginkatu 47. Café Tin Tin Tango at Töölöntorinkatu 7 is a café-bar-art gallery-laundry-sauna! A load of laundry costs about 30 mk (beer and sauna cost extra).

Helsinki Card

This pass gives free travel on all local transport (except bus No 615 to the airport); entry to more than 50 museums and attractions in and around Helsinki; a 1½ hour guided sightseeing tour; discounts on one-day excursions to Porvoo and Tallin; and various other discounts and gifts. If you keep busy, the Helsinki Card is definitely good value at 110/140/170 mk for one/two/three days (45/55/65 mk for children aged seven to 16). It is available from the city tourist office, the train station, some travel agencies and most hostels and hotels.

Toilets

So-called 'French toilets', self-cleaning toilet kiosks made in France, can be found throughout the city centre and cost 5 mk. Toilets in bus and train stations cost 10 mk – for free ones you might try a public library, the Stockmann department store or an upscale hotel.

Left Luggage

Lockers at the train station cost 10 mk per day (maximum four days). The left-luggage counter, open daily from 6.30 am to 10 pm, charges 10 mk per piece per day (maximum three months).

At the bus station, 24-hour lockers cost 10 mk. The left-luggage counter is open from 7 am to 7 pm Monday to Friday, 7 am to 5 pm Saturday and 9 am to 6 pm Sunday. It charges 15 mk per piece per day (maximum five days).

There are also small lockers at the Stockmann department store which are cheaper than those at the train and bus stations.

Medical Services

For medical assistance, English speakers should use the 24 hour clinic at Töölö Hospital (☎ 4711) at Töölönkatu 40.

Yliopistoni Apteekki (☎ 4178 0300) at Mannerheimintie 96 is the city's 24 hour pharmacy but the branch in the city centre at Mannerheimintie 5, open daily from 7 am to midnight, is more convenient.

Emergency

In a general emergency dial ☎ 112, for police call ☎ 10022 and for 24 hour medical advice call ☎ 10023.

The police have offices at the Helsinki train and bus stations.

WALKING TOUR

The thumping heart of Helsinki is the bustling **kauppatori** (market square), also known as the fish market (see Markets in the Shopping section later in this chapter). It is surrounded by graceful 19th century buildings – some of just the few remaining in the city after the devastation of WWII. One block west is the **Helsinki City Tourist Office** (see Information earlier in this chapter).

Havis Amanda, the lovely mermaid statue and fountain just west of the fish market, was designed in 1908 by one of Finland's most beloved artists, Ville Vallgren. The statue, also known as 'Manta', is commonly regarded as the symbol of Helsinki – if not all of Finland.

Across from the kauppatori is the **Presidential Palace** at Pohjoisesplanadi 1. This is the president's official residence – though current President Martti Ahtisaari's frequent absences have earned him the nickname Reissu-Mara (Travelling Mara).

The Orthodox **Uspenski Cathedral**, on a hill above the harbour, is one of the most recognisable landmarks in Helsinki (see Churches). It stands on the small island of Katajanokka, an upscale community with many fine old residential buildings. Several small bridges link Katajanokka with the mainland.

Senaatintori (Senate Square), just north of the fish market, is Helsinki's 'official' centre. Carl Ludvig Engel, a native of Berlin, was invited to design the square after the Finnish capital was moved from Turku in 1812. He had earlier worked in St Petersburg – so what you see today in Helsinki looks quite Russian, which may explain why Helsinki has been used by Hollywood to shoot 'Russian scenes', such as those in the films *Reds*, *White Nights* and *Gorky Park*. The **statue of Tsar Alexander II** in Senaatintori was cast in 1894 and symbolises the strong Russian influence in 19th century Helsinki.

The main **Helsinki University** building is at Senaatintori, though Engel's stately blue-domed **Tuomiokirkko** (Lutheran Cathedral) is the square's most prominent feature (see Churches).

Walk west on Pohjoisesplanadi along pleasant **Esplanade Park**, recently recobbled and spiffied up, to the city's broad main thoroughfare, Mannerheimintie. On the north-east corner is the famous **Stockmann department store**, where seemingly every Helsinkian buys, well, everything.

Continue two blocks north on Mannerheimintie to **Kiasma**, the newly opened Museum of Contemporary Art (see Art Museums). An **equestrian statue of** Marshal CGE Mannerheim, the most revered of Finnish leaders, dominates the square next to the museum. Protests by war veterans delayed the building of Kiasma by almost a decade because many felt that it would degrade Mannerheim's memory to build a modern art museum on the site – as it turned out, the Marshal was an avid collector of avant garde art in his day.

Detour two blocks east to the Soviet-sized Rautatientori (Railway Square), where you'll find the train station, naturally, as well as the National Gallery, **Ateneum** (see Art Museums). The museum building, long considered a masterpiece in progress, was completed in 1991.

Return to Mannerheimintie and continue walking north. The monolithic 1931 **Parliament House** dominates this stretch. Free guided tours are given at 2 pm Monday to Friday and at noon on Saturday and Sunday in July and August. In winter, tours are only given on weekends at noon.

On the other side of Mannerheimintie is one of Alvar Aalto's most famous works, the angular **Finlandia Hall**, a concert hall built in 1971. The Italian marble chosen by the great architect has not weathered the Finnish climate well and is being replaced at great expense!

A few blocks farther north is the 1993 **Opera House**, home of the Finnish National Opera. From the Opera House, turn right on Helsinginkatu to reach the tiny and manicured **City Winter Garden** and the **Linnanmäki amusement park**. Or, continue a short distance north on Mannerheimintie to the 1952 **Olympic Stadium**.

For some of the best views of Helsinki, take a lift to the top of the 72m **Stadium Tower**. It's open 9 am to 8 pm Monday to Friday, and 9 am to 6 pm on weekends. The cost is 10 mk (free with a Helsinki Card).

From the stadium, walk west to Sibelius park and the **Sibelius monument**. This kinetic modern sculpture was created by artist Eila Hiltunen in 1967 to honour Finland's most famous composer, Jean Sibelius. Bus No 24 from the park can take you north-west to the **Seurasaari Open-Air Museum** (see Museums), or south to the intersection of Mannerheimintie and Pohjoisesplanadi, its terminus.

For a good detour from Mannerheimintie, walk down posh Bulevardi all the way to the **Hietalahti flea market** (see Shopping) where even rich and famous Helsinkians have been known to sell some of their designer duds. **Sinebrychoff** at Bulevardi 40 is the museum of foreign art (see Art Museums).

Return to the fish market to catch one of the many ferries or water taxis that shuttle to nearby islands – don't miss a boat trip to **Suomenlinna island** or to the **Helsinki Zoo** on Korkeasaari island.

Another pleasant way to spend an afternoon might be a stroll south from the fish market along the waterfront to **Kaivopuisto park**, where you can rollerblade or bicycle – or simply laze away a few hours at the seaside **Café Ursula** (see the Cafés section in Places to Eat later in this chapter).

ART MUSEUMS

The painters, designers and architects mentioned in the Facts about Finland chapter earlier in this guide are well represented in Helsinki's galleries and museums.

Following are summer hours – opening hours are typically shorter in winter. The Helsinki Card gives free admission to all of the following museums.

In Espoo, the **Gallén-Kallela Museum** is one of the Helsinki area's top art museums. See the Around Helsinki section later in this chapter.

Kiasma Museum of Contemporary Art

Kiasma, at Mannerheiminaukio 2, opened to much fanfare in 1998. The quirky modern building, designed by American architect Steven Holl, exhibits a rapidly growing collection of Finnish and international art from the 1960s to the 1990s. It's open from 9 am to 6 pm Tuesday and Friday, 9 am to 8 pm

Wednesday and Thursday and 11 am to 5 pm Saturday and Sunday. Admission is 25 mk.

Ateneum

The list of painters at Ateneum (the National Gallery) at Kaivokatu 2 reads like a 'Who's Who'. It houses Finnish works from the 18th century to the 1950s, as well as a small collection of 19th and early 20th century foreign art. Hours are the same as at Kiasma. Tickets cost 10 to 40 mk, depending on the type of special exhibition on offer.

Sinebrychoff Museum of Foreign Art

The largest collection of Italian, Dutch and Flemish paintings in Finland can be found on the premises of the old brewery at Bulevardi 40 (catch tram No 6). It's open from 9 am to 5 pm Monday, Thursday and Friday, 9 am to 8 pm Wednesday, and 11 am to 5 pm Saturday and Sunday. Admission is 10 to 40 mk.

Finnish Museum of Photography

The Finnish Museum of Photography mounts interesting temporary exhibitions, usually grouped by artist or subject. It's located in **Kaapelitehdas**, a former cable factory in western Helsinki that is now full of studios, galleries and other businesses. Hours are noon to 6 pm Tuesday to Friday (until 8 pm Wednesday), noon to 5 pm on weekends. Admission is 15 mk. Catch tram No 8, or take the metro to Ruoholahti.

Cygnaeus Gallery

If you're looking for Finnish art from the 19th century, this is a great place to go. It opened in 1882 and is one of Finland's oldest art galleries. The attractive wooden building in Kaivopuisto park was built in 1870, and is open from 11 am to 7 pm on Wednesday and 11 am to 4 pm Thursday to Sunday. Admission is 15 mk.

Amos Anderson Art Museum

The collection of publishing magnate Amos Anderson, one of the wealthiest Finns of his time, includes Finnish and European paintings and sculptures. The museum, at Yrjönkatu 27, is closed for renovations until spring 1999.

Museum of Art and Design
This museum at Korkeavuorenkatu 23 hosts interesting special exhibitions. It's open from noon to 7 pm on weekdays (until 6 pm on weekends). Admission is 40 to 50 mk.

Museum of Finnish Architecture
This museum and its reference library are at Kasarmikatu 24. They're open daily (except Monday) from 10 am to 4 pm, and until 7 pm on Wednesday. Admission is 10 to 20 mk.

MUSEUMS
As with the art museums, these have shorter hours in winter, and are free with the Helsinki Card. **Heureka** is a fine science museum located in Vantaa (see the Vantaa section later in this chapter for details).

National Museum (Kansallismuseo)
The impressive National Museum building on Mannerheimintie is under renovation and will reopen in early 2000. Select pieces from the museum's collection of artefacts – which includes a throne of Tsar Alexander I dating from 1809 – are temporarily located near Kaivopuisto park at Laivurinkatu 3. Hours are 11 am to 8 pm on Tuesday, 11 am to 4 pm from Wednesday to Sunday. Entry is 15 mk for adults.

Mannerheim Museum
The fascinating home museum (☎ 635 443) of Mannerheim, former president and Civil War victor, is at Kalliolinnantie 14 in Kaivopuisto park. Among the souvenirs from Mannerheim's life are hundreds of military medals, as well as photographs from his trip to Asia, when he travelled 14,000km along the Silk Route from Samarkand to Beijing, riding the same faithful horse for two years. Some of the Asian artefacts are displayed – others are in the collection of the National Museum. The Mannerheim Museum is open from 11 am

CGE Mannerheim

to 4 pm Friday to Sunday, and by appointment. Admission is 40 mk (free on 4 June, Mannerheim's birthday) and includes a mandatory guided tour in one of six languages.

Seurasaari Open-Air Museum
West of the centre, Seurasaari island is an open-air museum (☎ 484 712) with 18th and 19th century houses from around Finland. Guides dressed in traditional costume demonstrate folk dancing, and crafts such as spinning, embroidery and troll-making. Admission to the open-air museum is 20 mk. Hours are 11 am to 5 pm daily (until 7 pm Wednesday) from June to August, shorter hours in May and September and closed 1 October to 14 May.

Urho Kekkonen Museum Tamminiemi
The large house at Seurasaarentie 15 in Tamminiemi was a presidential residence for 30 years, right up until Urho Kekkonen's death, when it was turned into a museum. The house is surrounded by a beautiful park. It's open from 11 am to 5 pm daily (closed Monday in winter). Admission is 20 mk.

From central Helsinki, take bus No 24, or tram No 4 and walk. Seurasaari is nearby.

Helsinki City Museum (Kaupunginmuseo)

Several small museums constitute the Helsinki City Museum. All are open from 11 am to 5 pm Wednesday to Sunday, and each charges a 20 mk entry fee

Burgher's House This historic house at Kristianinkatu 12, built in 1818, is the oldest wooden town house in central Helsinki (closed from October to March).

Helsinki City Museum The old villa opposite the National Museum was scheduled to reopen in early 1999, after extensive renovation.

Museum of Worker Housing This museum, at Kirstinkuja 4, shows how industrial workers in Helsinki lived earlier this century.

Sederholm House Helsinki's oldest brick building, at Aleksanterinkatu 16-18, dates from 1757 and is furnished to suit a wealthy 18th century merchant.

Tram Museum This delightful museum, in an old tram depot at Eino Leinonkatu 3, displays vintage trams and depicts daily life in Helsinki's streets in past decades.

Tuomarinkylä Museum & Children's Museum In the suburb of Tuomarinkylä, not far from the airport, this pair of museums occupies an 18th century manor house (closed from October to March). From central Helsinki take bus No 64 to its terminus and walk 1km.

Maritime Museum of Finland

The Maritime Museum, in a historic harbour building on Hylkysaari island, can only be reached by bridge from Korkeasaari island, home to the Helsinki Zoo (see Parks & Gardens later in this chapter). The exhibits – on shipbuilding and the sailor's life – are interesting. The museum is open from 11 am to 5 pm daily from May to September. Admission is 10 mk.

Natural History Museum

The University of Helsinki's collection of mammals, birds and other creatures numbers about seven million specimens. The museum, at Pohjoinen Rautatienkatu 13, is open from 9 am to 5 pm Monday to Friday (to 8 pm on Wednesday), and 11 am to 4 pm Saturday and Sunday. Admission is 25 mk.

Post Museum (Postimuseo)

The Post Museum, in the main post office building next to the train station, is free – and its stamp collections, computerised data banks and other hi-tech exhibits are fascinating. The museum is open from 10 am to 7 pm on weekdays (closed Tuesday) and from 11 am to 4 pm on weekends.

Sports Museum of Finland

The 1952 Olympic Stadium houses Finland's 'sporting hall of fame'. The museum is open from 11 am to 5 pm Monday to Friday and from noon to 4 pm on weekends. Admission is 10 mk. Tram Nos 3B, 3T, 4, 7A, 7B and 10 will get you to the stadium.

Military Museum

The Military Museum has an extensive collection of Finnish army paraphernalia. The museum is at Maurinkatu 1 and is open from 11 am to 4 pm daily (except Saturday). Admission is 10 mk.

CHURCHES
Lutheran Cathedral (Tuomiokirrko)

Tuomiokirrko, Helsinki's landmark Lutheran Cathedral, dominates the north side of Senaatintori. As with the square, it was designed by Engel and completed in 1852. The inside is surprisingly uninteresting – but make the climb up the staircase anyway for excellent views of old Helsinki. The cathedral is open daily in summer. Its crypt is now a café (see Cafés under Places to Eat).

Temppeliaukio Church

The Temppeliaukio Church (literally, Church in the Rock), designed by Timo and Tuomo Suomalainen in 1969, remains one of Helsinki's foremost attractions – and yes, it's hewn from solid rock. Concerts, both gospel and classical, are frequent, and English-language services are held Sundays at 2 pm. Hours are from 10 am to 8 pm weekdays, 10 am to 6 pm Saturday, and noon to 1.45 pm and 3.30 to 5.45 pm

Sunday. The church is at Lutherinkatu 3 – the entrance is at the end of Fredrikinkatu.

Uspenski Cathedral

This very photogenic red brick Orthodox cathedral, built in Byzantine-Slavonic style in 1868, has an interior lavishly decorated with icons. It is on Katajanokka island across from the fish market. Hours are 9.30 am to 4 pm Monday to Friday (until 6 pm Tuesday), 9 am to 4 pm on Saturday and noon to 3 pm on Sunday in summer (closed Monday in winter).

PARKS & GARDENS
City Winter Garden

The botanical gardens at Hammarskjöldintie 1 were founded in 1893 and contain cacti, palms and other sun-loving plants foreign to Finnish soil. Hours are from noon to 3 pm daily. Entry is free and there's a café. Take tram No 8 from Ruoholahti metro or Töölö.

University Botanical Gardens

The Botanical Gardens at Unioninkatu 44 comprise Finland's largest botanical collection, with greenhouses and a park. The greenhouses are open daily in summer, weekends only at other times. Admission is 10 mk. The garden is open longer, and has free entry.

Linnanmäki Amusement Park

The Linnanmäki amusement park has all the usual kid-pleasing rides and is on a hill just north of Kallio suburb (bus No 23 or tram No 3B, 3T or 8). Its profits are donated to child welfare organisations. Hours are daily until 10 pm from late April to September. Day passes are 90 mk (children 60 mk) but it is also possible to pay basic admission (15 mk; children 10 mk; free with Helsinki Card) and then buy individual ride tickets (6 mk).

HELSINKI ZOO

The Helsinki Zoo – one of the northernmost zoos in the world – is on Korkeasaari island. Established in 1889, it has animals from Finland and around the world housed in large natural enclosures. You can catch bus No 16 to Kulosaari, and then take bus No 11 or walk 1.5km through the island of Mustikkamaa and onto Korkeasaari – but the more pleasant way to arrive is by boat from the fish market; these depart from the passenger quay opposite the Presidential Palace. The 38 mk return boat ticket (children 21 mk) includes zoo admission. Regular zoo admission is 25 mk (children 15 mk), free with a Helsinki Card. The zoo is open daily May to September from 10 am to 8 pm, at other times until 4 pm.

ACTIVITIES

Rollerblading is popular in Helsinki, and K2 Skate Rental (☎ 040-525 7787) offers rentals at 25 mk for 30 minutes (10 mk per each additional 30 minutes), helmet, pads and wrist guards included. The K2 kiosk, at the north entrance to Kaivopuisto park, is open from 11 am to 10 pm daily in summer.

For information on bicycle rentals see the Getting Around section later in this chapter. The bike and skate route map, *Helsingin Pyöräilykartta*, is free at the city tourist office.

Helsinki has several public swimming pools with inexpensive admission. Most convenient is the outdoor Swimming Stadium near Hostel Stadion. It is open daily from May to the end of August. That said, the most impressive place to swim is the Itäkeskus swimming hall (take the metro to Itäkeskus Östra centrum station). The entire underground swimming hall – with several pools, saunas and a gym – is carved from rock and can also double as a bomb shelter for 3800 people. It is in the Itäkeskus shopping centre.

ORGANISED TOURS

A 1½ hour guided sightseeing tour by bus departs at 10 am daily from the Olympia Terminal on the south side of the kauppatori. Commentary is in English and Swedish, and the cost is 85 mk (its free with a Helsinki Card). In summer, additional English-language tours depart at 11 am and 2 pm daily from Pohjoisespanadi 15-17 at the kauppatori.

HELSINKI

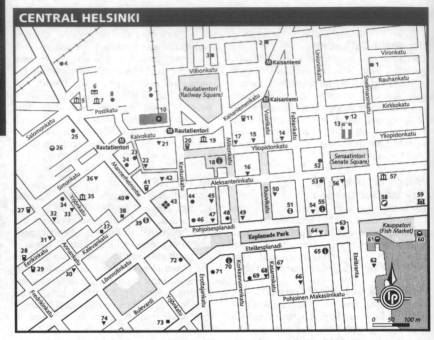

CENTRAL HELSINKI

There are also several types of guided walking tours in summer, usually given once each week. Inquire at the city tourist office.

Cruises

Strolling through the fish market in summer, you won't have to look for cruises – the boat companies will find you. Royal Line (☎ 170 488), Sun Lines (☎ 755 5488) and a number of smaller companies offer 1½ hour sea cruises (70 mk) with daily departures in summer. The trip around the island of Laajasalo, run by Sun Lines, is probably the most interesting.

A visit to the Helsinki Zoo or Suomenlinna sea fortress is a good way to combine a scenic boat ride with other sightseeing. There are also longer cruises from Helsinki to the Finnish cities of Inkoo and Porvoo; see the Getting There & Away section later in this chapter.

SPECIAL EVENTS

Vappu (May Day), the festival of students and workers, is taken seriously in Helsinki – on 30 April at 6 pm people gather in the centre around the Havis Amanda statue, which receives a white 'student cap'. Helsinki Day (12 June), celebrating the city's anniversary, brings many free and cheap activities to Esplanade Park; Helsinki's 450th anniversary will be celebrated in 2000.

The Regional Fair, held in early June, spotlights a different region of Finland each year. From late August to early September the Helsinki Festival is held, an elaborate arts festival with chamber music, jazz, theatre, opera and more. In early October the annual Baltic Herring Market, a 200-year-old tradition, takes place at the market square. Helsinki hosts an ethnic music festival, Etnosoi, in early November. Christmas

CENTRAL HELSINKI

PLACES TO STAY
1 Kongressikoti
2 Hotel Arthur
3 Omapohja
37 Sokos Hotel Torni & Ateljee
  Bar
38 Hotel Finn
73 Hostel Erottajanpuisto

PLACES TO EAT
12 Café Krypta
14 Porthania
15 Merhi's Snack Bar & Food
16 Hesburger
17 Planet Hollywood
21 Alepa Supermarket
22 Zetor
30 Lappi
31 Long Wall
32 Maithai
33 House of Sandwiches
36 Forum Shopping Centre,
  Golden Rax Pizza Buffet &
  Cinemas
42 Turkish Kebab Room
45 Tempura
47 Café Esplanade
49 Café Strindberg
50 Fazer
54 Café Ursula
56 Café Engel

62 Kauppahalli
64 Kappeli
66 Zucchini
67 Cantina West
68 Volga
74 Café Ekberg

OTHER
4 Greenbike
5 Kiasma Museum of
  Contemporary Art
6 Main Post Office, Poste
  Restante & Telephone Office
7 Postimuseo
8 Finnair Office & Finnair buses
9 Hotel Booking Centre
10 Train Station & Forex
11 Molly Malone's
13 Luthreran Cathedral
  (Tuomiokirrko)
18 Kompassi Youth Information
  Centre
19 Ateneum (The National
  Gallery)
20 Wall Street Bar
23 Kilroy Travels
24 Pharmacy
25 Lasipalatsi Multimedia Centre
26 Bus Station & Regional Buses
27 DTM
28 Corona Bar

29 Con Hombres
34 Finnish Youth Hostel Association (SRM)
35 Amos Anderson Art Museum
39 Forex
40 Viking Line
41 Vanha
43 Stockmann Department Store,
  Western Union & Kitchen
44 Eckerö Lines
46 Bookshop (Akateeminen
  Kirjakauppa)
48 Area Travel (AmEx office)
51 Forex
52 Helsinki University
53 Bookshop (Karttakeskus
  Aleksi)
55 Helsinki City Tourist Office &
  Tour Expert
57 Sederholm House
58 Swedish Embassy
59 Presidential Palace
60 Local Ferries
61 Cruise Boats
63 Havis Amanda Statue
65 Finnish Tourist Board
69 Rikhardinkadun Library
70 Finnish Forest & Park Service
  (Tikankontti)
71 Tallink
72 Silja Lines

is a special time in Helsinki, with the big Lucia parade taking place in mid-December.

PLACES TO STAY

Bookings are essential for Helsinki hostels and hotels from mid-May to mid-August. The Hotel Booking Centre (☎ 171 133, fax 175 524, hotel@helsinkiexpert.fi) in the west wing of the train station can help in a pinch – it's open Monday to Saturday from 9 am to 7 pm, Sunday from 10 am to 6 pm from June to the end of August, and weekdays from 9 am to 5 pm during the rest of the year. There is a second branch at the city tourist office. The booking charge is 20 mk, but room rates are often cheaper than you would be able to negotiate on your own.

PLACES TO STAY – BUDGET
Camping
Rastila Camping (☎ 316 551, fax 344 1578), 10km east of the centre in Vuosaari, is open all year. It charges 60 mk per head or 80 mk per group. Cabins cost 200 to 580 mk. Take bus No 90, 96 or 98 from Itäkeskus metro station. The trip takes about 15 to 20 minutes

Hostels
City Centre Helsinki has three year-round hostels and three that are open in summer only. The Finnish Youth Hostel Association (SRM) office (☎ 694 0377) is at Yrjönkatu 38B.

The HI-affiliated *Hostel Stadion* (☎ 496 071, fax 496 466, Pohjoinen Stadiontie 3B), at the Olympic Stadium, has 162 beds, with dorm beds from 70 mk as well as singles/doubles. Reception is open daily from 8 to 10 am and 4 pm to 2 am. A buffet breakfast costs 20 mk, and there is a well equipped kitchen, TV rooms and laundry. Take tram No 3T or 7A.

The high-rise *Eurohostel* (☎ 622 0470, fax 655 044, euroh@icon.fi, Linnankatu 9) on Katajanokka island near the Viking Line terminal is an HI hostel open all year. It charges 120 mk per bed in immaculate double rooms. The rate includes morning sauna and access to kitchen facilities, laundry and a café. Reception is open 24 hours. Take tram No 4 or 2 from the centre.

Hostel Erottajanpuisto (☎ 642 169, fax 680 2757, Uudenmaankatu 9), an HI hostel, is the closest and most convenient to the heart of the city. It charges 120 mk per bed in stylish six-bed dorm rooms and is open all year. It also offers singles and doubles.

Kallio Youth Hostel (☎ 773 3429, Kallio.kh@kallio2.pp.fi, Porthaninkatu 2), open from mid-June to August, is a tiny (35 beds) but extremely friendly place with dorm beds (70 mk; breakfast 20 mk) as well as a kitchen, TV room, laundry and café. Take the metro to Hakaniemi station (use the northern exit), or tram No 1, 2 or 3B.

A student apartment building in winter, the HI-affiliated *Hostel Academica* (☎ 1311 4334, fax 441 201, hostel .academica@hyy.fi, Hietaniemenkatu 14) is open to travellers from June to August. Rates for its 115 rooms with kitchenettes start at 90 mk per bed or 230/320 mk for singles/doubles, morning sauna and swimming included.

Satakuntatalo Hostel (☎ 695 85231, Lapinrinne 1A) is also a student apartment building that opens to travellers from June to August. An HI-affiliated hostel, it has beds for 70 mk. The six-bed dorms are equipped with kitchens, and an all-you-can-eat breakfast is 25 mk.

Airport *Vantaan Retkeilymaja* (☎ 839 3310, fax 839 4366, Valkoisenlähteentie 52), near the airport in Vantaa, is a clean HI-

affiliated hostel open year-round. Dormitory beds start at 55 mk, and there are singles and doubles, a sauna and laundry.

PLACES TO STAY – MID-RANGE
Guesthouses
Many guesthouses in Helsinki ooze sleaze, but not *Omapohja* (☎ 666 211, Itäinen Teatterikuja 3) near the train station. It offers spotlessly clean rooms from 220/295 mk – and it fills quickly.

Kongressikoti (☎ 135 6839, fax 728 6947, Snellmaninkatu 15A) is another small, very clean place in a residential area. The friendly owner offers rooms for 170/230 mk.

Hotels
City Centre *Marttahotelli* (☎ 646 211, fax 680 1266, martta@sui.fi, Uudenmaankatu 24) is pleasant. Its 45 rooms are 470/570 mk (360/460 mk in summer and on weekends) and include a superb buffet breakfast.

Close to the train station is *Hotel Arthur* (☎ 173 441, fax 626 880, Vuorikatu 19) with rooms from 400/500 mk (330/400 mk summer and weekends). *Hotel Finn* (☎ 640 904, fax 640 905, Kalevankatu 3B) is another central hotel, with rooms from 250/300 mk.

Hotel Anna (☎ 616 621, fax 602 664, Annankatu 1), in a lively neighbourhood, has rooms for 480/620 mk (310/420 mk summer and weekends).

Airport *Good Morning Hotels Pilotti* (☎ 329 4800, fax 329 48100, Veromaentie 1), 3km from the airport, has rooms from 310/410 mk (270/350 mk summer and weekends).

The *Airport Hotel Bonus Inn* (☎ 82 511, Elannontie 9), 5km south of the airport, has rooms for 440/550 mk (280/340 mk summer and weekends).

PLACES TO STAY – TOP END
Hotels
City Centre The lovely Art Nouveau *Lord Hotel* (☎ 615 815, fax 680 1315, Lönnrotinkatu 29) offers rooms for 680/840 mk

avis Amanda, symbol of Helsinki

Helsinki architecture

y dock, Suomenlinna shipyard

Helsinki café life

Pub Tram, Helsinki

Sibelius Monument, Helsinki

Sculptures in a Helsinki square

Summer drinking, Helsinki

(440/480 mk weekends and summer), breakfast and sauna included.

The highest building in the city centre is the *Sokos Hotel Torni* (☎ *131 131, fax 131 1361, Yrjönkatu 26)*, with rooms from 1075/1320 mk. Torni translates as 'tower'.

Radisson SAS Royal Hotel (☎ *69 580, fax 6958 7100, Runeberginkatu 2)*, one of the finest hotels in Helsinki, boasts a spectacular smorgasbord brunch. Rooms are from 1170/1290 mk (475/575 mk mid-June to late July).

In a renovated harbour building on Kata janokka island, *Scandic Hotel Grand Marina* (☎ *16 661, fax 664 764, Katajanokanlaituri 7)* has rooms from 790/990 mk (450/510 mk summer and weekends).

Airport The *Cumulus Airport Hotel* (☎ *4157 7100, fax 4157 7101, Robert Hubertintie 4)*, 3km south of the airport, has a pool and rooms for 670/810 mk (410/480 mk weekends and summer). Breakfast, sauna and shuttle service are included.

PLACES TO EAT
The *kauppahalli* (covered market) on Eteläranta has stalls selling 15 mk pizza slices and sandwiches. The *kauppatori*, also known as the fish market, is good for salmon chowder, cheap snacks and fresh produce.

Finnish
Konstan Möljä (Hietalahdenkatu 14) offers an excellent home-style lunch buffet – soup, salad, bread, meat and vegetable dishes – for 38 mk (dinner buffet 59 mk).

Kolme Kruunua (Liisankatu 5) is a relic of the 1930s, open daily from 4 pm. It is famous for its *lihapullat* (meatballs; 46 mk).

Zetor (Mannerheimintie 3-5) is a jokey Finnish restaurant with outrageous décor (open daily from 3 pm to 3 am). It's run by the Leningrad Cowboys, a local rock group.

Delightful *Lappi (Annankatu 22)* is a classy establishment with genuine Lappish specialities (lunch from 35 mk, dinner from 90 mk).

Mechelin (Mechelininkatu 7) is the training restaurant of Finland's oldest culinary institute. It offers a traditional Finnish

buffet lunch (38 mk) and dinner (45 to 85 mk) daily in summer.

Russian
Russia's best restaurants are said to be in Helsinki – try a blini (50 mk) at the romantic *Babushka Ira* (☎ *680 1405, Uudenmaankatu 28)* to judge for yourself. Its motto is 'fish from Finland – recipes from Russia'.

Volga (Richardinkatu 1) has a summer terrace and serves 40 mk weekday lunch specials. You'll find the place by looking for a life-sized plastic cow out the front.

Šašlik (☎ *348 9700, Neitsytpolku 12)* is Helsinki's top Russian restaurant (main courses from 70 mk). It offers live music nightly and seven private, themed dining rooms.

International
Fill up on ethnic food before leaving Helsinki – it doesn't really exist elsewhere in Finland.

Cantina West (Kasarmikatu 23) is a very popular Mexican restaurant and bar with a good buffet lunch.

Kitchen, in the basement of Stockmann department store, offers everything from 16 mk foccacia sandwiches to a 46 mk 'wok of the day'.

Persepolis (Pieni Roobertinkatu 7) offers a Middle Eastern buffet (with vegetarian choices) at 39 mk. *Ani (Telakkakatu 2)* has a good Turkish-Armenian buffet for 38 mk (daily from 10.30 am to 11 pm). The *Turkish Kebab Room* in the centre serves authentic Turkish food (30 to 45 mk).

Tiny *Maithai (Annankatu 31-33)* is a local favourite for Thai food, with lunch from 35 mk. Nearby *Long Wall (Annankatu 26)* is a large, popular Chinese restaurant that offers a 10% discount on takeaway.

Chico's All American Bistro (Mannerheimintie 68) is popular with families for its 'American' food – like pepperoni quesadillas and peanut butter chicken sandwiches.

Planet Hollywood is at Mikonkatu 9 – Renny Harlin, Finland's man in Hollywood, is an owner.

Golden Rax Pizza Buffet, on the 2nd floor of the Forum shopping centre at Mannerheimintie 20, isn't particularly good, but who could pass up all-your-can-eat pizza, pasta, salad and chicken wings for 43 mk? Children aged five to 10 pay 31 mk, and the ice cream buffet is an extra 5 mk.

Award-winning *Kynsilaukka Garlic* (☎ 651 939, Fredrikinkatu 22) offers an eclectic menu – including garlic beer. Appetisers are from 45 mk, main courses from 70 mk.

Near the Orthodox Church on Katajanokka island, *Sipuli* (☎ 179 900, Kanavaranta 3) offers fine views. It specialises in wild game (open for dinner only; main courses 90 to 160 mk).

Vegetarian

Helsinki's vegetarian restaurants are superb. *Tempura (Mikonkatu 2)* serves lunch only (from 25 mk) but *Kasvisravintola (Korkeavuorenkatu 3)* is open nightly to 8 pm, with generous 45 to 55 mk dinners. *Zucchini* on Fabiankatu is the city's 'vegetarian café'.

Cafés

There are a number of good cafés around Esplanade Park. In the park itself, *Kappeli*, established in 1837, is a café, restaurant and microbrewery/bar.

Café Esplanade (Pohjoisesplanadi 37) serves oversized Danish pastries at budget prices, while *Café Strindberg (Pohjoisesplanadi 33)* caters to snappy types, with 15 mk cappuccinos.

Café Ekberg (Bulevardi 9) is probably the oldest café in Finland, and was known as 'The Pit' when it opened in 1861.

Another historical café is *Fazer (Kluuvikatu 3)*. Founded in 1891 by the Finnish candy-making family, it does amazing ice cream sundaes.

Café Krypta (Kirkkokatu 18), in the crypt of Tuomiokirkko, is open from early June to mid-August daily until 4 pm. *Café Engel* at Senaatintori has a nice summer courtyard.

The seaside *Café Ursula* is popular year-round; its outdoor section affords good views of Suomenlinna. There is another branch by the same name in the centre, on Pohjoisesplanadi. *Café Tin Tin Tango* (see Laundry earlier in this chapter) is a unique café and art gallery – you can do your laundry or have a sauna here as well!

Fast Food

There are plenty of hamburger restaurants, pizza shops, kebab joints and grills in Helsinki – for the best selection head to the

---

Helsinki – *Kahvi* Drinking Capital of Europe

Time magazine recently predicted that Helsinki, with its street cafés full of coffee-guzzling, mobile-phone wielding go-getters, was poised to become the swinging London of the new millennium.

If mobile-phone ownership and coffee consumption have anything to do with success, this prediction could well come true. Finns consume 14kg of coffee per person annually, or the equivalent of nine cups a day each, and 50% of the Finnish population own a mobile phone.

Even outside the bustling big city, coffee is what drives Finland. There are dozens of cafés in every town and village; even petrol stations have cafés, and a cup of coffee is included with the lunch special at most restaurants.

Seldom will you visit a house without being served coffee. Traditionally you say 'no' three times and then accept, by saying 'OK, just half a cup', which in reality turns out to be four or five cups.

To do as the Finns do, pour your *kahvi* into a *kuppi* and add some *maito* (milk) or *kerma* (cream). Finns usually eat some *pulla* (wheat bun) with coffee.

basement level of the *Forum shopping centre*.

Merhi's Snack Bar & Food (Yliopistonkatu 5) has pita and kebab from 18 mk, and there's a *Hesburger* on Aleksanterinkatu.

The *House of Sandwiches*, on Yrjönkatu across from the Forum shopping centre, is a healthier alternative (closed Sunday and Monday).

University Eateries

Helsinki University operates several student cafeterias around the city, where a meal costs less than 20 mk. Each always offers a vegetarian main course. The best are *UniCafé* at Hostel Academica and *Porthania (Yliopistonkatu 11-13)*. Many foreign students eat at Porthania.

Self-Catering

The *Alepa supermarket*, in the train station pedestrian tunnel (Asematunneli), is open 8 am to 10 pm Monday to Saturday, 10 am to 10 pm on Sunday.

ENTERTAINMENT

For events, concerts and performances, see *Helsinki This Week* or inquire at the city tourist office.

The Symphony Orchestra of the Finnish Broadcasting Corporation (RSO) features popular concerts in *Finlandia Hall*. Ballet and opera are at the *Opera House (Helsinginkatu 58)*; performances of the Finnish National Opera are surtitled in Finnish.

Sports events in Helsinki are numerous. Many events are held at the *Olympic Stadium*, off Mannerheimintie, which has an indoor arena for ice hockey.

Bars & Clubs

In summer the bright red pub tram, *Pårakoff*, operates Monday to Saturday from 11 am to 3 pm and 5 to 10 pm with stops at the train station, Opera House and Kauppatori. The cost is 30 mk, first beer included.

The brewery pub in the cellar at *Kappeli* good, and its outdoor tables are always crowded in summer. Finnish composer Oskar Merikanto once wrote a song for Kappeli, his favourite drinking spot.

Ateljee Bar, atop the Sokos Hotel Torni, has the best views in the city.

Vanha (Mannerheimintie 3), in the 19th century students' house, is a perennial favourite for live music – there is a cover charge. *Molly Malone's (Kaisaniemenkatu 1C)* is a cosy Irish bar that is also popular for live music.

Storyville (Museokatu 8) is a jazz club with international acts.

Long popular with international travellers is the tiny *Wall Street Bar* on Yliopistonkatu. *Café Soda (Uudenmaankatu 16)*, a sleek spot with a DJ at night, is a hipster's hangout.

Corona Bar (Eerikinkatu 11) is famous for its billiard tables. *Pub Pete*, across the road from Hostel Academica, is a mellow student bar.

Groggy (☎ 454 4991, Pohjoinen Rautatienkatu 21) is a dance club with hip hop, techno, Finnish pop and disco (cover charge 20 mk). Most of the city's big hotels have upmarket dance clubs.

To experience first-hand the Finnish national passion for tango dancing, head to *Vanha Maestro (Fredrikinkatu 51-53)*. As one female reader notes, 'Finnish men are rather gallant – even if you do tread on their toes. As long as you're game for a dance, you'll have a ball.' The cover charge is 30 mk.

DTM (Annankatu 32) is a popular gay bar, and *Con Hombres (Eerikinkatu 14)* is also good.

Cinemas

Foreign movies (40 mk) are usually in English with both Finnish and Swedish subtitles – pick up a weekly schedule at the city tourist office. Next door to the Forum shopping centre there is a choice of seven cinemas.

The Finnish Film Archive's *Orion Theatre (Eerikinkatu 15)* is a rep house with a fondness for Woody Allen. You must purchase an annual membership card (20 mk), then admission is 17 mk.

SHOPPING

Prices are high at the shops on Pohjoisesplanadi, the main tourist street in town. Other notable shopping streets are Aleksanterinkatu and Fredrikinkatu. Mariankatu has many antiques shops, and Iso-Roobertinkatu is filled with funky boutiques.

Stockmann, the oldest and largest department store in Finland, is surprisingly reasonably priced for Finnish souvenirs and Sami handicrafts, as well as Finnish textiles, Kalevala Koru jewellery, Lapponia jewellery, Moomintroll souvenirs and lots more. It offers an export service.

The Arabia porcelain factory outlet and museum is rather bleakly located on the 9th floor of a suburban factory north of the centre at Hämeentie 135 (open daily). Take tram No 6 to its terminus and walk 200m farther north.

Markets

The famous fish market at the kauppatori is a must for anyone visiting Helsinki. Fish, strawberries and *makkara* (sausages) are on sale, and there is any number of stalls selling local handicrafts, weird hats, Sami dolls and T-shirts. The market is held daily from 6.30 am to 2 pm, and there are evening markets in summer.

The Hietalahti flea market (catch tram No 6) is the main second-hand centre in Helsinki: you'll find anything from used clothes to broken accordions. There is also a kauppahalli here.

The kauppahalli at the Hakaniemi metro stop has a mix of craft and food stalls.

GETTING THERE & AWAY

Air

There are flights to Helsinki from the USA, Europe and Asia on many airlines. Finnair offers international as well as domestic service, with flights to 20 Finnish cities – generally at least once a day but several times daily to Turku, Tampere, Rovaniemi and Oulu. The Finnair office (☎ 828 7750, 9800 3466 toll-free) at Asema-aukio 3, just west of the train station, is open from 8 am to 6 pm Monday to Friday, 9 am to 4 pm on

Saturday. The airport is in Vantaa, 19km north of Helsinki.

Bus

Purchase long-distance and express bus tickets at the main bus station (between Mannerheimintie and the Kamppi metro station) or on the bus itself. Local and regional buses also depart from this station. The station is open from 7 am to 7 pm weekdays, 7 am to 5 pm on Saturday and 9 am to 6 pm on Sunday.

Train

The train station is in the city centre and is linked by pedestrian tunnel with the Helsinki metro system. Helsinki is the terminus for three main railway lines, with regular trains from Turku in the west, Tampere in the north and Lahti in the north-east. There is a separate ticket counter for international trains, including those to St Petersburg and Moscow.

Car & Motorcycle

Turku is 166km west of Helsinki on road No 1. Take road No 3 north to Tampere (174km) and Vaasa (419km). Road No 4 goes north to Oulu (612km) and Rovaniemi (837km). Road No 7 east is the route to take for the Russian border, Vyborg and St Petersburg.

Boat

International ferries travel to Stockholm, Tallin, and Travemünde and Lübeck in Germany. There is also catamaran and hydrofoil service to Tallin. See the Getting There & Away chapter for more details.

Of the five ferry terminals in the city, four are just off the central kaupptori. Kanava and Katajanokka terminals are served by bus No 13 and tram Nos 2, 2T and 4, and Olympia and Makasiini terminals by tram Nos 3B and 3T. The fifth terminal, Länsiterminaali (West Terminal) is served by bus No 15.

Ferry tickets may be purchased at the terminal, from a ferry company's office in the centre or (in some cases) from the city tourist office. Avoid disappointment b booking in advance during the high season (late June through mid-August).

Ferry company offices in Helsinki include:

Eckerö Lines (☎ 228 8544)
 Keskuskatu 1, Länsiterminaali
Silja Lines (☎ 9800-274 552)
 Mannerheimintie 2, Olympia terminal
Tallink (☎ 2282 1211)
 Erottajankatu 19
Viking Line (☎ 12 351)
 Mannerheimintie 14, Katajanokka and Maka-
 siini terminals

A highly enjoyable way of leaving or entering Helsinki is on the MS *JL Runeberg* (☎ 019-524 3331), a historic steamship. The *JL Runeberg* runs west to Inkoo or east to Porvoo from June to mid-September. The cost is 150/200 mk return to Porvoo/Inkoo.

A speedier way to reach Porvoo is aboard the MS *Queen* operated by Royal Line. The cost is 155 mk return. All departures are from the kauppatori. See the Inkoo and Porvoo Getting There & Away sections in the relevant chapter for more information.

GETTING AROUND
To/From the Airport
Bus No 615 (15 mk; Helsinki Card not valid) shuttles between the airport and platform No 10 at the Rautatientori (Railway Square), east of the train station, every 20 to 30 minutes between 5 am and 10.30 pm.

Finnair buses (25 mk) depart from the Finnair office at Asema-aukio, next to the train station, every 20 minutes from 5 am to midnight.

There are also share taxis (☎ 2200 2500) at 70 mk per person. Standard taxis charge approximately 120 mk for a ride between central Helsinki and the airport.

Public Transport
The city transport system, Helsingin Kaupungin Liikennelaitos (HKL), operates buses, metro trains, local trains, trams and a ferry to the island of Suomenlinna. A single journey on any type of transportation within the HKL network costs 10 mk when the ticket is purchased on board, 8 mk when purchased in advance. A pack of 10 tickets costs 75 mk, which is very good value. Your ticket (which must be stamped) is valid for one hour from the time of stamping, or from the time of purchase if bought directly from the conductor, and allows unlimited transfers. A single tram-only ticket (no transfers allowed) is 8 mk on board, 6 mk in advance.

Tourist tickets are available at 25/50/75 mk for 24 hours/three days/five days. Alternatively, the Helsinki Card gives you free travel anywhere within Helsinki (though it is not valid on bus No 615, the airport express bus).

There are also regional tickets – for travel by bus or train to neighbouring cities such as Vantaa and Espoo – that cost 15 mk for a single ticket, 45 mk for 24 hours, and 120 mk for the 10 ticket pack. Children's tickets are half-price.

HKL offices at the Rautatientori and Hakaniemi metro stations (open weekdays) sell tickets and passes, as do many of the city's R-kiosks. Metro services run daily from about 6 am to 11.30 pm. The metro line extends to Ruoholahti in the western part of the city and north-east to Mellunmäki.

Timetables and a route map can be found on the city tourist office Web site at www.hel.fi/HKL/ and are available free of charge from HKL ticket offices.

Car & Motorcycle
Cars can be rented at the airport or in the city centre. Some of the more economical rental companies include Lacara (☎ 719 062) north of the centre at Hämeentie 12 and Budget (☎ 685 6500) at Malminkatu 24 near the Radisson SAS Royal Hotel. Motorbike rental is not common in Helsinki.

Parking in Helsinki is strictly regulated and can be a serious headache. Metered areas cost 3 to 6 mk per hour. There are a few free, long and short-term parking areas scattered around the city; for locations consult the *Parking Guide for the Inner City of Helsinki*, a free map available at the city tourist office.

Taxi

Vacant taxis are hard to come by during morning and evening rush hours. If you need one, join a queue at one of the taxi stands – at the train station, bus station or Senaatintori. A trip across town costs about 50 mk.

Bicycle

Cycling is practical in Helsinki with well-marked and good-quality bicycle paths. Greenbike (☎ 850 22850), just north of the train station at Mannerheimintie 13, rents bikes from 50 mk per day during spring and summer. Hostels also assist with bike rentals. *Helsingin Pyöräilykartta* is the free Helsinki bike route map, available at the city tourist office.

Around Helsinki

SUOMENLINNA

On a tight cluster of islands just south of Helsinki fish market is a UNESCO site, Suomenlinna, the 'fortress of Finland'. The fields around Suomenlinna's stone ramparts are a favourite picnicking destination for locals – the boozing can get pretty serious on Friday and Saturday evenings in summer. Some 900 people live on the island year-round. There are interesting museums and good restaurants, enough to occupy a full day of sightseeing.

Every evening at 6.30 pm dozens of people gather at Suomenlinna's main quay to wave as the Silja and Viking ferries sail through the narrow strait – it's quite a sight.

History

The greatest fortress of the Swedish empire was founded in 1748 to protect the eastern part of the empire against Russian attack. It was named Sveaborg (Swedish fortress).

At times, Sveaborg was the second largest town in Finland, after Turku. In 1806 it had 4600 residents whereas Helsinki had only 4200!

Sveaborg was surrendered to the Russians after the war of 1808, and renamed Viapori. Thanks in large part to the superb sea fortress, the Finnish capital was moved by the Russians from Turku to Helsinki in 1812. It remained Russian until Finland gained independence in 1917, and continued to have military significance until 1973.

The current name was chosen in 1918, after Finland's independence.

Things to See & Do

Most attractions are on two main islands, Iso Mustasaari and Susisaari, connected to each other by a small bridge. At the bridge is the **Inventory Chamber Visitor Centre** (☎ 668 800) which offers guided walking tours (25 mk) in summer and houses the Suomenlinna Museum (20 mk) of local history. Old bunkers, crumbling fortress walls and cannons are at the southern end of Susisaari island.

Suomenlinna's museums are open daily in summer and weekends only in winter. All except the Suomenlinna Museum are free with the Helsinki Card. There are two home museums: the interesting **Armfelt Museum** (15 mk), with furniture and exhibits brought from Joensuu Manor in south-west Finland and the **Ehrensvärd Museum** (10 mk) that preserves an 18th century officer's home with model ships and sea charts.

Opposite Ehrensvärd Museum is the **shipyard** where sailmakers and other workers have been building ships since the 1750s. As many as two dozen ships are in the dry dock at any given time. They can be from 12m to 32m long and from as far away as the United Kingdom.

Three museums relating to Suomenlinna's military history may be visited with a 20 mk combination ticket. **Manege** museum commemorates the battles of WWII and displays heavy artillery. The **Coastal Defence Museum** displays still more heavy artillery in a bunker-style exhibition. Finland was forbidden to possess submarines by the 1947 Treaty of Paris; the WWII-era **Submarine Vesikko** is one of the few submarines remaining in the country.

The delightful **Doll & Toy Museum** (15 mk) is the personal achievement of Piipp

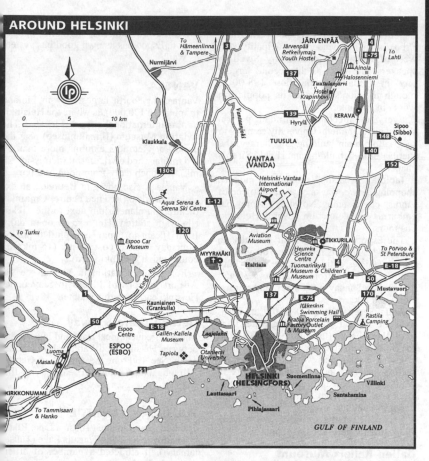

AROUND HELSINKI

HELSINKI

Tandefelt. Next to the main quay, the **Jetty Barracks Gallery** offers interesting temporary exhibitions (closed Monday).

Places to Eat

Bring picnicking supplies, or for light fare visit *Café Piper*, a delightful little wooden villa with superb sea views. *Suomenlinna Panimoravintola*, a good brewery restaurant at the main quay, makes a 'beer milkshake' (18 mk). *Walhalla* (☎ 668 552) is an upmarket place (its closed in winter,

and bookings are advised) with views of passing passenger ships from its open terrace.

Getting There & Away

HKL ferries depart every 35 minutes from the passenger quay at the fish market, opposite the President's Palace. Buy tickets (9 mk one way) for the 15 minute trip at the pier. There is a less frequent and more expensive direct service to the Inventory Chamber Visitor Centre and to Walhalla restaurant.

ESPOO

Espoo (pronounced EHZ-poe; Swedish: Esbo) is an independent municipality just west of Helsinki. It has many Swedish speakers and ranks as the second largest city in Finland (population 198,000), though the lion's share of its population works in Helsinki.

Every architecturally minded person should visit **Otaniemi University** campus to see Aalto's main building and library, the Pietiläs' student building and Heikki Siren's chapel.

Tapiola (Swedish: Hagalund), a modern shopping centre, was once a masterpiece of Finnish city planning. Now it is a somewhat embarrassing detour on several Helsinki bus tours.

The **Espoo Car Museum** at Pakankylän Kartano Manor has more than 100 vintage motor vehicles dating from the early 20th century. It's open from 11 am to 5.30 pm Tuesday to Sunday in summer, and admission is 20 mk.

Aqua Serena (☎ 8870 550), at Tornimäentie 10, is a truly amazing water park in northern Espoo (take bus No U339 from the Helsinki bus station). The indoor section operates year-round while the outdoor section becomes the Serena Ski Centre in winter, with marked and illuminated tracks. Hours are daily from 11 am to 8 pm. The day pass is 80 mk, evening pass 60 mk.

Espoo's annual **Jazz Festival** (☎ 8165 7234), held in late April, is topnotch.

Gallen-Kallela Museum

The most important sight in Espoo is the pastiche studio-castle of Akseli Gallen-Kallela, one of the most notable of Finnish painters. The Art Nouveau building was designed by the artist and is now a museum of his paintings. Take tram No 4 from central Helsinki to Munkkiniemi, then walk 2km or take bus No 33 (weekdays only). The museum is closed Monday in winter. Admission is 35 mk.

Getting There & Away

You can catch buses to various parts of Espoo from the bus terminal in Helsinki.

Local trains from Helsinki will drop you off at several stations, including central Espoo. Espoo has its own good bus system as well.

VANTAA

Vantaa, the fourth largest city in Finland (population 170,000), is where the **Helsinki-Vantaa international airport** is located. The **Aviation Museum** (Ilmailumuseo) near the airport at Tietotie 3 exhibits more than 50 old military and civil aircraft (admission 20 mk). It's open daily from noon to 6 pm.

Vantaa is also home to **Heureka**, an excellent hands-on science centre, Omnimax theatre and planetarium next to the Tikkurila train station. Heureka is open daily from 10 am to 6 pm, and until 8 pm on Thursday. Tickets cost 75 mk (15 mk discount with a Helsinki Card).

For accommodation in Vantaa see the Airport sections of Places to Stay under Helsinki earlier in this chapter.

Getting There & Away

There is frequent local train and bus service between Helsinki and Vantaa, 19km to the north. See To/From the Airport in Getting Around under Helsinki earlier in this chapter.

TUUSULAN RANTATIE

The Tuusulan Rantatie (Tuusula Lake Road) is a narrow road along Tuusula Lake (Tuusulanjärvi). It attracted a number of artists during the National Romantic era of the early 1900s. Sibelius, as well as the Nobel Prize winning novelist FE Sillanpää and the painter Pekka Halonen, among others, worked here. A major stop along the 'museum road' is **Halosenniemi**, the Karelian-inspired, log-built National Romantic studio of Halonen, now an art museum (closed Monday). Sibelius' home, **Ainola**, just north of the museum road is a worthwhile detour (open Tuesday to Sunday in summer). The building was designed by Lars Sonck, and built on this beautiful site in 1904. Hotel Krapinhovi doubles as the area tourist office.

Mika Häkkinen – 1998 Formula One World Champion

When Mika Häkkinen's Mercedes took the chequered flag at the 1998 Suzuka Grand Prix, he chalked up another victory for the McLaren team, accelerated fourteen points clear of his rival Schumacher, and took the 1998 Driver's Championship.

It took almost a decade for Häkkinen to achieve his success. His Formula One (F1) career began with the Lotus team in 1991, and in 1994 he joined Senna and Andretti on the McLaren team. In 1995 he was almost killed in a crash during practice for the Australian Grand Prix in Adelaide. Flag marshalls on the track pronounced him dead when he was carried from the wreckage. They revived him before the ambulance arrived, and he remained in a coma for several days. Häkkinen says of the experience, 'Something like that certainly opens your eyes, and maybe I don't take so many risks anymore. It's like beginning a second life.'

Häkkinen was born in Vantaa, just north of Helsinki, on 28th September 1968. He currently lives in Monaco with his wife Erja and pet tortoise Caroline.

Places to Stay & Eat

Järvenpää Retkeilymaja (☎ 287 775, marko rantala@dlc.fi, Stålhanentie 5) is a nice HI-affiliated hostel in Järvenpää on the western shore of Tuusulanjärvi. Beds are from 65 mk and there is a kitchen and sauna. This place is open year-round.

The unfortunately named *Hotel Krapin-hovi* (☎ 275 1501, fax 175 1548) at Rantatie 2 is an attractive 1883 manor hotel offering a fine restaurant and a rare chance to experience a traditional smoke sauna. Singles/doubles are from 460/580 mk (360/450 mk weekends and summer).

Getting There & Away

Tuusula Lake is about 40km north of Helsinki. Take a local train to Kerava or Järvenpää or a bus to Hyrylä and proceed from there by bicycle.

Turku

• pop 164,000   ☎ 02

The oldest city in Finland and its first capital, Turku (Swedish: Åbo) has much to offer the visitor. You can easily spend hours relaxing by the attractive riverside between visits to museums and the medieval Turku Castle. Indeed, Turku has more than 50 museums – more than Helsinki, as vocal locals are quick to point out. The long-standing joke among its loyal residents is that after Turku spread culture to the rest of Finland, it never returned.

Turku was named Åbo by Swedish settlers because it was a settlement (*bo*) on the Aura River (*å*). The Finnish name, Turku, means 'marketplace' – the city's market has long been one of the largest and finest on the south coast.

Due to the inexpensive ferries (free with some rail passes), Turku is by far the most popular gateway from Sweden to mainland Finland. It is the fifth largest city in Finland.

HISTORY

In 1229 a Catholic settlement was founded at Koroinen, near the present centre of Turku. Work soon started on the new church (consecrated in 1300) and the Turku Castle. Both the early Catholic Church and the Swedish administration ran what is present-day Finland from Turku, which was at times the second largest town in Sweden.

Fire destroyed Turku several times over the centuries, but the biggest blow to the town was the transfer of the capital to Helsinki in 1812. Locals still haven't forgiven Helsinki, or 'the village in the east', as it is called around Turku.

ORIENTATION

The centre of town is a few kilometres north-east of Turku harbour, and accessible by train or bus from each arriving ferry. The city centre is on both sides of the Aurajoki River, and everything is well within

HIGHLIGHTS

- Medieval Turku Castle with its dungeons and its magnificent banquet halls
- Luostarinmäki open-air museum, with costumed artisans and musicians in summer
- Classical music concerts at the Sibelius Museum
- Alfresco drinks and dining on Turku's glitzy boat restaurants
- The colourful Keskiajan Turku festival of medieval Turku in late July and early August
- Archipelago cruises – evening dinner-and-dance cruises as well as day trips around the islands
- Naantali, the most popular summer town in Finland
- Louhisaari Manor in Askainen village, built like a castle and containing a 'ghost room'
- The idyllic Päiväkulma Hostel, on an island south-west of Turku

walking distance. Aurakatu, Kauppiaskatu, Eerikinkatu and Yliopistonkatu around the market square are the main streets.

INFORMATION
Tourist Offices
The Turku City Tourist Office (☎ 233 6366 or 262 7444, fax 233 6488), at Aurakatu 4, is open from 8.30 am to 6 pm weekdays and from 9 am to 4 pm weekends. It's an excellent place to get information on the entire Turku region.

South-West Finland Tourism (☎ 251 7333), at Läntinen Rantakatu 13, is open from 9 am to 3 pm Monday to Friday. It handles cottage bookings and tours for the Turku region.

Money
Forex at Eerikinkatu 12 offers better rates than banks. It is open from 8 am to 7 pm Monday to Friday, and from 8 am to 5 pm Saturday. Several banks on the market square have 24 hour ATMs.

Post & Communications
The main post office, at Humalistonkatu 1, is open from 9 am to 8 pm Monday to Friday. The Telephonecompany is nearby at Humalistonkatu 7. There are two types of public telephones that accept phone cards in Turku – some accept a phone card that works nationally, and some require a card that works only in Turku. Both types of cards may be purchased at any city R-kioski.

Internet Resources & Library
Information on Turku can be found at www.turku.fi/ on the Web.

There are several Internet terminals on the second floor of the public library (☎ 262 3611) at Linnankatu 2. Hours are from 10 am to 8 pm Monday to Friday and to 3 pm Saturday.

Reading-Room Julin on the basement level at Eerikinkatu 4 offers an enormous selection of Finnish and foreign daily papers and periodicals, including the *International Herald Tribune*. It's open from 10 am to 8 pm on weekdays and to 4 pm on weekends.

Travel Agency
Kilroy Travels (☎ 273 7500) at Eerikinkatu 2 specialises in student and budget travel. It's open from 10 am to 6 pm Monday to Friday, and to 2 pm Saturday.

Bookshops
Akateeminen Kirjakauppa and Suomalainen Kirjakauppa bookshops are both within Hansa Shopping Arcade. They carry maps, English-language books and foreign periodicals.

You can find foreign newspapers also at the R-kioski at Aurakati 8, and at the train station.

Left Luggage
The train station offers a left-luggage counter and lockers. Lockers cost 10 mk per day (maximum five days).

Medical & Emergency Services
For a general emergency dial ☎ 112, for police call ☎ 10022 and for a doctor call ☎ 10023.

A 24 hour pharmacy is at the Hansa Shopping Arcade at Aurakatu 10.

TURKU CASTLE & HISTORICAL MUSEUM
The mammoth Turku Castle, near the ferry terminals, is a must for everyone visiting Turku. Recent renovations to the castle make it the most notable historic building in Finland – it's also one of the country's most popular tourist attractions. Founded in 1280 at the mouth of the Aurajoki, the castle has been growing ever since. Notable occupants have included Count Per Brahe, founder of many towns in Finland, who lived here in the 17th century, and King Eric XIV, who was imprisoned in the castle's Round Tower in the late 16th century, having been declared insane.

Highlights include two dungeons and magnificent banqueting halls, as well as a fascinating historical museum of medieval Turku. The castle and museum are open daily from 10 am to 6 pm from mid-May to mid-September. At other times, hours are

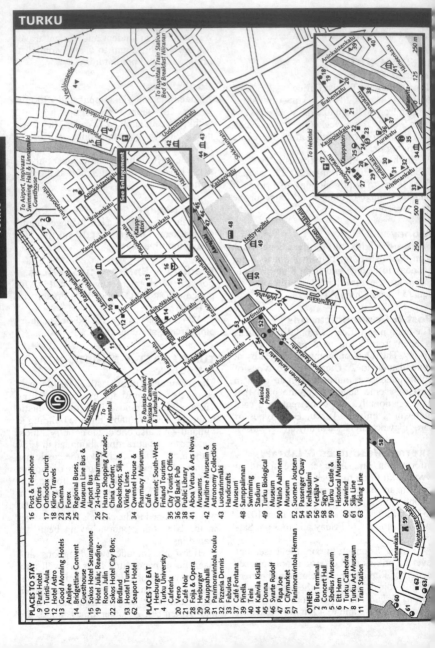

from 2 to 7 pm Monday and from 10 am to 3 pm Tuesday to Sunday. Entry is 30 mk. Bus No 1 from Kauppatori stops at the castle.

LUOSTARINMÄKI HANDICRAFTS MUSEUM

The only surviving 18th century area of this medieval town – Turku has been razed 30 times by fire – is now the open-air Luostarinmäki Handicrafts Museum. Almost every Finnish city has such a museum but this one is truly the best. Carpenters, stonemasons, jewellers and other workers built homes and shops in the area, beginning in 1779. When the great fire of 1827 destroyed most of Turku, the Luostarinmäki neighbourhood was one of the few that survived.

Since 1940 it has served as a museum. There are about 30 furnished workshops altogether, including a printing press, silversmith, watchmaker, bakery and cigar shop. In summer, artisans in period costume work inside the old wooden houses and musicians stroll its paths. The museum is open from 10 am to 6 pm daily from mid-April to mid-September. At other times it is open from 10 am to 3 pm Tuesday to Sunday. Admission is 20 mk.

TURKU CATHEDRAL

The most notable of all Finnish churches, the Turku Cathedral is the national shrine of the Evangelical-Lutheran Church of Finland. Its oldest parts date back to the 13th century. In the Middle Ages, the cathedral was extended by the addition of side chapels for Catholic bishops; these side chapels became resting places for Swedish war heroes after the Lutheran reformation. In one chapel rests Catherine Månsdotter, Queen of Sweden, wife of the unfortunate Erik XIV.

The **cathedral museum** displays models showing different stages of the cathedral's construction, as well as medieval sculptures and other religious paraphernalia.

TURKU

Finland's Oldest Towns

Residents of Turku have an ongoing rivalry with their neighbours to the east in Helsinki. Those who live in Turku like to point out that despite being the capital of Finland Helsinki is not the oldest town in the country! In fact, Helsinki, founded in 1550, doesn't even make it onto the list of Finland's five oldest cities; it's number six. Turku, on the other hand, is number one.

The oldest towns, in order of their founding, are as follows:

Turku (1200) – The oldest town in Finland, Turku boasts the stunning medieval Turku Castle and the Luostarinmäki Handicrafts Museum that preserves an 18th century artists' district.

Porvoo (1346) – The most charming of Finland's seaside towns, Porvoo features a neighbourhood of fine 19th century wooden buildings, with several museums and a historic medieval church.

Rauma (1442) – A UNESCO-protected town, 136km north of Turku, Rauma has 600 wooden buildings from the 18th and 19th centuries in its Vanha Rauma (Old Town) district, and a small medieval church.

Naantali (1443) – The most popular summer town in Finland, Naantali has a medieval convent church and attractive old wooden houses clustered around its harbour.

Ekenäs (1546) – This seaside town was founded as a trading port to rival Tallinn, just across the Gulf of Finland. It's small and charming, with narrow streets, wooden buildings and a greystone church.

The cathedral and museum are open from 9 am to 7 pm daily. Admission to the cathedral museum is 10 mk. Most Tuesday evenings the cathedral offers live music, and English-language services are held at 4 pm on the last Sunday of each month.

MUSEUM SHIPS

Four museum ships are anchored on the banks of the Aurajoki in the city centre.

Suomen Joutsen

The 'Swan of Finland', a 1902 sailing ship, was used by the Finnish Navy during WWII as a mother ship for submarines and as a hospital. Currently under renovation, it is open for guided tours by appointment (☎ 262 0400) from June to late August.

Sigyn

This beautiful three masted barque, anchored near Turku Castle, was first launched in the Swedish town of Gothenburg in 1887. Its cabins have been carefully preserved. Hours are from 10 am to 6 pm daily from mid-May to early September. Admission is 10 mk.

Keihässalmi

This WWII mine-layer is open for inspection from 10 am to 6 pm daily mid-June to late August. Admission is 10 mk.

Vetäjäv V

The Vetäjäv V is a steam tug first launched in 1891. Hours are 10 am to 6 pm daily mid-June to late August, and admission is 10 mk.

ABOA VETUS & ARS NOVA MUSEUMS

These twin museums (☎ 250 0552), under one roof, are at Itäinen Rantakatu 4-6. Ars Nova is a museum of contemporary art with permanent and temporary exhibitions. Aboa Vetus is a museum of archaeology that is built around an excavated housing plot from the 14th century. The museums are open from 10 am to 7 pm daily from late April to late August, and from 11 am to 7 pm Tuesday to Sunday at other times. The treasure hunt held at noon on Sunday is great for kids. Tickets are 50 mk for both wings, or 35 mk individually.

SIBELIUS MUSEUM

The Sibelius Museum, near the cathedral at Piispankatu 17, displays some 350 musical instruments from around the world, and exhibits memorabilia of the famous Finnish composer Jean Sibelius. It is the most extensive musical museum in Finland. You can listen to Sibelius' music on record or, better still, attend a Wednesday evening concert (40 mk). Hours are from 11 am to 3 pm Tuesday to Sunday (also from 6 to 8 pm Wednesday). Admission is 15 mk.

QWENSEL HOUSE

Qwensel House, on the Aurajoki at Läntinen Rantakatu 13, is the oldest wooden house in Turku. It was built in around 1700, and now houses the small Pharmacy Museum. You can see an old laboratorium with aromatic herbs, fine 18th century furnishings with hints of 'Gustavian' (Swedish) style, and an exhibition of bottles and other pharmacy items. Admission is 15 mk.

TURKU BIOLOGICAL MUSEUM

The Turku Biological Museum is surprisingly interesting and superbly presented, if you don't mind staring at stuffed beasts. Thirty mammal and 140 bird species native to Finland are displayed in their natural habitats – from the tundra of Lapland to the forests of Karelia. The museum is in a 1907 Art Nouveau building on Neitsytpolku. Hours are from 10 am to 6 pm daily from mid-April to mid-September, from 10 am to 3 pm Tuesday to Sunday at other times. Entry is 15 mk.

TURKU ART MUSEUM (TURUN TAIDEMUSEO)

The city Art Museum, with notable collections, is at Aurakatu 26. It's worth a look if you have an interest in Finnish art – works by the leading names of the National Romantic era are here, along with modern art from other Nordic countries. It is open from 10 am to 4 pm Tuesday to Saturday (also from 4 to 7 pm Wednesday and Thursday) and from 11 am to 6 pm Sunday. Entry is 30 mk.

MARITIME MUSEUM & ASTRONOMY COLLECTION

These two attractions are in an observatory building perched atop Vartiovuori Hill. On display are scale models of ships, paintings of ships and navigation equipment used in ships, plus lots of astronomy gear. Hours and entry fee are the same as for the Biological Museum.

ETT HEM MUSEUM

Ett Hem means 'a home'. The Ett Hem museum at Piispankatu 14 re-creates a wealthy 18th century home, with old furniture of various styles, valuable works by famous Finnish painters Albert Edelfelt and Helene Schjerfbeck, and collections of china and glass. It's open from noon to 3 pm Tuesday to Sunday from May to late September. Entry is 15 mk.

WÄINÖ AALTONEN MUSEUM

Wäinö Aaltonen was one of the leading sculptors of the 1920s, in the era of Finnish independence. The museum has permanent exhibitions of Aaltonen's paintings and sculptures; temporary exhibitions are of contemporary art. Near the river at Itäinen Rantakatu 38, the museum is open from 11 am to 7 pm Tuesday to Sunday. Entry is 15 mk (special fees may apply for temporary exhibitions).

ORTHODOX CHURCH

The Orthodox church, facing the market square, was designed in the 1840s by German architect CL Engel, who is best known for creating Senate Square in Helsinki.

ACTIVITIES
Cruises

Archipelago cruises are a popular activity in Turku during summer. There are day trips around the islands as well as evening dinner-and-dance cruises. Departures are from the quay at Martinsilta bridge and fares are from 45 mk.

The SS *Ukkopekka* charges 90 mk for its evening 'gourmet' cruise, departing at 8 pm Monday to Saturday from mid-June to late August.

Both the SS *Ukkopekka* and the MS *Summersea* offer pleasant cruises to Naantali. The MS *Summersea* also cruises to Dragsfjärd and north to Uusikaupunki. For more information see Getting There & Away later in this section.

Bicycling

The city tourist office assists with rentals, suggests routes and publishes an excellent free bike route map (*pyörätiekartta*) of the city and surrounding towns.

Swimming & Sauna

Samppalinnan outdoor swimming stadium charges 15 mk admission, and this includes a sauna. The 50m pool is open from late May to late August. In winter, go to the indoor Impivaara swimming hall for swimming and sauna, north of the city centre (take bus No 13 to Impivaara).

ORGANISED TOURS

Brightly coloured Museum Line buses make the rounds of Turku's top attractions from 10 am to 6 pm daily from June to mid-August. The 20 mk Museum Line bus ticket, good for 24 hours, entitles tourists to a 50% discount on admission to all sights along the route. You may get on and off these buses as often as you wish, for any length of time. Departures from the corner of Aurakatu and Eerikinkatu at the market square are every hour on the hour. Museum Line bus tickets are also valid on regular city buses.

TURKU

TURKU

SPECIAL EVENTS
The Turku Music Festival, held during the second week of August, is a feast of classical and contemporary music and opera. Venues include the Turku Castle and the cathedral. For further information contact the Turku Music Festival Foundation (☎ 251 1162, fax 231 3316, turku.music@tmf.pp.fi), Uudenmaankatu 1, 20500 Turku.

Quite different is Ruisrock (☎ 251 1596), Finland's oldest and largest annual rock festival, held since 1969. The festival takes place in late June at the recreational park on Ruissalo island.

Keskiajan Turku, held in late July or early August, is the festival of medieval Turku. It's a fantastic week of pageantry, banqueting, fencing and outrageous costumes. Events take place at the market square, Turku Castle, the cathedral and Aboa Vetus museum. Inquire at the city tourist office about programing and tickets.

PLACES TO STAY
Camping
Ruissalo Camping (☎ 258 9249, fax 262 3255), on Ruissalo island 10km west of the city centre, is open June through late August. Camping sites cost 70 mk. There are no cabins, but the places does have saunas, a cafeteria and nice beaches – including a nude beach. Bus No 8 runs from the market square in the centre to the camping ground.

Hostel
One of the busiest hostels in all of Finland is the HI-affiliated *Hostel Turku* (☎ 231 6578, fax 231 1708, Linnankatu 39), near the Aurajoki, which has 120 beds and is open year-round. It is very popular with Finnish school groups. Reception hours are from 6 to 10 am and from 3 pm to midnight daily. Facilities include a well equipped kitchen, 10 mk laundry and lockers. Beds cost 60 to 115 mk depending on the size of the room – the 60-mk beds are in dorms that sleep eight to 14 people. There are also single and double rooms. Linen is 30 mk, breakfast 20 mk. Bookings are advised in summer. From the train station take bus No 30, and from the bus station and harbour take bus No 1.

If Hostel Turku is full, consider taking a bus to a hostel in one of the nearby towns, such as Rymättylä (see Around Turku later in this chapter for more information).

Guesthouses & B&Bs
Bed & Breakfast Niiranan (☎ 237 7556, fax 237 7644, timo.niiranen@pp.inet.fi, Vanha Littoistentie 27), about 1km from the Kupittaa train station, has singles/doubles/triples for 100/150/200 mk.

The *Bridgettine Convent Guesthouse*, or Birgittalaisluostarin Vieraskoti (☎ 250 1910, Ursininkatu 15A), is a guesthouse kept by the nuns of this Catholic convent. The clean, simple rooms are 160/250/350 mk, breakfast included. To stay here you must be willing to respect the lifestyle of the convent – ie smoking, drinking and drugs are not tolerated.

Another good choice in this category is *Linnasmäki* (☎ 338 001, Lustokatu 7), run by the Turku Christian Institute. It has singles/doubles for 210/340 mk.

Near the train station, *Turisti-Aula* (☎ 231 1973, fax 233 4097, Humalistonkatu 13) has a dozen clean but not-so-stylish rooms for 150/220 mk.

Hotels
In the city centre, *Sokos Hotel City Börs* (☎ 337 381, fax 231 1010, Eerikinkatu 11) overlooks the market square. Rooms cost 460/560 mk regularly, but all are 405 mk during summer. Nearby *Hotel Julia* (☎ 336 311, fax 233 6699, Eerikinkatu 4) is one of the finest hotels in Turku. There are 130 rooms at 600/700 mk (400/480 mk in summer).

Sokos Hotel Seurahuone (☎ 337 301, fax 251 8051, Eerikinkatu 23) has rustic décor and the popular Memphis bar. Rooms are 390/490 mk on weekdays; on weekends and in summer all rooms are 330 mk.

Two blocks from the train station, and across the street from Turisti-Aula guesthouse, is *Hotel Astro* (☎ 251 7838, fax 251

5516, Humalistonkatu 18), with rooms for 230/290 mk. On the same road is **Good Morning Hotels Ateljee** (☎ 336 111, fax 233 6699, Humalistonkatu 7), in a landmark building designed by Finnish architect Alvar Aalto. Rooms are 420/520 mk (290/390 mk on weekends and in summer).

Also handy to the train station is **Park Hotel** (☎ 251 9666, fax 251 9696, Rauhankatu 1), in an Art Nouveau building dating from 1904. Rooms cost 600/800 mk (450/600 mk in summer).

The **Seaport Hotel** (☎ 230 2600, fax 230 2169, Matkustajasatama) is a pleasant place near the harbour, within walking distance of the ferry terminals. Rooms cost 340/460 mk. From mid-June to mid-August rates are discounted 20 mk.

PLACES TO EAT

Cheap eats abound in the city centre, in the *kauppahalli* (covered market) on Eerikinkatu and around the *kauppatori* (market square). In particular, the outdoor market (held daily in summer) is superb for produce and smoked fish. There are also plenty of fine restaurants and bars in the city, as well as popular boat restaurants in summer.

Finnish

Opposite the cathedral, **Pinella** is a cosy traditional restaurant set in a small park. The lunch menu ranges from 26 to 35 mk and dinners are from 70 mk.

Teini (Uudenmaankatu 1) is a city institution that is superb for traditional Finnish food. It has an enormous array of dining halls and smaller rooms. Starters are from 30 to 42 mk, vegetarian dishes 45 to 50 mk and main courses 50 to 90 mk.

Panimoravintola Koulu (Eerikinkatu 18) is in a former schoolhouse. Upstairs is an upmarket restaurant, downstairs is a brewery pub, beer garden and café serving fantastic, home-cooked 39 mk lunches.

Panimoravintola Herman (Läntinen Rantakatu 37) is another brewery pub/restaurant, near Hostel Turku.

International

Fabulosa on Linnankatu is a tiny place – a hole in the wall, really – that serves great 10 mk pizza slices. A step up is **Pizzeria Dennis** (Linnankatu 17). It's a traditional Italian pizza and pasta restaurant with options from 35 mk.

Inside the Hansa Shopping Arcade, **China Garden** (Aurakatu 10) offers meals from 45 mk, and there is a discount on takeaway. Also at the Hansa centre is **Foija**, a very popular place serving steaks, pastas and more. Food is good, portions are big and prices are OK at 40 to 60 mk. The entrance is on Aurakatu.

For an eclectic menu that includes pizza, schnitzel and chicken curry, visit **Café Noir** on Eerikinkatu. Lunch specials are 35 mk, à la carte dinners 40 to 60 mk.

Vegetarian

Verso (Linnankatu 3) is a nice vegetarian restaurant that offers filling 35 mk lunch specials from 11 am to 2 pm Monday to Friday. There are hot dishes as well as salads and home-made breads.

Boat Restaurants

Turku is more of a river town than any other in Finland, and a meal or a drink at one of its boat restaurants, just west of Auransilta bridge, is a must for anyone visiting in summer.

The **Donna** is one of the most popular and established of Turku's floating restaurants. **Svarte Rudolf** has a bar terrace on the upper deck, and its fine restaurant on the lower deck is well worth a visit. The **Papa Joe** serves American-inspired meals at reasonable prices. This once-sunken boat was found and rescued in the early 1990s.

Cafés

Café Fontana, on the corner of Aurakatu and Linnankatu in the heart of the city, is an Art Nouveau café with delicious pastries and pies.

Kahvila Kisälli is a large, cheery café in an 1851 building at the entrance to the Luostarinmäki Handicrafts Museum.

TURKU

Fast Food

Look for kebab stands and *grillis* around the market square, on Aurakatu and Yliopistonkatu.

Hesburger, the local burger chain, has an outlet at the Hansa Shopping Arcade (use the Eerikinkatu entrance) and another at the bus terminal.

University Eateries

Turku is a university city, so it is always possible to get a 15 mk breakfast or lunch at the Turku University *cafeteria*. The university campus is a short walk north-east of the cathedral.

Self-Catering

The *Citymarket* supermarket on the corner of Puistokatu and Matinkatu is convenient to Hostel Turku.

ENTERTAINMENT

For dancing, most locals flock to the chic nightclubs of the city's large hotels. For drinks, you can't beat the city's boat restaurants in summer – see Places to Eat.

Bars

The Irish pub *Old Bank* on the corner of Aurakatu and Linnankatu is worth a visit. The place was previously a bank, hence the name.

Also very good is *Panimoravintola Koulu* (see Places to Eat). The place makes its own brews, including a good stout (25 mk), and has a large, lively summer terrace.

At the Hansa Shopping Arcade there's *Opera*, a swank café and bar. The entrance is on Aurakatu.

Music Venues

The Turku Philharmonic Orchestra is one of the oldest in Europe – it was founded in the 1790s. The orchestra performs in the *Concert Hall (Aninkaistenkatu 9)*.

For live jazz, head to *Birdland* (*Kauppiaskatu 6*).

Cinema

A cinema with two screens is at Eerikinkatu 12. Foreign films are shown with Finnish and Swedish subtitles. Entry is 40 mk.

SPECTATOR SPORTS

Turku is a hot town as far as ice hockey is concerned. Games are played in Turkuhalli stadium, near Ruissalo island.

GETTING THERE & AWAY
Air

Finnair offers flights to Turku from 20 Finnish cities and many European capitals. Domestic flights are generally at least once a day but several times daily to Helsinki, Mariehamn, Tampere, Rovaniemi and Oulu.

The Finnair office (☎ 415 4909) is at the airport.

Bus

Purchase long-distance and express bus tickets from the bus terminal at Aninkaistentulli. There are express buses to Helsinki almost hourly, and express buses to Tampere and other points in southern Finland depart several times daily. To Helsinki the one-way fare is 95 mk, and the trip takes 2½ hours.

Regional buses depart from the market square.

Train

Turku is the terminus for the south-eastern railway line. The train station is a short walk north-west of the city centre; trains also stop at the ferry harbour and at the Kupittaa train station east of the centre. There are regular trains to Helsinki, Tampere and beyond. The trip to Helsinki tales two hours and costs 94 mk one way.

Bus No 30 shuttles between the city centre and train station.

Car & Motorcycle

From Turku, take road No 8 north to Rauma, Pori and Oulu, or road No 1 east to Helsinki. It's 166km to Helsinki and the drive takes about two hours.

Flying Finns

There's a proud dynasty of Flying Finns – athletes who have excelled in fields such as running, ski-jumping, motor racing, and ice hockey.

The first Flying Finn, the distance runner Paavo Nurmi, was born in Turku in 1897. He won the 10,000m and cross-country at the 1920 Antwerp Olympics, picked up four gold medals for various races in Paris in 1924, and scored another gold in the 10,000m in Amsterdam in 1928. From 1920 to 1931 he set 20 world records.

Nurmi is a hard act to follow, but successive generations of Finnish athletes have certainly tried. Finnish rally driving champions like Ari Vartanen, four-time world champion Juha Kankkunen, and the 1998 World Rally Drivers Champion Tommi Makinen have each in their time earned the nickname 'Flying Finn'. The Olympic ski-jumper Matti Nykanen, when he won gold in 1990, was known as a Flying Finn, as was the whole ice hockey team which beat Sweden in May 1995 to gain the world ice hockey championship. And these days when the 1998 Formula One Drivers Champion Mika Häkkinen signs an autograph, he signs himself 'The Flying Finn'.

Success in *Olympiakisat* (the Olympic Games) is the goal for many more would-be Flying Finns, and the towns of Helsinki, Lahti and Kuopio are currently dreaming of hosting the Winter Olympic Games. Even the smallest rowing boat competitions are treated with great enthusiasm. Every town has sports fields, indoor sports halls, swimming pools, tennis courts, downhill slopes and jogging and skiing tracks. Large crowds gather to watch locals compete in *pesis* (Finnish baseball), *futis* (soccer or football), *koris* (basketball), and especially *lätkä* (ice hockey).

Boat

Sweden & Åland Turku is the main gateway to Finland from Sweden and Åland. The harbour, south-west of the centre, has terminals for Silja Line (☎ 335 255), Viking Line (☎ 33311) and Seawind (☎ 210 2800). Ferries sail to Turku from Stockholm (9½ hours) and Mariehamn (6 hours). Prices vary widely according to season and class of service.

Purchase tickets from one of the offices at the harbour or from the Silja or Viking offices in the Hansa Shopping Arcade; you should book well in advance during the high season (late June through mid-August).

Bus No 1 travels between the market square and harbour.

See the earlier Getting There & Away chapter for more details about international ferry travel.

Mainland Finland The most enjoyable way to leave or enter Turku is aboard the MS *Summersea* (☎ 0400-523210) or the steamship SS *Ukkopekka* (☎ 233 0123). These offer a service to Naantali from late May to mid-August (70 mk return). The trip takes 1½ hours each way.

The MS *Summersea* also has a service to Dragsfjärd on Kemiö island (140 mk return, four hours one way) from Thursday to Sunday from mid-June to mid-August, and north to Uusikaupunki (160 mk return, 6½ hours one way) from Monday to Wednesday from late May to mid-August.

All departures are from the passenger quay just west of Martinsilta bridge.

GETTING AROUND
To/From the Airport

Bus No 1 runs between the market square and the airport, 8km north of the city, every 15 minutes from 5 am to midnight weekdays, from 5.30 am to 9.30 pm Saturday and from 7 am to midnight Sunday. The trip takes 20 to 25 minutes and costs 8 mk.

A shared taxi (☎ 020-830 3100) from the city centre to the airport will cost about 40 mk. Book at least three hours before pick-up.

Bus
City and regional buses are frequent and you pay 8 mk for a basic journey or 20 mk for a 24 hour ticket. Museum Line bus service tickets are also valid on regular city buses (see the Organised Tours section).

Important city bus routes include bus No 1 (harbour-market square-bus station-airport) and bus Nos 30, 32 and 42 (train station-market square).

Car & Motorcycle
Streets in the city centre have parking meters but these are free of charge in the evening and on Sunday.

Several rental car companies have offices at the airport, including Hertz (☎ 515 1200).

Around Turku

☎ 02
The area surrounding Turku is simply called 'Turku Land'. This region is among the most historical in Finland, with medieval churches every 10km or so.

NAANTALI
Naantali (Swedish: Nådendal) is an idyllic port town 13km north-west of Turku. Naantali is a popular day trip from Turku and a typical summer town – lively from June to mid-August and very quiet the rest of the year.

Twice in the 1990s (1993 and 1995) Finns have voted Naantali the 'best tourist town in the country'. The main attraction – at least for Finnish families – is Muumimaailma, a theme park celebrating characters from the popular storybooks by Helsinki-born Tove Jansson.

The population of Naantali is 12,500.

History
Naantali grew around the Catholic Convent of the Order of Saint Birgitta, which was founded in 1443. After Finland became Protestant in 1527, the convent was dissolved and Naantali had to struggle for its existence; the convent had been important not only spiritually but also economically. When the pilgrims no longer came to town, people had to find other means of making a living, notably by knitting socks, which became Naantali's main export!

Orientation
Naantali sprawls on both sides of the channel Naantalinsalmi. The island of Luonnonmaa is on the south-west side of the channel, accessible by bridge, and the mainland, with the town centre, is on the north-east side. The old part of Naantali surrounds the harbour, 1km west of the bus terminal.

Information
Tourist Office Naantali Tourist Service (Naantalin Matkailu, ☎ 435 0850, fax 435 0852), near the harbour at Kaivotori 2, is open from 9 am to 6 pm daily from June to mid-August (from 9 am to 4 pm Monday to Friday at other times). In addition to being a source of free tourist literature, the office serves as a reservation centre and a travel agent for regional tours.

Post The post office is at Tullikatu 11. Hours are from 9 am to 8 pm Monday to Friday.

Internet Resources & Library The library, on the second floor of the post office building, is open from 11 am to 8 pm Monday, from 11 am to 7 pm Tuesday to Friday and from 10 am to 3 pm Saturday. There is an Internet terminal.

The main site for Naantali is www.travel.fi/naantali/ on the Web.

Medical & Emergency Services There's a pharmacy at Luostarinkatu 25. Hours are from 9 am to 9 pm Monday to Friday, from 9 am to 3 pm Saturday and from 10 am to 2 pm Sunday.

The regional hospital is just north of the bus terminal, on the corner of Aurinkotie and Tuulensuunkatu.

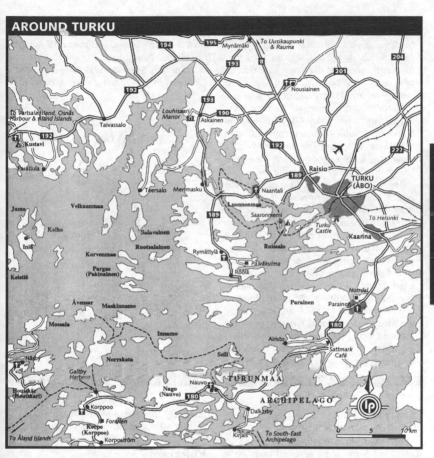

AROUND TURKU

For a general emergency call ☎ 112, for police call ☎ 10022 and for a doctor dial ☎ 10023.

Old Town

The Old Town of Naantali is like a big open-air museum. The town grew around the convent, without any regular town plan, and new buildings were always built on the sites of older ones. The result is a delightful district of narrow cobbled streets and low wooden houses – many of

which now house handicraft shops, art galleries and cafés. Only the old windmills and storehouses along the shore have disappeared.

Moomin World (Muumimaailma)

Even children who have not grown up reading the story books of Tove Jansson (or watching the Moomin film or TV series) will delight in the whimsies of the Muumimaailma of Naantali. This is not a single

Ms Moomin

Ms Tove Jansson, creator of the much-loved Moomin children's books, was born on 9 August 1914 in Helsinki to Swedish-speaking parents. The talented young Tove was an artist almost from birth – her first drawings were published in a magazine when she was a mere 14 years of age. The first book featuring Moomin trolls came out in 1945, and a new Moomin adventure followed every two years or so.

Despite almost immediate Moomin fever in Finland, more than 40 years elapsed before the lovable Moomin family attracted worldwide attention. The big break was a Japanese-made cartoon which has been shown on TV in several countries.

Today, the Moomin world comprises four picture books, eight novels and one short story collection, which have been translated into many languages – including English.

Tove has lived most of her life on various islands off the Finnish south coast. Whenever she tired of the journalists who frequently visited her studio, she moved to a more isolated island. Tove's original drawings – together with plenty of plush toy Moomins and Moomin CD-ROMs – are displayed at the Moomin Museum in Tampere, while the Moomin World theme park is the pride and joy of Naantali. The theme park is mobbed by Finnish families every summer.

theme park but rather a handful of attractions scattered across the town.

The **Moomin House of Surprises** at Kaivokatu 5 has a playground and 'do it yourself' radio station where kids can make their own broadcasts.

The **Moomin Strange House** at Mannerheiminkatu 21 is devoted to Moomin memorabilia.

On Kailo island is **Moomin Homevalley**, the main Moomin attraction, accessible by bridge from the mainland. Costumed characters inhabit its Moominhouse, Pirate Fort, Moominmama's Doughnut House and Whispering Woods. There is a safe swimming beach and a miniature golf course.

Muumimaailma is open from 10 am to 5 pm daily from June to mid-August. Admission is 80 mk adult, 60 mk child.

Kultaranta

The summer residence of the president of Finland is a fanciful stone castle on Luonnonmaa island, surrounded by a 56 hectare estate with beautiful, extensive rose gardens. For those without children, this is the top attraction in Naantali.

The Kultaranta grounds may be visited in summer by guided tour only; book through the tourist office.

Convent Church

The only building remaining from the Convent of the Order of Saint Birgitta is the

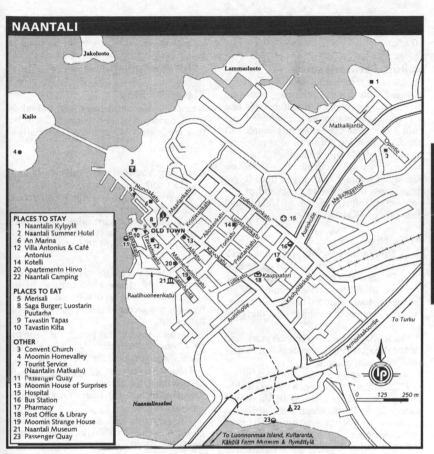

NAANTALI

PLACES TO STAY
1 Naantalin Kylpylä
2 Naantali Summer Hotel
6 An Marina
12 Villa Antonius & Café
   Antonius
14 Kotelli
20 Apartemento Hirvo
22 Naantali Camping

PLACES TO EAT
5 Merisali
8 Saga Burger; Luostarin
   Puutarha
9 Tavastin Tapas
10 Tavastin Kilta

OTHER
3 Convent Church
4 Moomin Homevalley
7 Tourist Service
   (Naantalin Matkailu)
11 Passenger Quay
13 Moomin House of Surprises
15 Hospital
16 Bus Station
17 Pharmacy
18 Post Office & Library
19 Moomin Strange House
21 Naantali Museum
23 Passenger Quay

OLD TOWN

TURKU

massive Convent Church, which towers above the harbour. The church was completed in 1462 and its fine stone tower dates from 1797. Until this century, the clock face on the tower had painted hands which always pointed to 11.30 – local people used to joke that the end of the world would come when the clock struck 12!

The church is open from noon to 7 pm daily from May to mid-August, and from noon to 3 pm daily in April and from mid-August to late September. At other times, it is open from noon to 3 pm on Sunday and holidays.

During summer the church offers a program of organ music; the tourist office can provide a schedule.

Naantali Museum

The Naantali Museum at Katinjäntä 1 is housed in three old wooden buildings dating from the 18th century. Displays include old furniture and exhibitions on the history of Naantali as a ritzy spa town. The museum is open from noon to 6 pm daily from mid-May to late August. Tickets are 10 mk.

Käkölä Farm Museum

On Luonnonmaa island, south-west of the centre, is this private museum – really an old farmhouse run by a man in his 80s and his son. Together they have assembled in a barn a charming 'museum' of hundreds of old farming tools. You can also purchase woodwork made with a chainsaw. The farm museum is open from noon to 6 pm on Sunday in summer and entry is free. To get there, cross the bridge to the island of Luonnonmaa, follow the sign to Käkölä and turn left onto Käköläntie.

Activities

Book **fishing trips** for pike, trout and perch at the tourist office or with local guide Erä-Divari Rantanen (☎ 049-619 464). These trips operate during summer months and are for one to four people. They aren't cheap, but your chances of catching something are quite good.

The tourist office also rents **bicycles**, and **motor boats** with equipment for water skiing or wake boarding.

Naantali's **spa** traditions go back as far as 1723, when people began taking health-giving waters from a spring in Viluluoto. Naantalin Kylpylä, the town's top-class spa hotel, allows nonguests to use its pool and sauna area – including several pools and a Turkish bath – during daytime hours. The charge for two hours is 85 mk adult, 55 mk child. Day packages are available.

Special Events

The week-long Naantali Music Festival, held in mid-June, features chamber music by Mozart, Bach, Rautavaara and others, with international participants. Many of the concerts are at the Convent Church. For ticket sales contact Lippupalvelu (☎ 09-6138 6246, fax 09-6138 6299).

One of the more unusual Finnish festivals is Sleepyhead Day (27 July), a Naantali tra-

dition that goes back over 100 years. Townspeople elect a 'Sleepyhead of the year' who is woken early in the morning by being thrown into the sea! A carnival with music, dancing and games follows.

Places to Stay

Naantali is one of the few towns in Finland to offer accommodation in quaint B&Bs but they are invariably expensive, especially in summer.

Camping *Naantali Camping (☎ 435 0855 or 435 0850, Kuparivuori)* is 400m south of the town centre and open year-round. This is an exceptional camping ground with good facilities, including a beachside sauna. Camp sites cost from 75 to 85 mk and cabins cost from 140 to 590 mk.

Guesthouses & B&Bs *Apartemento Hirvo (☎ 435 1619, Mannerheiminkatu 19)* has singles/doubles at 300/400 mk. Staff are friendly, the garden is quiet and you can use the kitchen.

Closest to the harbour, *An Marina (☎ 435 6066, Nunnakatu 5)* is a lovely little place with six rooms for 300/400 mk.

Villa Antonius (☎ 435 1938, Mannerheiminkatu 9) has about a dozen romantically decorated rooms (with hints of Art Nouveau) for 400/450 mk.

The very fine villa *Kotelli (☎ 435 1419, Luostarinkatu 13)* has singles/doubles/triples for 300/350/400 mk. The dining room has heaps of style and the garden is cosy.

Hotels The modern *Naantali Summer Hotel (☎ 445 5660, Opintie 3)* is open from June to mid-August. In June rooms are 180 mk per person Monday to Friday and 200 mk per person on weekends. In July rooms are 200 mk per person.

The town's top-end establishment is the sprawling spa hotel *Naantalin Kylpylä (☎ 44550, fax 445 5622, Matkailijantie 2)*, a few hundred metres north of the bus station. The spa is one of the finest in Finland, and the whole establishment will pamper you until you're limp and happy as a wet noodle – at prices from 540/640 mk.

Places to Eat

Naantali caters for tourists, with a great variety of places to sample good food. However, prices are higher than in other small towns in Finland.

The cheapest is *Saga Burger* on the waterfront, with 10 mk burgers, ice cream and a rousing motto – 'Burgers for People!'

Next door, *Luostarin Puutarha (Fleminginkatu 6)* is a combination beer cellar and open-air pizzeria. Pizzas are 40 mk, or slices for 25 mk.

Side by side at the harbour are *Tavastin Kilta* and *Tavastin Tapas*. In most respects they're identical, offering great outdoor seating, cold beer and 32 mk buffalo wings. Kilta has an international menu and is a bit more upmarket, while Tapas offers live music on summer nights and a Finnish spin on Spanish food, including tapas of smoked reindeer or salmon for 30 to 65 mk.

Without question the best on the Naantali dining scene is *Merisali (Nunnakatu 1)*, just below the Convent Church. The historic old place has a shaded terrace and a mind-blowing smorgasbord for lunch (45 mk) and dinner (55 mk), including staggering quantities of salads and fish. If you value your waistline, beware the 65 mk Sunday brunch.

Café Antonius in Villa Antonius *(Mannerheiminkatu 9)* is an unbeatable café with gingerbread made by the motherly proprietor, Lilja. The place has an endearing combination of style, kitsch and excellent pastries.

Getting There & Away

Bus There are buses to Naantali every 15 minutes from the bus terminal in Turku. Virtually all routes to Naantali go via Turku.

Car & Motorcycle From Turku, take road No 185 (Naantalin Pikatie) then follow signs to Naantali, 13km north-west.

Boat The MS *Summersea* and SS *Ukkopekka* sail between Turku and Naantali in summer. The SS *Ukkopekka* docks at the passenger quay by Naantali Camping and the MS *Summersea* halts at the Old Town passenger quay. For more information see the Turku Getting There & Away section earlier.

RYMÄTTYLÄ

Rymättylä, a sleepy island village 20km south-west of Naantali, is the ideal place to escape to when you've tired of big cities like Turku and Helsinki – particularly because it has one of the finest hostels in the entire country. The village church, at its centre, has one of the most colourful of all Finnish medieval church interiors. It's open daily from June to August.

Places to Stay

The excellent HI-affiliated hostel *Päiväkulma (☎ 252 1894, fax 252 1794, Kuristentie 225)* is in a big, old former schoolhouse on the seafront; it's a family-run place surrounded by farms. Dorm beds are from 70 mk, and there are private rooms and two cottages, as well as an excellent kitchen, laundry facilities and a seaside sauna. Guests have the use of several rowing boats. The house is on an unpaved road (but is clearly marked) about 3km from the village. Bookings are advised, as it's often full in summer. Päiväkulma is open from May to late August or by prior arrangement.

Getting There & Away

Rymättylä is on road No 189 south from Naantali. There are buses from Turku and Naantali every two hours or so.

LOUHISAARI MANOR

The village of Askainen, 30km north-west of Turku, is the setting for stunning Louhisaari Manor and its lavishly decorated rooms, including a 'ghost room', and its extensive museum and gardens. The manor, locally referred to as a castle, was built in

1655 in the Dutch Renaissance style. The five storey manor was purchased by the Mannerheim family in 1795, and Finland's greatest military leader and president, Marshal CGE Mannerheim, was born here in 1867. Soon after that the family lost its fortune and the property. Louhisaari was later acquired by the National Board of Antiquities; it's now an attraction rivalling the castles at Turku and Savonlinna. The manor is open daily from 11 am to 5 pm mid-May to the end of August and entry costs 15 mk. Tours are in Finnish only.

Getting There & Away

The village and manor are located just off road No 193. There are three to four buses daily from Turku to Askainen.

NOUSIAINEN

Nousiainen village is 25km north of Turku, and is worth a visit for the **Nousiainen church**. In a country with seemingly limitless medieval churches, this one is notable as the eternal resting place of St Henry, the first (Catholic) Bishop of Finland, who died in the early 15th century. The church was built in the 1300s and restored in the 1960s. It has a triple-aisled hall design with murals from the early 15th century. Hours are from noon to 6 pm Tuesday to Sunday.

Getting There & Away

The church is near road No 8 and there are buses from Turku almost every hour.

MYNÄMÄKI

The busy little village of Mynämäki is 17km north-east of Askainen and 15km north-west of Nousiainen. It's another town with a notable medieval stone **church** worth incorporating into a general tour of the area. This one dates from the early 14th century and is the largest stone church in Finland, with almost 1000 seats. There are numerous wooden statues, miniature ships, tombstones and coats of arms of the local

nobility. It's open daily from May to August.

Getting There & Away

Mynämäki is easy to reach, as it lies on busy road No 8. There are buses from Turku, Uusikaupunki and Rauma every two hours or so.

KUSTAVI

The island village of Kustavi (Swedish: Gustavs) offers scenic seascapes and freedom from anything approaching 'city life'. Its wooden **church**, built in 1783, features the miniature ships common in coastal churches – sailors offered these in exchange for divine blessings. The church is open daily from early June to mid-August.

For those heading to Åland via the northern archipelago route, Kustavi is one of the last stops before officially entering the Åland chain.

Places to Stay & Eat

Kustavin Lomakeskus ja Camping (☎ 876 230, *myyntipalvelu@lomaliitto.fi*) is a large holiday village to the south of Kustavi, open from late May to mid-August. It has 70 mk camp sites, a café-restaurant, many cottages and a host of activities.

Getting There & Away

Kustavi is on road No 192 from Turku, and there are many buses. To reach Åland, continue 8.5km west to the passenger pier of Osnäs (Finnish: Vuosnainen) on Vartsala island. From there ferries depart regularly for the island of Brändö.

Most buses from Turku travel direct to Osnäs, and some continue to Brändö. If you have a private vehicle, expect delays during the high season. Taking a car by ferry to Brändö will cost money; bicycles travel free. See the Åland chapter for more details.

TURUNMAA ARCHIPELAGO

The Turunmaa archipelago is a tightly clustered chain of islands that begins south of Turku, with Parainen, then stretches south-west to Korppoo. Free local ferries – especially for those travelling by bicycle or bus – can be taken all the way out to Galtby harbour on Korppoo island. From there, you can catch one of the frequent ferries plying the southern archipelago route to Mariehamn, Åland; see the Åland chapter for more details. Local ferries on the route between Parainen, Nauvo and Korppoo offer a continuous service.

Parainen

Parainen (Swedish: Pargas), about 25km south of Turku, is the de facto 'capital' of the archipelago. It's the largest town, with 12,000 residents and all facilities. There are paintings and old statues in the medieval church, open daily in summer. The old town with wooden houses is behind the church.

Places to Stay & Eat *Solliden* (☎/*fax 485 5955, Norrby*) is the seaside camping ground of Parainen, 1.5km north of the centre. It has both camp sites and cottages. At the same location, *Norrdal* is an HI-affiliated hostel in a rustic old building, with dorm beds from 70 mk, a kitchen and a TV room. Both places are open from June to mid-August.

Halfway between Parainen and the island of Nauvo, *Sattmark* is worth a stop. It is a café, in a charming 18th century red wooden cottage, that sells home-made wheat buns and cakes.

Getting There & Away Parainen is on road No 180 from Turku. There are one to three buses an hour from Turku to Parainen, and five or six buses a day from Helsinki.

Nauvo

Nauvo (Swedish: Nagu) is an idyllic island community between Parainen to the east and Korppoo to the west. It is connected to both by free continuous ferries. **Nagu church** dates from the 14th century and contains the

oldest Bible in Finland. It is open daily from June to late August.

Getting There & Away Nauvo is on road No 180, and is served by the same buses as Parainen and Korppoo.

From Nauvo it's possible to island-hop around the Turunmaa archipelago on free local ferries. The MS *Bastö* departs from Nauvo harbour for a small group of islands north of Nauvo. The MS *Fiskö* sails from the harbour at Kirjais (south of Nauvo) to a group of islands lying just south-east.

Korppoo

Korppoo (Swedish: Korpo) is the most distant island in the Turunmaa archipelago, and the final stop before entering the Åland archipelago. A highlight is the medieval **Korppoo church** built in the late 1200s. Treasures in this church include naive paintings on the ceiling and a statue of St George fighting a dragon. The church is open daily in summer.

Places to Stay & Eat *Forellen* (☎/*fax 463 1202, Kirkonkylä*), in the village centre, is a guesthouse open year-round that charges 110 mk per person. Meals and snacks are also served.

Getting There & Away Korppoo is 75km south-west from Turku on road No 180 and is connected to Nauvo by continuous ferry. This is a terminus for Saaristotie buses from Turku.

Galtby is the passenger harbour, 4km north-east of Korppoo centre. A number of free ferries depart from Galtby for Åland; as this is a popular route in summer, expect to wait a few extra hours on Friday going to Åland and on Sunday going to Turku if you are travelling with a car. There are also regular ferries to smaller, nearby islands of the Turunmaa archipelago, such as Houtskär.

Åland

• pop 25,000 ☎ 018

The Åland islands are unique, autonomous islands, with their own flag, culture and *lagting* (local government). Several dialects of Swedish are spoken, and few Ålanders speak Finnish. Though technically still a part of Finland, Åland took its own flag in 1954 and has issued its own stamps – prized by collectors – since 1984.

The islands are popular for cycling and camping, and for cabin holidays – and Midsummer celebrations are particularly festive here. There are medieval parish churches and quaint fishing villages, but Kastelholm castle, which was established in the 14th century, is Åland's most striking attraction.

Åland is also the name of the main island. Surprisingly, Åland translates as 'river land', although the region is better known for its islands and islets, which number more than 6400. You can take your wheels almost anywhere around the islands using the bridges or the network of car and bicycle ferries. Regular ferries connect Åland to both Sweden and the Finnish mainland.

The most striking feature in the Åland landscape is the Midsummer pole. It's a long flagpole decorated with leaves, miniature flags, small boats and whatever is available and seems appropriate. Each village usually has one or more poles, which are decorated in a public gathering the day before Midsummer. The pole then stands until the next Midsummer.

The centre of Åland is Mariehamn, a port with two harbours, in the south of the main island group.

History

The first settlers set foot on Åland 6000 years ago, and more than a hundred Bronze and Iron Age burial sites (*fornminne*) have been discovered. These are all clearly signposted, though they aren't much to look at. Åland was an important harbour and trade centre

ÅLAND

HIGHLIGHTS

• Free inter-island ferries

• A distinctive Swedish-speaking culture – this isn't Finland, but neither is it Sweden

• Superb cycling routes along scenic roads

• The medieval Kastelholm Castle in Sund

• Views of the archipelago from the observation tower at Café Uffe på Berget

• Åland pancakes with jam and cream

• The kitschy Ålands Sjöfartsmuseum

• Small, isolated, scenic villages and islands, which can only be reached by local ferry

• Churches dating from the 12th century, notably the Santa Maria Church in Kvarnbo

• Midsummer celebrations

• Archipelago safaris

• Colourful Mariehamn – town of a thousand linden trees

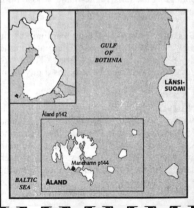

during the Viking era, and evidence of six fortresses from that time has been identified.

During the Great Northern War of 1700-21 (nicknamed the 'Great Wrath'), most of the population fled to Sweden to escape the Russians, who were bent on destroying Åland. The Russians returned during the 1740s (a period known as the Lesser Wrath), and again in 1809.

By the time Finland gained its independence in 1917, Ålanders were all too familiar with Russians and feared occupation by the Bolsheviks. There were moves for Åland to be incorporated into Sweden, which was not only the Ålanders' former mother country but also their source of cultural identity (not the case for the vast majority of Finns). But Finland didn't want to give up Åland. The Swedish-Finnish dispute only came to an end in 1921, when Åland was given its status as an autonomous, demilitarised and neutral province within the Republic of Finland by a decision of the League of Nations. Today Åland is almost like a Little Sweden, and locals are certainly more aware of events in Stockholm than in Helsinki.

Warning

Ticks carrying infectious diseases that may cause rash and fever (and may sometimes even lead to hospitalisation) are a concern in rural areas of Åland. The simplest way to deal with this problem is to take proper precautions – do not walk barefoot outside; wear trousers or long pants when hiking; and always conduct a swift 'tick check' after spending time outdoors.

Information

Money You can use both Finnish *markka* and Swedish *krona* in Åland. Branches of Merita Bank and Postbanken have ATMs that accept Visa cards – other types of ATM cards do not work in Åland.

Post & Communications The telephone code for Åland is 018. 'Tele' brand telephone cards purchased in mainland Finland will work in Åland (and vice versa), though other kinds will not.

Mail sent in Åland must have Åland postage stamps – Finnish ones won't work.

Medical & Emergency Services For emergencies call ☎ 112, for police ☎ 10022 and for medical service ☎ 10023.

Cabin Rentals For information about rental cabins all over Åland, visit Ålandsresor (☎ 28040, fax 28380) at Torggatan 2 in Mariehamn or check out www.alandresor.fi/ on the Web. The mailing address is Ålandsresor, Box 62, 22101 Mariehamn.

Getting There & Away

Air Finnair (☎ 24020) has a weekday direct service to Åland from Stockholm and a daily service from Helsinki via Turku. The airport is 4km north-west of Mariehamn and there is a bus service into the centre. A taxi to the centre costs about 50 mk. Skärgårdsflyg Air (☎ 13880) at Parkgatan 28 in Mariehamn has two regular flights on weekdays to Stockholm. The Finnair office is in Hotell Arkipelag at Strandgatan 31, Mariehamn.

Boat Viking and Silja lines have year-round daily ferries to Mariehamn from Turku as part of their links with Stockholm; you can stop off 'between' countries. Viking also sails to Mariehamn from Kapellskär (north of Stockholm) in Sweden. Birka Cruises sails only between Stockholm and Mariehamn.

Eckerö Linjen sails from Grisslehamn in Sweden to Eckerö – this is the cheapest and quickest route from Sweden to Åland. There are five connections a day from Grisslehamn during the high season and two or three during the low season. Most of the tours have a bus connection to/from Stockholm and Mariehamn. The boat trip takes two hours, and a combined boat and bus trip from Stockholm to Mariehamn takes five hours altogether.

Ferry fares vary widely by season and class of travel, so contact the local ferry offices for more information (see Getting There & Away in the Mariehamn section).

ÅLAND

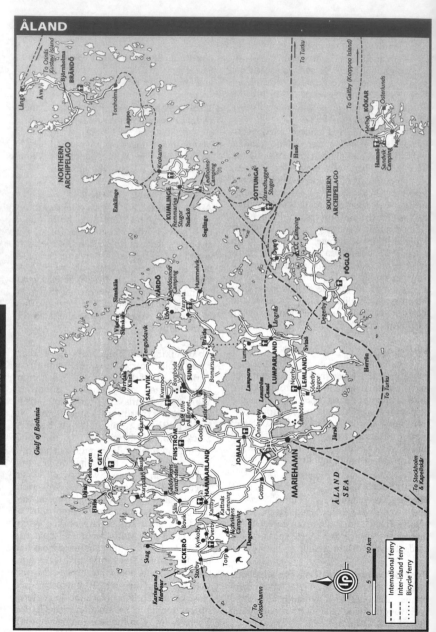

ÅLAND

Free travel for pedestrians and cyclists on the archipelago ferries all the way to the central Åland islands is possible from mainland Finland via Korppoo (southern route, from Galtby passenger harbour) or Kustavi (northern route, from Osnäs passenger harbour), but only if you break your journey to stay on one or more islands. Travelling nonstop costs 100 mk per person, plus 200 mk for a car.

Getting Around

Bus Five main bus lines depart from Mariehamn's regional bus terminal on Torggatan in front of the library, and go to Eckerö, Geta, Saltvik, Vårdö (Hummelvik) and Lumparland (Långnäs) fares are up to 30 mk.

Ferry There are three kinds of inter-island ferry. For short trips across straits, ferries ply nonstop and are always free. For longer routes, ferries run according to schedule, and take cars, bicycles and pedestrians. There are also three bicycle ferries in summer – a ride is 30 to 40 mk per person with bicycle. The bike ferry routes are Hammarland-Geta, Lumparland-Sund and Vårdö-Saltvik.

Timetables for all inter-island ferries are available at the main tourist office in Mariehamn and at the local transportation office, Ålandstrafiken at Strandgatan 25, Mariehamn.

Bicycle Cycling is a great way to tour these flat, rural islands. The most scenic roads have separate bike lanes that are clearly marked. RO-NO Rent has bicycles available at Mariehamn and Eckerö harbours with rates starting at 30 mk per day or 150 mk per week.

Mariehamn

Mariehamn will seem a bustling metropolis if you've arrived from some of the other entry points in Åland or have spent some time in the archipelago. But if you come directly to Mariehamn from either Sweden or mainland Finland, you are in for a pleasant surprise – if you like quiet little towns. Mariehamn is sometimes called the 'town of a thousand linden trees'. It is hectic here in summer, when it becomes the town of a thousand tourists, but in winter Mariehamn is quiet, with a population of only 11,000.

Mariehamn was founded in 1861 by Tsar Alexander II, who named the town after his wife, Tsarina Maria. Today, Mariehamn is the administrative and economic centre of Åland. It is the seat of the *lagting* and *landskapsstyrelse*, the legislative and executive bodies of Åland.

Orientation

Mariehamn is situated on a long, narrow peninsula and has two harbours – Västra Hamnen (West Harbour) and Östra Hamnen (East Harbour). Ferries from Sweden and mainland Finland dock at Västra Hamnen but just about everything else is at Östra Hamnen. Torggatan is the colourful pedestrian street. The airport is 4km north-west of the centre.

Information

Tourist Office The main tourist office is Ålands Turistinformation (☎ 24000) at Storagatan 8. It has material about the whole of Åland, and is open from 9 am to 6 pm daily June through August, and 9 am to 4 pm Monday to Friday, 10 am to 4 pm Saturday during the rest of the year.

The tourist information booth (☎ 531 214) at the ferry terminal is open daily in July, and Monday to Saturday in June and August (closed September through May).

Money Postbanken, at the main post office has an ATM that accepts Visa cards.

Post The main post office on Torggatan is open from 9 am to 5 pm from Monday to Friday and 11 am to 2 pm Saturday in summer.

Internet Resources & Library There are several Internet terminals Mariehamn Municipal Library at Östra Hamnen (these

MARIEHAMN

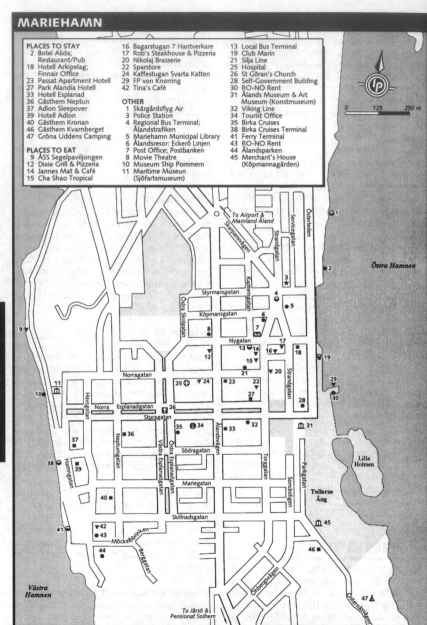

PLACES TO STAY
2 Botel Alida;
  Restaurant/Pub
18 Hotell Arkipelag;
  Finnair Office
23 Passat Apartment Hotell
27 Park Alandia Hotell
33 Hotell Esplanad
36 Gästhem Neptun
37 Adlon Sleepover
39 Hotell Adlon
40 Gästhem Kronan
46 Gästhem Kvarnberget
47 Gröna Uddens Camping

PLACES TO EAT
9 ÅSS Segelpaviljongen
12 Dixie Grill & Pizzeria
14 Jannes Mat & Café
15 Cha Shao Tropical

16 Bagarstugan 7 Hantverkare
17 Rob's Steakhouse & Pizzeria
20 Nikolaj Brasserie
22 Sparstore
24 Kaffestugan Svarta Katten
29 FP von Knorring
42 Tina's Café

OTHER
1 Skärgårdsflyg Air
3 Police Station
4 Regional Bus Terminal;
  Ålandstrafiken
5 Mariehamn Municipal Library
6 Ålandsresor; Eckerö Linjen
7 Post Office; Postbanken
8 Movie Theatre
10 Museum Ship Pommern
11 Maritime Museum
  (Sjöfartsmuseum)

13 Local Bus Terminal
19 Club Marin
21 Silja Line
25 Hospital
26 St Göran's Church
28 Self-Government Building
30 RO-NO Rent
31 Ålands Museum & Art
  Museum (Konstmuseum)
32 Viking Line
34 Tourist Office
35 Birka Cruises
38 Birka Cruises Terminal
41 Ferry Terminal
43 RO-NO Rent
44 Ålandsparken
45 Merchant's House
  (Köpmannagården)

Windmill and farm house in Jomala, Åland

Kastelholm Castle in Sund, Åland

Käringsund harbour boat houses in winter, Åland

In Eckerö even the tractors are Volvo, Åland

Mailbox in Finström, Åland

must be reserved in advance) and a few foreign newspapers. The library is open from 11 am to 8 pm Monday to Friday and to 3 pm on Saturday.

Travel Agency Ålandsresor (☎ 28040, fax 28380) at Torggatan 2 is a travel agency which specialises in summer cabin rentals (see Cabin Rentals earlier in this chapter). It also assists with hotel and guesthouse bookings around the archipelago, and organises tours.

Left Luggage You may store luggage in the lockers at the ferry terminal for up to 24 hours. The cost is 10 mk. Ålandstrafiken will store backpacks for longer periods, at 5 mk per day.

Medical & Emergency Services The hospital (☎ 5355) is at Norragatan 17. If you need a pharmacy, try Centralapotek (☎ 19714 or 19655) at Skarpansvägen 24, or Provinsial Apotek (☎ 16511) at Torggatan 10. You'll find the police on the corner of Styrmansgatan and Strandgatan.

Ålands Maritime Museum (Sjöfartsmuseum)

The stalwarts of Åland are mariners and the Maritime Museum at Hamngatan 2 in Västra Hamnen, a kitschy museum of fishing and maritime commerce, is devoted to them. There are heaps of items from old boats, including figureheads, model ships, ships in bottles, sea chests, all kinds of nautical equipment – and even a giant stuffed albatross. The museum is open daily from 10 am to 4 pm, except in June and August, when it's open until 5 pm, and in July, when it's open until 7 pm. Admission costs 20 mk.

Museum Ship *Pommern*

The *Pommern*, anchored behind the Maritime Museum, is one of the symbols of Mariehamn. The four masted sailing ship was built in 1903 in Glasgow, Scotland, and once carried tons of cargo and a 26 man crew on the trade route between Australia and England. The ship is open from 9 am to

5 pm daily from April to September (until 7 pm in July) and costs 20 mk.

Ålands Museum & Art Museum (Konstmuseum)

The fine Ålands Museum and the adjoining Art Museum are well worth a visit. Ålands Museum covers the history of Åland from prehistoric times to the present. It received the 1982 Council of Europe Award for the best new museum, and its exhibits are unusually lively and well presented. The Art Museum has a permanent collection of art from Åland, as well as temporary exhibitions. The museums are open daily from May to the end of August from 10 am to 4 pm (Tuesday to 8 pm). At other times of the year they keep the same hours but are closed on Monday. A joint admission ticket, good for both museums, is 15 mk.

St Göran's Church

The 1927 copper-roofed Sankt Göran's (St George's) Church is not as interesting as the medieval treasure-trove churches in Åland's villages. The design is Art Nouveau, by Lars Sonck. It is open from 10 am to 3 pm Monday to Friday.

Merchant's House (Köpmannagården)

The Köpmannagården on Parkgatan has trade and handicraft displays. It is open from 1 to 3 pm Monday to Friday from mid-June to mid-August. Admission is free.

Self-Government Building

The Self-Government Building, home of the Åland parliament, is on the corner of Österleden and Storagatan. Free guided tours are offered at 10 am every Friday from mid-June to mid-August. The tour ends with a slide show about Åland.

Ålandsparken

The small Ålandsparken amusement park, next to the ferry terminal, has rides best suited to small children. It is open from noon to 9 pm daily in July. Hours are shorter in May,

June and August, and the park is closed September through April. Entry costs 20 mk.

Tullarns Äng & Lilla Holmen

South of Östra Hamnen is Tullarns Äng, a small park that is prized for its spring wildflowers. Lilla Holmen island, connected to Tullarns Äng by a bridge, has a café, a good swimming beach and peacocks strolling through the grounds.

Järsö

The Järsö recreational area, 12km south of Mariehamn at the tip of the peninsula, is a good place for short bicycle and walking tours. The area is at its most beautiful in spring and early summer, when wildflowers cover the ground. Nåtö nature trail (trailhead at Nåtö Biological Station) and Järsö trail are two easy 2km walking tracks.

Activities

In additional to bicycles, RO-NO Rent (see Getting Around later in this section) rents all kinds of fun outdoor equipment. You can rent fishing rods for 40/80 mk per day/week; canoes for 50/100 mk per hour/day; rowing boats for 80/200 mk per two hours/day; and beach buggies for 130/250 mk per two hours/day. Scooters can be had for 90/140/200 mk per two hours/seven hours/day, including free mileage and a full tank.

Organised Tours

From mid-June to mid-August guided bus tours offer an alternative way to see Åland. On Wednesday and Thursday at 11 am tour buses depart Mariehamn for various attractions around the mainland, including Kastelholm Castle and the Bomarsund fortress ruins. A 'children's bus' departs Tuesday at 12.40 pm for a tour of a nearby toy factory and farm. Tour buses to the observation tower at Café Uffe på Berget in Finström depart from Mariehamn town square at noon on weekdays. Contact Ålands Turistinformation for more information.

RO-NO Rent, the bicycle rental company (see Getting Around later in this section), offers boat safaris to points around the archi-

pelago during summer. Departures are from the RO-NO stand at Östra Hamnen. The 10 am daily departure takes you to an uninhabited island for swimming, fishing and a picnic. Cost is 300 mk per adult, plus 60 mk for fishing rod and permit. The 11 am daily departure cruises around the most scenic parts of the archipelago and costs 150 mk per adult. A more costly option is an overnight camping safari to an uninhabited island.

Places to Stay

While hotel prices drop in mainland Finland during summer, Mariehamn's hotels raise their rates between mid-June and the end of August.

Places to Stay – Budget

The seaside camping ground *Gröna Uddens Camping* (☎ 19041) is on Östernäsvägen, just 1km south of the centre. Camping here costs 20 mk per person plus 15 mk per tent and 15 mk per car. The sites are pleasant if sometimes a bit cramped, and the beach is good for swimming. There are cooking and laundry facilities and a café – but no sauna and no cottages. Gröna Uddens is open from mid-May to the end of August.

Other than camping, the cheapest accommodation in Mariehamn is *Botel Alida* (☎ 13755), a boat hostel moored at the north end of Östra Hamnen, not far from the library and the bus station. Rates are 70 mk per bed in a basic two-bunk cabin, 15 mk for sheets (sleeping bags are allowed) and 25 mk for breakfast. There are no HI discounts. Arrive early in the day to be sure of getting a bed. The boat hostel is closed in winter. Alida's restaurant-pub, open year round, has cheap meals and outside seating on sunny days.

Places to Stay – Mid-Range

The best in this price bracket is *Gästhem Kronan* (☎ 12617, fax 19580, Neptunigatan 52), which has very friendly owners and is open year-round. It's close to the ferry terminal and charges 310/475 mk for singles/doubles in summer, less during other seasons. Two summer-only guesthouses with similar prices are run by the same family: *Gästhem Kvarnberget* (☎ *13785, Parkgatan 28C)* is a modern house on a quiet street opposite Tullarns Äng park, and *Gästhem Neptun* (☎ *12617, Neptunigatan 41)* is two blocks from Kronan. Reception for all three is at Kronan.

Ideal for small groups is *Adlon Sleepover* (☎ *15300, Hamngatan 7)*, across the street from Hotell Adlon (see later in Places to Stay). Rooms are bigger than those in the hotel and can accommodate up to six people. Guests may use all the facilities of Hotell Adlon, including the sauna and the swimming pool. Reception is at Hotell Adlon. In summer, rooms are from 260/320 mk, including breakfast. Each extra bed is 195 mk.

One of the quiet places to stay in Mariehamn is *Pensionat Solhem* (☎ *16322, fax 16350)*, pleasantly situated by the sea on Lökskärsvägen, 3km south of the centre. Rooms cost 310/445 mk, less outside the summer high season. Guests can use the rowing boats free of charge, and there's a sauna.

Passat Apartment Hotell (☎ *15555, fax 21077, Norragatan 7)* has only 12 rooms, and should be reserved in advance. The keys can be obtained from a shop nearby. Rooms are from 300/350 mk.

Another cheap hotel in Mariehamn is *Hotell Esplanad* (☎ *16444, fax 14143, Storagatan 5)*, open from mid-June to the end of August. Rooms are 420/525 mk.

Places to Stay – Top End
Hotell Adlon (☎ *15300, fax 15077, Hamngatan 7)* is a nice, modern hotel not far from the ferry terminal. Rooms cost 585/735 mk in summer.

Overlooking Östra Hamnen, *Hotell Arkipelag* (☎ *24020, fax 24384, Strandgatan 31)* is the largest hotel in Åland and one of the brighter lights of Mariehamn's nightlife. Rooms in this impressive hotel cost from 615/825 mk year-round, and suites are from 1485 mk.

Park Alandia Hotell (☎ *14130, fax 17130, Norra Esplanadgatan 3)* is very close to the centre. There are 80 rooms, with rooms from 500/720 mk during the high season.

Places to Eat
Many cafés, including *Tina's Café* opposite the ferry terminal, serve the local specialty, *Ålandspannkaka* (Åland pancakes), for 15 mk. The best place to try one is at cosy *Kaffestugan Svarta Katten* on Norragatan. Coffee is served here in copper pots. Another tasty local specialty, Åland dark bread, is available at local markets, such as the *Sparstore (Torggatan 14)* (closed Sunday). This type of bread takes four days to make!

Two popular restaurants on Torggatan serve daily lunch specials from about 35 mk: *Cha Shao Tropical (Torggatan 10)* has pastas and stir-fries and *Nikolaj Brasserie (Torggatan 13A)*, inside the shopping centre, has huge pizzas. Ordinary meals are dearer. Both places offer vegetarian dishes. Also on Torggatan, *Jannes Mat & Café* has pleasant outdoor seating, and the home-made food is good value.

Rob's Steakhouse & Pizzeria (Strandgatan 12) and *Dixie Grill & Pizzeria (Ålandsvägen 40)* are down-to-earth eateries with burgers and such from 30 mk. The restaurant at the Alida boat hostel is similar (see Places to Stay).

Bagarstugan 7 Hantverkare (☎ *19881, Ekonomiegatan 2)* is the town's most charming café, with home-made soups and sandwiches. It is a favourite local meeting place. Handicrafts are also sold here (see Shopping later in this section).

The boat restaurant *FP von Knorring* (☎ *16500)* at Östra Hamnen has classy seafood meals, plus a busy beer terrace on the deck. North of the Maritime Museum at Västra Hamnen, *ÅSS Segelpaviljongen* (☎ *19141)* is the oldest restaurant in town, and also one of the nicest. It's in a lovely old wooden building. À la carte options are from 60 mk.

There are restaurants and pubs in the many Mariehamn hotels, but these are not necessarily good value.

Entertainment
Hotell Arkipelag has a lively disco and casino (see Places to Stay). *Club Marin* is an attractive harbour pavilion that serves

beer and meals, and is very popular on weekend nights in summer when there's live music. The *movie theatre* on the corner of Nygatan and Ålandsvägen, just west of the centre, usually shows films in English with Swedish subtitles.

Shopping

Mariehamn is one of the best places in Finland to shop for quality handicrafts – pick up a map of craft shops in Mariehamn and around mainland Åland at Ålands Turistinformation. Jussis Keramik (☎ 13606) at Nygatan 1 sells lovely ceramics and glassware, and visitors can watch the objects being made. Svalan Art & Handicrafts (☎ 13470), around the corner at Torggatan 5, specialises in knitting, needlework and related items. Bagarstugan 7 Hantverkare is a crafts collective representing nearly a dozen artists. It also has a superb café (see Places to Eat). Fäktargubben (☎ 19603) at Norragatan 13 sells assorted Åland handicrafts.

Getting There & Away

See the main Getting There & Away section at the beginning of this chapter for information on travelling to and from Mariehamn by plane or ferry.

Viking and Silja ferries depart from the ferry terminal at Västra Hamnen. Just north of it is a smaller terminal used only by Birka Cruises.

All ferry lines have offices in Mariehamn: Viking Line is at Storagatan 2, Silja Line is at Norragatan 2, Eckerö Linjen is at Torggatan 2 and Birka Cruises is at Östra Esplanadgatan 7.

Regional buses depart from the terminal on Torggatan in front of the library; for route and fare information see the main Getting Around section at the beginning of this chapter, or contact Ålandstrafiken (☎ 25155) at Strandgatan 25.

Getting Around

A local bus services the town, departing from Nygatan.

For bicycles, RO-NO Rent is the largest rental firm, with offices at Västra Hamnen

(☎ 12821) and Östra Hamnen (☎ 12820). There are daily/weekly rates for bicycles (30/150 mk), three-speed models (40/200 mk) and mountain bikes (70/350 mk). RO-NO Rent is open from 9 am to noon and 1 to 6 pm daily from June to the end of August. At other times, arrangements can be made by phone.

Mainland Åland & Around

The largest islands of the archipelago form a group which is the most popular destination in the province. This is where many of the oldest historical landmarks in Finland are found. Bicycle tours are popular in summer, and bridges or ferries connect the various islands here to make up an area large enough for an interesting week of touring.

ECKERÖ

The island of Eckerö (population 800) is the westernmost municipality in Finland, just a two hour ferry ride from mainland Sweden. Eckerö has been a popular holiday spot since the 1800s. Today this area of Åland is almost a Little Sweden, and vacationing Swedes constitute the majority of the population during the summer season.

Eckerö has also been an important communication link across the Baltic since Viking times. In 1638, the farmers of Eckerö were divided into *rotas*, groups of eight men who were responsible for maintaining mail services between Eckerö and mainland Sweden. Mail was transported in small boats until 1910. Over the 272 years that the post rota system operated, more than 200 men lost their lives. On the second Saturday in June in odd-numbered years old-fashioned boats are rowed to Eckerö from Grisslehamn in Sweden.

Storby (Big Village), at the ferry terminal, is the main centre. The distance from Mariehamn to Storby (40km) makes this suitable day trip by bicycle.

Things to See & Do

The historic **Post and Customs House (Post och Tullhuset)** in Storby (☎ 38689) was designed by German architect Carl Ludwig Engel, who also designed parts of central Helsinki. It was completed in 1828, during the era of Tsar Alexander I of Russia. The building was meant to be a bulwark against the west and, for that reason, is far more grandiose than a post office in a small village should be. It now houses a café, bank, art gallery and the small **mailboat museum** in addition to the post office. The museum (7 mk) and café are open from 10 am to 4 pm daily from June to mid-August. The post office, bank and art gallery are open daily in summer and weekdays only in winter.

Also in Storby, the **Labbas Homestead & Bank Museum** is the local museum of Eckerö. It has old archipelago houses with local furniture, plus a section devoted to banking history. The museum is open from noon to 4 pm Tuesday and Thursday from late June to early August (admission 7 mk).

Just north of Storby is the attractive **Käringsund harbour**. Especially on summer evenings the quiet small-boat harbour, with its rustic old wooden boathouses, is so scenic it's almost unreal. There's an 800m **nature path** (*naturstig*) from Käringsund west to the larger ferry harbour. The **Ålands Hunting and Fishing Museum** at Käringsund harbour is open from 10 am to 6 pm daily June through August (weekends only in April, May and September). Admission is 20 mk.

Viltsafari (☎ 38000) at Käringsund harbour is a fenced-in forest with typical Finnish fauna like red and fallow deer, black swans and wild boar, as well as a few ostriches. The 45 minute tour (25 mk) departs from the Hunting and Fishing Museum hourly in summer and by arrangement during other seasons.

In the village of Kyrkoby, about 5km east from Storby on the road to Mariehamn, the 13th century **Sankt Lars Church of Eckerö**, open daily in summer, has beautiful 18th century interior paintings and a 14th century Madonna sculpture.

Kyrkoby is also home to the **Kyrkoby golf course** (☎ 38370), a short-hole course with 18 holes. You must have a Green Card to play.

Degersand, approximately 9km south of Storby beyond the village of Torp, has a good **beach** for swimming and sunning, and it's also possible to camp right on the beach.

A good way to see Eckerö is by bicycle. See the Mariehamn Getting Around section for details of bicycle hire.

Places to Stay

Camping *Käringsunds Camping* (☎ 38309, fax 38455), at Käringsund harbour, is a down-to-earth place with 35 mk camp sites and many cabins. There are all kinds of activities available, and the restaurant is busy at weekends with Swedes dancing to live music. Other amenities include a *grilli* and sauna. Käringsunds is open from mid-May to the end of August.

From Överby village on road No 2, turn south and go 2km to reach *Notvikens Camping* (☎ 38020, fax 38329). Camp sites cost 35 mk and there are cabins. The camping ground has a café and sauna and also rents boats and fishing equipment. It's open from May to the end of September.

In the isolated village of Skag on the northern coast, *Uddens Camping* (☎ 38670, fax 38547), open from May to the end of September, charges 9 mk per tent, plus 9 mk per person and 9 mk per vehicle.

Guesthouses In an 18th century wooden house in Storby, *Ängstorps Gästhem* (☎ 38665) is one of the best places to stay on Åland, but it's often full. There are just six rooms, and they're well equipped and attractive. Singles/doubles cost 200/300 mk in high season. Ängstorps is open from April to the end of October.

Granbergs Gästhem (☎ 39462) in Storby is an attractive place open April through November. Its five doubles cost 240 mk in high season, breakfast included. Opposite the Labbas Museum, *Storby Logi* (☎ 38469) is another central guesthouse with 10 rooms that are reasonably priced.

Alebo Stugor (☎ *38575, fax 38543)*, in Storby, 200m north of the main road, has 10 cabins starting from 250 mk per day. In July most of its cabins are rented by the week, however.

Hotels Between the Post and Customs House and the sea, *Hotell Havsbandet* (☎ *38200, fax 38305)*, closed January, is a 29 room hotel with a nice restaurant and rooms from 370/430 mk in high season. Guest rooms in the historic *Post and Customs House* itself are available April through October and cost 300/340 mk. Book these through Hotell Havsbandet.

Also in Storby is *Hotell Eckerö* (☎ *38447, fax 38247)*, a favourite of visiting Swedes. It has 40 rooms from 330/400 mk on weeknights during the high season (weekend rates are slightly higher), and a restaurant with daily specials.

On the quiet beach of Torp, *Österängens Hotell* (☎ *38268, fax 38356)* has a good restaurant and sea views. Rooms cost 300/400 mk during the high season.

Places to Eat

In addition to the places mentioned in Places to Stay, you can eat in Storby village at *Pirjo Café* at the Esso petrol station opposite the Mathis supermarket, or at the *Hem Bagarn* bakery, which is a bit closer to the harbour. *Jannes Bodega* is an attractive little café at the Käringsund harbour. *Café Lugn & Ro* at the Post and Customs House serves sandwiches and hamburgers.

Rusell (☎ *38499)*, one of the best eateries in the whole province, is in Kyrkoby on road No 2 – just look for the pink house. Lunch (45 mk) is available until 3 pm, but evenings see plenty of locals gossiping downstairs at the pub.

Getting There & Away

Road No 2 runs from Mariehamn to Eckerö. If you use public transport, take bus No 1. The trip takes 40 minutes. For information on ferries between Eckerö and Grisslehamn, Sweden, see Getting There & Away at the beginning of this chapter.

SUND

Sund (population 950), just east of the main island group, is one of the most interesting municipalities in Åland. Attractions include a medieval castle and a church, the ruins of a Russian stronghold and a large open-air museum. Sund is just 30km from Mariehamn, which makes it an ideal first overnight stop on a slow-paced bicycle tour. Finby is the largest town, with all services.

Things to See & Do

The small but impressive **Kastelholm** castle is one of Åland's top sights. Its exact age is not known, but it was mentioned in writings as early as 1388. To visit the castle you must join a guided tour (20 mk). Hours are from 10 am to 6 pm daily May to late September.

Nearby is Åland's oddest tourist attraction, the **snail safari** run by Alandia Escargots (☎ 43964). The one-hour tours are held several times daily from 16 June to 22 August and include tastings.

Also near Kastelholm is the **Jan Karls gården Museum**, a magnificent open-air museum. Traditional buildings from the archipelago have been gathered here, and the old Åland culture is alive and well. It's one of the best places in all Finland to witness the Midsummer festival. The museum is open from 10 am to 5 pm daily May to September and admission is 10 mk.

Close to the entrance to the Jan Karls gården Museum is **Vita Björn**, a prison museum that's worth a visit. The building was used as a jail from 1784 to 1974. Hours are the same as the open-air museum, and admission is 10 mk.

Åland's first **golf course** (☎ 43883), with 36 holes, is across the bay from Kastelholm Castle. You must have a Green Card to play.

North of Kastelholm, the **Sankt Johannes Church** is the biggest church on Åland. It is 800 years old and has beautiful paintings. Note the stone cross with the text 'Wenn E'. According to researchers, it was erected in memory of the Hamburg bishop Wenni who died here when on a crusade in 936. The church is open daily in summer.

East of Kastelholm are the ruins of the Russian fortress at **Bomarsund**. After the war of 1809, Russian troops began to build Bomarsund as a defence against the Swedes. Construction was halted during the Napoleonic Wars – when Russia allied itself with Sweden against France – but the mammoth building was finally completed in 1842. Ultimately Bomarsund was destroyed by the French and the English during the Crimean War. The ruins of Bomarsund can be seen on both sides of road No 2 between Kastelholm and Prästö island.

The small **Bomarsund museum** is on Prästö island, which is joined to the mainland island by a bridge. The museum is open from 10 am to 5 pm Tuesday to Sunday in summer (shorter hours in winter). Admission is free.

There are four **graveyards** – Greek Orthodox, Jewish, Muslim and Christian – on the island of Prästö. All date to the Russian occupation.

Prästö is also an entry point to the main island group from the island of Vårdö.

Places to Stay & Eat

Puttes Camping (☎ 44016 or 44040, fax 44047), at Bomarsund, charges 10 mk per tent, 12 mk per person and 10 mk per vehicle, and also rents cabins. A café and sauna are on the premises. Puttes is open from May to the end of August.

On Prästö island, *Prästö Stugor & Camping* (☎/fax 44045), open mid-June to mid-August, is another camping ground with cabins. Tents are 10 mk, plus 15 mk per person and 10 mk per vehicle. There is a grilli and a sauna.

Kastelholms Gästhem (☎ 43841), 1.5km from Kastelholm in Tosarby village, gives good value for money. It charges 180/300 mk for singles/doubles in high season and is open April through October. Breakfast is brought to guests' rooms.

The *restaurant* opposite the Jan Karlsgården Museum serves both light snacks and real meals. This is one place to stuff yourself with those incredibly tempting Åland pancakes!

Getting There & Away

Road No 2 and bus No 4 from Mariehamn to Vårdö will take you to Sund. The bus goes via Kastelholm, Svensböle and Prästö.

The bicycle ferry *Nadja* operates between Prästö, Sund and Lumpo, Lumparland, from June to mid-August. There is one departure daily in June and August, and two daily departures in July. Cost is 30 mk one way.

FINSTRÖM

Finström (population 2150) is the central municipality in Åland. Godby is the island's second biggest town and offers all facilities.

Things to See

The medieval **Sankt Mikael Church**, with a wealth of frescoes and sculptures, is in a small village 5km north of Godby along a picturesque secondary road and is perfect for a stopover on a bicycle tour. It's open weekdays in summer.

The Café Uffe på Berget (see Places to Stay & Eat), just south of the bridge to Sund, has a new, 30m-high **observation tower** with superb views of the archipelago. Across the road is **Godby Arboretum**, a tiny park with native and exotic trees along a short, marked nature trail. There is no charge to visit the tower or the park.

Places to Stay & Eat

Bastö Hotell & Stugby (☎ 42382, fax 42520) on a headland at Bastö, 12km northwest of Godby, has cottages and hotel rooms for 355/450 mk for singles/doubles, a sauna and a restaurant. *Café Uffe på Berget*, on the main Mariehamn-Sund road, is a popular spot with outdoor seating and great views.

Getting There & Away

Road No 2 from Mariehamn takes you to Godby. Bus Nos 2, 3 and 4 from Mariehamn all go via Godby. To get to other parts of Finström, take bus No 6.

GETA

The northern municipality of Geta (population 450) is quiet and isolated. The only real attraction is **Getabergen** – at 98m above sea level, the archipelago's second highest 'mountain'. Explore the surroundings via a 2km marked nature trail.

On the island of Dånö is an open-air **museum** with well preserved old buildings. It's open only in summer and charges 5 mk admission.

Places to Stay & Eat

Granqvist Stugor (☎/fax 49610), on road No 4, has five clean two- and four-bed cottages. *Soltuna (☎ 49530)*, at the top of Getabergen, is a pleasant, well located group of eight cottages that is popular with cyclists. The *restaurant* at the top of Getabergen serves breakfast, lunch and dinner.

Getting There & Away

Road No 4 from Mariehamn via Godby takes you to Geta. To get to Geta from Mariehamn, take bus No 2.

The bicycle ferry *Silvana* travels between Hällö, Geta and Skarpnåtö, Hammarland, from 1 June to 20 August. There is one departure daily from 1 June to 19 June and two daily departures during the rest of the season. Cost is 30 mk one way.

HAMMARLAND

The north-western section of mainland Åland is called Hammarland (population 1200). This is one of the oldest inhabited areas in Åland; almost 40 burial mound sites have been discovered. Kattby is the main village, with all facilities.

Things to See & Do

The **Sankta Catharina Church** in Kattby was probably built in the 12th century. It's open daily in summer. There's an **Iron Age burial site** to the west of the church, with over 30 burial mounds.

North of Kattby, on the road to Skarpnåtö, is the **Ålands Wool Spinnery** and shop. It sells homespun yarn and handmade sweaters. The spinnery is in the town of Mörby, 1.5km

north of road No 1 to Eckerö. Farther north in Lillbostad is a ceramics shop, **Lugnet Ceramics**. All products are handmade. West of the village of Sålis, **Bovik** is a nice fishing harbour.

Activities in Skarpnåtö centre around **Södergård Estate**, a museum and handicrafts shop (closed in winter). The owners of the estate rent fishing boats.

Places to Stay & Eat

Kattnäs Camping (☎ 37687) is 3km south of the Eckerö-Mariehamn road, a bit west of Kattby. It has a café and sauna and charges 9 mk per tent, plus 9 mk per person and 9 mk per vehicle.

Sålis Gästhem (☎/fax 37613), in the village of Sålis, has clean but simple rooms for 130/260 mk for singles/doubles in high season. *Gäddvikens Turisthotell (☎ 37650)* north of Sålis, has a restaurant and sauna. Rooms are 200/340 mk in high season.

Kvarnhagens Stugor (☎/fax 37212) a Skarpnåtö has six cottages.

Getting There & Away

Bus No 1 from Mariehamn to Eckerö runs through Hammarland. For information or the bicycle ferry between Hammarland and Geta, see Getting There & Away under Geta.

JOMALA

The Jomala region (population 3000) jus north of Mariehamn has two main centres Jomala village has all facilities, while Gottby is smaller and quieter.

The locally famous painter Victor Westerholm had his summer house in Önningeby a tiny village in eastern Jomala. Other artist followed him there, and for two decade around the turn of the 20th century, the are was known as the 'Önningeby colony' There's a small **museum** here that is dedi cated to the artist, open from noon to 3 pn Tuesday to Sunday from mid-June to mid August. Admission is 10 mk.

Getting There & Away

From Mariehamn, catch bus No 5 to Ön ningeby or bus No 1 to Gottby.

LEMLAND

Lemland municipality (population 1300) is between Lumparland and the Lemström canal, which is 5km east of Mariehamn on road No 3. The canal was built in 1882 by POWs. Norrby village is Lemland's centre.

In Norrby, the **Sankta Birgitta Church** has 13th to 14th century wall paintings that were rediscovered in 1956. It is open weekdays in summer. **Burial mounds** from the Iron Age are nearby.

Herrön, at the southernmost tip of Lemland, is a popular picnic spot. There is a small observation tower here for watching birds.

Places to Stay & Eat
Söderby Stugor (☎/fax 34310), south of Norrby, has 12 cottages and a café.

Getting There & Away
To get to Lemland from Mariehamn, take bus No 5.

LUMPARLAND

Many travellers pass through Lumparland (population 300) in south-east Åland because of its two ferry harbours, Svinö and Långnäs. Otherwise, there's little reason to visit.

The **Sankt Andreas Church**, built in 1720, is one of the newer churches of Åland. This little wooden church, in a beautiful spot at the seaside, is open daily in summer. It's along the road to Lumparby village.

Places to Stay & Eat
Långnäsbyn (☎ 35557), next to the Långnäs ferry terminal, has nine reasonably priced cottages. In Svinö, *Café Ingela* serves light meals.

Getting There & Away
From Mariehamn take bus No 5 to Svinö and Långäs (45 minutes).

For information on the bicycle ferry to Prästö see Getting There & Away under Sund.

For information on the ferry service to Kumlinge and Föglö see the relevant Getting There & Away sections later in this chapter.

SALTVIK

Was the 10th century Viking capital, Birka, situated in Saltvik? Though there's no real evidence of this – and stronger proof exists that the legendary Viking stronghold was located near the Swedish Lake Mälaren – one Ålandese archaeologist is convinced of Saltvik's former glory.

Whatever the case, many signs of Viking occupation have been unearthed around Saltvik (population 1600), more so than elsewhere on the Åland archipelago. There just isn't much to look at.

East of Kvarnbo, the central village of Saltvik, is the Viking fortress of **Borgboda**. On the main Saltvik bicycle route, it is thought to have been built at the end of the Iron Age (400-1000 AD). Some stone outcroppings remain, but otherwise it's just a cow field with a nice view.

Kvarnbo has the large **Sankta Maria Church** that dates from the 12th century. It is probably the oldest church in Finland. There are some wall paintings and sculptures from the 13th century, but most of the paintings are from the Lutheran era, from the 1500s.

Opposite the church look for the **Birka monument** on an old *tingsplats* (meeting and cult site).

Orrdals Klint
The highest mountain in Åland, 129m above sea level, is really no more than a big hill. Two short, well marked walking tracks lead to the top, where there's a viewing tower and a four bed hut. One trail is 1km long and the other is about 2.5km. There is no charge to sleep in the hut. Bring sheets or a sleeping bag, a torch (flashlight), water and food, and do not take wood from living trees. There is no public transportation to Orrdals Klint.

Getting There & Away
Bus No 3 runs from Mariehamn to Kvarnbo and other villages in Saltvik.

The bicycle ferry *Kajo* travels between Tengsödavik (Saltvik) and Västra Simskäla (Vårdö) from Monday to Saturday from 23 June to 9 August. There are two daily departures in June and August, and four daily departures in July. The fare is 40 mk one way.

VÅRDÖ

The island of Vårdö (population 400) was on the old mail route from Sweden to Finland, and some of the ancient 'milestones' have been resurrected for tourists.

The main settlement is Vargata, which has a bank, a shop and a post office. Northeast of Vargata, Lövö village was the scene of a peace conference in 1718 between representatives of King Karl XII of Sweden and Tsar Peter I (Peter the Great) of Russia, during the Great Northern War. Judging by what has been dug from the earth here, the 1200 participants in this high-class event consumed French wine and oysters in frightening quantities. The event ended with few positive results, and there was no peace until 1721.

On the main road between Vargata and Lövö, **Seffers Homestead Museum** has a windmill and a Midsummer pole on display. The museum is open Tuesday, Thursday and Saturday from noon to 3 pm in June and July. Entry is 5 mk.

Places to Stay

Sandösunds Camping (π/fax 47750) has a beautiful seaside location in the north of the island. The large camping ground charges 10 mk per tent, 15 mk per person and 10 mk per vehicle, and also rents pleasant two- and four-bed cottages. There is a café and restaurant as well as canoe and bike rentals.

Getting There & Away

Bus No 4 will take you to Vårdö from Mariehamn. Ferries on the northern archipelago route depart from the village of Hummelvik on Vårdö. For more details see Getting There & Away under Brändö. For information on the bicycle ferry between Saltvik and Vårdö, see Getting There & Away under Saltvik.

Northern Archipelago

The northern group of Åland islands consists of the archipelago municipalities of Brändö and Kumlinge. They are very quiet and offer less for the traveller than the southern group.

BRÄNDÖ

The municipality of Brändö (population 550) consists of a group of 1180 islands, the largest and most important of which are connected by bridges. Banks and other services are on the main island and in the villages of Lappo and Torsholma on smaller islands.

The particular shape of the main island makes for interesting cycling – no matter where you go, you will always be riding by the sea. A signposted bike route runs from the harbour at Torsholma north across the main island to the harbour at Långö.

Things to See

St Jakobs Church, the wooden church on the main island of Brändö, dates from 1893. On Lappo island farther south (and connected to the main island by ferry), the **Archipelago Museum** has exhibits of local history. Hours are from 10 am to noon and from 2 to 4 pm daily from mid-June to early August. Entry is 10 mk.

Places to Stay & Eat

The top-end *Hotell Gullvivan* (π 56350, fax 56360) on Björnholma island has 16 rooms for 270/420 mk for singles/doubles in high season. A restaurant and mini-golf course are on the premises. In Lappo, *Pellas Gästgård* (π 56692, fax 56720) is a guesthouse and café.

Getting There & Away

From Mariehamn, take bus No 4 to Hummelvik harbour on Vårdö Island. There are three ferry connections a day from Vårdö to Lappo and Torsholma. The trip from Hummelvik takes about three hours.

From Turku on mainland Finland, take a bus to Kustavi, and on to Vartsala Island to reach the harbour of Osnäs (Finnish: Vuosnainen). There are five to seven connections a day from Osnäs to Långö on the northern Brändö island of Åva.

KUMLINGE

Kumlinge municipality (population 450) isn't exactly a thrumming tourist mecca. The main island, Kumlinge, is flanked by Enklinge island to the north and Seglinge island to the south. All services may be found on Kumlinge, and a bank is on Eklinge. There is no accommodation on Seglinge and no restaurant – only a shop in the main village.

The local ferry to Seglinge departs from the island of Snäckö, 8km from Kumlinge village. Local ferries to Enklinge from the main island depart from the village of Krokarno.

A marked bike route runs from Snäckö north to Krokarno, with bridges between the islands. On Enklinge island there is a signposted bike route from the harbour to the local museum.

Things to See & Do

Many consider the Sankta Anna Church on Kumlinge island to be one of Finland's most beautiful churches, with lovely 500 year old Franciscan-style paintings. The church is some 2km north of Kumlinge village and is open daily in summer.

Enklinge island boasts the small Hermas Farm Museum, 3.5km from the pier, with 20 buildings that are all original to this island. The museum is open weekdays from mid-June to early August, and entry is 10 mk.

On Seglinge island there is a fishing village near the ferry pier, and a 2km nature trail.

Places to Stay & Eat

On the island of Snäckö near the ferry pier, Ledholms Camping (☎ 55647) is open May through August and charges 10 mk per tent, plus 15 mk per person and 10 mk per

vehicle. It also has cheap cabins and a small grocery.

Remmarina Stugor (☎ 55402), at the guest harbour 2km from Kumlinge village, has 12 clean, reasonably priced cottages on a small hill, plus a sauna and a small canteen for snacks.

Formerly a hospital building, Värdshuset Remmaren (☎ 55402, fax 55032) on Kumlinge island is now a guesthouse with the only restaurant in the entire archipelago municipality. Call ahead to make sure it's open.

Getting There & Away

Ferries on the route between Hummelvik and Torsholma stop at both Enklinge and Kumlinge islands. The trip from Hummelvik to Enklinge takes an hour, and the trip to Kumlinge is 1½ hours.

One or two ferries a day go from Långnäs in Lumparland to Snäckö in Kumlinge, via Överö in the Föglö island group. See the Föglö Getting There & Away section for more details. The trip takes two hours.

There are weekend ferry connections between Kumlinge and Sottunga.

Southern Archipelago

The southern group of Åland islands consists of the municipalities of Föglö, Kökar and tiny Sottunga. Kökar Island is the most quaint.

FÖGLÖ

The Föglö island group is sleepy, with only 600 permanent inhabitants. The island was first mentioned in 1241 by a Danish bishop who landed here en route to Tallinn. An inn was founded in 1745 at Föglö, at the Enigheten Estate. The local population lived by fishing and farming, and were subjected to the taxes and demands of two governments, Swedish and Russian.

A signposted bike route runs from Degerby north-east to Överö, and there is a regular bus service. Both villages are served by archipelago ferries. Degerby has a bank, post office and grocery.

Things to See

The 'capital' of Föglö is Degerby, a small village that is noted for its unusual architecture. Many Föglöites have traditionally been civil servants, not farmers, and have chosen to build their houses in Art Nouveau or Empire styles instead of the traditional archipelago style.

In the red building right at the harbour, you will find the local museum. It is open from 11.30 am to 2.30 pm and from 3 to 6 pm Tuesday to Sunday from mid-June to early August (admission 5 mk).

The Sankta Maria Magdalena Church is on an island south from Degerby, connected by a bridge. Getting there is half the fun, as the road is scenic. The simple 14th century church is not very impressive but the way it rises from the plain rock bed is dramatic. It is open weekdays in summer.

Places to Stay & Eat

CC Camping (☎ 51440), on the small Finholma island north-east of Degerby, is open June through August and charges 10 mk per tent, plus 15 mk per person and 10 mk per car. It's on the Degerby-Överö bike route.

The rustic Enigheten Gästhem (☎/fax 50310), 1km from the Degerby ferry terminal, is a fine place to stay (open summer only). Single rooms cost 175 to 205 mk, doubles are 230 to 290 mk and booking is essential. It has a café and good breakfasts.

Also in Degerby is Seagram (☎ 51092), a guesthouse with six rooms and a restaurant. Room rates are lower than at Enigheten and breakfast is included.

Getting There & Away

From Mariehamn, bus No 5 goes to the Svinö and Långnäs ferry harbours, both in Lumparland. A dozen or so ferries a day make the one hour trip between Svinö and Degerby. They can be crowded during the high season. There are one or two ferries a day on the Långnäs-Överö-Kumlinge route.

KÖKAR

The Kökar island group, with its strikingly barren landscape, is one of the most interesting in Åland. Its population is about 300. The main town is Karlby, which has a bank, post office and grocery. It's a quaint little place.

Though it feels quite isolated from the rest of the world, Kökar is not difficult to reach by ferry. A signposted bike route runs from the harbour to Karlby and Hellsö.

Things to See & Do

Historic Hamnö island is connected to the main island by a bridge. Since time immemorial, boats have been anchored at its shores, many of them plying the Hansa trade route between Germany and Turku. A very small – a dozen members at most – Jesuit Franciscan community built a monastery here in the 14th century. The main building is long gone, but the present church, from 1784, was built on the same site (open daily in summer).

The small Kökar Homestead Museum of local history is on the east side of the main island, in the village of Hellsö. The museum is open from noon to 5 pm Tuesday to Sunday from mid-June to mid-August. Entry is 10 mk.

A short nature trail starts near Hellsö.

Places to Stay & Eat

Sandvik Camping (☎ 55911), at the harbour, is open from May to the end of September. Tent sites are 40 mk, and there are cabins, a grilli and bike rentals.

Antons Gästhem (☎ 55729, fax 55938) is a red building along the road south from the harbour. Open year-round, it has simple singles/doubles for 230/330 mk during the high season.

In Karlby, the homestay Kökar Logi (☎ 55889) has five rooms and is open from mid-June to the end of July.

The year-round Hotell Brudhäll (☎ 55955, fax 55956) in Karlby has an impressive location on the waterfront. Rooms are 450/610 mk. It has a nice restaurant with dancing on summer evenings.

Getting There & Away

On mainland Finland ferries depart for Kökar once or twice daily from the harbour of Galtby on Korppoo Island, 75km from Turku (take the Saaristotie bus from Turku). This is a popular route – if you're travelling with a car expect to wait a few extra hours on Friday going to Åland and on Sunday going to Turku. The trip from Galtby to Kökar takes two hours.

It is much easier to get to Kökar from mainland Åland. There are three to five connections a day from Långnäs (bus No 5 from Mariehamn) to Kökar, via Föglö and Sottunga. The ferry also stops at the tiny island of Husö. Travel time is 2½ hours from Långnäs.

SOTTUNGA

Sottunga island has fewer than 130 permanent residents – in fact, there are more cows than people here. Despite the small population, the island has its own bank, shop, school, health care centre, library and church.

The wooden **Sankta Maria Magdalena Church** in Sottunga was built in 1661 and renovated in 1974. The **fishing harbour** is at the southern end of Sottunga. A short **nature trail** starts at the harbour, and a marked bike route runs north from the harbour to the village of Skaget.

Places to Stay & Eat

Strandhuggets Stugor (☎ 55255 or 55108) near the harbour has six cottages for overnight or longer stays and a café.

Getting There & Away

Ferries on the southern archipelago route, as well as occasional ferries from Kumlinge, will take you to Sottunga.

ÅLAND

The South Coast

The Swedes settled the southern coast of Finland in medieval times, bringing their language and Scandinavian traditions with them. The area remained predominantly Swedish until 1550, when King Gustav Vasa of Sweden established Helsingfors (Helsinki) at rapids on the Vantaa River, north of today's Helsinki.

Another boost for the region came in 1812 when Finland's capital was transferred from Turku to Helsinki – only since then have Finns moved to the province in a big way. That said, to this day many towns east and west of Helsinki remain predominantly Swedish-speaking.

Any of the following towns can be seen on a day trip from Helsinki.

Porvoo

- **pop 43,000**   ☎ **019**

Porvoo (Swedish: Borgå), 50km east of Helsinki, is the second oldest town in Finland after Turku. Officially it has been a town since 1346, but even before that Porvoo was an important trading centre. There are three distinct sections to the city: the old town, the new town and the 19th century Empire quarter, built in the Russian style under the rule of Tsar Nicholas I of Russia. The old town is one of the most attractive in Finland. Over one-third of the residents in the Porvoo area speak Swedish as their mother tongue.

If you have time for only one day trip from Helsinki, Porvoo is an excellent choice, particularly when combined with a cruise on the MS *JL Runeberg*.

Information
Tourist Office The tourist office (☎ 580 145, fax 582 721, pia.hogstrom@porvoo.fi), at Rihkamakatu 4, is open from 10 am to 6 pm Monday to Friday, and to 4 pm Saturday and Sunday, from mid-June to the end of

HIGHLIGHTS

- Hamina, with its unusual octagonal town plan
- Fly-fishing at the Imperial Fishing Lodge at Langinkoski, in Kotka
- Summer evenings at the Mill Restaurant in Ruotsinpyhtää
- The rapids of Imatra
- Steamship cruises from Helsinki to Porvoo or Inkoo
- An overnight stay in one of the Russian villas of Hanko
- The Old Town section of Porvoo, second-oldest city in Finland
- Raseborg castle ruins, near Ekenäs
- The seaside hostel in Dragsfjärd
- The idyllic old seaside town of Ekenäs and the Ekenäs Archipelago National Park
- Sibelius House, the summer home of the famous composer in Loviisa
- Runeberg House, former home of the poet Johan Ludvig Runeberg

August. At other times, hours are from 10 am to 4.30 pm Monday to Friday, and to 2 pm Saturday. A tourist information kiosk at the harbour is open from 11 am to 5 pm daily from June to mid-August.

Post The post office is on the corner of Mannerheiminkatu and Rauhankatu. Porvoo's post code is 06100.

Internet Resources & Library The public library at Mannerheiminkatu 14 is open from 10 am to 8 pm Monday to Friday and from 9 am to 2 pm Saturday. There are plans to install an Internet terminal in 1999.

For more information about Porvoo visit www.porvoo.fi/ on the Web.

Medical & Emergency Services For a general emergency call ☎ 112, for police ring ☎ 10022 and for a doctor call ☎ 10023. There are pharmacies on Piispankatu at Nos 30 and 34.

Porvoo Old Town

The old town district north of Mannerheiminkatu was largely built after the Great Fire of 1760. It's a beautiful area of narrow, winding cobblestone alleys and brightly coloured wooden houses. Craft boutiques and antique shops line the main roads, Välikatu and Kirkkokatu. The distinctive row of storehouses along the Porvoonjoki River were first painted with red ochre to impress the visiting King of Sweden, Gustavus III, in the late 18th century.

Porvoo Cathedral

The striking medieval cathedral on Kirkkotori, overlooking the old town, has an important place in Finnish history: this is where the first Diet of Finland assembled in 1809, convened by Tsar Alexander I. It's open from 10 am to 6 pm Monday to Friday, to 2 pm Saturday, and from 2 to 5 pm Sunday from May to September; reduced hours at other times.

Linnamäki Hill

North-west, and within walking distance, of the cathedral, Linnamäki Hill (Swedish: Borgbacken) was once a Viking defence post. Today, thick pine trees grow on this hill which offers a fine view of Porvoo.

Porvoo Museum

The town museum has two sections, in adjacent buildings on the Vanha Raatihuoneentori (Old Town Hall Square). The more interesting of the two is the **Edelfelt-Vallgren Museum** at Välikatu 11. It has paintings by Albert Edelfelt and sculptures by Ville Vallgren, two of Porvoo's most famous artists – Ville Vallgren designed the Havis Amanda statue that graces Helsinki's kauppatori.

The **Porvoo Historical Museum**, in the town hall building across the square, has old furniture and other paraphernalia.

Hours for both museums are from 11 am to 4 pm daily May through August, and from noon to 4 pm Wednesday to Sunday at other times. The 20 mk admission ticket is good for both museums.

Doll & Toy Museum

There are over 800 dolls and other toys in the museum at Jokikatu 14, the largest museum of its kind in Finland. Hours from May to the end of August are from 11 am to 3.30 pm Monday to Saturday, from noon to 3.30 pm Sunday.

Runeberg House

National poet Johan Ludvig Runeberg wrote the lyrics to the Finnish national anthem, *Maamme* (Our Country). His former home, at Aleksanterinkatu 3, has been a museum since 1882. The interior has been preserved as it was when Runeberg lived in the house, and the house itself is one of the best preserved buildings in the Empire part of the town centre. At Aleksanterinkatu 5 is the **Walter Runeberg Sculpture Collection**. It has 150 sculptures by Walther Runeberg, JL Runeberg's eldest son. Hours for both are from 10 am to 4 pm Monday to Saturday and 11 am to 5 pm Sunday from May to August (closed

THE SOUTH COAST

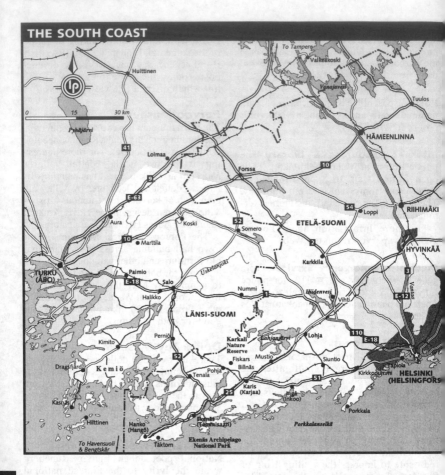

Monday and Tuesday at other times). The 15 mk admission is good for entry to both museums.

Organised Tours

Guided walking tours of old Porvoo take place at 2 pm on Saturday from late June to late August. Tours begin at the passenger harbour and last about an hour; they cost 30 mk.

In winter, Saaristolinja Ky (☎ 523 1350 or ☎ 0400-840 001, contact is Ari Kautto)

offers snowmobile safaris. Departures are from the Porvoo bus station at 1 pm on Tuesday and Thursday from January to March, and bookings must be made at least three hours in advance. A two hour trip ending with snacks by a bonfire costs 360 mk per person, minimum two people.

Cruises The MS *Barkassi Bo* and the MS *Fredrika* depart from the passenger harbour at noon, 1.45 and 3.30 pm daily from June to the end of August for 1½ hour river

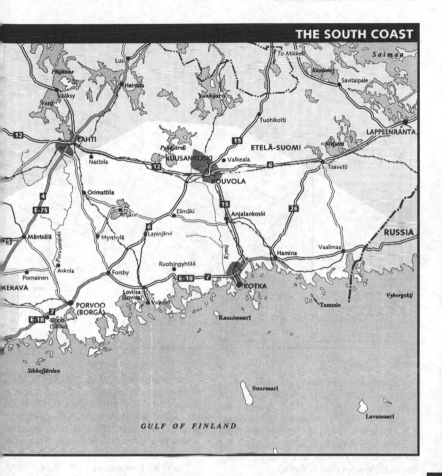

THE SOUTH COAST

cruises that include good views of old Porvoo. Cost is 30 mk per adult.

For information on cruises between Porvoo and Helsinki aboard the MS *JL Runeberg* see the Getting There & Away section that follows.

Places to Stay

Camping Kokonniemi (☎ 581 967, *myynti palvelu@lomaliitto.fi*) is 2km south of Porvoo town. Tent sites cost 75 mk, cabins from 290 to 325 mk. It's open from June to mid-August.

The HI-affiliated hostel *Porvoon Retkeilymaja* (☎/fax 523 0012, *Linnan-koskenkatu 1-3*), 800m south-east of Mannerheiminkatu, is open year-round and very popular. You should book in advance during summer. Dormitory beds cost 65 mk and there are also private rooms. The kitchen is clean and well equipped. Guests at the hostel may use the indoor pool and sauna complex across the street for a fee.

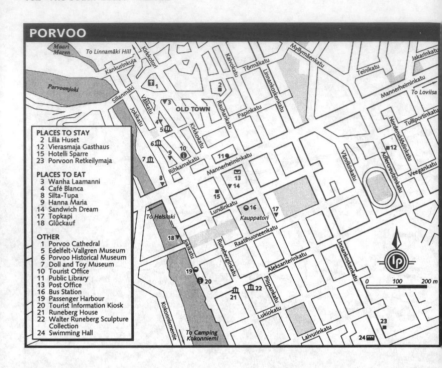

PORVOO

PLACES TO STAY
2 Lilla Huset
12 Vierasmaja Gasthaus
15 Hotelli Sparre
23 Porvoon Retkeilymaja

PLACES TO EAT
3 Wanha Laamanni
4 Café Blanca
8 Silta-Tupa
9 Hanna Maria
14 Sandwich Dream
17 Topkapi
18 Glückauf

OTHER
1 Porvoo Cathedral
5 Edelfelt-Vallgren Museum
6 Porvoo Historical Museum
7 Doll and Toy Museum
10 Tourist Office
11 Public Library
13 Post Office
16 Bus Station
19 Passenger Harbour
20 Tourist Information Kiosk
21 Runeberg House
22 Walter Runeberg Sculpture
   Collection
24 Swimming Hall

Vierasmaja Gasthaus (☎ 524 4454, Adlercreutzinkatu 29) is a family-run place with five rooms, at 150/200 mk for singles/doubles. The bed-and-breakfast *Lilla Huset (☎ 524 8120, Itäinen Pitkäkatu 3)*, open mid-April to late September, is in an 18th century house in the heart of old Porvoo. Doubles cost 450 mk.

Hotelli Sparre (☎ 584 455, Piispankatu 34) is a no-nonsense hotel with 290/340 mk rooms in summer (350/420 mk at other times).

Places to Eat

The cheapest places to eat are in the modern centre of town. *Topkapi*, on the market square, serves kebab and pizzas for under 30 mk. *Sandwich Dream (Piispankatu 19)* is a tiny place with Danish open sandwiches that are quite good.

In the old town, *Hanna Maria (Välikatu 6)* is a local favourite for its hearty, home-cooked food. Lunch specials are 28 to 35 mk. *Silta-Tupa (Mennerheiminkatu 2)*, right at the bridge, specialises in steak and fish dishes priced from 50 to 80 mk. Meals can be had on its terrace on sunny summer days.

Wanha Laamanni (☎ 523 0455, Vuorikatu 17), the Old Judges' Chambers, is the gourmet restaurant of Porvoo. It's in a splendid late 18th century building with a fireplace for winter nights and a terrace for summer days. Game is a speciality, and prices are as steep as the alley it is found in.

In summer you will find *beer terraces* along the eastern riverfront, as well as the boat restaurant *Glückauf*. Meals are from 30 to 80 mk in this 19th century sailing ship, which is also a popular drinking spot.

Cafés are a speciality of old Porvoo. The best is the cheery *Café Blanca (Välikatu 13)*, on the old town hall square and open daily all year round.

Getting There & Away

Bus Buses depart for Porvoo from the Helsinki bus station every 30 minutes or so, and the trip takes about an hour. There are also frequent buses to/from towns farther east, including Kotka. The one-way fare from Helsinki is from 40 mk.

Train The historic Porvoo Museum Train runs between Helsinki and Porvoo on Saturdays in summer. The train departs from Helsinki at 10.12 am and from Porvoo at 4.30 pm. Cost is 90 mk return; purchase tickets at the Helsinki or Porvoo train station or on board the train. The 1½ hour train ride can also be combined with a cruise on the MS *JL Runeberg* for 130 mk return.

Car & Motorcycle Porvoo is 50km east of Helsinki and 90km west of Kotka. From Helsinki take road No E18, a 45 minute drive.

Boat The MS *JL Runeberg* (☎ 524 3331), a former steamship, travels between Helsinki and Porvoo in summer. As a day trip, it's highly recommended. The boat runs on Monday, Wednesday, Friday, Saturday and Sunday, departing Helsinki at 10 am and returning at 4 pm. The trip takes 3½ hours and costs 150 mk return. See Getting There & Away under Helsinki for more information.

The speedy MS *Queen*, operated by Royal Line (☎ 09-170 488), travels from the Helsinki fish market at 11 am on Tuesday, Thursday, Saturday and Sunday from mid-June to mid-August. The trip takes 2½ hours each way and allows for two hours of sightseeing in Porvoo, returning to Helsinki by 6 pm. Cost is 155 mk per adult.

The South-West

The south-west is the most historic part of Finland, with medieval stone churches in every other village, and some notable castles and manor houses. The area also has plenty of idyllic little islands that are fun for camping, cycling and general island-hopping. Many of the ferries that travel to these islands are free.

HANKO

* pop 10,600   ☎ 019

Hanko (Swedish: Hangö) blossomed as a spa town in the late 19th and early 20th century, when it was a glamorous retreat for Russian nobles, tsars and artists. The grand seaside villas built by these wealthy summer visitors are now the town's star attraction – locals refer to the villas as 'the old ladies' as each has been given a woman's name. Many now operate as fancy guesthouses which are Finland's most unique accommodation and very popular with tourists in summer.

Even before Hanko was founded, in 1874, the peninsula on which the town lies had been an important anchorage. Hanko has also been a major point of departure from Finland: between 1881 and 1931, approximately half a million Finns left for the USA and Canada via the Hanko docks. During WWII, Hanko was annexed by the Soviet Union for one year.

Hanko is 127km south-west of Helsinki and is the southernmost town in Finland. The majority of its residents speak Finnish.

Orientation

The main streets are Bulevardi and Esplanaadi, although Vuorikatu is the main shopping street. The East Harbour is the centre of the town's activity in summer; the West Harbour handles only commercial traffic. Russian villas are on Appelgrenintie, east of the East Harbour. Most things are within walking distance of the bus and train stations.

HANKO

PLACES TO STAY
2 Pensionat Garbo
6 Villa Doris
7 Villa Elisa
8 Villa Eva
11 Villa Maija
12 Villa Tellina
26 Hotel Regatta

PLACES TO EAT
9 Café Plage
20 Satamaruokala
22 Origo

24 Jonathan
25 Ari's Snack Bar &
 Bicycle Rentals

OTHER
1 Hospital
3 Bus Station
4 Train Station
5 Paul Feldt's Bicycle
 Shop
10 Casino
13 Hanko Church
14 Water Tower

15 Public Library
16 Tourist Office
17 Grönan Restaurant &
 Blues Club
18 Pharmacy
19 Post Office
21 Fortress Museum
 (Linnoitusmuseo)
23 Pirate Bar & Restaurant
27 Harbour Tourist
 Information
28 Passenger Harbour

Information

Tourist Office The tourist office (☎ 2203 411, fax 248 5821, rita.lagerroos@victorek .com) at Bulevardi 10 is open from 9 am to 5 pm Monday to Friday year-round. There's also a tourist information booth at the East Harbour, open daily in summer until almost midnight.

Post The post office is at Bulevardi 19, and is open from 9.30 am to 6 pm Monday to Friday. Hanko's post code is 10900.

Internet Resources & Library The public library is centrally located at Vuorikatu 3-5 and is open from 11 am to 8 pm Monday to Friday and to 2 pm Saturday. It has an Internet terminal. Check the Web site www.hanko.fi/ for information about the town.

Left Luggage There are 24-hour lockers for 10 mk at the train station.

Medical & Emergency Services For a general emergency ring ☎ 112, for police ring ☎ 10022 and for a doctor call ☎ 10023.

The pharmacy at Nycanderinkatu 18 is open from 8.30 am to 8 pm Monday to Friday, from 8.30 am to 3 pm Saturday and from 11 am to 2 pm Sunday. A hospital is on Esplanaadi.

Things to See

Take a lifzt to the top of the 50m **water tower** on Vartiovuori for an excellent view across town and out to sea. It's open daily from mid-May to the end of August, and admission is 5 mk. The neogothic **Hanko church**, built in 1892, was damaged in WWII but has been thoroughly renovated. It's open daily in summer. The **Fortress**

Museum (Linnoitusmuseo) is the local museum at Nycanderinkatu 4 near the East Harbour. It has only temporary exhibitions. Hours are from 11 am to 4 pm Tuesday to Sunday (also from 6 to 7 pm Thursday) and admission is 10 mk. Inquire at the tourist office if you are interested in visiting any of the half-dozen art galleries scattered around town.

Activities

Hanko offers 30km of sand beaches good for swimming and sunning. The beach next to the Casino is the best. Bicycles are ideal for exploring the parkland and Russian villas east of the town centre; see Getting Around for information on rentals. The tourist office rents motorboats, and Café Plage rents rowboats and canoes. Eight outdoor tennis courts adjacent to Café Plage are open to the public for a fee.

Organised Tours

Cruises From mid-June to the end of August the MS Marina (☎ 2411 733) sails at noon daily to Bengtskär island and at 6 pm daily to Hauensuoli strait. Tours depart from the East Harbour. The six hour tour to Bengtskär costs 190 mk. The tour to Hauensuoli lasts 1½ hours and costs 60 mk. The MS Anna (☎ 4692 500) also travels to Bengtskär, with departures from the East Harbour at 11 am daily from July to mid-August. This tour lasts seven hours, costs 200 mk and includes a light lunch. Purchase tickets on board. See the Around Hanko section for more information on Bengtskär and Hauensuoli.

Special Events

Hanko's most important annual event is the Hanko Regatta in which over 200 boats compete. The regatta takes place on the first weekend of July and attracts thousands of viewers.

Places to Stay

Bookings are advised during summer months, particularly at any of the Russian villas. Many places raise their prices during the annual Hanko Regatta, and bookings must be made well in advance.

Camping Hanko Camping Silversand (☎ 248 5500, myyntipalvelu@lomaliitto.fi), about 3km north-east of the town centre, is set on a long beach. Camp sites cost 75 mk per person and cabins for six to eight people cost 320 to 390 mk per night. Silversand has a café and sauna and is open from June to mid-August.

Guesthouses & Hotels Pensionat Garbo (☎/fax 248 7897, Raatimiehenkatu 8) is a quirky place, essentially a museum of kitsch. Each room commemorates a particular Hollywood star. The 10 rooms, priced from 120/185 mk for singles/doubles, are open in summer (other times by prior arrangement).

The only hotel in Hanko is Hotel Regatta (☎ 248 6491, fax 248 5535, Merikatu 1). It's popular with tour groups. Singles cost 290 to 490 mk and doubles are 390 to 590 mk, breakfast included. Higher prices apply for rooms with sea views.

Villas A unique feature of Hanko is its selection of old villas that have been meticulously renovated and converted to guesthouses.

Villa Maija (☎ 248 4917, Appelgrenintie 7), built in 1888, is open year round. It's a real beauty, with fine verandah windows and loads of ornate trim. Rooms are from 190/350 mk, or 240/400 mk with private bath. The reception and dining room is in Villa Tellina at Appelgrenintie 2.

Built in 1914, Villa Eva (☎ 248 6356, Kaivokatu 2) is a less showy villa open from June to mid-August. The 19 rooms cost 200/340 mk.

Villa Elisa (☎ 248 7201, Appelgrenintie 17), more like a motel, has 15 rooms and is open all year round. Toilets and showers are shared, and there is a sauna that costs 20 mk per hour. Rooms are from 180/280 mk.

The charmingly old-fashioned pensionat Villa Doris (☎ 248 1228, Appelgrenintie 23) has old furniture from various decades in all 12 rooms. The house was built in 1881 and is open year-round. Prices start at

200/350 mk per night in summer, and 150/250 mk during other seasons. Rates are negotiable for longer stays.

Places to Eat

The best choice for reasonably priced food is plain little *Satamaruokala* on Satamakatu, with home-style dishes at 20 to 40 mk. The place is open till 5 pm Monday to Friday. *Ari's Snack Bar*, at the East Harbour, is good for hamburgers and such but is open only in summer. *Leipäsatama (Esplanaadi 34)* is a small bakery and café. *Café Plage*, open May to September, is a nice place by the sea, on Appelgrenintie.

Several gourmet restaurants are in a row of quaint red wooden buildings at the East Harbour. *Origo (☎ 2485 023)* is the most charming, and is especially known for its excellent fish dishes from 80 mk. Salads and soups are 35 mk. Origo is open from April to September. Another place, *Jonathan*, serves meat dishes in a rustic stone-walled room. It is open May through August, and prices are comparable to those at Origo. The adjacent *pizzeria*, under the same management, is open in summer and offers good value.

On Little Pine Island, 1.5km east of the centre, *Neljän Tuulen Tupa* (House of the Four Winds) is where folks went to imbibe so-called 'hard tea' (alcohol) during the Finnish prohibition (1919-32). At the time, Field Marshal CG Mannerheim had his summer cottage on the neighbouring island. He found the merry-making disturbing and solved the problem by buying the whole joint in 1926 – he fired the chef, imported tea sets from France and ran the place himself until 1931. The café is open from mid-May to mid-August; Little Pine Island is now connected to the mainland by a bridge.

Entertainment

The *Casino (☎ 2482 310, Appelgrenintie 10)* is the most famous nightspot in Hanko, with dancing and a roulette table. The cover charge is 25 to 30 mk depending on the day, and the food is expensive but good.

It's open April through September. *Grönan Restaurant & Blues Club (Bulevardi 17)* is open from 6 pm daily and features live jazz. At the East Harbour, *Pirate Bar & Restaurant* is a music bar that also serves good pizzas and pastas; it's open year-round.

Getting There & Away

Bus There are five to seven daily express buses from Helsinki. The trip takes 2¼ hours and costs 90 mk one way.

Train Seven to nine trains travel daily from Helsinki or Turku to Karjaa (Swedish: Karis), where they are met by connecting trains to Hanko (via Ekenäs). From Helsinki it's a two hour trip that costs 70 mk one way.

Car & Motorcycle Hanko is on road No 53, a 1¾ hour drive from Helsinki.

Boat The MS *Franz Höijer* travels between Hanko and Uusikaupunki on weekdays from mid-May to mid-August. The trip takes 10 hours one way and costs 60 mk.

Getting Around

At the East Harbour, bicycles can be rented for 50 mk per day at Ari's Snack Bar, open from May through September. In the centre, Paul Feldt's bicycle shop (☎ 2481 860) at Tarhakatu 4 is open year-round and has slightly lower rates.

AROUND HANKO
Hauensuoli

The narrow strait between the islands of Tullisaari and Kobben, called Hauensuoli (Pike's Gut), is a protected natural harbour where sailing ships from countries around the Baltic Sea used to wait out storms in days of yore. Many of the sailors who passed through here paused to carve their initials or tales of bravery on the rocks, earning Hauensuoli its other name, 'The Guest Book of the Archipelago'. Some 600 rock carvings dating back to the 17th century remain. Hauensuoli can only be reached by sea; see Cruises earlier in this section for more information.

Bengtskär

This isolated island, 25km and two hours south of Hanko by boat, is the southernmost inhabited island in Finland. Its lighthouse, built in 1906, is the tallest in Scandinavia. For information on transportation to Bengtskär see the Cruises section.

EKENÄS

• pop 14,700   ☎ 019

The seaside town of Ekenäs (Finnish: Tammisaari), 96km south-west of Helsinki, is one of Finland's oldest – King Gustav Vasa conceived of it in 1546 as a trading port to rival Tallin, Estonia. The idea failed, and many local business people were soon forcibly transferred to the newly founded Helsinki.

Present-day Ekenäs is an idyllic little seaside town, popular with Finnish and Swedish holiday-makers. It has many well preserved old buildings, and parts of the adjacent archipelago – with some 1300 islands – are a national park. Nearby there are the 14th century Raseborg castle ruins, the area's most impressive sight.

The majority of Ekenäs' residents speak Swedish.

Orientation

Ekenäs is situated on the Barcken peninsula, the tip being the oldest part of town. Rådhustorget is the main square, and the partly pedestrianised Kungsgatan is the main commercial street. The train and bus stations are north-east of the centre and within walking distance.

Information

Tourist Offices The tourist office (☎ 263 2100, fax 263 2212, tourist.office@ ekenas.fi) at Rådhustorget is open from 8 am to 5 pm Monday to Friday and from 10 am to 2 pm Saturday in summer. During other times of the year, hours are from 8 am

to 4.15 pm Monday to Friday. It has tourist information for the entire Ekenäs region.

At the harbour, the Gamla Gnägget Nature Centre (☎ 241 1198) provides information on Ekenäs Archipelago National Park, including a free slide show. It's open from 10 am to 7 pm daily from May to the end of August.

Post The post office, at Ystadsgatan 12, is open from 9.30 am to 6 pm Monday to Friday. Ekenäs' post code is 10600.

Internet Resources & Library The public library, just east of the centre at Raseborgsvägen 6-8, has an Internet terminal. Hours are Monday to Friday from 10 am to 8 pm, and to 2 pm Saturday. The main site for Ekenäs is www.ekenas.fi/ on the Web.

Left Luggage The bus station has a left-luggage counter, and the train station has 24-hour lockers for 10 mk.

Medical & Emergency Services For a general emergency ring ☎ 112, for police call ☎ 10022 and for a doctor call ☎ 10023. There is a pharmacy on Rådhustorget. The regional hospital is south of the town centre on Carpelansvägen.

Things to See

The **Old Town** (Gamla Stan) is well preserved. Wooden houses from the late 18th and early 19th century line narrow streets that are named after hatters, combmakers and other artisans who once worked in the precinct. Some buildings contain artisans' shops, open in summer. The oldest buildings are on Linvävaregatan.

The pretty stone **church** in Gamla Stan has a tower that can be seen from most parts of town. It was built between 1651 and 1680 and was last renovated in 1990. The church is open daily in summer.

The **Ekenäs Museum** is at Gustav Wasas gata 13. The main building, built in 1802, exhibits the lifestyle of a wealthy artisan family in the 1800s. Other buildings have temporary exhibitions of modern art and photography, and permanent displays on

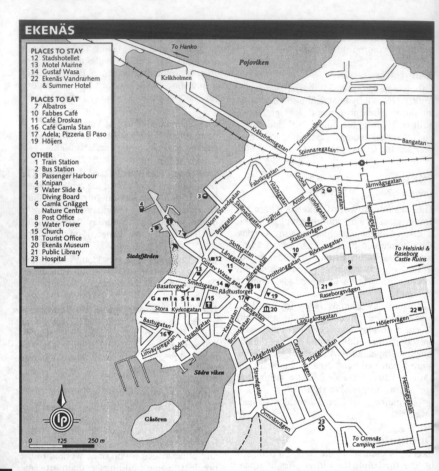

EKENÄS

PLACES TO STAY
12 Stadshotellet
13 Motel Marine
14 Gustaf Wasa
22 Ekenäs Vandrarhem
     & Summer Hotel

PLACES TO EAT
7 Albatros
10 Fabbes Café
11 Café Droskan
16 Café Gamla Stan
17 Adela; Pizzeria El Paso
19 Höijers

OTHER
1 Train Station
2 Bus Station
3 Passenger Harbour
4 Knipan
5 Water Slide &
    Diving Board
6 Gamla Gnägget
    Nature Centre
8 Post Office
9 Water Tower
15 Church
18 Tourist Office
20 Ekenäs Museum
21 Public Library
23 Hospital

---

local history. On the grounds is a fine collection of life-sized cow statues. The museum is open from 11 am to 5 pm daily in summer. Admission is 10 mk.

The old **water tower has** the best view of the town; ask for the keys at the tourist office. Cobbled **Kungsgatan**, the first pedestrian street in Finland, has some nice boutiques.

Activities

The water slide, diving board and swimming beach at the harbour are the most popular stops for Finnish families. Rent

rowboats (20 mk for one hour, 8 mk for each additional hour) and bikes (10 mk for one hour, 8 mk each additional hour or 40 mk per day) at Ormnäs Camping.

Organised Tours

Basatorget square, in Gamla Stan, is the starting point of free walking tours on some summer afternoons. Ask at the tourist office about the current schedule.

For information on boat cruises to Ekenäs Archipelago National Park, see the Around Ekenäs section.

Places to Stay

Camping *Ormnäs Camping (☎ 241 4434 or in winter ☎ 0400-471 548)* is at the seaside 1km from the town centre, next to Ramsholmen Natural Park. Camping costs 50 mk per tent or 35 mk per individual traveller. There are cottages for two/four for 160/220 mk. The sauna costs 50 mk per hour. It's open from May to the end of September and on weekends in October.

Hostel The cheapest place to stay is the HI-affiliated hostel *Ekenäs Vandrarhem (☎ 241 6393, fax 241 3917, Höijerintie 10)*, with tidy, modern rooms. It's open from mid-May to mid-August. Single/double/triple rooms are 115/75/65 mk per person. Breakfast is an additional 25 mk. There is a sauna and a laundry. A *summer hotel* on the premises has singles/doubles for 150/270 mk, breakfast and bed linen included.

Guesthouses & Hotels At *Gustaf Wasa (☎ 241 1551)*, on Rådhustorget in the town centre, rooms cost 160/240 mk. There are just seven rooms, all with shared toilets and showers.

There are two hotels near the harbour and Gamla Stan. Best in town is *Stadshotellet (☎ 241 3131, fax 246 1550, Norra Strandgatan 1)*, which has a swimming pool. Its 20 rooms cost 390/490 mk, breakfast and sauna included. Double rooms have balconies.

The 29 rooms at *Motel Marine (☎ 241 3833, fax 241 3837, Kammakaregatan 4 6)* are neat, and cost 180 to 430 mk for singles, 290 to 530 mk for doubles, breakfast and sauna included. Cheaper rooms have no showers; pricier ones have kitchenettes.

Places to Eat

During summer, *Albatros* at the harbour does a booming business in takeaway hamburgers (20 mk), hot dogs and ice cream. The Albatros beer terrace has good food at higher prices.

Höijers (Drottninggatan 1) is a simple, pleasant place with tempting 30 to 49 mk lunch specials from 11 am to 2 pm daily.

Of the many restaurants on the main square, Rådhustorget, *Adela* is good for cheap pizza and kebabs, while *Pizzeria El Paso* has pizza and more pizza, with daily lunch specials from 30 to 55 mk.

Knipan at the harbour has the nicest restaurant in town; see the Entertainment section following.

Fabbes Café (Skillnadsgatan 16) is a cosy nook that serves meals. Better still is *Café Droskan (Gustav Wasasgatan 6)*, a café and handicraft shop. It serves homemade pies with berries, and summer seating is in a garden.

Even nicer is *Café Gamla Stan (Bastugatan 5)*. The small house is somewhat hard to find and has just a few seats, but the private garden is superb. The café is open daily from May to the end of August.

Entertainment

At the harbour, *Knipan (☎ 241 1169)* is a swank dance club and restaurant open from May to mid-September. It was built on poles over the water because local laws allowed only one bar on town ground! Live music in the evenings has a 15 to 25 mk cover charge, and main courses range from 50 to 130 mk.

Getting There & Away

Ekenäs is 96km south-west of Helsinki (a 1½ hour drive) on road No 53. There are five to seven buses a day from Helsinki, Turku or Hanko; the one-way fare from Helsinki is 70 mk. There are seven to nine daily trains to Ekenäs from Helsinki (55 mk) or Turku, continuing on to Hanko. See the Hanko Getting There & Away section for more information.

AROUND EKENÄS
Raseborg Castle Ruins

The Raseborg castle ruins (Finnish: Raasepori), dating from the late 14th century, are fairly impressive thanks to restorations starting as early as 1890. The castle was of great strategic importance in the 15th century, when it protected the important trading town of Tuna. Karl Knutsson Bonde, three times the King of Sweden, was one of its most prominent residents. By the mid-1500s, Raseborg's importance declined, and it was left empty for over 300 years.

Free tours are given at 3 pm on weekends from mid-May to mid-June (also 3 pm Wednesday from mid-June to the end of July), but you can visit the area at any time. During July there are evening concerts at Raseborg; contact the Ekenäs tourist office for details.

The castle is 15km east of Ekenäs in the town of Snappertuna. There is no public transport, so come on foot, by bicycle or in a car.

Ekenäs Archipelago National Park

The beautiful archipelago surrounding Ekenäs includes a scattering of some 1300 islands, 50 sq km of which is a national park. The best way to visit the park is by boat from the Ekenäs harbour. Boats depart at 1 pm daily for the four hour tour, from mid-June to the end of August. The cost is 90 mk return. Once on Älgö island, you can see the old fishing house, use the cooking facilities or stay overnight at the camping ground. There are also camping grounds on the islands of Fladalandet and Modermagan. Visit the Gamla Gnägget Nature Centre in Ekenäs for more information about the park.

POHJA

- **pop 5000**   ☎ 019

The Pohja area, north of Ekenäs, includes several small villages that can be visited in a single day. In the tiny village of Pohja (Swedish: Pojo) is a medieval **stone church** that houses sculpture from the Middle Ages. The **Fiskars ironworks**, in Fiskars village (Finnish: Fiskari), is one of the quaintest of all *bruk* (old factory areas). There's a local history **museum**, open daily from May to September. Fiskars village also has a host of shops selling souvenirs and handicrafts. In Billnäs village (Finnish: Pinjainen), you will find the **Billnäs ironworks**. Founded in

1641, they were important in the development of Finland's metal industry.

The tourist information office in Fiskars is open Monday to Saturday from May to the end of August.

Getting There & Away

There are hourly buses from Ekenäs to all three villages. There are also a few direct buses to Fiskars from Helsinki.

INKOO

- **pop 4800**   ☎ 019

Inkoo (Swedish: Ingå) is a small, attractive seaside town where locals predominantly speak Swedish. Look for the unusual bell tower atop the **medieval church** which was founded in the 13th century (open daily in summer). There are rich paintings on the church walls. Across the river, **Ingå Gammelgård** is the local museum.

Just west of Inkoo on road No 105 is the **Fagervik factory** (☎ 221 221), the most attractive bruk in Finland. It was established in 1646 by the Swedes. The Russian army destroyed the area during the Great Northern War in the 1720s, but the factory was later rebuilt before ultimately closing in 1902. Guided tours of the grounds are available, and there is a café.

Getting There & Away

Inkoo lies south-west of Helsinki on road No 51. There are several direct buses each week from Helsinki.

The MS *JL Runeberg*, a former steamship, travels between Helsinki and Inkoo on Thursdays in summer. The boat departs Helsinki at 10 am and Inkoo at 4 pm. The trip takes five hours each way and costs 200 mk return. See the Helsinki Getting There & Away section for more information.

LOHJA

- **pop 18,800**   ☎ 019

Lohja (Swedish: Lojo), on the eastern side of Lake Lohjanjärvi, has been a mining town since 1542. There were initially only a few small iron mines, but since 1897 limestone has been the area's most important product. The **Tytyri Mining Museum**, in the mining area just north of the town centre, offers tours of the working mines daily from mid-May to mid-August. **Lohja church** was built during the 15th century. Its lively murals depict torture, demons and saints. The church is open daily in summer. The **local museum** behind the church has a dozen old buildings and some prehistoric items (closed Monday). The café in the museum garden is pleasant.

The tourist office (☎ 320 1309) is at Sepänkatu 7.

Getting There & Away

Lohja is on road No 53 that connects Ekenäs and Hanko with Helsinki. There are frequent buses to Lohja from the Helsinki bus terminal. The 60km trip takes one hour.

SALO

• pop 22,000 ☎ 02

The industrial town of Salo, roughly halfway between Turku and Helsinki, is generally known in Finland as the place where Salora television sets come from. For travellers, this is mainly a transportation hub. There's nothing particularly worth seeing in the town itself, although it's pleasant enough.

Information

The tourist office (☎ 733 1274, ssmy@ netti.fi) is at Rummunlyöjänkatu 2. The post office is at Turuntie 6. There are pharmacies on Vilhonkatu at Nos 4, 8 and 14 and at Helsingintie 6. Inquire at the tourist office or the train and bus stations about bicycle rentals.

Places to Stay & Eat

Vuohensaari Camping (☎ 731 2651), open June to late September, is 5km from the centre on Vuohensaari island, accessible by bridge. It has camp sites for 55 mk, and cabins.

Laurin Koulu (☎ 778 4409, Venemestarinkatu 37) is an HI-affiliated hostel in a school building, open to travellers from June to early August. Beds are from 45 mk and you can use the kitchen. The hostel is a short walk from the train station.

Penan Saluuna (Helsingintie 10) is a down-to-earth restaurant with good food.

Getting There & Away

All buses and trains in the area stop at Salo. The bus station, in the Anttila building close to the train station, has several daily departures to Kemiö Island.

AROUND SALO
Halikko
☎ 02

Halikko, a historical centre just north-west of Salo, is close enough for rewarding bicycle tours from the Salo bus and train stations (rent bicycles at either place, or through the Salo tourist office).

The most prominent natural feature is long and narrow Halikonlahti Bay, which is vaguely reminiscent of a Norwegian fjord. It is believed that this was once the mysterious Portus Tavastorum, a free port for pre-Christian fur traders from the Finnish interior.

In the area are three old **estates** that have belonged to just two families, first the Horns and later the Armfelts. Although they are not open to the public, they're worth looking at from the outside. Vuorentaka Manor, from the 14th century, is the oldest of them. Its unusual tower is visible from the main road. Originally established in medieval times, Joensuu estate has a manor dating from the 1780s. Viurila, from the early 19th century, is now the Viurila golf course, with public access. The clubhouses, with their distinctive columns, were designed by CL Engel, the German architect responsible for designing Senate Square in Helsinki.

The 15th century **Halikko church** is a legacy of the wealth of the Swedish nobility in the area. The Horn and Armfelt families have their crests hanging on the walls here.

The nearby **Halikon Museo**, a local museum, is certainly worth a visit. Count CG Armfelt has donated his gun collection, which is unusually extensive for a local museum. Next to the museum, **Taitojen Tupa** is a handicrafts shop and café. The museum and Taitojen Tupa are open from 11 am to 5 pm on Sunday.

Getting There & Away There are buses from Salo to Halikko every 30 minutes on weekdays and every hour on weekends.

KEMIÖ
- pop 3400   ☎ 02

Kemiö (Swedish: Kimito) is the main village on the island of the same name. Swedish is still predominantly spoken here, so you'll find the name Kimito commonly used. The village has a 14th century **church** with a grandiose interior, open to the public daily from mid-May to mid-August. The **Sagalund Museum**, 2km west of the church, has over 20 old buildings. The museum is open from noon to 5 pm Tuesday to Sunday. Admission is 15 mk and there are guided tours every hour.

Getting There & Away
To get to Kemiö, take road No 52 south from Salo to road No 183. There are three to five buses a day from Turku, or from Salo, 50km north-east.

DRAGSFJÄRD
- pop 3800   ☎ 02

Dragsfjärd, in the south-west of Kemiö Island, is a quiet, rural place with a **church** dating from the 1700s. **Söderlångvik** is a manor house that belonged to a local newspaper magnate until 1961. There are paintings, furniture and special exhibitions in this beautiful manor, as well as an extensive garden and a café. The manor is open from 11 am to 6 pm daily in summer. Admission is 20 mk. The best reason to come to Dragsfjärd, however, is the excellent hostel.

Places to Stay
The HI-affiliated hostel *Pensionat och Van-drarhotell (☎/fax 424 533, Kulla)* is open

year-round and excellent value for money. It is beautifully furnished like a private home. Beds are from 70 mk, and guests have access to a kitchen, sauna and rowing boats. The sea is just steps away.

Getting There & Away
Dragsfjärd is on road No 183, 18km south of Kemiö village. Take a bus from Salo, Turku or Kemiö village; there are several daily.

KASNÄS
☎ 02

The Kasnäs harbour, on a small island south of Kemiö Island, is the main jumping-off point for regional archipelago ferries. Visit **Sinisimpukka (☎ 466 6290)** in summer, daily from 10 am to 6 pm, for information on the South-West Archipelago National Park. The centre, also known as Naturum, organises tours to some of the islands in June, July and August, depending on demand. There's also a nature trail from Sinisimpukka.

Getting There & Away
There are just one or two daily bus-and-ferry connections from Dalsbruk (Taalintehdas) on Kemiö Island, about 3km south of Dragsfjärd on road No 183.

HIITTINEN
☎ 02

The people of this small island group (Swedish: Hitis) make their living primarily by fishing. In 1995, an extensive archaeological excavation revealed a Viking Age trading place at **Kyrksundet**, on the main island. Nearby, the colourful archipelago **church** from 1686 ranks among the oldest wooden churches in Finland. The main community is **Rosala**, which offers accommodation in small huts.

Högsåra island has an old fishing village with houses from the 18th century.

Getting There & Away
To get to the main island, take a bus or drive to Kasnäs, then take the MS *Aura* ferry

which runs every one to two hours. The ride is free. If you want to visit any of the other islands, board the MS *Falkö*.

The South-East

The south-east region is where Russian influence is at its strongest in Finland, and forts and ruins remain from battles between Sweden and Russia. Best is the town of Hamina with its fortifications and unusual town plan.

Sadly, industrial pollution is also omnipresent in the south-east. On windless days, the region's many pulp factories can give off a pretty big stink.

LOVIISA
- **pop 7700**   ☎ 019

Loviisa (Swedish: Lovisa) is a humble town that is pleasant to visit at the height of summer, when its picturesque marina is in full swing. It was established in 1745 and named after the Swedish Queen Lovisa Ulrika. In the 18th century Loviisa was one of three towns in Finland allowed to engage in foreign trade, and by the 19th century it was a flourishing port and spa town. Loviisa was devastated by fire during the Crimean War.

Information
The tourist office (☎ 555 234 or in summer ☎ 555 446, matkailu@loviisa.fi) at Mannerheiminkatu 10B is open from 9 am to 4 pm Monday to Friday (longer hours and including Saturday in July).

The post office is at Kuningattarenkatu 13. The library, down the road at No 24, has two Internet terminals.

Loviisa Regional Hospital is just east of the centre at Öhmaninkatu 4, and a pharmacy is at Kuningattarenkatu 15.

Things To See & Do
The **old town** section of Loviisa, south of Mannerheiminkatu, contains the buildings that were saved from the disastrous fire of 1855. The narrow streets around the restaurant Degerby Gille are the quaintest in town, and the restaurant itself is in the town's oldest building (dating from the 1600s).

On the market square, the impressive neogothic **Loviisa church**, built in 1865, is the first thing you will see on arrival from Helsinki. It's open daily in summer.

The summer home of the family of Jean Sibelius, the great Finnish composer, is now the **Sibelius House** museum at Sibeliuksenkatu 10. Sibelius House is open only in summer. The **Loviisa Town Museum**, Puistokatu 2, is in an old manor house that is open year-round.

The most attractive part of town is **Laivasilta marina**, half a kilometre south of the centre. In summer you may rent bicycles here or catch a boat to Svartholma sea fortress (see the Around Loviisa section).

Archipelago cruises past the fort and nuclear power plant take two hours and cost 45 mk; four-hour cruises on the open sea cost 55 mk.

Places to Stay
You can camp for 85 mk at *Casino Camping* (☎ 530 244, Kapteenintie 1), south of the marina by the sea. Cabins are 100 mk per bed. Casino is open mid-May to mid-September.

Open year-round, *Helgas Gasthaus* (☎ 531 576, Sibeliuksenkatu 6) is run by a family and has 18 rooms for 100/180 mk for singles/doubles. There's a quiet garden.

Hotelli Degerby (☎ 50651, fax 505 6200, Brandensteininkatu 17) is the finest of the three hotels in town. Singles and doubles cost 335 mk in summer (370/480 mk at other times).

Places to Eat
In the centre, *Mexmarié (Mariankatu 20)* is festive and cheap. It serves beer, coffee and Mexican and international food. Lunch specials are 35 to 40 mk. *Vaherkylä (Aleksanterinkatu 2)* is a bakery and a pleasant café.

At Laivasilta marina, *Saltbodan Café & Restaurant* serves coffee and snacks in a rustic room and meals in a pleasant dining hall. It's open summer only.

Degerby Gille *(☎ 505 6300, Sepänkuja 4)* is the most famous restaurant in Loviisa. It has stylish, old-fashioned dining rooms and dinners from 90 to 150 mk.

Kappeli is an old wooden villa, built in 1865, in Kappelinpuisto park. It's usually lively in summer evenings and you can dance there.

Getting There & Away

Loviisa is 90km east of Helsinki, reached by road No E18 or 7. There are up to 25 buses a day to/from Helsinki, as well as a regular bus service to/from Kotka and Porvoo.

AROUND LOVIISA
Svartholma Sea Fortress

The sea fortress lies on an island 10km from the town centre. It was established in 1748 soon after Sweden had lost control of the eastern part of Finland. The fort was destroyed by the British during the Crimean War in 1855, but has since been renovated. There are daily launches from Laivasilta marina from June to late August. Return tickets cost 50 mk (65 mk with guided walking tour of the island). **Pirate cruises** to the fort are held daily in summer, complete with treasure hunt – terrific for families. Tickets cost 50 mk (no discounts for children).

Loviisa Nuclear Power Plant

This power plant on Hästholmen island, 15km from the centre, opens its doors to visitors for two-hour tours on Sunday in summer. A bus leaves at 12.30 pm from Loviisa's bus terminal.

LAPINJÄRVI
• pop 3100   ☎ 019

The small lakeside town of Lapinjärvi (Swedish: Lappträsk), north of Loviisa, is named for the Lapp population who dwelt in the region before they were pushed further north by Swedish settlers in the 13th

century. The idyllic village centre features two **churches** built side by side in 1744. In 1742, lightning struck and burnt down the original Swedish and Finnish churches. A fierce two-year construction boom followed. The Finnish church was finished first and became known as 'the small church', as the slower Swedes were able to build a slightly bigger one! The churches are open in summer. **Kycklings** is the local museum and tourist information office. The village also has a number of shops selling handicrafts and pottery.

Places to Stay

The excellent HI-affiliated ***Embom Hostel*** *(☎ 616 354, Embomintie 164)* is in the neighbouring Swedish-speaking community of Liljendal, 2km west of the No 6 (Helsinki-Kouvola) road. The owners are friendly and the hostel is pleasantly located close to a river. There are two saunas, a café and laundry. Dorm beds in the old wooden villa cost 60 mk (open May to late September or by agreement).

Getting There & Away

To get to Lapinjärvi, take one of the slower buses between Helsinki and Kouvola. There are 10 such buses per day.

ELIMÄKI
☎ 05

Elimäki is a green little village 20km northeast of Lapinjärvi. In 1608 the whole area became the property of the Wrede family and there are surviving historical landmarks from various centuries.

The **Moisio Manor** (☎ 377 6331 or 779 011) in Elimäki was built in the 1820s by the architect CL Engel. It hosts fairs and cultural events in summer.

Just off road No 6, **Arboretum Mustila** was founded in 1902 when State Secretary AF Tigerstedt planted the first foreign trees in the Mustila Estate area. The original purpose of the arboretum was to pit foreign trees against miserable Finnish winters, then observe the results. The botanical garden is at its most beautiful when the rhododendrons and azaleas blossom in June, and in September during the *ruska* (autumn). There are several short walking tracks. The entry fee is 15 mk.

The **Elimäki Homestead Museum** in Elimäki village, half a kilometre west of road No 6, consists of farm equipment and half a dozen old farm buildings.

The **Elimäki church**, built in 1638, is one of the oldest wooden churches in Finland still in regular use.

Places to Stay & Eat
Puustelli (*☎ 377 7713, Meijeritie 1*) in Elimäki village is a guesthouse open from June to mid-August. Rooms are from 110 mk per person.

There are a few places on road No 6 to eat and shop: *Alppiruusu*, a collection of pyramid-shaped glass structures at a petrol station, serves food and sells handicrafts. Across the road, *Piika ja Renki* is a former granary offering coffee and snacks, a handicrafts shop and an art exhibition.

Getting There & Away
Elimäki is on road No 6, 25km south-west of Kouvola. Buses between Helsinki and Kouvola stop here.

AROUND ELIMÄKI
Anjala Manor
The large estate of the influential Wrede family dates back to 1606, but the wooden main building is from the late 18th century. On display is the sculpture collection of Carl Henrik Wrede, as well as items relating to local history. The family has played an important role in regional history – improving school and prison conditions – mostly through the work of the Wrede family women. The manor is east of Elimäki on road No 359, just outside Anjalankoski, and is open daily from mid-May to mid-August. Admission is 15 mk.

KOUVOLA
- **pop 32,000**   ☎ 05

Kouvola, 20km north-east of Elimäki, is the capital of the province of Kymi. It's the only provincial capital in Finland that you could skip yet miss almost nothing. The reason for this is that it is barely 100 years old, and when its landmarks were built, the ideas on how a town should look are now those that prescribe how a town should *not* look. The Kouvola rail junction is one of the busiest in Finland, however.

Orientation
Most of the services in Kouvola are south of road No 6, on or near Kauppalankatu at the centre of town. This main street runs south from road No 6 to the bus and train station. West of this is the old town area, Kaunisnurmi, where most attractions are to be found.

Information
The tourist office (☎ 829 6558 or 829 6561, tourism@kouvola.fi) at Torikatu 10 is open Monday to Saturday in summer (to Friday at other times).

There's a post office on the main street, at Kauppalankatu 13. The public library at Salpausselänkatu 33 has an Internet terminal and is open from 10 am to 8 pm Monday to Friday, and to 3 pm Saturday. At the train station, the lockers cost 5 mk (24 hour maximum) and there is a left-luggage counter.

There are pharmacies near the post office at Kauppalankatu 15 and at Torikatu 5.

Things to See & Do
The unusual **town hall (kaupungintalo)** in the town centre next to the tourist office was designed by award-winning architect Juha Leiviskä.

The modern **Kouvolatalo** west of the centre, houses an art museum with modern Finnish paintings. The museum is open Tuesday to Friday and admission is free.

The **Kaunisnurmi Museum Quarter**, west of the centre, contains many old wooden houses that have been renovated to form a cultural and shopping district. There are two small museums here, the **Pharmacy Museum (Apteekkimuseo)** at Varuskuntakatu 9 and the **Railwayman's Museum (Rautatieläisko-timuseo)**, the preserved home of a railway worker. Both museums are open Tuesday to Sunday in summer. Several artisans live in other houses, and their shops are open Monday to Saturday in summer.

North of Kaunisnurmi on Sakaristonkatu, the **Greek-Orthodox Church,** with its beautiful icons, was built in 1915 for the Russian army. Long used as a Lutheran church, it was only in 1982 that it was turned back into an Orthodox church. The church is open in summer.

Tykkimäki Amusement Park, 5km east of the centre, has 20 rides and more than 100 games, as well as a terrarium with snakes, crocodiles and turtles. A dance hall hums on Friday evenings in summer. Tykkimäki is open daily from late May to mid-August.

Places to Stay

Käyrälampi Camping (☎ 321 1226), 5km east of the town centre along road No 6, is open year-round. It is set on a lake close to the Tykkimäki Amusement Park. The camping fee is 75 mk. There are cottages from 210 mk, and you can rent boats and canoes.

Turistihovi (☎ 311 5661, fax 371 3917, Valtakatu 23) is a cheap but clean hotel in the centre with singles/doubles from 150/220 mk.

Cumulus Kouvola (☎ 789 911, fax 789 9299, Valtakatu 11) is also centrally located and has 107 nice rooms, four restaurants and two saunas. Rooms are from 550/640 mk, with discounts possible in summer.

Places to Eat

There are several pleasant cafés on Kauppalankatu, including *Juho Manner Kahvila* at No 3. *Hesburger* is across the street.

Another place to look for a cheap meal is the *kauppatori* (market square) on Torikatu, one block west of Kauppalankatu. At the market square, *Wiener Café* has wonderful pastries, and *Sip Pub* downstairs has a meal

package for 40 mk, including salad, coffee and drink.

Getting There & Away

Kouvola is on road No 6. Most buses travelling west to Lahti and Helsinki or east to Lappeenranta stop at the Kouvola bus terminal. Trains depart hourly for Helsinki and Lahti; the journey from Helsinki generally takes less than two hours. Eastbound trains go to Russia. Trains to Kotka are small electric ones, and you can buy your ticket on the train.

RUOTSINPYHTÄÄ

• pop 3200   ☎ 019

If you are looking for somewhere quiet and beautiful to stay for a day or two, the tiny village of Ruotsinpyhtää (Swedish: Strömfors) is for you. The long name means 'Pyhtää of Sweden', as it was here that the Swedish-Russian international border cut the town of Pyhtää into two. The western oddly shaped section was Swedish property; Pyhtää proper was to become Russian for some time. The municipal and provincial border follows the river, and nobody has had the courage to unite these areas. Perhaps locals think that Finns are not supposed to unite what Swedes and Russians have separated.

Things to See & Do

The **Strömfors ironworks,** founded in 1695, is one of the oldest of its kind in Finland. Today it's an extremely picturesque open-air museum, surrounded by forest, brooks and farm buildings, and open June to mid-August.

The **Forge Museum** consists of an old smith's workshop and equipment. Adjacent are several **craft workshops** – potters, silversmiths, textile makers and painters. One of the ironworks buildings serves as an **art gallery** in summer.

The octagonal wooden **church** dates from 1770; its altarpiece was painted in 1989 by Helene Schjerfbeck, a famous Finnish painter.

Beautiful wooden buildings in Porvoo

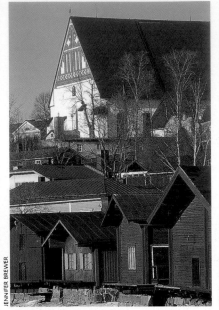

Porvoo riverfront in winter

Salmon smoking, Laukontori, Tampere

Kuopio town hall & market square

The area is ideal for **canoeing**, and you can rent canoes from either the tourist information office adjacent to the Forge Museum or the hostel.

The village of Pyhtää, across the river, is only worth visiting for a look at its 15th century greystone **church**.

Places to Stay & Eat

Adjacent to the ironworks, the HI-affiliated *Finnhostel Krouvinmäki (☎ 618 474 or 0400-492 161, fax 618 475)* is a superb hostel in a renovated former tavern house. The hostel is open from June to mid-August or by prior arrangement. Accommodation costs 120 mk. Krouvinmäki has a kitchen and laundry.

Kulma Kahvila is a café and *grilli* about 100m from the hostel. Also in the ironworks area, *Myllyravintola* (the Mill Restaurant) is in a 17th century former mill on a lovely quiet pond. In summer the restaurant has a terrace with live music and dancing.

Getting There & Away

Ruotsinpyhtää is 115km east of Helsinki, just north of road No 7. Many buses run from Helsinki, Loviisa and Kouvola. There are one or two connections a day from Helsinki via Porvoo, three to five from Loviisa and one to three from Kouvola.

KOTKA
• **pop 56,000**   ☎ 05

Kotka, 132km east of Helsinki, is Finland's most important port and is sometimes called the Sea Town. Massive pulp factories and oil tanks are features of Kotka – which makes for a stinky town on windless days. For the traveller, Kotka's greatest appeal may be as a jumping-off point for visits to outlying tiny islands and to the Langinkoski Imperial fishing lodge.

Orientation

The city centre is on Kotkansaari island. Keskuskatu and Kirkkokatu are the two main streets in the centre. To the west is the more rural island of Mussalo, a suburb of Kotka.

Information

The tourist office (☎ 234 4424, matkailu@kotka.fi) at Keskuskatu 17 is open from 9 am to 5 pm Monday to Friday.

The main post office at Kapteeninkatu 16 is open Monday to Friday from 9 am to 5 pm. The postal code is 48100.

The library, at Kirkkokatu 24, has an Internet terminal. The Kotka site is www.kotka.fi/matkailu on the Web.

The city hospital is on Keskuskatu, south-west of the centre. A pharmacy is at Kirkkokatu 10.

Things to See

The **St Nicholas Orthodox Church** in Isopuisto Park was built in 1801 and is the only building in Kotka to survive the Crimean War of 1853-56. It is believed to have been designed by architect Yakov Perrini, who also designed the St Petersburg Admiralty. The church is open daily in summer.

The **museum ship** *Tarmo* is an icebreaker that once kept Finnish shipping lanes open. Built in 1907, it's now the oldest of its kind. The *Tarmo* is open daily in summer and admission is 15 mk.

Kymenlaakso Provincial Museum (Maakuntamuseo) at Kotkankatu 13 is the museum of regional history. It's open from noon to 6 pm Tuesday to Friday and to 4 pm weekends. Entry is 10 mk.

Sapokka Water Park at Sapokka harbour is a lovely green oasis perfect for picnicking. The Rose Terrace garden is lit every evening.

Activities

Archipelago cruises of all types depart from Sapokka harbour in summer – ask for timetables at the tourist office, and see the Around Kotka section.

The travel agency Ykköslaituri (☎ 213 284) at Keskuskatu 17 offers **white-water rafting** trips on the nearby Kymijoki. You can go **fly-fishing** at Langinkoski (see the Around Kotka section).

THE SOUTH COAST

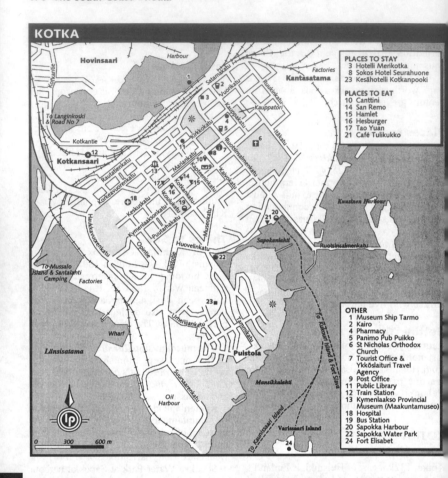

KOTKA

PLACES TO STAY
3 Hotelli Merikotka
8 Sokos Hotel Seurahuone
23 Kesähotelli Kotkanpooki

PLACES TO EAT
10 Canttini
14 San Remo
15 Hamlet
16 Hesburger
17 Tao Yuan
21 Café Tulikukko

OTHER
1 Museum Ship Tarmo
2 Kairo
4 Pharmacy
5 Panimo Pub Puikko
6 St Nicholas Orthodox Church
7 Tourist Office & Ykkőslaituri Travel Agency
9 Post Office
11 Public Library
12 Train Station
13 Kymenlaakso Provincial Museum (Maakuntamuseo)
18 Hospital
19 Bus Station
20 Sapokka Harbour
22 Sapokka Water Park
24 Fort Elisabet

Special Events

The Kotka Maritime Festival (Kotkan Meripäivät) is held annually at the beginning of August. Events include boat racing, concerts, cruises and a market.

Places to Stay

Santalahti Camping (☎ 260 5055), 5km from the centre, is on Mussalo island by the sea. Camping costs 70 mk per family or 35 mk per person; cottages cost 150 to 340 mk. The camping ground has every imaginable

amenity and is open from May to late September. There is a *summer hotel* (☎ 260 4333) here as well. Bus Nos 13 and 14 will take you to Santalahti.

Kesähotelli Kotkanpooki (☎ 218 1945 or 228 2484, Urheilijankatu 2B) is a summer hotel, open from mid-June to mid-August. Rooms start at 100 mk, and bookings are advised.

Hotelli Merikotka (☎ 15222, fax 15414 Satamakatu 9) is a small, friendly hotel. Singles/doubles are 250/320 mk.

Sokos Hotel Seurahuone (☎ 35035, fax 350 0450, Keskuskatu 21) is the finest hotel in town and the most popular night spot. All rooms are 365 mk in summer. An annexe has cheaper rooms.

Places to Eat

The *Hesburger (Kotkankatu 11)* in the Sokos shopping centre keeps hamburger-lovers happy. *Hamlet (Kymenlaaksonkatu 16)* has a more eclectic menu, with Danish sandwiches for 30 mk.

Canttiini (Kaivokatu 15) is good for pasta from 45 mk and other, more substantial meals, and is quite popular among locals. Also good is *San Remo (Keskuskatu 29)*, a real Italian place with chianti and large portions.

Tao Yuan (Mariankatu 24) is a nice Chinese restaurant with options from 50 mk. For coffee and snacks at Sapokka harbour, try *Café Tulikukko*.

Entertainment

Kotkankatu has a great number of pubs if you want to go bar-hopping with locals.

Kairo (Satamakatu 7) is an old sailors' pub with outrageous paintings on the walls, a large terrace in summer and frequent live music. There are more tourists than sailors among its clientele these days.

Panimo Pub Puikko (Ruotsinsalmenkatu 14) translates as a brewery but, no, they don't have their own home-brew.

Getting There & Away

Bus There are regular express buses from Helsinki, via Porvoo, Loviisa and Pyhtää. It's just over two hours to Helsinki, and around 85 mk one way. Hourly buses make the 45 minute trip to Hamina, 26km east.

Train There are between four and six trains a day to Kouvola and they take 40 minutes to cover the 50km. From Kouvola trains run to all major Finnish cities.

Car & Motorcycle From Helsinki take road No 7 east for 1¾ hours.

AROUND KOTKA
Langinkoski

The **Imperial fishing lodge** at the Langinkoski rapids, 5km north of the centre, is Kotka's most interesting attraction. The wooden lodge was built in 1889 for Tsar Alexander III, who visited Langinkoski frequently. Most of the original furniture has been retained and the rooms look as they did at the turn of the century. **Fishing** is allowed at Langinkoski rapids – for permits and equipment rentals visit the Lohikeskus Kotka recreation centre adjacent to the lodge.

The Imperial lodge and the recreation centre are open from 10 am to 7 pm daily from May to late August and weekends in September and October. Admission to the Imperial lodge is 15 mk. You can get almost all the way to Langinkoski on bus No 13 or 27. Alternatively, get off at the sign at the *pikavuoro* (express) bus stop and walk 1.2km.

Islands

Three interesting islands off the Kotka coast make for good day trips during the warm months. There are several boat connections daily to each from Sapokka harbour during summer. Return tickets cost 20 to 35 mk.

Fort Slava, also known as the Fortress of Honour, is on **Kukouri** island. The fort was built by Russians and was finished in 1794, then was destroyed by the British in 1855. It was renovated in 1993.

Fort Elisabeth on **Varissaari** was built by the Russians as part of a fortification to defend the coast against the Swedes, but was abandoned in the late 19th century. It is now a popular venue for festivals, dances and open-air performances, and a favourite picnic spot.

On **Kaunissaari**, there is a fishing village and a local museum, as well as a camping ground with some cabins. Special cruises to Kaunissaari with singing and live music depart at 7 pm Wednesday from late May to late August.

HAMINA

- pop 10,000 ☎ 05

Just 40km west of the Russian border, Hamina (Swedish: Fredrikshamn) is a small town with an unusual octagonal plan.

Hamina was founded in 1653, when Finland was a part of Sweden. The crumbling fortifications that surround it were begun by panicky Swedes in 1722 after they lost Vyborg to Russia. Shortly thereafter they lost Hamina, too.

For much of its existence Hamina has been an important garrison town. The cadet school of imperial Finland was here, and today Hamina is known as the home of the Finnish Reserve Officers School.

The unique town plan and pleasant, small-town atmosphere make Hamina one of the most enjoyable tourist stops on the south coast. It is a favourite place for Russians to visit.

Information

Tourist Offices The tourist office (☎ 749 5251) at Pikkuympyräkatu 5 is open from 9 am to 4 pm Monday to Friday. A second office at the Lipputorni (Flagtower) in the kauppatori is open from Monday to Friday from 9 am to 5 pm and Saturday to 1 pm from June to mid-August.

Post The post office is at Maariankatu 4.

Internet Resources & Library The public library at Rautatienkatu 8, just north of the bus station, is open from 1 to 7 pm Monday to Friday and from 10 am to 2 pm Saturday. You'll need to book the Internet terminal well in advance.

Medical & Emergency Services In a general emergency ring ☎ 112, for a doctor call ☎ 10023 and for police call ☎ 10022. There are pharmacies at Isoympyräkatu 13 and Sibeliuskatu 36.

Things to See & Do

Restored 19th century wooden buildings grace the eight radial streets of Hamina's octagonal town plan. At the centre is the 18th century **town hall**. The tourist office, one block west on Fredrikinkatu, distributes a free guide, *Walking in Old Hamina*, that is very helpful.

Highlights of Old Hamina include the neoclassical **Hamina church**, built in 1843, and directly opposite, behind the town hall, the **Orthodox Church of Saints Peter and Paul**. Hamina church was designed by CL Engel, and the 1837 Orthodox church is thought to have been created by architect Louis Visconti, who designed Napoleon's monument in France. Both churches are open to tourists during summer.

The **Town Museum (Kaupunginmuseo)** at Kadettikoulunkatu 2 is the museum of local history. King Gustav III of Sweden and Catherine II (the Great) of Russia held negotiations in one of the rooms in 1783.

The **Merchant's House Museum (Kauppiaantalomuseo)** is a former merchant's store and residence at Kasarminkatu 6, and one of the best house museums in Finland. Nearby is the bakery **Resenkovin Rinkeli Leipomo**, owned by the Resenkovs who came from Russia. They still run this bakery at Kasarminkatu 8, which has a 100-year tradition.

The **Reserve Officers School Museum (RUK-museo)** at Mannerheimintie 7 is devoted to military uniforms and weapons. Nearby, **Gallery Ruutikellari**, an old gunpowder warehouse on Roopertinkatu, has been converted to an art gallery.

All Hamina museums are open from 11 am to 3 pm Wednesday to Saturday and from noon to 5 pm Sunday from May to August. Admission to each is 10 mk.

Around Old Hamina are remnants of the 18th century **Hamina Fortress**, including 3km of crumbling stone walls, but there really isn't much left to see.

South-west of the centre, Tervasaari harbour has the **SS Hyöky**, a 1912 steamship that is now a museum, hotel and café (all open only in summer). From Tervasaari there are summer cruises to Tammio and Ulkotammio islands (see the Around Hamina section later).

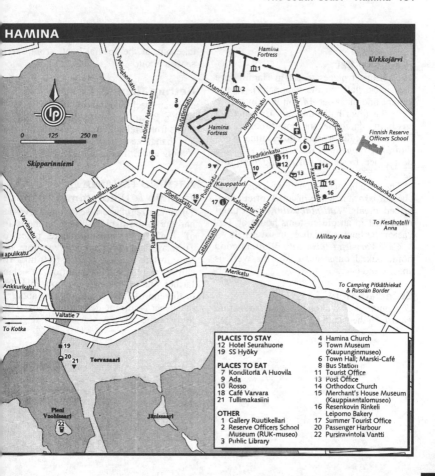

HAMINA

PLACES TO STAY	4 Hamina Church
12 Hotel Seurahuone	5 Town Museum
19 SS Hyöky	(Kaupunginmuseo)
	6 Town Hall; Marski-Café
PLACES TO EAT	8 Bus Station
7 Konditoria A Huovila	11 Tourist Office
9 Ada	13 Post Office
10 Rosso	14 Orthodox Church
18 Café Varvara	15 Merchant's House Museum
21 Tullimakasiini	(Kauppiaantalomuseo)
	16 Resenkovin Rinkeli
OTHER	Leipomo Bakery
1 Gallery Ruutikellari	17 Summer Tourist Office
2 Reserve Officers School	20 Passenger Harbour
Museum (RUK-museo)	22 Pursiravintola Vantti
3 Public Library	

Special Events

Every two years in July, Hamina celebrates military music during the one-week Hamina Tattoo, an international event. Concert tickets range in price from 50 to 220 mk. Contact the tourist office for ticket purchase information.

Places to Stay

Camping Pitkäthiekat (☎ 345 9183) is 6km east of Hamina at Vilniemi, open May to late August. Pitching a tent costs 60 mk per family. Cottages cost 180 to 400 mk. It's on a beach, offers rowboat rentals, and has a sauna and laundry.

Kesähotelli Anna (☎ 344 7747, Annankatu 1) is a summer hotel with singles/doubles from 125/160 mk. You can also choose to sleep in one of the 16 cabins of the SS Hyöky moored in Tervasaari harbour for 150/200 mk.

Hotel Seurahuone (☎ 3500 263, Pikkuympyräkatu 5) in the heart of Old Hamina is full of olde world ambience. Rooms cost

350/400 mk, with summer discounts available.

Places to Eat

The cheapest places to eat in Hamina are the snack stalls in the kauppatori, or the kebabs and pizzas at *Ada* on Puistokatu.

In the town hall building, *Marski-Café* has both a large elegant dining room and a less formal café. Also in Old Hamina, *Konditoria A Huovila (Fredrikinkatu 1)* is the best place to enjoy coffee and tempting cakes.

There's a branch of the Finnish restaurant chain *Rosso* at Isoympyräkatu. It offers mid-priced meals. *Tullimakasiini*, the quaint restaurant in an old customs house at Tervasaari harbour, specialises in fresh fish.

Café Varvara (Puistokatu 2) offers good home-baked buns and cakes, as well as snacks and beer.

Entertainment

On summer weekends, *Pursiravintola Vantti*, on the island of Pieni Vuohisaari just off Tervasaari harbour, is the place to go fo dancing to live music. To get to the island take one of the special boats from Terva saari harbour.

Getting There & Away

You can reach Hamina by hourly bus from Kotka, 26km to the south-west. Expres buses from Helsinki make the 153km trip in less than three hours. Eastbound buses go t Vyborg and St Petersburg, Russia.

AROUND HAMINA
Tammio & Ulkotammio Islands

There are regular cruises from Tervasaar harbour to the fishing village on the islan of Tammio. Departures take place o Tuesday, Saturday and Sunday from lat May to late August, and cost 60 mk. Yo can also reach Ulkotammio, an islan farther south, on weekends from mid-Jun to the end of July. Expect to pay about 7 mk. Check current departure times at th tourist office.

The Lakeland

The Lakeland is a popular tourist destination among Finns, who come here en masse in summer to rent holiday cottages and enjoy fishing and boating. Foreign travellers, who usually head to Lapland for their Finnish adventure, will find this region fascinating.

This region – much of it is the Savo district – is where you'll find numerous lakes, islands, narrow straits, canals and beaches. Here, too, are the most popular steamboat routes. No pulp factories pollute the pristine landscape in most of the region – only the town of Varkaus manages to spoil it.

This watery area would not be what it is without its people, the *savolaiset*. No other group in Finland seems to make so much fuss about themselves, but with good reason: these are witty, open-hearted and easy-going people. Finns from elsewhere joke about the Savo dialect, but perhaps they just envy the locals their beautiful Lakeland.

The ideal way to get around this region is by car, but public transportation is fast, efficient and relatively cheap. Trains connect the major cities, but buses are better for getting to smaller towns, particularly in the area surrounding Savonlinna.

Savonlinna

• **pop 28,700**   ☎ 015

If you want to see just one place outside Helsinki, Savonlinna is a good choice in summer. Set on two islands between Lake Haapavesi and Lake Pihlajavesi, it offers the prettiest of waterscapes and the most dramatic medieval castle in Finland.

In July, Savonlinna hosts the Opera Festival, the most popular of all Finnish festivals. It's a delightful experience, despite the high prices and crowds.

History

The slow growth of Savonlinna began in 1475 with the building of Olavinlinna Castle on a tiny island between two large

THE LAKELAND

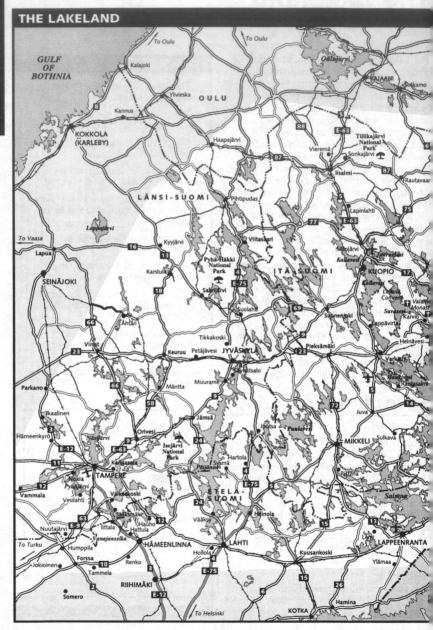

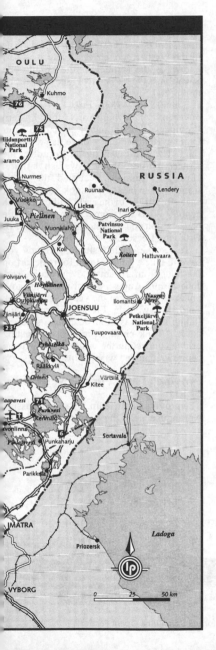

lakes. In 1639, Savonlinna received a municipal charter at the instigation of Count Per Brahe, the founder of numerous towns around Finland. In 1743, this small market town was annexed to Russia; it was returned to the Finnish grand duchy in 1812. By the 1920s, Savonlinna was important as the major hub for steamboat traffic in the Lakeland, and has retained this important role to the present day.

Information

Tourist Office The tourist office, Savonlinna Tourist Service (☎ 273 492 or 273 458, fax 514 449, savonlinna@touristservice-slv.fi), is at Puistokatu 1, just west of the *kauppatori* (market square). It provides information about most places in the region, sells festival tickets, reserves accommodation and organises tours. Hours are 8 am to 6 pm daily from early June to mid-August (until 10 pm daily during the Opera festival). At other times, hours are 9 am to 4 pm Monday to Friday.

Closer to the town centre there is a post office inside the K-Market supermarket at Koulukatu 10, 57130 Savonlinna. Hours are 9 am to 8 pm Monday to Friday, 9 am to 4 pm Saturday.

Internet Resources & Libraries The small public library is on Tottinkatu. It has an Internet terminal and is open from 11 am to 7 pm Monday to Friday, 10 am to 2 pm Saturday.

The city also has a music library at Kirkkokatu 12, open 1 pm to 7 pm Monday to Thursday, 10 am to 4 pm Friday. It has a good collection of CDs, including opera.

The main Web site for Savonlinna is www.travel.fi/int/Savonlinna/.

Bookshops Suomalainen Kirjakauppa at the Kauppalinna shopping centre has an extremely limited selection of English-language paperbacks.

Left Luggage Neither the bus nor the train station has lockers, but the train station has a left luggage counter with limited opening hours.

THE LAKELAND

What's In A (Watery) Name?

Ten percent of Finland is water. Many of its 187,888 lakes are linked by rivers, and the towns, villages, factories and hydro-electric plants along these lakes and rivers rely on them for drinking water, and as a means of transportation. Finns cross them by boat in summer and snowmobile in winter.

Finnish lakes are shallow – only three are deeper than 100m. This means their waters warm quickly in summer, but it also makes them susceptible to pollution.

Throughout Finland you will often hear the words *järvi* (lake), *saari* (island), *ranta* (shore), *niemi* (cape), *lahti* (bay), *koski* (rapids), *virta* (stream) and *joki* (river). All these words form some of the most common Finnish family names, especially Järvinen, Saarinen, Rantanen, Nieminen, Lahtinen, Koskinen, Virtanen and Jokinen.

Medical & Emergency Services The Central Hospital is south of Savonkatu (road No 14) on Keskussairaalantie. Pharmacies are on Olavinkatu at Nos 40, 41 and 56.

In a general emergency call ☎ 112, for police call ☎ 10022 and for a doctor dial ☎ 10023.

Olavinlinna Castle

Olavinlinna, the principal sight of Savonlinna, is the best preserved medieval castle in the northern countries. Today it is best known as the setting for the month-long Savonlinna Opera Festival (see the section on Special Events).

Founded in 1475 by Erik Axelsson Tott, governor of Vyborg and the Eastern Provinces, Olavinlinna was named after Olof, a 10th century Norwegian Catholic saint. The castle was meant to protect the eastern border of the Swedish empire. However, Russians occupied the castle from 1714 to 1721, and took control of it again from 1743 to the early half of the 20th century. Two museums within the castle have exhibits on its history plus displays of Orthodox treasures.

To see the castle's stunning rooms you have to take a guided tour. Tours depart on the hour from 10 am to 5 pm daily from June to mid-August, and from 10 am to 3 pm at other times of the year. Guides speak English, Swedish, French, German and Italian as well as Finnish. Entry is 20 mk adult, 10 mk child. A motorised floating bridge connecting the castle with the town centre is removed when ships pass.

Provincial Museum & Museum Ships

The provincial museum, in an old Russian warehouse near the castle, has exhibits

Olavinlinna Castle, the setting for the Savonlinna Opera Festival

SAVONLINNA

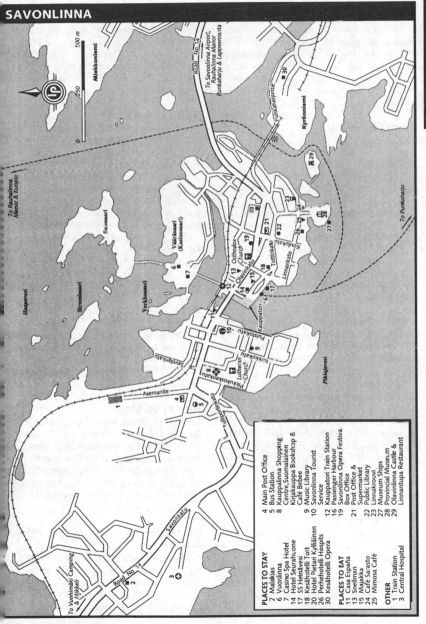

500 m

250

0

Miekkoniemi

To Savonlinna Airport,
Rauhalinna Manor,
Punkaharju & Lappeenranta

Road No 14

30

Punkahaljuntie

Kyrönniemi

To Rauhalinna
Manor & Kuopio

To Punkaharju

29

23

30
21
22
26 25
27 28

Haapavesi

Strennsaari

Suosaari

Vääräsaari
(Kasinosaari)

6
7

Orthodox
Church

Olavinkatu

31
19
18
15
14
17
16

12 13

Tottinkatu

Linnankatu

Koulukatu

Pihlajavesi

11

Puistokatu

Kauppatori

6
10

9

Kirkkokatu

Savonlinna

Lutheran
Church

8

Pikuskoskenkatu

Asemantie

4

Tulppokatu

1

9 5

To Voehimäki Camping
& Mikkeli

Road No 14

2

3

Savonkatu

PLACES TO STAY
2 Malakias
6 Vuorilinna
7 Casino Spa Hotel
14 Hotel Seurahuone
17 SS Heinävesi
18 Kesähotelli Tott
20 Hotel Pietari Kylliäinen
26 Perhehotelli Hospits
30 Kesähotelli Opera

PLACES TO EAT
11 Casa España
13 Snellman
15 Majakka
24 Café Sarasto
25 Mimosa Café

OTHER
1 Train Station
3 Central Hospital
4 Main Post Office
5 Bus Station
8 Kauppalinna Shopping
   Centre,Suomalainen
   Kirjakauppa Bookshop &
   Café Bebee
9 Music Library
10 Savonlinna Tourist
   Service
12 Kauppatori Train Station
16 Passenger Harbour
19 Savonlinna Opera Festiva.
21 Post Office &
   Box Office
22 Supermarket
23 Public Library
   Linnakrouvi
27 Museum Ships
28 Provincial Museum
29 Olavinlinna Castle &
   Linnantupa Restaurant

related to local history. Tethered alongside the museum are the historic ships *Salama*, *Mikko* and *Savonlinna*, all with exhibitions. The museum and ships can all be seen with a single 25 mk ticket. Hours are 10 am to 8 pm daily in July and 11 am to 5 pm daily in August. At other times, hours are 11 am to 5 pm Tuesday to Sunday.

Rauhalinna Villa
This romantic Moorish-style wooden villa was built in 1900 by Nils Weckman, an officer in the Tsar's army, as a wedding anniversary gift for his wife. It features a beautiful wooden lattice trim and has a serene lakeside setting.

These days Rauhalinna houses a restaurant, café and hotel, open in summer only. For a real treat, try the excellent buffet. The cost is 135 mk per person in July, 75 mk per person in June or August.

The villa is at Lehtiniemi, 16km north of Savonlinna. The best way to visit is by boat from Savonlinna passenger harbour (see the Lake Cruises section that follows). Alternatively, there are a few buses from the Savonlinna bus terminal to within half a kilometre of the manor from Monday to Saturday.

Activities
The area around Savonlinna, with its quiet country lanes and gently sloping hills, is terrific for **bicycle touring**. If you'd like to combine cycling with some lake scenery, it's possible, for a small fee, to bring bikes on board local ferries. The tourist office rents bicycles in summer, as does the camping ground. To rent **canoes and rowing boats**, visit the camping ground.

Organised Tours
Lake Cruises In summer, the Savonlinna passenger harbour is one of the busiest in Finland. There are a number of scenic cruises to choose from, with dozens of daily departures during the high season. These include cruises around the castle, to Rauhalinna villa, or through the archipelago. Cruises are typically one to two hours long and cost about 40 mk per person. Additionally, there is a regular ferry service from Savonlinna to Punkaharju and Kuopio (see the Getting There & Away section that follows). Purchase tickets from the tourist office or from the ticket kiosk at the passenger harbour.

Special Events
The Savonlinna Opera Festival is the most famous and popular festival in Finland. It offers four weeks of high-class opera performances with an array of international performers. The setting is the most dramatic location in Finland: the courtyard of Olavinlinna Castle. The festival is from early July to early August; tickets average 400 mk but can be as low as 100 mk.

Tickets for same-night performances are sold after 6 pm from the booth near the bridge. No last-minute discounts are available. The Savonlinna Tourist Office also sells tickets.

In August the castle hosts a beer festival and in September a theatre festival takes place.

For more information and advance ticket purchase see www.operafestival.fi/ or contact the Savonlinna Opera Festival (☎ 476 750, fax 476 7540), Olavinkatu 27, 57130 Savonlinna.

Places to Stay
Savonlinna is notoriously expensive in any season, and prices actually *rise* in summer for the Opera Festival, when beds are scarce. Book accommodation well in advance – at least six months for hotels, slightly less for hostels – if you plan to visit during opera season. The tourist office assists with reserving accommodation.

Places to Stay – Budget & Mid-Range
Camping *Vuohimäki Camping* (☎ 537 353, *myynitpalvelu@lomaliitto.fi*), 7km west of the town centre, has tent sites for 75 mk and cabins for 280 to 420 mk. It's open from late May to mid-August.

Hostels There are no year-round hostels in Savonlinna. However, *Vuorilinna* (☎ 739 5495, fax 272 524, casino.myynti@svlkylpylaitos.fi, Kylpylaitoksentie), an HI-affiliated hostel near the spa hotel on Kasinosaari (Casino Island), is open from June to late August. Beds are from 110 to 170 mk and there is access to all kinds of facilities: kitchen, laundry, sauna, café and restaurant.

The HI-affiliated summer hostel *Malakius* (☎/fax 533 283, casino.myynti@svlkylpylaitos.fi, Pihlajavedenkuja 6), 2km west of the town centre, is open during the Opera Festival only (early July to early August). It has shared rooms from 110 to 170 mk per person. Each room has cooking facilities and two beds, and there is a sauna and laundry here.

Other Accommodation In summer, the cheapest accommodation option is *SS Heinävesi*, a ferry boat. You can sleep here after the last cruise in the evening for 120 to 180 mk per person. The 30 beds are rarely full; however, facilities are basic and the traffic around the harbour is a bit noisy. Inquire at the tourist office for more information.

Places to Stay – Top End
Hotels Hotel prices rise approximately 100 mk during the Opera Festival.

The best of Savonlinna's few hotels is cosy *Perhehotelli Hospits* (☎ 515 661, fax 515 120, Linnankatu 20), near the castle. It has a pleasant garden with access to a small beach. Singles/doubles are from 250/350 mk.

Another good option is the *Casino Spa Hotel* (☎ 73950, fax 272 524, casino.myynti@svlkylpylaitos.fi) on Kasinosaari near the Kauppatori train station. Guests have unlimited access to the pool, sauna and Turkish bath. Rooms are from 450/630 mk, higher during opera season. *Hotel Seurahuone* (☎ 5731, fax 273 918, Kauppatori 4-6) is on the kauppatori, in the heart of town. It has rooms from 460/580 mk.

Also near the kauppatori, *Kesähotelli Tott* (☎ 575 6390, fax 514 504, Satamakatu 1) is open only from early June to late August. Rooms are from 330/440 mk. Some rooms are apartment-style, with kitchens.

Hotel Pietari Kylliäinen (☎ 739 5500, fax 534 873, Olavinkatu 15) is a nondescript hotel with 49 rooms. Rooms are from 280/340 mk.

Open from mid-June to early August, **Kesähotelli Opera** (☎ 521 116 or 476 7515, fax 476 7540, marikki.arponen@operafestival.fi, Kyrönniemenkuja 9) is a 43-bed hotel 1.5km from the town centre. Doubles are 400 mk, or 360 mk with shared facilities.

Places to Eat
Head to the dozen or so stalls at the colourful kauppatori, next to the passenger harbour, to enjoy cheap snacks such as *omena-lörtsy* (apple turnover) and coffee. There are also several *grilli* in the town centre serving fast food or simple meals, and a *supermarket* at Koulukatu 10.

In the Kauppalinna shopping centre, *Café Bebee* is popular with locals for its lunch specials – heavy on the potatoes – from 30 mk.

Majakka, overlooking the harbour, is a family restaurant with a nautical motif. It serves good *kotiruoka* (home-made food) at reasonable prices – from 30 mk for lunch and 35 mk for dinner.

Casa España (Olavinkatu 39) has Spanish and Finnish food, and there are vegetarian options. Lunch specials, from 30 to 48 mk, are served from 11 am to 2 pm weekdays. Dinner is priced a bit higher.

Snellman on Olavinkatu is the town's top restaurant, open summer only.

Near the castle there are a few cafés, including *Mimosa Café* (Linnankatu 12) and *Café Surasto* (Linnankatu 10) which has a pleasant garden.

Inside the castle, *Linnantupa* serves traditional Finnish food for 50 mk, or soup for around 30 mk, until 3 pm.

Entertainment

Majakka restaurant is a popular drinking spot in the evening (see Places to Eat). *Linnakrouvi* near the castle has a beer terrace; the house is old and has heaps of style.

Shopping

At the kauppatori you'll find a lively market with handicrafts and souvenirs on sale. It is open daily in July, and from Monday to Saturday during the rest of the year. There are shops selling Finnish handicrafts at outrageous prices in a row of old wooden houses on Linnankatu near the castle. At No 10, Markun Savipaja sells local pottery and Marja Putus has fine clothes made of wool, linen and silk.

Getting There & Away

Air There are two to three flights a day from Helsinki to Savonlinna, and daily flights from other big cities.

Bus Savonlinna is the major travel hub for the south-eastern Savo bus network. There are several express buses a day from Helsinki to Savonlinna (6 hours), and buses run almost hourly from Mikkeli (1¼ hours).

Train From Helsinki there are daily trains via Parikkala (5 to 6 hours). Train tickets and passes are valid on certain buses from Parikkala.

The main train station is a long walk from the centre, so get off at the Kauppatori station instead.

Car & Motorcycle Savonlinna is 338km north-east of Helsinki, accessible via road Nos 6 or 14.

Boat In summer there is scheduled ferry service from the Savonlinna passenger harbour to Punkaharju and to Kuopio. The SS *Heinävesi* travels to the Retretti jetty in Punkaharju daily from mid-June to mid-August. It departs from Savonlinna at 11 am and from Punkaharju at 3.40 pm. The two-hour trip costs 85/130 mk one-way/return

for adults, 40/60 mk for children. The on-board buffet costs 70 mk.

Two ferries, the MS *Kuopio* and the MS *Puijo*, travel on the Savonlinna-Kuopio route from mid-June to mid-August. There are departures from both cities at 9.30 am Tuesday to Sunday. The trip takes just under 12 hours and costs 250 mk one way (125 mk child). Meals costs 70 mk – so consider bringing your own food! Accommodation on board is available for 120 to 180 mk per person.

For information on scenic cruises from Savonlinna, see the earlier Lake Cruises section.

Getting Around

To/From the Airport The Savonlinna airport is 15km north-east of the centre. An airport shuttle bus meets arriving flights; in town it picks up at the bus station and Hotel Seurahuone. The 20-minute trip costs 35 mk one way.

Bus The city bus service costs 11 mk per ride within the Savonlinna area.

Car & Motorcycle Several car rental agencies have offices in the centre and at the airport, including Europcar (☎ 520 605) and Budget (☎ 514 320 or 514 321).

AROUND SAVONLINNA

The area around Savonlinna, with its scenic islands, peninsulas, bays and straits, is the most beautiful part of the Lakeland.

Punkaharju

• pop 4500   ☎ 015

Between Savonlinna and Parikkala is Punkaharju, the famous pine-covered sand esker (sand or gravel ridge) that is one of the most overrated attractions in Finland. The village of Punkaharju has a tourist office, post office, bus and train stations, and several shops.

Punkaharju Ridge During the Ice Age, formations similar to this 7km-long sand ridge were created all over the country. Because the Punkaharju ridge crosses a

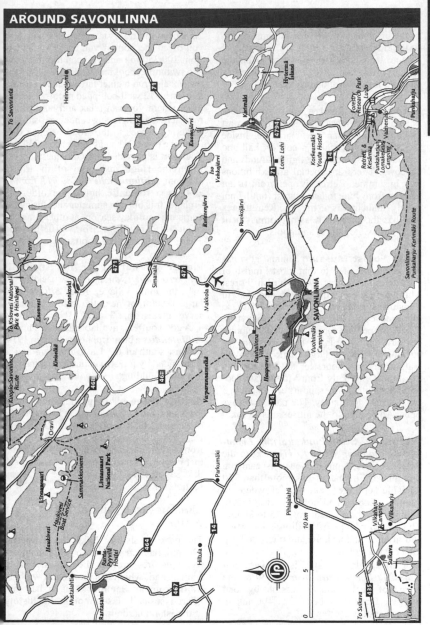

AROUND SAVONLINNA

large lake, it has always been an important travelling route. Just a few hundred metres of the original unsealed road along the top of the ridge remain – this was once part of a route to Russia. To take a stroll on the famous Punkaharju Ridge, get off at the Retretti train station and walk east.

Retretti Art Centre An unusual but popular tourist attraction, Retretti is an art exhibition inside an artificial cave. Inside the cave are waterfalls, a concert hall and special effects, including lights, sounds and shadows. There are special art exhibitions here in summer. Retretti is open from 10 am to 6 pm from June to late August (until 7 pm in July) and entry is 65 mk. The Retretti area also has the popular **Kesämaa amusement park**, with water slides and pools.

Lusto Forest Museum Finland now has a museum devoted to that most Finnish of industries, forestry. The Finnish Forest Museum is actually quite good, and close to Punkaharju ridge and the Retretti centre, so all three could be visited on a day trip. Wood, timber and forestry-related technology are on display. The museum is surrounded by a large park area with walking tracks. Hours for the museum are 10 am to 6 pm daily from May to late September. At other times, hours are 10 am to 5 pm Tuesday to Sunday. The park is always open. Admission to the museum is 35 mk.

Places to Stay *Punkaharjun Loma-keskus Camping* (☎ 739 611), next to the Retretti centre, is one of the largest camping grounds in Finland. It has more than 150 lakeside cottages and is crowded in summer. Cabins and cottages cost 175 to 580 mk. Pitching a tent costs 75 to 85 mk. There's every type of facility and sporting activity imaginable here, and plenty to keep kids busy as well.

A cheap place to stay is *Punkaharjun Kurssi ja Leirikeskus* (☎ 644 189) on the island of Vaahersalo (accessible by road bridge). Dormitory beds cost 100 mk in summer, but it is often full.

In the village proper, *Gasthaus* (☎ 441 371, Palomäentie 18) is a clean guesthouse 2km from the train station (buses will drop you off at the door if you ask). Rooms are from 200/350 mk and you can use the sauna and swimming pool for an additional fee. The owners also run a quiet farm estate, *Naaranlahti*, with 12 well-equipped rooms. This is a place where you can relax and take part in rural activities, including canoeing, fishing or gathering berries in the woods. Canoe trips (with the owner's son as guide) cost 230 mk. Transport is provided from the guesthouse.

On the ridge just west of the Lusto museum, *Valtionhotelli* (☎ 739 611, fax 441 784) is a romantic hotel, the oldest in Finland. It is open in summer and during the Christmas holiday season, at other times on request. Rooms are from 310/460 mk. There are also two-bed cottages.

Places to Eat At the bus station is *Punkero Baari*, which serves snacks.

In the main village, go to *Siltavahti*, a large restaurant near the train station. It serves meals from 35 mk.

A good buffet is available daily in summer at *Finlandia*, a beautiful house built in 1914. It's just south of the Lusto museum and is surrounded by forest; a geriatric hospital is in the same building.

Getting There & Away All trains between Parikkala and Savonlinna stop in the village of Punkaharju, as well as the Lusto and Retretti train stations. There are also buses from Savonlinna and Parikkala. In summer there is ferry service from Savonlinna; see the Savonlinna Getting There & Away section for more information.

Linnansaari National Park
☎ 015

The park consists of Lake Haukivesi and 130 uninhabited islands, but the main activity centres around the largest island, Linnansaari, which has three short **walking trails** from its Sammakkoniemi harbour. There is a small **museum of natural history** at the island harbour.

Rare birds, including osprey, can be seen and heard in the park. Lurking in the park's waters is a population of the rare Saimaa ringed seal.

The village of Rantasalmi, on the west side, is the main gateway to the park. On the lake's east shore is Oravi village, a smaller jumping-off point.

The best way to see the park is to pack camping gear and food, then rent a rowing boat in Rantasalmi or Oravi and spend a few days exploring on your own.

Information The Lakeland Centre (Järviluonnonkeskus; ☎ 737 1552) in Rantasalmi is the main information centre. It also has exhibits relating to the natural history of the area. It is open daily in summer, and from Monday to Friday at other times of the year.

Places to Stay & Eat In Rantasalmi, the HI hostel *Ranta-Pyyvilä (☎ 440 124, Pyyviläntie 240)* gets mixed reports. Its lakeside location is 4km east of the village just outside the national park boundaries. The hostel is open year-round, with dormitory beds from 75 to 85 mk.

On the island you can stay at the established *camping grounds* for free, or reserve a bed in a *cottage* (call ☎ 0500-275 458 for bookings). You can rent the sauna for a fee. A canteen at Sammakkoniemi harbour sells provisions.

Several smaller islands also have designated camping sites.

Getting There & Away The main entrance to Linnansaari National Park is Mustalahti quay, but there is not a bus stop, only boat conections.

Bus There are regular buses to Oravi and Rantasalmi from Savonlinna. From Rantasalmi, it's an extra 3km to Mustalahti quay – hitch, walk, or catch a taxi.

Boat There is regular boat service to Linnansaari Island from Mustalahti quay in Rantasalmi and from Oravi.

Kolovesi National Park
☎ 015

This fine national park was founded in 1990 and covers several islands which feature unusually well preserved pine forests. There are high hills, rocky cliffs and caves, and even prehistoric paintings on rocks. The rare Saimaa marble seals live in the park's waters.

Motor-powered boats are prohibited in the park. A rowing boat is practically the only way to see the fantastic scenery, and groups get to travel in an old *kirkkovene* or 'church longboat' with up to 10 pairs of oars. A guide is an unavoidable expense if you want to find the best places.

Kolovesi Retkeily (☎ 673 628) is the main tour operator for the park. It also rents boats and canoes, as well as cottages in the park area. To get to the Kolovesi office, drive north from Savonlinna towards Heinävesi on road No 471 and look out for the sign 'Kolovesi Retkeily' after Enonkoski village.

Inside the national park there are just two *camping grounds*, one at Lohilahti near the southern access road No 471, and the other on the island of Pitkäsaari.

Kerimäki
• pop 6500   ☎ 015

The first thing that strikes you in Kerimäki is the huge church. Kerimäki is a small place, yet it has the largest wooden church in the world. The small tourist information booth next to the church sells souvenirs, but information about the church and town is always free. The info booth is open daily in summer.

Kerimäki Church Dominating the entire village, this wooden church was built in 1847 to seat 3300 people. The church's size was not a mistake (one version says 'feet' on the plan were read as 'metres') but was quite deliberately inflated from original plans when built by overexcited locals. Worshippers would come to the church from across the lake in their *kirkkovene* longboats. For 10 mk, you can climb the *tapuli* (bell tower). The church is open from 9 am to 8 pm daily (until 6 pm Saturday) from June to mid-August.

Hytermä This protected island celebrates one of the weirdest of human achievements: it has a monument to Romu-Heikki (Junk Heikki), a man who built large structures with millstones. The island is also quite beautiful, so you should try to visit it, perhaps by hiring a rowing boat in the village.

Places to Stay *Loma Lohi* (☎ 541 771), 7km from Kerimäki going towards Savonlinna, is worth checking out. This popular, down-to-earth camping ground has tent sites for 65 mk and a few cottages.

In the village of Kerimäki, *Gasthaus Kerihovi* (☎ 541 225, Puruvendentie 28) is an attractive old wooden house with rooms from 160/200 mk. Meals are available.

The best value in Kerimäki is the HI-affiliated *Korkeamäki Hostel* (☎ 544 827, Ruokolahdentie 545), 8km south of Kerimäki village on the road to Punkaharju. This quiet farmhouse, run by a friendly Savonian couple, provides accommodation from June to late August in three old houses. Rates are from 65 to 125 mk per person.

Getting There & Away There are hourly buses along route 71 between Savonlinna and Kerimäki.

Sulkava

- pop 3800   ☎ 015

Scenic Sulkava is known for its rowing-boat competitions – it's water sports that count here. The village of Sulkava is a sleepy litle place, with many attractive wooden houses around the small commercial centre near the bridge.

Church The church was built in 1822 and has an attractive interior. It is open daily in summer. The bell tower dates from 1770.

Vilkaharju Ridge This protected ridge along road No 438 has two *luontopolku* (nature trails), 3km and 3.6km long, and marked by yellow ribbons. On Lake Pöllälampi you can rent boats and purchase fishing permits to fish for salmon.

Linnavuori Fortress Ruins This prehistoric fortress is probably the most interesting sight in the Sulkava area. It's well signposted. The view from the top is of ideal lakeland scenery and old fortifications. At the bottom, there's a covered barbecue area.

Places to Stay In the Vilkaharju area 7km from the village, *Vilkaharju Camping* (☎ 471 223) is located on a scenic headland across a pedestrian bridge (road access is possible). There are tent sites for 70 mk and cottages for 150 to 230 mk.

Partalansaaren Lomakoti (☎ 478 850, Hirviniementie 5) is an HI-affiliated hostel not far from the Sarsuinmäki WWII battery site. Dormitory beds cost 75 mk, and there are also cottages. Facilities include a sauna, meals, and bicycles and boats for hire.

The best value restaurant is *Ravintola Alanne* at the village harbour, 500m from the bus terminal. There are *supermarket* near the bus terminal.

Getting There & Away There are regular buses to Sulkava from Savonlinna, 39km away.

Tampere

- pop 186,000   ☎ 03

The proud city of Tampere is Finland's third largest. It is the largest Nordic city without access to the sea.

Long known for its textile industries, Tampere has often been called 'the Manchester of Finland'. Dozens of tall red-brick chimneys from 19th century textile factories point skyward in the centre.

Tampere is one of the most visited cities in Finland due to good transport connections and plenty of attractions. One of the most popular with foreign visitors is the Lenin Museum. Särkänniemi, just north of the centre, is one of Finland's most popular amusement parks.

Tampere also boasts two universities, a national television station (TV2) and some interesting architecture.

History

In the Middle Ages, the area around Tampere was inhabited by the notorious Pirkka tribe who collected taxes as far north as Lapland. At that time, the 'town' consisted of a number of Swedish-run estates around the forests and the two lakes that surround Tampere. Modern Tampere was founded in 1779 during the reign of Gustav III of Sweden.

In the 19th century, the Tampere Rapids Swedish: Tammerfors), or Tammerkoski Rapids, which today supply abundant hydroelectric power, were a magnet for textile industries. Finnish and foreign investors flocked to the busy town, including the Scottish industrialist James Finlayson, who arrived here in 1820.

The Russian Revolution in 1917 increased interest in socialism amongst Tampere's large working-class population. It became the capital of the 'Reds' during the Civil War that followed Finnish independence.

Orientation

Tampere is set between Näsijärvi and Pyhäjärvi lakes, which are connected by the Tammerkoski Rapids. Hämeenkatu, the main street, runs west from the train station through the heart of the city.

Information

Tourist Offices The Tampere City Tourist Office (☎ 3146 6800, fax 3146 6463, touristbureau@tampere.fi) is at Verkatehtaankatu 2. From June to late August it's open from 8.30 am to 8 pm Monday to Friday, 8.30 am to 6 pm Saturday and 11 am to 6 pm Sunday. At other times it's open from 8.30 am to 5 pm Monday to Friday. Drop by to pick up the useful, free guide *This is Tampere & Sur-*

roundings, with information on accommodation, restaurants and attractions in the Tampere area. The office's hotel booking hotline (☎ 342 5700, fax 342 5736) is open from 8.30 am to 4.30 pm Monday to Friday.

The international youth centre Vuoltsu, at Vuolteenkatu 13, provides tourist information and free luggage storage. It is open daily from late June to September.

Money Forex currency exchange office at Hämeenkatu 1 is open from 9 am to 7 pm Monday to Friday and 9 am to 5 pm Saturday year-round, with additional hours 10 am to 4 pm Sunday in summer.

Post The main post office at Rautatienkatu 21, 33100 Tampere, near the train station, is open from 9 am to 7 pm Monday to Friday, 10 am to 2 pm Saturday and noon to 5 pm Sunday.

Internet Resources & Library The Tampere City Library at Pirkankatu 2 – called 'Metso' (Wood Grouse) by locals because of its unusual organic architecture – is open from 9.30 am to 8 pm Monday to Friday, 9.30 am to 3 pm Saturday and noon to 6 pm Sunday during most seasons. In summer, it is closed on Sunday and has shorter hours. It has three Internet terminals.

The Newspaper Reading Room at Puutarhankatu 1, by the river, has some magazines and newspapers in English. Opening hours are similar to those of the public library.

Nettikahvila Vuoltsu (nettikahvila@info1.info.tampere.fi), adjacent to the Vuoltsu youth centre, is an Internet café open from noon to 6 pm Monday to Friday.

The main Web site for Tampere is www.tampere.fi/.

Travel Agencies The student travel agency Kilroy Travel (☎ 223 0995) at Tuomiokirkonkatu 36 is open from 10 am to 6 pm Monday to Friday and 10 am to 2 pm Saturday.

TAMPERE

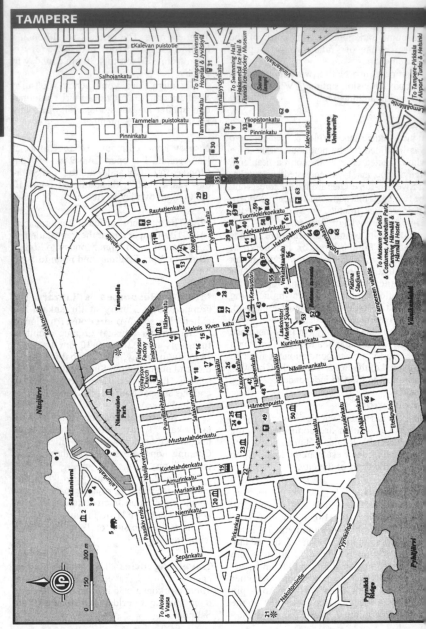

TAMPERE

PLACES TO STAY
11   Hostel Tampere YWCA
13   Sokos Hotel Tammer
22   Hostel Uimahallin Maja
30   Hotelli Victoria
33   Ramada Hotel Tampere
36   Scandic Hotel Tampere
60   Iltatähti

PLACES TO EAT
12   Ohveli Kahvila
14   Panimoravintola Plevna
15   Aleksin
16   Tira-mi-su
17   Anttila
18   Ohranjyvä
32   Attila House
39   Café Leivonpesä
40   Linkosuo
41   Punjab Tandoor
44   Keskustori Market & Local
       Buses
45   Hesburger
46   Kauppahalli
47   Tây-Dô
48   Thai Non Khon
51   Strøget

53   Laukontori Market
56   Koskikeskus Shopping Centre
       & Bio Bio Cinema
59   Salud
61   Donatello
66   Klingendahl

OTHER
1   Särkänniemi Amusement Park
2   Sara Hildén Art Museum
3   Aquarium & Planetarium
4   Näsinneula Observation Tower
       & Revolving Restaurant
5   Children's Zoo & Dolphinarium
6   Mustalahati Quay
7   Häme Museum
8   Central Workers' Museum
9   Bike Rentals (Keskuspyörä)
10   Tampere Cathedral
19   Pyynikki Swimming Hall
20   Amuri Museum of Workers'
       Housing
21   Old Observation Tower
23   Hiekka Art Museum
24   Tampere City Library
25   Moominvalley Museum &
       Mineral Museum

26   Student House
27   Old Wooden Church
28   Newspaper Reading Room
29   Main Post Office
31   Salhojankadun Pub
34   Tulliklubi
35   Train Station & R-Kioski
37   Forex (Currency Exchange)
38   Bookshop (Akateeminen
       Kirjakauppa)
42   Vanha Posti & Henry's Pub
43   Liikennelaitos- Bus Station
       Ticket Office
49   Aleksanteri Church
50   Lenin Museum
52   Laukontori Quay
54   Kehräsaari
55   Verkaranta Arts and Crafts
       Centre
57   Tampere City Tourist
       Office
58   Kilroy Travels
62   Tampere Hall
63   Orthodox Church
64   Vuoltsu Youth Centre &
       Nettikahvila Vuoltsu
65   Bus Station

Bookshops Akateeminen Kirjakauppa at Tuomiokirkonkatu 28 has an extensive selection of English-language fiction and non-fiction.

The R-Kioski at the train station sells foreign newspapers and magazines.

Left Luggage The train station has lockers for 10 mk and 15 mk per day, depending on size, that may be used for a maximum of seven days. It also has a left-luggage counter. Lockers at the bus station cost 10 mk and may be used for a maximum of 24 hours. Vuoltsu (see Tourist Offices above) offers free luggage storage for young travellers.

Medical & Emergency Services
Tampere University Hospital (☎ 247 5111), 2km east of the train station, deals with medical emergencies. There are pharmacies on Hämeenkatu at Nos 14, 16 and 31. Call ☎ 100 176 for 24 hour pharmacy service.

In a general emergency call ☎ 112, for police call ☎ 10022 and for a doctor dial ☎ 10023.

Särkänniemi Amusement Park
The Särkänniemi amusement park (☎ 248 8111, www.sarkaniemi.fi) just north of the city centre is *enormously* popular with Finnish families. A day pass good for all sights and unlimited rides costs 130 mk (a pass for rides only costs 90 mk adult, 65 mk child). Alternatively, you can pay admission for each attraction separately as you go along – they range in price from 15 to 30 mk. The park is open generally from 10 am to 8 pm from mid-May to mid-August. To get to Särkänniemi quickly, take bus No 4 from the train station.

Inside the amusement park are 30 **carnival rides**, plus cafés and restaurants. The **aquarium** is the largest in Finland, with 200 species of sea creatures. The **children's zoo**, with gentle domestic animals, and a planetarium, with daily shows, are nearby. The planetarium is open year-round.

The **Dolphinarium** – Finland's only dolphin show – is also open year-round. There are one to five dolphin shows in summer and an entertaining dolphin training show (in Finnish) daily at other times.

At 124m, **Näsinneula Observation Tower** is the tallest in Finland and has a revolving restaurant at the top (see the Places to Eat section). The tower is open from noon to midnight daily.

Lenin Museum

The Lenin Museum, at Hämeenpuisto 28, is the city's most fascinating attraction and is packed with relics from the life of the Russian revolutionary. Since 1946, the museum has been maintained by the Finnish-Soviet Friendship Society, which still runs the place. There's an equally fascinating gift shop.

Lenin lived in Finland from November 1905 to December 1907, and the museum displays the couch that he slept on in the Helsinki Library. The building itself is where Lenin convened Russian revolutionaries in 1905 and 1906. See also www.tamper.fi/culture/lenin/.

Hours are 9 am to 5 pm Monday to Friday and 11 am to 4 pm Saturday and Sunday. Admission is 15 mk adult, 5 mk student or child.

Moominvalley Museum

Tove Jansson, the Finnish artist and writer, created her Moomin figures decades ago, but the popularity of the funny cartoon figures never seems to wane – at least not in Finland! The museum, in the public library building at Hämeenpuisto 20, contains original drawings by Ms Jansson, plus models, computer displays, toys and other memorabilia. There's also a gift shop. Hours are 9 am to 5 pm weekdays and 10 am to 6 pm weekends in summer, closed Monday at other times. Admission is 15 mk adult, 5 mk student or child.

Adjacent is the small **Mineral Museum** (Kivimuseo), a museum devoted to rare stones and fossils. Hours and admission fees are the same as for Moominvalley.

Sara Hildén Art Museum

The museum on the shore of Lake Näsijärvi contains a collection of international and Finnish modern art and sculpture amassed by Sara Hildén, a local business person and art collector. The concrete building was designed by Pekka Ilveskoski and was opened in 1979. There are good views from the café, which has Alvar Aalto furniture. The museum is open from 11 am to 6 pm daily, and entry is 20 mk. Bus No 4 or 16 will take you to the museum.

Hiekka Art Museum

The Hiekka museum (☎ 212 3975), at Pirkankatu 6, contains the collection of Kustaa Hiekka, a wealthy industrialist. There are paintings, furniture and fine old gold and silver items in the impressive building. Hours are 3 to 6 pm Wednesday and Thursday, noon to 3 pm Sunday and by prior arrangement. Admission is 20 mk.

Central Workers' Museum

The Central Workers' Museum (Työväen Keskusmuseo), at Kuninkaankatu 3, is dedicated to revolutionary aspects of the workers' movement. It is open from 11 am to 6 pm Tuesday to Sunday. Entry is 15 mk. The museum is in the old **Finlayson Factory**, a massive red-brick building that was once a textile mill. This was the first building in northern Europe to have electric lighting, which was installed on 15 March 1882.

Amuri Museum of Workers' Housing

The Amurin Työläismuseokortteli, at Makasiinikatu 12, preserves an entire block of 19th century wooden houses, including 32 apartments, a bakery, a shoemaker, two general shops and a café. It is the most realistic home museum in Finland – many homes look as if the tenant had left just moments ago to go shopping. The museum is open from 9 am to 5 pm Tuesday to

Friday and 11 am to 6 pm Saturday and Sunday from mid-May to mid-September. Entry is 15 mk.

Finnish Ice Hockey Museum

The largest ice hockey museum in Europe is east of the centre at Hakametsä Ice Hall. It has photos, trophies, pucks, jerseys and other hockey memorabilia. Museum hours are 5 to 6.30 pm Thursday, 3 to 6 pm Saturday and 2 to 4 pm Sunday in winter, or by appointment (☎ 212 4200). Entry is 10 mk. Take bus No 25.

Häme Museum

The 'Castle of Näsi' (Näsilinna) in Näsinpuisto Park houses this museum of local history, with exhibitions covering medieval times to the 19th century. A traditional farmhouse, called a *savupirtti* (literally 'smoke cottage') was transferred here during the 1910s and is a good example of how people used to live without modern conveniences such as chimneys and flush toilets. The museum is open from 10 am to 6 pm Tuesday to Sunday. Entry is 15 mk.

Museum of Dolls & Costumes

The fascinating doll and costume museum, at Hatanpää Manor south of the city, has more than 4000 dolls. The oldest and rarest of these date from the 12th century. Museum hours are 10 am to 5 pm Tuesday to Saturday, noon to 5 pm Sunday from May to August. At other times, hours are noon to 5 pm Tuesday to Sunday. Entry is 30 mk.

The old manor house is surrounded by the large Arboretum Park with about 350 species of flora. Bus No 21 runs from the city centre to Hatanpää.

Churches

Old Church The landmark old wooden church just north of Keskustori Square has occasional gospel concerts on Saturday evenings. It's open daily in summer.

Tampere Cathedral The cathedral on Tuomiokirkonkatu is one of the most notable examples of National Romantic architecture in Finland. It was designed by Lars Sonck and was finished in 1907. Inside are the weird frescos of Hugo Simberg. Hours are from 10 am to 6 pm daily.

Orthodox Church The small but ornate, onion-domed Orthodox church is near the train station. It's open from 9.30 am to 3 pm Monday to Friday from May to August.

Aleksanteri Church There is nice woodwork in this landmark church at the western end of Hämeenkatu. It's open daily, year-round.

Activities

Cycling Keskuspyörä (☎ 212 4074), at Lapintie 6, rents out bicycles by the day or by the week.

Swimming The indoor *uimahalli* (swimming pool), at Joukahaisenkatu 7, is open 6 am to 7.45 pm weekdays and 10 am to 4.45 pm on weekends. It is closed on Tuesday mornings.

The older Pyynikki swimming hall, at Kortelahdenkatu 26 adjacent to Hostel Uimahallin Maja, is closed in summer and on Wednesday and Sunday.

At both, the fee is 18 mk adult, 10 mk child.

Fishing To fish in the Tammerkoski Rapids in the town centre, you will need a daily or weekly permit, available from the tourist office.

Boating You can rent rowing boats and canoes from Camping Härmälä (see the following Places to Stay section).

Hiking Pyynikki Ridge offers nice views of both lakes, and the surrounding pine forests stretch to the suburb of Pispala. There's an old observation tower on the ridge, open from 9 am to 8 pm daily. Entry is 3 mk. You can also take westbound bus No 15 to its terminus and walk back from there along the ridge.

Organised Tours

Lake Cruises Lake cruises on Tampere's two beautiful lakes are popular in summer and there are many options.

Two-hour cruises around Lake Näsijärvi on the MS *Finlandia Queen* (☎ 212 1565), a paddle-steamer, depart from Mustalahti quay at noon, 2 pm and 4 pm daily from mid-June to mid-August and cost 55 mk per adult/25 mk per child.

Tammerlines Cruises (☎ 214 1078) offers short cruises on Lake Pyhäjärvi from mid-June to mid-August, with departures from the Laukontori quay on Monday, Friday and Saturday. Tickets for the 1½ hour cruise cost 35/10 mk, and tickets for the 3½ hour cruise cost 60/20 mk.

Tammerlines Cruises also has shuttle service to nearby **Viikinsaari Island**, a pleasant picnic spot, from Tuesday to Sunday in summer. Departures from Laukontori quay are every hour on the hour and the trip costs 22 mk adult, 17 mk senior, 10 mk child.

The SS *Tarjanne* (☎ 212 4804), a steam ship, departs from Mustalahti quay for eight-hour excursions on Lake Näsijärvi three times a week in summer. The route, from Tampere to Ruovesi and Virrat, is known as the **Poet's Way**. It is one of the finest lake cruises in Finland. A one-way ticket costs 167 mk to Ruovesi, 226 mk to Virrat. For 100 mk per person, you can sleep in this old boat before or after your trip. The boat transports bicycles for about 30 mk.

For information about cruises with Finnish Silverline between Tampere and Hämeenlinna see the Getting There & Away section that follows.

Special Events

There are festivals and annual events in Tampere almost year-round. Usually held in March, the Tampere Film Festival is a respected international festival of short films. The Tampere Biennale is a festival of new Finnish music, held in the spring of even-numbered years only. The Pispala Schottishce, an international folk-dance festival, takes place in early June. In July, Pirkan Soutu is a widely attended rowing competition. The Tampere International Theatre Festival, held during a week in mid-August, is a showcase of international and Finnish theatre. Most works are in Finnish. October brings the Tampere Jazz Happening.

Places to Stay

Camping *Camping Härmälä* (☎ 265 1355, myyntipalvelua@lomaliitto.fi, Leirintäkatu 8) is 5km south of the city centre (take bus No 1). Tent sites cost 77 mk per night, cabins from 130 to 300 mk. It is open from mid-May to late August.

Hostels The clean *Hostel Tampere YWCA* (☎ 254 4020, fax 254 4022, Tuomiokirkonkatu 12A), open from June to mid-September, is affiliated with HI and charges 70 to 140 mk per bed. There is a kitchen here.

The HI-affiliated *Domus Summer Hotel* (☎ 255 0000, hermica@pp.tpo.fi) will move from Pellervonkatu to a new location in summer 1999. Beds start at about 150 mk. The city tourist office can provide more information.

Hostel Uimahallin Maja (☎ 222 9460, fax 222 9940, aris@sci.fi, Pirkankatu 10-12) also HI-affiliated, is Tampere's only year-round hostel but is overpriced and very poorly kept. Despite this, it's often fully booked by Finnish student groups. Beds cost 95 to 190 mk.

Adjacent to the camping ground of the same name, the HI-affiliated *Härmälä Hostel* is open from June to late August. Beds cost 130 to 170 mk, and there is kitchen, laundry and sauna.

Guesthouse Convenient to the train station, *Iltatähti* (☎ 222 0092, Rautatienkatu 18) has singles/doubles from 150/220 mk. Sheets are extra.

Hotels There are many fine hotels in the city centre. The modern *Hotelli Victori* (☎ 242 5111, fax 242 5100, Itsenäisyydenkatu 1) near the train station offers rooms for 340/400 mk in summer, 410/480 mk at other times.

Scandic Hotel Tampere (☎ *244 6111, fax 222 1910, Hämeenkatu 1*) has rooms for 430/480 mk in summer and 600/720 mk at other times. It's just opposite the train station.

One of the oldest hotels in Tampere, *Sokos Hotel Tammer* (☎ *262 6265, fax 262 6266, Satakunnankatu 13*) charges 410 mk for all rooms on weekends and in summer. At other times rooms cost 470/590 mk.

Ramada Hotel Tampere (☎ *245 5111, fax 245 5100, Yliopistonkatu 44*) has excellent facilities, including a fine sauna. Rooms cost 395/470 mk in summer and 720/865 mk at other times.

Places to Eat

The scary-looking Tampere speciality, *mustamakkara*, a thick black sausage made with cow's blood, can be had at any of the city's several markets. Locals think mustamakkara tastes best with milk and cranberry jam

Finnish The most enjoyable place to eat in Tampere is *Panimoravintola Plevna (Itäinenkatu 8)*, on a small street extending north from Satakunnakatu. It's a brewery pub and restaurant in the old Finlayson textile mill. Wash down a plate of bratwurst (35 mk) or other hearty fare with a pint of Plevna's award-winning stout.

Ohranjyvä (Näsilinnankatu 15) serves good home-made lunches on weekdays, for 35 mk.

Klingendahl (Hämeen puisto 44), southwest of the centre, is open for lunch only; the extensive buffet is 26 to 40 mk.

Näsinneula (☎ *248 8212*) is the revolving restaurant atop the observation tower at Särkänniemi amusement park. It serves gourmet Finnish cuisine.

International *Thai Non Khon (Hämeenkatu 29)* and *Tây-Dô*, a Vietnamese restaurant across the street, offer good vegetarian dishes. Tây-Dô is a very basic place, while the Thai restaurant is more upmarket.

Donatello (Aleksanterinkatu 37) sets out a lavish all-you-can-eat pizza and pasta buffet (39 mk) from 10.30 am to 3 pm on weekdays.

Punjab Tandoor (Verkatehtaankatu 5) is an attractive restaurant serving good Indian food, including many vegetarian options, priced from 45 to 50 mk. The vegetarian thali is 75 mk. Lunch specials, served from 10.30 am to 3 pm weekdays, are good value.

Salud (☎ *223 5996, Tuomiokirkonkatu 19*) is a long-running favourite for gourmet Spanish food. The signature dish is 'coyote casserole' – made with pork, chicken and alligator, but not coyote! The salad buffet is terrific.

Aleksin (☎ *272 0241*) on Puutarhakatu is a classy Russian restaurant with authentic cuisine from 60 mk.

Cafés There are dozens of cafés on Hämeenkatu, including *Café Leivonpesä* (Lark's Den) next door to the bookshop. It has sunny outdoor tables in summer.

Linkosuo (Hämeenkatu 9) is a traditional bakery with sandwiches and such for 15 to 20 mk, plus superb sweets.

Tira-mi-su on Kuninkaankatu is a cute little café with fresh breads and pastries.

Ohveli Kahvila (Ojakatu 4) is a quaint place in a well-to-do neighbourhood.

Fast Food The *Koskikeskus Shopping Centre*, on Hatanpään Valtatie just south of the tourist office, is good for fast food – it has pizza, kebab, taco and hamburger outlets.

Hesburger, the booming chain with tasty burgers, is on Hämeenkatu opposite the kauppahalli.

Strøget (Laukontori 10) is a tiny place serving excellent Danish open sandwiches, burgers, and American-style tuna and club sandwiches, priced from 20 to 40 mk. Food can be packaged to go.

University Eateries The Tampere University student cafeteria at *Attila House* just north of the main campus on Yliopistonkatu is a good place to eat with and talk to local students. Substantial meals can be had for less than 25 mk. Coffee and snacks are also inexpensive.

Self-Catering *Anttila* is a large supermarket and department store on Puutarhakatu. It is closed Sunday. The cheapest food stores in Tampere are the numerous *Vikkula* shops, which have a *tarjous* (special price) on almost everything.

Markets From Monday to Saturday, visit the *kauppahalli* (indoor market) at Hämeenkatu 19 for fresh produce and quick, cheap meals.

The *Laukontori market* is a produce and fish market at Laukontori, also called *alaranta* (lower lakeside). It's open until about 2 pm from Monday to Saturday.

Keskustori, the central market, is busy only on the first Monday of each month, and on weekday evenings in summer.

Entertainment

Bars *Salhojankadun Pub*, on Salhojankatu east of the train station, has Guinness on tap and has been beloved by Finnish Anglophiles since 1969.

Panimoravintola Plevna (see Places to Eat) has award-winning brews, including a stout named 'best beer in Europe' in 1998.

There are many bars on Hämeenkatu, including *Vanha Posti (Hämeenkatu 13A)*, which serves beer from the local PUP brewery. On the basement level in the same building, *Henry's Pub* has country & western and rock acts.

Clubs & Live Music Tampere is a centre for the performing arts – check the current program at the tourist office.

Tampere Hall (☎ 243 4500) has classical concerts by the Tampere City Orchestra on Friday, except in summer; tickets are available on the spot. Take bus No 5, 13, 22 or 24 to the concert hall.

Tulliklubi near the train station is popular for its nightly rock concerts, and rock or blues concerts are frequently held in the *Student House* (Ylioppilastalo) at Kauppakatu 10.

For dancing, locals flock to the chic nightclubs of the city's large hotels. The Russian restaurant *Aleksin* has dancing to live music on weekends. Cover charge is 30 mk.

Cinema There are several cinemas around the city, including *Bio Bio* at the Koskikeskus shopping centre. Films are usually recent American releases subtitled in Swedish and Finnish.

Spectator Sports Tampere has two ice hockey teams in the national league. The *Hakametsä Ice Hall* is the venue for matches on Thursday and Sunday from September to March. Take eastbound bus No 25.

Football (soccer) is played in summer at *Ratina stadium*.

Shopping

Kehräsaari, a converted brick factory building just east of the Laukontori market square, is your one-stop souvenir shopping centre, with many boutiques selling authentic Finnish glassware, handicrafts, knitted clothing and T-shirts.

The Verkaranta Arts and Crafts Centre Verkatehtaankatu 2, a smaller former factory building near the tourist office, exhibits and sells beautiful textiles and handicrafts.

Anttila (see the earlier Places to Eat section) has a music department with a good selection of Finnish CDs, both traditional and pop.

The gift shop at the Lenin Museum sells McLenin T-shirts and the Lenin Museum's own label of coffee.

Getting There & Away

Air You can fly to Tampere direct from Stockholm; all other international flights are via Helsinki. There are several daily Finnair flights to Tampere from Helsinki and other major Finnish cities.

Bus The station is at Hatanpäänvaltatie 7 about 500m south of the tourist office. There are several express buses daily to Helsinki (4½ hours) and Turku (2½ 3 hours).

Regional buses are most conveniently taken from Keskustori (central square).

Train The train station is at the city centre. There are hourly trains from Helsinki (. hours) during the day and several trains a day from Turku (2 hours), Jyväskylä (1½ hours), Pori (2 hours) and Oulu (5 to 7 hours).

Car & Motorcycle Tampere is on road No 3, 174km north-west of Helsinki. From Tampere it's 155km to Turku, 275km to Lappeenranta, 355km to Savonlinna and 712km to Rovaniemi.

Boat Suomen Hopealinja (Finnish Silverline; ☎ 212 4804) cruises on Lake Pyhäjärvi to Hämeenlinna from the Laukontori quay in Tampere daily from June to mid-August. The eight-hour trip costs 202 mk per person one way.

There is also the 'Poet's Way' cruise that goes to the nearby villages of Ruovesi and Virrat; see the earlier Lake Cruises section for information.

Hitching To reach Helsinki or Turku, try hitchhiking from the Viinikka roundabout near the university campus. For Jyväskylä or Lahti, walk east 2km to the hospital.

Getting Around

To/From the Airport The Tampere-Pirkkala airport is 15km south-west of the city centre. Each arriving flight is met by a bus to Tampere. Bus No 61 to the airport stops at Pyynikintori and several points in the city centre. The trip takes from 30 to 45 minutes and costs 15 mk one way.

There are also shared taxis (☎ 10041) that cost 50 mk per person.

Bus The city transport and ticket office is Liikennelaitos at Keskustori 5A. Local bus service is extensive and a one-hour ticket costs 9 mk. A 24 hour Traveller's Ticket is 25 mk, and each additional day is 16 mk.

You can pick up a free bus-route map at the city tourist office or at Liikennelaitos.

Car & Motorcycle Several major car rental agencies have offices in the centre and at the airport, including Budget (☎ 253 2588) and Hertz (☎ 214 3341).

AROUND TAMPERE
Vammala

- **pop 15,790**   ☎ 015

Vammala, south-west of Tampere, isn't much of a tourist destination, but it might be worth a quick stop if you're on the way to Turku. **Tyrvää Museum**, at Jaatsinkatu 2, is a museum of local history. Entry is 10 mk. **Tyrvää church**, at the northern end of Puistokatu, was the first in Finland to have two towers. The **Jaatsi House** on Asemakatu is the childhood home of Akseli Gallen-Kallela, the most famous Finnish painter. It houses the art collection of the town of Vammala and is open daily. At Vehmaanniemi, 3km east of the town centre, there is a 2km marked **nature path** through a preserved area in which Iron Age graves have been found.

Places to Stay & Eat *Tervakallio Camping* (*☎ 514 2720, Uittomiehenkatu*), north-west of the centre, has cottages from 180 mk. It's open from 1 May to 15 August.

Gasthaus Liekoranta (*☎ 514 3662, Asemakatu 34*) near the train station has reasonably priced rooms and a good all-you-can-eat buffet lunch.

Pyymäen Leipomo near the kauppatori is a pleasant place for coffee and snacks.

Getting There & Away There are regular buses from Tampere and Turku. Trains between Tampere and Pori stop at Vammala, and there are five or six trains each day.

Hämeenkyrö

- **pop 9600**   ☎ 03

Hämeenkyrö, north-west of Tampere, is best known as the birthplace of FE Sillanpää, winner of the Nobel prize for literature in 1939. He was born in a small house known as **Myllykolu**. The setting is very picturesque. Follow the Maisematie road south of the village of Hämeenkyrö and turn towards Heinijärvi, then Kierikkala. The house is open from Tuesday to Sunday in summer.

In the village centre there is a **local museum** in the old red brick building beside the church, open daily in summer.

Places to Stay & Eat *Pinsiön Majat* (☎ *340 6191, Sasintie 400)*, open year-round, is 5km from the Tampere to Vaasa road – follow the 'Pinsiö' signs. It is affiliated with the HI and has beds from 50 mk, plus boats and bicycles for hire.

In the village there is a herb garden by the river, and the *Kehäkukka café* serves home-made herb tea.

Getting There & Away Hourly buses make the 36km trip between Tampere and Hämeenkyrö.

Ikaalinen
• pop 8000   ☎ 03

Further north-west of Tampere, this small town, surrounded by Lake Kyrösjärvi, is on a peninsula off the main Tampere to Vaasa road. The main street has a number of banks, supermarkets and other businesses. Every year in early June, Ikaalinen celebrates accordion music during the Sata-Häme Soi Festival.

Vanha Kauppala, the 'old township', has a few remaining wooden houses. A small **museum** on Valtakatu displays old musical instruments. It is open in June and July. The beautiful cross-shaped **church** was built in 1801 and is open daily in summer.

A huge **spa** 10km north of the town centre is the pride of Ikaalinen.

Places to Stay *Ikaalisten Spa* (☎ *4511, fax 451 2032)* is the largest spa in Scandinavia. There are five hotels as well as restaurants and sports facilities. Admission to the pool and sauna section costs 50 to 60 mk. Accommodation is available in singles/doubles from 435/590 mk, with discounts available.

Getting There & Away Several buses a day make the one hour trip from Tampere to Ikaalinen and the spa area.

Nokia
• pop 26,000   ☎ 03

Nokia, Tampere's western neighbour, is the home of the Nokia mobile phone company. The phones are not manufactured here, and it's not exactly a pretty town, but it's large enough to have an extensive range of services.

The **wooden church** was designed by Engel and was completed in 1838. Opposite the church on Nokianvaltatie, **Hinttala** is a local museum with several buildings and items relating to peasants life. Both places are open daily in summer.

Places to Stay *Viinikanniemi Camping* (☎ *341 3384)* has cottages from 190 mk. It is open from early May to early September.

Getting There & Away There are buses from Tampere to Nokia every 10 to 30 minutes from Monday to Friday.

Vesilahti
☎ 03

Once an important settlement for Lapps, Vesilahti is now a sleepy but fairly scenic town south of Lake Pyhäjärvi. An established 'tourist' route, the **Klaus Kurjen Tie** (named after a historical character who lived in Laukko Manor, now one of the attractions along this route) is a nice road for cycling if the weather is fine.

According to the *Kanteletar* epic, Klaus Kurki killed the young girl Elina here. 'The Murder of Elina' is one of the oldest legends in Finland.

The village of Vesilahti has a full range of services.

Getting There & Away There are buses from Tampere, and some ferries in summer.

ROUTE 66

Road No 66, which starts north-east of Tampere and winds north, is one of the oldest roads in Finland. When the famous song – the chorus of which goes 'Get your kicks on Route 66' – was translated into

Techno-Finland

The first Global System Mobile (GSM) network in the world was inaugurated in Finland in 1991 – and in the years that have followed, this small nation has gone for modern technology in a big way. Local operators offer more services than operators in most countries. To capitalise on the phone craze, a company in Helsinki has invented a vending machine that, instead of accepting coins, is activated by using a mobile phone; the cost of a chocolate bar or drink is added to the caller's telephone bill!

According to recent surveys, Finns are the highest per capita users of mobile phones – 425 of every 1000 Finns has one – followed by Norwegians and Swedes. Not surprisingly, Nokia, Finland's most successful company, is one of the world's leading manufacturers of cellular phones, with a 20% share of the world market and sales totalling more than 52 billion mk in 1997. In Finland, it's no longer a novelty to find wilderness guides leading thrilling whitewater rafting or snowmobile safaris while nattering away on their trim mobile phones. Likewise, the Sami of Lapland now use cellphones and snowmobiles to speed up their annual reindeer roundups.

Finnish students are among the most enthusiastic Internet users in the world, while computers, telefaxes and other modern gadgets are common in even the smallest of Finnish companies. It's estimated that in Finland there are 56 Internet-linked computers for every 1000 persons, compared to 38 in the USA and 43 in Norway. What do the Finns do with so much cyber time? According to a survey, the most frequently entered word on one Finnish Internet search engine was – just as you'd expect – 'sex'.

innish, the popular rock star Jussi Raittinen adapted the lyrics to this national highway.

Orivesi

☎ 03

Road No 66 begins in Orivesi. There's nothing spectacular in the village itself, but it is at a major crossroads. You can get tourist information at the Auvinen handicrafts shop in the village centre.

The village's silo-like modern **church** was controversial when built, one reason being the Kain Tapper woodcarving in the altar. The old bell tower remains, with its *vaivaisukko* (pauper statue). The church is open on weekdays in summer.

Getting There & Away Orivesi is 43km from Tampere on the main Tampere to Jyväskylä road. There are frequent buses from either city. Trains stop at the small station several kilometres from the village centre.

Kallenautio Roadhouse

This wooden roadhouse (☎ 335 8915) is the oldest building along Route 66 and dates back to 1757. It has always been a *kievari*, or roadside guesthouse. Two hundred years ago kievari were nearly as common as petrol stations are today. However, there are few such places left.

The building houses a café and museum. There are sometimes handicraft exhibitions – you can see how *päre* is made from wood. Päre is a thin sheet of wood once burnt to shed light in a house. It was often the main reason for the devastating fires that destroyed entire towns.

Siikaneva Marshland

This large protected marshland accommodates some unusual bird species, including owls. Staying overnight is not allowed, but if you have a vehicle of any kind, it may be worth driving to either starting point of the 6km loop path, which can be walked in a few hours. The entrance is at the 'Varikko' sign on the Orivesi to Ruovesi road.

Kalela House

The most celebrated artist of the National Romantic Era, Gallen-Kallela painted most of his famous *Kalevala* works in this studio set in the wilderness. There are exhibitions every summer. To get here, follow main road No 66 5km south from the village of Ruovesi, then turn east. It's 3km to Kalela along a gravel road. Kalela is open daily from late June to early August. Admission is 30 mk.

Ruovesi

☎ 03

Once voted the most beautiful village in Finland, Ruovesi retains much of its charm. There is not much to see or do in the village, but the journey through the surrounding wilderness is scenic. The **local museum** is in a house dating from the 18th century. Entry is 10 mk.

Places to Stay *Haapasaari Camping* (☎ 486 1388), open from mid-May to early September, is on the small islet north of the village. Tent sites are 80 mk and cottages are 95 to 800 mk. There are two small hotels in the village.

Getting There & Away Several buses a day connect Ruovesi with Tampere and other places in the region. There are also direct buses from Helsinki. The 'Poet's Way' ferries from Tampere stop at Ruovesi; see the Tampere Lake Cruises section for more information.

Helvetinjärvi National Park

The main attraction of this national park, often called 'the Hell' for short, is a narrow **gorge**, probably created as the ice moved the huge rocks apart some 10,000 years ago. The scene inspired the design of the Finnish pavilion at the Seville World Exhibition in 1992. There are a few trails to follow and you can pitch a tent for the night.

Toriseva

One of the most spectacular gorges in th region surrounds three lakes, which togeth er constitute a nice 5km **walking trail**. Sta from the small café on the top of the hil near the parking area, 5km south of th town of Virrat. The café has a trail map.

Virrat

• pop 9000   ☎ 03

The town of Virrat is the end point for som ferry cruises from Tampere. It is useful t have a bicycle with you to continue explo ing the region.

The first church of Virrat was built i 1651, and the present-day red-coloure wooden **church** dates from 1774. Its simpl interior reflects the original plan.

Places to Stay & Eat Outside the tow centre, *Lakarin Camping* (☎ 475 8639) ha tent sites and cabins, open from late May t late August.

Located quite near the harbour and th church, the HI-affiliated *Domus Virr* (☎ 475 5600, Sipiläntie 3), open from Jun to mid-August, has beds from 65 mk.

There's the standard *grilli* at the kaupp. tori, and nearby is *Pub Kahvila 66*. A *ca* at the harbour serves snacks.

Getting There & Away Several buses day connect Virrat to Tampere and oth towns in the region. The 'Poet's Way cruises from Tampere end here; see th Tampere Lake Cruises section for more i formation.

Perinnekylä

☎ 03

The 'Tradition Village' features fo museums, handicraft shops and a restaura with a lavish buffet lunch. Most attractio are open daily from late May to la August.

The **Talomuseo** has furniture, tradition Sunday decorations from the 1840s and smoke sauna. The **Metsäkämppämuseo** fe tures a large house and two small huts on used by loggers. The **Sotaveteraanie**

useo-huone, or War Veteran Museum
Room, has guns and other things that were
sed during WWII. The **Kanavamuseo** has
n exhibition relating to the canal.

Tuulimylly, a windmill dating from 1828,
as been renovated and is in working con-
ition. The nature trail or the gravel road
old road No 66) will take you to **Herrasen
intutorni**, a birdwatching tower that pro-
ides a good view of birdlife on Lake
oisvesi bay.

Kenttälinnoitusalue, the area near the
anal, was used by Russian troops as a depot
uring the war in 1808. In 1915, when
inland was part of tsarist Russia, a ditch
ystem was dug as a large strategic defence
ystem against expansionist Germany.
oday the area has renovated ditches and a
unker. A French 19th century cannon com-
letes the attraction. The Perinnekylä area is
km north-west of Virrat, at the Herraskos-
i Canal. Set aside half a day for this area
nd bring a picnic if the weather is fine.
here's also a *camping ground* here.

Western Lakeland

LAHTI
pop 95,000   ☎ 03

 major venue for winter sports in
inland, Lahti has hosted five world
hampionships in Nordic skiing. It's not
ery interesting in other respects. Founded
 1905, it lacks anything that could be
alled 'old town'.

The 10,000 Karelian refugees who
rrived here after WWII have contributed
heir entrepreneurial spirit to what the locals
all the 'Business City'.

Surrounded by a network of bicycle
outes, Lahti does make a good base for
isiting nearby attractions. Its location by
ake Vesijärvi (which is connected to Lake
äijänne) makes it *the* place to start a ferry
ip to Jyväskylä. One of the largest lakes
 Finland, Päijänne provides Helsinki with
rinkable tap water and everyone else with
cenic waterways.

Information
Tourist Office The tourist office (☎ 814
4566, matkailu@lahti.fi) is on the 2nd floor
at Torikatu 3, near the kauppatori. It's open
from 8 am to 6 pm Monday, 8 am to 5 pm
Tuesday to Friday and 9 am to 2 pm Saturday from June to late August. At other
times it's open 8 am to 5 pm Monday, 8 am
to 4 pm Tuesday to Friday.

Post The most central post office is at Mariankatu 17, 15110 Lahti. Hours are 8 am to
6 pm Monday to Friday.

Internet Resources & Library The public
library at Kirkkokatu 31 has two Internet
terminals. Hours are 10 am to 7 pm Monday
to Friday in summer. At other times it's
open until 8 pm on weekdays, and 10 am to
3 pm Saturday.

Travel Agency Lahti Blue Lakes Tours
(Päijät-Hämeen Matkailu; ☎ 783 4400,
fax 752 3385) at Aleksanterinkatu 4 is the
place to go to book cottages or sign up for
tours and activities in the southern Lake
Päijänne region. The office rents bikes for
60 to 80 mk per day. Canoes and kayak
rentals are from 60 mk per day. Hours are
from 9 am to 6 pm weekdays, 10 am to 2
pm Saturday in summer. At other times
it's open from 9 am to 5 pm Monday to
Friday.

Left Luggage The bus station has a left
luggage counter and lockers for 10 mk that
may be used for a maximum of 24 hours.
The train station also has a left luggage
counter, and lockers for 5 or 10 mk.

Medical & Emergency Services There
are pharmacies near the market, including
those at Torikatu 1, Aleksanterinkatu 13 and
Vapaudenkatu 12. In a general emergency
call ☎ 112, for police call ☎ 10022 and for
a doctor dial ☎ 10023.

Things to See
At the Sports Centre, the **Ski Jump Observation Terrace** is open daily in summer and

LAHTI

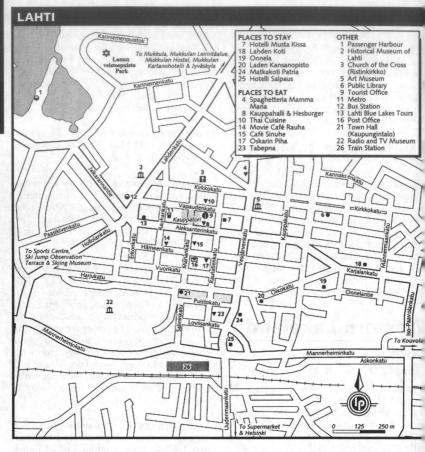

PLACES TO STAY
7 Hotelli Musta Kissa
18 Lahden Koti
19 Onnela
20 Laden Kansanopisto
24 Matkakoti Patria
25 Hotelli Salpaus

PLACES TO EAT
4 Spaghetteria Mamma Maria
8 Kauppahalli & Hesburger
10 Thai Cuisine
14 Movie Café Rauha
15 Café Sinuhe
17 Oskarin Piha
23 Tabepna

OTHER
1 Passenger Harbour
2 Historical Museum of Lahti
3 Church of the Cross (Ristinkirkko)
5 Art Museum
6 Public Library
9 Tourist Office
11 Metro
12 Bus Station
13 Lahti Blue Lakes Tours
16 Post Office
21 Town Hall (Kaupungintalo)
22 Radio and TV Museum
26 Train Station

on weekends in winter. You can ride a chair-lift to the top. Entry to the terrace is 20 mk, chairlift 15 mk, or 30 mk for both.

The small **Skiing Museum** at the Sports Centre is worth a visit. There are skis that were used 2000 years ago and skis that belonged to the Samis of Lapland. The ski jump simulator is great fun.

The **Historical Museum of Lahti** (Lahden Historiallinen Museo) at Lahdenkatu 4 is in a beautiful old manor house. Exhibits include the Klaus Holma collection of

French and Italian furniture and medieva and Renaissance art.

The **Art Museum** (Taidemuseo) at Ves järvenkatu 11 has temporary exhibitions.

The **Radio and TV Museum** on Radic mäki Hill has a collection of old radios an a working broadcasting studio from th 1950s.

At present all museums in Lahti hav similar opening hours: 10 am to 5 pm week days, and 11 am to 5 pm weekends. Entr to each is 15 mk.

The **Ristinkirkko** (The Church of the Cross) was designed by Alvar Aalto and finished in 1978. Although the exterior is made of brown brick, the interior is typically Aalto: wooden benches, white walls and, on the ceiling, four concrete structures which look like rays emanating from the cross. The church, at Kirkkokatu 4, is open from 10 am to 3 pm daily.

Kaupungintalo (town hall) at Harjukatu 31 was designed by another famous Finnish architect, Eliel Saarinen. There are guided tours of the building at 2 pm on Friday.

Activities

The **Sports Centre** just west of the centre has three sky-high ski jumps that are the landmark of Lahti. These are not open to the general public! However, there's still plenty to do. In winter, there is an ice-skating hall and a total of 145km of cross-country ski tracks, 35km of which are illuminated. Skiing and skating gear can be rented in the main building. In summer the centre offers bike trails and a large outdoor swimming pool (entry 15 mk).

At the **Mukkula Manor** area, by Lake Vesijärvi 5km north of the centre, there is mini-golf, tennis and archery, plus bike and boat rentals. There are also enjoyable lakeside saunas, and a number of accommodation options (see the Places to Stay section following). On Wednesday evenings in summer there is dancing at the pier. Take bus No 30 to Mukkula.

Places to Stay

Camping *Mukkulan Leirintäalue (☎ 882 3500, Ritaniemenkatu 10)* has tent sites from 70 to 85 mk and cabins from 200 to 450 mk. It is in the scenic grounds of Mukkula manor house (see the previous Activities section).

Hostels The local folk college, *Laden Kansanopisto (☎ 752 3344, Harjukatu 46)* is affiliated with the HI and open to travellers from June to mid-August. Beds are from 95 mk, and there is a kitchen.

Adjacent to the camping ground at Mukkula, the HI-affiliated *Mukkulan Hostel* is open year-round and also has beds from 95 mk. It offers many facilities: kitchen, sauna, café and restaurant.

Onnela (☎ 883 3300, Onnelantie 10) is an independent hostel with a very eccentric owner; you sleep in sheds in the backyard. Singles/doubles are from 90/150 mk.

Guesthouse *Matkakoti Patria (☎ 782 3783, Vesijärvenkatu 3)* is a bit run-down but close to the train station. Rooms cost 100/160 mk.

Hotels *Lahden Koti (☎ 522 173, Karjalankatu 6)* is a renovated apartment building which has been converted into a very nice small hotel. All apartments are tastefully decorated and come with a well-equipped kitchen and a bathroom. Studios and two-room apartments are from 250 mk. In summer prices are lower.

Hotelli Musta Kissa (☎ 85122, fax 851 4477, Rautatienkatu 21) is in the heart of town and has rooms from 245/340 mk.

Mukkulan Kartanohotelli (☎ 882 3500, fax 882 3522, Ritaniemenkatu 10) is in the old manor house at Mukkula, 5km north of Lahti. It is a romantic place to stay, and the lakeside location is superb. Rooms are from 210/330 mk.

Hotelli Salpaus (☎ 813 411, fax 813 4711, salpaus@salpauslahti.fi, Vesijärvenkatu 1) is closest to the train station, with rooms at 490/550 mk, and a restaurant and two saunas. All rooms are 395 mk in summer.

Places to Eat

Lahti has a number of good eating and drinking places on Aleksanterinkatu near the market, including a *Hesburger*. The market itself, and the nearby *kauppahalli* (indoor market), are probably the cheapest places to eat in town.

Tabepna (Rautatienkatu 3) is a Greek place that is very popular for its 32 mk lunch feast. On the kauppatori, *Thai Cuisine (Vapaudenkatu 10)* has many vegetarian options. Most entrées are in the 40 to 40 mk range. *Spaghetteria Mamma Maria (Vesijärvenkatu 32)* is run by an

THE LAKELAND

Italian woman and a Finnish man and has delicious, authentic food from 30 mk. It's closed Monday.

Movie Café Rauha (Rauhankatu 9) has an art gallery and hip decor, and is the place where the cool crowd gathers. *Café Sinuhe (Mariankatu 21)* is a pleasant street-style café with fantastic pastries. *Oskarin Piha (Hämeenkatu 17)* is a café, handicrafts shop and art gallery with lovely things for sale. *Metro* at the kauppatori is an unusual bar and club, part underground.

There is an enormous *supermarket* on the Lahti to Helsinki road. The sports complex has a *café* and *restaurant*.

Getting There & Away

Bus Each day there are more than 35 buses from Helsinki (102km south), at least 10 buses from Tampere (128km) and about 10 each from Jyväskylä (171km) and Turku (214km).

Train There are at least 15 direct trains per day from Helsinki and Riihimäki. Travellers from Tampere change trains at Riihimäki.

Boat Ferries to Heinola depart from Lahti on Thursday and Sunday from early to mid-June, and daily from mid-June to mid-August. A one-way ticket to Heinola costs 90 mk adult, 45 mk child. A return ticket is 130 mk adult, 65 mk child. The trip takes 4½ hours each way.

For information about the Lake Päijänne ferries to Jyväskylä, see the Getting There & Away section for that city, later in this chapter.

HOLLOLA
☎ 03

Hollola, west of Lahti, is the most historical place in this area. It's close enough to Lahti for a leisurely bicycle tour – take the narrow road around Lake Vesijärvi. In the village centre, a small tourist office (☎ 880 111) provides information about local attractions.

Messilä Estate

Messilä, just east of Hollola, is a fine old estate with a golf course and a guest harbour (see also the following Places to Stay & Eat section). Messilän Pajat is a separate building featuring local craft (and a bakery).

Pirunpesä (Devil's Nest) is a steep rock cliff near Messilä. A marked trail takes you there, or you can walk the entire 7km *luontopolku* (nature trail) which goes via a series of hills and offers some good views. One of these hills, **Tiirismaa**, is a downhill-skiing resort in winter.

Between Pirunpesä and the other attractions in Hollola lies **Lake Kutajärvi**, a resting place for migratory birds. In May plenty of local people gather to scan the lake for rare species.

Pyhäniemi Manor

The manor house (☎ 788 1466) in Pyhäniemi is one that deserves a visit.

This wooden mansion, dubbed the 'Hollywood of Hollola' in the 1930s, when many films were staged here, has had quite a colourful history. It was established in the 15th century. Swedish king Gustav II granted the estate to the Schmiedefelt family in 1780 and even visited it himself in 1783.

The estate grew to enormous proportions; its industries included a sawmill, a wheel factory and a Swiss-run dairy that exported its products to St Petersburg.

The wealth of this empire was lost by gambling in Monte Carlo in 1912, and during the Civil War it remained neutral property as a consulate under the Dutch flag.

Finns are today attracted by its interesting art exhibitions in summer. It is open daily from June to August. Admission is 40 mk.

Hollola Church

This large church (☎ 788 1351) dates from 1480. The enormous door to the main hall has been depicted on a Finnish 8-mk postage stamp. In the main hall, you will see 10 sculptures from the 15th century, and coats of arms from the von Essen family. The bell tower from 1831 was designed by CL Engel.

The church is not far north of Pyhäniemi. It's marked 'Hollola kk' on signs and bus timetables. The church is open to visitors from 11 am to 6 pm daily from June to mid-August. During the rest of the year it's open from 11 am to 4 pm on Sunday.

Opposite the church you will find the Marian Portti gallery, which opens daily in summer. Nearby is a food store and, up a short alley, Astra Pulkinnen's handicrafts shop. The alley and gardens here are well preserved.

Hollola Museums

The local museum of Hollola actually consists of two museums. Esinemuseo, the large red building not far from the church, contains a collection of local paraphernalia, including a Stone Age axe. Hentilä museum features old buildings which have been transferred from nearby locations. Both places are open Tuesday to Sunday. Entry costs 25 mk.

A map is available of a 3km *luontopolku* (nature trail) around the area.

Rälssipiha Horse Farm

This private farm estate is one of Hollola's major horse-breeding centres. It's a kilometre from the church (follow the signs behind the museum).

Formerly an old Swedish *frälse*, or tax-free estate, it now has a summer café, sales of local handicraft, and horse and carriage rides. The estate is closed on Monday.

Places to Stay & Eat

Messilä (☎ *86011, fax 860 123*) offers plenty of choices. There are modern rooms for 400/480 mk, plus a holiday village with well-equipped cottages. The several restaurants here serve everything from gourmet cuisine to burgers and beers, and this is a popular venue in summer for live music and dancing.

Getting There & Away

The attractions of Hollola are 15 to 18km west of Lahti. Regular buses from Lahti stop at all attractions as well as at the commercial centre, Salpakangas.

PÄIJÄNNE NATIONAL PARK

This national park was founded in 1994 to protect some of the impressive nature in the southern part of Lake Päijänne. The narrow **Pulkkilanharju ridge** offers good lake views from its crest. However, the main feature of the national park is **Kelvenne Island**, an unusually long ridge in the middle of southern Lake Päijänne. There is a 10km trail from one end of the island to the other, with designated camping grounds along the way, plus a few lagoon beaches and beautiful pine forests. This is a popular place in summer.

Look for park information at Padasjoki, Asikkala, Sysmä and Pulkkilanharju ridge.

There's a regular summer boat service to the island from the pier at Kullasvuori near Padasjoki town. Check the information booth at Pulkkilanharju ridge for information on other regular boats.

VÄÄKSY
☎ 03

Vääksy is mostly known for Vääksy Canal, the busiest canal in Finland – over 15,000 vessels pass through it every summer. A local tourist office (☎ 888 6232) in the commercial centre has information about local attractions, and arranges accommodation in the pleasant lakeside surroundings. **Vääksyn Vesimyllymuseo** (☎ 766 0860) is a small water-mill museum open in summer.

There's a museum in the **Danielson-Kalmarin huvila**, a very fine wooden building that is over 100 years old. It's open in summer and charges 15 mk entry.

Automuseo in the centre has an exhibition of vintage cars and motorcycles. The museum is open daily in summer; entry is 25 mk.

The **Urajärven Kartano estate** (☎ 766 7191), one of the finest in Finland, was the property of the von Heideman family. It has a museum, a café and an attractive garden, all open daily from June to August. You'll need a private car to visit the estate as it is east of the Vääksy Canal.

Places to Stay & Eat

One kilometre east of the bus station, *Tallukka* (☎ 88811, Tallukantie 1) is a large hotel which plays a role in the local nightlife. There are 100 rooms from 270/390 mk.

At the canal, *Kanavan Kahvila* is a 1950s-style restaurant serving home-made food. Right at the waterfront, *Sulkuportti* is a summer-only restaurant. The commercial centre of Vääksy has several *supermarkets*.

Getting There & Away

Vääksy is busy in summer, with plenty of buses, or you can catch one of the canal boats which ply their way between Lahti and Heinola in summer (see the Lahti Getting There & Away section).

HEINOLA

- pop 16,000   ☎ 03

Heinola is today overshadowed by Lahti to the south but is a much older town. It has a scenic waterfront setting, with the Jyrängönvirta River flowing through it. In addition to summer cultural attractions, Heinola serves as a starting point for scenic summer lake cruises. The tourist office (☎ 849 3615) is at Kauppakatu 10-12.

Heinola Ridge

The ridge has a few attractions. The 1900 **Harjupaviljonki pavilion** is meant to look like a Japanese temple. In summer there is an art exhibition here, open daily. Nearby, the **tower** is also open daily in summer and offers good views.

Museums

Heinola has three museums on Kauppakatu. **Heinolan kaupunginmuseo**, at Kauppakatu 14, is in an 1830s Empire-style building and contains antique furniture and temporary exhibitions (10 mk).

Taidemuseo at Kauppakatu 4 is the local art museum and includes a permanent collection. There is a fee during special exhibitions; entry is free at other times.

Aschanin talo at Kauppakatu 3 is the oldest house in town, dating from the late 18th century (10 mk). The museums are open Tuesday to Sunday.

Churches

The **Lutheran church** on Siltakatu was built in 1811 and is open Tuesday to Sunday. The **Orthodox church** contains icons from the Valamo Monastery.

Places to Stay & Eat

Heinäsaari Camping (☎ 715 3083) is on Heinäsaari island, 1.5km from the town centre. Cottages are from 150 mk. It's open from June to mid-August.

The HI-affiliated *Finnhostel Heinola* (☎ 714 1655, Opintie 3) is open from June to early August. The cost is 80 mk for a bed.

Hotelli Kumpeli (☎ 715 8214, fax 715 8899, Muonamiehenkatu 3) is the top establishment in Heinola. Rooms are from 490/590 mk regularly, all rooms are 410 mk in summer.

Harjupaviljonki on the hill is a most attractive place to enjoy a cup of coffee in summer. There are several *restaurants* on Kauppakatu, the main road.

Getting There & Away

There are buses roughly every half-hour from Lahti. Heinola is 136km north of Helsinki. Ferries from Lahti sail to Heinola in summer. See Lahti for details.

SYSMÄ

☎ 03

The village of Sysmä is on the eastern shore of Lake Päijänne. A series of classical concerts, *Sysmän suvisoitto*, take place here in early July.

The highlight of Sysmä will be **Vanha Kerttu** as long as 'old' Kerttu Tapiola keeps entertaining visitors in her art gallery. She's very funny and friendly. In the same building, **Suomen Harmonikka-museo** houses a large collection of accordions. This private collection is open from Monday to Saturday year-round. Entry is 25 mk.

The 15th century stone **church** is open daily from June to late August. The local **museum** is open on Sunday only.

Also in the centre is a bookshop with some material in English and a health-food shop with coffee and snacks.

Places to Stay & Eat

Sysmä Camping (☎ 717 1386, Anne .kurvnen@sci.fi, Huitilantie 3) is good value, with two-bed cottages from 80 mk per night. It's very close to the shops and services of Sysmä and has rowing boats and canoes for rent. Camping is 60 mk and there's every facility, including a sauna and a café. It's open from June to late August.

Finding a place to eat is no problem in Sysmä, especially in summer. Hamburgers are available at *grillis* and there are *cafés* and a few beer-drinking *baaris* on Sysmäntie and Uotintie.

Getting There & Away

Sysmä is well connected to Helsinki by express buses.

AROUND SYSMÄ
Onkiniemi
☎ 03

This small village is on the Hartola to Heinola road. The **balancing rock** near the main road is its landmark and its main attraction is the Musta and Valkea Ratsu Nukketalot (Black and White Horse Puppet House; ☎ 718 6959). *Nukketalot*, or **Puppet Houses**, are extremely popular with Finnish kids. A very eccentric couple and their talented son have created more than 350 hand puppets – some appearing regularly on TV – and give daily performances (30 mk). Most people fall in love with the place, the people and the puppets. Some items are for sale, and the building has a self-service café. Hours are noon to 4 pm daily, year-round.

JYVÄSKYLÄ
• pop 75,300   ☎ 014

Jyväskylä (pronounced YUHvahskuhllah) was founded in 1837. Its reputation as a nationalistic town goes back to the earliest days, when the first Finnish-language schools were established here. In 1966 the University of Jyväskylä was inaugurated; it was to become renowned for its architecture. Indeed, the whole town is well known for its architecture, many of its buildings having been designed by Alvar Aalto (see boxed text). This reputation could come as a surprise to the traveller, who might be more inclined to think that the town consists of a cluster of boring cement boxes!

Today, Jyväskylä is a bustling town with its university and a large number of young people.

Information

Tourist Office The tourist information office (☎ 624 903, matkailu@jkl.fi) is at Asemakatu 6 near the train station. It publishes an excellent free guide to events and activities in the region, rents bicycles and sells fishing permits.

Hours are from 9 am to 6 pm weekdays and 9 am to 3 pm weekends from June to late August. At other times it is open from 9 am to 5 pm weekdays, and 9 am to 2 pm Saturday.

Post The main post office is at Vapaudenkatu 60, 40100 Jyväskylä. It is open from 9 am to 8 pm Monday to Friday.

Internet Resources & Libraries The public library in Jyväskylä is located at Vapaudenkatu 39-41. It has three Internet terminals on the third floor, and also stocks fiction in English. The library is open from 11 am to 8 pm Monday to Friday, and 11 am to 3 pm Saturday.

The Jyväskylä University library is also good.

The main Web site for information on Jyväskylä is www.jkl.fi/.

Bookshop Head to the Suomalainen Kirjakauppa bookshop in the Torikeskus shopping centre at Väinönkatu 11, if you're looking for English-language fiction and non-fiction and periodicals.

JYVÄSKYLÄ

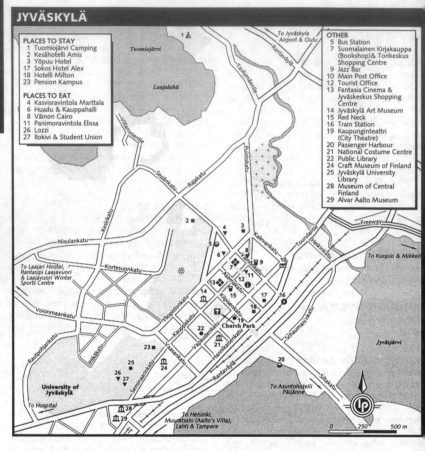

PLACES TO STAY
1 Tuomiojärvi Camping
2 Kesähotelli Amis
3 Yöpuu Hotel
17 Sokos Hotel Alex
18 Hotelli Milton
23 Pension Kampus

PLACES TO EAT
4 Kasvisravintola Marttala
6 Huadu & Kauppahalli
8 Väinon Cairo
11 Panimoravintola Elissa
26 Lozzi
27 Ilokivi & Student Union

OTHER
5 Bus Station
7 Suomalainen Kirjakauppa (Bookshop)& Torikeskus Shopping Centre
9 Jazz Bar
10 Main Post Office
12 Tourist Office
13 Fantasia Cinema & Jyväskeskus Shopping Centre
14 Jyväskylä Art Museum
15 Red Neck
16 Train Station
19 Kaupunginteattri (City Theatre)
20 Passenger Harbour
21 National Costume Centre
22 Public Library
24 Craft Museum of Finland
25 Jyväskylä University Library
28 Museum of Central Finland
29 Alvar Aalto Museum

Left Luggage The train station has lockers for 10 mk that may be used for a maximum of 24 hours.

Medical & Emergency Services The Central Hospital (Keski-Suomen Keskussairaala; ☎ 626 400 or 691 811) is at Keskussairaalantie 19-21. There are pharmacies at Puistokatu 4 and on Kauppakatu at Nos 13, 35 and 39. In a general emergency call ☎ 112, for police call ☎ 10022 and for a doctor dial ☎ 10023.

Architecture

At times Jyväskylä is crawling with architecture buffs pointing wide-angled lenses at every Alvar Aalto building. The list of Alvar Aalto buildings includes the university's main building and the theatre at Vapaudenkatu 36. The building housing Panimoravintola Elissa (see Places to Eat), at Väinönkatu 7, was designed by Alvar Aalto in 1952 to be a workers' club. If you're into architecture, the best time to visit Jyväskylä is Tuesday to Friday, as many

Alvar Aalto – Architect, Designer, Sculptor

'It is still the architect's duty to attempt to humanise the age of machines.' Alvar Aalto 1955

The churches, town halls, museums and concert halls designed by Alvar Aalto can be seen from Helsinki to Rovaniemi. Aalto's buildings tread the line between the unadorned functionalism of the International Style (so-called because its designs spoke the universal language of the machine) and the people and materials orientation of the Organic Style. His designs emphasise the qualities of wood, brick and glass, the role of the building and its relation to the people using it.

Aalto was born in 1898 just outside Seinäjoki in the town of Kuortane. He practised in central Finland, Turku and Helsinki until gaining an international reputation for his pavilions at the World Fairs of 1937 (Paris) and 1939 (New York). He was professor of architecture at the Massachusetts Institute of Technology from 1945-49, and president of the Academy of Finland from 1963-68.

His most famous work is probably Helsinki's Finlandia Hall (1962-71), but the House of Culture (1952-58), with its convex wall of wedge-shaped bricks, and the Helsinki University of Technology in Espoo (1953-66) are also fine examples of his work. Jyväskylä is chock-a-block with Aalto-designed buildings including the Workers' Club (1952) and the Alvar Aalto Museum (1971-73). A comparison of the Civic Center in Seinäjoki with the Church of the Three Crosses (1955-58) in Imatra highlights the range of Aalto's work.

Aalto also achieved a reputation as an abstract painter, sculptor and furniture designer. In 1925 he married Aino Marsio, with whom he collaborated on Artek furniture designs. Their work on bending and laminating wood revolutionised furniture design. Marsio died in 1949 and Aalto in 1976.

FINNISH TOURIST BOARD

---

buildings are closed on weekends and the Aalto Museum is closed on Monday. You can pick up a brochure with details in English on Aalto-designed buildings at the Alvar Aalto Museum.

Museums

Jyväskylä has five museums, all of which are open from 11 am to 6 pm Tuesday to Sunday (to 8 pm in August). A joint ticket – good for entry to all the museums – costs 20 mk. Individual tickets cost 10 mk adult, free for students and children. Admission is free to all museums on Friday.

Alvar Aalto Museum Alvar Aalto is without a doubt Finland's most famous architect. The museum at Alvar Aallon katu 7, in a building designed by the man himself, contains models and photographic exhibits relating to Aalto's work, life and philosophy. Even for those totally uninterested in architecture the museum is engaging and worthwhile.

Museum of Central Finland The Keski-Suomen Museo, adjacent to the Alvar Aalto Museum, has artefacts and displays from various parts of the province, including an exhibition on the history of Jyväskylä. The building was designed by Alvar Aalto and finished in 1961.

Jyväskylä Art Museum Opened in 1998, the Jyväskylän Taidemuseo, at Kauppakatu 23, houses the modern art and sculpture collection of Ester and Salo Sihtola. There are Finnish and international works on display, with changing exhibitions.

Craft Museum of Finland The Suomen Käsityön Museo is at Seminaarinkatu 32. The permanent collection is about Finnish handicrafts and their history. There are also temporary displays, and a room with materials for children to play with.

National Costume Centre The Kansallispukukeskus, at Gummeruksenkatu 3, displays regional costumes from around Finland. There is a small permanent collection plus temporary exhibitions.

Activities

Skiing The Laajavuori Winter Sports Centre (☎ 624 885), north-west of the city centre, has four modestly sloped ski runs, illuminated cross-country skiing trails and a number of very scary ski jumps (for which it is famous). There is a good ski area for children. A day pass to the ski centre costs 110 mk, and equipment hire is 100 mk per day for downhill and 50 mk per day for cross-country skiing.

Organised Tours

Lake Cruises Jyväskylä is a popular cruise centre in summer due to the recently opened Keitele route north of town. This runs through some impressive canals constructed by Russians in the early 1990s. You can return to Jyväskylä the same day for 212 mk, or travel one way to Suolahti for 141 mk. Short cruises on northern Lake Päijänne are also available from early June

to early August, with daily departures. Some of these are evening cruises with dinner and dancing. The city tourist office can furnish specific schedules and prices.

For information about the Jyväskylä to Lahti route, see the Getting There & Away section that follows.

Special Events

The Jyväskylä Winter Festival in February features concerts and dance performances. In early June, the Jyväskylä Arts Festival has concerts, exhibitions, theatre and dance.

Places to Stay

Camping The pleasant *Tuomiojärvi Camping* (☎ 624 896, Taulumäentie 47) has several four-bed cottages scattered in the lakeside woods. These cost 200 to 280 mk per night. Tent sites are 75 mk. Take bus No 8 to get there.

Hostel The HI-affiliated hostel *Laajari* (☎ 624 885, fax 624 888, Laajavuorentie 15) is at the skiing complex north-west of the centre (take bus No 25). It's open year-round and has dorm beds from 85 mk. There's a sauna, kitchen and a cafeteria on the premises.

Guesthouse *Pension Kampus* (☎ 211 723, Vaasankatu 29) is a clean, pleasant guesthouse that is very centrally located. There are just eight rooms priced at 210/300 mk, and guests may use the kitchen.

Summer Hotel *Kesähotelli Amis* (☎ 443 0100, fax 443 0121, Sepänkatu 3) is open from June to mid-August. Each room has a toilet, shower and kitchen. Rooms are 200/290 mk.

Hotels *Hotelli Milton* (☎ 213 411, fax 631 927, Hannikaisenkatu 27-29) is a family hotel opposite the train station. Rooms are from 250/350 mk, with discount prices on weekends from mid-June to late July.

Asuntohotelli Päijänne (☎ 444 6311, fax 444 6360, Salmirannantie 5) has small rooms with shared kitchen and bathroom at 250/300 mk. It's located several kilometres south-east of Jyväskylä; take bus No 19.

Yöpuu Hotel (*☎/fax 620 588, ravintla .yopuu@co.inet.fi, Yliopistonkatu 23*) is an old-fashioned hotel with two fine restaurants and plenty of style. With only 26 rooms, the place is often full. Rooms are from 390/570 mk, in summer 350/450 mk.

Sokos Hotel Alex (*☎ 651 211, fax 651 200, Hannikaisenkatu 35*) is just across from the train station. Rooms are from 550/720 mk, except in summer and on weekends, when all rooms are 320 mk.

Rantasipi Laajavuori (*☎ 628 211, fax 628 500, Laajavuorentie*) is near the skiing complex north-west of the centre, and has sports facilities in and around the hotel. There are 196 rooms, with rooms from 620/710 mk.

Places to Eat

The cheapest meals in town are available at university restaurants. The building housing **Lozzi** was designed by Alvar Aalto. Meals, available in summer, are excellent value.

Ilokivi in the Student Union building has meals from 25 mk.

Väinon Cairo in the Vänönkeskus shopping centre at Väinönkatu 26 serves superb 30 mk lunches from 10.30 am to 2 pm on weekdays.

Kasvisravintola Murttala, on the 2nd floor at Väinönkatu 36B, is a vegetarian restaurant open for lunch only, from 11 am to 2 pm on weekdays.

For Chinese food, head to **Huadu** (*Yliopistonkatu 15*). It has very filling lunch specials from 11 am to 3 pm on weekdays. Adjacent is the town's **kauppahalli** (covered market), with produce and snacks.

Panimoravintola Elissa (*Väinönkatu 7*) is a brewery pub and restaurant in a landmark Alvar Aalto-designed building. Most dishes are 50 to 80 mk, although lunch can be cheaper.

Entertainment

With so many university students around, Jyväskylä has a thriving nightlife. The best area for bar-hopping is along Kauppakatu, the pedestrian section of the main street. **Jazz Bar** (*Kauppakatu 32*) has good live jazz.

Red Neck (*Asemakatu 7*) is a bar with Finnish music and a heavy farming motif. Happy hour is from 3 to 9 pm daily.

The university restaurant **Ilokivi** hosts rock concerts on some evenings.

A six-screen movie complex, **Fantasia**, is in the Jyväskeskus shopping centre.

Getting There & Away

Air There are several flights from Helsinki to Jyväskylä each weekday and fewer on weekends.

Bus The bus terminal just north of the town centre serves the entire southern half of Finland, with many daily express buses connecting Jyväskylä to the big cities.

Train The train station is between the town and the harbour. There are direct trains from Helsinki, Turku, Joensuu and Vaasa.

Boat There is regular ferry service on Lake Päijänne between Jyväskylä and Lahti, operated by Päijänne Risteilyt Hildén Oy (*☎ 263 447, fax 665 560*). Boats depart from either town at 10 am on Tuesday, Wednesday, Friday and Saturday from June to mid-August; the trip takes 10 hours and cost 210 mk one way. Try to catch the SS **Suomi**, one of the oldest steamers still plying the Finnish lakes.

Getting Around

To/From the Airport The Jyväskylä airport is 21km north of the town centre. Buses meet each arriving flight. In the centre, catch the airport bus on Vapaudenkatu. Fare is 22 mk one way.

Bus Catch local buses on Vapaudenkatu, south of the church park. Tickets cost 11 mk adult, 6 mk child. A one-day tourist ticket costs 30 mk adult, 15 mk child.

AROUND JYVÄSKYLÄ
Säynätsalo
☎ 014

The large **Säynätsalo Civic Centre** southeast of Jyväskylä is one of Alvar Aalto's most famous works, the architect winning an international competition in 1949 to design it. The building was completed in 1952. The library is open every afternoon from Monday to Friday; the municipal office opens during office hours. On the small island of **Juurikkasaari**, just off Säynätsalo, Alvar Aalto's boat (his own design) features a humble note 'Nemo Propheta in Patria' (No-one is a prophet in one's own land). Follow the sign that says 'Aallon vene'.

On the island of **Muuratsalo**, accessible via Lehtisaari, Aalto's villa was a test building, on which the architect tried out various brick materials. For opening times, contact the Alvar Aalto Museum (see Museums in the earlier Jyväskylä section). Admission is 30 mk.

Getting There & Away Bus Nos 16, 17M and 21 run regularly from Jyväskylä to Säynätsalo.

Muurame
☎ 014

If you are driving along the main Tampere to Jyväskylä road, you might want to stop in Muurame – 13km south of Jyväskylä – to have a look at the **Sauna Village** (Saunakylä). This open-air museum, open from 10 am to 6 pm daily in summer, has a variety of old saunas. Entry is 15 mk. A white **church** designed by Alvar Aalto during the 1920s is open in summer from 10 am to 6 pm.

Riihivuori Hill is a local downhill **skiing centre** some 5km from the main Tampere to Jyväskylä road, just south of Muurame.

Places to Stay *Kultakenkä Asuntohotelli* (☎/fax 631 294, Mäkijärventie 6B) is a resort hotel, with rates from 110 mk per person. Serious skiers should try *Riihivuoren Lo-*makylä (☎ 311 0911, fax 311 0921) on the top of Riihivuori Hill. Beds are from 85 mk.

Tikkakoski
☎ 014

This small village is an air-force base, but there are several attractions. To reach Tikkakoski there, go along the narrow road towards Uurainen. The scenic route is great for cycling.

Aviation Museum of Central Finland
The Aviation Museum of Central Finland (Keski-Suomen Ilmailumuseo) is the highlight of Tikkakoski. Despite its name it's more of a military museum and will be of interest to students of WWII. Rare planes include a fighter from the 1920s; a Russian Polikarpov U2 that was shot down with a single shot in December 1939; and a self-made aeroplane belonging to Raimo Päätalo, who was punished for the 'unforgivable crime' of flying it without a proper licence. The aviation museum is open from 10 am to 8 pm daily in summer, and from 11 am to 5 pm daily at other times. Admission is 30 mk.

Central Finland Firearms Exhibitions
Once a cow shelter, the Tikkamannila building now houses a museum of Finnish guns, ammunition and gunsmiths. There's also an art gallery and a tourist information booth here. Hours are 10 am to 7 pm daily in summer and 10 am to 6 pm Tuesday to Sunday at other times. Admission is 20 mk. Tikkamannila is 500m from the Jyväskylä to Oulu road.

Places to Stay & Eat *Ränssi Kievari Inn* (☎/fax 311 0086) is at a beautiful lakeside location near the village of Kuikka, 5km west of Tikkakoski. The large yellow house dates from 1820 and has been a guesthouse for more than 100 years. These days, beds cost 150 mk per person, and there are activities ranging from horseback riding to cross-country skiing. There is a smoke sauna which can be heated on request, but this is very expensive unless you are part of a large group.

PETÄJÄVESI
☎ 014

This rural municipality lies 35km west of Jyväskylä. Its highlight is a cross-shaped wooden church, which was the third Finnish attraction to be placed on the UNESCO World Heritage List. Petäjävesi is also the starting point for the Wanhan Witosen paddling route along the waterways to Jämsänkoski.

Petäjävesi Church

Built in 1764, this church is probably the most notable example of 18th century peasant architecture in Finland. Prior to its construction, there had been some debate about whether this village should get a church at all. While a reply to applications (sent to Stockholm for approval) was delayed, one Jaakko Leppänen started the job minus permission and properly drawn instructions. The result was a combination of Renaissance and Byzantine architecture. It's a marvellous, though rather awkward, wooden building with fine details. Since 1879, the church has functioned only as a museum. Hours are from 10 am to 6 pm from June to mid-August. Admission to the museum is 10 mk.

Getting There & Away

There are hourly buses between Jyväskylä and Petäjävesi. You can also take one of the express buses between Tampere and Jyväskylä via Keuruu.

KEURUU
☎ 014

The little town of Keuruu is on the northern shore of Lake Keurusselkä and boasts one of the most interesting wooden churches in Finland. There is a tourist office (☎ 751 7144) in the town hall at Multiantie 5, open in summer.

Things to See & Do

Keuruu's fascinating old **wooden church**, built in 1758, has superb portraits of Bible characters, and photos of the mummified corpses that are buried below the chancel. The church is open from 10 am to 5 pm daily from June to mid-August. Admission is 5 mk.

Ulkomuseo is an open-air museum, open from Tuesday to Sunday in June, July and August. Entry is 5 mk.

There are **lake cruises** on the MS *Elias Lönnrot*, a paddle boat, from early June to mid-August. It has service to the town of Mänttä once weekly, more frequent service to other destinations.

Places to Stay & Eat

Camping Nyyssänniemi (☎ 751 7719, Nyyssänniementie 7-8), is open from June to late August. Cottages cost 150 to 240 mk. A café, *Katariinan Kamari*, is located in a log house almost opposite the church.

Getting There & Away

Buses to Keuruu can be caught from Jyväskylä or Tampere. There are several trains a day from Jyväskylä and Haapamäki.

MÄNTTÄ
• pop 7200   ☎ 03

The main reason for visiting the industrial town of Mänttä is to see the Serlachius Art Museum, one of the best art collections in Finland. The tourist information booth at the Makos hamburger restaurant on Ratakatu is open daily.

Things to See

Mänttä is dominated by the huge Serlachius paper factory. The Art Nouveau 1928 **church** was financed by the factory, and has unique wood carvings on the altar and pulpit. It is open daily.

Joenniemi Manor, the private home of the late industrialist Gösta Serlachius, now houses the **Gösta Serlachiuksen Taidemuseo**. Its large collection features art from various European countries but the highlight is the Finnish section, which includes all the major names from the 'Golden Age' of Finnish art. The museum is open from 11 am to 6 pm Tuesday to Sunday in summer.

THE LAKELAND

At other times the hours are from noon to 5 pm on weekends.

Honkahovi is another mansion belonging to the Serlachius family. It's a 1938 Art Deco structure containing temporary art exhibitions and open year-round. You can walk between Honkahovi and the Joenniemi Manor via a trail around Lake Melasjärvi.

Places to Stay & Eat

The HI-affiliated *hostel (☎ 488 8641, Koulukatu 6)* is in the modern dormitory building of a school, not far from the centre. There are beds from 80 mk. It is open from June to early September. There are two hotels right in the centre of Mänttä, with restaurants that serve good if pricey meals. Around the central square are a few grillis, such as *Makos Burger*.

Getting There & Away

In summer, you can catch the MS *Elias Lönnrot* from Keuruu. Otherwise, there are several buses a day to Mänttä from Tampere, via Keuruu. The bus station is 700m west of the centre.

SAARIJÄRVI
☎ 014

The small town of Saarijärvi is surrounded by water on almost all sides. This is where the Karstula to Saarijärvi canoeing route ends. In the main village, there's a **museum** at Lake Herajärvi and an impressive old **church** from 1849. North of town, the **Säätyläismuseo** (also known as the Upper Class Residence) is the former home of Finland's national poet, JL Runeberg, where he worked in the 1820s. Now a museum, it's open daily in summer. Farther north, **Julmat Lammit** is a nature conservation area, with deep lakes of crystal-clear water. South-east of Saarijärvi on Summassaari island, there's a reconstruction of an authentic **Stone Age village** – a settlement which was here approximately 5000 years ago. The village is open from Tuesday to Sunday in summer.

Places to Stay

North-west of the centre, *Ahvenlahti Camping (☎ 439 583)* has tent sites (60 mk) and cottages (80 to 380 mk), and is open from June to mid-August. The nearby hotel has good rooms and rents canoes.

Getting There & Away

Many of the westbound buses from Jyväskylä will take you to Saarijärvi.

KARSTULA
☎ 014

The remote village of Karstula is in a beautiful setting, surrounded by lakes. It is here that one of the most exciting canoeing routes starts. You can rent canoes in Karstula or at the other end, in Saarijärvi.

Evankelinen Kansanopisto (☎ 462 151) is open year-round and has rooms from 100 mk per person.

Getting There & Away

Karstula is a few kilometres west of the main Jyväskylä to Kokkola road. There are express buses that cover the 100km from Jyväskylä.

VIITASAARI
• pop 8000   ☎ 014

Midway between Oulu and Tampere is Viitasaari. The setting is scenic, but there's not much to see in the village itself – it's a quiet little place. Viitasaari is known for its unique taste in art and music, and there is a **modern art exhibition** in two school buildings off the main road. It's open daily in summer.

Viitasaari is known for the **Time of Music Summer Festival** (☎ 573 195, fax 579 3515, time.music@festivals.fi) in mid-July – this is modern, experimental music definitely outside the mainstream. Tickets cost 50 mk.

Places to Stay & Eat

Hännilänsalmi Camping (☎ 572 550) is in a beautiful lakeside location 4km south of Viitasaari. Cottages start at 170 mk.

Viitasaari has just one hotel, *Hotel Pihkuri (☎ 571 440, fax 571 198, Kappelintie 5)* with rooms for 250/340 mk in summer.

On the main Jyväskylä to Oulu road, 14km north of Viitasaari village, is *Wiikin Kartano* (☎ 530 242, fax 530 121). It is an old estate mansion, but its stone-walled guest rooms are in a magnificently renovated cowshed! Rooms are 200/300 mk. There are also small cottages from 250 mk, and good meals from 40 mk.

You'll find several *supermarkets* in the village centre.

Getting There & Away

Viitasaari is well connected by bus to all major towns in central Finland.

Häme Region

The Häme (Swedish: Tavastland) district is a place of great contrasts: from the busy towns of Hämeenlinna and Tampere to the old villages of Hattula and Kangasala; from the wilderness of the north to the flat farmland in the south.

In addition to historic towns and villages, Häme offers opportunities for short treks and canoe trips.

History

The people of Häme built a chain of fortresses that had its heyday approximately 1000 years ago. In 1249 Earl Birger, on a Catholic crusade, arrived in Häme. He attacked the fortress at Hakoinen and founded the Swedish stronghold of Tavastehus (Hämeenlinna in Finnish). The Swedish settlers who followed him established large estates – causing irritation among locals who had traditionally been hunters and fishers. During the 19th century a workers' movement sprang up in industrialised Tampere, which consequently spread to other provinces.

HÄMEENLINNA
- pop 44,500   ☎ 03

Hämeenlinna (Swedish: Tavastehus), is the capital of the Province of Häme and the oldest inland town in Finland, founded in 1649. However, there had been a trading settlement at this location on Lake Vanajavesi from the 9th century. Häme Castle was built in the 13th century by Swedes on a crusade to Finland. Later, Hämeenlinna developed into an administrative, educational and garrison town.

These days Hämeenlinna's many attractions and its proximity to Helsinki make it a popular place to visit. Many visitors arrive by lake ferry from Tampere.

Orientation

Hämeenlinna lies on both sides of Lake Vanajavesi. The town centre is a compact area between the lake in the south and east, the main Helsinki to Tampere road in the west and Häme Castle in the north. Raatihuoneenkatu is the main street and part of it is only open to pedestrians.

Information

Tourist Office Häme Tourist Service (☎ 621 2388, fax 621 2716, hml.matkailu@htk.fi) is the tourist office at Sibeliuksenkatu 5. It offers information on attractions in town and in surrounding villages, sells tickets for lake cruises and books accommodation at hotels and cabins throughout the region. Hours are 9 am to 5 pm Monday to Friday, plus 9 am to 2 pm Saturday from mid-June to mid-August.

Post The post office is at Palokunnankatu 13-15, 13100 Hämeenlinna. Hours are 9 am to 8 pm Monday to Friday.

Internet Resources & Library The public library at Lukiokatu 2 is open from 10 am to 8 pm Monday and Tuesday, to 7 pm Wednesday to Friday and to 3 pm Saturday. It has six Internet terminals on the basement level.

Left Luggage Lockers at the train and bus stations cost 10 mk for a maximum of 24 hours.

Medical & Emergency Services There are pharmacies on Sibeliuksenkatu at Nos 3 and 11. In a general emergency call ☎ 112, for police call ☎ 10022 and for a doctor dial ☎ 10023.

HÄMEENLINNA

PLACES TO STAY
4 Matkustajakoti Vanaja
5 Sokos Hotel Vaakuna
21 Hotelli Emilia

PLACES TO EAT
12 Pauliina
17 Piparkakkutalo
18 Dragon
19 Popino
22 Laurell

OTHER
1 Häme Castle
2 National Prison Museum
3 Train Station
6 Museum Gallery House of Cards
7 Palander House
8 Public Library
9 Passenger Harbour
10 Rantakasino
11 Hämeenlinna Art Museum
13 Sibelius Museum
14 Roadhouse
15 Metropol
16 Hämeenlinna Church
20 Tourist Office
23 Post Office
24 Bus Station

Häme Castle

Häme Castle (☎ 675 6820) is the symbol of Hämeenlinna town and also its most significant attraction. Construction of the castle was started during the 1260s by Swedes, who wanted to establish a military base in Häme. In 1837 the castle was converted to a jail. The last prisoners were moved out in the 1980s and extensive renovation of the castle was completed in 1991.

The red-brick castle now houses a museum of local history and is also a venue for local events. Castle hours are from 10 am to 6 pm daily from May to mid-August, and 10 am to 4 pm daily at other times. Admission is 20 mk.

Varikonniemi Park, across a narrow channel from the castle, is where a trading settlement was established in the 9th century.

National Prison Museum

The old prison block near the castle has been converted into a museum where you can visit a solitary confinement cell or

Jean Sibelius

Born in 1865 in the town of Hämeenlinna, Jean Sibelius started playing piano when he was nine and composed his first notable work at age 20. During the cultural flowering that inspired Finland's independence, Sibelius provided the nation with music that complemented its literature and visual arts. Sibelius was fascinated by mythology and one of his greatest inspirations was the *Kalevala*, the Finnish epic compiled by Elias Lönnrot in 1833.

In 1892 Sibelius gained international recognition for his tone poem *En Saga*, and in 1899 composed the *Finlandia* symphony, a piece which has come to symbolise the Finnish struggle for independence.

Sibelius experimented with tonality and rejected the classical sonata form, building movements from a variety of short phrases which grow together as they develop. His work, particularly the early symphonies, is notable for its economical orchestration and melancholic mood.

In 1892 he married Aino Järnefelt (sister of the painter Eero Järnefelt) and together they had six daughters. The family moved to a new home, Ainola, north of Helsinki, in 1904; this is where Sibelius composed five of his seven symphonies. Ainola is now preserved as a museum that is open to the public in summer.

Sibelius studied in Berlin and Vienna and visited the USA in 1914 as an honorary doctor at Yale University. In later life he wrote incidental music for plays and a number of choral works and songs. He died in 1957, at the age of 92.

Sibelius' birthplace in Hämeenlinna, the family's summer residence in Loviisa, and his former home, Ainola, in the town of Järvenpää, now function as museums. The excellent Sibelius Museum in Turku is devoted to the composer and his musical instruments, and frequently holds concerts. It's a terrific introduction to the music of Finland's greatest composer.

admire the graffiti left by former inmates. This building was last used as a prison in 1997. Hours are from 11 am to 5 pm daily. Admission is 10 mk.

Sibelius Museum

Jean Sibelius, the most famous of Finnish composers, was born in Hämeenlinna and went to school here. His childhood home, at Hallituskatu 11, has been converted into a small museum where you can see Sibelius' piano. You may hear recordings of his music on request. The museum is open from 10 am to 4 pm daily in summer and from noon to 4 pm daily at other times. Admission is 15 mk.

Hämeenlinna Art Museum

The town's art museum, at Viipurintie 2, has an interesting collection of Finnish art from the 19th and 20th centuries, including some well-known works. The building's ceiling frescos are by famous Finnish painter Akseli Gallen-Kallela. The museum hours are from noon to 6 pm Tuesday to Sunday (to 8 pm Thursday). Entry is 20 mk.

Museum Gallery House of Cards

Hundreds of postcards are displayed at this small, quirky museum of postcards at Niittykatu 1. Some of the cards on display date back almost a century. The museum gift shop sells reproductions of the best postcards in the collection, as well as stamps. Hours are from 10 am to 4 pm Tuesday to Sunday from June to August. Entry is 10 mk.

Palander House

The historic Palanderin Talo (Palander House) at Lukiokatu 4 is an upper-middle class home built in 1861 and filled with period furnishings, including Art Nouveau furniture and copper utensils. Guided tours are given from noon to 3 pm daily in summer and cost 15 mk.

Hämeenlinna Church

The town church on Linnankatu dates from 1798 and was designed by Jean-Luis Desprez, the court painter for King Gustav III of Sweden. It is modelled after the Pantheon Temple in Rome. It is open daily all year round.

Organised Tours

Lake Cruises Hämeenlinna is on Lake Vanajavesi at the southern tip of a lake network that stretches north to Tampere. See the Getting There & Away section that follows for details.

Places to Stay

There is a hostel and a camping ground in Aulanko (see the Around Hämeenlinna section that follows).

Matkustajakoti Vanaja (☎ 682 2138, Hämeentie 9), 100m south-west of the train station, is a dark, run-down old guesthouse, with rooms for 100 mk per person.

Hotelli Emilia (☎ 612 2106, fax 616 5289, Raatihuoneenkatu 23) is a pleasant small hotel on the pedestrian street in the heart of town. Singles/doubles are 300/400 mk, or 220/320 mk in summer.

Sokos Hotel Vaakuna (☎ 65831, fax 658 3600, Possentie 7), near the train station, is a large modern hotel that vaguely resembles Häme Castle. There are 121 rooms, three saunas and several restaurants. Rooms cost 445/530 mk except in summer when all rooms cost 365 mk.

Places to Eat

Pauliina (Linnankatu 3) is such a popular lunch place that you have to step lively to get a table. It's open for lunch from noon to 4 pm weekdays. The food is good and a full meal costs 35 to 80 mk.

Popino, on Linnankatu between the church and the bus station, is one of the most popular pizza and pasta restaurants. It's especially good value during lunch hours.

Piparkakkutalo (Kirkkorinne 2), one block east of the church, is everyone's favourite for a gourmet meal. The restaurant is in an historic 1906 shingled house with old-fashioned decor. Salads and entrees range in price from 25 to 80 mk.

Dragon (Raatihuoneenkatu 8A) is a good Chinese restaurant in a cellar. Rice and noodle dishes are from 40 mk, and seafood dishes are 55 mk and up.

Laurell (Raatihuoneenkatu 11a) serves filled croissant (15 mk), but most folks come here for the pastries and coffee.

Entertainment

Metropol, on Sibeliuksenkatu at the kauppatori, is a lively bar (closed Monday). Around the corner, *Roadhouse* is a club with live rock music. Cover is 25 mk.

At the lakefront, *Rantakasino*, open summer only, has outdoor tables and is a great place to enjoy a pint of beer.

Getting There & Away

Bus The bus terminal is at Palokunnankatu 25 in the centre. Hourly buses between Helsinki and Tampere stop in Hämeenlinna. From Turku, there are eight buses daily.

Train The train station is 1km north-east of the town centre. Hourly trains between Helsinki and Tampere stop at Hämeenlinna. From Turku, change trains in Toijala.

Boat The MS *Wanaja* cruises between Hämeenlinna and the village of Hauho on Tuesday and Wednesday in summer. Book at Häme Tourist Service.

See the Tampere Getting There & Away for information about the Hämeenlinna-Tampere ferry that operates in summer.

The passenger harbour is just north of the Rantakasino beer terrace.

AROUND HÄMEENLINNA
Aulanko Park
☎ 03

This beautiful park, north-east of Hämeenlinna, was founded early in the 20th century by Hugo Standertskjöld, who dreamt of a Central European-style park with ponds, swans, pavilions and exotic trees. He spent a fortune to achieve his goal and the result was Aulanko. In 1930, it was declared a nature conservation area and today is one of the most varied parks in Finland. Although the best way to move around it is on foot, the sealed one-way road (loop) is accessible by private car. An observation tower is open daily in summer. You can play golf and ride horses in Aulanko, and there is a nature trail.

Places to Stay *Rantasipi Aulanko* (☎ 658 801, fax 682 1922) has a long tradition and is considered one of the finest hotels in the region. Its lakeside location could not be better. There are 245 rooms, five saunas and lots of other facilities. Singles/doubles are 720/860 mk, with discounts in summer.

Getting There & Away Bus Nos 2, 13 or 17 will take you to Aulanko from Hämeenlinna centre.

Vanajanlinna Mansion
☎ 03

The hunting mansion of Vanajanlinna (☎ 619 6565), on the Lahti road 10km from the village of Harviala, was built between 1919 and 1924 by the wealthy Rosenlew family. Many of the rooms are richly decorated. Vanajanlinna was long used as the school of the Finnish Communist Party. It can be visited from Monday to Friday year-round, and there is accommodation at the mansion.

Getting There & Away Hourly buses from Hämeenlinna stop at Harviala.

Hattula Church
Pyhän Ristin kirkko (Church of the Holy Cross) in Hattula was built in the 14th century. It is one of the oldest churches in mainland Finland and has beautiful paintings and a number of old statues. The church is 5km north of Hämeenlinna. It is open daily in summer. Entry is 15 mk. The old grain store built in 1840, close to the old church, houses the tourist office and sells handicrafts.

Getting There & Away Take bus No 5 or 6 from Hämeenlinna.

Hauho
This small village has a finely preserved wooden township called **Vanha Raitti**. It includes a small museum and a medieval stone church built in the 15th century. There are several old wooden statues inside.

A bit isolated from the daily life of Hauho, **Hauho-seuran kotimuseoalue** is an open-air museum with several old houses and a windmill. The museums are open daily in summer.

Getting There & Away Hauho is 32km north-east of Hämeenlinna; there are hourly buses. Buses that run between Tampere and Lahti also stop at Hauho.

IITTALA
Iittala is a village 23km north-west of Hämeenlinna along the main Helsinki to Tampere road. It is best known for its glass factory, which sells its products under the brand name 'Iittala'.

The **Glass Centre** is opposite the bus terminal. It is open from 10 am to 8 pm daily in summer and until 5 pm daily at other times. The interesting glass museum exhibits objects designed and manufactured locally. It also gives an insight into the history of Finnish design. Admission is 10 mk. However, you don't have to pay to watch craftspeople blowing glassware in the back room. There is an **art exhibition** at the Glass Centre in summer, with separate entry fee. The glass shop sells second grade products at 35% below normal price. Nearby is a small **chocolate factory** and shop.

Getting There & Away
Iittala is 23km north of Hämeenlinna, and there are frequent buses.

SÄÄKSMÄKI
This historical and scenic area north-west of Hämeenlinna on the main road to Tampere is one of the highlights of the region.

Rapola Hill
Rapolan Linnavuori on Rapola Hill is the largest prehistoric fortress in Finland. There are fine views and you can follow a marked **trail** that will take you to 100 burial mounds on the western side of the hill. You can get to Rapola either by following the signs from the main road, or by taking the narrow road, Rapolankuja, that passes by the privately owned Rapola estate.

Sääksmäki Church
This fine stone church was built at the end of the 15th century and reconstructed in 1933. In addition to the interesting paintings inside, there is a small church museum.

Visavuori
Once the studio of Emil Wickström, a sculptor from the National Romantic era, this is the best-known sight in the region. Visavuori consists of three houses, the oldest of which is the **home of Emil Wickström**, built in 1902 in Karelian and Art Nouveau styles. There is fantastic Art Nouveau furniture. The beautiful **studio** with hundreds of sculptures was built in 1903 and later expanded.

The astronomical observatory also gives a glimpse of the attractive lake scenery. **Kari Paviljonki** is dedicated to Kari Suomalainen,

Emil Wickström's grandson. He is one of the most famous political cartoonists in Finland, and in the early 1960s he received an award from the US National Cartoonist Society for his daring cartoons on communism. The museum is open daily in summer and Tuesday to Sunday during the rest of the year. Admission costs 30 mk. There are ferries from Tampere and Hämeenlinna in summer.

Getting There & Away
Sääksmäki can be reached via private car, or by ferry from Tampere or Hämeenlinna.

NUUTAJÄRVI
The well known Nuutajärvi glass manufacturer is based in the small village by the same name, 4km west of the Turku to Tampere road. **Glass blowing** can be seen and there is a factory outlet store with inexpensive second quality glassware. The **Prykäri Glass Museum** exhibits old glassware and tools. The museum is open daily and charges 10 mk entry.

OX ROAD
One of the oldest roads in Finland and still partly unpaved, the Ox Road (Härkätie) winds through rural landscape.

Renko
Renko, 15km south-west of Hämeenlinna is the first stop along the Ox Road. The local museum, **Härkätien museo**, is devoted to the Ox Road and its history.

Tammela
Tammela village is on the shores of Lake Pyhäjärvi. The old **Tammela church** dates from the early 1500s. It was enlarged in 1785 and is almost like a museum: there are medieval sculptures and old coats of arms. The church is open daily in summer.

Tammela provided King Gustav II Adolf of Sweden with 24 soldiers during the Thirty Years' War in 1630 (the largest number of such soldiers from anywhere in Finland) and the 'Hakkapeliitat' are now honoured by a **statue** near the church.

North of Tammela village, the impressive **Mustiala Manor** was originally owned in the 16th century by Marshal Klaus Horn, a Swede. Now the estate houses an agricultural school and there is a small museum devoted to farming tools (open Sunday).

Places to Stay & Eat *Tammelan Krouvi* (☎ 03-436 0647) has just two rooms at 200/260 mk, including breakfast. The place serves meals and tasty lager brewed at Mustiala Manor.

Saari Park

The scenery in Saari Park, south of Tammela, inspired many painters during the National Romantic era. The attractive sand ridge is part of the estate of Saari, which includes a private manor nearby. The park allows public access to anyone, any time. For the best view, climb the 20m **observation tower**. You can get the keys from the restaurant on the eastern side of the park.

Hämeen Pirtti is a cultural centre and café. There is information available on walks in the surrounding forest.

Somero

The Ox Road town of Somero was founded in the 15th century. The **kivisakasti**, a stone building on the grounds of the old **church**, dates from that time. The church dates from 1859. **Someron torpparimuseo**, the local museum, includes a windmill and some very old peasants' houses. The museum, north of the centre, is open only in summer.

Ateljee Hiidenlinna is the isolated home of Reino Koivuniemi, a local artist, who built this castle-like studio to exhibit his sculpture. To get there, take your wheels first to the village of Somerniemi and follow signs from there. It's open a few days each week from June to September.

Jokioinen

The town of Jokioinen has a unique history. In the 16th century, King Erik XIV of Sweden (who later went insane) gave exclusive rights to the Swedish war hero Klaus Horn to establish an estate in the Jokioinen region. At the time of independence, in 1917, it had grown to be the largest such estate in Finland. The main estate, in the town centre, now houses an agricultural research institute. There is also an odd-looking red granary, with three floors and a clock tower. The granary was stolen from the nearby Humppila in the 18th century. Today it's open in summer as a gallery.

The little **church** of Jokioinen (1631), a kilometre past the granary, is the second oldest wooden church in Finland but renovations hide the original architecture. The church is open daily in summer.

A **museum train** runs from Jokioinen to Humppila. The 14km trip takes one hour and runs on summer Sundays.

There's also a **vicarage museum**, which looks like a haunted house, near the Jokioinen centre.

Getting There & Away

There are regular buses from Hämeenlinna to Renko, the first village on the Ox Road route. At the other end, there are buses between Jokioinen and Helsinki. Local buses connect the rest of the towns, mainly coming from the large industrial town of Forssa. However, it's easiest to explore the Ox Road by private car.

Central Lakeland

KUOPIO
* pop 85,250   ☎ 017

Kuopio is an attractive, vital city surrounded by forests and lakes. There is a wide variety of things to see and do in this centre of the Savo region, on Lake Kallavesi. Views from Puijo Hill are as unforgettable as the bustling Kuopio kauppatori or the treasures of the Orthodox Church Museum – and just south of the town centre is the world's largest smoke sauna!

History
The first Savonian people entered the area at the end of the 15th century, and in 1552 the first church was built. In 1652 the ambitious

THE LAKELAND

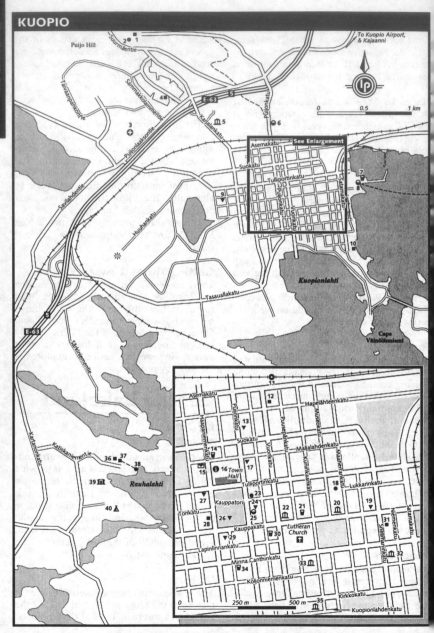

KUOPIO

Count Per Brahe founded the 'church village' of Kuopio, which had little significance until 1775, when Gustav III of Sweden incorporated Kuopio as a provincial capital. Several important figures of the National Romantic era lived here from the 1850s, but the main growth of Kuopio has occurred during the 20th century.

Information

Tourist Office The tourist office, Kuopioinfo (☎ 182 585, fax 261 3538) at Haapaniemenkatu 17, is next to the town hall. It is open from 9 am to 6 pm Monday to Friday, 9 am to 4 pm Saturday from June to mid-August. At other times it's open from 9 am to 5 pm Monday to Friday. It has information on attractions and accommodation in the entire Kuopio region.

Post The most convenient post office (70110 Kuopio) is on Haapaniemenkatu across from the tourist office. Hours are 9 am to 6 pm weekdays.

Internet Resources & Library The public library at Maaherrankatu 12 is open from 10 am to 8 pm weekdays, 10 am to 3 pm Saturday. There is an Internet terminal on the 2nd floor, but you'll probably need to book several days in advance.

The main Web site for Kuopio is www .travel.fi/kuopio/.

Left Luggage The train station has lockers for 10 mk that may be used for a maximum of 24 hours.

Medical & Emergency Services There's a pharmacy on the kauppatori at Puijonkatu 23. The University Hospital (Yliopistollinen Sairaala) is in Puijo, just north-west of the centre.

In a general emergency call ☎ 112, for police call ☎ 10022 and for a doctor dial ☎ 10023.

Puijo Hill

The pride of Kuopio is Puijo Hill, and the spectacular views from the 75m **Puijo Tower**. The lift to the top of the tower costs 15 mk and is open year-round. At the top is a revolving restaurant (summer only) with views of Lake Kallavesi and beyond (see Places to Eat).

Surrounding Puijo Hill is one of the best-preserved **spruce forests** in the region (see Activities). Take bus No 6 from the town centre to reach Puijo.

Jätkänkämpällä Smoke Sauna

Not to be missed is the world's largest smoke sauna at Jätkänkämpällä, a former

Sauna – Smoke and Steam but no Sex

The ancient Romans had their steam and hot-air baths, and the Finns have their sauna (pronounced 'SOW-oo-nah' not 'SAW-nuh'). It's one of the most essential elements of Finnish culture. Finns will prescribe a sauna session to cure all ills, from a head cold to sunburn!

The earliest written description of the Finnish sauna dates from chronicles of Ukrainian historian Nestor in 1113. There are also numerous references to sauna-going in the Finnish national epic, the *Kalevala*.

Today there are 1.2 million saunas in Finland, which means that practically all Finns have access to one. Most are private, situated in Finnish homes. An invitation to bathe in a family's sauna is an honour, just as it is to be invited to a person's home for a meal.

There are also public saunas, often found on the edge of a lake or by the sea. Usually these have separate sections for men and women and if there is just one sauna the hours are different for men and women. In unisex saunas you will be given some sort of wrap or covering to wear. Indeed, Finns are quite strict about the nonsexual character of the sauna bath and this point should be respected. The sauna was originally a place to bathe, meditate and even give birth. It's not, as many foreigners would believe, a place for sex. Travellers Mark and Maria Anderson note, 'If the sauna's hot enough, sex would be impossible anyway'. The ideal temperature for a sauna is about 90°C.

The traditional *savusauna*, or 'smoke sauna', is marvellous if you can find one; the modern electric sauna stoves used by most hotels and hostels are very dry and lack the authentic smell of burning wood, heated stones and *löyly* (steam). Look for authentic, log-heated savusauna in the countryside. The world's biggest savusauna at Jätkänkämpällä is adjacent to the Rauhalahti camping ground and hostel in Kuopio – it seats 60 and is unisex.

Proper sauna etiquette dictates that you use a *kauha* (ladle) to throw water on the *kiuas* (sauna stove), which then gives off the löyly. At this point, at least in summer in the countryside, you might take the *vihta* or *vasta* (a bunch of fresh, leafy *koivu* (birch) twigs) and lightly strike yourself. This improves circulation and gives your skin a pleasant smell. When you are sufficiently warmed, you'll jump in the sea, a lake, river or pool. The swim is such an integral part of the experience that in the dead of winter, Finns cut a hole in the ice and jump right in!

loggers' camp near the Rauhalahti tourist centre. The 60-person, mixed sauna is open to the public from 2 pm to 8 pm Tuesday and Friday year-round. It is heated a full 24 hours in advance with a great big indoor bonfire, hence the name 'smoke sauna'. Entry is 50 mk per person and guests are given wraps to wear. Bring a swimsuit to swim in the lake – devoted sauna-goers do so even when it is covered with ice!

There is a restaurant on the premises, and live music and storytelling at a small outdoor theatre on summer evenings. Take bus Nos 16, 19, 20 or 21 to Rauhalahti, or take a lake ferry in summer.

Rauhalahti Tourist Centre

The tourist centre has grown around the former **Rauhalahti Manor**, an area which has been converted into a children's park called Uppo-Nalle after the bear in Elina Karjalainen's fairy tales. The whole Rauhalahti area is full of amusements and activities for children and adults. The children's park is open from noon to 8 pm daily in summer. Bus Nos 16, 19, 20 and 21 connect the Rauhalahti area with the town centre. There are lake ferries from the passenger harbour in the town centre during summer.

Orthodox Church Museum

The Orthodox Church Museum, at Karjalankatu 1, is one of the most interesting museums in Finland. Its collections were brought to Finland from monasteries, churches and *tsasouni* (chapels) in USSR-occupied Karelia. Today it is the most notable collection of Eastern Orthodox icons, textiles and religious objects outside Russia. The oldest artefacts date from the 10th century.

The museum is in a plain brown building a kilometre west of the train station. It's open from 10 am to 4 pm Tuesday to Sunday from May to late August (until 5 pm in July). Admission is 20 mk adult, 10 mk senior and student, 5 mk child. Take bus No 7.

VB Photographic Centre

The Photographic Centre at Kuninkaankatu 14-16 is devoted to Victor Barsokevitsch, who was a local portrait photographer. His studio is now a photo gallery, but there are enough old cameras and photos to call this a museum. In the garden, you can enjoy a cup of coffee in summer, and be astounded by the camera obscura. Hours are from 10 am to 7 pm weekdays, noon to 4 pm weekends from mid-June to late August. During May and September, hours are 11 am to 5 pm Tuesday to Friday (until 7 pm Wednesday) and noon to 4 pm Saturday and Sunday. Entry is 10 mk.

The Old Kuopio Museum

This block of old town houses (entrance at Kirkkokatu 22) forms another of Kuopio's delightful museums. It consists of several homes – all with period furniture and décor – seven of which are open at present. Apteekkimuseo in building No 11 contains old pharmacy paraphernalia. There is also a nice museum café, where you can have coffee and taste the delicious *rahkapiirakka* (a local pastry). Hours are 10 am to 5 pm daily from mid-May to mid-September until 7 pm Wednesday). At other times it's open from 10 am to 3 pm Tuesday to Sunday. Entry is 15 mk.

Kuopio Museum

The beautiful Art Nouveau 'castle' at Kauppakatu 23 houses the Kuopio Museum, with interesting archaeological and cultural displays. There are also frequent special exhibitions. Hours are 9 am to 4 pm Monday to Saturday (until 8 pm Wednesday) and 11 am to 6 pm Sunday from May to late August. At other times, the museum is open 9 am to 4 pm weekdays. Entry is 15 mk.

Kuopio Art Museum

The art museum at Kauppakatu 35, near the Kuopio Museum, features mostly modern art in temporary exhibitions. It is open from 9 am to 4.30 pm Monday to Friday (until 8 pm Wednesday) and 11 am to 6 pm Sunday. Admission is 15 mk.

Snellman Home Museum

The Snellman Home Museum, at Snellmaninkatu 19, is a branch of the Kuopio Museum. At this old house JV Snellman, an important cultural figure during the National Romantic era of the 19th century, used to live. The museum is similar to the Old Kuopio Museum, but really only interesting to students of Finnish history. It's open from 10 am to 3 pm daily (until 7 pm Wednesday) from mid-May to late August. Entry is 10 mk.

Activities

At the Rauhalahti centre, bike rentals are 10 mk per hour or 50 mk per day, mountain bikes 20 mk per hour or 80 mk per day. Rowing boats cost 15 mk per hour, and canoes 35 mk per hour or 120 mk per day. You can also rent roller skates or play minigolf on the extensive grounds. Nearby is a riding stable that offers trail rides on gentle Icelandic ponies.

Activities at Rauhalahti during winter include ice skating, cross-country skiing and ice fishing. Ice fishing tackle rents for 10 mk per day, and snowshoes or cross-country skis are 25 mk for two hours or 50 mk per day.

At Puijo Hill, there are also mountain-biking and walking tracks, including a marked nature trail. During winter there are cross-county ski trails, and equipment rentals are available.

Organised Tours

Lake Cruises During summer months there are daily departures for several different types of lake cruises, ranging in price from 30 to 60 mk. Most are two to three hours in length. Special theme cruises are dinner and dancing, wine tasting, or a trip to a local berry farm. There are also daily cruises to Rauhalahti tourist centre; the best deal is the smoke-sauna cruise on Tuesday, which costs 75 mk for the cruise, sauna and towel rent.

Tickets for all cruises are available at the passenger harbour. Schedules are available at the harbour or the tourist office.

Longer cruises go to Savonlinna and to the monastery at Uusi-Valamo; for more information, see the Getting There & Away sections for those towns.

Special Events

Tanssii ja Soi is the Kuopio Dance Festival in late June and early July, the most international and the most interesting of Kuopio's annual events. This is where you'll see folks like the Finnish All Star Afro-Cuban Jazz Orchestra, as well as talented performers from many other countries.

In addition to performances, dance lessons are also given during the festival, but these must be booked well in advance (☎ 182 586).

For more information contact Kuopio Dance Festival (☎ 282 1541, fax 261 1990, kuopio.dance.festival@travel.fi), Torikatu 18, 70110 Kuopio. For advance ticket sales see www.lippupalvelu.fi/.

The Kuopio International Wine Festival, held in early July, celebrates a different wine-producing region each year.

Places to Stay – Budget & Mid-Range

Camping The lakeside *Camping Rauhalahti* (☎ 361 2244, fax 262 4004, jukka.makkonen@kuopio.fi, Kiviniementie),

adjacent to the Rauhalahti tourist centre, is open from June to late August and charges from 65 to 90 mk for tent sites and 130 to 420 mk for cabins. There are 90 cabins, and a large reduction is available for subsequent nights. Bus Nos 16, 19, 20 and 21 go to the camping ground.

Hostels *Hostelli Rauhalahti* (☎ 473 111, fax 473 470, Katiskaniementie 8) is an HI-affiliated hostel next to the spa hotel in the Rauhalahti tourist centre complex, 5km south-west of the centre. Take bus No 16, 19, 20 or 21 from the town centre to get there. The hostel is open year-round and has beds from 120 to 230 mk per person. Groups of two to four rooms share a well-equipped kitchen and bath, and guests may use the spa facilities for a fee. This hostel is very popular, so advance bookings are advised.

The lake ferry SS *Leppävirta* at the harbour rents cabins during summer at a cost of 100 mk per person. There are no HI discounts.

Guesthouses Of the several *matkakot* (guesthouses) near the train station, *Puijo Hovi* (☎ 261 4943, Vuorikatu 35) is the cleanest and most pleasant. Singles/doubles cost 170/220 mk.

At the train station itself, the *Station Boarding House* (☎ 580 0569, Asemakatu 1) has singles/doubles/triples for 250/400/525 mk.

Hotel *Hotel Kievari Matias* (☎ 282 8333, Hiihtäjäntie 11) is a small, private hotel north-west of the town centre. It has modern, clean rooms for 220/320 mk, breakfast and morning sauna included. On weekends all rooms are 20 mk less.

Places to Stay – Top End

Hotels – Central *Hotel Atlas* (☎ 21 2111, fax 211 2103, Haapaniemenkatu 22) is a Best Western hotel right on the kauppatori. Rooms cost 440/520 mk regularly, 390/420 mk on weekends and 365/395 in summer.

Near the passenger harbour, *Hotel Jahti* (☎ 264 4400, fax 264 4444, Snellmaninkatu 23) is a pleasant, intimate small hotel with a good restaurant. It's a 500m walk to the kauppatori. Rooms cost 350/430 mk, 270/340 mk on weekends and in summer.

Scandic Hotel Kuopio (☎ 195 111, fax 195 170, Satamakatu 1) is a large place on the shores of Lake Kallavesi, 900m from the kauppatori. There are 134 rooms, several restaurants and saunas, and a pool. Singles/doubles are from 520/620 mk regularly, 420/460 mk on weekends and 365/395 mk in summer. Suites cost 1500 mk.

Hotel – Rauhalahti *Hotel-Spa Rauhalahti* (☎ 473 111 or 473 473, fax 473 470, Katiskaniementie 8) at the Rauhalahti tourist centre is a superb place to stay. Rooms cost 440/600 mk (summer 320/420 mk). In addition to the spa facilities, the hotel has a restaurant, café and very popular dance club. Advance bookings are advised.

Hotel – Puijo The *Hotel Puijo* (☎ 209 111, fax 209 109) on top of Puijo Hill was originally built in the 1920s. Rooms are from 270/340 mk, including free entry to the observation tower.

Places to Eat
At the kauppatori you'll find stalls selling fresh produce, coffee and snacks. Look for *kalakukko*, a sandwich, eaten hot or cold, that is made with locally caught fish baked inside a rye loaf. The *kauppahalli* (covered market) is at the southern end of the kauppatori.

Trube Torinkulma at the Sokos building near the kauppatori has the best pastries and cakes, as well as sandwiches and other light fare.

For good Turkish food, try *Pamukkale Kebab (Puijonkatu 27)*. This is a pleasant place, a cut above your typical kebab joint. Meals are from 25 mk.

Zorbas (Puijonkatu 37) is a Greek restaurant with a weekday lunch special for 37 mk, salad, bread and coffee included. The lunch menu changes daily.

Another good place for lunch is *Lounas-Salonki (Kasarmikatu 12)*, a charming place in a neighbourhood of wooden houses just west of the centre. There are choices from 30 mk.

Golden Rax Pizza Buffet, on the 2nd floor at Puijonkatu 45, overlooks the kauppatori. The food isn't particularly good, but who could pass up all-you-can-eat pizza, pasta, salad and chicken wings for 40 mk? The special buffet is served at lunch and dinner.

For a truly local taste, visit *Vapaasatama Sampo (Kauppakatu 13)*. This place – the town's oldest restaurant – has been in Kuopio for almost 70 years. It serves *muikku* (whitefish) in various forms and charges 50 to 70 mk for a meal. The room is plain, and most of the staff do not speak English. Still, it's a unique experience.

Puijon Torni (☎ 209 111) is the revolving panorama restaurant at the top of the Puijo observation tower, open in summer only. Buffet lunch or dinner is 60 to 90 mk.

Just south of the kauppatori, *Burts Cafee (Kauppakatu 28)* is the town's most charming café.

Entertainment
Wanha Satama at the passenger harbour is a lively pub with a large beer terrace in summer, plus plenty of live music and dancing.

Kummisetä (Minna Canthinkatu 44) is a very popular pub-cum-restaurant, a rustic place like a little red barn. On sunny summer days its terrace is really packed. *Vanha Trokari (Kauppakatu 29)* is a stylish pub and brewery, also with outdoor tables in summer. On the narrow alley of Käsityönkatu, you'll find *Henry's Pub*, the best place in town for live music, usually rock.

Antura Pub (Maljalahdenkatu 35) is a bar and club on the kauppatori.

Getting There & Away
Air There are half a dozen direct flights from Helsinki to Kuopio daily.

Bus The busy bus terminal, just north of the train station, serves the entire southern half of Finland, with regular departures to all major towns and villages in the vicinity. Each destination has its own platform.

Train Five trains a day run to Kuopio from Helsinki. The fastest connection takes just 4½ hours. Kouvola, Pieksämäki, Iisalmi and Kajaani also have direct trains to Kuopio.

Boat Ferries and cruise boats depart from the passenger harbour, about 600m east of the kauppatori. There is regular service to Savonlinna and to the Valamo Orthodox Monastery during summer (see the Getting There & Away sections for those towns).

Getting Around

To/From the Airport The Kuopio airport is 17km north of town. Airport buses depart from the kauppatori. The 30 minute trip costs 22 mk one way. Airport taxis (☎ 106 400) cost 50 to 70 mk and must be booked at least three hours in advance.

Bus The local bus network is extensive. A single ticket costs 11 mk Monday to Saturday, 13 mk Sunday. Some buses travel beyond Kuopio city limits, with higher rates.

HEINÄVESI
☎ 017

The most beautiful lake route in Finland passes by the village of Heinävesi. The main village lies amid hilly country, and canals provide a means of local transport.

Climb up to the **church** for views over Lake Kermajärvi. The church, built in 1892, seats 2000 people and is open daily in summer.

Down the hill from the church is the **local museum**. Entry is 5 mk.

There is a **handicrafts centre** opposite the museum. If you don't want to buy anything, you can have a go at making your own rug. The handicrafts centre is open Monday to Friday.

Places to Stay

Gasthaus (☎ 562 411), in the centre opposite the bus terminal, has clean and comfortable rooms that are reasonably priced. The place serves an excellent breakfast.

The friendly hostel *Pohjataipaleen Kartano* (☎ 566 419) is by the lake, about 13km south of the centre. Call ahead to be picked up at the bus or train station by hostel staff, and be prepared for a long sauna session once you arrive. Beds cost 65 to 75 mk.

Getting There & Away

The bus terminal in the village centre has departures for villages around the lake. The train station is 5km to the south. You must buy your ticket on the train.

In summer, passenger ferries from Kuopio or Savonlinna call at the Heinävesi jetty, just below the village. See the Savonlinna Getting There & Away section for more information. There are also local ferries across the lake to Karvio.

KARVIO
☎ 017

Attractive rapids are the highlight of Karvio village, and the canal serves as a jetty for ships. The rapids are good for fishing (a permit is required). The Neste petrol station doubles as the Matkahuolto bus station, and tourist information and pottery are also available there.

Karvio is central enough to serve as a base for covering the northern side of Heinävesi. You can rent bicycles and rowing boats here, and obtain fishing permits.

Places to Stay & Eat

Karvio Camping (☎ 563 603, Takunlahdentie 2) is a clean place, open from May to mid-September, with cottages from 100 to 350 mk and tent sites for about 70 mk. Across the road is *Uittotupa* (☎ 563 519, which has cabins and cottages priced from 100 to 300 mk. Uittotupa is renowned for its homemade bread, which can be sampled at lunch or purchased by the loaf. Across the bridge is **Karvion Kievari** (☎ *563 504*), a pleasant old manor house with reasonably priced rooms. For a splurge, try the excellent buffet lunch.

Getting There & Away

You can get to Karvio by bus or ferry from Heinävesi. There are two direct buses daily from Varkaus.

LINTULA ORTHODOX CONVENT
☎ 017

The only Orthodox convent in Finland, Lintula is much quieter than the popular Valamo monastery (see below). It's a serene place that is well worth visiting.

Lintula was founded in Karelia in 1895 and transferred during WWII to Savo and then Häme. The nuns founded a convent at the present location in 1946. You can visit from 9 am to 6 pm daily from May to late August. A small shop on the premises sells wool and candles which are manufactured at the convent.

Places to Stay

Lintulan Vierasmaja (☎ *563 106*) is a small red house at the back of the convent. There are simple but clean rooms, with separate bathroom. Both sexes may stay here from 100/160 mk for singles/doubles.

Getting There & Away

A visit to Lintula convent is included on the Monastery Cruise from Kuopio. There are also regular ferries from Valamo to Lintula. See the Valamo Getting There & Away section for more information.

VALAMO ORTHODOX MONASTERY
☎ 017

The Valamo monastery – an Orthodox monastery, the only one in Finland – is one of Savo's most popular attractions. Its history goes back 800 years to the island of Valamo on Lake Lagoda.

The original Valamo monastery was annexed by the Red Army during WWII.

Most of its treasures were brought to Finland, and some of them remain here (others are in Kuopio).

The Valamo monastery has grown considerably over the last several decades, partly because of increased tourism, which is the monastery's only source of income. In fact, it's become a somewhat commercialised place, with crowds of summer tourists flocking to buy souvenir beeswax candles, icons and CDs at the Tuohus gift shop. If you're looking for something more peaceful you might want to visit Lintula convent (see above).

The two churches at the monastery contain a number of priceless icons. The new church was finished in 1977, while the old one was built in 1940. Down at the riverside, the small *tsasouna* (chapel) of St Nicholas, is also worth a look.

Guided tours of the monastery are conducted regularly in English for 15 mk per person. Services are open to the public and there are several daily.

The grounds around the monastery make Valamo an attractive place to relax – take a picnic. However, taking photos in the churches, or of the monks, is forbidden unless you get permission at the gate. Women are asked not to wear shorts within the complex.

For more information contact Valamo Monastery (☎ 570 1504, fax 570 1510, valamo@mpoli.fi), Valamontie 42, 79850 Uusi-Valamo, or see www.mpoli.fi/valamo/index.html/.

Places to Stay & Eat

You can stay in the monastery itself, in the **Valamo Guesthouse** (☎ *570 1504*), where beds are 95 mk per person in shared rooms (with two to five persons), or 110 mk for a single room. The **Valamo Hotel** has rooms from 175/320 mk. All accommodation prices include breakfast.

The monastery café-restaurant, **Trapesa** has snacks, good meals for 30 mk and a tempting lunch or dinner buffet for 50 mk. A Russian-style 'high tea' in the evenings costs 35 mk, but must be pre-booked.

Pulp Fiction and Fact

Finland, a country that is incredibly green and covered with trees, appears at first glance to be quite ecologically conscious. Some 70% of Finland is forested, the highest percentage anywhere in the world. Indeed, according to the Finnish Forest Industries Federation (FFIF), Finland's forests are healthier than ever, with many thriving species of flora and fauna. Any logging which goes on, FFIF argues, merely imitates the effects of natural forest fires.

Environmentalist groups dispute the FFIF's upbeat claims. This is, after all, a country that depends heavily on logging – wood and paper products account for about one-third of all Finnish exports. Over the past 30 years or so, ancient woodlands have dwindled or disappeared in all parts of the country except sparsely populated north-eastern Finland: the regions of North Karelia, Kainuu and Lapland. The World Wide Fund for Nature (WWF) and Finland's own environment ministry point out that only about 3% of Finland's native woodlands maintain the level of biodiversity of its ancient forests. Most forest areas are now planted only with trees of commercial value, chiefly pine and birch.

The WWF and Greenpeace argue that short-sighted commercial practices have placed some 692 species of Finnish plants and animals at risk of extinction. These include the flying squirrel, osprey and white-backed woodpecker, as well as fungi, mosses, lichens and invertebrates which need a variety of tree species of all ages, plus large quantities of dead or decaying wood, in order to survive.

Despite the impending environmental havoc, much of the paper produced from Finnish timber bears an eco-friendly label: 'This comes from sustainably managed Finnish forests'. The WWF argue the word 'sustainable' is used in the narrowest of senses – by concentrating on a couple of commercial species, the Finns have been able to maintain their timber yield but they certainly aren't sustaining the forest as a whole.

Fortunately, the mid and late 1990s have brought some signs of change. Demonstrations against environmentally damaging forestry practices in Scandinavia took place throughout Europe in 1995. That year, the Finnish government undertook its first extensive forest surveys (it was the first country in the world to begin doing so). A landmark Forest Act, with stricter measures for protection of biodiversity, followed in 1997. Since then, timber harvesters on both public and private land have made greater efforts to preserve the richest forest habitats – such as areas around rivers, springs and gorges – when cutting.

Environmentalists are pleased with the improvements – particularly since similar guidelines issued a decade earlier were largely ignored – although they do remain cautious. Those who care about saving Finland's forests know that as long as the timber export trade brings in billions of markkaa each year, conservation measures are always likely to be unpopular in many quarters.

Getting There & Away

Bus There are regular buses from Heinävesi, Joensuu, Mikkeli and even Helsinki.

Ferry You can reach Valamo monastery from Kuopio on a Monastery Cruise. The service is available three times a week in summer and costs 240 mk return. The cruise includes a visit to the Lintula Convent.

There are also local cruises from Valamo to Lintula.

LEPPÄVIRTA
☎ 017

Soisalo, the largest island in Finland, is surrounded by lakes, canals and rivers. Leppävirta is one of the canal towns that make the trip around Soisalo possible.

Stop at both **churches** along the main street in Leppävirta, and check out the **museum** at the larger church, which opens daily except Monday in summer. There is also the **Unnukka tourist centre** just off the main road. The historic **Konnus Canal**, 6km from the village, has an exhibition and offers fishing opportunities.

Places to Stay
Camping Mansikkaharju (☎ 554 1383, *Kalmalahti*), 500m south of Unnukka tourist centre, has 70 mk tent sites and some cottages.

The HI-affiliated *Hirvola Hostel* (☎ 558 188, *ikka.kanniainen@pp.inet.fi*, *Timoantie 100*) is open year-round. There are 16 beds, all costing 150 mk per person.

Getting There & Away
Buses between Varkaus and Kuopio stop in Leppävirta; there are several buses daily.

SUONENJOKI
pop 8600   ☎ 017

Strawberry Town attracts crowds of strawberry pickers every summer, and travellers might be able to earn some extra cash if there is a labour shortage. There is a **local museum** and a **church** near the train station, as well as all the essential services.

Places to Stay
Suonenjoen Ammatti-Instituutti Maatlousoppilaitos (☎ 513 511, *Jalkalantie 60*) is open year-round and has rooms for 100 mk per person. *Mansikkupaikka*, or Strawberry Place, (☎ 511 761, *Koulukatu 2*) has rooms at slightly higher prices.

Getting There & Away
Some Kuopio-bound trains stop at Suonenjoki. There are buses from Mikkeli, Kuopio and Pieksämäki.

VARKAUS
pop 24,000   ☎ 017

The town of Varkaus has a superb location, surrounded by water, but its centre is rather depressing, due to several huge factories that dominate the view. Much of the population works for local paper and pulp industries. Although *varkaus* means 'stealth', Varkaus is not a dangerous place to visit.

Orientation
Varkaus has grown over several islands and headlands, and is surrounded by water. The main commercial centre is close to the central station, and the main street is Keskuskatu. The Taipale canal is 2km east.

Information
The tourist office (☎ 552 7311) is at Kauppatori 6. There are post offices near the train station, and near the tourist office.

Museum of Mechanical Music
If you have a vehicle, it is well worth driving the 2km from the town centre to the Mekaanisen Musiikin Museo at Pelimanninkatu 8. A Finnish-German couple runs this delightful collection of 250 unusual musical instruments. It has been voted the best museum in Finland in years past. The two floors of old, carefully renovated mechanical instruments from the USA and Europe are presented in a hilarious way. There are guided tours every half-hour if there is demand, and admission is 40 mk. The museum is open Tuesday to Sunday from early March to mid-December.

Taipale Canal
East of the town centre is a canal area. The new canal was built by Russians, and the old canal area includes **Keskuskanavamuseo**, a canal museum with information on the history and use of Finnish canals. The new canal is worth a look when logs are floated through it. There are canal cruises on weekends in summer.

Places to Stay & Eat
Camping Taipale (☎ 552 6644, *Leiritie*) has tent sites from 50 to 90 mk and cottages from 200 to 510 mk. It's open from late May to mid-August.

The HI-affiliated *Varkauden Retkeilymaja* (☎ 579 5700, *Kuparisepänkatu 5*) is a hostel that is open from June to mid-August. It has beds from 65 to 100 mk.

Hotel Oscar (☎ 579 011, fax 579 0500, Kauppatori 4) has rooms from 620/760 mk, but all rooms are 420 mk in summer.

Kauppakatu near the train station is a street with several eateries, such as *Herkkupizza* and *Kahvila Aaretti*.

Getting There & Away

There are daily flights from Helsinki to Varkaus. Keskusliikenneasema is the central station, which includes train and bus stations. Trains between Joensuu and Turku stop in Varkaus.

JUVA

☎ 015

The village of Juva, midway between Mikkeli and Varkaus at Lake Jukajärvi, spans several kilometres, from the main road No 5 in the west to the Partala area in the east. The village centre is along the main street, Juvantie. You can get travel information from the tourist office (☎ 755 5224) at the town hall building at Juvantie 13.

History

Juva was one of Savo's first inhabited areas during the 14th century. The centre of a large administrative area, it had a wooden Catholic church and large estates gradually emerged – some manor houses still remain. Unfavourable border changes during the 18th century meant a blow for Juva's trade contacts with the east, and the area has since declined.

Things to See & Do

Just at the crossing on road No 5, **Puutaitonäyttely** has a collection of 500 wooden sculptures made by 40 artists. It is open daily from June to September, and admission is 30 mk. East from here, the **water tower** is open daily in summer, and its café serves coffee and snacks.

Central Juva is a mainly commercial area, but has an imposing 1863 stone **church**. Nearby, **Käsityökeskus** sells and exhibits local handicraft.

East of the centre, **Suomen Mehiläis museo** is a national museum devoted t bee-keeping. There are 500 exhibits an you'll find honey and other bee-keeping related items on sale. The museum is ope daily in summer. **Vihertietokeskus** is an in formation centre which promotes 'green ideas in farming and gardening.

The imposing Partala manor area house two museums: **Juvan museo** is a museum o local history, and **Karjalaisten museo** dis plays items from Soviet-occupied Karelia These museums are open from Tuesday t Sunday in summer.

Canoeing the Vesiluontopolku Route

Previously known as Oravareitti, the Juva t Sulkava canoeing route has been rename the 'Aquatic Nature Trail'. It's a 52kr scenic route that travels via lakes, rivers an rapids. Only one section is unpassable – ɛ Kuhakoski rapids, where canoes must b carried 50m past a broken dam. Otherwis the rapids are relatively simple, though th water level drops 25m between Juva an Sulkava. A waterproof map in English an German is available, and includes all esser tial information. Contact Juva Camping fɒ canoe rentals.

Places to Stay

Juva Camping (☎ 451 930) has cottage from 160 to 290 mk and tent sites for 6 to 75 mk. It is open from early June t mid-August and is not far from the mai road. You can rent rowing boats an canoes here.

The HI-affiliated *Hostel Toivio (☎ 45 622)* is approximately 10km from th village, on the Sulkava road. Dormitor beds are 75 to 85 mk. It's open from June t late August.

There are a number of pubs, grillis an cafés in Juva, including a *café* at the b station. The *restaurant* next to the touri office in the town hall building serve wholesome and inexpensive mea throughout the day.

Getting There & Away

There are express buses to Juva from Mikkeli. The village itself is 3km from the main road, so hitchhikers will probably end up walking all the way.

MIKKELI
☎ 015

Mikkeli was the headquarters of the Finnish army during WWII, and some of its attractions relate to those years. The friendly Mikkeli tourist office (☎ 151 444) is at Hallituskatu 3 on the kauppatori.

Things to See

Päämajamuseo (closed in winter) was the army's command centre, and Jalkaväkimuseo is one of the largest military museums in Finland. Kenkävero, outside the centre at Pursialankatu 6, is a handicraft centre where you can get involved and create something for yourself.

Fishing

The Mikkeli district is one of the best in Finland for freshwater fishing – its many lakes teem with perch, salmon and trout. In winter, ice-fishing is popular. For information on fishing permits, locations, guides and equipment rental contact the tourist office.

Places to Stay & Eat

The summer hotel *Metsätähti* (☎ 173 777, *Metsäkouluntie 10*) has beds from 85 mk per person. There are several expensive hotels in the centre.

The *kauppahalli* (covered market) is entered from an alley next to the tourist office, and adjacent is *Kahvila Matkahuolto*, good for a quick, cheap meal.

The market is one of the best in the region – it's especially lively in summer and a source of delicious local specialties.

Getting There & Away

There are up to five trains daily from Helsinki and a similar number of connections from towns in the north. From other directions, change at Pieksämäki or Kouvola.

There are lake cruises between Mikkeli and Ristiina in summer; the Mikkeli tourist office has schedule and fare information.

RISTIINA
- pop 5200   ☎ 015

Ristiina, one of the region's historic villages, was founded by Count Per Brahe in 1649 and named after Kristina, his wife (subsequently the queen of Sweden). Little remains of the village's glorious past, though there are several places that reflect Per's aspirations.

The main attractions of Ristiina municipality lie 20km from the village. The tourist office will provide a map, and you can rent bicycles from the Brahe hotel.

Ristiina Village

There's quite a distance between the main road and Ristiina's principal attraction, the castle ruins, but most shops and places to stay and eat are situated along the main street, Brahentie. Information is provided by the Klemmari shop at Brahentie 16, 500m from the main road.

Brahelinna is the castle that was built by Per Brahe; its ruin is on a hill 2km from the main road. The castle's high walls and the surrounding forest are lovely.

A sign saying 'Dunckerin kivi' points to a stone that was erected to honour a local, Mr Duncker, who fought and died during the 1809 battles against Russia. The view from the memorial is excellent. Gränna talo, which was transferred here from Mikkeli, has art exhibitions in summer, normally from late June to July only. There's also an open-air summer theatre and a windmill in the area.

Working back towards the main road, the 1775 church is unique in terms of interior decoration as no other church in Savo exhibits so many paintings from the heyday of the Swedish empire. The count and his wife Kristina are more prominently displayed than Jesus Christ himself. The church distributes a leaflet in English, and is open daily in summer.

Nearby, **Käsityökeskus** is a handicraft centre and souvenir shop where mats and other goods are made using traditional methods.

The Rock Paintings of Astuvansalmi (Astuvansalmen Kalliomaalaukset)

The rock paintings of Astuvansalmi are some of the finest prehistoric rock paintings in Finland. They are on a steep rock cliff, 20km east of Ristiina village. Their age is estimated to be 3000 to 4000 years, and the paintings as a whole span 60m. There's a walking track from the road.

Pien-Toijolan Talomuseo

A visit to this open-air museum should be combined with a look at the rock paintings; there is a marked trail from here. The estate dates from 1672, and consists of over 20 old houses, some of them from the 18th century. The museum is open daily in summer.

Places to Stay & Eat

Rosalie (☎ *661 078, Brahentie 54*) is affiliated with HI and is the only place to stay in Ristiina itself. It's on the main street and is open year-round. Rooms are from 70 to 150 mk per person. This place also has a decent restaurant and provides some local nightlife. The rooms are in a separate building, previously used as a school dormitory. There are bicycles, boats and canoes to rent.

Löydön Kartano (☎ *664 101, Kartanontie 71*), 5km north of Ristiina near the village of Löytö, is a pleasant HI-affiliated hostel in an old manor house. Beds cost from 75 to 130 mk per person. There's a bus stop at Kartanontie, the gravel road that takes you to the hostel.

Getting There & Away

There are regular buses from Mikkeli to Ristiina, but express buses only stop at the road crossing. There are also lake cruises between Ristiina and Mikkeli in summer.

Northern Lakeland

LAPINLAHTI

- **8000**   ☎ **017**

Lapinlahti enjoys a scenic location surrounded by Savonian waters.

Eemil Halosen Museo

The Halonen family lived in Lapinlahti, and several members became known nationally some 100 years ago. Pekka Halonen was the most famous of them, and this museum displays sculptures by Pekka's cousin Eemil Halonen, who was one of the most notable Finnish sculptors of the early 20th century. The museum is on Eemil Halosentie, not far from the village centre. An enormous number of sculptures are on display in an old cow shed. The museum is open from 10 am to 8 pm daily (to 6 pm Saturday) from June to late August. At other times, hours are noon to 6 pm Tuesday to Friday, noon to 4 pm Saturday. Admission is 20 mk. The nearby **Taidemuseo** (art museum) on Suistamontie arranges temporary exhibitions and has similar opening hours and an admission fee of 15 mk, higher during special exhibitions.

Artisan Centre (Käsityöläisaukio)

The 'artisan centre' across the tunnel from the centre, at Juhani Ahontie 5, has a number of studios and handicraft shops. Käsityökeskus is the central sales exhibition, and across the pedestrian street you will find the TBK gemstone studio with precious stones.

Special Events

The Finnish cattle-calling championships are held in Lapinlahti on a weekend in early August.

Places to Stay & Eat

The HI-affiliated ***Nerkkoon Retkeilymaja*** (☎ *735 281, Iisalmentie 770*) is in a school building 8km north of Lapinlahti. It is open from June to early August, with beds from 60 to 80 mk. There's a café, art exhibition and a well-equipped kitchen.

The HI-affiliated hostel *Portaanpää* (π 768 860) is an old manor-like building 2km south-west from the train station. Beds are 70 to 80 mk and meals are available. The place is open from June to mid-August.

In the centre, *Iloinen Viivi (Asematie 3)* is a good place for coffee and light meals.

Getting There & Away

All trains between Kuopio and Iisalmi stop at the Lapinlahti train station, and there are buses.

IISALMI

pop 24,000   π 017

Iisalmi, 85km north of Kuopio, is a centre for the northern part of the Lakeland district. It is known for its Olvi Brewery and annual beer festival, but there are also several historic places around the town. During the 18th century, the area became known for the Runni 'health springs', and in 1808 a successful battle against the Russians was fought in Koljonvirta, near Iisalmi.

Orientation

Savonkatu, directly opposite the train station, is the main street and in summer is partly pedestrianised. The lakeside area near the brewery is home to several restaurants. Koljonvirta, 5km north of Iisalmi, is another tourist centre.

Information

The tourist office (π 830 1391) at Kauppakatu 22 is open from 8 am to 6 pm Monday to Friday, 10 am to 2 pm Saturday in summer. At other times it's open from 8 am to 4 pm Monday to Friday.

The post office is at the market at Riistakatu 5, 74100 Iisalmi.

You can store your bag in a locker at the train station for 10 mk.

Things to See

The **Karelian Orthodox Cultural Centre**, at Kyllikinkatu 8, displays icons and miniature models of Orthodox churches and *tsasouni* (chapels) from Russian Karelia. Some of the icons had lain forgotten in attics and barns, and were later discovered to be valuable. Hours are 9 am to 6 pm daily. The adjacent **Orthodox church** has beautiful illustrations which were painted in 1995 by a Russian. It is open from 10 am to 4 pm Tuesday to Sunday in summer.

The **Brewery Museum** at the harbour was the first museum of beer to open in the Nordic countries. It's open from 11 am to midnight Sunday to Thursday and 11 am to 2 am Friday and Saturday from May to late August.

Special Events & Strange Festivals

The Beer Festival (Oluset) is held in Iisalmi in early July, and features plenty of you-know-what. The Iisalmi region seems to specialise in strange festivals – in early May there's a 'Fishing By Hand' competition in the Rajajoki river, and then there's the Wife-Carrying World Championships in Sonkajärvi (see the later section on Sonkajärvi). The nearby village of Pielavesi is host to the annual Finnish Boot-Throwing Championships, usually in July. Lapinlahti is proud to hold the annual Cattle-Calling Finnish Championships (see the Lapinlahti section earlier).

Places to Stay

Cheap and clean, the HI-affiliated *YMCA Hostel* (π 823 940, Sarvikatu 4C) is open from June to late July. Accommodation costs 100 to 150 mk per person, and you can use the sauna for an additional fee. There is a shared kitchen and bathroom for every three rooms.

Hotel Artos (π 812 244, fax 814 941, Kyllikinkatu 8) has rooms from 250/310 mk. The 'backpacker package' includes dinner and breakfast, and is available for an additional fee. The hotel is run by the Orthodox Church, and has loads of atmosphere.

Places to Eat

The cheapest meals are available at the train station.

Savonkatu is the best place to look for restaurants, including *Blue Moon (Savonkatu 17)*, which does lunch for about 30 mk, including all extras. Game and smoked food are the specialities.

Kultainen Peura (Pohjolankatu 5) is another good place for reasonably priced meals.

At the harbour, *Kauppi* bills itself as the 'world's smallest restaurant' – it has four seats.

Olutmestari at the harbour is not very cheap, but its has a very large terrace area and the brewery museum is upstairs. Nearby, *Oluthalli* (Beerhouse) is a grand place with a large beer hall and a fine-dining restaurant.

Getting There & Away

Bus Iisalmi is a centre for bus traffic in the region, and a link between the West Coast and North Karelia, so you can catch buses from Joensuu in the east or from Oulu in the west.

Train There are five trains a day from Helsinki to Iisalmi, via Lahti, Mikkeli and Kuopio. Coming from the north, you can reach Iisalmi from Oulu or Kajaani.

AROUND IISALMI
Sonkajärvi
* pop 5800   ☎ 017

This isolated village is becoming known for its most unusual summer event, the **Wife-Carrying World Championships**, held in early July. The winning couple takes home the wife's weight in beer. There are competitors from all over Europe.

Sonkajärvi's other major blockbuster sight is the **International Bottle Museum** (Pullomuseo; ☎ 761 470). There are hundreds of bottles from many countries, and the display is well set out. The museum is open from 10 am to 8 pm Tuesday to Sunday from June to late August. Admission is 10 mk.

The 30km **Volokki Nature Trail** begins in the village and travels through the country side.

Ameriikka

When 'everybody' was leaving Finland to travel to America, the distant and promising new land, a strange restlessness attacked a poor peasant in the northern wilderness of Vieremä village, 24km north-west of Iisalmi. One morning, the uneducated farmer took his horse and left for America. Late in the evening he grew tired and decided that this must be America. He settled down, and lived there until his death. Since then, the place has been called Ameriikka (`AH-meh-reek-kah').

The only attraction in Ameriikka, 10km west of Vieremä, is a **Horse-Carriage Museum**, open daily from mid-May to late August.

North Karelia

There is no area in Finland like North Karelia, or *Karjala* as it is called in Finnish. When Finland lost the Karelian Isthmus and the Salla region to the Soviet Union after WWII, this province was the only part of Karelia to remain Finnish territory. Some 500,000 Karelian refugees had to be settled in Finland after WWII.

Under the shadow of the Soviet Union, Karjala was a taboo subject. Starting a discussion about how and when Karelia should be returned to Finland was a definite end to any political career.

All nations have their symbols and their nationalistic dawn. For Finns, Karelia provided both. The wild Karelian 'outback' inspired artists during the National Romantic era, from Sibelius, the composer, to Gallen-Kallela, the painter. This sparsely populated frontier region (population 175,000) does its best to live up to all Karelian legends.

For the traveller, it is a unique region where you can meet friendly people, visit beautiful Orthodox churches and explore wilderness trekking paths.

History

In 1227, a crusade from Novgorod (in present-day Russia) forcibly baptised Karelians to the Orthodox faith, sparking skirmishes that did not end until the Treaty of Nöteborg in 1323 established Novgorod's suzerainty over the region.

Karelians have survived constant war with both Sweden and Russia. In 1617 Swedes annexed much of Karelia. North Karelia was constantly attacked by Russia and religious intolerance forced Orthodox believers across the border into Russia. The Treaty of Uusikaupunki in 1721 saw North Karelia remain Swedish territory and South Karelia fall to Russian feudalism.

JOENSUU

pop 50,000   ☎ 013

Joensuu is both the capital of the Province of North Karelia and its major travel centre. Its university, lively cultural life, good market and abundant services compensate for the lack of any major tourist attraction. That said, you might find yourself in Joensuu anyway as it is a jumping-off point for hikes in surrounding wilderness areas.

History

Joensuu was founded in 1848 at the mouth of the Pielisjoki River, hence its name ('joen' is a genitive form of joki, or river; 'suu' means 'the mouth').

Joensuu soon became an important trading post for the region, and an international port after the completion of the Saimaa Canal in the 1850s.

Orientation

The Pielisjoki rapids divide Joensuu into two parts. Train and bus stations are in the east, the town centre in the west. Siltakatu and Kauppakatu are the two main streets.

Information

Tourist Office The tourist office (☎ 267 300, or 225 114 for cottage rentals, fax 123 933) is at Koskikatu 1 near the kauppatori. It handles tourism information for the town

and the region. The office is open from 8 am to 6 pm Monday to Friday, 9 am to 2 pm Saturday in summer. At other times it's open 9 am to 4 pm weekdays.

Post The post office is at Rantakatu 6, 80100 Joensuu. Hours are 8 am to 8 pm Monday to Friday.

Internet Resources & Libraries The public library at Koskikatu 25, near the university campus, has several Internet terminals. It is open from 10 am to 7 pm weekdays, 9 am to 3 pm Saturday in summer. At other times, it closes at 8 pm on weekdays.

Carelia House, on the university campus, also has an excellent library that is open on weekdays.

Left Luggage The train station has a luggage room and 5 mk lockers that may be used for 24 hours maximum. Lockers at the bus station are 10 mk.

Medical & Emergency Services Pharmacies are at Siltakatu 14, Koskikatu 7 and Kirkkokatu 18. The Siilainen Health Care Centre is at Noljakantie 17.

In a general emergency call ☎ 112, for police call ☎ 10022 and for a doctor dial ☎ 10023.

Things to See

The imposing **town hall** at Rantakatu, designed by Eliel Saarinen, was built in 1914.

Just east, the small **North Karelian Museum** on Ilosaari island features old furniture and artefacts from Russian and Finnish Karelia. It has been under renovation and is scheduled to reopen in 1999.

Near the kauppatori, the **Joensuu Art Museum** at Kirkkokatu 23 has art from the Mediterranean, Asia and Scandinavia, including a few old religious icons. Hours are 11 am to 4 pm Tuesday to Sunday (also 4 pm to 8 pm Wednesday). Entry is 15 mk. Admission is free on Wednesday.

The most interesting church in Joensuu is the wooden **Orthodox church** of St

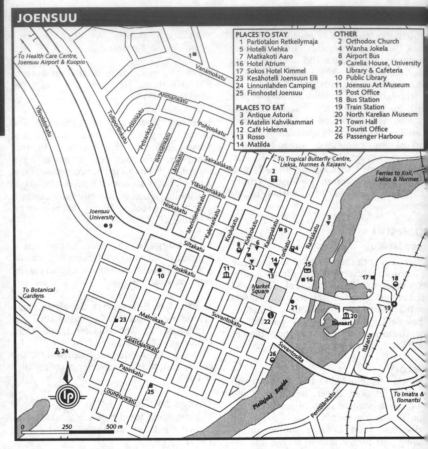

JOENSUU

PLACES TO STAY
1 Partiotalon Retkeilymaja
5 Hotelli Viehka
7 Matkakoti Aaro
16 Hotel Atrium
17 Sokos Hotel Kimmel
23 Kesähotelli Joensuun Elli
24 Linnunlahden Camping
25 Finnhostel Joensuu

PLACES TO EAT
3 Antique Astoria
6 Matelin Kahvikammari
12 Café Helenna
13 Rosso
14 Matilda

OTHER
2 Orthodox Church
4 Wanha Jokela
8 Airport Bus
9 Carelia House, University
  Library & Cafeteria
10 Public Library
11 Joensuu Art Museum
15 Post Office
18 Bus Station
19 Train Station
20 North Karelian Museum
21 Town Hall
22 Tourist Office
26 Passenger Harbour

Nicholas, built in 1887. The icons were painted in St Petersburg in the late 1880s. The church is at the north end of Kirkkokatu and is open from noon to 6 pm weekdays from mid-June to mid-August.

The world's northernmost **tropical butterfly garden** (Trooppinen Perhospuutarha) is at Avainkuja 2, north of the centre. It's open from 10 am to 6 pm weekdays, 10 am to 4 pm weekends in summer. At other times, it's open from 10 am to 4 pm daily. Admission is 30 mk.

The Joensuu University **Botanic Garden** is at Heinäpurontie 70, close to the camping ground. Its greenhouses showcase close to 1000 plant species. The gardens are open from 10 am to 6 pm Wednesday to Saturday, noon to 6 pm Sunday in summer. At other times, the hours are Monday to Friday from 10 am to 3 pm (to 8 pm Wednesday) and noon to 4 pm Sunday. Admission is 20 mk.

In summer, the **kauppatori** is a good place to shop for Karelian handicrafts.

Organised Tours

Cruises In summer there are scenic cruises on the Pielisjoki, a centuries-old trading route. These cost 60 mk, take about two hours and leave from the passenger harbour south of Suvantosilta bridge. Check current timetables and rates at the city tourist office.

For ferry cruises to Koli, Lieksa and Nurmes, see the Getting There & Away section that follows.

Special Events

Joensuu's Midsummer festival at the end of June and its Ilosaari Rock festival in mid-July are highly spirited events – these are good times to visit.

Places to Stay

Camping *Linnunlahden Camping* (☎ 126 72, *Linnunlahdentie 1*) has a superb lakeside location near a vast open-air stage, so expect occasional free concerts and lost sleep! There are tent sites for 50 to 75 mk and cabins for 140 to 240 mk.

Hostels There are three options in Joensuu; all are affiliated with the HI. The year-round *Finnhostel Joensuu* (☎ 267 5076, fax 267 5075, *Kalevankatu 8*) has excellent rooms – each with kitchen and bath – for 160 to 220 mk per person.

Kesähotelli Joensuun Elli (☎ 225 927, *Länsikatu 18*) is a student apartment building that doubles as a summer hotel, open to travellers from mid-May to mid-August. Cost is 80 to 200 mk per person, and there a sauna and laundry.

Partiotalon Retkeilymaja (☎ 123 381, *Vanamokatu 25*) is somewhat run-down, but certainly has character. It's open from June to late August. Beds are from 55 to 75 mk.

Guesthouse Very central is *Matkakoti Karo* (☎ 148 1051, *Kirkkokatu 20*), with singles/doubles for 110/200 mk. Reception on the 3rd floor.

Hotels *Hotelli Vlehka* (☎/fax 221 450, *Kauppakatu 32*) is very central, and its nightclub is one of the most popular in

town. Rooms are 290/390 mk, with a 40 mk discount on weekends and in summer.

Hotel Atrium (☎ 126 911, 226 969, *Siltakatu 4*) has 53 rooms, a restaurant, a sauna and a friendly, talking pet parrot in the lobby. Rooms cost 350/470 mk, in summer 330/380 mk.

The largest hotel in Joensuu, *Sokos Hotel Kimmel* (☎ 277 111, fax 277 2112, *Itäranta 1*) is close to the bus and train stations. Rooms are regularly 595/720 mk, but in summer and on weekends all rooms are 385 mk.

Places to Eat

At the kauppatori look for Karelian sweets such as *Karjalan piirakka*, a rice-filled pastry.

The University of Joensuu has several student cafeterias, most notably *Carelia* in the main building. It is open for lunch from 11 am to 2 pm Monday to Friday. A meal costs less than 20 mk, milk, bread and salad included.

Matilda (*Torikatu 23*) is a restaurant, bakery and café. The restaurant, on the 2nd floor, is terrific for well-priced lunches of sandwiches, soups and salads. The café and bakery on the ground floor have terrific breads and cakes.

Rosso, near the kauppatori, is popular, and has a menu in English. Pizza, pasta and steaks are from 40 mk, and there is a hot buffet.

Antique Astoria (*Rantakatu 32*) in a small building on the riverside, is an intimate Hungarian restaurant with a terrace and live music. Most things on the menu are 70 to 150 mk, but you can also order pizzas for 30 mk.

Café Helenna (*Siltakatu 16*) has light meals and tempting sweets, while *Matelin Kahvikammari* (*Niskakatu 9*) is a café and handicrafts shop.

Entertainment

There are many, many bars and clubs on Torikatu, heavily patronised by local students. Of these, *Wanha Jokela* (*Torikatu 26*) is one of the most popular evening pubs, with occasional singing.

Getting There & Away

Air There are several flights a day between Helsinki and Joensuu. The airport is 11km west of town; bus service is 20 mk one way and departs from Kirkkokatu 25.

Bus There are regular buses to all towns in the Lakeland and North Karelia, departing from the bus terminal east of the centre. Tickets are sold from 8 am to 4 pm Monday to Friday, but you can pay the fare on the bus. If you arrive by bus, you can also get off at a bus stop in the town centre.

Train Direct trains run frequently from Turku, Jyväskylä and Helsinki, but from Savonlinna you have to change at Parikkala.

Boat A ferry runs north to Koli (140 mk one way) and Lieksa (160 mk) on Saturday from June to August, making the return trip to Joensuu on Sunday. There are also cruises farther north to Nurmes during summer months; see the Nurmes Getting There & Away section for more information.

OUTOKUMPU

- **pop 9000**   ☎ 013

Outokumpu, about 50km west of Joensuu, was a wealthy mining town until the 1980s, when all three mining operations were permanently closed. Outokumpu was on the verge of becoming a ghost town. Its property prices plunged to the lowest level in Finland and its unemployment rate exceeded the national average. However, a new industrial area attracted several companies to the town, and employment figures are now close to the national average. The main attraction in town is a mining museum.

Vanha Kaivos Mine

On a hill overlooking the town centre lies an abandoned mine, which was re-opened to the public in 1985. There is an extensive mining museum and an adjacent tunnel with mining equipment. You can climb the tower for a superb view, or watch the hourly slide show. For children, there is a fun park at the bottom of the valley. An underground restaurant and a café with a good view offer refreshment. The entire area takes several hours to explore. It's open daily from 10 am to 6 pm. Admission to the museum is 1 mk, or 40 mk for all attractions.

Lake Sysmäjärvi Bird Sanctuary

One of the best bird-nesting lakes in Finland lies south of Outokumpu. Sysmäjärvi was declared dead in the 1950s, due to polluted mining deposits that flowed freely into the lake. Since recovered, the lake is now surrounded by lush vegetation, and birds have returned here in large numbers; a recent study found 72 species. There are several birdwatching towers. May and June are the best months to visit.

Places to Stay & Eat

Särkiselän Leirintäalue (☎ 553 03?, *Rikkarannantie 36*), a camping ground 5km north-west of town, has tent sites for 65 mk and cottages from 160 to 200 mk. It is open from June to late August.

The only hotel in Outokumpu *Malmikumpu* (☎ 550 333, fax 521 190, *Asemakatu 1*) is easy to find in the town centre. Rooms cost 320/420 mk. The hotel restaurant and café serve the best food in town.

Getting There & Away

All buses between Kuopio and Joensuu call at the Outokumpu bus terminal.

LAKE VIINIJÄRVI LOOP
☎ 013

Roads around Lake Viinijärvi are scenic, with beautiful churches and old houses. In August, you can find blueberries in the nearby forests. If you have a bicycle, you can bring it to Viinijärvi by train or bus from Joensuu, Varkaus or Kuopio, and ride the 60km loop between Viinijärvi, Sotkuma, Polvijärvi and Outokumpu in a single day. Another option is to take a bus from Joensuu to Polvijärvi, bypassing Sotkuma.

Viinijärvi

There are a few banks, many shops and a post office in the village of Viinijärvi, on the southern shore of the lake. Viinijärvi is quite famous domestically, as its women's *pesäpallo* (baseball) team won the national championship a while back. The town is really packed on Sunday during matches. A colourful Praasniekka Festival (a Karelian religious holiday) is held on 26 June each year.

The beautiful **Orthodox church** is west of the village centre. Its 19th century icons are copies of those in Kiev Cathedral.

Getting There & Away All buses between Joensuu and Kuopio stop in Viinijärvi.

Sotkuma

The narrow road from Viinijärvi north to Sotkuma is scenic. Sotkuma is not much of a village, but the small *tsasouna* (chapel), built in 1914, has interesting 19th century icons inside; note the large ones on the side walls. If you want to go in, phone ahead (☎ 638 522) to get the warden to open the door for you. The Praasniekka Festival is held here on 20 July each year.

Polvijärvi

Polvijärvi has an interesting history. When a canal was being constructed at the southern end of Lake Höytiäinen in 1859, the embankment collapsed and the water level sank 10m, revealing fertile land. Polvijärvi was soon incorporated as a municipality and its population soared, although the current figure of almost 5800 is lower than it used to be. The village has a bus terminal, a few banks, a post office and several food stores.

The beautiful **Orthodox church**, built in 1914, is not far from the village centre. The key is kept by the Mutakatti restaurant in the centre. Someone will show you around, if they have time, but the church is most interesting from the outside. Its icons are from St Petersburg and were probably painted in the early 20th century. The church has its Praasniekka Festival on 24 June each year.

Don't mistake the Orthodox church for the less appealing **Lutheran church** in the centre of the village. Polvijärvi also has a **local museum**, north of the village centre.

Getting There & Away There are several buses a day from Joensuu and a few others from Kuopio and Juuka. Buses from Outokumpu run on school days only.

ILOMANTSI
☎ 013

Ilomantsi, Finland's most Karelian, Orthodox and eastern municipality, is one of the three regions in Finland with a non-mainstream indigenous culture (the two others being Åland and the Sami culture of north Lapland). Indigenous Karelians see themselves as distinct from both Russians and Finns. Its inhabitants are some of the friendliest in Finland, and its forests contain brown bears and moose. However, the commercial centre of Ilomantsi is one of the ugliest in Finland, and has nothing to do with the Karelian heritage.

Information
The tourist office (☎ 881 707) at Mantsinkatu 8 assists with cottage reservations, fishing permits, maps, equipment hire and other trekking necessities. Hours are 9 am to 5 pm Monday to Friday, 9 am to 2 pm Saturday in July. At other times, hours are 8 am to 4 pm Monday to Friday.

Parppeinvaara
One of the most famous of Ilomantsi's historical characters was Jaakko Parppei (1792-1885), a bard and a player of the *kantele*, a traditional Karelian stringed instrument. He is the namesake of this hill (where he lived), which now features a **Karelian village** with several attractions. Built since the 1960s, it is the oldest of the Karelian theme villages in Finland and probably the most attractive. To qualify for their job, guides wearing *feresi* (traditional Karelian work dress) must know how to

play the kantele and be fluent in several languages. Runonlaulajan pirtti, the main building, has exhibitions on the *Kalevala* epic and Orthodox arts.

An **Orthodox tsasouna** (chapel) stands behind the **Matelin museoaitta**, a tiny museum commemorating female rune singer Mateli Kuivalatar, renowned in the 19th century for her renditions of the *Kanteletar* epic.

To get to Parppeinvaara, leave Ilomantsi village and proceed south towards Joensuu. Turn left and follow the 'Runonlaulajan pirtti' sign. The place is open from 10 am to 8 pm daily from mid-June to mid-August and from 10 am to 6 pm. Tickets are 15 mk and include admission to all buildings.

Peltohermanni Wine Tower

The local water tower was reborn as a *viinitorni* (wine tower) when a local company, Peltohermanni, started a café at the top in 1994. Strawberry and blackcurrant are used as raw materials to produce the wine sold here. Viinitorni is open from 10 am to midnight daily from June to late August, and 10 am to 10 pm daily in August. Admission is 10 mk.

Churches

Ilomantsi features two interesting churches. Pyhän Elian Kirkko is the large and beautiful Orthodox church of Ilomantsi, a kilometre west of the village centre, towards Lake Ilomantsinjärvi. The *kalmisto* (graveyard) sign near the church will lead you to the old graveyard at the waterfront. It is a silent place, where old trees give shade to a few graves.

The large Lutheran church, dating from 1796, is almost as impressive as the Orthodox church. Following the Swedish conquest, a Lutheran congregation was established here in 1653 and the new religion soon overshadowed the eastern one. Colourful paintings from 1832, an achievement of Samuel Elmgren, are the highlight of this church.

Special Events

As Ilomantsi has so many (Russian) Orthodox believers, several Praasniekka festivals are held here. Originally, these were strictly religious events, but these days they also attract tourists. Sometimes there is dancing afterwards. Ilomantsi village celebrates Petru Praasniekka on 28 to 29 June and Ilja Praasniekka on 19 to 20 July every year.

Places to Stay

Lomakeskus Ruhkaranta (☎ 843 161, *Ruhkarannantie 21)* is a year-round camping ground 9km east of Ilomantsi. Located in thick pine forest, it has spectacular views of several lakes. Cottages are from 100 mk with discounts outside the high season. Tent sites are 60 mk. Its traditional smoke sauna is expensive unless you have a large group. A large restaurant is open daily and serves at the reception outside the high season.

On a hill 3km south of the village centre towards Joensuu, 500m off the main road, is *Anssilan Monola* (☎ 881 181), where a very friendly family rents rooms in their farmhouse. Rooms are 80/165 mk (bring your own sheets). There are cows, so fresh milk is served at breakfast. Bicycles can be rented.

In the village itself, *Hotel Ilomant* (☎ 882 533, fax 883 643) is a pleasant and clean hotel with rooms for 320/450 mk.

Places to Eat

There are several *grillis* in the centre, and *bakery*. For a real Karelian buffet (*pitopöytä*) go to *Parppeinpirtti* in Parppeinvaara. The Karelian buffet is 80 mk. Taste the excellent mushroom salad and vatruska pies, and the slightly sweet vuašša malt drink. There's also a standard lunch buffet for 50 mk, and snacks are served in the *café*.

Getting There & Away

Buses run frequently between Joensuu and Ilomantsi on weekdays. There are fewer buses on weekends. The bus terminal is in the village centre. From here, there are infrequent connections to nearby villages.

HATTUVAARA
☎ 013

Hattuvaara, north-east of Ilomantsi, is a convenient base for exploring easternmost Finland. The village is the main landmark along the little-travelled *Runon ja rajan tie* route. Experiencing a summer night in this quaint little village is a highlight: birds sing and cow bells tinkle. Winter is quieter, with a great deal of snow falling.

Gold was recently discovered on both sides of Hattuvaara village, so mining activity may grow during the next couple of decades.

Jouni Puruskainen runs much of the village and almost any tour around the region. His wife speaks English and they can be contacted at Taistelijan Talo (see below).

Orthodox Tsasouna
Hattuvaara has the oldest Orthodox *tsasouna* (chapel) in Finland. Built in the 1720s, it has several old Russian icons inside. Its small tower was used as a watch-tower during WWII. Behind the chapel, many of the old graves at the **kalmisto** (graveyard) have a wooden *grobu* (marker) above them.

Fighter's House (Taistelijan Talo)
The modern 'Fighter's House' is down the road from the tsasouna. Designed by Joensuu architect Erkki Helasvuo, this house symbolises the meeting of East and West. There is a WWII museum downstairs, with interesting photos, guns and handi-crafts *(puhde-esineitä)* made by Finnish soldiers during wartime. The house serves food and is open daily in summer. Entry to the museum costs 20 mk.

Special Events
On 29 June, a colourful Praasniekka festival takes place here, with a *ristinsaatto*, or Orthodox procession commemorating a saint, beginning at the tsasouna.

Places to Stay & Eat
Arhipanpirtti (☎ 830 111, Hatunraitti 5B) is the only place to stay in Hattuvaara. There are rooms in several buildings, plus a cottage. Rates start at 100 mk per person. There are bicycle, canoe and rowing boat rentals.

For a good buffet, go to *Taistelijan Talo*; for 50 to 65 mk you can eat as much as you like. In summer, the place serves food all day until 10 pm.

You can get food supplies at the only *shop* in the village, near the tsasouna.

Getting There & Away
Hattuvaara is the largest village between Ilomantsi and Lieksa along the Runon ja rajan tie route. There are one or two buses daily from Ilomantsi village.

AROUND HATTUVAARA
Lake Virmajärvi
☎ 013

Lake Virmajärvi, the easternmost point of Finland (and the European Union) is now open to visitors. You must go there with Jouni Puruskainen, who will arrange a special permit at the Border Guards' Station next to Taistelijan Talo. You must provide the authorities with passport details. The permit is free and usually provided in less than 24 hours.

Jouni has a 4WD minibus that takes seven people. The minimum charge is approximately 200 mk; to reduce costs, try to join a group or wait until enough people show up. It seems Jouni is willing to include a meal in the wilderness with the tour so negotiate first. It's an interesting journey, passing a few WWII *sotapaikka* (battle locations) at Sikrenvaara, and the *hauta* (grave) of a Russian female soldier. Ask for these, as Jouni speaks little English.

Tapion Taival Trekking Route
The easternmost trekking route in Finland gives you the choice of a 13km wilderness track along the Koitajoki river, or an 8km northern extension across the Koivusuo Nature Reserve, or yet another extension north of Koivusuo to Kivivaara. The Koita-joki section is certainly the highlight. The path is marked by orange paint on tree trunks.

The Koivusuo track starts at the northern end of Koivusuo Reserve, on an old gravel road that takes you via Pirhu Research Station (everything's locked), and through an open bog that is the only thing really worth seeing along the Koivusuo leg.

South of Koivusuo, you join the original Tapion Taival path near the Polvikoski rapids. After the first campfire place (20 minutes or so), you reach the river and follow its twists and turns. There are unusually large trees, mostly pine and fir, varied vegetation and abundant birdlife. There are rumours of bears and other big mammals. After Hanhikoski, the track leaves the river (which flows into Russia) and crosses a few bogs until it parallels the yellow-marked border. A parking area marks the end of the trek at Tapionaho.

Getting There & Away You will need a private car and good local map to reach the trekking area, or you can negotiate with Jouni Puruskainen in Hattuvaara about transport and its price.

Lake Hoikan Kylkeinen
For fishing, try Lake Hoikan Kylkeinen, where salmon are released. Fishing permits are sold in Hattuvaara, and you can rent boats at Taistelijan Talo restaurant.

RÄÄKKYLÄ
- pop 3400   ☎ 013

This small isolated place boasts beautiful scenery on the shores of Lake Orivesi, but offers little else for the traveller. The only time to visit is during the Kihaus festival, a four-day folk music festival in July. The festival features the band Värttinä, Rääkkylä's own contribution to the world music scene. During the white nights (when the sun doesn't set) there's music well beyond midnight.

In the centre, the large yellow **church** from 1851 seats 1200 people and is open daily in summer.

If you have an interest in birds, there are several **bird-watching towers** at good locations in Rääkkylä, including Ruokosalmi

(5km from the centre), and at Lake Kiesjärvi where a 2km **nature trail** has been set up.

Places to Stay & Eat
Koivuniemen Lomakylä (☎ 661 182 Koiveniementie 20) just outside the village centre is an attractive camping ground, and its fine manor house serves good meals. Tent sites cost 50 mk, and there are also cottages and reasonably priced hotel-style rooms in the main house.

Getting There & Away
Rääkkylä is a 31km side trip from the busy Imatra to Joensuu road No 6. Several buses run Monday to Friday from Joensuu, 66km to the north.

KITEE
☎ 013

Kitee is a small town with a huge **church**. It's among the 10 largest in Finland and seats 2200 people. Made of grey stone, it was built in 1886 and is open daily from June to August. The **local museum** on the main road in the centre is open Tuesday to Friday and Sunday from mid-June to mid August. Just next door, downstairs at the town hall, **Pienoisrautatie** is a 250m long model railway that is viewable daily in July and on weekdays in June and August. Entry is 10 mk.

About 4km from the centre is **Savikon maakauppa**, the oldest general store in Finland. It is open for tourists weekdays from mid-June to early August.

Places to Stay & Eat
Likolampi (☎ 422 222) is a fine lakeside camping ground approximately 1.5km from the train station along the road to Rääkkylä. There are reasonably priced cottages as well as tent sites, and you can rent a boat or bathe in one of the saunas. The reception doubles as a restaurant.

Getting There & Away
All trains stop at Kitee train station (also known as Tolosenmäki), but it is far from the town centre.

There are buses to Kitee from Savonlinna (88km west) and Joensuu (67km north). Most of them go via Tolosenmäki.

Lake Pielinen Region

Some of the most interesting attractions in North Karelia are around this lake, one of the largest in Finland.

For information on the unique culture and history of North Karelia, see the preceding North Karelia section.

NURMES

- pop 11,000   ☎ 013

Nurmes, at the north-west tip of Lake Pielinen, is probably the most pleasant of the Karelian-heritage eastern towns. It's a good base from which to explore the Lake Pielinen region.

The terraced old town section of Nurmes is attractive, with traditional wooden houses and views of two surrounding lakes.

Nurmes was founded in 1876 by Tsar Alexander II of Russia and the old town still has the character approved of by the 19th century Russian ruler.

The surrounding area features genuine wilderness and good fishing waters.

Orientation

Train and bus stations are in the town centre, opposite Kauppatori. The main street is Kirkkokatu, with its beautiful birches. Old Nurmes is north-west of Kauppatori, while the Bomba (a Karelian theme village) and most places to stay are a few kilometres south-east of the centre. Porokylä is a commercial neighbourhood at the north end of town.

Information

Tourist Office The excellent tourist information services are run by Loma Nurmes (☎ 481 770, fax 481 775) at Hyvärilä, south-east of the town centre. Hours are 8 am to 10 pm daily from June to mid-August, 8 am to 4 pm Monday to Friday at other times.

Post The post office is at Torikatu 5, 75500 Nurmes. Hours are 9 am to 6 pm Monday to Friday.

Internet Resources & Library The public library is in the Nurmes-talo building at Kötsintie 2. It has an Internet terminal and a collection of the *Kalevala* in various languages. Library hours are 10 am to 8 pm Monday to Friday, 10 am to 3 pm Saturday and noon to 4 pm Sunday.

Medical & Emergency Services In a general emergency call ☎ 112, for police call ☎ 10022 and for a doctor dial ☎ 10023.

Things to See

Just north of the kauppatori, the **Lutheran church** from 1896 is the largest in North Karelia, with 2300 seats. Inside there are miniature models of earlier Lutheran churches. The church is open in summer from 10 am to 6 pm.

Continue north-west from the church to reach **Puu-Nurmes**, the old town area on the esker above the train station. In this neighbourhood there are traditional wooden houses which are protected by law and surrounded by birch trees.

Kötsi Museum, the local museum of history, is in the Nurmes-Talo building with the public library. Artefacts on display include some from the Stone Age. The museum is open from noon to 6 pm Tuesday to Friday, 10 am to 3 pm Saturday and noon to 4 pm Sunday. Admission is 5 mk.

The biggest tourist attraction in Nurmes is **Bomba House**, 2.5km south-east of the town centre. The imposing main building – with its high roof and ornate wooden trim – is a copy of a typical Karelian family house that was built in 1855 by Jegor Bombin, a farmer from Suojärvi (now in Russian Karelia). It houses a hotel and restaurant. The surroundings include a delightful re-creation of a Karelian village,

THE LAKELAND

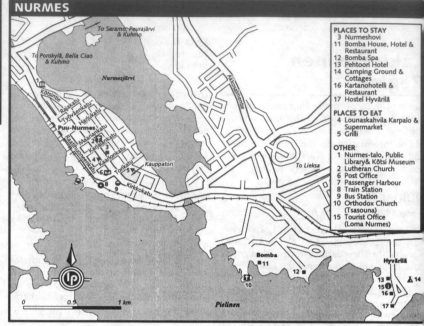

NURMES

PLACES TO STAY
3 Nurmeshovi
11 Bomba House, Hotel &
    Restaurant
12 Bomba Spa
13 Pehtoori Hotel
14 Camping Ground &
    Cottages
16 Kartanohotelli &
    Restaurant
17 Hostel Hyvärilä

PLACES TO EAT
4 Lounaskahvila Karpalo &
    Supermarket
5 Grilli

OTHER
1 Nurmes-talo, Public
    Library& Kötsi Museum
2 Lutheran Church
6 Post Office
7 Passenger Harbour
8 Train Station
9 Bus Station
10 Orthodox Church
    (Tsasouna)
15 Tourist Office
    (Loma Nurmes)

with an Orthodox *tsasouna* (chapel) and a summer theatre.

Activities & Organised Tours

Perfect for those with money but little time, Nurmes offers a well organised schedule of tours with daily departures – dog sledding, snowmobiling, ice-fishing and cross-country skiing from January to the end of March, and canoeing, rapids-shooting at Ruunaa and farmhouse tours from June to the end of August. Nurmes is a popular holiday spot for Finns so there are usually enough people to form a tour. Cost is from 75 mk up to 900 mk per person, depending on the type of tour and number of people participating.

Contact the Loma Nurmes tourist office for an updated schedule, pricing information and other details. Bookings at least 24 hours in advance are often required for the tours.

Special Events

The Bomba Festival Week, held in early o mid-July, is a Finno-Ugrian cultural specta cle, with theatre performances and concerts It's a fascinating event for those who have a special interest in Finnic cultures.

Places to Stay

Nurmes Centre In the town centre *Nurmeshovi (☎/fax 480 750, Kirkkokat 21)* is a bit of a travelling salesperson' joint, with a popular nightclub, but the 30 rooms are good. Singles/doubles start a 200/350 mk.

Hyvärilä The best place to stay is *Hyväril Tourist Centre (☎ 481 770, fax 481 775 Lomatie)*, 4km south-east of the town centre The lakeside resort area has a hotel, a hostel a camping ground and over 30 bungalows There's also a beach, sauna, tennis court. and mini-golf, plus bike, canoe and boa entals, and many other activities. You can walk from here to Bomba along marked walking routes. Not surprisingly, this is a very popular vacation destination for Finnish families and school groups.

The *camping ground* is open from mid-May to mid-September and has tent sites for 70 mk. Cabins cost 180 to 250 mk.

Hostel Hyvärilä is open year-round. Dorm beds are from 55 mk, and there's access to all facilities: kitchen, laundry, sauna, café and restaurant.

The yellow *Pehtoori Hotel* has rooms for 150/200 mk. *Kartanohotelli* has just 14 deluxe rooms, from 200/300 mk.

Hyvärilä staff will also help you arrange to rent a private cottage in the Nurmes area.

Local buses run from the kauppatori to the Hyvärilä crossing a few times each morning on weekdays.

Bomba *Bomba Hotel* (☎ 687 200, fax 687 2100, Suojärvenkatu 1), at the Karelian theme village 2.5km south-east of the centre, has 50 attractive rooms in Karelian cabins decorated by local artisans. Rooms are from 350/440 mk.

The *Bomba Spa* (*Tuulentie 10*), just east of Bomba Hotel, has 37 modern rooms and suites; prices are the same as those at Bomba Hotel. Non-guests can use the gym, solarium, saunas, Turkish steam rooms and swimming pools for 50 mk.

Farmhouses Several farmhouses in the countryside around Nurmes offer B&B accommodation, a unique opportunity to meet local people and experience their way of life.

Koivula (☎/fax 440 066, Joensuuntie 50) is a farmhouse with 16 beds, at 75 mk per person. Breakfast and sauna are extra. *Männikkölän Pirtti* (☎ 481 873, Pellikan-lahdentie 1) has accommodation at the farmhouse for six to eight people, plus two cabins for rent. Cost is 120 mk per person, breakfast included.

Places to Eat

In the town centre, you can rely on the *grilli* at the kauppatori, or do your grocery shopping at the *supermarket* on Kirkkokatu.

Lounaskahvila Karpalo (*Kirkkokatu 18*) is in the same building as the supermarket. It is an unpretentious place that serves burgers, pizzas, kebabs and steaks.

In the commercial centre of Porokylä, *Bella Ciao* (*Porokylänkatu 14*) is a good Italian restaurant, popular with families. Meals are from 35 mk.

The *Bomba House restaurant* has a Karelian smorgasbord abounding in Karelian pies, *muikku* (fried whitefish) and varieties of *karjalanpaisti* (stew). The buffet (80 mk) is served all day, and is good value. There's also a café here. Bomba is generally open from 7 am to midnight daily.

At Hyvärilä, the hotel *restaurant* offers a reasonably priced buffet. There's also a summer café.

Getting There & Away

Bus Buses run regularly to Nurmes from towns in the region, including Joensuu, Kuhmo, Kuopio and Lieksa.

Train Nurmes is the terminus for the eastern railways, with service via Joensuu twice a day. Connections from Kajaani are by bus but train passes are valid.

Boat Saimaa Ferries (☎ 481 244 or 481 248) offers a summer cruise service twice weekly from Joensuu to Nurmes via Koli, a 10½ hour trip. A one-way ticket is 160 mk from Joensuu and 100 mk from Koli. Current timetables are available from most local tourist offices. See the Joensuu Getting There & Away section for more information.

AROUND NURMES
Saramo
☎ 013

This small, remote village, 24km north of Nurmes, is where the *Korpikylien tie* (Road of Wilderness Villages) begins. At the far end of the village, the Kalastajatalo, or 'Fisher's House', serves as an information centre and restaurant. Kalastajatalo is open daily in summer and on weekends during the rest of the year. There is a shop and a post office in Saramo.

Saramo Jotos Trek Saramo can be used as a base for this 75km trekking route, which covers all the interesting places around Saramo. Between Saramo and Peurajärvi, there are two campfire sites in addition to Kourukoski, a spot named after rapids there. Between Peurajärvi and road No 75, at Jalasjärvi, there's a *laavu* (open-air shelter). Between road No 75 and Lake Mujejärvi, there are three laavu sites. South of Lake Mujejärvi, there's a laavu at Markuskoski and cottages for rent at Paalikkavaara. The marked trail was established in 1996. Ask for details in Nurmes or Saramo.

Canoeing the Saramojoki There are two possible routes. Peurajärvi is not a bad lake to start paddling from (there are few difficult rapids), although July might not be the best month because of low water levels. If you start from Lake Mujejärvi, beware of Pitkäkoski rapids. The river drops 19m over 900m, so carry your canoe. Just half a kilometre later at Louhikoski, there's another drop of 5m. Other than these two rapids, this route is fine. Contact Kalastajatalo in Saramo for canoe rentals and transport.

Getting There & Away Saramo village is 24km north of Nurmes, and there are infrequent buses. A shared taxi is less hassle, and can be cheap if you have a group.

Peurajärvi Fishing Area
☎ 013

Carefully planned and well kept, this area has good, economical services to keep you busy for days and enough peace and quiet to keep you relaxed for weeks. Go first to the service cabin, which has a café and an information booth. It's open daily from June to mid-August. Three hour fishing permits allow you to catch one salmon and unlimited numbers of other species, or you can get a one day permit; see the Fishing section in the Activities chapter for more information about permits. The service-cabin rents rowing boats and holds keys to a lakeside sauna. The fishing area is managed by the Forest and Park Service, which releases 6000kg of salmon into the local waters every spring, for the benefit of licensed amateur fishers.

Apart from the fishing, there's a network of trekking routes (marked by orange paint on trees) running west to Hiidenportti National Park, east to the main road and further to Lake Mujejärvi.

Places to Stay Camping is allowed in many places – get a free map that shows the locations. *Peurajärvi Centre* (☎ 453 011) has several six-bed cottages for 375 mk. You must reserve in advance. There are *luppokota* huts, small Lappish-style houses, with room for three trekkers, at the southern and northern end of Lake Peurajärvi and at the shores of Lake Iso-Valkeinen. They can be used for free year-round and are always open.

Getting There & Away Peurajärvi is west of the Nurmes to Kuhmo highway. From Peurajärvi, a marked trail due east crosses the highway; from there, you can hitchhike or catch a bus to Nurmes or Kuhmo. The only sealed road is road No 75.

LIEKSA
• pop 16,000   ☎ 013

The small centre of Lieksa, on Lake Pielinen about 100km north of Joensuu, will be important if you wish to hike, bicycle, fish or paddle in the region. It has transport links, accommodation and services.

History
Count Per Brahe founded the town of Brahea in 1653 but it didn't survive long. The present Lieksa township was founded in 1936 and incorporated as a town in 1972.

Information
Lieksan Matkailu Oy (☎ 520 2400) at Pielisentie 7 is the local tourist office, open from 8 am to 6 pm Monday to Friday, 9 am to 2 pm Saturday from mid-June to mid-August, plus 11 am to 3 pm Sunday in July. At other times it is open from 8 am to 4 pm

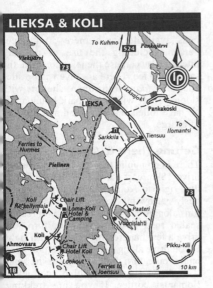

LIEKSA & KOLI

Lieksan Church
The modern Lieksa church (also known as the Church of Lake Pielinen) was built in 1982 to replace the old wooden church that burnt down on a freezing New Year's night in 1979. It was designed by contemporary Finnish architects Reima and Raili Pietilä. The huge cross-shaped ceiling dominates the hall, and large windows at the altar enable you to view the surviving bell tower. The church is open daily in summer.

Sarkkilan Manor
The privately owned Sarkkila Hovi at Sarkkilantie 45B is an Empire-style manor that has been carefully renovated. It was originally built in 1840 and was purchased in a dilapidated condition by the Kilpeläinen family, the present owners, in 1978. All houses on the estate have been meticulously rebuilt and decorated. In summer, when the estate is open to visitors, there are regular art exhibitions. Entry is 30 mk. Sarkkilan Hovi is 20km south of Lieksa.

Activities
Pony-trekking on hardy Icelandic horses can be arranged through the tourist office or directly with Loma-Ravila stables (☎ 535 123) at Tiensuuntie 23 in the village of Tiensuu, 11km south of Lieksa. A half-day tour and picnic lunch costs 250 mk.

In winter, husky dog and snowmobile **expeditions** along the Russian border are popular – Lieksan Matkailu Oy has a list of tour operators.

Special Events
The Lieksa Brass Week festival, held during a week in late July, attracts quite a number of international players. There are several concerts each day, with prices ranging from 20 to 60 mk. For further details, contact Lieksa Brass Week (☎/fax 523 133, brass .week@lieksa.inet.fi), Koski-Jaakonkatu 4, 81700 Lieksa.

Places to Stay
You can get a cabin at the river mouth at *Timitraniemi Camping* (☎ 521 780), open

Monday to Friday. It has information on accommodation, fishing, paddling, smoke saunas and national parks, and sells trekking maps for local routes.

The post office (81700 Lieksa) is at the north end of Pielisentie, the main street. Hours are 9 am to 8 pm Monday to Friday.

Pielisen Museo
The Pielisen Museo at Pappilantie 2 is a complex of almost 100 Karelian buildings and open-air exhibits, divided into several sections according to the century or the trade featured (eg farming, milling, firefighting, forestry). The collection of Pielisen Museo totals 100,000 objects and 15,000 photographs. This is probably the best open-air museum in Finland! A separate indoor museum handles folk history. Hours for the open-air museum are 10 am to 6 pm daily from mid-May to mid-September. The folk history museum is open year-round, from 10 am to 3 pm Tuesday to Friday outside of the summer season. Entry is 15 mk, or 10 mk for the indoor museum during winter.

from June to late August. Cabins cost 150 to 480 mk and tent sites are 70 mk.

The riverside *Hotelli Puustelli* (☎ 525 544, Hovileirinkatu 3), in the centre, is a pleasant hotel with rooms for 320/400 mk in summer, including breakfast and sauna.

Places to Eat

In the town centre, *Café Sanna (Pielisentie 2-6)* offers reasonably priced home-cooked lunches. Across the street, *Brahea Pizza* has pizzas from 30 mk. There are several *supermarkets* on Pielisentie.

Getting There & Away

Buses from Joensuu are frequent, up to 10 per day. There are two trains a day to Lieksa from Helsinki, via Joensuu. The scenic mode of transport is by ferry from Joensuu, via Koli; see the Joensuu Getting There & Away section for more information.

PATVINSUO NATIONAL PARK
☎ 013

Patvinsuo is a large marshland area between Lieksa and Ilomantsi. Swans, cranes and other birds nest here, and bears and other mammals can be seen if you're lucky. With the excellent *pitkospuu* (boardwalk) network, you can easily hike around, observing the life of a Finnish marshland.

If you have little time, go to the southern shore of Lake Suomu. It is 3.5km from the main road to Teretin lintutorni, a birdwatching tower. This is a good walk through forests and wetlands, and you will see some birds. Get a free map at the park headquarters and use it for planning. There are lakes and pine forests between the wetlands. Come in May or June to hear birds sing, or from June to September for the best trekking conditions.

There are three nature trails and several good hiking routes along the boardwalk path. You can walk around Lake Suomujärvi or follow pitkospuu trails through the wetlands.

Places to Stay

Suomu Park Centre (☎ 548 506) has a warden in attendance from May to mid-

September, for advice, fishing permits and free maps. There is a dormitory with nine beds available for a mere 50 mk per person, including the use of a small kitchen. You can use the telephone and the sauna for a fee. There are seven camp sites and one *laavu* (an open shelter with sloping roof) within the park boundaries, all have toilets and firewood and are free of charge.

Getting There & Away

There is no public transport. From Lieksa, drive 18km east towards Hatunkylä, then turn right to Kontiovaara. It is a dangerously narrow but very scenic road, which runs along small ridges. When you reach a sealed road (Uimahar-juntie), turn left, drive a few hundred metres and turn right. If you drive along the eastern Runon ja rajantie route, turn west as you see the small 'Uimaharju' sign, just south of the Lieksa-Ilomantsi border. If you are trekking, Bear's Path and Suden taival (Wolf Trail) both lead here, as the park is where these trails meet.

RUUNAA RECREATION AREA
☎ 013

Ruunaa, 30km north-east of Lieksa, is currently the most popular destination east of Lake Pielinen. A great variety of outdoor activities make Ruunaa a rewarding place to visit. It boasts 38km of waterways with six white-water rapids, plus unpolluted wilderness, excellent trekking paths and good fishing. The area is run by the Forest and Park Service, which puts over 6000kg of fish into the waters every year. Designated camping sites (with fire rings) are also provided and maintained.

There's an observation tower at Huuhkajavaara.

Information

The Ruunaa Visitor Centre (☎ 533 165) is near the bridge over the Naarajoki, which is where most boat trips start. It's open from 9 am to 7 pm daily in summer (until 9 pm in

July). There are exhibitions, maps, a library and a slide show in English.

Activities

Ruunaa is busy all year round, as it hosts skiing and other snow sports in winter.

Boating & Canoeing There are six rapids, and you can shoot them in wooden or rubber boats. There are several launches daily in summer from Naarajoki bridge, where all tours start. Prices range from 150 to 160 mk and include all equipment and a lunch. The easiest way to organise a tour is to go to Lieksan Matkailu (the tourist office in Lieksa), as they can bargain a bit for you. Transport is available from Lieksa to Naarajoki bridge. Canoeing is also possible here.

Fishing Ruunaa is one of the most popular fishing spots in North Karelia. Those using a wheelchair can reach the water along a long wooden walkway. One-day fishing permits cost 48 mk and are available in Lieksa and Ruunaa. There is also a fishing permit machine near the Neitijoki rapids. Fishing is allowed from June to early September and from mid-November to late December.

Trekking There are two trekking routes in the Ruunaa area. **Bear's Path**, a longer trekking route, runs across Ruunaa. You will find it just 50m north of the Naarajoki bridge. The path is marked with round orange symbols on trees.

Around the river system, and over two beautiful suspension bridges, runs **Ruunaan koskikierros**, a 29km loop along good pitkospuu paths, with good signs along the way and beige paint on trees. If you have more time, there are another 20km of side trips you can take.

If you start at the Naarajoki bridge, you will have to walk 5km along the Bear's Path to reach the Ruunaan koskikierros trail. Another 3.3km brings you to the Neitikoski rapids, where you'll find commercial services. Neitikoski has road access.

Organised Tours

Highly recommended is Ismo Räsänen (☎ 533 111), who is something of a Crocodile Dundee of the Karelian wilderness. He can tailor a boat trip to your needs, and has a picturesque island where you can stop for a picnic lunch. His family prepares typical Karelian dishes, and he catches his own salmon.

Places to Stay & Eat

There are at least 10 laavu shelters and another 10 designated camp sites in the area. Camping and sleeping in a laavu is free of charge. Get the free *Ruunaa Government Hiking Area* map and guide for accommodation information. You will need a lightweight mattress, a sleeping bag and some mosquito repellent. Lighting a fire is allowed, except during fire alerts (watch for posted signs).

Lomapirtti Sillankorva (☎/fax 533 121) offers superb accommodation right at the Naarajoki bridge. You can rent the entire farmhouse if you have a large group, or either floor for about 400 mk. Everything is extremely clean and nice with wood panelling on the walls. There is a smoke sauna and a summer restaurant.

Ruunaan Matkailu (☎/fax 533 130, Siikakoskentie 47), 5km east of Naarajoki bridge, has cabins and rooms starting at 70 mk per person. It has a café, lakeside sauna, smoke sauna, rental boats and various snowmobile and boating tours.

Near the Neitikoski rapids, the *Ruunaa Hiking Centre* (☎ 533 170, fax 521 149) has a wide range of accommodation in log cabins. Rates start at 450 mk per night for a four-person cabin. Tent sites are 50 mk. This is a modern place, with public telephones and a TV, and you can use the kitchen, washing machines and showers at no extra cost. There are mountain bikes, canoes and rowing boats for hire, and a sauna. You can eat in the restaurant or buy sausages and other items at the shop. The Ruunaa Hiking Centre is open daily from May to late October.

Getting There & Away

There are infrequent mini-buses from Lieksa – inquire at the tourist office. The best way to reach the area is on an organised rafting tour from Lieksa, by hitching or by private car.

NURMIJÄRVI AREA
☎ 013

Known for its canoeing routes, the Nurmijärvi area is wild and remote. Nurmijärvi village has enough services to get you to the Jongunjoki or Lieksajoki canoeing routes, or to the Änäkäinen area for fishing and trekking.

Änäkäinen Fishing Area

Änäkäinen is a government fishing area, with the Bear's Path running through it. The Forest and Park Service controls fish quantities in three lakes in the area. Fishing is allowed all year round, except in May. The Aunen Kahvila (see later Places to Stay & Eat section) and the Karjalan Eräkeskus and the Jongunjoen Lomapirtti have boats and fishing permits for 48 mk per day. Permits are also available in Lieksa.

Änäkäinen saw fierce fighting during the early weeks of the Winter War in December 1939. Finnish soldiers held their positions here, leaving a large number of Russian soldiers dead. In order to stop enemy tanks, the Finns built large rock barriers; when the war erupted again in 1940, even larger rocks were added.

To get to Änäkäinen, turn right as you drive north from Nurmijärvi, and proceed 6km. To your left is the fishing area, with a *korsu* (a rebuilt underground bunker used by Finnish soldiers during WWII), and the Korsukierros area, with *juoksuhauta* (circular) trenches opposite.

Canoeing the Pankasaari Route

While in Nurmijärvi, you can rent a canoe from the Erästely Company (☎ 546 550) at Nurmijärventie 158A. The paddle route starts across the road. Get yourself a free route guide, which is widely available at brochure outlets (tourist offices or roadside shopping areas), or at Lieksan Matkailu. The route follows the Lieksajoki downstream to Lake Pankajärvi. From there, you paddle south-east under a road bridge to Lake Pudasjärvi. Avoid the dangerous Pankakoski power station in the south and paddle upstream to the upper part of the Lieksajoki. Heading north-west from this point, you first reach Naarajoki at Ruunaa and then pass a few tricky rapids, especially Käpykoski (pull the canoe with a rope here, unless you are experienced), before returning to Nurmijärvi.

Canoeing the Jongunjoki

This beautiful wilderness river has over 40 small rapids, but none of them are very tricky. Lieksan Matkailu has a good English-language guide to the route. You can start at Jonkeri up north (in the municipality of Kuhmo), or further south at Teljo bridge, or at Aittokoski, or even at Lake Kaksinkantaja. Allow four days if you start at Jonkeri and one day from the last point. The Räsänen shop in Nurmijärvi will take care of transportation to Jonkeri, Teljo or Kaksinkantaja, and will also rent canoes.

Places to Stay & Eat

Erästely Ky (☎ 546 500, Nurmijärventie 158A), the main canoe rental company, also offers accommodation in the village. Bed cost about 60 mk, including a sauna, but bring your own sheets.

If you come by bus, you can walk to *Jongunjoen Lomapirtti* (☎/fax 546 531, Kivivaarantie 21), 2km from the main road towards Änäkäinen and the Russian border. There is also a connecting 5km path from the Bear's Path to the Lomapirtti. The overnight charge is 100 mk per person in spotless four-bed rooms. You can also pitch a tent here. There are two smoke saunas available, as well as bicycles, canoes and boats for rent.

Aunen Kahvila is a popular roadside café in Nurmijärvi, 15km from the Russian border. It is visited by locals as well as by tourists. There are reasonably priced home-made meals, and you can buy fishing permits and pick up keys for the Änäkäinen rented fishing boats. Aunen Kahvila is open every day till 7 pm.

Getting There & Away

The Nurmijärvi area can be reached by catching the weekday bus from Lieksa to Kuhmo. It passes the villages of Nurmijärvi, Teljo and Jonkeri.

VUONISLAHTI

☎ 013

Vuonislahti, a completely rural village, has a train station and a hostel – one of only two hostels in the Lieksa area.

There is a **war memorial** on a small hill across the road, as you come from the train station. This is where Russians were stopped by Finnish soldiers in 1808. The nearby *tanssilava* house has dancing in summer on Saturday evenings.

Places to Stay & Eat

The HI-affiliated *Kestikievari Herranniemi (☎/fax 542 110, tn@kestik.pp.fi)*, south of the Vuonislahti centre, is a very quaint hostel, open year-round, and a good choice for those wanting to stay in an old farmhouse. The main building is over 200 years old. There are cheap dormitories in an old *aitta* (storage) building; beds cost 70 mk. There are also hotel rooms and a few cabins. The place sells coffee and snacks, exhibits local handicrafts and rents bicycles and boats. You can also bathe in a sauna. To get to Herranniemi, walk straight from the Vuonislahti train station to the main road, turn left and proceed 500m.

Isäntärenki (Vuonijärventie 2) serves traditional Karelian dishes. There are also handicrafts for sale.

Getting There & Away

There are daily trains to Vuonislahti from Joensuu and Lieksa. The small Vuonislahti train station keeps short hours, but you can always buy tickets on the train.

AROUND VUONISLAHTI
Paateri
☎ 013

Paateri is best known for the church and gallery at the studio-home of Eva Ryynänen, a respected woodcarver. Born in 1915, she has been a sculptor since her teens and is still active. This isolated property, surrounded by pine trees, is the childhood home of her husband, Paavo. The Paateri wilderness church was built in 1991 with walls and floor made of Russian pine, and huge doors carved from Canadian cedar. The altar was created using a stump that once belonged to the largest fir tree in Finland. The place also has a café. The gallery is open daily from May to September. Inquire about hours on ☎ 520 2400. Entry is 25 mk for adults and 15 mk for children..

Getting There & Away The most exciting way to get to Paateri is to row a boat from the Herranniemi hostel. Ask for a map to avoid getting lost. If you are driving or cycling, follow the road signs from the main road or from the secondary road north of Vuonislahti. You can also rent a bicycle at the Herranniemi hostel.

KOLI
☎ 013

Koli Hill, south of Lieksa across Lake Pielinen, has been dubbed the first-ever tourist attraction in Finland. Several Finnish artists of the National Romantic era drew their inspiration from this place. The composer Jean Sibelius is said to have played a grand piano at the top of the hill to celebrate his honeymoon.

Koli hill was declared a national park in 1991 after hot debate between environmentalists and landowners. The owners agreed to sell their land and environmentalists dropped their demand that the Hotel Koli, up on the hill, be demolished. Most of the area is relatively pristine and there are many walking tracks.

Things to See & Do

Near the hotel on the hill is **uhrihalkeama**, a large crack in the rock that once served as a sacrificial site.

Ukko-Koli is the highest point and 200m further is **Akka-Koli**, another peak. **Mammutti** is a huge stone with a 'Temple of Silence', which is used for religious events. The solid rock peak nearby is called **Pahakoli**, or 'Evil Koli'. Further south is **Mäkrävaara**, a hill which has the best views.

Pirunkirkko (Devil's Church) is an area of rocks, cliffs and small caves. The site, south of the Koli area on the lakeside road, is signposted.

All of the above attractions are linked by trails.

Places to Stay

You can stay one night free in the cosy *Ikolanaho* hut with a pleasant meadow setting in the national park. The door is locked, but you should have no problem signing for the key at Hotel Koli. There are four bunks with mattresses, a fireplace and wood.

The HI-affiliated hostel, *Kolin Retkeily-maja* (☎ 673 131, Niinilahdentie 47) is a family-run place that stays open year-round. It is 5km from the main road and bus stop, so you have to hitchhike or walk. This magnificent, quiet hostel must be one of the most relaxing places to stay in Finland. A bed costs 65 mk and the sauna costs 10 mk. Bring food to prepare in the kitchen.

Hotel Koli (☎ 672 221, fax 672 240, Ylä-Kolintie 39), at the top of Koli hill, is a typical 1970s concrete box with rooms from 300/380 mk. Services are good as are the views from the café and restaurant.

Loma-Koli Holiday Centre (☎ 673 211, fax 673 201, Merilän-rannantie 68) is near the Hiisi Hill slopes, where there is downhill skiing. There are rooms and apartments with rates starting at 185 mk per person. Nearby, *Loma-Koli Camping* (☎ 673 212) has excellent camping facilities, including cottages, and rents sturdy mountain bikes that are excellent for exploring the area.

Tent sites cost 55 to 70 mk. The camping ground is open from June to late August.

Getting There & Away

Bus The Koli area is served by regular buses from Joensuu, Juuka and Nurmes.

Boat There is ferry service in summer to Joenssu and Lieksa; see the Joensuu Getting There & Away section for more information. Buses to the Koli hilltop meet all arriving ferries.

JUUKA
☎ 013

Juuka is a vital link on the route around Lake Pielinen. It is famous for its soapstone mining and handicrafts, and has two nice museums and a small, wooden old town. The village itself is off main road No 18, equidistant from Nurmes and Koli.

Puu-Juuka

Puu-Juuka (Wooden Juuka) in the village has at least 60 wooden houses, some over 100 years old. They were preserved from demolition largely through the efforts of local individuals. Many have been beautifully renovated.

Mill Museum

The Myllymuseo is in a beautiful natural riverside setting. The museum includes an old grain mill, which has served the villagers since 1870. There are four buildings with old tools and machines, including a genuine smoke sauna. In the old days, logs were floated downriver past the rapids through the *uittoränni* (a specially constructed chute for floating logs past rapids). The museum is open daily from June to late August. Entry is 15 mk, and the ticket is also valid in Pitäjänmuseo.

Pitäjänmuseo

This big red wooden house with 'Museo' written on it is visible from the main road and houses the Juuka village museum. It was built in 1825 with double walls to prevent thieves from stealing the grain that was stored inside. The museum has an impressive collection of local and regional artefacts, some up to 200 years old. Opening hours are similar to the mill museum, and the same 15 mk entry ticket is valid for both.

Places to Stay & Eat

On the shore of Lake Pielinen, *Piitterin Lomakylä* (☎ *472 068, Piitterintie 144*) has tent sites for 65 mk and cabins from 180 to 220 mk. There is a typical Finnish *huvilava* (dancing stage), where minor Finnish celebrities sometimes sing on Saturday nights; tickets cost about 50 mk.

In the village centre, *Hotel Petra* (☎ *472 700, Piokolantie 2*) has five rooms at 260/320 mk. The hotel restaurant offers fine dining, while *Katrilli Lounas-Kahvila* (*Väyryläntie 9*) offers inexpensive home-cooked meals until 6 pm Monday to Friday.

Getting There & Away

Regular buses between Joensuu and Nurmes stop in Juuka.

PAALASMAA ISLAND

☎ 013

The largest island in Lake Pielinen is connected to the mainland by a free ferry that winds through smaller islands. The island is noted for its scenery and peaceful atmosphere, and is the highest island in Finland – its tallest point is 132m above water level. There is a wooden **observation tower** on the island, 3km from the camping ground via a marked trail. If you follow the signs that say 'tornille', you will see some **old houses** that tell of the long history of Paalasmaa. Boat tours and fishing are popular activities on the island, with rentals available.

Near the ferry terminal on the mainland is **Ritoranta**, a *savipaja* or small pottery studio. You can purchase handicrafts made by local artists.

Places to Stay & Eat

At the east end of the island there's *Paalasmaan Lomamajat* (☎ *479 516*), open June to late August. It's a camping ground with a nice lakeside spot. There are two/four bed cottages that cost 180/250 mk, tent sites for 50 mk and two saunas. On the island you can buy food supplies at a small *shop*, open daily in summer.

Getting There & Away

To get to Paalasmaa, drive 2km north of Juuka village and turn right. It is 15km to the ferry dock.

VUOKKO

☎ 013

The northern bicycle route from Juuka follows the parallel road through Keski-Vuokko. The locals are sure to remind you that Keski-Vuokko was used as the beautiful setting in the 'blockbuster' Finnish movie *Kivenpyörittäjän Kylä*.

The old Orthodox monastery at Pyötikkö, south of Vuokko, is long gone but there is a fine **tsasouna** (chapel), open daily in summer.

Places to Stay & Eat

Vuokonjärven Loma (☎ *477 096, Vuokontie 1035*) is the camping ground with the best location in the Juuka area. There are just 10 cottages hidden among trees and the shallow lake is pleasant to swim in if the weather is warm. Rent a rowing boat and visit the cave in the steep cliff on an island across the strait. Two bed cottages are 150 mk, camping costs 55 mk. There are several saunas, including a smoke sauna. There are showers, a very nice kitchen in the service building and a laundry.

Kosken kioski in the village sells food and some is available at the camping ground, but you're best off bringing your own supplies.

Getting There & Away

Buses travelling north from Juuka to Nurmes pass Vuokko once daily, but a bicycle or car is more reliable.

AHMOVAARA
☎ 013

The village of Ahmovaara is little more than a blip along road No 18. The place is known (and hated) for its modern architecture (which has been called 'modern Karelianism'). The main reason to stop is to visit the **Kolinportti tourist information centre** (☎ 671 333) at Kolintie 10. You can eat, fill the car with petrol, book cottages, buys maps, drink a few beers at the bar, stock up on provisions, or shop for tacky souvenirs. There's also an exhibition on natural attractions in the Lake Pielinen region. Kolinportti hours are 9 am to 5 pm Monday to Friday, 9 am to 3 pm Saturday in summer. In winter it's open from 9 am to 5 pm weekdays.

VAIKKOJOKI

The Vaikkojoki river has been restored to its original state and is no longer used for floating logs. It is now promoted as a 50km canoeing route. There are 40 rapids of varying difficulty and a few accommodation options along the route. Get a free copy of the *Vaikkojoki* brochure (English and German text) and buy a waterproof route map (25 mk) at the Kolinportti tourist office in Ahmovaara. The route starts 25km west of Juuka village, at the Ahmonkoski rapids, and ends near the village of Kaavi. You can rent canoes at holiday villages in Kaavi or Juuka.

South Karelia

If you study the map, you may come to the conclusion that just a tiny fraction of South Karelia is Finnish territory. There is barely 10km between Lake Saimaa and the Russian border at the narrowest point, near Imatra. The once busy South Karelian trade town Vyborg (Finnish: Viipuri) and the Karelian isthmus reaching to St Petersburg are now part of Russia.

Wars have been a feature in this troublesome region, and Russian fortifications are to be seen in South Karelia.

LAPPEENRANTA
• pop 57,000   ☎ 05

Lappeenranta (Swedish: Villmanstrand) is an old spa and garrison town at the southern end of Lake Saimaa, near the Russian border. Thanks to its interesting sights, beautiful location and friendly people, Lappeenranta is one of the most frequently visited cities in Finland. Increasingly, it is popular with Russian visitors shopping for luxury goods.

The building of the Saimaa Canal in 1856 made this an important trading port, and Lappeenranta is now the largest inland port in Finland. The waterway from Lake Saimaa to the Gulf of Finland is 43km long and has eight locks.

A day cruise along the Saimaa Canal to Vyborg, Russia – Finland's second-largest city until it was lost in World War II – is one of Lappeenranta's main attractions.

Lappeenranta is the capital of South Karelia.

History
The early Lappeenranta area on the shores of Lake Saimaa was a busy Karelian trade centre. It was officially established as a town by Count Per Brahe in 1649. Queen Kristina of Sweden accepted the coat of arms, which depicts a rather primitive man, after whom the Swedish Villmanstrand was unflatteringly named (Villmanstrand means 'Wild Man's Shore' in Swedish). Apparently jealous Vyborg businesses lobbied against their emerging rival, and Lappeenranta lost its town status in 1683.

Following a Russian victory on 23 August 1741 and the town's complete destruction, Lappeenranta was ceded to Russia in 1743 and it remained part of tsarist Russia until independence in 1917. Fortified during the 1780s, Lappeenranta remained a small village, numbering only 210 people in 1812. A spa was founded in 1824, but it was only after railways and industries were developed that Lappeenranta started its growth. Today the beautiful lakeside setting is marred by oversized industries that provide work and wealth to many.

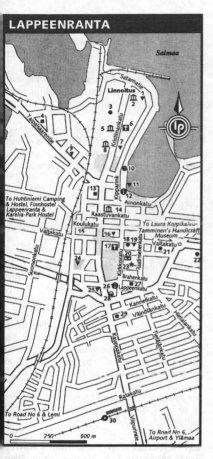

LAPPEENRANTA

PLACES TO STAY
4 Hotelli Pallo
13 Scandic Hotel Patria
27 Sokos Hotel Lappee
29 Gasthaus Turistilappee

PLACES TO EAT
1 Majakka
7 Kahvila Majurska
9 Pallon Pizzariina
11 Prinsessa Armaada, SS Suvi-Saimaa
15 Wing Wah
16 Café Galleria, Old Park
19 Tassos, Wild & Happy Cannibals
24 Kauppatori
25 Drive-In Elvis

OTHER
2 South Karelia Museum
3 Artists' Workshops
5 South Karelia Art Museum
6 Orthodox Church
8 Cavalry Museum
10 Passenger Quay
12 Summer Tourist Information
14 Wolkoff Talomuseo
17 Lappee Church
18 Pharmacy
20 Post & Telephone Offices
21 Public Library
22 Water Tower
23 Police Station
26 Tourist Office
28 Bus Station
30 Train Station

Orientation

Kauppakatu and Valtakatu are the main streets. The train station is approximately 1 km south of their intersection. The cheapest places to stay are west of the town centre.

Information

Tourist Office The tourist information office (☎ 667 788, matkailuoy@lappeenranta fi) at the bus station complex is open from 9 am to 6 pm Monday to Friday from June to late August. At other times it's open from 9.30 am to 4.30 pm Monday to Friday.

A summer tourist information booth at the harbour is open from 9 am to 9 pm daily June to late August.

Post & Communications The main post office is at Pormestarinkatu 1, 53100 Lappeenranta. There is a Tele office next door.

Internet Resources & Library The public library at Valtakatu 47 is open from 10 am to 8 pm Monday to Friday, 10 am to 3 pm Saturday and noon to 3 pm Sunday.

The Internet terminal books up quickly – arrive early in the morning to sign up.

Left Luggage The train station has 10 mk, 24-hour lockers and a left-luggage counter.

Medical & Emergency Services In a general emergency, ring ☎ 112. For a doctor, call ☎ 10023 and for police ☎ 10022. The police station is adjacent to the post office.

The pharmacy at Valtakatu 37 is open daily from 8 am to 10 pm.

Linnoitus

The fortifications in Linnoitus (Fortress) area of Lappeenranta above the harbour were started by the Swedes and finished by the Russians in the 18th century. Some of the fortress buildings have been turned into museums and one 20 mk ticket (15 mk seniors, 10 mk students and children) is valid for all three. From June to late August they are open from 10 am to 6 pm Monday to Friday and 11 am to 5 pm on weekends. From September to late May 11 am to 5 pm Tuesday, Thursday, Saturday and Sunday (with the exception of the Cavalry Museum, which is open by appointment only during the winter months).

The Fortress has many **artists' workshops** selling ceramics, paintings and handknitted garments; these shops are open daily in summer.

Riders in old cavalry costumes parade between the fortress and the kauppatori for several hours each day from Tuesday to Friday between June and mid-August.

South Karelia Museum The historical museum at the northern end of the fortress displays folk costumes and a scale model of Vyborg as it looked before it fell to the Russians in 1939. Before WWII, Vyborg was the capital of Karelia and the second biggest town in Finland.

Cavalry Museum The cavalry tradition is cherished in Lappeenranta – from the 1920s to the 1940s, cavalrymen in their red trousers and skeleton jackets were a common sight on town streets. The town's oldest building (built in 1772), a former guardhouse, houses the Cavalry Museum which exhibits uniforms, saddles and guns.

South Karelia Art Museum This museum has a permanent collection of paintings, as well as temporary exhibitions.

Orthodox Church The jewel-like Orthodox church is Finland's oldest. It was built in 1785 by Russian soldiers. Hours are noon to 4.30 pm Tuesday to Sunday from June to mid-August.

City Centre

The city centre has several attractions worth exploring, although the fortress area is the prime tourist attraction.

Wolkoff Talomuseo The Wolkoff House Museum, at Kauppakatu 26, is the preserved home of a Russian emigrant family. The house, built in 1826, was owned by the Wolkoff family from 1872 to 1986. Ten rooms have been maintained as they were; you must join one of the hourly guided tours to see them. The museum is open from 10 am to 5 pm Monday to Friday and 11 am to 5 pm on weekends from June to late August. During other times, hours are 11 am to 5 pm Friday and Saturday. Admission is 20 mk (10 mk seniors and students, 7 mk children).

Laura Korpikaivo-Tamminen's Handicraft Museum This museum at Kantokatu 1 has a permanent collection of over 2000 handmade pieces, donated by the late Laura Korpikaivo-Tamminen. It's open from 11 am to 6 pm daily from June to late August. Hours at other times are 11 am to 3 pm from Tuesday to Thursday and 11 am to 5 pm on weekends. Admission is 10 mk (7 mk seniors, students and children).

Lappee Church The Lappee church in the middle of town was built in 1794. It's open to the public daily from June to mid August.

Water Tower The water tower, near the intersection of Valtakatu and Myllykatu, has a café at the top with good views of Lake Saimaa. It's open daily from June to August.

Organised Tours

Two-hour sightseeing tours that take in the fortress, city centre and surrounding area are given by the tourist office starting at 2 pm Monday to Friday from June to late August and at 2 pm Saturday from late June to early August. Tours are by bus and cost 30 mk per adult.

Half-day bus tours of attractions near Lappeenranta – such as the Imatra rapids and Ylämaa Jewel Village – take place every Wednesday from June to late August; contact the tourist office for more information.

Cruises Cruises on Lake Saimaa and the Saimaa Canal are popular and there are daily departures from late May to late August – current schedules are available at the city tourist offices. All departures are from the passenger quay near the fortress.

Most interesting are the day cruises down the Saimaa Canal to **Vyborg, Russia** aboard the MS *Karelia*. A return ticket costs 110 to 150 mk. A Russian visa is not required. The Karelia Lines (π 453 0380) office at the harbour sells tickets.

Half-day cruises on Lake Saimaa aboard the MS *Katrilli* and the more spacious MS *Camilla* are also run by Karelia Lines. Cost is 50 mk for a cruise on MS *Katrilli* and 60 mk for those on MS *Camilla*. There are also island cruises on most evenings.

Saimaa Risteilyt (π 415 6955) at the harbour offers cruises aboard the 95-passenger MS *El Faro*, either around the archipelago or down the Saimaa Canal for 50 mk per adult. This company also operates the SS *Suur-Saimaa* ferry between Lappeenranta and Savonlinna. See the Getting There & Away sections for both cities for more details.

Places to Stay

Camping The well-kept camping ground, *Huhtiniemi* (π 453 1888, Kuusimäenkatu 18) is on the shores of Lake Saimaa about 2km west of the centre (take bus No 5, 6 or 7). Sites cost 75 mk and cottages 150 to 390 mk. Eight cottages on the island of Nuottasaari, just north of Huhtiniemi, have cooking facilities and include the use of a rowing boat and lakeside sauna.

Hostels The most inexpensive accommodation in Lappeenranta is HI-affiliated *Huhtiniemi Hostel* (π 451 5555, fax 451 5558, huhtiniemi@loma-oksa.inet.fi), next to the Huhtiniemi camping ground. It is open from June to mid-August and has dorm beds for 55 mk, plus a café, kitchen, laundry and indoor swimming pool. The charge for linen is 20 mk, breakfast 25 mk.

Finnhostel Lappeenranta on the same site is open all year and has beds in single and double rooms from 100 mk per person, linen included. Breakfast costs 25 mk. This hostel is also affiliated with III.

Karelia-Park (π 675 211, fax 452 8454, Korpraalinkuja 1), 300m west of Huhtiniemi, is a summer hostel that charges 90 mk per person for dorm beds. Linen and breakfast are an additional 20 mk each. The HI-affiliated hostel is open from June to late August and has kitchen, sauna and laundry.

Guesthouses *Gasthaus Turistilappee* (π 415 0800, Kauppakatu 52), not far from the train station, is a homey place that offers tidy singles/doubles/triples at 180/280/320 mk, breakfast and sauna included.

In a quiet residential area west of the fortress, *Hotelli Pallo* (π 411 8456, Pallonkatu 9) is a small and pleasant guesthouse with rooms from 160/250 mk, including breakfast.

Hotels The best hotel in Lappeenranta is *Scandic Hotel Patria* (π 677 511, fax 451 2441, Kauppakatu 21), which overlooks the fortress park. There are 135 rooms, three restaurants and two saunas. Singles/doubles are regularly 550/650 mk, in summer 400/460 mk.

Sokos Hotel Lappee (☎ *67861, fax 678 6545, Brahenkatu 1)* is convenient to the centre and is the largest hotel in town, with all rooms priced at 435 mk in summer. Rooms are 635/760 mk at other times.

Farmhouses Many farmhouses in the countryside around Lappeenranta offer B&B accommodation, a unique opportunity to meet local people and participate in their way of life.

Lahtela Farmhouse (☎ *457 8034, Lahtelantie 120)* in Ylämaa, 43km south of Lappeenranta, is a dairy farm run by Hellevi and Lauri Lahtela. It is open to guests year-round. The cost of 130 mk per person includes breakfast, sauna and use of a rowing boat.

Asko's and Maija's Farmhouse (☎/fax *454 4606, Suolahdentie 461)* is a dairy farm 27km north of Lappeenranta in the village of Peltoi. Run by the Saikko family, it offers accommodation from mid-May to late September in a traditional log outbuilding for 130 mk per person, breakfast included.

Farmhouse Päivänkakkara (☎ *454 4621, Suolahdentie 360)*, also in Peltoi, is a sheep farm that charges 140 mk per person for B&B accommodation in the old farmhouse. The hosts offer bicycle and cross-country skiing trips. Päivänkakkara is open from June to late September or by prior arrangement.

Places to Eat

Lappeenranta offers many good dining options in all price ranges.

At the *kauppatori* stalls sell local specialities such as *vety* (meat pie with ham, eggs and butter), a local favourite, or waffles with jam and whipped cream. There are a dozen more snack stands at the harbour during summer.

Drive-In Elvis on Kauppakatu near the bus station is a grilli with plenty under 15 mk, including the 'Hound Dog' for 12 mk.

Pallon Pizzariina, on Taipalsaarentie west of the fortress area, is a nice little neighbourhood place where you can fill up on pizza for less than 20 mk.

Café Galleria, on the basement level at Koulukatu 15, offers home-cooked lunches – salad, coffee and dessert included – for 40 mk.

There are several ethnic restaurants in the town centre that will make you believe you're in another country. One is the Chinese restaurant *Wing Wah* in the Kauppakanava shopping centre, with dinners from 50 to 80 mk. *Tassos (Valtakatu 41)* is a fine Greek place with mid-priced dinners. Their 45 mk lunch special served from 11 am to 2.30 pm Monday to Friday is good value.

At the harbour, the restaurant ship *Prinsessa Armaada* offers fine dining in summer. Just north of the harbour and also open in summer, *Majakka (Samatie 4)* is a nice little restaurant with Finnish cuisine and hints of maritime atmosphere.

Kahvila Majurska, in an 18th century wooden building at the fortress complex, is easily one of the most charming cafés in all of Finland. The place is cosy and furnished with antiques. Home-baked cakes and pies are a speciality, as are the delicious quiches.

Entertainment

At the harbour, the SS *Suvi-Saimaa* is an old steamship turned summer beer terrace.

There are many bars and pubs on Valtakatu in the centre, including the Irish pub *Old Park* at No 36, and *Wild & Happy Cannibals* at No 41.

Getting There & Away

Air Finnair operate daily flights to Helsinki and many other major Finnish cities. Bus No 34 travels between the city centre and the airport, 3km west of the centre.

Bus All buses along the eastern route between Helsinki and Joensuu, stop in Lappeenranta. Buses run hourly from Lappeenranta to Imatra, 37km north-east

There are handy connections to smaller places in South Karelia, although some buses only run once a day, Monday to Friday.

Train Seven to eight trains a day between Helsinki and Joensuu will take you to Lappeenranta. The trip from Helsinki takes a bit more than 2½ hours.

Car & Motorcycle Lappeenranta is on road No 6, about 220km east of Helsinki.

Ferry From mid-June to mid-August, the SS *Suur-Saimaa* sails three times a week between Savonlinna and Lappeenranta. A one-way ticket costs 250 mk. For more information see the Savonlinna Getting There & Away section.

Getting Around

There is an extensive bus network, and you can catch a local bus at the train station. The tourist office assists with bicycle rentals.

AROUND LAPPEENRANTA
Ylämaa
• pop 1650　　　☎ 05

Ylämaa, 21km south of Lappeenranta, is a rural municipality best known for the gemstone spectrolite, a special kind of labradorite found only here. Spectrolite is a dark stone which glitters in all the colours of the spectrum.

The **Jewel Village**, on the No 387 Lappeenranta to Vaalimaa road, is Ylämaa's main attraction. The village consists of two stone grinderies, quarries, a goldsmith's workshop and a gem museum. The gem museum has a collection of spectrolites and other precious stones; admission is 15 mk. The museum and shops are open daily from June to late August.

The **Ylämaa church**, in the municipal centre, was built in 1931 and has an unusual façade made of spectrolite. The church is open daily in summer.

The local tourist information office (☎ 613 4259) is in Jewel Village.

Getting There & Away In summer, catch the afternoon bus from Lappeenranta, which runs Monday to Friday only.

Lemi

This small village 25km west of Lappeenranta is known for its *lemin särä* (roast mutton). This traditional dish – cooked in a wooden trough – has been described as 'one of the seven wonders of Finland'!

You can try lemin särä at *Säräpirtti Kippurasarvi* (☎ 414 6470) at Rantatie 1, on the lakeside. The dish takes nine hours to cook so it must be ordered at least two days in advance.

Getting There & Away Half a dozen buses run between Lappeenranta and Lemi from Monday to Friday, as well as one on Saturday.

IMATRA
• pop 32,000　　　☎ 05

North-east of Lappeenranta is Imatra, a strange city situated on Lake Saimaa that bears a legacy of wars, industrial pollution and human greed. The city is justifiably proud that in 1894 one of its citizens invented a revolutionary machine for gutting herring.

Among Imatra's four centres, scattered across a large area, are fine attractions unfortunately marred by embarrassments of the first degree. Take the waterfall, for example – once the prime 19th century tourist attraction in Finland. In 1929, its raging waters were harnessed to produce hydroelectricity.

The famous Alvar Aalto church looks fine from inside, but outside you have to put up with the smell from the nearby pulp factory – incidentally also designed by Aalto and for a long time hailed for its 'beauty'.

Despite these industrial woes, Imatra and its foaming rapids (which once again foam daily in summer) remain popular with vacationing Finns.

IMATRA

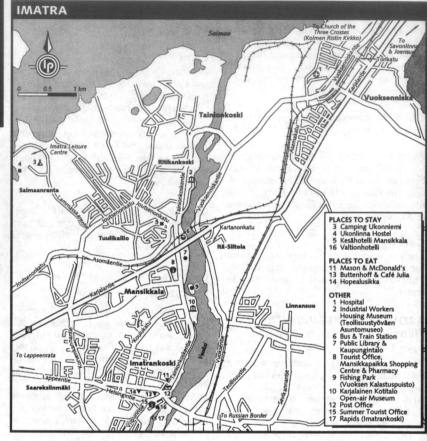

PLACES TO STAY
3 Camping Ukonniemi
4 Ukonlinna Hostel
5 Kesähotelli Mansikkala
16 Valtionhotelli

PLACES TO EAT
11 Mason & McDonald's
13 Buttenhoff & Café Julia
14 Hopealusikka

OTHER
1 Hospital
2 Industrial Workers
 Housing Museum
 (Teollisuustyöväen
 Asuntomuseo)
6 Bus & Train Station
7 Public Library &
 Kaupungintalo
8 Tourist Office,
 Mansikkapaikka Shopping
 Centre & Pharmacy
9 Fishing Park
 (Vuoksen Kalastuspuisto)
10 Karjalainen Kotitalo
 Open-air Museum
12 Post Office
15 Summer Tourist Office
17 Rapids (Imatrankoski)

Orientation

There are four centres. Imatrankoski at the rapids (or the power station) is where people want to spend their time shopping and dining. Lappeentie is the main street. Mansikkala is the administrative centre, with architecture not dissimilar to the Soviet ideal. That's where you'll find the bus and train station and the isolated shopping centre, which houses the tourist office. Vuoksenniska, to the north-east, is an industrial area (surrounded by two gigantic pulp factories) and former independent municipality.

Information

Tourist Office The tourist office (☎ 681 2500, info@imatranmatkailu.inet.fi) is in the Mansikkapaikka shopping centre in Mansikkala, not far from the bus and train station. It's open from 9 am to 5 pm Monday to Friday and 10 am to 2 pm Saturday in summer. At other times it's open 9 am to 4.30 pm Monday to Friday.

A second tourist office at Torkkelinkatu 1 in Imatrankoski is open from 10 am to 8 pm daily in summer. This office rents bicycles.

Post There's a post office in Imatrankoski at Tainionkoskentie 1, 55100 Imatra.

Internet Resources & Library The public library is in Mansikkala, in the Kaupungintalo (Cultural Centre). It has an Internet terminal.

Left Luggage The 10 mk lockers at the bus and train station are good for 24 hours.

Medical & Emergency Services In a general emergency, ring ☎ 112. For a doctor, ☎ 10023 and for police ☎ 10022. You'll find a pharmacy in the Mansikkapaikka shopping centre. The hospital is on Honkaharju in Vuoksenniska (take bus No 1).

Things to See & Do

Probably the highlight in Imatra is the 3km stroll along the mighty **Vuoksi River**, from the bus and train station in Mansikkala to the power station in Imatrankoski. Until the hydroelectric power station was built in 1929, Imatra's **rapids** were one of the highest waterfalls in Finland and drew hundreds of tourists (as well as a fair number of people bent on committing suicide by jumping). These days, the water is allowed to flow free at 7 pm on weekdays and 3 pm on Sundays during summer. Imagine how things were in the past!

Vuoksen Kalastuspuisto is a fishing park on Varpasaari island in Mansikkala. Spike and salmon can be caught here. A kiosk sells permits and rents equipment and boats. The park is open daily in summer.

Karjalainen Kotitalo, signposted as 'Ulko-museo', is an open-air museum with a dozen Karelian houses gathered at the riverfront. The museum is open Tuesday to Sunday in June and July.

The **Kolmen Ristin Kirkko** (Church of the Three Crosses) on Ruokolahdentie in Vuoksenniska was designed in 1957 by Alvar Aalto, the famous Finnish architect. As an interesting detail, only two of the 103 windows of the church are identical. The church is open daily year-round. Bus No 1 runs to Vuoksenniska.

The **Teollisuustyöväen Asuntomuseo** (Industrial Workers' Housing Museum) in Ritikankoski portrays the housing conditions of industrial workers in the 1890s. It's open Tuesday to Sunday in June and July.

Vuoksen Lautturi operates **cruises** daily in summer on the Vuoksi River from Imatrankoski. Some cruises go as far as the Russian border. Ask at the tourist office for a current schedule.

Places to Stay

Camping Ukonniemi (☎ 472 4055, myyn-tipalvelu@lomaliitto.fi, Leirintie 1), in the Imatra Leisure Centre complex, is open from June to early August. Sites at the lakefront camping ground cost 65 mk, cabins 140 to 250 mk. Bus No 3 travels from the bus station to the Imatra Leisure Centre every hour or so.

The cheapest beds in town are at HI-affiliated hostel **Ukonlinna** (☎ 432 1270, Leirintie 8), also in the leisure centre (take bus No 3). The setting is fantastic, the rooms are tiny, and the place has a kitchen and sauna. Dorm beds cost 60 mk.

Kesähotelli Mansikkala (☎ 682911, Rastaankatu 3A), a summer hotel open from June to early August, is convenient to the train station. Rooms cost 120/240 mk.

The Art Nouveau **Valtionhotelli** (☎ 68881, fax 688 8888, Torkkelinkatu 2) overlooks the rapids in Imatrankoski and is the city's most famous building. Built in 1902 and called 'The Grand Hotel Cascade', it was a favourite spot of the St Petersburg aristocracy. Rooms in the fancy castle hotel are from 530/700 mk.

Places to Eat

Grillis and a number of good, reasonably priced restaurants are clustered in Imatrankoski, along Lappeentie and Helsingintie.

For inexpensive lunch, **Hopealusikka** (Lappeentie 18) is highly recommended. Lunch specials are served from 10 am to 3 pm Monday to Friday. Also good is **Mason**

(Tainionkoskentie 10), and a **McDonald's** is adjacent.

The best place to sample rare cuisine is **Buttenhoff** (☎ 476 1433, *Koskeparras 4*) near the rapids. This is the most legendary restaurant in Imatra, with a 100 year history. Those with a sweet tooth might want to head downstairs to **Café Julia** – the place for coffee and tempting cakes.

Getting There & Away

Imatra is well served by eastbound trains and buses from Helsinki, and by hourly buses from Lappeenranta. There are seven trains a day from Helsinki to Imatra (3 hours). The central train station at Mansikkala, just north of the tourist office, also has four bus platforms for various destinations and a number of travel-related services.

Western Finland

Western Finland comprises a region known as Pohjanmaa in Finnish, Österbotten in Swedish and sometimes as Ostrobothnia (from the Latin).

Swedes first developed trading towns on the west coast in the 17th century to exploit the rich surrounding forests – sources of tar for Sweden's war fleet. After the tar trade dried up many Swedish settlers remained, and in the centuries since a proud farming culture has grown up in the flat but fertile Pohjanmaa.

This is a flat, dry and unremarkable-looking region, a region that many travellers may decide is one of the dullest on the planet. True, it lacks the mystery and grandeur of Lapland or the riverine beauty of the Lakeland. But skipping the coastal towns – from Uusikaupunki in the south to charming Jakobstad in the north – would be a mistake for anyone wanting to get a full picture of Finland. Two of Finland's finest music festivals are here, in Pori and Kaustinen. The seaside towns are quaint, peaceful and well-preserved, and nearby islands offer numerous opportunities for short or long cruises.

Geology

Some 7000 years ago, most of what is now western Finland was covered by the waters of Lake Litorina. The heavy ice layer that had once covered all of Scandinavia, including Finland, compressed the landmass. As the ice melted, the land slowly expanded and rose. Even today, the lands of western Finland continue to rise almost one centimetre each year!

Vaasa

▶ pop 55,000   **☎ 06**

Vaasa (Swedish: Vasa), the largest town on the west coast, has a culture all of its own. Some 27% of the population speak Swedish and the surrounding countryside is largely

HIGHLIGHTS

- The Pori jazz festival in July, one of Europe's best celebrations of jazz
- The Old Town district of Rauma – Finland's first entry on the UNESCO World Heritage List
- Lake Puurijärvi, one of the best birdwatching lakes in Western Finland
- Wasalandia, the 'Finnish Disneyland', in Vaasa
- Bicycling around the fishing villages of Replot island
- Jakobstad with its old town (Skata), eccentric museums and beautiful waterfront setting
- In July, the Kaustinen Folk Music Festival – 300 bands and 250 concerts in eight days!
- Kalajoki Beach, a Mediterranean holiday experience at a latitude of 64°
- Getting away from it all on Maakalla and Ulkokalla Islets – no roads, no shops and no electricity

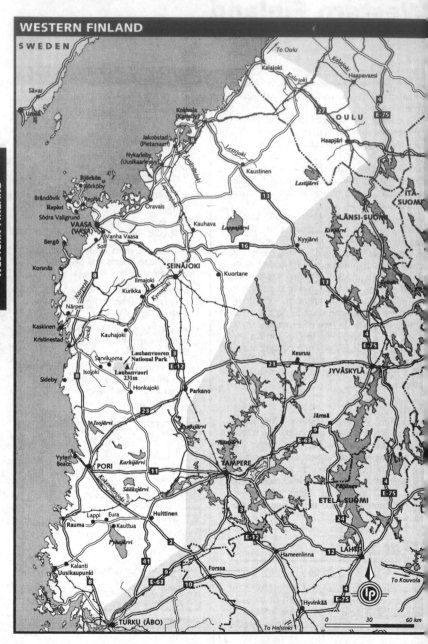

WESTERN FINLAND

rn, Häme Province

nset on a frozen lake, Lahti

Vanha Rauma (Old Rauma)

Cyclists, Vanha Rauma

Window decorations, Vanha Rauma

inhabited by Swedish speakers, making Vaasa the biggest distinctively bilingual town in Finland.

History

The town began in the 14th century as a village called Korsholm. In 1606 Swedish King Charles IX created Vasa, named after the royal Swedish Wasa family. During the Civil War that followed Finnish independence, Vaasa was the capital of the 'Whites'.

Orientation

Vaasanpuistikko is the main street through the centre of Vaasa. Vaskiluoto to the west and Pikisaari to the north are two islands connected to central Vaasa by bridges. The town centre is small enough to walk around.

Information

Tourist Office The tourist office (☎ 325 1145), at Hovioikeudenpuistikko 11, is open from 8 am to 7 pm on weekdays and from 10 am to 7 pm on weekends from June to August. At other times, it's open from 8 am to 4 pm Monday to Friday.

Post The main post office is opposite the train station at Hovioikeudenpuistikko 23A, 55100 Vaasa. Hours are 10 am to 6 pm Monday to Friday

Internet Resources & Library The public library is on the 3rd floor of Rewell Shopping Centre at Raastuvankatu 19. It has an Internet terminal. Hours are from 11 am to 8 pm Monday to Friday and from 10 am to 3 pm Saturday.

Left Luggage The train station has a left-luggage counter, and lockers that cost 10 mk for 24 hours.

Medical & Emergency Services There are pharmacies at Hovioikeudenpuistikko 9 and 20. The city hospital (☎ 323 1111) is at Hietalahdenkatu 2-4. In a general emergency call ☎ 112, for police call ☎ 10022 and for a doctor ☎ 10023.

Things to See & Do

Vaskiluoto island is a big holiday tion for Finnish families, with beaches, boating, a popular camping ground and **Wasalandia** (☎ 312 5888) amusement park, the Finnish equivalent to Disneyland (though much smaller). Hours are noon to 8 pm daily from late June to early August. From early May to mid-June and from mid to late August the park runs on an abbreviated schedule. During summer holidays, the park has extended hours. A day pass costs 80 mk (children 35 mk), though you may also buy an entry ticket for 15 mk (children 10 mk) and individual ride tickets for 8 mk.

About 200m south of the amusement park is the 'tropical bathing paradise' **Tropiclandia** (☎ 312 5988), a water amusement park and spa. Entry is 70 mk (children 40 mk) and the place is open daily from mid-June to mid-August and keeps similar hours to Wasalandia.

The **Museum of Ostrobothnia**, in the centre at Museokatu 3, boasts one of the best collections of art from Finland's Golden Era. The general collection displays some of the cultural wealth for which Pohjanmaa is famous: decorations, traditional wedding items and colourful artefacts. Hours are 10 am to 5 pm daily (also 5 pm to 8 pm Wednesday) and entry is 10 mk (free on Wednesday).

The **Water Tower**, at Raastuvankatu 30, has good views from the top and is open from 11 am to 5 pm daily from mid-June to mid-August (entry 3 mk). The exterior doubles as a climbing wall – contact Magnus Sundelin (☎ 0400-867 201) to use it (10 mk per person).

Bragegården is an open-air history museum a kilometre south of the centre, at Hietalahti. There are old saunas and other buildings. It is open from 1 pm to 6 pm Tuesday to Friday and noon to 4 pm on weekends from June to late August (10 mk entry).

Tikanoja Art Gallery, at Horioikeudenpuistikko 4, has a good collection of Finnish and international paintings, and is well worth a visit. It's open from 11 am to

WESTERN FINLAND

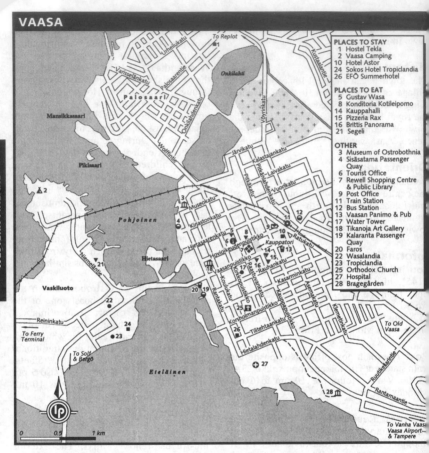

VAASA

PLACES TO STAY
1 Hostel Tekla
2 Vaasa Camping
10 Hotel Astor
24 Sokos Hotel Tropiclandia
26 EFÖ Summerhotel

PLACES TO EAT
5 Gustav Wasa
8 Konditoria Kotileipomo
14 Kauppahalli
15 Pizzeria Rax
16 Brittis Panorama
21 Segeli

OTHER
3 Museum of Ostrobothnia
4 Sisäsatama Passenger Quay
6 Tourist Office
7 Rewell Shopping Centre & Public Library
9 Post Office
11 Train Station
12 Bus Station
13 Vaasan Panimo & Pub
17 Water Tower
18 Tikanoja Art Gallery
19 Kalaranta Passenger Quay
20 Faros
22 Wasalandia
23 Tropiclandia
25 Orthodox Church
27 Hospital
28 Bragegården

4 pm Tuesday to Saturday and from noon to 5 pm Sunday (20 mk entry).

The **Orthodox Church** at Kasarmintori has some old icons brought from St Petersburg; contact the tourist office if you'd like to see them.

Organised Tours

Cruises The MS *Captain Waasa* cruises the Vaasa archipelago at 1 pm and 4 pm daily from mid-June to mid-August, departing from the Kalaranta passenger quay. Cost is 50 mk (childen 15 mk).

Berny's Cruising offers combination boat/bus tours to Replot Bridge (see th Around Vaasa section that follows) on Tuesday, Thursday and Sunday from mid June to early August. Tours depart at 3.15 pm from Sisäsatama passenger quay and cost 7(mk (children 30 mk).

Special Events

The Korsholm Music Festival, an interna tional chamber music festival, is held in lat June; see www.festivals.fi/korsholm or cal ☎ 322 2390 for more information.

During the Vaasa Carnival in early August, there is dancing, music and beer drinking.

Places to Stay

Camping On Vaskiluoto island, *Vaasa Camping* (☎ 317 3852), 2km from the town centre, has 85 mk camp sites and 170 to 250 mk cabins, and is open June to late August. It is well kept and has good kitchens. It also rents bicycles and boats, and offers discount coupons for the Tropiclandia spa and free admission to Wasalandia amusement park.

Hostel *Hostel Tekla* (☎ 327 6411, fax 321 3989, Palosaarentie 58) on Palosaari island in northern Vaasa (take bus No 1 or 3) is the only hostel – but it's more like a hotel for business travellers. Beds start at 150 mk in summer. During the rest of the year singles/doubles cost 210/340 mk.

Guesthouse The *EFÖ Summerhotel* (☎ 0400-668521, Rantakatu 21-22), open mid-June to mid-August, is run by an evangelical folk school. Singles/doubles/triples cost 200/250/280 mk and must be booked in advance. Use of kitchens, gym and sauna is included in the price.

Hotels The classy *Hotel Astor* (☎ 326 9111, fax 326 9484, Asemakatu 4) has just 32 rooms and is popular with foreign tour groups in summer and well-to-do business types in winter. Rooms cost 490/630 mk, 390/490 mk in summer. Rooms with private sauna cost 100 mk more.

Sokos Hotel Tropiclandia (☎ 212 7111, fax 312 1239, Lemmenpolku 3), next to Wasalandia on Vaskiluoto island, is a large spa hotel. Rooms are from 550/650 mk and include all kinds of spa and resort activities.

Places to Eat

There are cheap grillis, pizzerias and hamburger restaurants around the *kauppatori* (market square) and in the *Rewell shopping centre*. The *kauppahalli* (covered market) in Kauppapuistikko has a few stalls selling fresh bakery products.

Brittis Panorama, at Vaasanpuistikko 16, is a popular lunch restaurant with a panoramic view over the market square; it's open to 4 pm on weekdays and to 3 pm Saturday. Generous lunch specials are from 25 mk.

Pizzeria Rax at Kauppapuistikko 13 offers an anytime 'megabuffet' of pizza and pasta for 42 mk – good value if you're very hungry.

Around the corner from the tourist office, *Gustav Wasa*, at Raastuvankatu 24, is a cellar restaurant with gourmet Finnish cuisine (and steep prices).

Vaskiluoto island has a few summer restaurants, such as *Segeli* at Niemeläntie 14, south-east of the camping ground.

On the market square in the city centre, *Konditoria Kotileipomo* is a pleasant café that has outdoor seating in summer.

Entertainment

Vaasan Panimo & Pub at Vaasanpuistikko 22 serves its own brewery beer. *Faros*, a boat restaurant near Kalaranta passenger quay, offers live music and is always packed when the sun is shining (open only in the summer).

Getting There & Away

Air There are daily flights from Vaasa to Helsinki, Turku and other major Finnish cities. The airport is 12km south-east of the centre; airport buses depart from the city bus station.

Bus There are daily bus services from all major western and central towns, and several express buses a day from Helsinki and Turku via Pori. Buses run along the west coast on weekdays almost hourly.

Train Vaasa is off the main railway lines, but there is a connecting line from Seinäjoki to Vaasa and there are half a dozen trains per day. The fastest IC train to/from Helsinki covers the 420km in four hours.

Car & Motorcycle Vaasa is on road No 8, 318km south of Oulu and 348km north of Turku. To Helsinki it is 419km.

Boat There are one to four daily Silja Line ferries between Vaasa and the Swedish town of Umeå (Finnish: Uumaja); the crossing takes 3½ hours. The ferry terminal is on the west side of Vaskiluoto island (take bus No 10).

Getting Around

Bus Local buses come in handy if you want to reach areas of town outside the centre. Take bus No 10 to Vaskilouto island and bus No 1 or 3 to the hostel on Palosaari island. The fare is 10 mk (12 mk on Sunday). The Lilliputti tram runs between the kauppatori and Wasalandia (15 mk) daily in summer.

Bicycle Bicycles can be rented at the tourist office or Vaasa Camping for 10 mk per hour or 30 mk per day.

AROUND VAASA
Vanha Vaasa

The old town of Vaasa developed around a harbour south-east of the modern centre that became unfit for large vessels. The medieval church is now in ruins, and although the old fortress area has been protected not much remains. Probably the most interesting sight is the **Church of Korsholm**, built in 1786. It looks very pompous; it was originally a judges' palace. **Köpmanshuset Wasasferne** is a museum of local history, open daily from mid-June to mid-August. Entry is 10 mk.

Getting There & Away Bus Nos 7 and 9 travel between Vanha Vaasa and the town centre.

Solf

One of the most attractive villages in Finland, Solf (Finnish: Sulva) is best known for its **Stundars Handicraft Village** (☎ 344 0282). The open-air museum, boasting 50 traditional wooden buildings, is open from noon to 6 pm daily from mid-May to mid-August, and noon to 6 pm on weekends from mid to late August. The whole place hums with activity in summer, when artisans demonstrate crafts such as wool dyeing and wood carving. On some days the workers dress up in national costume (call for schedule). Lots of handcrafted items are available for sale. The 15 mk entry includes a guided tour.

Places to Stay & Eat *Solf Gästgiveri* (☎ 344 0999, fax 344 0508, Solfvägen 199) is a meticulously renovated old house. Pleasant rooms cost 250/300 mk and include breakfast and sauna.

Fredrikas is a good restaurant in the village centre.

Getting There & Away Regional buses from Vaasa make the 15km trip south to Solf.

Bergö

This little island, a former fishing community, offers quaint archipelago vistas. The **church**, dating from 1802, was rebuilt in 1853. The **local museum** in Bergö is open on Wednesday from 6 to 8 pm. **Handarbetsstugan** sells handcrafted items and is open Monday to Saturday.

Getting There & Away A bus departs from Vaasa Monday to Friday at 2.10 pm. It arrives at Bergö, 53km away, two hours later. If you are driving, it's best to go via Molpe; there's a ferry across the strait to the island.

Replot

Replot (Finnish: Raippaluoto) is a large island that lies just off the Vaasan coast. It's easy to reach and ideal for exploring by bicycle. On the island there are several small fishing communities in addition to the main village, which is also called Replot. The total population is 2000.

Södra Vallgrund village is at the southwestern corner of the island, some 10km from the village of Replot. It has a small museum. **Klobbskat** village, at the western end of the island, is in a barren, Lappishlike setting. **Björkön** (Swedish: Björköby) is a fishing village on a smaller, northern island, accessible from Replot by bridge.

In 1997 a 1045m bridge – the longest bridge in Finland – was completed connecting Replot with the mainland.

Places to Stay & Eat The *Bullerås Holiday Village* (☎ *352 7613, Bulleråsvägen 30*) in Södra Vallgrund has camp sites for 40 mk, cottages from 200 to 300 mk and a restaurant in a 1920s villa.

On Björkö, the *Björkö Inn* (☎ *352 4149*), run by Tom and Markia Ohls, is a lovely small hotel with rooms from 210/280 mk (breakfast included) and dorm beds for 100 mk. Rooms with all meals will cost you from 360/550 mk.

Getting There & Away Regional buses from Vaasa make the 15km trip south to Solf. Guided boat/bus tours also travel to Replot; see the Vaasa Cruises section earlier in this chapter.

The South-West

The south-west region is known as Vakka-Suomi, and refers to the wooden bowls (*vakka*) that have been made here for centuries. For travellers, this is one of the most appealing areas of western Finland, and its cities are easily visited from Turku.

UUSIKAUPUNKI
pop 17,600   ☎ 02

Uusikaupunki (Swedish: Nystad) is an idyllic seaside town to the north of Turku. The name translates as 'New Town' – ironic because Uusikaupunki is now one of the oldest towns in Finland, first founded in 1617 by Gustav II Adolf, the king of Sweden.

Uusikaupunki's main claim to fame is the treaty of 1721 which brought an uneasy peace between Sweden and Russia after the devastating Great Northern War. Today, almost nobody in the town speaks Swedish and Nystad is merely a historical name – use Uusikaupunki!

Information
Tourist Office The tourist office (☎ 842 1225 or ☎ 8451 5443), at Rauhankatu 10, is open from 8.30 am to 6 pm Monday to Friday, 9 am to 3 pm Saturday and 10 am to 3 pm Sunday from late June to early August. At other times, it's open from 8.30 am to 4 pm Monday to Friday.

Post The post office, on the corner of Rauhankatu and Alinenkatu (23500 Uusikaupunki), is open from 9 am to 8 pm Monday to Friday.

Internet Resources & Library The public library at Alinenkatu 34 has an Internet terminal and a newspaper room that subscribes to *Time*. The library is open from 11 am to 7 pm on weekdays and 10 am to 2 pm Saturday.

The Web site for Uusikaupunki is www.uusikaupunki.fi/.

Left Luggage The bus station's left-luggage counter charges 15 mk per bag per day.

Medical & Emergency Services The pharmacy on Alinenkatu 28 is open from 8.30 am to 9 pm Monday to Friday, 9 am to 6 pm Saturday and 11 am to 4 pm Sunday and holidays. The regional hospital is at Terveystie 4.

In a general emergency call ☎ 112, for police call ☎ 10022 and for a doctor call ☎ 10023.

Things to See
Is the **Bonk Dynamo Centre**, at Siltakatu 2, a science and history museum, or a practical joke? The creation of local artist Alvar Gullichsen, this one-room museum tells the story of a Mr Per Bonk (who made a fortune on 'Garum Superbe' anchovy spice in 1900) and his strange machines. It's Finnish humour – don't expect to get it. The museum is open from 11 am to 6 pm daily from mid-May to late August and admission is 25 mk.

The **Kulttuurihistoriallinen museo** (Museum of Cultural History), at Ylinenkatu 11, is in an old house built by a powerful

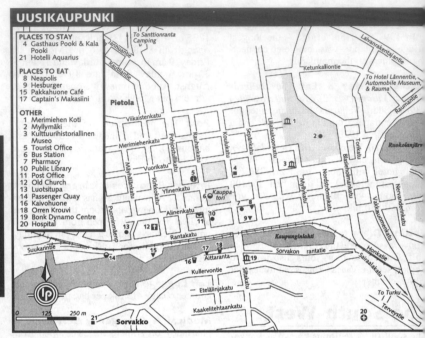

UUSIKAUPUNKI

PLACES TO STAY
4 Gasthaus Pooki & Kala Pooki
21 Hotelli Aquarius

PLACES TO EAT
8 Neapolis
9 Hesburger
15 Pakkahuone Café
17 Captain's Makasiini

OTHER
1 Merimiehen Koti
2 Myllymäki
3 Kulttuurihistoriallinen Museo
5 Tourist Office
6 Bus Station
7 Pharmacy
10 Public Library
11 Post Office
12 Old Church
13 Luotsitupa
14 Passenger Quay
16 Kaivohuone
18 Orren Krouvi
19 Bonk Dynamo Centre
20 Hospital

shipowner and tobacco manufacturer. Rooms are furnished in the style of a wealthy 19th century home. Admission is 10 mk.

Merimiehen Koti (Sailor's Home) at Myllykatu 18 is a home museum of a local sailor. **Luotsitupa** (Pilot Museum) at Vallimäki hill is a small house devoted to maritime navigation. Admission to each is 5 mk.

Hours for the Museum of Cultural History, Pilot Museum and Sailor's Home are 11 am to 3 pm Tuesday to Friday and noon to 3 pm on weekends from June to mid-August, and from noon to 3 pm on weekends only during the rest of the year.

The **Automobile Museum**, at Autotehtaantie 14, includes a collection of old Saab cars. If you're a fan of Scandinavian automobiles, you'll love it. The museum is open from 11 am to 5 pm daily from May to late August, 11 am to 5 pm on weekends

only during the rest of the year. Admissio is 25 mk.

The **Vanha Kirrko** (Old Church), a Kirkkokatu 2, is worth a look. Completed i 1629, it's the town's oldest building. It ornate barrel-vaulted roof is meant to re semble a ship's hull. Hours are 11 am to pm Monday to Saturday, noon to 4 pr Sunday from June to mid-August.

Myllymäki (the Windmill Hill), north east of the centre, is a hilltop park with fou lovely windmills – the sole survivors of th dozens that used to exist in Uusikaupunk

Activities

The quiet rural roads surrounding Uusi kaupunki are terrific for bicyclists; th tourist office rents bicycles for 10 mk pe hour or 30 mk per day. Those looking t fish should pick up a permit at the pos office and a local fishing map at the touris office, which also assists with equipment rentals and arranges charter fishing trips.

The MS *Franz Höijer* cruises to Isokari, an island with a lighthouse, on Saturday and Sunday from mid-May to mid-August. On summer weekdays it travels between Uusikaupunki and Hanko; see the Getting There & Away section that follows. You may book tickets for these trips through the tourist office.

Places to Stay

A kilometre north-west of the town centre, the seaside *Santtionranta Camping* (☎ 8451 5218, heli.kruuna-rauvola@uusikaupunk.fi, Kalalokkikuja 14) has 90 camp sites that cost 50 mk each, and cottages from 150 to 220 mk. Santtionranta is open from late May to mid-August.

East of the centre on the road to Rauma, *Hotel Lännentie* (☎ 841 2636, fax 841 2651, Levysepänkatu 1) provides basic accommodation in neat rooms from 290/370 mk. There are cheaper dorm beds for approximately 100 mk per person. There is no HI discount.

Gasthaus Pooki (☎ 841 2771, fax 841 2772, Ylinenkatu 21) is a charming inn in the centre. It has just four rooms for 340/450 mk, including breakfast.

Hotelli Aquarius (☎ 841 3123, fax 841 3540, Kullervontie 11) is the largest hotel in town, in a park-like setting with tennis courts and a pool. All rooms are 380 mk in summer, 420/480 mk at other times.

Places to Eat

The kauppatori (market square) is in full swing from Monday to Saturday in summer. Otherwise, the *Hesburger* stand at Rantakatu 25 is the cheapest place to grab a quick snack.

Neapolis, in the centre at Alinenkatu 28, serves pizza and pasta at good prices.

Kala Pooki, at Gasthaus Pooki on Ylinenkatu (see Places to Stay, above) is a gourmet restaurant and local favourite. Weekday lunch specials range from 30 mk (salad only) to 48 mk (the works). Dinner

options are from 50 mk. You can also sit on the pleasant terrace and have a beer or two.

If you want to have just one big meal in Uusikaupunki, head for *Captain's Makasiini* in the red saltbox buildings on Aittaranta, across the bridge from the centre. The menu ranges from 35 mk salads and hamburgers to 80 mk steaks – but you're really here to soak up the terrific nautical atmosphere.

Pakkahuone Café, at the guest harbour, is the town's best café, with a nice waterfront terrace.

Entertainment

Orren Krouvi is a fun pub associated with Captain's Makasiini, while *Kuivohuone* at Sorvakonrantatie 20 is a large waterfront establishment which is best for dancing and live music (nightly in summer).

Getting There & Away

Bus Buses to/from Turku run from the Kauppatori in the centre of town once or twice per hour on weekdays, less frequently on weekends. There are five to eight buses per day from Rauma. Buses from Helsinki run via Turku.

Car & Motorcycle Uusikaupunki is 75km north of Turku and 50km south of Rauma, off the main north-south road (road No 8). From road No 8 take road No 43 west to reach Uusikaupunki.

Boat The MS *Franz Höijer* travels between Uusikaupunki and Hanko on weekdays from mid-May to mid-August. The trip takes 10 hours, and costs 60 mk one way.

AROUND UUSIKAUPUNKI
Kalanti

The village of Kalanti, considered a suburb of Uusikaupunki, is where the first sizable party of Swedes, led by Bishop Henry of the Catholic Church, arrived on a crusade in 1155. Thus, the Swedish chapter of Finland's history began. The medieval **Kalanti Church** dates from the late 1300s; its interior paintings depict Bishop Henry meeting a pagan on the Finnish coast. The church is open from 9 am to 5 pm daily in summer.

Kalanti is a few kilometres east of Uusikaupunki on road No 43; catch an Uusikaupunki to Laitila bus.

RAUMA

• pop 38,000   ☎ 02

Rauma (Swedish: Raumo) was founded in 1442 and came of age in the 18th century, when it became famous throughout Europe for its production of beautiful handmade lace. Citizens still celebrate their heritage of lace making with an annual festival.

Although Rauma is not as attractive as many south coast seaside towns, it merits a stop for its **Vanha Rauma** (Old Rauma) district. The old town area of more than 600 low wooden houses won a spot on the UNESCO World Heritage List as Finland's first entry. It is the largest wooden town preserved in the Nordic countries.

Vanha Rauma is not a museum but a living centre, with low-key cafés, hardware shops, residences and a smattering of artisans and lace makers working in small studios (see Vanha Rauma section).

Orientation

Rauma is really two towns – Vanha Rauma (the old town), with historic houses and shops, and the new district where all of the services are located. The main street is Valtakatu in the new part of town.

Information

Tourist Office The tourist office (☎ 834 4551 or 834 4552, matkailu@Rauma.fi), at Valtakatu 2, publishes a free map and a self-guided walking tour. It also rents bikes for 10 mk per hour or 40 mk per day. Hours are from 8 am to 6 pm Monday to Friday, 10 am to 3 pm Saturday and 11 am to 2 pm Sunday from June to late August. At other times it's open from 8 am to 4 pm Monday to Friday.

Post The main post office, at Valtakatu 15 (26100 Rauma), is open from 9 am to 8 pm Monday to Friday.

Internet Resources & Library The public library, at Ankkurikatu 1, is open from 10 am to 7 pm Monday to Friday, 10 am to 2 pm Saturday and has two Internet terminals.

The Web sites for Rauma are www .rauma.fi/ and www.satanet/fi/rsm/.

Medical & Emergency Services Pharmacies are at Kauppakatu 11 and Valtakatu 9-11. There's a hospital at Uotilantie 2. For general emergency ring ☎ 122, for police call ☎ 10022 and for a doctor call ☎ 10023.

Vanha Rauma

Most of the low wooden buildings of Vanha Rauma (Old Rauma) were erected in the 18th and 19th centuries. The old town has 600 houses and 180 shops, and each building has a name – look for it on a small oval sign near the door.

The **kauppatori** is the heart of Old Rauma, and the Vanha Raatihuone (town hall), built in 1776, is its most imposing building. The town hall houses the **Rauma Museum**, with exhibits relating to seafaring.

The **Marela** house museum at Kauppakatu 24 is the most popular museum in Rauma. At the turn of the century it belonged to a wealthy shipowner.

Kirsti, at Pohjankatu 3, is another house museum – this was once the home of a sailor.

Savenvalajan Verstas, at Nummenkatu 2, is a small museum of pottery. Here you can watch how pottery is made and try making some yourself.

The preceding museums are open from 10 am to 5 pm daily from mid-May to mid-August and from 10 am to 5 pm Tuesday to Saturday during other seasons. A 15 mk ticket is good for admission to all.

The **Art Museum**, at Kuninkaankatu 37, features temporary exhibitions. Hours are from 10 am to 6 pm Monday to Friday, 10 am to 4 pm Saturday and noon to 6 pm Sunday from June to late August (closed Monday at other times). Admission is 15 mk.

The attractive stone **Pyhän Ristin Kirkko** (Church of the Holy Cross), at Luostarinkatu 1, is a 15th century Franciscan church; a Catholic monastery functioned

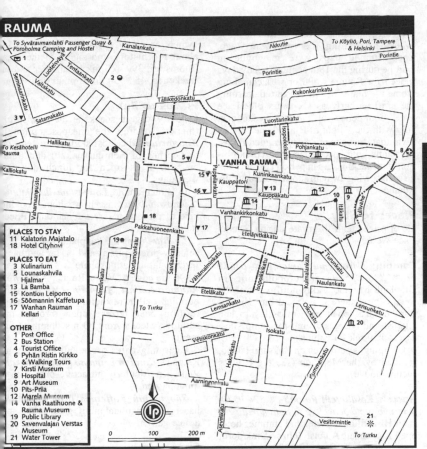

RAUMA

To Syväraumanlahti Passenger Quay &
Poroholma Camping and Hostel

Kanalankatu

Akkutie

To Köyliö, Pori, Tampere
& Helsinki

Portintie

Portintie

Luostarintie

Tentaankatu

Valtakatu

Seminaarinkatu

Kukonkarinkatu

Tallikedonkatu

Satamakatu

Luostarinkatu

Hallikatu

Isopökikikatu

To Kesähotelli
Rauma

Pohjankatu

Kalliokatu

VANHA RAUMA

Kuninkaankatu

Pappilankatu

Kauppatori

Kauppakatu

Vähämalminkatu

Vanhankirkonkatu

Itäkatu

Tullivahe

Pakkahuoneenkatu

Eteläpitkäkatu

Torninkatu

Kulmalankatu

Naulankatu

Alfredinkatu

Nortamonkatu

Savilankatu

Eteläkatu

Olkikatu

Lensunkatu

To Turku

Lemsankatu

Isokatu

Paimenkatu

Vähämalminkatu

Vetiskonkatu

Hakinkatu

Aarninnnkatu

Asevelikatu

Vesitornintie

To Turku

LP

0   100   200 m

PLACES TO STAY
11 Kalatorin Majatalo
18 Hotel Cityhovi

PLACES TO EAT
3 Kulinarium
5 Lounaskahvila
  Hjalmar
13 La Bamba
15 Kontion Leipomo
16 Söömannin Kaffetupa
17 Wanhan Rauman
  Kellari

OTHER
1 Post Office
2 Bus Station
4 Tourist Office
6 Pyhän Ristin Kirkko
  & Walking Tours
7 Kirsti Museum
8 Hospital
9 Art Museum
10 Pits-Prlia
12 Marela Museum
14 Vanha Raatihuone &
  Rauma Museum
19 Public Library
20 Savenvalajan Verstas
  Museum
21 Water Tower

here until 1538. The church is open daily from May to September. On a hill just south of the old town is the town **water tower**, which doubles as an observation tower. Entry costs 5 mk, and hours are noon to 6 pm daily from May to late August.

Organised Tours
Cruises During summer the MS *Pujo* offers two-hour cruises around the Rauma archipelago – with a 30 minute stop at the holiday island of Reksaari. Departures are at 11 am and 5 pm daily from mid-June to mid-

August, from the passenger quay at Syväraumanlahti, the bay north of Poroholma Camping and Hostel. Service is on weekends only during the first half of June. The cost is 40 mk return.

Organised Tours
Walking tours of Vanha Rauma are coordinated by the city tourist office. Tours in English are at 4 pm on Tuesday from mid-June to early August. The 1½ hour tour costs 10 mk per person and departs from Pyhän Ristin Kirkko.

Special Events

The biggest annual event is Rauma Lace Week, celebrating the town's heritage. Lace-trimmed caps were in vogue in Europe during the 18th century, heady days indeed for Rauma's 600 or so lacemaking women – many of whom started learning the craft as early as six years old. Lace Week commences on the last weekend in July with the 'Night of Black Lace', a carnival that draws many party-minded Finns. Museums hold special lace-related exhibitions, and lacemakers in period costume can be seen sewing away in shops around Vanha Rauma.

Places to Stay

Hotel prices tend to inflate during Rauma Lace Week.

Camping *Poroholma Camping* (☎ 83881 or ☎ 8388 2500), at Poroholmantie on Otanlahti bay about 2km north-west of the town centre; there is no local bus service. Poroholma is open from mid-May to late August and charges 75 mk for camp sites, 210 to 250 mk for cabins.

Camping is permitted on Reksaari island, reached by the MS *Pujo* (see the Cruises section above).

Hostels *Kesähotelli Rauma* (☎ 824 0130, pentti.voipio@penvoi.pp.fi, Satamakatu 20) is an HI-affiliated hostel and summer hotel open June to late August. It has 55 mk dorm beds and rooms from 130/220. A kitchen and sauna are on the premises.

The HI-affiliated *Poroholma Hostel* is part of Poroholma Camping, and rooms are in a nice old villa that also houses a café. Beds are from 70 mk. Kitchen, sauna and laundry are available.

Hotels *Hotel Cityhovi* (☎ 822 3745, fax 822 3742, Nortamonkatu 18) is a small town hotel with rooms for 300/320 mk on weekends and in summer. Ordinary rates are 320/390 mk.

The most pleasant hotel in town is *Kalatorin Majatalo* (☎ 822 7111, fax 822 2535, Kalatori 4) in a beautifully renovated Art Deco warehouse in Vanha Rauma. The owners are very friendly and know a lot about the history and sights of the area. Rooms are 390/420 mk in summer and on weekends, 450/550 mk at other times.

Places to Eat

Unless you grab snacks at the *kauppatori* (market square), the cheapest option is *Kulinarium*, the local student cafeteria on the corner of Seminaarinkatu and Satamakatu. It is open for lunch only on weekdays.

In Vanha Rauma, *Lounaskahvila Hjalmar* (Kuninkaankatu 6) is a hearty home-cooking kind of place that serves lunch only. Prices start at 26 mk.

La Bamba at the kauppatori serves reasonably prices pizzas and pastas and has a festive, family atmosphere.

On the edge of Vanha Rauma is *Wanhan Rauman Kellari* (Anundilankatu 8), a very popular cellar restaurant with a terrific rooftop beer terrace open through the summer. Steaks from 50 mk dominate the menu.

Charming cafés are plentiful in Vanha Rauma – *Kontion Leipomo* (Kuninkaankatu 9) is a particularly attractive one, with a quiet garden.

Söömannin Kaffetupa (Kauppakatu 8) has a strong nautical motif, great coffee and a nice garden.

Shopping

Rauma is famous for its bobbin lace. The best place to buy lace is at Pits-Priia at Kauppakatu 29, where you can see the bobbin lace being made. Prices start at around 200 mk.

Getting There & Away

Bus There are daily direct buses between Helsinki and Rauma. Between Rauma and Pori, there are buses every hour or so. From the south, Turku and Uusikaupunki are connected by buses every two hours or so. The bus station is north-west of Vanha Rauma, a block north of the main street Valtakatu.

Train Get off the Tampere-to-Pori train at the Kokemäki railway station, and transfer to a connecting bus. Your train pass will be valid on the bus.

AROUND RAUMA
Lappi

The small village of Lappi (Finnish for Lapland) is particularly pleasant, with the Lapinjoki running through it. An old stone bridge survives, and nearby is a church that dates from 1760. It has medieval sculpture and a separate bell tower.

The main attraction is the prehistoric site, by the name **Kirkonlaattia** (Church Floor), which is a plain stone tableau in a seemingly Lappish setting. The prehistoric site is 4km from the main road No 12 – turn north to Eurajoentie and then follow signs.

Joki-Pub, in the village at the riverside, serves food and beer.

Getting There & Away Lappi is 18km east of Rauma on road No 12. Buses between Rauma and Helsinki stop at Lappi, and there some direct buses from Rauma.

Köyliö

Köyliö, now a quiet hamlet, was an important estate in medieval times. It also was the scene of a terrible crime: in 1156 a local peasant, Lalli, killed the crusading Bishop Henry – the first Catholic bishop to voyage into the Finnish wilderness – on frozen Lake Köylionjärvi. In the local church are paintings – created later and intended to teach a lesson – that depict Lalli under the foot of a saint, his inevitable fate in the afterlife. The church and its paintings are on an island in Köyliönjärvi lake and are accessible by a small causeway. This is the finishing point of Catholic pilgrimages from Turku.

Another attraction to this place is its name, which serves as a good introduction to tongue-twisting spoken Finnish – ask a local to tell you how to pronounce it.

Getting There & Away Köyliö is about 35km east of Rauma, south from road No 12 at the town of Eura. There is no bus service.

PUURIJÄRVI-ISOSUO NATIONAL PARK

Lake Puurijärvi, 65km due east of Rauma, is one of the best birdwatching lakes in Western Finland. The lake and surrounding marshlands have been protected since 1993 and are a favourite nesting site for migrating waterfowl of many varieties, totaling about 500 pairs in season. The lake itself can be reached by a 800m nature trail from the main road. A boardwalk makes a loop of the open marshland, where there's an observation tower. The Näköalapaikka (a viewing cliff) also offers a good general view. Visitors are required to stay on marked paths during breeding season, and camping is not allowed in the park at any time.

Getting There & Away There is no bus service to the national park. By car, there are two ways to access the park from road No 2: to reach Lake Puurijärvi, take the Kauvatsa to Äetsä road No 2481; to reach the marshlands and boardwalk, head 3km south from the Lake Puurijärvi parking area, then follow signs to Karhiniemi. Proceed about a kilometre towards Karhiniemi and turn right to Mutilahdentie following the Ala-Kauvatsa signs. The national park boundary (with the boardwalk path) is 2km away.

PORI
- **pop 76,500**   ☎ 02

Pori (Swedish: Björneborg) is one of the most important deep-water harbours in Finland. The textile industry has a long tradition in the town, but now various timber-related industries, oil-related industries, and manufactures of household appliances and goods are the town's major employers. Pori has more recently become famous for its annual jazz festival in July, recognised as one of the finest in Europe.

The best time (or really, the only) to visit Pori is during the festival.

Pori has few Swedish speakers. The Swedish name Björneborg translates as Fort of the Bear.

History

In 1558, Duke Juhana, who was then ruler of Finland, decided to establish a trading town on the eastern coast of the Gulf of Bothnia. As a result, Pori was founded at the mouth of the Kokemäenjoki.

For a brief shining moment in 1726 a Professor Israel Nesselius championed Pori as the new capital of Finland – but it was not to be. Since then, Pori has been a regional centre for trade, shipping and industry.

Information

Tourist Office The city tourist office (☎ 621 1273, matkailu@pori.fi or elinkeino@ pori.fi), in the old town hall at Hallituskatu 9, is open from 8 am to 6 pm Monday to Friday and 9 am to 1 pm Saturday from June to mid-August. At other times of the year it's open from 8 am to 4.15 pm Monday to Friday.

Post The main post office is at Yrjönkatu 8, 28100 Pori. Hours are 9 am to 8 pm Monday to Friday.

Internet Resources & Library The public library, at Gallen-Kallelankatu 12, has three Internet terminals (bookings required). The hours are 10 am to 7 pm Monday to Friday (also 10 am to 3 pm Saturday from September to late April).

Pori is on the Web at www.pori/fi/.

Bookshops Suomalainen Kirjakauppa at Yrjönkatu 13 has a small selection of paperbacks in English.

Left Luggage The train and bus stations both have 10 mk lockers which may be used for 24 hours maximum.

Medical & Emergency Services The pharmacy in the Bepop Shopping Centre on Isolinnankatu is open from 8 am to 10 pm daily. West of the centre is the city hospital on Maantiekatu. For general emergency call ☎ 112, for police call ☎ 10022 and for a doctor ring ☎ 10023.

Things to See

Pori, despite being one of the oldest towns in Finland, has few historic buildings or other attractions.

The **Pori Taidemuseo** (Pori Art Museum on Eteläranta is a very fine modern art museum with a good permanent collection. Finnish and international art is exhibited in the airy, elegant space, a former warehouse. The museum is open from 11 am to 6 pm Tuesday to Sunday (also 6 pm to 8 pm Wednesday). Admission is 15 mk. Adjacent is **Poriginal Gallery**, Eteläranta 6, an art gallery.

The neo-Gothic **Keski-Pori Church** on Yrjönkatu was built in 1863 and lovingly renovated in 1998. It has a steeple with unusual iron fretwork. Keski-Pori is open from 9 am to 6 pm daily from June to late August, and from 10 am to 1 pm at other times.

The **Satakunta Museum** at Hallituskatu 11 is a museum of regional history and archaeology – it has an interesting miniature of Old Pori. Hours are from 11 am to 5 pm Tuesday to Sunday, and entry is 15 mk.

The **Juselius Mausoleum** at Käppärä Cemetery, west of the centre on Maantiekatu is the most poignant sight in Pori. FA Juselius, a wealthy businessman, had the mausoleum built as a memorial to his daughter, who died of tuberculosis at the age of 11. The original frescoes were painted in 1898 by famous Finnish artist Akseli Gallen-Kallela (who had just lost his own daughter). The ones you see now were painted by Akseli's son, Jorma Gallen-Kallela, after his father's death. The mausoleum is open from noon to 3 pm daily in summer.

Special Events

The **Pori Jazz Festival**, spanning nine days in mid-July, is one of the most appreciated summer events in Finland. The festival

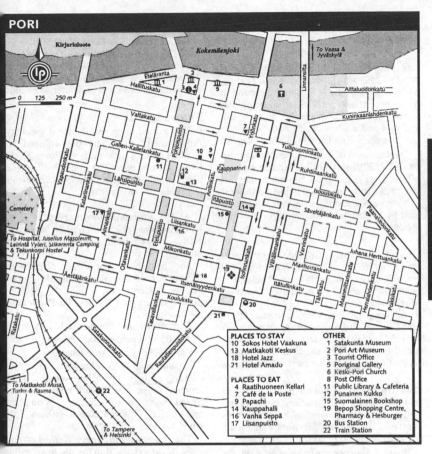

PORI

PLACES TO STAY
10 Sokos Hotel Vaakuna
13 Matkakoti Keskus
18 Hotel Jazz
21 Hotel Amado

PLACES TO EAT
4 Raatihuoneen Kellari
7 Café de la Poste
9 Papachi
14 Kauppahalli
16 Vanha Seppä
17 Liisanpuisto

OTHER
1 Satakunta Museum
2 Pori Art Museum
3 Tourist Office
5 Poriginal Gallery
6 Keski-Pori Church
8 Post Office
11 Public Library & Cafeteria
12 Punainen Kukko
15 Suomalainen Bookshop
19 Bepop Shopping Centre,
   Pharmacy & Hesburger
20 Bus Station
22 Train Station

started in 1966 when some local musicians arranged a two-day event with an audience of 1000 people. Nowadays the Jazz Festival features more than 100 concerts held in tents, outdoors or in old warehouses. Performers – and thousands of visitors – pour in from all over the world, and hotels are fully booked a year in advance.

Ticket prices range from 40 to 300 mk but most concerts cost about 80 mk. The popular open-air concerts on Kirjurinluoto cost 220 mk.

For more information and to purchase tickets contact Pori Jazz (☎ 550 5550, fax 550 5525), Pohjoisranta 11, 28100 Pori, or see www.porijazz.fi/.

Places to Stay

If you are planning to visit Pori during the Jazz Festival you must book your hotel a year in advance, and hostel or guesthouse about six months in advance. Otherwise, the city tourist office offers basic accommodation – typically a mattress on the floor of a classroom building – during the festival on a first-come, first-served basis. The cost is 85 mk per person.

Camping *Leirintä Yyteri (☎ 638 3778 or ☎ 633 5250, Marjaleena.Raunela@Pori.fi)*, on Yyterinsatojentie is a camping ground at Yyteri beach (take bus No 32 from the market square). It offers camp sites for 80 to 90 mk and four and six-bed cabins for 250 to 640 mk. It is open from late May to mid-August.

On Reposaari island, *Siikaranta Camping (☎ 638 4120)*, open mid-May to late August, offers camp sites for 69 mk and cabins for 185 to 200 mk. The island is just north-west of Yyteri beach and is connected to the mainland by bridge; take bus No 30 or 40 from the centre.

Hostel The HI-affiliated *Tekunkorpi (☎ 637 8400, fax 637 8125, Tekniikantie 4)* has a kitchen, sauna and laundry, and is open from 7 am to 10 pm daily from mid-May to mid-August. Dorm beds cost 75 to 95 mk per person; hotel-style rooms start at 160/240 mk. From the centre, take bus No 32 or 42 towards Yyteri, get off at Ammatillinen kurssikeskus, cross two streets and follow signs for the next 200m.

Guesthouses *Matkakoti Keskus (☎ 633 8447, Itäpuisto 13)* is a very basic guesthouse with decent singles/doubles/triples for 160/220/300 mk. Showers and toilets are shared and no breakfast is available.

Some 3.5km west of the centre, in the Musa area, *Matkakoti Musa (☎ 637 0153, Putimäentie 69)* is a guesthouse with pleasant rooms that cost 110 mk per person (150 mk with breakfast).

Hotels Close to the bus station, *Hotel Amado (☎ 633 8500, Keskusaukio 2)* is the most reasonably priced of the city's hotels, with rooms from 340/420 mk during the festival, 280/330 mk the rest of the summer and on winter weekends.

The snazzy, stylish *Hotel Jazz (☎ 529300, fax 529333, Itsenäisyydenkatu 41)* has rooms from 340/450 mk and is a centre of festival activity.

Sokos Hotel Vaakuna (☎ 528100, fax 528182, Gallen-Kallelankatu 7) in the town centre, has rooms from 440/570 mk during the jazz festival. Rooms are 345 mk for the rest of the summer and on winter weekends.

Places to Eat

Grillis around town sell the local specialty, *Porilainen* (Pori burger), best enjoyed late at night after a few pints of Porin Karhu (Bear of Pori) beer. The finest Porilainen is made with *Korpelan Metsästäkänwurst* (Korpela onion sausage), pickles and a fluffy bun.

At the *kauppahalli* (market hall) on Isolinnankatu look for another local specialty, smoked river lamprey (a fish that looks like an eel).

For cheap hamburgers and such, there's *Hesburger* inside the futuristic Bepop Shopping Centre on Yrjönkatu, and for pizza and kebap try the popular *Papachi* on the kauppatori.

The *cafeteria* at the public library offers 25 to 30 mk lunch specials from 11 am to 1 pm on weekdays – a true bargain.

Liisanpuisto (Liisankatu 20) is run by a catering college and offers superb 39 mk lunches, while just down the street *Vanha Seppä (Liisankatu 12)* has very good pizza and steaks. This restaurant is in a little white house.

The classy *Raatihuoneen Kellari (☎ 633 4804, Hallituskatu 9)* in the old town hall is a vaulted, elegant cellar restaurant with a superb weekday buffet luncheon.

Café de la Poste, across from the Post Office, is a sunny café with a piano and light meals from 30 mk.

Entertainment

Pori is fairly quiet when the Jazz Festival isn't in town – except for the Hotel Jazz, which offers live jazz and dancing nightly in summer.

Punainen Kukko is a lively dance club on Pohjoispuisto.

Getting There & Away

Air There are daily flights between Pori and Helsinki. There are also daily flights to/from Turku.

Bus There are 16 buses daily between Helsinki and Pori. There are 12 buses a day between Rauma and Pori on weekdays and seven on weekends. There are also a few buses from Turku and Tampere. The bus station is at the south end of Isolinnankatu.

Train All trains to Pori go via Tampere, where you often have to change. There are five or six trains a day between Tampere and Pori, all of which have good connections with trains from Helsinki.

Car & Motorcycle Pori is on road No 8, about 135km north of Turku. To Tampere, drive 110km east on road No 11.

Getting Around

Bus An extensive bus service operates in the town area; route maps are available at the tourist office. Most buses pass the market square.

Bicycle Ask at the tourist office about special deals for bicycle rental.

AROUND PORI
Yteri Beach

Yteri beach., 15km north-west of Pori town centre, is still something of a playground in summer, though all Finnish beach resorts have been in a decline ever since charter flights to Spain were invented. Stands at the beach offer all kinds of activities, and the white sand stretches quite a distance. There is a good camping ground here; see the Pori Places to Stay section earlier in this chapter.

Getting There & Away To get here from Pori, take bus No 32 from the market square.

Leineperi

This fine village received the Europe Nostra award in 1993 for careful preservation of 18th century buildings. The area was first developed in 1771 by the Swedish as a *bruk* (factory) for making household items, and was in operation for about a century. Today it is a lively place, at least on summer weekends. Attractions along the scenic Kullaanjoki riverside include **Masuuni ironworks**, now renovated, a blacksmith's shop, now a **museum**, and some **artisans' workshops**. **Museo Kangasniemi** is devoted to Kaarlo Kangasniemi, the 1968 Olympic weight-lifting champion (he is Finnish, of course). On weekends you may be lucky enough to meet the champion. Most of these museums charge a 5 mk admission and are open on summer weekends. Free town maps are available at most attractions.

Getting There & Away Leineperi is on an unpaved road that runs parallel to the Tampere to Pori road No 11. Buses between Pori and Kullaa stop at Leineperi; there are usually two daily.

Swedish Coast

The 'Swedish Coast' is a predominantly Swedish-speaking area south and north of Vaasa. The landscape is typically flat but there are dense forests and hundreds of islands off the coast.

Very neat old houses typify the coastal region, as do numerous long houses where animals that will eventually be slaughtered for the annual fur auctions near Helsinki are reared.

Language is the distinctive feature here; a magazine booth in a local supermarket will have a collection of imported Swedish papers that keep locals gossiping about Sweden's TV stars, and the radio station is more likely to be playing Stockholm's 'P3' than the Finnish Rundradion. People from Sweden treat this region of lost brethren with curiosity and call it *Parallelsverige*, or 'Parallel Sweden'.

KRISTINESTAD

• pop 8600   ☎ 06

Kristinestad (Finnish: Kristiinankaupunki) is a small, idyllic seaside town. Like many other towns in the area, it is bilingual. Some 57% of the inhabitants speak Swedish.

History

Kristinestad, named after Queen Kristina of Sweden, was founded in 1649 by the great Count Per Brahe. By the 1850s, the town had become one of the main ports in Finland and an important centre for shipbuilding. With the arrival of steamships, Kristinestad's importance declined, and many of its inhabitants moved to Sweden.

Orientation & Information

Kristinestad is quite small, and everything except the camping ground is within a block or two of the market square. There is no tourist office per se, but folks around here are very friendly, and glad to speak with travellers!

The post office is at Parmansgatan 11, 64100 Kristinestad.

There's a pharmacy on the market square at Salutorget 3.

Things to See

The most interesting thing in Kristinestad is the town itself, with its rows of colourfully painted old wooden houses. In olden times, every traveller entering the town had to pay customs duty, collected at the **Old Customs House** on Staketgatan.

Adjacent to the customs house is the fantastic **Old Church**, Ulrika Eleonora Kyrka, which was constructed from 1698 to 1700 and has many of its original details. The church, named after the 17th century Swedish Queen Ulrika Eleonora, wife of Karl XI, is now among the oldest wooden churches in Finland. The church is open Tuesday to Saturday from mid-May to late August.

The **Sjöfartsmuseet** (Maritime Museum) at Salutorget 1 contains sea-related items collected by an old sea captain – the whole town seems to have pitched in to help put this place together, and they've done a fine

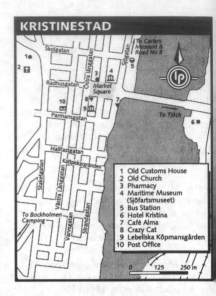

KRISTINESTAD

1 Old Customs House
2 Old Church
3 Pharmacy
4 Maritime Museum (Sjöfartsmuseet)
5 Bus Station
6 Hotel Kristina
7 Café Alma
8 Crazy Cat
9 Lebellska Köpmansgården
10 Post Office

job. It's open from noon to 4 pm Tuesday to Sunday from May to late August and charges 5 mk admission.

Lebellska Köpmansgården at Strandgatan 51, a block south of the market square, is a house museum that once belonged to a wealthy merchant. Dating from the early 19th century, it's an excellent representation of upper-class life in old Kristinestad. Hours are the same as for the Maritime Museum, and admission is 10 mk.

Three blocks south of the market square is **Kattpiskargränden** (Cat Whipper's Alley). It's the narrowest street in town, a mere 299cm wide. In the 1880s the town employed a cat catcher, whose job was to kill sick cats in order to prevent the spreading of plague – hence the name of the street.

Places to Stay

Bockholmen Camping (☎ 221 1484, Salavägen 32) is 1.5km south-west of the town centre. This pleasant place at a small beach is open from June to mid-August. Camp sites cost 70 mk, cabins 130 to 280 mk. There are bicycles for rent.

Hotel Kristina (☎ *221 2555, fax 221 3250, Stortorget 1)*, across the bridge from the town centre, offers comfortable accommodation with a nice view over the bay. Rooms cost 290/390 mk in summer, 310/420 mk at other times. There is dancing and live music here in the evenings.

Places to Eat

Café Alma is a great big airy café at the bridge. It offers a terrific home-cooked buffet lunch from 11 am to 5 pm weekends – for 25 mk you get just salads, and for 40 mk you get the full monty. *Crazy Cat* on Östralånggatan at the market square is a small pizzeria. You're in luck if you show up in time for the 35 mk pizza buffet, 11 am to 3 pm on Tuesday.

Getting There & Away

Kristinestad lies on road No 662, about 100km south of Vaasa. Five buses a day running between Pori and Vaasa stop at Kristinestad. The bus station is on Sjögatan, just north of Café Alma. The trip from either Vaasa or Pori takes approximately 1½ hours. There are two buses a day from Tampere, a trip of over five hours.

AROUND KRISTINESTAD

The **Carlsro Museum** is in an old villa and is quite delightful, with a collection of bric-a-brac from the tsarist era. The museum is 5km north of town (2km from road No 662), and is open from noon to 6 pm Tuesday to Sunday.

The **Tjöckå River** winds through pleasant rural scenery. You can rent a canoe for 80 mk in Tjöck Bilservice on road No 8 at Tjöck and paddle the 7km along the river to Kristinestad. There are a few rapids along the route and lots of fish in the river. Ask for further details at the post office, Maritime Museum or Hotel Kristina in Kristinestad.

KASKINEN

• pop 1650   ☎ 06

If you want to visit a truly peaceful island town, Kaskinen (Swedish: Kaskö) is the place to go – it is mainland Finland's smallest town, with a population of only 1650. Finnish is spoken by the majority of people, many of whom work in the enormous pulp factory at the south end of Kaskinen. This may be the only factory area in Finland which is actually larger than the town itself.

The town's friendly hostel alone is worth the trip.

Orientation & Information

Two bridges connect the island town to the mainland. There is no tourist office, but you can get advice and brochures from the town hall at Raatihuoneenkatu 34 or at the excellent hostel. There's a post office, a supermarket and a pharmacy on the market square. Raatihuoneenkatu is the main road, and runs north-south.

Things to See & Do

There's not a lot to see in Kaskinen – and that's the point. Relax, and make arrangements at the hostel to rent a boat and fishing gear. If you must sight-see, there's a **local museum** at Raatihuoneenkatu 48. A small **fishing museum** is at the north end of the island, at the Kalaranta boat dock. These museums are typically open one or two days a week during summer months – usually Sunday and Wednesday. The old wooden **boat sheds** at Kalaranta are also worth a look, and there's a nice old **windmill** on a nearby wooded hill.

Places to Stay & Eat

Marianranta Camping (☎ *222 7589)* is small, but pleasantly located by the seaside at the north-eastern tip of the island. Camp sites cost 65 mk and there are a few cottages.

The HI-affiliated *Björntrå Vandrarhem* (☎*/fax 222 7007, Raatihuoneenkatu 22)* is a superb hostel with six rooms almost of hotel standard costing 85 to 95 mk per person. The place is run by Erik and Annikki Björndahl, a Swedish-speaking husband and wife team who are wise, funny and wonderfully kind. Guests have use of a well-stocked kitchen and TV room. Bjorrnträ is open from June to mid-August or by prior arrangement.

Café Kung Gustab is on the market square and does triple duty as the town's only café-pub-restaurant.

Getting There & Away
Kaskinen is on road No 67, 95km south of Vaasa and 12km south of Närpes. There are a few buses daily from Närpes, mostly on weekdays.

NÄRPES
- pop 10,000   ☎ 06

Närpes (Finnish: Närpiö), 85km south-west of Vaasa, is the tomato basket of Finland. It also has one of the highest ratios of Swedish to Finnish speakers in the country – 93% of the inhabitants speak Swedish as their native language, with a local accent that is hard to understand.

Things to See
Some 150 *kyrkstallar*, or 'church stables' (though they are in fact for the use of people not horses), surround the medieval **Närpes Church**. This is the only place in Finland where these temporary shelters have been preserved. In the past, people from outlying districts used these to stay overnight when visiting the church. The interior of the church is beautifully decorated.

Öjskogsparken, just down the road from the church, includes a pharmacy museum, a dozen old wooden houses and a 'country store' with goods that are 100 years old. Admission is 10 mk.

Getting There & Away
Four buses a day, from Turku to Vaasa via Kristinestad and Pori, stop at Närpes.

ORAVAIS
- pop 2432   ☎ 06

Oravais (Finnish: Oravainen) is known for its Vallonic (Belgian-French) minority, now assimilated, who arrived during the 17th century to develop ironworks in the village

of Kimo. As many as 85% of the local population speak Swedish.

The **Oravais Slagfält** site, 2km from the village, commemorates the battle of 14 September 1808 in which Finnish and Swedish soldiers fought Russians. At least 12,000 soldiers fought here and hundreds lost their lives.

Furirbostället on the Minnestods 'museum road' is a historic house that has a café.

Getting There & Away
There are several buses daily between Vaasa and Jakobstad that stop at Oravais, 48km from both.

NYKARLEBY
- pop 7650   ☎ 06

Nykarleby (Finnish: Uusikaarlepyy) is a small town 20km south of Jakobstad where 91% of the population speak Swedish, making it the most Swedish of all mainland Finnish towns.

The town was founded in 1620, the same year as Karleby (Kokkola); despite the identical founding dates, this place got the name Nykarleby which means 'new Kokkola'.

In 1995 a Finnish newspaper estimated that the happiest people in Finland live in Nykarleby. It is also a pleasant place for travellers to pass a day or afternoon.

Orientation & Information
The town centre is on the west bank of the Nykarleby River, which divides the town into two parts. The bus terminal, post office, banks, pharmacies, shops and library are all on the main street, Topeliusesplanaden, at the market square.

In summer, you can get tourist information and excellent town maps from the Kyrktuppen café.

Nykarleby Church
The beautiful yellow church on the riverside was built in 1708. Its walls, pulpit and ceiling are covered with 18th century paintings. It's open from 9 am to 6 pm daily in summer.

Nykarleby Museum

Also known as Herlers Museum, this old red house, to the north along the main street, has plenty of local flavour. It features bric-a-brac, old costumes and furniture, and is open from noon to 5 pm Sunday to Friday.

Kuddnäs Museum

This museum preserves the birthplace of writer Zacharias Topelius, whose fairy tales are much loved. He was born in 1818. The large house has fantastic furniture and a nice garden. The place is open from 10 am to 5pm Tuesday to Sunday from May to August. Admission is 10 mk.

Places to Eat

Café Kyrktuppen is a pleasant little café, and *Brostugan*, across the river opposite the church, is also worth a visit. *Våfflor* (waffles) with cream and strawberry jam is the speciality at both places.

Getting There & Away

Kokkola, Jakobstad and Vaasa are the main gateways to Nykarleby; there is a regular bus service from all these towns. Nykarleby is 7km off the main road, road No 8.

JAKOBSTAD

• pop 20,000   ☎ 06

Jakobstad (Finnish: Pietarsaari) is a delightful little town that is distinctively Swedish; 55% of the population speak Swedish. It has great museums and a well-preserved historic area filled with 18th and 19th-century wooden houses, and in summer is linked by ferry with Sweden. Beware the nearby pulp factory and its distinctive bad smell.

History

The Swedish town of Jakobstad was founded in 1652 by Ebba Brahe, wife of war hero Jacob de la Gardie. The surrounding region, Pedersöre, gave the town its Finnish name, which translates as Peter's Island. Russians sacked Jakobstad twice in 1714; despite the repeated drubbings, it became the leading shipping town in Finland during the 18th century. Later, in 1844, Finland's first round-the-world sailing expedition started from the Jakobstad harbour.

Information

Tourist Office The tourist office (☎ 723 1796) is at Rådhusgatan 7, near the market square. It is open from 8 am to 6 pm Monday to Friday and 9 am to 3 pm Saturday from June to late August. At other times it's open from 8 am to 4 pm Monday to Friday.

The tourist office rents bicycles for about 30 mk per day.

Post The post office is at Stationsvägen 4, 68600 Jakobstad. Hours are 9 am to 8 pm Monday to Friday.

Internet Resources & Library The public library at Rådhusgatan 3 has an Internet terminal on the 2nd floor, and is open 11 am to 7 pm Monday to Thursday, 11 am to 4 pm Friday in summer. At other times, hours are 11 am to 8 pm Monday to Friday.

Left Luggage There is a left-luggage counter at the bus station.

Medical & Emergency Services There are pharmacies at Köpmansgatan 16, Storagatan 16 and Skolgatan 21. In a general emergency call ☎ 112, for police call ☎ 10022 and for a doctor ☎ 10023.

Museums

Jakobstad has a truly eclectic collection of small private museums, some of the quirkiest in Finland. Museums in Jakobstad are generally open from noon to 4 pm Tuesday to Sunday in summer.

Jacobstad Wapen In Gamla Hamn (the old harbour area) is the pride of Jakobstad, the *Jacobstad Wapen*, modelled after a 17th century sailing vessel. It is open to visitors when in dock, daily from mid-May to late August (entry 10 mk). Cruises on the *Jacobstad Wapen* cost 150 to 290 mk; inquire at the tourist office.

Motorcycle Salon The Motocykelsalongen at Alholmsgatan 8 is a private museum with a collection of over 120 motorcycles – from old Harley Davidsons to funny little motor-powered bicycles. Admission is 20 mk.

Nanoq Arctic Museum The Nanoq Arctic Museum is at Pörkenäsintie 60, 7km west of Jakobstad in the village of Fäboda. While the concept might seem incongruous here (the Arctic Circle is, after all, several hundred kilometres to the north), this little museum is surprisingly good, and worth a detour. The collection is the private achievement of Pentti Kronqvist who has made several expeditions to the Arctic. There are Eskimo tools, fossils, authentic Arctic huts from Greenland and elsewhere, and various other Arctic souvenirs. Nanoq is open noon to 7 pm daily in summer and 11 am to 5 pm Monday to Friday at other times. Admission is 25 mk.

Weapons Museum The Vapenmuseum, also at Alholmsgatan 8, is the small private collection of Bengt Ena, a resident of Jakobstad. There are more than 300 old guns, hunting rifles and military pistols dating back to the 1740s. Admission is 20 mk.

Tobacco Museum The Tobaksmuseum museum at Alholmsgatan 9 is associated with the local tobacco industry. It is open by prior arrangement (☎ 785 1370). Entry is 5 mk.

Westmansmors Stuga This small museum, at Visasbacken 4, was once a private school dating from 1794. The *vindskammare* (upstairs room) was where JL Runeberg, Finland's national poet, was taught (JL Runeberg was born in Jakobstad in 1804). Admission is 5 mk.

Jakobstadsmuseum This museum at Storagatan 2, open year-round, includes the old main building, Malmska Gården, and several other houses filled with furniture, paintings and objects relating to local maritime culture. Admission is 5 mk.

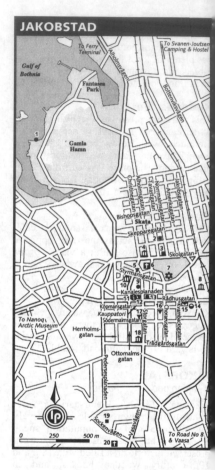

Skata

The old town section of Jakobstad has 300 or so wooden houses that have been beautifully preserved. Most of them were built in the 19th century; the 18th century houses along Hamngatan are the oldest in town.

School Park

The Skolparken, a botanical garden, is delightful in summer – and admission is free. At its western end is **Pietarsaari Church**,

JAKOBSTAD

PLACES TO STAY
2   Westerlund Resandehem
3   Park Hotel Vanadis
19 Bodgärdet

PLACES TO EAT
5   Visa Grande
12 Korv Görans
16 Café Ludvig
17 Saigon City

OTHER
1   Jacobstad Wapen
4   Motocykelsalongen & Vapenmuseum
6   Pietarsaari Church
7   School Park (Skolparken)
8   Tobaksmuseum
9   Pharmacy
10 Westmansmors Stuga
11 Tourist Office & Silja Line
13 Public Library
14 Bus Station
15 Post Office
18 Jakobstadsmuseum
20 Pedersöre Church

dating from 1731. The church is open daily in summer.

Fantasea Park

This amusement park at Gamla Hamn has water slides, arcade games, pools and a good swimming beach. The park is open from 11 am to 7 pm daily from June to mid-August. Entry is 18 mk (children 12 mk).

Pedersöre Church

Pedersöre Church at Vasavägen 118 was originally built in the 1400s, but the bell tower dates from the 1760s. During the reign of King Gustav III the church was greatly enlarged to become a cross-shaped church. Thankfully, the architect thumbed his nose at the king's plan to demolish the 85m spire. Contact the tourist office if you wish to see the interior.

Places to Stay

Camping *Svanen-Joutsen Camping (☎ 723 0660 or ☎ 723 1796, Luodontie 50)* is 6km

north of town, in Nissasörn (take a local bus from the city bus station). It's open from mid-May to late August; camp sites cost 65 mk and cabins cost 95 to 330 mk. You can hire bicycles (30 mk per day), boats and canoes.

Hostels The HI-affiliated *Svanen-Joutsen Hostel* is at the same location as the camping ground. Reception is open from 9 am to 10 pm daily in summer. Beds in double rooms cost just 50 mk.

A kilometre south of the town centre is *Bodgärdet (☎ 724 6610 or ☎ 0500-510608, Sockenvägen 5)*, an HI-affiliated hostel open from June to early August. Dorm beds cost 60 to 80 mk.

Both hostels have kitchen, sauna and laundry facilities.

Bed & Breakfast For accommodation in old Jakobstad, try *Westerlund Resandehem (☎ 723 0440, Norrmalmsgatan 8)*, run by a friendly Swedish-speaking lady. Spotless rooms cost 130/210 mk, including breakfast.

Hotel The small, elegant *Park Hotel Vanadis (☎ 723 4700, Skolgatan 23)*, on the edge of the old town, is the town's nicest hotel. Rooms cost 340/450 mk in summer and on weekends, or 460/570 mk at other times.

Places to Eat

Korv Görans on Kanalesplanaden is a zippy little pizza and kebab restaurant that has been in business more than 25 years. Most options are under 25 mk.

Saigon City (Storgatan 8) is an appealing Asian restaurant – possibly the only one in the world to offer wok-fried fillet of reindeer! Lunch specials, from 11 am to 3 pm weekdays, range from 30 to 35 mk.

Visa Grande (Storgatan 20) is an authentic Italian place with a good pizza and pasta buffet for 40 to 50 mk.

Café Ludvig (Köpmansgatan 8) near the bus station is a large café with a good selection of pastries.

Getting There & Away

Air The nearest airport is at Kronoby, 32km north-east of Jakobstad. There are several daily flights from Helsinki. Regional buses offer transport into town.

Bus There are regular buses to Jakobstad from Vaasa and other towns along the West Coast.

Train Bennäs (Finnish: Pännäinen), 11km away, is the closest railway station to Jakobstad. A shuttle bus meets arriving trains.

Car & Motorcycle Jakobstad is on a large island north-west of the main road (road No 8) and is connected by bridge to the mainland – use road No 741 or 749 to reach town. The distance to Vaasa is about 100km.

Boat Silja Line offers service on the MS *Fennia* from Jakobstad to Skellefteå and Umeå in Sweden from late May to early September. Purchase tickets at the Silja Line counter in the tourist office.

The Jakobstad harbour is 6km north of the town centre; buses to each departing ferry leave the market square 30 minutes prior to the ferry's departure.

KOKKOLA

• pop 35,500   ☎ 06

Seen from the train station, Kokkola (Swedish: Karleby) looks very boring. It *does* have a small, pleasant old town area hidden behind the box-like supermarkets – but that's about it. This is primarily a transportation hub.

In 1620, Kokkola was founded as Karleby on the west coast of Finland. The village was an essential port for the tar trade, which flourished in the 17th century. Today only a small number of the population are Swedish-speakers.

Orientation

The train station is south of the centre on Rantakatu, the main street. The market square is at the intersection of Rantakatu and Torikatu, and everything is within easy walking distance.

Information

The tourist office (☎ 831 1902) is on Mannerheiminaukio in the heart of Kokkola. The main post office is at Rantakatu 4, 67100 Kokkola. There is an Internet terminal at the public library, Isokatu 2, one block north of the train station. There are 24-hour lockers at the train and bus stations – they're cheaper (10 mk) at the bus station. You'll find pharmacies at Rantakatu 10, Mannerheiminaukio 1 and Mariankatu 19.

Things to See

Neristanis is the old town district. The most colourful streets are Itäinen Kirkkokatu, Läntinen Kirkkokatu and Isokatu. In the area are several museums: the **Historical Museum** at Pitkänsillankatu 28, the **Renlund Art Gallery** at Pitkänsillankatu 39, and adjacent to the gallery, the **Camera Museum**. All are closed on Monday and have free admission. At the riverside is an old British **barge**. It was captured during the Crimean War of the 1850s; despite efforts by the British to buy it back, it remains on display in Kokkola. The riverfront area is nice for strolling.

Places to Stay

Suntinsuu (☎ *831 4006, Pikiruukki)* is a camping ground north-west of the centre that charges 60 mk for tent sites and 140 to 300 mk for cabins. It's open from June to late August.

Tankkari (☎ *831 4006)*, near the camping ground, is an HI-affiliated hostel open from June to late August. Beds cost 85 to 100 mk. There are many hotels in the centre, including *Hotelli Kantarellis* (☎ *822 5000, fax 822 5490, Kauppatori 4)*, with rooms for 340/380 mk in summer and 450/540 mk at other times.

Places to Eat

Hesburger is on Rantakatu near the train station. There's also *Yöpizza (Rantakatu 17)* with 15 mk slices and a 4 am closing time.

Wanha Lyhty & Kellari (Pitkänsil-lankatu 24) is a café, restaurant and beer cellar cheerfully decorated in the spirit of the old town. The beer cellar offers live music on weekends.

Around the corner from Wanha Lyhty, *Café Kahvipuu (Isokatu 11)* is a lovely little café with home-made pastries, strong cappuccino and a summer terrace which serves beer.

Getting There & Away

Air The Kronoby airport is 22km south-east of Kokkola and served by regional bus. There are several flights a day from Helsinki.

Bus Regular buses run to/from all coastal towns, especially Vaasa and Jakobstad. The bus station is one block west of the train station.

Train There is a major train station in Kokkola and all trains using the main western railway line stop here. The journey from Helsinki takes less than five hours in daytime.

Getting Around
The hostel rents bicycles for 50 mk per day or 180 mk per week.

KALAJOKI
• pop 10,000   ☎ 08

Most Finns know Kalajoki for its long, sandy beaches. Over the years, as package charter flights to Spain have become cheaper than a holiday in Kalajoki, the region has sought new ways to attract Finnish tourists. Consequently, Kalajoki provides many services for tourists, including an amusement park and expensive hotels. Skip all this, if you like, but don't miss the side trip to the rocky, windswept Maakalla and Ulkokalla islets.

Orientation & Information
You'll find the bus terminal, supermarkets, banks, a post office and a pharmacy in Kalajoki village, on the banks of the Kalajoki.

The Kalajoki beach area is 6km south of the village.

The tourist office (☎ 460 505, katariina .peltola@kalajoki.fi) is at Kalajoentie 5, at the southern end of the beach area. It's open daily in summer.

Things to See
A kilometre north of Kalajoki village, the Plassi area has 17th-century wooden houses and a small **fishing museum** (Kalastus-museo). A kilometre south of the bus terminal is the **local museum**. Both places are open from Tuesday to Sunday in summer.

Kalajoki Särkät (Kalajoki Beach), 6km south of Kalajoki village, is one of the most popular holiday spots for Finns. It has a lot to offer: an amusement park, a spa, a golf course, holiday villas, sandy beaches, restaurants and cafés, good hotels and discos. If you would like to have a Mediterranean-style holiday experience at a latitude of 64°, this is just the ticket.

Places to Stay
The beach, 6km south of the village, is the place to look for accommodation.

Camping Hiekkasärkät (☎ 469 2300 or ☎ 469 2380, raija.makela@hiekkasarkat.fi) charges 70 to 80 mk for camp sites, 140 to 450 mk for cabins. It's open from mid-May to late August.

Tapion Tupa (☎ 466 622), near the main road, is a HI associated hostel with beds from 100 mk per person, and good rooms from 400 mk (100 mk less during off-season weeks).

There are many hotels at the beach, including *Hotelli Rantakalla (☎ 466 642, fax 466 617)*, with rooms from 310/350 mk.

Getting There & Away
There are several buses a day from Oulu, Raahe, Kokkola and other coastal places to Kalajoki and the beach. There are weekday bus connections from both Oulainen and Ylivieska railway stations.

AROUND KALAJOKI
Maakalla & Ulkokalla Islets

An isolated islet that has only existed since the 15th century, Maakalla has retained a genuine fishing-village image. There are no roads, shops or electricity – in fact, there are no permanent human inhabitants – but you will find an interesting wooden **church**, abundant plant and bird life and some weathered **fishing huts**. The owners of the tiny fishing huts gather regularly and vote to keep the islet exactly as it is.

For the most isolated accommodation in Finland, ask the boat operator about cottages on the island of Ulkokalla, a rocky islet 5km west of Maakalla. There is no electricity, and fresh water for the sauna stove is brought from the mainland!

Getting There & Away Book your boat ride (60 mk return) in Kalajoki at the pier or through the local tourist office. There are daily departures from early June to early August.

Central Pohjanmaa

What's Central Pohjanmaa? It's flat – as flat as can be. Farmer's fields stretch as far as the eye can see, each one dotted with dozens and dozens of grey weathered hay barns.

It's an unlikely area for travellers – but if you find yourself passing through, pause to enjoy some of its subtle delights.

The undisputed capital of the area is Seinäjoki, although the outstanding Kaustinen Folk Music Festival in July probably makes Kaustinen the most lively and exciting of the central towns.

SEINÄJOKI
• pop 29,,000   ☎ 06

Seinäjoki, the commercial centre of the region and the most important inland town in western Finland, is for travellers primarily a railway junction. It is known for the modern town centre designed by Finnish ar-

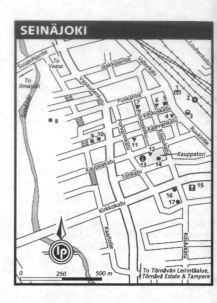

chitect Alvar Aalto, and for its large open-air museum area at the southern edge of town. Otherwise, there's little reason to linger. Only 0.2% of the population speak Swedish.

Information

Tourist Office The tourist office or Seinänaapurien Matkailu (☎ 414 3890, matkailu@tietoraitti.fi), is on the 2nd floor of the Torikeskus Shopping Centre. Although this is the regional tourist office, there is little information in English. Hours are 9 am to 5 pm Monday to Friday.

Post The main post office is near the train station, at Valtionkatu 1, 60100 Seinäjoki. Hours are 8 am to 8 pm Monday to Friday.

Internet Resources & Library The public library at Koulukatu 21 has three Internet terminals. It is open from 10 am to 7 pm Monday to Friday and 11 am to 3 pm Saturday.

The Web site for Seinäjoki is www.tietoraitti.fi/matkailu/.

SEINÄJOKI

PLACES TO STAY
- 8   Marttilan Kortteeri
- 9   Matkustajakoti Vuorela
- 10 Perhehotelli Nurmela
- 14 Sokos Hotel Vaakuna

PLACES TO EAT
- 4   Istanbul Kebab
- 6   Rosso
- 7   Juulia
- 11 Kotipulla
- 12 Hesburger

OTHER
- 1   Post Office
- 2   Train Station
- 3   Bus Station
- 5   Pharmacy
- 13 Seinänaapurien Matkailu (Regional Tourist Office) & Torikeskus Shopping Centre
- 15 Lakeuden Risti Church
- 16 Town Hall
- 17 Public Library

Left Luggage The train station has a left-luggage counter and 24-hour lockers that cost 5 mk. The bus station charges 10 mk for 24-hour lockers.

Medical & Emergency Services In a general emergency call ☎ 112; for a doctor ☎ 10023. There are pharmacies at Keskuskatu 3 and Koulukatu 11.

Aalto Centre

The monumental Aalto Centre, built in 1960, is one of the most important works of architect Alvar Aalto, who was born in this province in 1898. It's a must-see for students of modern architecture but a likely miss for ordinary travellers. The complex's stark white buildings include the **Lakeuden Risti Church**, the **town hall** and the **public library**. The massive church, with its oddly secular steeple, is the most famous building of them all. The church is open from noon to 6 pm daily. Most of the other buildings can be seen weekdays until 3 pm.

Törnävä Estate

South of the town centre on road No 64 is the leafy suburb of Törnävä. The wealthy Wasastjerna family first settled this area in 1806 and built a mansion, Törnävä, that is still standing. Elsewhere on the grounds, a large number of old wooden buildings, including some that have been transferred from elsewhere, constitute an open-air museum.

On your right, when coming from the town centre, is the **Agriculture Museum** and the **Mill Museum**. On your left in the old yellow building is the **Gunpowder Museum**. Behind is a smoke house and a smith's house from the 17th century. The area around the museum houses is well-kept and perfect for picnicking.

The museums are open from 11 am to 7 pm Tuesday to Sunday from mid-May to late August. During the rest of the year, they're open from 9 am to 2.30 pm on weekdays. Local bus Nos 1 and 5 run the 7km from Seinäjoki bus station to Törnävä.

Special Events

The time to visit Seinäjoki is during its summer festivals: Provinssirock, a festival of international rock music held in mid-June, and Tango Markkinat, a festival of all things tango held in mid-July. These events attract some of the largest crowds at Finnish summer festivals – though you're likely to be one of only a few foreigners.

Places to Stay

Törnävän Leirintäalue (☎ 412 0784, Törnäväntie 29) is a camping ground south of the centre. You can pitch your tent for 60 to 70 mk, or rent a cabin for 130 to 230 mk.

Seinäjoki's hostel is the HI-affiliated **Marttilan Kortteeri** (☎ 420 4800, Puskantie 38), a student dormitory open to travellers from June to early August. Most rooms are priced at 160/200 mk.

Two very attractive places are on Kalevankatu west of the centre. **Perhehotelli Nurmela** (☎ 414 1771, Kalevankatu 29) is a family-run hotel with rooms from 180/300 mk, breakfast included. Cheaper and more

Tango

Seinäjoki is the undisputed tango capital of a country that's tango-mad. In the rest of the world the tango craze was swept away by Elvis, but in Finland it never died.

The world's first tango was danced in the suburbs of Buenos Aires toward the end of the 1900s. Argentinian musicians and dancers brought tango to Europe in the 1910s. A Finnish version of tango developed soon after, championed by the composer Unto Mononen and Olavi Virta, the Finnish king of tango-dancing.

No other music could epitomise the melancholic Finn better than this Argentinian music. If Finns lack the electrifying tension that Latin Americans bring to the tango, they lack none of the enthusiasm. Finnish tango music is best heard on long bus journeys through the Finnish wilderness, passing by abandoned farm houses. The Finnish lyrics deal with loneliness, unrequieted love and desperation. The best place and time to dance is during the *Tangomarkkinat* festival held in Seinäjoki every July. However, many younger Finns might disagree about tango being the thing; they would rather stick to *rokki* or *jatsi* or *tekno* or whatever the latest dance craze may be.

basic is *Matkustajakoti Vuorela* (☎ 423 2195, Kalevankatu 31).

There are many big hotels in Seinäjoki, including the *Sokos Hotel Vaakuna* (☎ 419 3111, fax 419 3112, Kauppatori 3). Singles/doubles are from 430/550 mk, though in summer all rooms are 360 mk.

Places to Eat

Just opposite the train station, *Istanbul Kebab* serves pizzas and kebap plates from 30 mk, and there's a *Hesburger* at the Torikeskus Shopping Centre.

Juulia (Puistopolku 15) is a pleasing little lunch place that closes at 4 pm Monday to Friday and 2 pm Saturday. The home-cooked specials range from 22 to 40 mk.

Rosso (Keskuskatu 7) is part of a national chain and has a standard menu available in English. Meals start around 35 mk. *Kotipulla (Kalevankatu 14)* is a bakery and café.

Getting There & Away

Bus There are bus connections to towns and villages throughout Western Finland.

Train Seinäjoki is the train hub of Pohjanmaa. The fastest trains from Helsinki cover the 346km in three hours.

Car & Motorcycle Seinäjoki is on road no 18. To reach Seinäjoki from the coastal road No 8, take road No 16 east from Vaasa and follow signs.

AROUND SEINÄJOKI
Ilmajoki

The small village of Ilmajoki, on the banks of the Kyrönjoki, makes a nice side trip from Seinäjoki. It has many museums and entry to each is 10 mk.

Visit **Merita Bank** in the centre of town during opening hours to see a unique collection of old Roman coins and a large number of German, Russian, Finnish and other European banknotes from between WWI and WWII.

The **Ilmajoki Museum** has 15,000 items relating to local history. The museum is open daily from June to August.

Yli-Laurosela Museum is in an 1849 house that has been carefully renovated by the National Board of Antiquities. It is open daily in summer and on weekends during the rest of the year.

Ilmajoki Church dates from 1766 and is full of old statues and paintings. The church is open daily in summer.

Kantri in the town centre serves a decent lunch from 35 mk.

The village is a few kilometres off road No 67, the main Seinäjoki to Kurikka road. There are regular buses from Seinäjoki, 15km away.

WESTERN FINLAND

Kurikka

Kurikka, 34 km south-west of Seinäjoki, is an excellent place to learn something about Pohjanmaa's traditions. The **local museum** on Museotie has an extensive coverage of local traditions, including a collection of *kurikka* tools, items used to dry clothes. Samuli Paulaharju, an important 'cultural explorer', was born in Kurikka in 1875 and there's a special room devoted to his travels. The museum is open Sunday to Friday from June to August; admission will set you back 5 mk.

Eveliina is a decent lunch restaurant in the post office building. Two nearby *cafés* create tempting bakery products.

Most buses that travel south from Seinäjoki stop at Kurikka.

Kauhava

• pop 8500

Knife-making industries are the main attraction in the village of Kauhava. You can purchase a knife for use during treks in the Finnish wilderness. There's also a **knife museum** in the library on Kauppatie. Otherwise, what you'll see here is a lot of hay barns and a very flat landscape.

Most trains on the Helsinki to Oulu line stop at Kauhava railway station, which is a kilometre west of the centre. There are buses from Seinäjöki, 40km south on road No 19.

Kuortane

The town of Kuortane was the birthplace of architect Alvar Aalto in 1896. Although his childhood home still exists, it is privately owned and not open to visitors.

The **Kuortane Church** is exceptionally beautiful and dates back to 1777. The yellow bell tower is equally attractive, and there's an old longboat nearby. The church is open daily in summer. Nearby, the **Talomuseo** is a collection of a dozen old houses, including one from the 16th century. The museum is closed Monday; entry is 10 mk.

Kuortane is surrounded by a wealthy farming region with several examples of the typical *kaksifooninkinen* farmhouse (literally 'one house with two floors').

Places to Stay & Eat The camping ground *Aholankangas* (☎ 525 4104, Kirkkotie 25) is just north of the church. Sites cost 40 to 60 mk, and there are cabins.

The HI-affiliated *Finnhostel Virtaniemen Lomatila* (☎ 525 6689, Virtala), open year-round, has a café, sauna, laundry and kitchen, and charges 100 mk and up for beds.

Getting There & Away Kuortane is on road No 66, about 40km east of Seinäjoki. There is bus service between the two towns.

KAUSTINEN

• pop 4500   ☎ 06

Kaustinen is a small inland village 47km south-east of Kokkola. There isn't much to see in the village itself, so plan your visit around the superb Kaustinen Folk Music Festival in July. Incidentally, the Peanuts cartoon character 'Woodstock' is called 'Kaustinen' in the Finnish version.

Orientation

The bus terminal and most shops and banks are along Kaustintie in the village centre and can be reached on foot.

Information

The small tourist information office is easy to find at Kaustintie 1 in the centre. Nearby is the festival office, which handles accommodation during the festival. The bus station, shops and services are all easily reached on foot.

Things to See

The **Folk Music Instrument Museum** at the festival area is small but interesting. Hours are from 10 am to 7 pm daily during summer. Admission is 5 mk. **Pauanne** is an off-beat centre that combines shamanism, handicrafts and much more. The place has a popular smoke sauna that costs 15 mk per person. Pauanne is on a small hill about 3km from the centre of Kaustinen.

Special Events

The Kaustinen Folk Music Festival is one of the most loved summer festivals in

Finland, attracting huge crowds. It's *the* place to be if you're interested in Finnish folk music and dance, since some 300 Finnish bands (and many internatonal acts) perform more than 250 concerts during the week in mid-July. At any time from 10 am to 3 am there are several official concerts and half a dozen impromptu jam sessions going on. Daily festival passes cost 70 to 120 mk. For more details visit www. lesti.kpnet.fi/kaustinen/ktk.htm/ or contact the Kaustinen Folk Music Festival (☎ 860 4111, fax 860 4222, folk.fest@ kaustinen.inet.fi) PL 24, 69601 Kaustinen.

Places to Stay & Eat
The festival office organises accommodation during the busy periods. Camping and dormitory beds cost around 60 mk, home accommodation is 175/250 mk for singles/ doubles, and hotel-style doubles cost around 350 mk. Advance bookings are advised.

Pauanteen (☎ 861 1881, fax 735 735 023) at the Pauanne centre offers beds from 150 mk per person.

The HI-affiliated *Koskelan Lomatalo (☎ 861 1338, Känsäläntie 123)*, 5km north of Kaustinen, is open year round. Beds cost between 75 and 95 mk. It offers kitchen, sauna and laundry facilities.

Marjaana (☎ 861 1211, fax 861 1213, Teerijärventie 1) is a hotel with rooms for 220/340 mk, which includes breakfast.

There are some *grillis* in the centre, and the festival area has a busy *restaurant*, which serves hearty meals for around 40 mk.

Getting There & Away
Catch a bus from Kokkola, which has a railway station and is just 47km away. There are several buses every day. There are express buses from other cities during festival season.

AROUND KAUSTINEN
Lake District Museum (Järviseudun museo)
The Järviseudun museo, or Lake District Museum, is one of the largest open-air museums in Finland. On display are several houses, dating from the 1600s to the mid-1800s, and thousands of artefacts. The museum is open daily in summer.

There is no bus service to the museum, 40km south-west of Kaustinen on road No 63. It's possible to take a bus from Kaustinen, Seinäjoki or Kokkola to the village of Evijärvi, then hitchhike the remaining 10km west.

LAUHAVUORI NATIONAL PARK
This small national park (36 sq km) was founded in 1982 to protect the area around Lauhavuori hill, which at 231m above sea level is western Finland's highest point. There are many springs and bogs in the park, and pine forest atop the hill.

An **observation tower** at the top of Lauhavuori hill is staffed from 5 am to 10 pm daily in summer and has nice views as well as a kiosk selling cool drinks.

There are 10km of walking and cross-country skiing trails within the park: one track leads to Lake Kaivoslampi in the north and one to Lake Spitaalijärvi in the south. From Lake Spitaalijärvi, an extension to the west takes you to a marshland area.

Camping is permitted in the park at the three locations (two are next to the lakes). You can stay at *Lauhan kämppä (☎ 06-132 221)*, a kilometre north of the tower, if you reserve the whole hut in advance.

If you want to get to the national park by public transport you'll have to walk 5km from the Honkajoki to Kauhajoki road (No 669) or 12km from Isojoki, via Sarviluoma. There are buses to both crossings.

Lapland & Oulu

Covering almost half of the entire country, the sparsely populated province of Lapland **is *the* great adventure** in Finland. Together with Oulu, the province just south of Lapland, this is some of the best preserved wilderness in Europe. Whether you just drive through it or do extensive trekking around the region, set aside enough time to get off the main roads and into the wilderness.

Lapland has a population of 200,000, or 2.1 people per sq km. Much of the population lives in towns in southern Lapland. The true wilderness is farther north. Rovaniemi is the capital of Lapland and the best place to start a tour.

Oulu Province can be divided into several regions. The town of Oulu, the provincial capital, is surrounded by a flat, fertile farming region. Kainuu, to the east, is a wilderness area with a recorded history going back to the 16th century. Just south of Lapland is the rugged Koillismaa area, one of the natural highlights of Finland.

LAPLAND HISTORY

Finnish Lapland was inhabited as early as the Stone Age, but was probably not as heavily settled as the Finnmark region in northern Norway. Discoveries have been made dating back to the Stone Age. When Sami peoples were pushed north by migrating Finns, traditions evolved and developed. Many legends remain, including those of miracle-working witches who could fly and transform themselves into strange creatures. Conspicuous lakes or rocks became *seita* (holy sites), the island of Ukko on lake Inarinjärvi being the best known of these.

The banks of the Tornionjoki river, as well as the mouth of the Kemijoki river nearby, developed into busy trade centres during medieval times. Some traces of Viking contacts have been found. The king of Sweden granted the Pirkka people (of Häme) exclusive rights to collect taxes among Lapps in

HIGHLIGHTS

- Excellent fell walking in the north of Lapland
- The Karhunkierros route in Oulanka National Park – best scenery in Finland!
- A cruise on the *Sampo*, an authentic Arctic icebreaker
- Bird-watching in Liminka Bay during the 'great migration' of May, August and September
- Fishing for salmon, trout and perch at Hossa, Finland's 'fisher's paradise'
- Cross-country and downhill skiing
- Husky and reindeer safaris during winter twilight
- Canoeing and kayaking on the Kitkajoki and Oulankajoki rivers near Kuusamo
- Midnight golf in Tornio
- The village of Inari, centre of Sami culture
- The chamber music festival in the lively wilderness town of Kuhmo

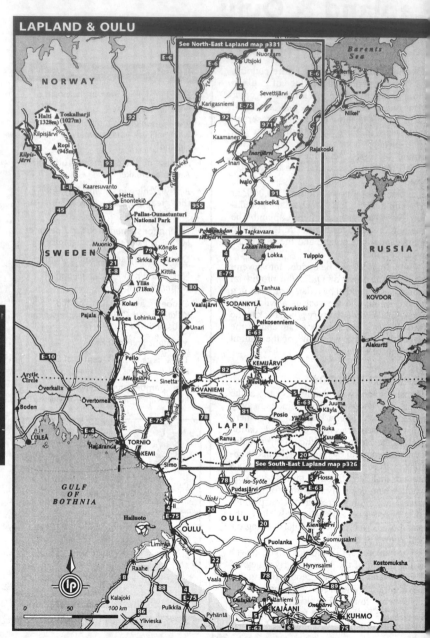

LAPLAND & OULU

he 13th century, and their centre grew at Tornio. Finns moved farther north along the rivers.

Inari was an important Sami trade centre from the early 1500s, when there were Sami settlements around the vast territory. During the 1600s, Swedes increased their presence throughout northern Finland (the Tornionjoki valley remained Swedish until 1809). In 1670, cult sites and religious objects of the Sami were destroyed by one Gabriel Tuderus, who represented the Lutheran Church. Wooden churches were built throughout Lapland, the oldest remaining in Tornio, Sodankylä and Tervola.

During the next centuries, more Finns were attracted to the vast province, adopted reindeer herding and were assimilated into the Sami communities (or vice versa), especially in southern Lapland. In 1800, there were 463 Samis in Inari and only 18 Finns. One hundred years later, there were 800 Samis and 585 Finns. At that time, there were only paths to the northernmost parts of Lapland. The first gravel road to Ivalo was built in 1913, to Inari in 1924 and to Karigasniemi during WWII.

The area of Petsamo, north-east of Inari, was annexed to Finland in 1920 as a result of the Treaty of Tartu and a nickel mine was opened in 1937. Russians attacked the area in the Winter War and the whole area was evacuated on 4 September 1944. The Soviet Union annexed the mineral-rich area and has kept it ever since. The Scolt Samis from Petsamo were settled in Sevettijärvi, Nellim and Virtaniemi in north-eastern Lapland.

The peace agreement of 1944 between Finland and the Soviet Union stated that Germans had to leave Finnish territory immediately, but while retreating to northern Norway the troops of Nazi Germany burned and destroyed all buildings in their path. Apart from a few churches and a few villages, only a few isolated houses in Lapland date back to the period before WWII.

Lapland has eventually emerged from this devastation as one of the most affluent regions in Finland, benefiting from booming tourism and generous subsidies from the south.

Pirkka tribe in Lapland, 13th century. The king of Sweden granted the Pirkka people (from Häme) the right to collect taxes from the Lapps

SAMIS

Samis (Lapps) have traditionally been nomads, herding their reindeer in the large area of Lapland spanning the region from the Kola peninsula in Russia to the southern Norwegian mountains. Their traditional dwelling, the *kota*, resembles the tepee or wigwam of native North Americans, and is easily set up as a temporary shelter. Now that old traditions are vanishing, most Samis live in houses and use motor vehicles while still herding their reindeer.

Reindeer wander free around the large natural areas within each *paliskunta* (reindeer cooperative), which is bordered by enormous fences that cross the wilderness. Reindeer are slaughtered after the annual reindeer roundup, during which each family recognises its own stock by ear marks. Some Finns also herd reindeer in Lapland.

Samis have been subjected to humiliation in the past. Samis inhabited all of Finland 6000 years ago but have been pushed farther north ever since. They were forcibly converted to (Protestant) Christianity in the 1600s, and their religious traditions were made illegal. This has led to an awkward situation whereby many Samis define themselves not as Samis but as ordinary Finns.

Officially, Samis in Finland number 6500, and speakers of Sami languages about 1700. These days, Sami rights are defended, and their language is prominently displayed officially in Sami regions in Finnish Lapland.

The universal right to 'Sami territory' (a somewhat blurry definition) is continuously disputed. No 'homeland' or 'reservation' has been created so far. The Sami area of Finland is larger than, say, Belgium.

Norway is the strongest preserver of Sami culture today, and Finnish Samis keep close contacts with their Norwegian counterparts across the border. The National Museum in Helsinki, Arktikum in Rovaniemi, Ainola in Oulu, Maakuntamuseo in Tornio and Saame-laismuseo in Inari are some of the museums that cover Sami culture extensively.

SAMI LANGUAGES

Sami languages are related to Finnish and other Finno-Ugric languages. There are three Sami (Lapp) languages used in Finland today, although there are under 2000 regular users. Sami is taught in local schools, and legislation grants Samis the right of Sami usage in offices in North Lapland. In Utsjoki Sami speakers constitute almost the majority of the population. You will find another seven Sami languages in Norway, Sweden and Russia.

Fell Sami

The most common of Sami languages (also known as Northern Sami or Mountain Sami), Fell Sami, is spoken by Utsjoki and Enontekiö Samis, and tens of thousands of Sami in Norway. Fell Sami is considered the standard Sami, and there is plenty of literature printed in Utsjoki or in Karasjok (Norway).

Written Fell Sami includes several accented letters but does not directly correspond to spoken Sami. In fact, many Samis find written Sami difficult to learn. For example, *giitu* (for 'thanks') is pronounced 'GHEECH-too', but the strongly aspirated 'h' is not written. Likewise, *da* is pronounced as 'tah-ch'. You should ask Samis to read these words out loud, to learn the correct pronunciation.

Hello	*Buorre beaivi*
Hello (reply)	*Ipmel atti*
Goodbye	
(to the one who leaves)	*Mana dearvan*
(to the one who stays)	*Báze dearvan*
Thank you	*Giitu*
You're welcome	*Leage buorre*
Yes	*De lea*
No	*Ii*
How are you?	*Mot manna?*
I'm fine	*Buorre dat manna*
library	*girjerádju*
airport	*girdingieddi*
1	*okta*
2	*guokte*
3	*golbma*
4	*njeallje*

JOHN BORTHWICK

...ot the mosquito

JENNIFER BREUER

...mi Church

JENNIFER BREUER

Oulu architecture

JOHN BORTHWICK

A ZZ Top fan at the Arctic Circle

JENNIFER BREWER

Basket maker's shop, Oulu

JOHN BORTHWICK

'You'll have someone's eye out with those!'

5	*vihta*	3	*koumm*
6	*guhta*	4	*nellj*
7	*cieza*	5	*vitt*
8	*gávcci*	6	*kutt*
9	*ovcci*	7	*ciccâm*
0	*logi*	8	*kääu'c*
		9	*ååuc*
		10	*loé*

nari Sami

lthough spoken by some people in the egion around Lake Inarinjärvi, Inari Sami s rarely written and seems to be heading for xtinction.

ello	*Tierva*
ioodbye	*Mana dearvan*
hank you	*Takkâ*
es	*Kal*
o	*Ij*
low are you?	*Maht mana?*
m fine	*Pyereest mana*

1	*ohta*
2	*kyeh'ti*
3	*ulma*
4	*nelji*
5	*vitta*
0	*love*

icolt Sami

'his rare language (Finnish: *kolttasaame*) is poken by approximately 600 Sami people /ho live in Sevettijärvi and Nellim villages. Seing refugees from the Petsamo region which was annexed by the Soviet Union), ley maintain Russian Orthodox traditions. colt Sami contains some Russian loan vords.

iello	*Tiõrv*
ioodbye	*Kuáddu teárvan*
hank you	*Spässep*
es	*Kaéll*
lo	*Ij*
low are you?	*Mä'htt maan?*
m fine	*Puârast maan*

1	*õhtt*
2	*kue'htt*

WARNING

Visitors to Lapland should keep in mind the region's history – German troops destroyed much of Lapland during WWII – as it's a reason why many Lapps are inclined to treat foreigners with suspicion. Even though Finnish trekkers may cause more harm, it is always foreigners who are accused.

When using wilderness huts or camping sites, be careful with fire, replace all wood and food you take from open huts, carry out all rubbish – and don't tease the reindeer.

Rovaniemi

• pop 22,000 ☎ 016

Rovaniemi is the capital of and gateway to Lapland. The town itself is relatively uninteresting, built from a plan by Alvar Aalto (with the main streets radiating out from Hallituskatu in the shape of reindeer antlers) after its complete destruction by Germans in 1944. Until that time, Rovaniemi had been classified as a *kauppala*, or a trade centre. Hidden landmines remained for years following WWII.

Rovaniemi's proximity to Napapiiri (the Arctic Circle) means that tour buses thunder through year-round. Rovaniemi is also a good base for activities such as dog or reindeer sledding, white-water rafting, skiing and touring by snowmobile. It's a friendly place for the budget traveller.

Information

Tourist Offices The Rovaniemi tourist office (☎ 346 270) at Koskikatu 1 is an excellent source of information for all of

LAPLAND & OULU

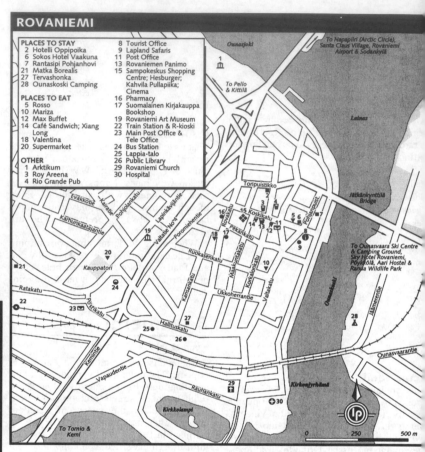

ROVANIEMI

PLACES TO STAY
2 Hotelli Oppipoika
6 Sokos Hotel Vaakuna
7 Rantasipi Pohjanhovi
21 Matka Borealis
27 Tervashonka
28 Ounaskoski Camping

PLACES TO EAT
5 Rosso
10 Mariza
12 Max Buffet
14 Café Sandwich; Xiang Long
18 Valentina
20 Supermarket

OTHER
1 Arktikum
3 Roy Areena
4 Rio Grande Pub

8 Tourist Office
9 Lapland Safaris
11 Post Office
13 Rovaniemen Panimo
15 Sampokeskus Shopping Centre; Hesburger; Kahvila Pullapiika; Cinema
16 Pharmacy
17 Suomalainen Kirjakauppa Bookshop
19 Rovaniemi Art Museum
22 Train Station & R-kioski
23 Main Post Office & Tele Office
24 Bus Station
25 Lappia-talo
26 Public Library
29 Rovaniemi Church
30 Hospital

Lapland. It's open from 8 am to 6 pm weekdays, and from 11.30 am to 4 pm weekends from June to late August. At other times, hours are from 8 am to 4 pm weekdays.

Etiäinen (☎ 362 526) at Napapiiri (see the Around Rovaniemi section) is the information centre for the national parks and trekking regions, with information on hiking and fishing in Lapland. The office also sells maps and fishing permits, and books cottages. It is open from 10 am to 5 pm daily.

Post & Communications The main post office is at Postikatu 1, near the train and bus stations. The telephone office is next door. More central is the post office at Koskikatu 9.

Internet Resources & Library The public library at Hallituskatu 9 has two Internet terminals and a newspaper reading room with foreign periodicals. Hours are from 11 am to 8 pm weekdays, and from 10 am to 4 pm Saturday; the reading room is also open from noon to 4 pm Sunday.

Travel Agencies Lapland Safaris (☎ 331 200, fax 331 1222), next door to the tourist office, is the largest and best established of Rovaniemi's tour operators. It has a weekly tour program for winter and summer. There are many other tour operators near the main hotels, offering river cruises, white-water rafting, fishing, visits to reindeer farms and so on.

Bookshop Suomalainen Kirjakauppa at Rovakatu 24 sells English-language paperbacks, and Lapland maps. The R-kioski at the train station has imported newspapers and magazines.

Left Luggage The train station has a left-luggage counter and large 24-hour lockers that cost 20 mk. The bus station has small lockers and a luggage room.

Medical & Emergency Services The pharmacy at Rovakatu 11 is open from 9 am to 5.30 pm weekdays. There is a hospital at Sairaalakatu, near the Rovaniemi church.

In a general emergency call ☎ 112, for police call ☎ 10022 and for a doctor dial ☎ 10023.

Arktikum

The glass-roofed Arktikum at Pohjoisranta (☎ 317 840) is one of the best museums in Finland. It's really two superb museums under one roof: the Provincial Museum of Lapland, and the Arctic Centre. Exhibits and interactive displays focus on Arctic flora and fauna as well as the Sami and other people of Arctic Europe, Asia and North America. Arktikum is open from 10 am to 8 pm daily in July and August, and to 7 pm daily in May and June. At other times it's open from 10 am to 6 pm Tuesday to Sunday. Entry is 50 mk for adults (40 mk for students, 20 mk for children).

Lappia-talo

Lappia-talo (☎ 322 2745) on Hallituskatu is a concert hall designed by Alvar Aalto. Guided tours, given from 10 am to 2pm Monday to Friday in summer, are 10 mk.

The adjacent library and town hall were also designed by Aalto.

Rovaniemi Art Museum

The museum at Lapinkävijäntie 4 has temporary exhibitions of contemporary art. It is open from 10 am to 5 pm Tuesday to Sunday. Admission is 20 mk.

Rovaniemi Church

The church at Kirkkotie 1 was completed in 1950, replacing the one destroyed during WWII. The fresco above the altar depicts a Christ figure emerging from Lappish scenery. The church is open from 9 am to 9 pm daily from June to late August.

Activities & Organised Tours

Providing that you have the funds for it, Rovaniemi is a terrific base from which to sample 'typically Lappish' activities. The large numbers of tourists here means that tours go out daily during the summer and winter high seasons.

To tour a **reindeer farm**, you must book with any of the operators that have offices near the main hotels. Snowmobile, husky and reindeer **safaris** are popular in winter. Summer tours include river cruises, **white-water rafting** and **fishing** expeditions. Tours range from 200 to 700 mk per person.

For bookings contact one of the travel agencies in town (see the Travel Agencies section earlier) or the tourist office.

Special Events

Rovaniemi is as busy in winter as it is in summer – and perhaps even busier. With the Arctic Circle – and Santa Claus – close by, there are plenty of festive activities in December celebrating Christmas. The Northern Lights Festival in February offers a variety of sports and arts events. In March Rovaniemi hosts the Ounasvaara Winter Games, with skiing and ski jumping competitions. Jutajaiset, a festival in June, showcases folk music, dance and other Lappish traditions.

LAPLAND & OULU

The Northern Lights

The northern lights, or aurora borealis, are a vibrant, beautiful sight, and they are visible at most times of year to observers standing at or above the Arctic Circle (latitude 66°), which includes a large portion of Lapland. They're especially striking during the long, dark nights of a Finnish winter.

The aurora appears as curtains of greenish-white light stretching east to west across the sky for thousands of kilometres. At its lower edge, the aurora typically shades to a crimson-red glow. Hues of blue and violet can also be seen. The lights seem to shift and swirl in the night sky – they can almost be said to dance.

The Northern Lights have a less famous southern counterpart, the aurora australis or southern lights, which encircles the South Pole. Both are oval in shape with a diameter of approximately two thousand kilometres.

These auroral storms, however eerie, are quite natural. They're created when energy particles (called photons) from the Sun bombard the Earth. The photons are deflected towards the the north and south poles by the Earth's magnetic field. There they hit the earth's outer atmosphere, 100 to 1,000 km above ground, causing highly charged electrons to collide with molecules of nitrogen and oxygen. The excess energy from these collisions creates the colourful lights we see in the sky.

The ancients had other explanations for the spectacle: the Greeks described it as 'blood rain'; the Inuit attributed the phenomenon to 'sky dwellers'; and the ancient inhabitants of Lapland believed it was caused by a giant fox swishing its tail above the Arctic tundra.

Places to Stay

Camping *Ounaskoski Camping* (☎ 345 304, Jäämerentie 1), on the river front opposite the town centre, charges 95 mk per camp site. It's open from June to late August.

There is also a small *camping ground* (☎ 369 045) at Ounasvaara Ski Centre open during summer (see the Around Rovaniemi section).

Hostels HI-affiliated *Tervashonka* (☎/fax 344 644, Hallituskatu 16), open year-round, is a very basic hostel with dorm beds from 85 mk and a kitchen. Reception is closed daily from 10 am to 5 pm.

In the south-eastern suburb of Pöykkölä, HI-affiliated *Aari Hostel* (☎/fax 362 906), open from June to mid-August, charges 105 to 135 mk per person and has a kitchen and sauna. Take bus No 6.

Guesthouse *Matka Borealis* (☎ 342 0130, Asemieskatu 1), opposite the train station, is a simple guesthouse, clean and friendly with singles/doubles from 180/250 mk.

Hotels There are a dozen big hotels i Rovaniemi. *Hotelli Oppipoika* (☎ 338 811, Korkalonkatu 33) is one of the cheapes charging 410/490 mk for rooms (340/42 mk in summer and on weekends).

Rantasipi Pohjanhovi (☎ 33711, fa 313 997, Pohjanpuistikko 2) is the olde hotel in Rovaniemi. It has a legendar restaurant with live music. Rooms ar from 620/710 mk (390/520 mk summe and weekends).

The *Sokos Hotel Vaakuna* (☎ 332 21, fax 332 2199, Koskikatu 4) is probably th finest hotel in town, with rooms fro 540/640 mk. All rooms are 450 mk i summer.

Sky Hotel Rovaniemi (☎ 335 3311, fa 318 789, Ounasvaarantie) is 3km east (the town centre at the top of Ounasvaa Hill. Rooms cost 450/560 mk, with dis counts in summer.

Places to Eat

Rovaniemi has plenty of grillis and hamburger restaurants, including *Hesburger* in the Sampokeskus shopping centre. Also here is *Kahvila Pullapiika*, a café that's *the* meeting place in Rovaniemi, for all ages.

Café Sandwich (Koskikatu 11) is good for 20 mk sandwiches. Next door, *Xiang Long* serves reasonably priced Chinese food.

Cheery *Mariza (Ruokasenkatu 2)* serves excellent, home-cooked Finnish food from 35 mk. It is only open weekdays until 3 pm.

Jux Buffet (Koskikatu 9) isn't particularly good, but offers all-you-can-eat pizza, pasta, salad and chicken wings for 40 mk (pizza and salad only, 30 mk).

Rosso (Koskikatu 4) offers good pizza, pasta and steaks from 45 mk. *Valentina (Rovakatu 21)* is a pleasant café.

There is a *supermarket* on the kauppatori (market square), which is near the train and bus stations.

Entertainment

Rovaniemen Panimo on Koskikatu is a popular pub that makes its own 20 mk brews. However, the best spot for a beer under the midnight sun is the *Roy Areena* terrace, next to the Sampokeskus shopping centre.

Rio Grande (Korkalonkatu 32) bills itself as 'the Arctic Circle rock pub'.

Inside the Sampokeskus shopping centre you'll find a *cinema*, usually offering recent American releases subtitled in Swedish and Finnish.

The town's big hotels offer nightclubs and dancing. Cover charge is around 30 mk on weekends.

Shopping

Sami handicrafts made of reindeer skin and horn, or of Arctic birch, are popular souvenirs. Trekkers may want to buy a *kuksa* (carved birch cup). The traditional Sami costume, which is very colourful, and handmade Sami hats, mittens and shoes are also swift-selling souvenirs.

The widest selection of souvenirs (and decent prices) can be found in shops at the Arctic Circle (see the Around Rovaniemi section). In the centre, try Lauri-Tuotteet at Pohjolankatu 25.

J Marttiinin Puukkotehdas at Marttiinintie 6 is the most famous knife manufacturer in Finland. The shop is connected to the factory. You can buy *puukkos* (knives) cheaper here than in other places.

Getting There & Away

Air Finnair has daily flights from many Finnish cities. There are four or five flights a day between Helsinki and Rovaniemi, some going via Oulu.

Bus Rovaniemi is the major bus travel hub in Lapland. Express buses travel to Muonio, Enontekiö (Ounas-Pallas National Park) and Kilpisjärvi in the west, to Sodankylä, Inari, Karigasniemi and Utsjoki in the east, and north to Norway. There is a daily bus between Oulu and Rovaniemi (3½ hours).

Train There are four trains daily from Helsinki via Oulu, two of which are night trains. The trip from Helsinki takes approximately 12 hours. All trains terminate in Rovaniemi. There is one train connection daily to Kemijärvi, farther north.

Car & Motorcycle Rovaniemi is on road No 4, approximately 840km north of Helsinki.

Getting Around

To/From the Airport The Rovaniemi airport is 10km north of the town centre. Buses meet each arriving flight; the trip costs 20 mk. Airport buses leave the bus station 50 minutes before flight departure, picking up at several hotels in the centre.

Car & Motorcycle Most major car rental agencies are represented, and have offices in the centre and at the airport. Try Hertz (☎ 313 300) at Pohjanpuistikko 2 or Budget (☎ 312 266) at Koskikatu 9.

LAPLAND & OULU

Around Rovaniemi

☎ 016

NAPAPIIRI (THE ARCTIC CIRCLE)

The Arctic Circle is the southernmost line where the midnight sun can be seen. Napapiiri (the Arctic Circle) crosses the main Rovaniemi-Sodankylä road about 8km north of Rovaniemi (take bus No 8 or 10). The official **Arctic Circle marker** is here, and so is the 'official' **Santa Claus Village**. Gift shops offer a surprisingly good selection of handicrafts and souvenir trinkets. The **Santa Claus Main Post Office** (address: FIN-96930 Arctic Circle) receives close to a million letters each year from children all over the world.

For kids, there are computerised portraits with jolly ol' St Nick, and for adults, there is a hokey 'Arctic Circle Initiation Ceremony'. Groups have great fun crossing the line painted on the asphalt (supposedly marking the circle) in order to be awarded their Arctic Circle certificates. Note that in reality, since all celestial bodies affect each other, the Arctic Circle can shift several metres daily. By 2000 the 'real' Arctic Circle will be near the Rovaniemi airport.

Also here is Etiäinen, the information centre for national parks and trekking regions (see the earlier Tourist Offices section).

The Santa Claus village is open from 8 am to 8 pm daily June to mid-August, from 9 am to 6 pm daily from mid-August to late September, and from 10 am to 5 pm daily at other times. Admission is free.

Santapark, a Christmas-themed amusement park, opened in 1998 at Syvasenvaara Mountain, 2km west of the Rovaniemi Airport on the Rovaniemi to Ivalo main road. Local buses connect the park with the city centre. Additionally, there is free shuttle service between Santa Claus Village and Santapark, or in winter you can pay a fee to travel by snowmobile or reindeer sleigh between the two attractions. Santapark is build inside a cavern in the mountain and features a Magic Sleigh Ride, a Christ-

mas Carousel, a theatre, a cafeteria and, course, Santa Claus himself. Hours are 1 am to 8 pm daily from early December 1 mid-January and from early June to lat August, as well as during the Easter holida period. A more limited schedule is in effe during other times of year. Admission is 9 mk adult, 65 mk child, and discount tick packages are available for families. See th Web site www.santapark.com/ for more in formation.

OUNASVAARA SKI CENTRE

The Ounasvaara Ski Centre, 3km east the town centre, is open year-round. I winter it offers five downhill ski slop and three ski jumps, plus a total of 123k of cross-country skiing tracks. The longe downhill run is 600m with a vertical dro of 140m. Skiing equipment can be rente at the Sky Hotel Rovaniemi, downhi equipment at the Ounasvaara Slalo Centre. In summer, Ounasvaara has a t bogganing run, open from noon to 8 p daily from mid-June to mid-August. chairlift ride up and a toboggan run dow costs about 20 mk.

RANUA WILDLIFE PARK

The town of Ranua, 80km south o Rovaniemi on road No 78, is home to th excellent Ranua Wildlife Park (☎ 35 1921), the northernmost of all such park and a popular day trip from Rovaniemi. I 30 mammal and 30 bird species – incluc ing brown bears, forest reindeer, owls an wolverines – are native to Finland an Scandinavia and are housed in spaciou natural enclosures. It might be your onl chance to see *hirvi* – the elusive Finnis moose. The park is open daily year-roun Hours are from 9 am to 8 pm daily fro June to mid-August, with shorter hou during the rest of the year. Admission 50 mk.

There are daily buses to Ranua fro Oulu and Kajaani, and several daily co nections from Rovaniemi.

Is Santa Finnish?

Santa Claus, a.k.a. Jolly Ol' Saint Nick, is popularly known as a roly-poly fellow with a long white beard, clad in a red, fur-trimmed suit, who drives a sled and lives at the North Pole. With this kind of lifestyle Santa certainly seems Finnish. However, the historic St Nicholas – the real man behind the Santa myth – wouldn't have know a reindeer from a rhinoceros and would have melted in a typical Santa suit, as he lived in temperate present-day Turkey!

The story of the real St Nicholas is this: many centuries ago, a poor peasant, father of three daughters, did not have enough money for their wedding dowries. To ensure that at least two of the daughters would have money enough to attract husbands, the man decided that he would have to sell the youngest daughter into slavery. One sad day the heartsick father announced his decision: the youngest daughter would leave the following morning. The soon-to-be-sainted Nicholas, who may or may not have been a chimney sweep, got word of the terrible situation, crept into the family's house while they were sleeping and magically filled a sock with golden coins. The youngest daughter was saved, all three daughters were joy-fully married and the whole family lived happily ever after.

Since then Santa Claus (Santa means saint; Claus is an abbreviation of Nicholas) has been filling socks with presents every Christmas season. In Finland, Uncle Markus, a famous radio announcer since the 1930s, established the Finnish legend that a gift-giving Santa Claus lived in the Korvatunturi Hill, right at the Russian border. Long before that, in pagan times, Finns had believed in an evil male goat spirit that demanded gifts on the shortest day of the year. The two stories, of Santa and the evil goat, eventually blended, which is why the Finnish name for Santa is *Joulupukki*, which literally translates as 'Christmas stud goat'.

These days Santa Claus is big business, with many nations claiming to be the homeland of the generous Father Christmas. But Finland seems to be a strong contender as the *real* home of the jolly fat man. Just north of Rovaniemi, right on the Arctic Circle (Finnish: Napapiiri), is a post office – officially named Santa Claus' Main Post Office – that to date has received more than five million children's letters addressed to 'Santa Claus' in dozens of languages. In 1996 alone, there were almost a million letters, arriving at rates from 100 per day in the middle of the year to about 3200 per day during the holiday season. The countries with the most letter writers are Great Britain, Poland and Japan, but children from countries such as Pakistan, Brazil and Kenya also send wish lists. How could that many children be wrong?

If Santa really *is* Finnish, he must have a Web site – and he does at www.santaclaus.posti.fi/ Here you can email a letter to Santa and get one in return. But ho, ho, ho – the service isn't free.

West Lapland

Lapland is not all wilderness and fell-walking. The south-west corner of Lapland is usually referred to as Sea Lapland, and is relatively urban, industrialised and prosperous. Moving north, the region is dominated by the mighty Tornionjoki and Muonionjoki rivers, and the highest mountains in Finland.

This section covers the western route to Norway, from Kemi to Kilpisjärvi. The main road (road No 21) follows the Finnish border with Sweden, and there are numerous crossing points. See the Getting There & Away chapter at the start of the book for more details on border crossings.

KEMI

- **pop 25,000**   **☎ 016**

Kemi is an industrial town surrounded by huge pulp factories – avoid visiting on windless days. Although the town itself hardly sounds attractive, it is home to one of Lapland's blockbuster attractions: the *Sampo*, an authentic Arctic icebreaker ship. A cruise on the *Sampo* is expensive, but fascinating.

Information

Tourist Office The Kemi tourist office (☎ 259 467, fax 259 468), in the tall town hall building at Valtakatu 26, is open from 8 am to 4 pm daily from early June to late August. At other times it's open from 8 am to 4 pm Monday to Friday.

Post The post office is at Asemakatu 12 near the train station. It's open from 9 am to 8 pm Monday to Friday.

Internet Resources & Library The public library, at the kauppatori, is open from 11 am to 8 pm Monday to Thursday, from 11 am to 6 pm Friday and from 10 am to 4 pm Saturday. There are two Internet terminals.

Medical & Emergency Services In a general emergency call ☎ 112, for police call ☎ 10022 and for a doctor dial ☎ 10023.

There is a pharmacy (☎ 223 135) on Va takatu.

The Arctic Icebreaker *Sampo*

The highlight of a visit to Kemi is a tri aboard the *Sampo*, an authentic Arctic ice breaker ship – the only one in the world tha accepts passengers. The four hour cruise ir cludes, for the very brave, ice swimming i special drysuits. It's a truly remarkable ex perience.

The *Sampo* sails at noon on Thursday Friday and Saturday from mid-Decembe to late April. The best time to go is when th ice is thickest, which is usually in Marcl The cost is 820 mk per person and booking are advised.

For more information contact Samp Tours (☎ 256 548, fax 256 361), Kaup pakatu 19, 94100 Kemi, or see www .sampotours.com on the Web.

Departures are from Ajos Harbour, 15k south of Kemi.

Gemstone Gallery (Jalokivigalleria)

The Gemstone Gallery in an old seasid customs house at Kauppakatu 29 has a internationally notable collection of ove 3000 beautiful and rare stones and jeweller including a crown that was meant for th king of Finland. The crown was made in th 1980s by the gallery's founder, who create the 'first and only' crown of the king ⟨ Finland from the original drawings. Th gallery is open from 10 am to 8 pm daily i summer and from 10 am to 6 pm daily ⟨ other times. Admission is 25 mk (student and seniors 20 mk, children 10 mk).

Local History & Culture Museun (Kotiseutumuseo)

The open-air museum of local history is i Meripuisto park, near the harbour. Its thre floors of exhibits include historical item from prehistory to more recent tools ar farming equipment. The museum is ope from noon to 6 pm daily from June to lat September, and admission is free.

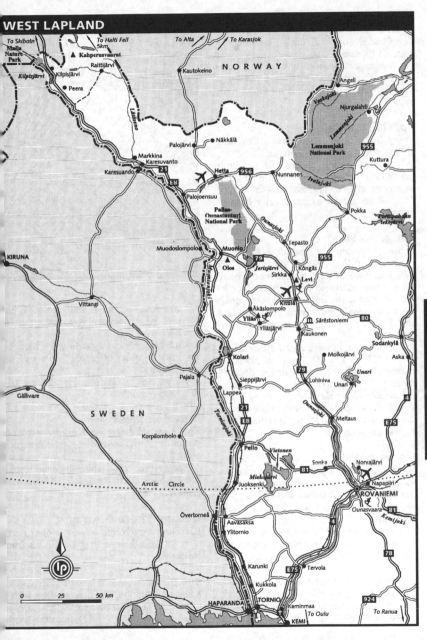

Kemi History Museum (Historiallinen Museo)

The Kemi History Museum at Sauvosaaren-katu 11 does not have permanent collections, just frequently changing exhibitions. It's open from noon to 6 pm daily. The admission fee depends on the current exhibition.

Special Events

Every May, Kemi hosts 'Arctic Comics', an international cartoon festival.

In 1996, the good citizens of Kemi built the 'World's Largest Snow Castle', 13,500 sq metres in size. This has become something of an annual event, usually held in February.

Places to Stay

There are no camping grounds in Kemi.

The HI-affiliated hostel *Turisti* (☎ *250 876, Valtakatu 21-23)*, diagonally opposite the tall town hall, is the cheapest place to stay in Kemi. It doesn't look like much from the outside, but rooms are clean and cost from 90 to 120 mk per person, linen included.

The pleasant, modern *Hotel Palomestari* (☎ *257 117, fax 257 118, Valtakatu 12)* is the cheapest hotel in the centre. Singles/doubles are from 310/370 mk.

Summer Hotel Relletti (☎ *233 541, Miilukatu 1)*, located 2km south of the centre, has rooms from 115/185 mk. It is open from June to mid-August.

Places to Eat

There are plenty of grillis and pizzerias on Valtakatu, but for a break from that routine, *Hoa Phong Lan-Orkidean Kukka* is a good Vietnamese restaurant with lunch specials for 35 mk.

Hullu Pohjola (Meripuistokatu 9) is an 'authentic' Tex-Mex restaurant (open for dinner only). Burritos and fajitas are from 30 mk.

Raatihuone, the finest restaurant in town, is in a charming old villa in Meripuisto park near the local museum. The buffet lunch, served weekdays from 11 am to 2 pm, costs

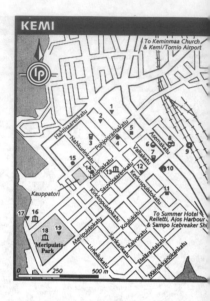

45 mk. Another fine-dining option is the *Sampo*, which serves as a restaurant in summer.

Café Seilari is a tiny café at the harbour. Its outdoor tables offer good views of the pulp factory!

Across the street from Hoa Phong is a large *supermarket*.

Entertainment

The *Kemi Brewery* on Keskuspuistokatu doesn't brew its own beers, but it is a good pub.

For a typical old-fashioned dance restaurant, check out *Ravintola Meripuisto (Valtakatu 22)*.

Getting There & Away

Air The Kemi/Tornio airport is 6km north of town, and there are regular flights from Helsinki.

Bus Buses from Tornio will take you to Kemi train station, and they are free with a train pass. There are also some departures to Muonio to the north and Oulu to the south.

KEMI

PLACES TO STAY
5   Hotel Palomestari
11 Turisti

PLACES TO EAT
1   Supermarket
2   Hoa Phong Lan-Orkidean Kukka
12 Hullu Pohjola
17 Café Seilari
19 Raatihuone

OTHER
3   Kemi Brewery
4   Pharmacy
6   Bus Station
7   Ravintola Meripuisto
8   Post Office
9   Train Station
10 Tourist Office
13 Kemi Historical Museum (Historiallinen Museo)
14 Sampo Tours
15 Public Library
16 Gemstone Gallery (Jalokivigalleria)
18 Local History & Culture Museum (Kotiseutumuseo)

Train There are trains from Helsinki and Rovaniemi to Kemi.

Car & Motorcycle Kemi is on road No 4 116km south of Rovaniemi and 24km south-east of Tornio.

AROUND KEMI
Keminmaa Church

North of Kemi, the 16th century stone Keminmaa Church, opposite the power station on the Kemijoki river, is worth a visit. It contains the mummified Reverend Nikolaus Rungius, who died in 1629. He is reported to have said: 'If my words are untrue, my body will rot. If they are true, my body shall not rot'. So far, only the wooden coffin has rotted – it has had to be changed several times. The church is open from 10 am to 6 pm daily in summer.

Getting There & Away All buses between Kemi and Tornio stop in Keminmaa village,
but the old church is 2km from the bus stop; get off just after the river.

TORNIO
• pop 23,200   ☎ 016

Tornio (Swedish: Torneå) has a twin across the Tornionjoki river – the Swedish town of Haparanda (Finnish: Haaparanta). These towns share tourist brochures, and even a famous golf course – which is probably the main attraction in Tornio. Nearby, the rapids at Kukkolankoski are another highlight. Otherwise there's little to see. Tornio's population is spread over an area that is 10 times larger than Kemi, but Swedish day-trippers help to keep it busy.

Don't forget – Finland's clocks are one hour ahead of those in Sweden.

History

The area along the Tornionjoki has been inhabited since medieval times, when it was the centre for Pirkka tax collectors (who worked for the king of Sweden). The town of Tornio was founded in 1621, and the entire Tornionjoki valley was administered by Sweden until 1809, when it was incorporated into Finland, under Russian suzerainty. In 1821, Haparanda was founded as a Swedish trading town to replace the loss of Tornio to Russia.

Information
Tourist Office The Tornio tourist office (☎ 432 733, matkailu.tourist@tornio.fi) is at the Green Line Centre at the border. It's open from 8 am to 8 pm weekdays, and from 10 am to 8 pm weekends, from June to mid-August. At other times it's open from 8 to 11.30 am and from 12.30 to 4 pm weekdays.

The Haparanda tourist office, with information about Sweden, is also in the Green Line building.

Money There's a 24 hour automated money exchange facility at the Green Line Centre at the border.

Post The post office is at Puutarhakatu 3. Hours are from 9 am to 8 pm weekdays.

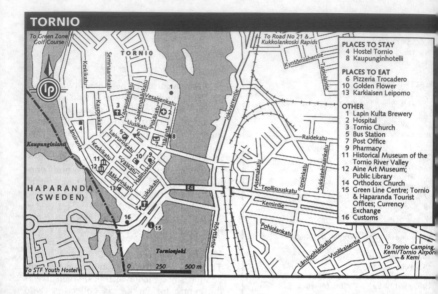

TORNIO

To Green Zone Golf Course

To Road No 21 & Kukkolankoski Rapids

Kyntömiehentie

TORNIO

Keskikatu
Seminaarinkatu
Kauppakatu
Länsiranta
Keskikatu

Kaupunginlahti

HAPARANDA (SWEDEN)

Torniojoki

To STF Youth Hostel

Saarenpäänkatu
Vesaisenkatu
Uusikatu
Lukiokatu
Hallituskatu
Laivurinkatu
Eväliänkatu

Yliaki

Raidekatu

Kokinniementie
Tapiolakatu

Asemakatu
Teollisuuskatu
Röyttänitie
Pohjolankatu
Kemintie

Lansipohjankatu
Vuolukaisentie

Torinkatu
Sukkaltehtaankatu

E4

To Tornio Camping, Kemi/Tornio Airport & Kemi

0   250   500 m

PLACES TO STAY
4 Hostel Tornio
8 Kaupunginhotelli

PLACES TO EAT
6 Pizzeria Trocadero
10 Golden Flower
13 Karkiaisen Leipomo

OTHER
1 Lapin Kulta Brewery
2 Hospital
3 Tornio Church
5 Bus Station
7 Post Office
9 Pharmacy
11 Historical Museum of the Tornio River Valley
12 Aine Art Museum; Public Library
14 Orthodox Church
15 Green Line Centre; Tornio & Haparanda Tourist Offices; Currency Exchange
16 Customs

Internet Resources & Library The public library is at Torikatu 2, next to the Aine Art Museum. It's open from 10 am to 8 pm Monday to Thursday, to 4 pm Friday and to 3 pm Saturday. There are two Internet terminals.

The town's Web site is www.tornio.fi/.

Medical & Emergency Services In a general emergency call ☎ 112, for police call ☎ 10022 and for a doctor dial ☎ 10023.

There is a hospital at Sairaalakatu 1 and a pharmacy at Hallituskatu 14.

Things to See

The **Tornio church** was completed in 1686 and is one of the most beautiful wooden churches in Finland. It is dedicated to the Swedish Queen Eleonora. The church is open weekdays from late May to late August.

The 19th century **Orthodox church** was constructed by order of Tsar Alexander I of Russia. It is open only on request.

The **Aine Art Museum** (Aineen Taide-museo) at Torikatu 2 features a private collection of Veli Aine, a local business tycoon. It features Finnish art from the 19th and 20th centuries. Hours are from 11 am to 7 pm weekdays, and to 5 pm weekends in summer. It is closed Monday at other times. A 5 mk donation is requested.

The **Historical Museum of the Tornio River Valley** (Torniolaakson Maakunta-museo) at Keskikatu 22 has a collection of interesting old artefacts and costumes, although all displays are in Finnish. It is closed on Saturday. Entry is 10 mk.

The **Lapin Kulta Brewery** was founded in 1873, and is situated just north of the centre. Free tours of the brewery plant are offered on weekdays only; call ☎ 43366.

Activities & Organised Tours

Tornio and Haparanda share the 18 hole **Green Zone Golf Course** (☎ 431 711). You can't play golf at midnight (with the sun shining) anywhere else: if you start from the Finnish side at, say, 12.30 am you can hit the next ball in Sweden, yesterday! In all, you cross the international border and time zone four times during a game.

LAPLAND & OULU

Salmon have recently returned to the Tornionjoki which runs through town, and expert local guide Risto Mämmioja (☎ 470 093 or 040-551 1283) will take you **fishing** maximum two persons).

River-rafting trips are popular in summer on the Kukkolankoski rapids (see the Around Tornio section). Rafting tours from 00 mk per person are run by Safaris Unlimited (☎ 253 405 or 040-552 8235), which also offers winter excursions such as snowmobile, reindeer and husky **safaris**. The Tornio tourist office also books rafting trips.

Places to Stay

Tornio Camping (☎ 445 945, Matkailiantie), 2.5km east of the town centre, is open from June to mid-August. Camp sites costs 80 mk, cabins 200 to 260 mk. The place also offers tennis, minigolf, bicycles, boats, canoes and fishing.

Hostel Tornio (☎ 481 682, fax 480 048, Kirkkokatu 1), a kilometre from the train station, was under renovation at the time of writing. It is scheduled to reopen for summer 1999. In Haparanda there's the *STF Youth Hostel* (☎ 0046 611 71, fax 0046 61784, Strandgatan 26), open year-round.

The *Kaupunginhotelli* (☎ 43311, fax 482 020, Itäranta 4) is *the* hotel in Tornio – it's absolutely enormous. Singles/doubles start at 390/490 mk.

Places to Eat

You'll have your choice of *grillis* on Halli-tuskatu and Länsiranta. On Länsiranta you'll also find a few *supermarkets*.

Pizzeria Trocadero (Kemintie 11) has lunch specials (20 mk and up) from 11 am to 3 pm weekdays. *Golden Flower (Eliakenkatu 8)* is a Chinese restaurant that also serves pizza. Weekday lunch specials are 36 mk.

Karkiaisen Leipomo (Länsiranta 9) is an attractive café with superb fresh pastries and *donitsi* (doughnuts) made on the premises.

Getting There & Away
Air The Kemi/Tornio airport is 18km south of town, and there are regular flights to and from Helsinki.

Bus There are a few daily buses from Rovaniemi, and buses from Kemi run almost hourly. Most continue to Haparanda. There are also frequent buses between Haparanda and Tornio, although the distance is so short you could actually walk.

Car & Motorcycle Tornio is 24km northwest of Kemi on road No 4. North from Tornio is road No 21 (E8) which runs along the Swedish border to Norway.

AROUND TORNIO
Kukkolankoski Rapids
The Kukkolankoski rapids on the Tornionjoki, 15km north of Tornio on road No 21, are the longest free-flowing rapids in Finland. The length is 3500m and the fall is just under 14m. For information on whitewater rafting at Kukkolankoski, see the Activities & Organised Tours section under Tornio.

Kukkolankoski has been a favoured fishing place since at least the Middle Ages. Today, local folk still catch whitefish the traditional way, using long-handled nets. An annual whitefish festival is celebrated on the last weekend of July.

You can sample grilled *siika* (whitefish) at either Café Myllynpirtti or Kukkolankoski Grill Café.

On the Swedish side of the rapids is a fishing museum, open daily in summer, but there's no bridge across the river here.

PELLO
• pop 5500   ☎ 016

Pello is a border village with a twin village on the Swedish side of the Tornionjoki. The Pello tourist office is near the bridge to Sweden.

North of Pello is a **monument** to the French expedition that did scientific research and measurements on Kittisvaara

Hill in 1736. The team was able to determine from these measurements – together with similar ones taken in Peru – that Newton had been right about the globe not being perfectly round.

The biggest annual event in Pello is the **Poikkinainti Festival**, held during a week in July to celebrate cross-border marriages. A wedding ceremony is conducted in the middle of the river.

Places to Stay
Camping Pello (☎ *512 494, Nivanpääntie 58*), north-west of the centre, has 80 mk tent sites, and some cabins. It's open from June to late August.

Motelli Jätkänkolo (☎ *513 131, fax 512 855, Pellontie*) has rooms from 120 mk per person and is open year-round. There are several other guest houses and hotels in and around the centre.

Getting There & Away
There are three daily buses from Kemi (150km away) via Tornio. The same buses return from Muonio.

LAPPEA
☎ 016

There are **rapids** worth seeing in Lappea, where the Tornionjoki and Muonionjoki meet. Sweden is just a stone's throw away.

Lappean Loma (see Places to Stay & Eat) organises **raft tours** along the Tornionjoki, which marks the international border between Sweden and Finland. If you get a group together, you can float down the river on a large raft, fish for salmon from the river, prepare your meals aboard and even bathe in a raft sauna. The rafts can even negotiate the Kukkolankoski rapids farther south!

Places to Stay & Eat
One of the best hostels in Lapland, the HI-affiliated *Lappean Loma* (☎ *563 155, fax 563 165*) has beds from 80 to 110 mk, and a heavenly smoke sauna. Other amenities include a café that serves full meals, plus a kitchen and laundry. The place is open year-

round and arranges a number of activities including white-water rafting, canoeing and fishing.

Getting There & Away
Lappea is only accessible by private vehicle. From the main road (road No 21) follow signs to the minor road that runs between Pello and Kolari along the river.

KOLARI
☎ 016

For travellers, Kolari is chiefly a gateway to the busy skiing centre of Ylläs, 35km north-east of the village centre. It is also possible to cross over the Tornionjoki to Sweden from Kolari.

The village of Kolari has a bank, a post office and some supermarkets. The tourist office (☎ 561 721) is at Isonpalontie 2.

Places to Stay
The quiet and friendly *Vaattovaaran Retkeilymaja* (☎ *561 086*), open year-round, is an HI-affiliated hostel about 700m from the village centre. Rooms are clean and have a TV. The sauna is free for guests and there is a well equipped kitchen and a laundry. Beds cost 70 to 100 mk.

Getting There & Away
Bus Buses run between Kolari and Rovaniemi every weekday. There are two buses a day between Kemi and Kolari.

Train During the winter holiday season from mid-February to mid-April, there are trains from Helsinki to Kolari (the last stop for the northbound train). The train station is approximately 3km north-east of the village centre.

YLLÄS
☎ 016

Ylläs, 35km north-east of Kolari, is the highest fell in Finland to offer downhill skiing. Not surprisingly, it is also one of Finland's most popular skiing centres. There are plenty of events in winter, and a music festival in July. Mountain biking is a popular summer activity in the Ylläs area.

Keep in mind that many restaurants and some hotels in Ylläs are only open during the winter ski season.

Orientation

On either side of the mountain are the villages Äkäslompolo and Ylläsjärvi. Both are typical ski resort towns filled with upscale hotels and holiday cottages, although Ylläsjärvi tends to be the quieter of the two.

Information

For tourist information, contact Ylläksen Matkailu Oy (☎ 561 721, fax 561 337) or Ylläs Holiday Service (☎ 569 666). For accommodation booking, get in touch with Ylläs Majoituspalvelut (☎ 482 000 in Ylläsjärvi, ☎ 0208-692 585 in Äkäslompolo).

Skiing

Ylläs, one of the largest ski resorts in Finland, boasts 34 downhill slopes and 17 lifts, plus special areas for snowboarders. The vertical drop is 463km and the longest run is 3km. Cross-country skiing trails total some 250km.

Lift passes are 80 mk per day or 360 mk per week. Renting equipment also costs 80 mk per day or 350 mk per week.

The ski season usually runs from November to May.

Mountain Biking

In summer Ylläs is a mecca for mountain-biking enthusiasts. Hotel Ylläshumina (☎ 569 501) in Äkäslompolo rents bikes for 90 to 180 mk per day. It also sells maps and arranges guided mountain-biking tours.

Ylläs Holiday Service (☎ 569 666) also rents mountain bikes and offers guided biking tours.

Places to Stay

There are plenty of empty hotel rooms and cottages around Ylläs during summer. In winter, accommodation is harder to come by, and also is more expensive. Budget trav-

ellers might want to consider staying at the hostel in Kolari.

Hotel Seitapirtti (☎ 569 211, fax 569 360) in Äkäslompolo is one of the most reasonably priced hotels, with singles/doubles from 170/340 mk. Also in Äkäslompolo, *Äkäshotelli* (☎ 553 000, fax 553 368) has 41 rooms and 44 cottages, with rates from 385/540 mk in high season and 300/360 mk at other times.

In Ylläsjärvi, *Ylläsrinne* (☎ 565 441, fax 565 451) has rooms from 285/370 mk, while nearby *Yllästokka* (☎ 565 421, fax 565 422) offers rooms and cottages from 250/300 mk.

Finnair has package arrangements with local hotels; inquire at a travel agency for more information.

Getting There & Away

Air During the ski season, there is a shuttle service from Kittilä airport to Ylläsjärvi (40 mk one way) and Äkäslompolo (60 mk one way).

Bus If you arrive in Kolari by train there will be a connecting bus that goes first to Ylläsjärvi, then to Äkäslompolo.

A few long-distance buses travel via Äkäslompolo each week. For Ylläsjärvi, catch one of the post buses that run on weekdays between Kolari and Kittilä

KITTILÄ

● **pop 3000**   ☎ 016

According to legend, Kittilä was named after Kitti, a daughter of the mighty witch Päiviö, who appears in local fairy tales.

The village is one of the main centres of Lapland: its airport is served by regular flights and road connections are good. Kittilä is a good base for those heading 20km north to Levi for skiing and other outdoor activities.

Things to See

The old wooden **church** of Kittilä was designed by CL Engel and completed in 1831. It's open weekdays in summer. The **Taidemuseo Einari Junttila** in central Kittilä commemorates a local artist, who once lived in that place (closed Sunday). The Kittilä **open-air museum**, 3km south of the village, features a collection of traditional buildings. It's open from Tuesday to Sunday in summer.

Special Events

At the beginning of July, Kittilä hosts a traditional market that attracts folks from all over Lapland.

Early September sees a marathon race, which is probably the northernmost regularly organised such event in the world.

Places to Stay & Eat

The HI-affiliated *Retkeilymaja Majari* (☎ *642 238, Valtatie 5)* is conveniently situated in the centre of Kittilä. It is open from mid-June to mid-August and has dormitory beds from 70 to 90 mk.

Hostel Kittilä (☎ 642 002 or 0400-962 915, Valtatie 220) is also HI-affiliated, and open from June to mid August. It charges 75 mk per person. Meals are available, and there is a kitchen and sauna.

At the northern end of the village, *Hotelli Kittilä (☎ 643 201, fax 643 222, Valtatie 49)* has doubles priced from 370 mk.

Leilan Pihvi ja Pizza is a grilli, pizzeria and café that also sells fresh bakery products.

Getting There & Away

There are daily flights between Helsinki and Kittilä. The airport is 4km north of town.

Four buses a day run between Rovaniemi and Kittilä. All buses stop at the K petrol station.

AROUND KITTILÄ
Molkojärvi

This beautiful, remote village, south-east of Kittilä, has 100 inhabitants, an old village shop and the excellent *Kittilän Eräkeskus* (☎/*fax 016-655 323)* with bed-and-breakfast accommodation in very clean rooms, each with TV. Singles/doubles cost 105/140 mk. The estate has two small museums and a café. Activities include fishing, hunting, berry picking, skiing and snowmobile safaris. There are also reindeer.

To reach Molkojärvi from Kittilä, exit the main road No 79 at Lohiniva and follow the signs along the minor road for 22km.

Särestöniemi

Visiting this unusual museum makes for a fine day trip from Kittilä. Reidar Särestöniemi, who died in 1981, was the best-known painter from Lapland. Except for the years when he studied painting in Helsinki and in Leningrad (now St Petersburg), he always lived in Särestö in Kittilä. His home has been converted into a museum, where his big, colourful paintings are exhibited, together with some drawings and graphic works. You can visit Reidar's studio and gallery, and have coffee in the café.

To get there, drive 20km south of Kittilä to Kaukonen village, then proceed 9km east. The museum is open daily from mid-February to mid-October. Tickets cost 30 mk adult, 15 mk student.

SIRKKA & LEVI
☎ 016

Levi is a major skiing centre that lies just east of Sirkka, a typical Lappish village. Both places are about 20km north of Kittilä.

Skiing is the main activity in the winter months, and the ski season usually runs from November to May. In summer and autumn, trekking and mountain biking are the main outdoor activities.

Many independent tour operators are in Sirkka and Levi, making this a good place to join organised tours – from canoeing in summer to dog sledding in winter – although these types of activities tend to be priced out of reach of the average budget traveller.

Orientation

Sirkka has all services, including a post office and shops. Levi has three hotels, 11 restaurants and a nightclub.

Information

The tourist office (☎ 644 555, fax 643 469) is at Myllyojantie 2 in Sirkka. For accommodation booking contact Levin Matkailu Oy (☎ 643 466, fax 643 469), a travel agency in Levi. It also books snowmobile safaris, dog sled treks and reindeer rides.

Skiing

Levi ski centre (☎ 641 246, fax 641 247) has 36 downhill slopes and 16 lifts. The vertical drop is approximately 325m, and the longest run is 2500m. There are two half-pipes for snowboarders and several ski runs for children.

Opportunities for cross-country skiing are also good, with cross-country trails totalling 230km. There are routes to Aakenustunturi Hill, Särestöniemi and other places. On longer ski treks, you can stay overnight in wilderness huts, which have supplies of firewood.

Downhill skiing tickets are 95 mk per day or 455 mk per week. Equipment rental costs 80 mk per day or 350 mk per week. Downhill, telemark, and cross-country skis, snowboards, sleds and snowshoes are all available for rental.

Canoeing

The long Ounasjoki is one of the best canoeing routes in Lapland. The river runs from Hetta in the north to Rovaniemi in the south, and passes the small villages of Raattama, Sirkka, Kittilä and Kaukonen. Equipment can be rented at Pole Star Safaris (☎ 641 688 or 049-391 090, fax 641 687) at the Levin Portti tourist centre. Companies in Kittilä also offer equipment rentals.

Places to Stay & Eat

Levi is one of Finland's most popular winter holiday centres. If you're on a budget or are looking for relative solitude, avoid the busy holiday weeks in February and March.

Levin Matkailumaja (☎ 641 126, fax 641 543) in Sirkka is a pleasant, clean guesthouse with slightly lower rates than regular hotels. Its restaurant serves home-cooked traditional meals.

Hullu Poro (The Crazy Reindeer; ☎ 641 506, fax 641 568), a bit off the main Sirkka to Levi road, has 44 apartments and six cabins, plus a very popular restaurant. Rooms are from 360 to 860 mk.

Levitunturi Spa (☎ 646 301, fax 641 434, myyntipalvelu@levinmatkailukeskus.fi), opposite the tourist office near the main Sirkka to Levi road, is a spa with a pool and Turkish bath. This large establishment has a restaurant and singles/doubles from 380/480 mk.

Sirkantähti (☎ 640 100, fax 641 494) is a good hotel and restaurant in Sirkka, with rooms from 380/480 mk.

Getting There & Away

Sirkaa and Levi are on road No 79, 170km north of Rovaniemi. Some buses between Muonio and Rovaniemi stop at Sirkka. From the airport at Kittilä (15km to the south) you would need to take a taxi.

AROUND SIRKKA & LEVI
Köngäs
☎ 016

Köngäs is an attractive little village 8km north of Sirkka. If you're interested in the world of **Arctic sled dogs**, that's a good reason to visit Köngäs. Polar Speed Tours (☎/fax 653 447 or 657 111), 99140 Köngäs, has a husky farm a few kilometres east of Köngäs on the road to Inari. In summer you can take a guided tour of the farm or just visit the huskies. In winter, it offers one to five-day dog sledding safaris, with accommodation in wilderness huts. Two-hour sled tours with a husky team, including a meal at a camp fire, cost approximately 300 mk per person, while three-day tours with the huskies, including transport, accommodation, all meals, equipment, sauna and a guide, cost about 3000 mk per person.

Places to Stay & Eat The HI-affiliated hostel *Sillankorva* (☎ 653 428) is situated in Köngäs near the river. It's open year-round and charges 115 mk per person for beds in pleasant cottages. The hostel serves meals, and also has a kitchen and a sauna.

LAPLAND & OULU

MUONIO
☎ 016

This small village offers more commercial services than anything north of here until Norway. The wooden **church** in Muonio dates from 1817. When the village was burned during WWII, the church was somehow spared. A local **museum** is nearby.

The Muonio tourist office (☎ 534 305 or 534 213) is in the village centre at Puthaanrannantie 15.

South of the centre on road No 21, the *Harriniva Holiday Centre* (☎ 532 491, fax 532 750) rents out canoes and kayaks for exploring the Muonionjoki, as well as fishing equipment for those who'd like to catch salmon or grayling. There are mountain bike rentals, and guided mountain bike or hiking tours. Harriniva has a husky farm with 160 huskies, and a guided tour is 35 mk. In winter, dog sledding safaris are possible. In summer, the centre offers daily guided white-water rafting trips, that last approximately one hour and cost 110 mk. After rafting, you get a 'diploma' and coffee. The owner is a lot of fun and speaks good English. Harriniva has rooms and cottages from about 150 mk per person.

In the centre of Muonio, the HI-affiliated *Lomamaja Pekonen* (☎/fax 532 237, Lahenrannantie) has rooms and cottages from 130 mk per person. It is open year-round, and has a kitchen and sauna.

Getting There & Away
There are two buses a day between Rovaniemi and Muonio. The trip takes approximately four hours. From Kemi and Tornio, there are two buses each weekday and one on Saturday.

HETTA
☎ 016

Hetta, previously known as Enontekiö, is the centre of the municipality of Enontekiö (population 2450, of which 400 are Sami), and a good place to start trekking and exploration of the nearby area. Connections to Norway are good, too. Hetta is not a big place, with just a few dozen houses on either side of the road, but travel services are good. The popular Pallastunturi Trek brings many travellers to the village.

Information
There is a municipal tourist office (☎ 556 211) at the crossroads of the Hetta main road and the road to Norway. It's open daily in summer.

The Fell Lapland Nature Centre (☎ 533 056) at Peuratie provides information about Pallas-Ounastunturi National Park.

Things to See
In the centre of Hetta is **Enontekiö church**, built in 1952 with the financial help of American churches. The organ was a gift from Germany. The church has an altar mosaic that pictures Christ blessing Lapland and its people. On the eastern side of Hetta, 3km from the church, there is an interesting **Sami museum**. Both places are open daily in summer.

Places to Stay & Eat
In the centre, *Hetan Majatalo* (☎ 521 351, fax 521 362) is a year-round guest house with singles/doubles from 145/210 mk.

Ounasloma (☎ 521 055 or 049-396 510) is open year-round and has cottages and camping facilities at the river near the tourist office.

Farther east beyond the village, *Hotelli Hetta* (☎ 521 361, fax 521 049) has rooms from 340/420 mk. It is affiliated with the HI, and offers some hostel beds for 120 to 170 mk per person.

Getting There & Away
Air Finnair flies to Enontekiö regularly, sometimes via Rovaniemi. The airport is 7km west of Hetta.

Bus There are two buses a day from Rovaniemi to Hetta, one of which continues in summer to Kautokeino in Norway. To get to Kilpisjärvi from Hetta, you have to change buses at Palojoensuu.

PALLAS-OUNASTUNTURI NATIONAL PARK
☎ 016

Pallas-Ounastunturi National Park, established in 1938, is one of the oldest national parks in Finland. It protects the area surrounding Pallastunturi Fell. The main attraction is the excellent 60km trekking route from the village of Hetta to Hotel Pallastunturi inside the park. There's good skiing here in winter.

Information

The Pallastunturi Visitor Centre (☎ 532 451) at Pallastunturi Fell sells trekking maps, makes reservations for locked huts (50 mk per night) and provides facts about the region, and its flora and fauna. It has slide presentations in several languages. The centre is open daily from June to late September. There is also a park information centre in Hetta (see that section earlier in the chapter).

Trekking Route

The 60km trek from Hetta village to Hotel Pallastunturi is one of the easiest in the country. It takes three to four days to complete. The route is well marked, with poles every 50m or so, and there are several wilderness huts along the way.

The popularity and ease of this trek means that in some huts (especially Hannukuru hut), there may be up to 60 people staying at one time!

Day 1 – Starting from Hetta village, you must cross a lake to get to the national park. There is a boat-taxi that costs approximately 40 mk. Walk 5km through a forest to Pyhäkero hut, then ascend the high Pyhäkero, which is part of Ounastunturi Fell. It's 7km to Sioskuru hut.

Day 2 – This section of the trail is mostly treeless plateau with good visibility. You might want to take a detour to Tappuri hut for lunch before continuing to Pahakuru hut (10km). If it's full, continue 2km farther to Hannukuru, the 'capital' of the Pallastunturi Fell area.

Day 3 – The first leg is 5km over relatively difficult terrain to a small *laavu* (simple shelter) where you can cook lunch. Another 9km takes you through pleasant mountains to the small

hut of Montelli. If it is full, continue a kilometre farther to Nammalankuru hut.

Day 4 – The final day takes you through some magnificent high mountains. There is only one place to stop, a simple *laavu* and campfire place 2.5km from Nammalankuru. From here, it's a 10km uphill walk to Hotel Pallastunturi.

Skiing

In winter, Pallastunturi Fell is a popular place for both cross-country and downhill skiing. The longest slope is 2km long, and lift passes cost 85 mk per day or 360 mk per week.

Places to Stay

Hotel The impressive *Hotel Pallas (☎ 532 441, fax 532 741)* is up in the fells, 50m from the national park information centre. The first hotel in Lapland was built on this site in 1938. Singles/doubles are from 350/450 mk, including a good all-you-can-eat breakfast. Prices are highest during the skiing season.

Wilderness Huts For trekkers in the Pallas-Ounastunturi National Park, free accommodation is available in wilderness huts. Following is a list of huts from north to south.

Pyhäkero – This hut is 5km from the lake. You cannot sleep here, but there is a gas stove and a toilet. In March and April there is also a café.
Sioskuru – Sioskuru is 7km from Pyhäkero hut and accommodates up to 16 people. There are mattresses, a gas stove, a telephone and dry firewood.
Tappuri – This nice hut is a kilometre off the main path. It accommodates six people, and has a gas stove and good water from a nearby creek.
Pahakuru – This hut is 10km from Sioskuru. It sleeps up to 10 people, and has a gas stove and a toilet. You'll need to walk a few hundred metres to get water.
Hannukuru – Just 2km from Pahakuru, this hut has room for 16 people, but it is often full. There are mattresses, a gas stove and a telephone here, plus plenty of firewood and a lakeside sauna.
Montelli – This nice hut on the high fells has a fireplace and sleeps five people.
Nammalankuru – A kilometre beyond Montelli hut is this large hut that accommodates 16 people. There is a gas stove, a telephone and excellent fell scenery. A café is open in March and April.

Finnish Jokes

Norwegians have created a fine category of humour based on their understanding of Finnish traits, and *Finskevitser* (Norwegian for 'Finnish Jokes') are told in Norwegian pubs to anyone who cares to listen. Many *Finskevitser* involve two manly Finnish heroes, Pekka and Toivonen.

One joke about Finnish *sisu* (guts or endurance) goes like this: The two Finnish heroes, Pekka and Toivonen, are known for their skill and stamina in various pursuits, including sexual ability. After Pekka returned from battle in the Winter War, he boasts about what he did first with his wife. 'What did you do next?' asks the curious listener. 'Then,' replies Pekka, 'I took off my skis.'

Small talk is not common among Finns. When Pekka and Toivonen meet again after a long time apart, they go to a sauna in the woods. They drink vodka for a couple of hours. Pekka asks how Toivonen has been doing. Toivonen says nothing, but continues drinking for a couple of hours. Then, slowly, he replies: 'Did we come here to babble, or did we come here to drink?'

A real 'accident' happened once on Lake Inarinjärvi while Pekka and Toivonen were fishing on ice. Both men were wearing thick fur hats. Pekka had a bottle of vodka, and he uttered: 'Toivonen, do you want a sip of vodka?' Because of his thick fur hat, Toivonen did not hear the offer, and was left without. This was the big 'accident' on Lake Inarinjärvi.

Finns in *Finskevitser* have an awkward relation with the Soviet Union. We learn that Finns use double-ply toilet paper because they had to send a copy of anything they produced to the USSR.

Finskevitser first became popular among Norwegian soldiers because they often spent their leave in Finnish Lapland. Liberal consumption of intoxicating liquids on these occasions may give rise to quite a number of new Finnish legends, if you dare set foot in a local pub during the Arctic winter.

Getting There & Away

There is a bus from Rovaniemi to Pallastunturi Fell every Saturday morning. You can also catch the post bus from Kittilä or from Muonio on weekdays.

KILPISJÄRVI
☎ 016

The village of Kilpisjärvi, the northernmost place in the 'arm' of Finland, is right in the 'thumb'. It is a tiny place between lake Kilpisjärvi and the magnificent surrounding fells, which are the highest fells of Finland. Both Norway and Sweden are next door, and a popular trek reaches the joint border of these three countries.

Every midsummer, the folk of Kilpisjärvi put on a ski race at Saana Fell, where the snow may not melt until mid-July.

Orientation

Kilpisjärvi consists of two 'villages' several kilometres apart – one has a pair of hotels and a supermarket, and the other has the Kilpisjärvi Trekking Centre (Kilpisjärven Retkeilykeskus) and a petrol station.

Information

Kilpisjärven Retkeilykeskus is a central meeting place for all trekkers (see Places to Stay & Eat). It's the place to find trekking partners, get advice on routes, and buy maps and supplies. The centre also sells fishing permits and handles wilderness huts that must be booked in advance (35 mk per person per night).

Trekking

The area around Kilpisjärvi offers fantastic trekking. Routes range from easy day treks to demanding two-week treks into the mountains.

A marked loop route to **Saana Fell** starts at Kilpisjärven Retkeilykeskus. This route takes one full day.

Another very popular day trek is the 15km route through **Malla Nature Park** to the joint border post of Finland, Sweden and Norway. At the border is a free wilderness hut, if you want to stay overnight.

If you are interested in learning more about the Sami people, make a trek to **Raittijärvi**, a traditional Sami village. There is no road, so walking is the only way to get there. A path starts at the village of Saarikoski, 35km south of Kilpisjärvi, and is approximately 40km long.

For experienced trekkers, a one to two-week trip from Saana Fell to **Halti Fell**, the highest point in Finland (there is snow in June), is a demanding but rewarding trip. The scenery is magnificent, and there are excellent fishing possibilities and free wilderness huts along the way. At two points you will have to ford rivers.

If you are interested in the trek to Halti Fell but are not quite sure of your capabilities, join one of the groups organised by Kilpisjärven Retkeilykeskus – there are a few departures every year.

All trekking routes and wilderness huts around the Kilpisjärvi area are clearly displayed on the 1:100,000 *Käsivarsi* map (50 mk). The 1:50,000 *Kilpisjärvi* topographical sheet (25 mk) covers a small area.

Scenic Flights

There is a heliport at the southern end of the village of Kilpisjärvi. Helicopter flights cost a minimum of 200 mk per person. For information, call Polar Lento Oy (☎ 537 810) or Helijet (☎ 537 743).

Places to Stay & Eat

Peeran Retkeilykeskus (☎/fax 532 659) is an HI-affiliated hostel definitely in the middle of nowhere, 25km south of the village of Kilpisjärvi. It is a pleasant place by the fell, open from late February to late October. Beds are from 95 to 135 mk per person. Amenities include kitchen, sauna, laundry, and a café serving full meals.

More convenient to trekking routes, *Kilpisjärven Retkeilykeskus (☎ 537 771, fax 537 702)* on the main road through Kilpisjärvi, is open from early August to late September. It has singles/doubles from 125/190 mk and some cottages. If you have

a tent, you can pitch it here for 60 mk. The restaurant serves an all-you-can-eat buffet lunch daily in the high season.

Kilpisjärven Matkailuhotelli (☎ 537 761, fax 537 767) also on the main road through Kilpisjärvi, is a bit far from Saans Fell, and has rooms from 260/350 mk.

Prices at the **supermarket** in Kilpisjärvi are in both Finnish and Norwegian currencies, and you can pay in either.

Getting There & Away

Bus There is a daily bus connection between Rovaniemi and Kilpisjärvi via Kittilä and Muonio.

Car & Motorcycle The road to Kilpisjärvi is excellent – just make sure your car is in good shape (there are no repair shops around) and that you have enough petrol.

East Lapland

East Lapland offers some of Finland's most rewarding and demanding treks. Here, as in other areas of eastern Finland, proximity to the Russian border gives villages a frontier character. This is the region of the Sami people, the gold rush and the famous Arctic Road, taken every summer by thousands of Europeans on their way to Nordkapp, the northernmost point in Europe.

KEMIJÄRVI
• pop 12,000   ☎ 016

As the northernmost town in Finland with a train station, and as the gateway to the north-eastern part of Lapland, Kemijärvi gets a steady flow of travellers. That said, it is a disappointment to anyone expecting to see genuine Lappish life, complete with reindeer and so on.

Information
Tourist Office The tourist office (☎ 813 777), in the Torikeskus building at Kuumaniemenkatu 2A, is open from 8 am to 6 pm Monday to Friday, and from 9.30 am to 3 pm Saturday from June to mid-August. At

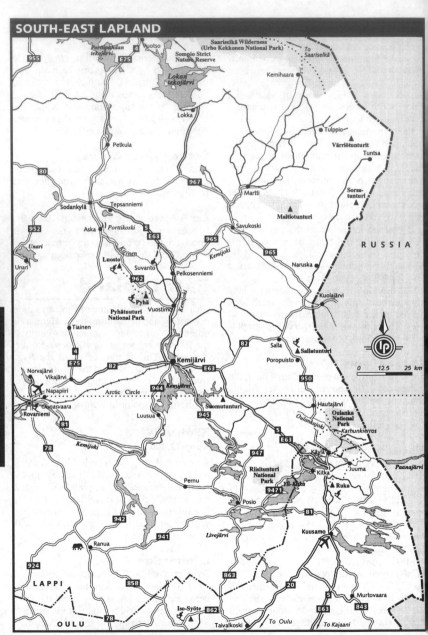

SOUTH-EAST LAPLAND

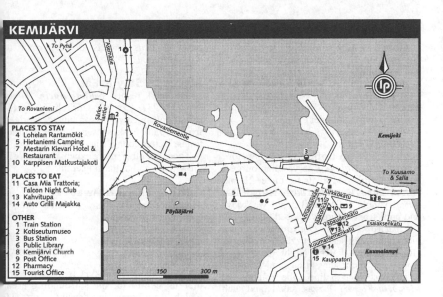

KEMIJÄRVI

PLACES TO STAY
4 Lohelan Rantamökit
5 Hietaniemi Camping
7 Mestarin Kievari Hotel &
   Restaurant
10 Karppisen Matkustajakoti

PLACES TO EAT
11 Casa Mia Trattoria;
   Falcon Night Club
13 Kahvitupa
14 Auto Grilli Majakka

OTHER
1 Train Station
2 Kotiseutumuseo
3 Bus Station
6 Public Library
8 Kemijärvi Church
9 Post Office
12 Pharmacy
15 Tourist Office

other times, it's open from 8 am to 4 pm Monday to Friday.

Post The post office is at Hallituskatu 5. It's open from 8.30 am to 8 pm Monday to Friday.

Internet Resources & Library The public library at Hietaniemenkatu 3 has an Internet terminal – and a cosy fireplace. Hours are from 11 am to 7 pm Monday to Thursday, to 5 pm Friday and to 3 pm Saturday.

Medical & Emergency Services In a general emergency call ☎ 112, for police call ☎ 10022 and for a doctor dial ☎ 10023. There's a pharmacy at Vapaudenkatu 8.

Things to See
The **local museum** (Kotiseutumuseo) features a collection of artefacts and old houses – including a *kota* (Lappish hut). The museum is open from 10 am to 4.30 pm Monday to Friday and from 10 am to 6 pm weekends, from June to late August. Entry is 10 mk.

The **Kemijärvi church**, built in 1951, has a wooden bell tower dating from 1774. The church is open daily in summer.

Special Events
The Kemijärvi Sculptural Week, a festival of woodcarving, is held during July. It draws artists from many European countries and is an interesting event as all the woodcarvers work outside, in view of the public.

In mid-September, Kemjärvi hosts Ruksa Swing, a festival of swing dancing and swing music. Participants are from around the world, and there is a special 'Swing Train' from Helsinki.

Places to Stay
Camp sites cost 75 mk at *Hietaniemi Camping* (☎ 813 640) on Pöyliöjärvi lake just 200m west of the town centre. The place also rents bicycles. It's open from March to late September.

Just 300m west of the camping ground, *Lohelan Rantamökit* (☎ 813 253, Lohelankatu 1) is an HI-affiliated hostel, open year-round, that charges 85 to 150 mk per person. It has a kitchen and sauna.

Karppisen Matkustajakoti (☎ 813 061, Hallituskatu 2) is a nice guesthouse with singles/doubles for 85/170 mk.

Hotels include *Mestarin Kievari (☎ 813 577, fax 814 104, Kirkkokatu 9)*, a fine place with rooms from 330/400 mk (310/370 mk in summer).

Places to Eat

Next to the tourist office and kauppatori, *Auto Grilli Majakka* serves hamburgers and other fast-food treats for under 25 mk.

Kahvitupa (Vapaudenkatu 6) is a café that serves simple meals until 5 pm weekdays and until 1 pm Saturday (closed Sunday).

Casa Mia Trattoria (Jaakonkatu 2-4) is a nice Italian spot serving pizzas from 40 mk. Upstairs is the Falcon Night Club, open from 9 pm Wednesday, Friday and Saturday.

The best place to dine is the restaurant at *Mestarin Kievari*. Pizzas, salads and such are from 30 mk, while gourmet fish and game dishes are from 75 mk.

There are several *supermarkets* at or near the centre of town.

Getting There & Away

Bus The bus terminal is in the centre of town. There are several buses each weekday to Pyhä (50km), Rovaniemi (85km), Sodankylä (110km), Salla (71km) and Kuusamo (160 km). Bus services are less frequent on weekends.

Train A direct daily train makes the 14 hour journey from Helsinki to Kemijärvi, arriving in Kemijärvi in the morning and leaving again in the early evening.

AROUND KEMIJÄRVI
Salla
☎ 016

Salla was entirely rebuilt after WWII, when it was destroyed, and its 1951 **church** is an attractive example of post-war architecture. The village offers a host of tourist services.

Sallatunturi, 10km from the village, is a small downhill skiing area. It also offers activities such as reindeer sleigh rides. The tourist office (☎ 832 141) is called Yritys-palvelukeskus and is on the road to Sallatunturi.

Places to Stay & Eat

At the ski resort, *Sallatunturin Tuva (☎ 831 931, fax 837 765)* has a café-restaurant and two-person cottages priced from 330 mk in ski season, 245 mk at other times. Better cottages have a sauna.

There are other, more expensive *hotels* in the village and at the ski centre.

Getting There & Away

There are regular buses from Kemijärvi, 64km west of Salla.

SODANKYLÄ
☎ 016

The village of Sodankylä is a busy commercial centre for the surrounding area, which has a population density of just 0.9 people per sq km!

The tourist office (☎ 618 168) at Jäämer-entie 9 is open weekdays. Also in the tourist office building, the **Andreas Alariesto Art Gallery** displays paintings by the famous Lapp painter who favoured a primitive style. There are many images of Sami life.

The **old wooden church** near the Kitiner riverside is Lapland's oldest – it was built in 1689. It's one of the few buildings in Lapland to survive the massive destruction of WWII, and is open daily in summer.

Several kilometres south of the village, the **local museum** exhibits typical Lappish arts and crafts, tools and such in weathered old buildings. Hours are noon to 5 pm daily from early June to late August and entry is 10 mk.

Places to Stay

Camping Sodankylä Nilimella (☎ 612 181, fax 611 503), open from June to mid-August, is across the river from the village. It charges 70 to 80 mk for tent sites, 160 to 500 mk for cabins. The café serves meals.

Adjacent to the camping ground is the HI-affiliated hostel *Lapin Opisto*, open

June to mid-August, with 80 mk dorm beds. The place has a kitchen and sauna.

About 10km south of Sodankylä, *Orakoski* (☎ *611 965, Jäämerentie 68)* is a pleasant riverside camping ground with 50 mk tent sites and a large number of cottages.

Majatalo Kolme Veljestä (☎ *611 216, Ojennustie 19)*, a guesthouse in the village centre, has tidy singles/doubles for 120/200 mk.

Hotel Sodankylä (☎ *617 121, fax 617 177, Unarintie 15)* has 54 rooms, two saunas and two restaurants, and is close to the bus station. Rooms are from 320/360 mk.

Places to Eat

For something quick and cheap try one of the *grillis* near the hotels. *Pizza Pirkko (Jäämerentie 35)* near the bus station is reasonably priced. Just south of the bus station, *Seita-Baari (Jäämerentie 62)* offers inexpensive home-made food, including Lappish specialities such as *poronkäristys* (sautéed reindeer). *Café Lapponia (Sompiontie 4)* is open daily and serves snacks and coffee. It also sells handicrafts.

Getting There & Away

Sodankylä is on the main Rovaniemi-Ivalo road (road No 4), and there are regular buses from either town (70 to 90 mk one way). The bus terminal is slightly off the main road.

PYHÄ-LUOSTO REGION
☎ 016

The area between the fells of Luosto (514m) and Pyhä (540m) forms a popular winter sports centre, and high season extends from February to May. In summer the region is excellent for trekking, particularly in the Pyhätunturi National Park that surrounds Pyhä Fell. Pyhä and Luosto each have resort 'villages' with full services. The Pyhä-Luosto region lies halfway between Kemijärvi and Sodankylä.

Information

In Luosto, the travel agency Pyhä-Luosto Matkailu (☎ 020-838 4248, fax 624 261) at Pyhä-Luostontie 2 has accommodation and tourist information for the region, and books cottages.

In Pyhä, the Pyhähippu Reservation Centre (☎ 882 820, fax 882 853) also offers tourist information and books accommodation at 130 cottages and apartments. It has a café-restaurant, showers, sauna and laundry.

For information on Pyhätunturi National Park, as well as about summer activities such as hiking and fishing, drop by the park's Pyhätunturi Nature Centre (☎ 882 773, fax 882 824), adjacent to the Pyhä downhill ski centre; follow signs from the main Kemijarvi-Sodankylä road (road No 5).

Korpikutsu Amethyst Mine

The amethyst mine on Lampivaara Hill in Luosto is the only working amethyst mine in Europe. The mine is open 10 am to 5 pm daily from early June to late August, and there are guided tours hourly on the hour. The mine is accessible by forest road from Luosto; follow the signs.

Pyhätunturi National Park

The 43 sq km park is one of the oldest national parks in Finland, established in 1938. The most notable sight is the steep Pyhäkuru Gorge between the Kultakero and Ukonhattu peaks. According to local legend, Lake Pyhänkasteenlampi (Lake of Holy Baptism), in the gorge, was where EM Fellman, the 'Apostle of Lapland', forcibly baptised the Sompio Samis in the 17th century to convert them to Christianity.

There is a birdwatching tower at the south-east corner of the park, about 3km from the Nature Centre.

Skiing

At Pyhä there are 10 ski runs and seven lifts. The longest run is 1.8km, with a vertical drop of 280m. At Luosto, there are seven runs and four lifts, plus a halfpipe and special slopes for snowboarders. The longest ski run is 1.5km, with a vertical drop of 230m.

Pyhä has 50km of trails for cross-country skiers (15km of which are lit), and Luosto has 95km of trails (25km are lit). You can rent equipment from the ski centre at either location.

Trekking

Within Pyhätunturi National Park there are 24km of marked hiking trails, including a 10km loop trail to Pyhäkuru Gorge. Some 16km of trails are open in winter to cross-country skiers. There is also a 35km trekking route between Pyhä and Luosto, which travels through the national park and the protected forest area of Luosto. All trails start at the Nature Centre.

For an overnight trek, a good map is highly recommended, such as the 1:40,000 *Luosto-Pyhätunturi* map, which can be purchased at the Nature Centre and in local hotels and resorts. Shorter walks are possible without a map.

Places to Stay & Eat

There are many designated *camping areas* within a short walk from the Pyhä Nature Centre.

The only hut where you can overnight inside the national park is the modern *Huttuloma* wilderness hut that sleeps six; *Karhunjuomalampi* hut, 5km from the Nature Centre, is for day use only. On the Pyhä-Luosto trail, accommodation is possible at *Kapusta* and *Rykimäkuru* wilderness huts.

The hotels in Pyhä and in Luosto are busiest in ski season, when rates rise. *Hotelli Pyhätunturi (☎ 856 111, fax 882 740)* is the best hotel in Pyhä, with doubles from 400 mk in summer. There is a good view from the hotel's restaurant.

In Luosto, *Scandic Hotel Luosto (☎ 624 400, fax 624 410, Ellitsantie 5)* has rooms, cottages, restaurants and saunas. Doubles are from 490 mk in summer. *Hotelli Ravintola Luostonhovi (☎ 624 421, fax 624 297, Ellitsantie 6)* is a bargain, with doubles from 180 mk in summer. The restaurant here is also good value.

Pyhän Asteli (☎ 852 141, fax 852 149) is a charming resort on the Pyhä-Luosto road. There are cottages (from 80 mk per person

in summer), plus bike and canoe rentals. The restaurant offers a daily dinner buffet.

For *cottage* bookings in the region, contact one of the agencies listed in the earlier Information section. Prices are from 150 mk per day.

Getting There & Away

The easiest connection to the Pyhä Nature Centre is the morning bus from Kemijärvi, which operates Monday to Saturday. There are buses between Luosto and Sodankylä on school days only (ie Monday to Friday, from mid-August till the end of May).

SAARISELKÄ REGION
☎ 016

The Saariselkä region includes villages and towns surrounding the Saariselkä Wilderness and Urho Kekkonen National Park, the most popular trekking area in Finland. These outposts offer national park information centres, as well as shops and supermarkets where you can stock up on trekking supplies.

The Saariselkä region does not have the greatest downhill skiing, but it is still among the most popular winter resort areas in Finland.

Saariselkä

Saariselkä village is a winter sports centre and also a base for trekkers heading into the Saariselkä Wilderness area, so beware: this is one of the busiest yuppie resorts in the whole of Lapland. That said, Saariselkä village is not a bad place to start hiking – all necessary trekking supplies are available in local sports shops and supermarkets and there are superb transport connections to/from town.

Information For tourist and accommodation information, contact Pohjois-Lapin Matkailu Oy (☎ 668 400, fax 668 405) at Honkapolku 3.

The Forest Research Institute operates the Saariselkä Information Cabin (☎ 668 122), with plenty of free information for trekkers.

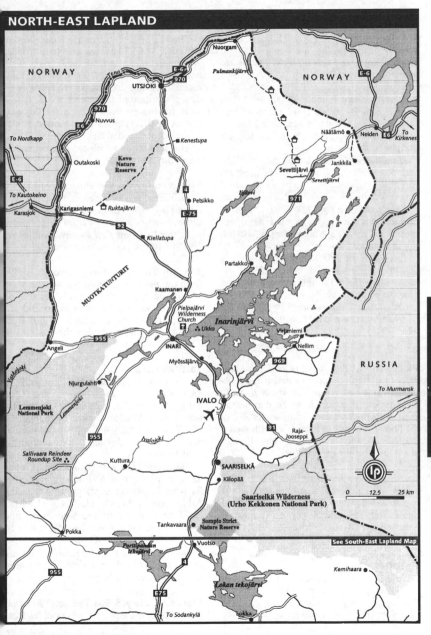

NORTH-EAST LAPLAND

NORWAY

NORWAY

Nuorgam

E-6

E-6

970

Pulmankijärvi

E-6

UTSJOKI

970

Nuvvus

E6

To Nordkapp

Kenestupa

Nätämö

Neiden

E6

To Kirkenes

Kevo
Nature
Reserve

Jankkila

Outakoski

Sevettijärvi

Sevettijärvi

To Kautokeino

E-6

Karigasniemi

Ruktajärvi

Petsikko

E-75

Iijärvi

971

Karasjok

92

Kiellatupa

Partakko

MUOTKATUNTURIT

Kaamanen

Pielpajärvi
Wilderness
Church

Inarinjärvi

Ulkko

Virtaniemi

955

INARI

Nellim

Angeli

Myössäjärvi

969

RUSSIA

Njurgulahti

To Murmansk

Lemmenjoki
National Park

IVALO

955

Ivalojoki

91

Raja-
Jooseppi

Sallivaara Reindeer
Roundup Site

Kuttura

SAARISELKÄ

Kiilopää

0   12.5   25 km

Pokka

Tankavaara

Sompio Strict
Nature Reserve

Saariselkä Wilderness
(Urho Kekkonen National Park)

See South-East Lapland Map

955

*Porttipahdan
tekojärvi*

Vuotso

Kemihaara

E75

4

Lokan tekojärvi

To Sodankylä

kka

Skiing Saariselkä offers 12 downhill slopes served by six lifts. The longest run is 1300m and the vertical drop is 180m. Cross-country trails in the area total 250km. Cross-country and downhill ski rentals are available in the village.

Places to Stay Finnair sometimes offers special package tours from Helsinki that include a few nights in Saariselkä hotels, usually at bargain rates. Prices are highest during the ski season.

Hotelli Teerenpesä (☎ 668 001, fax 668 002, Saariseläntie 5) is one of the most affordable places in Saariselkä, with singles/doubles for 150/200 mk in summer.

Saariselkä Spa (☎ 6828, fax 682 328) is an enormous spa hotel with a number of activities and services. Rooms start at 340/450 mk in summer.

Laanihovi (☎ 668 816, fax 668 894), a few kilometres south of Saariselkä village, has doubles from 320 mk and is not a bad place to begin a trek.

Saariselän Tunturihotelli (☎ 68111, fax 668 771) is a fine old hotel with rooms from 475/595 mk in high season, 400/500 mk at other times.

Places to Eat Saariselkä is one of the best places to sample gourmet Finnish food, although high-season prices are notorious. *Pakkasukko* is a simple place that serves pizza. *Petronella* is good value and probably the finest restaurant in Saariselkä, although it may be closed in summer. You can self-cater at any of several *supermarkets*.

Getting There & Away Each flight arriving at Ivalo airport is met by a shuttle bus to Saariselkä (30 mk one way). Northbound buses from Rovaniemi stop on request at Saariselkä, and some buses make a loop through the village.

Kiilopää

Kiilopää, 18km south-east of Saariselkä village, is another major trekking centre for the region. It's probably the best place to start your trek: you can dine well and stay

overnight. Buy food elsewhere, though, as it is not that cheap in Kiilopää.

The Kiilopää Fell Resort (Tunturikeskus Kiilopää; ☎ 667 101, fax 667 121, kiilopaa .suomenlatu@co.inet.fi) takes care of all accommodation and services. It rents mountain bikes, rucksacks, sleeping bags, skiing equipment and much more. It also sells fishing permits, runs a left-luggage service and dispenses good, sound advice on trekking. Guided treks are possible.

The area around Kiilopää is excellent for mountain biking.

Places to Stay & Eat Hostel Ahopää is the HI-affiliated hostel, open year-round, with dormitory beds from 85 mk. A kitchen, sauna, laundry and café are on the premises.

At the *Kiilopää Fell Resort*, doubles are 360 to 580 mk and there are cottages.

Getting There & Away Kiilopää is 6km from the main road (road No 4). The Matti Malm company has several buses that do the one-hour trip between Ivalo and Kiilopää. If you are travelling by bus from Rovaniemi, check whether the bus runs to Kiilopää: some do and some don't.

Tankavaara

Tankavaara, approximately 30km south of Saariselkä, is locally famous as the 'Gold Village'. It also has an **Urho Kekkonen National Park Visitor Centre** (☎ 626 251), which is open daily with plenty of information about activities and sights within the wilderness area.

The **Gold Museum** (Kultamuseo), open daily, displays tools and other paraphernalia from Lapland's crazy gold-fever years. Admission is 35 mk adult, 10 mk child. Gold panning is offered year-round and costs 20 mk. Gold-related events and festivals are held throughout the summer.

Several **nature trails** around Tankavaara are suitable for short walks. Some routes require waterproof boots.

Places to Stay & Eat The hotel *Korundi (☎ 626 158, fax 626 261)* has doubles from

300 mk and a dozen cottages. There's a *café* in summer, and the year-round restaurant *Wanha Waskoolimies* (Ye Olde Goldpanner).

Getting There & Away Tankavaara is on the main Rovaniemi-Ivalo road. All northbound buses pass the village, stopping on request.

Savukoski

The village of Savukoski serves as a base for visits to the isolated south-eastern part of the Saariselkä Wilderness. The **National Park Visitor Centre** (☎ 841 401) at Samperintie 32 is open daily and has a superb wilderness exhibition and slide show. It offers park information, and sells maps and permits.

Joulupukin Muorin Tupa, a shop that sells local handicrafts as well as Christmas paraphernalia, is the 'official workshop' of Santa Claus' wife. According to Finnish legend, Santa Claus' home is in the Korvatunturi Fell, a remote, inaccessible mountain near the Russian border. Fortunately, Santa has an 'official workshop' at Napapiiri (the Arctic Circle), just north of Rovaniemi (see the Around Rovaniemi section earlier in this chapter).

Places to Stay & Eat Savukoski's *camping ground* has campsites for 30 mk, and cabins from 150 mk per person. The top-end choice in Savukoski village – not that there's much to chose from – is *Samperin Savotta* (☎ 841 351, fax 841 386), a modern hotel and restaurant at the Kemijoki waterfront. Singles/doubles are from 230/350 mk. A *café* at the camping ground sells snacks only.

Getting There & Away Savukoski is on road No 965, 95km north of Kemijärvi. Post buses and Möllärin Linjat buses run daily from Kemijärvi to Savukoski via the village of Pelkosenniemi.

Tulppio

As the Savukoski wilderness, the south-east pocket of Urho Kekkonen National Park, continues to attract more visitors, Tulppio is becoming more popular. The village is just south of the national park boundary, and is a stepping stone to one of the most interesting natural fishing rivers in Finland, the Nuorttijoki (see Fishing, in the Urho Kekkonen National Park section that follows).

In the early 20th century, the old **steam locomotive** now on display in the centre was transported in pieces from the United States, first by ship to Hanko, then by rail to Rovaniemi, and finally from Rovaniemi to Tulppio by horse sledges over frozen bogs and forests, with temperatures reaching -30°C. It was used by loggers for many decades.

Tulppio was a busy logging station right up until WWI, but little of this legacy remains, as Finnish troops burned down the houses during the Winter War of 1939-40 to prevent the Russians making bases in them.

Places to Stay & Eat *Tulppio* (☎ 844 101) has Spartan but clean rooms in cottages; doubles start at 200 mk. The *café* is a popular beer-drinking bar for locals, but there are also meals available.

Getting There & Away A private vehicle is the easiest way to reach Tulppio. Alternatively, you could take a bus to Martti (south-east of Tulppio), then call the Tulppio cottages (see Places to Stay & Eat) for a lift. They may charge for pick-up. Hitchhiking is easiest on weekend afternoons, when people drive to Tulppio for the Tisko, a sort of lumberjacks' disco.

SAARISELKÄ WILDERNESS (URHO KEKKONEN NATIONAL PARK)

☎ 016

The Saariselkä Wilderness – which includes Urho Kekkonen National Park, the Sompio Strict Nature Reserve, Nuortti Recreational Fishing Area and also large tracts of protected forestry lands – extends all the way to the Russian border. It is by far the most

The Princess of Itäkaira

After days of solitary trekking in the eastern frontier area of Saariselkä – also known as Itäkaira – a man might be thankful to chat up anything living, even a reindeer. But imagine running across a woman with little or no clothes on, frolicking around like a fairy-tale creature. If you meet such a woman, you will have found the mysterious Princess of Itäkaira.

Although nobody has seen her, the 'princess' has left her signature in every trekking book, in every hut or shelter in the region. The entries show up a few months apart on average. She writes at length and in detail in each of the trekking books – rhapsodising about the beauty of Lapland, as well describing how she spends her days running around in the wilderness, half naked, sometimes with no clothes at all, chasing after ermines and butterflies and singing songs of joy. Between all these stories are innumerable remarks by lonely male trekkers: 'Where are you, Princess?' or 'Who are you, Princess of Itäkaira?' And, optimistically, 'When are we going to meet?'

One theory about the princess' origins is that she is in reality a married, middle-aged lady who has a home near Oulu and who treks in Lapland with her spouse at every opportunity. If that's the case, she is a princess with a wicked sense of humour – as the following story, also written in one of the trekking books, will attest.

A lonely man once quite innocently placed an advertisement in a Finnish newspaper, looking for a partner to share a long trek in the eastern part of Saariselkä. From the plethora of replies, he chose one applicant, who described herself as a somewhat bulky and hairy – but very enthusiastic – female trekker. The man ordered plenty of parachute cloth from a Pietarsaari factory to ensure enough material for a double sleeping bag.

After a lengthy correspondence, and vivid fantasies of his zaftig lady, the man finally had a date. A final note read: 'See you at the Tahvon Tupa hut, at 6 pm, and do have the sauna heated and your sleeping bag open and warmed.' After walking for days in a dream-like state of excited anticipation, the lonely trekker arrived at the Tahvon Tupa hut. There was no one there. Bitterly the man recorded the tale of his betrayal in the trekking book – and then left.

In the same trekkers' book six months later, a playful note appears: 'Now that I'm here, where are you? I obviously came six months too late.' The note is signed by the Princess of Itäkaira.

popular trekking area in Finland. The large network of excellent wilderness huts is one reason for the area's popularity; another is the beauty of the low *tunturi* hills.

Orientation

Zone Division The park is divided into four zones, each with different rules. The basic zone is the area closest to main roads. Camping and fires are only allowed in designated places. In the wilderness zones of Saariselkä (in the west) and Nuortti (south-east, between Tulppio and Kemihaara), camping is allowed everywhere except in certain gorges and on

treeless areas. In the Kemi-Sompio wilderness zone (east), camping and fires (using dead wood from the ground) are allowed everywhere.

Maps A map and compass are *essential* for the most remote areas of the park. There are three maps available for the area: for short treks around the village of Saariselkä, the 1:50,000 *Sompio-Kiilopää* map will do; the 1:50,000 *Sokosti-Suomujoki* map will take you beyond lake Luirojärvi; the entire park is shown on the 1:100,000 *Koilliskaira* map.

SAARISELKÄ WILDERNESS (URHO KEKKONEN NATIONAL PARK)

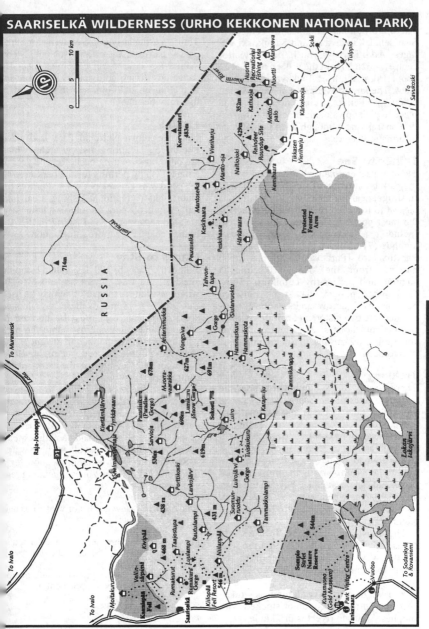

Information

There are national park visitor centres in Saariselkä, Tankavaara and Savukoski villages. Additionally, you'll find a visitor centre (☎ 626 241) in the village of Vuotso, about 15km south of Tankavaara on road No 4. The largest is the one at Tankavaara.

Kiilopää Fell Resort in Kiilopää is a good place to pick up valuable practical information on trekking, although it isn't an official information centre.

Things to See

There are several natural attractions within the park boundaries, of which the **Rumakuru Gorge**, near the hut of the same name, is closest to the main road. **Lake Luirojärvi** is the most popular destination for any trek, including a hike up the nearby **Sokosti summit** (718m), the highest in the park. **Paratiisikuru** (Paradise Gorge), a steep descent from the 698m Ukselmapää summit, and the nearby **Lumikuru** (Snow Gorge) are popular day trips between Sarvioja and Muorravaarakka huts.

There are two historical **Scolt fields**, with restored old houses, 2km south of Raja-Jooseppi, and 2km west of Snelmanninmaja hut, respectively.

Trekking

There are a large number of possible walking routes in the Saariselkä area. Use wilderness huts as bases and destinations, and improvise according to your ability: an experienced, fit trekker can cover up to 4km per hour, and up to 25km per day.

The four to six-day loop from the main road to lake Luirojärvi is the most popular route, and can be extended beyond the lake. To reach areas where very few have been, take a one-week walk from Kiilopää to Kemihaara.

The most remote route follows old roads and walking routes through the fells all the way from Raja-Jooseppi in the north to Kemihaara or Tulppio in the south-east.

You will need to carry all food, as wilderness huts in the park are not stocked with supplies. Water in rivers is drinkable.

Note that despite its popularity, Saariselkä can be tough going for the less experienced. Trails – particularly in the eastern part of the park – can be faint or almost nonexistent. Winter ski safaris can become especially dangerous during cold spells. For more information on trekking, see that section in the Activities chapter.

Fishing

Urho Kekkonen National Park is divided into three recreational fishing areas, which are open on a rotating basis for one year at a time. Fishing permits for the park cost 48 mk per day or 185 mk per week. Permits for Nuorttijoki recreational fishing area, partially within the park's south-east boundary, are sold separately. See Fishing in the Activities chapter for more information.

Places to Stay

Within the park are 200 designated camping sites; all are free. There are close to 30 wilderness huts in the park that may be used free of charge. Some of these have locked areas with beds that must be booked in advance, and a few cabins within the park which must also be booked in advance. The charge is 50 mk per bed per night. Book cabins or beds at any of the park visitor centres.

A few wilderness huts close to the main road are for day use only – you can overnight at one of these in an emergency. More distant huts usually have comfortable mattresses, gas or wood-burning stoves and sometimes telephones or saunas. Almost all are near water.

See the earlier Orientation section for a description of the park zones, including regulations for each.

Basic Zone Below is a list of wilderness huts in the basic zone:

Rumakurut – Day use only; the most popular cabin in Saariselkä, with over 200 skiing visitors on busy April days.
Luulampi – Day use only; tourist information centre and café (open in spring only).
Taajostupa – Sleeps six.
Vellinsärpimä – Day use only.
Kivipää – Sleeps 10.

Niilanpää – Day use only.
Rautulampi – Day use only.
Suomunruoktu – Sleeps 10 in the open section, 10 in the reserved; telephone.
Tammakkolampi – *Kammi* (earth-covered hut); sleeps three; must be reserved in advance.
Lankojärvi – Accommodates 10 open/10 reserved; telephone.
Porttikoski – Sleeps 10; sauna.
Snelmanninmaja – Sleeps five.

Saariselkä Wilderness Zone The hilly Saariselkä region is busy during the winter holidays, in August before school starts and during the ruska (autumn) weeks in late September.

Tuiskukuru – Sleeps 10 in the open section/10 in the reserved; firewood.
Luirojarvi – Sleeps 16 open/16 reserved; sauna, telephone.
Luirojarvi/Kuusela – Sleeps five; must be reserved in advance.
Luirojarvi/Porokämppä – Sleeps six.
Luirojarvi/Raappana – Kammi; sleeps two; must be reserved in advance.
Hammaskuru – Sleeps 10 open/10 reserved; telephone.
Hammaskota – Kammi; sleeps three; must be reserved in advance.
Siulanruoktu – Dramatic position halfway up a ridge; sleeps six.
Tahvontupa – Sleeps six; sauna, firewood.
Peuraselkä – Sleeps six.
Jyrkkävaara – Sleeps 10 open/10 reserved.
Kiertämäjärvi – Sleeps five.
Sarvioja – Sleeps 10 open/10 reserved; telephone.
Muorravaarakka – Sleeps 10 open/10 reserved; telephone.
Anterinmukka – One of the best huts in the park; accommodates 15; sauna.
Karapulju – Sleeps five.
Vongoiva – Kammi; sleeps two; must be reserved in advance.

Kemi-Sompio Wilderness Zone This area gets few trekkers. The terrain is flatter than that of Saariselkä, and there is little water available in summer. It is easy walking country, and large bogs can be crossed on *pitkospuu* (board walk) paths.

Peskihaara – Former border guard hut; sleeps five.
Manto-oja – Sleeps eight; telephone.

Mantoselkä – Sleeps six in the open section/six in the reserved.
Vieriharju – Sleeps six; sauna.
Härkävaara – Sleeps 10; sauna.
Tammikämppä – Sleeps six.

Nuortti Wilderness Zone The Nuortti region is popular for fishing. Tulppio is used as a starting point for exploring the area.

Kärkekeoja – Sleeps six in the open section/three in the reserved.
Mettopalo – Accommodates four.
Karhuoja – Sleeps six open/six reserved; sauna.
Naltiojoki – Accommodates 10.
Nuortti – Sleeps six open/six reserved.
Tikkasen Vieriharju – Sleeps four; may be reserved in advance in Tulppio; sauna.

Getting There & Away

It is easy to start trekking from Saariselkä or Kiilopää. Tankavaara is not a good starting point for longer treks, but does have short nature trails nearby. From Savukoski you can catch a post taxi to Kemihaara village, a kilometre from the park boundary. From Tulppio you'll have to negotiate with locals for a ride closer to the park boundary. (See the relevant earlier sections for more information.)

The Raja-Jooseppi border station is another good starting point for a trek, as it takes you directly into the real wilderness. (See the Around Ivalo section for more information.)

IVALO
- **pop 3500**   ☎ 016

Ivalo (Sami: Avvil) is the undisputed administrative and commercial centre of the surrounding region, and its airport makes it the major transport hub for East Lapland.

Ivalo has all the services you would expect in a small Finnish town, but little else to recommend it; even its unusual looking church is bleak on the inside.

That said, there *is* a unique subculture here – gold panners. Ivalo is the nearest 'big city' for hermits who spend their time panning the Ivalojoki for gold chips. Hotel Kultahippu is one place where any gold found is traded for booze and where incredible tales are told before panners return to their solitary, secretive hunt for the mother lode.

Information
The tourist office is at Neste petrol station on the main street. It's open daily in summer. The public library in the town centre has some English-language magazines.

Dog Sledding
One of the best (but not the cheapest) ways to experience the Finnish wilderness in winter is on a husky safari. In Ivalo, Kamisak (☎ 667 736, fax 667 836), 99800 Ivalo, run by Eija and Reijo Järvinen, offers just such a tour. Safaris range in length from five hours to six days and cost from 690 to 5900 mk per person. The price includes transportation, equipment, insurance and meals, plus accommodation in wilderness cabins on overnight tours. Participants are taught how to drive their own husky team of five to 12 dogs. The Järvinens take solo travellers as well as groups.

Places to Stay
Näverniemen Lomakylä (☎ 677 601, fax 677 602) just south of Ivalo is a year-round camping ground with tent sites for 50 to 90 mk and cottages from 75 to 350 mk.

North of Ivalo, *Ukonjärvi (☎ 667 501, fax 667 516)*, at the lake of the same name, is a camping ground with terrific services. It's open from May to late September and has tent sites for 80 mk, cabins for 150 to 700 mk.

The closest Ivalo comes to offering budget accommodation is *Motelli Petsamo (☎ 661 106, fax 661 628, motelli.petsamo @pp.ukolo.fi, Petsamontie 16)*, 500m off the road to Murmansk (Russia). It has singles/doubles from 190/300 mk, or 150/240 mk in low season. The place is affiliated with the HI and gives a discount to members.

South of town, *Hotelli Ivalo (☎ 688 111, fax 661 905, Ivalontie 34)* is a fine establishment with doubles from 225 mk in high season, 175 mk low season.

Hotel Kultahippu (☎ 661 825, fax 66: 510, Petsamontie 1), at the riverside in the north, has rooms from 270/340 mk.

Places to Eat
Lauran grilli, the most popular eatery in Ivalo, stays open till 3 am serving kebab and *poronkäristys* (reindeer stew). Across from the grilli is *Anjan Pizza (Ivalontie 12)* with pizzas and such. *Casa Mia* at the bus station is the most typical Finnish restaurant in town. *K-Halli Supermarket* in the centre is open daily.

Getting There & Away
There are daily flights from Helsinki to Ivalo, and regular air services from many other Finnish towns.

Buses from Rovaniemi always stop in Ivalo. There are daily departures.

Getting Around
To/From the Airport The airport is 12km south of Ivalo. A connecting bus to the centre meets each arriving flight, and cost 18 mk one way.

Car & Motorcycle Car rental companie with offices at Ivalo Airport include Avis Budget, Hertz and Europcar. Rates are the same as elsewhere in Finland.

AROUND IVALO
The **Raja-Jooseppi border station**, 53km south-east of Ivalo, is a crossing point to Russia for travellers to Murmansk, 250km away. It's also a good starting point for trek into the Saariselkä Wilderness. A post taxi travels between Ivalo and the borde station, departing Ivalo early in the after noon from Monday to Saturday.

INARI
• pop 550   ☎ 016

The small village of Inari (Sami: Anár) i the main Sami community in the region The village has supermarkets, banks an handicrafts shops, and is a good base for ex ploring northern Lapland.

You can easily spend a day sight-seeing around Inari's interesting attractions – take a morning trek to the Wilderness Church, an afternoon cruise on lake Inarinjärvi and then visit Saamelaismuseo in the evening.

Information

The tourist office, Inari Info (☎ 661 666, fax 661 777, northern-lapland.tourism@co.inet.fi) is open from 9 am to 8 pm daily from mid-June to mid-September. At other times it's open from 9 am to 5.30 pm Monday to Friday. The office has tourist information for all of northern Lapland, and sells maps.

Pielpajärvi Wilderness Church

The *erämaakirkko* (wilderness church) of lake Pielpajärvi is accessible from Inari by a marked walking track (7km one way). The church area has been an important marketplace for the Sami over the centuries, with the first church erected here in 1646. The present church was built in 1760, and was restored in the 1970s. The trail starts from the parking area at the Sami Museum.

Sami Museum (Saamelaismuseo)

The superb Sami Museum of Inari should not be missed: it is one of the best open-air museums in Finland, with unique Sami handicrafts, old buildings and local artefacts on display. The museum is open from 9 am to 9 pm daily from June to August. At other times it's open from 10 am to 5 pm Tuesday to Sunday. Admission is 20 mk.

Sami Church

This church was built in 1952 with American financing. The altar painting depicts a wandering Sami family meeting Christ. Inari Sami and Fell Sami are spoken in this church. The church is open daily in summer.

Organised Tours

Lake Cruises There are regular cruises on Inarinjärvi from mid-June (as soon as the ice melts from the lake) to late August. Departures are at 2 pm daily, with additional departures in July at 10 am and 6 pm. The fare is 50 mk.

The destination is **Ukko Island** (Sami: Äjjih), sacred to the Sami for at least 1000 years. During the brief (20 minute) stop, most people climb to the top of the island,

Sami witch drums, 16th century. When the Samis were forcibly converted to Christianity in the 17th century, their traditions were outlawed

but there are also cave formations at the island's north end.

Places to Stay & Eat

For those on a budget, there is a free *wilderness hut* near the Pielpajärvi church. Note that lighting an open fire anywhere in the church area is strictly forbidden.

About 3km from Inari on the road to Lemmenjoki is a small, free *camping ground* with firewood and a pit toilet.

Hotel Inarin Kultahovi (☎ 671 221, fax 671 250), also on the road to Lemmenjoki, has singles/doubles from 330/400 mk. The hotel restaurant serves *siika* (whitefish) by weight.

Several bungalow villages are to be found to the south of the village. *Lomakylä Inari (☎ 671 108, fax 671 480)* is open year-round and is within walking distance of the bus station. It has cottages from 120 mk.

Uruniemi Camping (☎ 671 331, fax 671 200), open March to late September, is a bit farther south.

Inari-keskus is a local scene with an excellent lunch, beer, a grilli and all kinds of souvenirs for sale.

There is a *café* at Samekki (see the following Shopping section).

Shopping

Inari is a centres for *sámi duodji* (Sami handicrafts). Samekki, the studio of Petteri Laiti – the most famous artisan among Finnish Sami – is open daily. Sápmelaš Duodjarat is a handicrafts shop next to the tourist office. Inarin Hopea sells handworked silver items.

Getting There & Away

Heading north on the much-travelled Arctic Road (road No 4), Inari is the next stop after Ivalo. Several buses a day make the 40km trip between the two villages.

LEMMENJOKI NATIONAL PARK
☎ 016

At 2855 sq km, Lemmenjoki (Sami: Leammi) is the largest national park in Finland. Saariselkä is probably more popular with trekkers, but the Lemmenjoki experience is more diverse: slush through desolate wilderness rivers, explore the rough Arctic landscape and bump into lonely gold panners in the middle of nowhere. The Morgamjoki is the main gold panning area, and there are several old huts where gold panners still sleep in summer.

Information

An information hut (☎ 673 411) at the village of Njurgulahti, 50km south-west of Inari, is open from June to late September. You can purchase maps and fishing permits here. All services are available in Njurgulahti village.

Sallivaara Reindeer Roundup

The Sallivaara Reindeer Roundup site, 70km south of Inari, was used by Sami reindeer herders twice yearly until 1964. Roundups were an important social event for the people of northern Lapland, usually lasting several weeks and involving hundreds of people and animals. The Sallivaara reindeer corrals and cabins were reconstructed in 1997, and there are plans to once more have roundups here in autumn and spring. To reach the site, park at Repojoki parking area then follow the marked trail 6km one way. You can sleep overnight in one of the Sallivaara huts.

Trekking

Almost all trails start from Njurgulahti, including a 4km marked nature trail suitable for families with children. The majority of the trekking routes are within the relatively small area between the Lemmenjoki and the Vaskojoki rivers. A 18km loop between Kultala and Ravadasjärvi huts takes you to some of the most interesting gold panning areas. As you can do this in two days, many trekkers head over Ladnjoaivi Fell to Vaskojoki hut and back, which extends the trek to four to five days. For any serious trekking, you will need the 1:100,000 *Lemmenjoki* map, available at the Njurgulahti information hut.

Organised Tours

River Cruises In summer, a local boat service cruises the Lemmenjoki valley, from Njurgulahti village to the Kultahamina wilderness hut at Gold Harbour. A 20km marked trail also follows the course of the river – so you can take the boat one way, then hike back. You can also get on or off the boat at other jetties along the route. There are daily departures from mid-June to mid-September. Fares are 60 mk one way, 120 mk return.

Places to Stay

In the village of Njurgulahti, *Ahkun Tupa* (☎ 673 435) offers accommodation in rooms and cottages, from 80 mk per person. The owners book river cruises and also rent canoes and rowboats.

Inside the park, half a dozen wilderness huts along the most popular trekking routes provide free accommodation. Several are along the river-boat route.

Getting There & Away

There are usually one or two post buses daily from Inari to Njurgulahti village. If you have very little time, and want to take a river cruise, the afternoon bus waits in the village until the boat has made the return trip, then drives back to Inari.

ANGELI

☎ 016

This remote village of 70 inhabitants can be used as a base for exploring the northern section of Lemmenjoki National Park. There are walks nearby, and the quiet Sami culture can be experienced here.

The village's greatest claim to fame is as home to Angelin Tytöt. The duo has been responsible for getting the loud *yoik* singing – the traditional Sami music style – listed in the 'world music' chart, by combining it with the driving energy of Finnish hard rock.

Places to Stay

An Alaskan couple, Todd and Gerry Nolen, runs *Hello Holidays* (☎/fax 672 434, *rry.nolen@pp.inet.fi*), a superb, isolated farmhouse that has good food and lots of sheep. The place accommodates up to 40 visitors in authentic log cabins.

Four people is the minimum, and advance bookings are essential, but you will be picked up from Ivalo airport or in Inari by the admittedly funny host. Full board is about 250 mk per person. Hello Holidays is 2km north of Angeli village.

Getting There & Away

Angeli is 70km west of Inari. No buses run to the village, and hitchhiking can be slow.

KAAMANEN

☎ 016

The village of Kaamanen is little more than the crossing point of three northern roads. The Kotipuoti shop has postal services and a petrol station.

All post buses – and most local folk for that matter – call at *Kaamasen Kievari*, a busy roadhouse a few kilometres north of the Sevettijärvi crossing. Some 5km north is the Karigasniemi crossing.

The HI-affiliated *Hostel Jokitörmä* (☎ 672 725, fax 672 745), open year-round, has rooms and cottages from 95 to 155 mk per person. It has a kitchen and a sauna for guests' use.

Getting There & Away

Kaamanen is 25km north of Inari on road No 4. From Kaamanen, there are bus connections available to various villages in the north.

KEVO NATURE RESERVE

☎ 016

Kevo Nature Reserve was established in 1956 and is 712 sq km in size. Within its boundaries you'll find some of the most breathtaking scenery in Finland (although it's nothing spectacular if you've spent your life in Norway or near the Grand Canyon) along the splendid gorge of the Kevo River (Sami: Geävu), which also has some spectacular waterfalls.

Rules for visiting the Kevo reserve are stricter than those concerning national

parks: hikers cannot hunt, fish or collect plants and berries, and *must* stay on marked trails. The gorge area is off-limits from April to mid-June.

The main trail is 63km long and runs through the canyon, from the Utsjoki-Kaamanen road to the Karigasniemi-Kaamanen road. The trek is rough and takes about four days one way. Use the 1:100,000 *Kevo* topographical sheet, which costs about 50 mk.

Places to Stay

You will need a tent if you plan to hike through the canyon, as there is only one wilderness hut within the boundaries of the nature reserve. *Camping* is permitted within the reserve only at designated camp sites, of which there are many.

There are three free wilderness huts along a north-western path that does not descend into the gorge. From south to north, the huts are: *Ruktajärvi*, at the southern end of the gorge route (accommodates eight people and has a telephone and an oven); *Njavgoaivi* (10 people, telephone); and

Kuivi, inside the park (10 people, oven). It best to do these as a round-trip trek, fro Sulaoja trailhead to Kuivi hut and back.

For those who hike through: *Kenestup* (☎ 678 531), on the Utsjoki-Kaamane road, rents cabins and has a sauna. End yo trek here so you can take advantage of th sauna!

Getting There & Away

Bus The preferred route is to start from th south-west; catch the Karigasniemi-boun bus from Inari and ask the driver to dro you off at the Sulaoja trailhead. From Ke estupa you can catch buses to Inari Nuorgam.

Car & Motorcycle Those with a car ca leave their vehicle at Kenestupa, catch th afternoon bus to Kaamanen and change the Karigasniemi-bound bus.

KARIGASNIEMI
☎ 016

The small village of Karigasniemi (Sam Gáregasnjárga) is a crossing point fro Finland to Norway along the popular Nor kapp route. It has services such as a bar and a post office. Fell Sami, the language the local people of Karigasniemi, is dialect spoken across the border in Norwa

Camping Tenorinne (☎ 676 113) has e cellent cottages at a pleasant locatio ranging in price from 160 to 230 mk. Te sites are 70 mk. Tenorinne is open fro June to mid-September.

Getting There & Away

Two buses a day travel from Ivalo to Kar gasniemi, continuing on to the Norwegia town of Karasjok. A shared taxi travels Sami villages north of Karigasniemi alor the Teno River on Tuesday and Friday.

UTSJOKI
☎ 016

It would be misleading to call the village Utsjoki (Sami: Ohcejohka) an attractiv place, but it has a certain interest as

order town and as the home to a relatively large Sami population. There are two
anks, a post office and several shops in the
village.

Information

The tourist office, Utsjoki Info (☎ 686 234
or 686 111) is jointly run by the municipality and Metsähallitus (the Forest and Park
ervice). There are maps for sale. The
ffice is open daily from June to late Sep-
ember.

Places to Stay & Eat

Utsjoki Camping, at the southern end of the
village, has cabins and tent sites in summer.
There is a kitchen and coin-operated
howers.

Hotel Utsjoki (☎ *677 121, fax 677 126,
uossatie)*, behind the post office, has
ingles/doubles from 260/320 mk, or from
80/250 mk in low season. There is a
estaurant serving full meals.

Tšarssi promises 'pizza, food, café and
nusic' and is essentially a place where
oung Samis learn to rock'n'roll.

Getting There & Away

The daily post bus leaves Rovaniemi each
norning, stopping at Ivalo, Inari and Kaa-
nanen on the way to Utsjoki. There are also
uses from Polmak (Norway) and Nuorgam
o Utsjoki.

NUORGAM
☎ 016

Nuorgam (Sami: Njuorggan) is the north-
rnmost village of Finland. The fact that it's
ne John O'Groats of Finland may be its
nly true appeal. Services, including a bank
nd a postbox, as well as shops that sell
acky clothes to Norwegians, are scattered
long the narrow main road. Prices are typ-
cally given in Norwegian kroner.

The majority of Nuorgam's 200 residents
re Sami.

Nuorgam is the northern end of a
rekking route from Sevettijärvi (see the
rekking Around Sevettijärvi section).

Fishing

The Teno River and its salmon are a good
reason to stop in Nuorgam. Most fishers
gather near Boratbokcankoski and
Alaköngäs rapids, 7km south-west of the
village centre.

Places to Stay

Holiday villages in Nuorgam and along the
river are booming due to good fishing
prospects along the Teno River. There are
almost a dozen possibilities along the road
from Utsjoki to Nuorgam. These places
have mid-range prices, cater mostly to
people fishing the Teno River, and are
usually open from June to August only.

In the village, *Nuorgamin Lomakeskus*
(☎ *678 312)* has hotel-style rooms, cabins
and tent sites, plus boat rentals and a sauna.
You may purchase fishing permits here.

Ala-Jalven Tuvat has cabins at the
popular fishing rapids of Alaköngäs.

Places to Eat

Tenon Lohikellari is a roadside café west of
the village that serves mostly meat dishes.
Some fish dishes are available – after all,
almost everyone here catches their own
fish. In Nuorgam, *Staalonpesä* is a very
nice restaurant with beer and meals, but it
ain't cheap.

Getting There & Away

A daily post bus travels to Nuorgam from
Rovaniemi, and there is an additional bus
on weekdays. When coming from Norway,
it is a 2km walk or hitch from the Norwegian village of Polmak to the border, and
another 4km to the village of Nuorgam.

SEVETTIJÄRVI
☎ 016

One of the roads heads from Kaamanen
eastwards along the shore of Inarinjärvi to
the village of Sevettijärvi (Scolt Sami:
Ce'vetjäu'rr), in the far north-east of
Finland. The inhabitants are a distinctive
Lappish group called Scolt Lapps *(koltta-
lappalaiset)*; some of the Scolts speak
Scoltish, Finnish and Russian.

Things to See

The Orthodox **tsasouna** (church), built in 1951, is dedicated to Father Trifon from Petsamo (now part of Russia). The altar has beautiful icons, some of which were brought from the Soviet-occupied monastery of Valamo. The oldest graves in the church cemetery have a wooden *grobu* (marker) above them, with a wooden bird attached. The church is open on weekdays; knock first at the warden's door.

Perinnetalo is a small museum devoted to Scolt traditions. It, too, is open on weekdays.

Organised Tours

The only person who takes tourists on guided tours is a Dutch man, Ernest Dixon. He has guided his 'Lapland Pulka Treks' and 'Lapland Ruska Treks' for over 30 years, and has the best local knowledge in the region. Ernest takes trekkers to local Lappish homes or out to the fells in search of reindeer herds, and provides food that he prepares over an open fire – he buys fresh salmon from the Lapps!

Write well beforehand to J Ernest Dixon, SF-99930 Sevettijärvi, Finland, or contact Travel North (☎ 31-023 537 7573), Duinlustparkweg 48 A, 2061 LD Bloemendaal, Holland.

Places to Stay & Eat

Sevettijärven Lomamajat (☎ 672 215), behind the church, has rooms and four-bed cabins. The reception is in an adjacent private home.

Farther south from Sevettijärvi are several holiday villages. The modern *Nili-Tuvat* (☎ 672 240), 4km to the south, has cabins and a food kiosk but is close to the road.

Some 26km south of Sevettijärvi, *Koltta-majat* (☎ 673 531) has several modern cabins. There is good fishing in the nearby lake.

Sevetin Baari is the only place that offers meals, snacks and coffee. There is a single **supermarket** in the village.

Getting There & Away

The nearest airport to Sevettijärvi Kirkenes in Norway. The nearest Finnis airport is in Ivalo.

You can hitchhike from Ivalo, but traffi is sparse beyond the Kaamanen crossin There is a post bus connection betwee Ivalo and Sevettijärvi on weekdays.

TREKKING AROUND SEVETTIJÄRVI
☎ 016

The Sevettijärvi region has more lakes p square kilometre than any other region Finland. Very few trekkers explore th remote wilderness, yet it is worth the effo it takes to reach it.

Sevettijärvi to Nuorgam

This is an established trekking route, an the most popular from Sevettijärvi. You' need the 1:50,000 trekking maps for th area, available at Karttakeskus in Helsink There are two places to start the trek, th better one just north of Sevettijärvi, Saunaranta. You'll see a sign readir 'Ahvenjärvi 5', and a trekking sign – 12k to Opukasjärvi, 69km to lake Pulmank järvi. There are six mountain huts along th route; from the final wilderness hut you ca walk to Nuorgam along a road, or make phone call from a local home for a taxi Nuorgam village.

Sevettijärvi to Kirakkajärvi

This is the shortest trekking route in th area, and there are two huts along the wa There is a 1:20,000 trekking map for th route. You can walk the route in two day or set a more leisurely pace and do it three days. The route takes you across th rocky, hilly region on the other side of lak Sevettijärvi. Cross the narrow strait ju south of the Siitapirtti. Follow the rou north-east, and you'll end up on the oth side of lake Sevettijärvi. At the other en preferably at the western side of Lak Kirakka, you'll come to a minor road th will take you to the main road to Kirakka järvi village.

Näätämö to Sevettijärvi

This exciting route starts at Näätämö village in the Norwegian border and goes via Jankkila, Routasenkuru, Vätsäri, Tuulijärvi and Sollomisjärvi to Sevettijärvi, taking you to an area where very few people go. There are a few huts along the way, all clearly marked on major trekking maps.

First head for Näätämö, right at the border. There is a marked path from there south to Jankkila house (14km). From Jankkila, along the Pakanajoki, there is a path to a large lake, and you have the choice of two routes around the lake. The northern one is easier.

The beautiful gorge, Routasenkuru, is easy to find, as it extends north-south for over 5km. You may camp near the campfire places, or stay at the border guards' hut, which has shelter for two to three trekkers. The following day, trek south along Routasenkuru Gorge to the Vätsäri Fells, then turn west again. There is no path, so have your compass ready. You'll find a mountain hut to the west of Vätsäri, and another at Tuulijärvi – one route has a path, the other does not. Farther west is Sollomisjärvi hut. From this hut, there is a short walk through the wilderness or a slightly longer trek along a path, back to Sevettijärvi.

NORDKAPP (NORWAY)

☎ 00 47

Nordkapp (North Cape), a high, rugged coastal plateau at 71°10'21", is the northernmost point in Europe. The best way to experience it is a walk along the stark cliffs under the midnight sun. Keep in mind that there's often heavy fog – the northernmost fog in Europe – which can foil photo-taking. That said, Nordkapp is a popular pilgrimage for visitors to Lapland, so be prepared for crowds. **Nordkapphallen** is the touristy complex with exhibits, eateries, souvenir shops and a post office. There is an entry fee of 130 kr (discounted by 15 kr if you arrive before 6 pm). Champagne, caviar and a midnight buffet are served at very steep prices.

Getting There & Away

Bus Nordkapp can be visited on a marathon bus ride from Rovaniemi: depart Rovaniemi in the morning, change buses at Lakselv (Norway) and you'll arrive in Nordkapp just before midnight. This bus route is only run from early June to mid-August.

Car & Motorcycle From Karigasniemi, you can drive via Karasjok (the Sami centre) and Lakselv, a small settlement on the shores of the Arctic Sea. From Hetta (in Enontekiö), you can drive via Kautokeino (another Sami centre) and Alta (which has an excellent museum and several hotels). There is a ferry crossing from mainland Norway to the small Magerøya island, where Nordkapp is.

Oulu Region

The province of Oulu can be broken up into three areas: Kainuu to the east, Koillismaa in the north-east, and the town of Oulu and its surrounds.

Finns entered the Kainuu region in the 16th century, violating the earlier border treaty between Sweden and Russia. In the late 16th century, the region witnessed fierce frontier wars between Russians and citizens of the Swedish Empire. After these bloody wars, Swedish territory was pushed further east, to where the border stands today.

By the 19th century tar had become the salvation of the economically depressed Kainuu region, but most of the profits were sent along downriver to Oulu, along with the barrels of tar. During WWII, bloody battles were fought against the Red Army in the area around Kuhmo, and soon after the war an enormous flood of emigrants escaped poverty-stricken Kainuu for Sweden and elsewhere. The region has only recently recovered from this exodus but remains sparsely populated.

Kainuu is a heavily forested wilderness area traversed by the famed UKK trekking route close to the border with Russia.

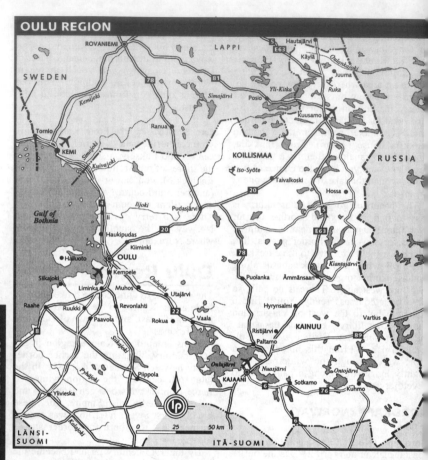

OULU REGION

Koillismaa, near the Russian border, is the transitional region between the south and Lapland, and includes the rugged Kuusamo area, one of the natural highlights of Finland. It is an area of tumbling rivers, isolated lakes and dense forests. Fells and reindeer make this the most Lappish area of Oulu Province. This is also where northern and southern fauna meet, and there are more species to be found here than almost anywhere else. Add to this the fierce local pride and excellent services and you have a most interesting region

to explore. The town of Kuusamo is th centre of the Koillismaa region.

Oulu is the provincial capital, and is sur rounded by a flat region with man historical attractions.

OULU

• pop 113,500   ☎ 08

Oulu (Swedish: Uleåborg) is a lively, fast growing university town, the largest city o Finland's west coast. Its extraordinar number of outdoor bars and terrific networ

f bike paths, plus a generous dollop of fes-
vals, make this a fun place to visit in
ummer. In June and July, it never gets dark
n Oulu, even at night.

Locals often say that Oulu is the only
own with 'a university built on a swamp, a
neatre on the sea, a ship in the marketplace
nd a science centre in a factory'.

High-tech companies love Oulu for its
rainy Oulu School of Technology gradu-
tes and have settled here en masse. This
eing Finland, there's also a stinky pulp
actory not too far from the city centre.

History

)ulu was founded by King Karl IX of
weden in 1605. Shortly thereafter, hard-
vorking Swedish pioneers descended upon
ne Kainuu forests in search of tar, which
vas floated in barrels to Oulu – the sticky
tuff was essential to the building of unsink-
ble wooden ships. By the late 19th century
)ulu boasted the largest fleet in Finland.

In 1822 Oulu burned, and was rebuilt, al-
hough very few old buildings now remain.

Orientation

)ulu is situated at the mouth of the Oulujo-
i, with bridges connecting the riverbanks
nd several islands. Although the entire city
overs a very large area, you can easily
valk from the train and bus stations to most
laces in the centre.

The main street is Kirkkokatu, which
uns north-south. It has a pedestrian section
alled Rotuaari. Kauppurienkatu is also
edestrianised from Isokatu to the kauppa-
ori (market square).

Information

ourist Office The tourist information
ffice (☎ 314 1294 or 314 1295,
aatti.backstrom@ouka.fi) at Torikatu 10 is
pen from 9 am to 6 pm Monday to Satur-
ay and from 10 am to 4 pm Sunday from
ate June to mid-August. At other times it's
pen from 9 am to 4 pm Monday to Friday.

ost & Communications The main post
ffice is near the train station at Hallitus-

katu 36. Hours are from 9 am to 8 pm
Monday to Friday. The telephone office is
next door.

Travel Agency Kilroy Travels (☎ 534
5900) at Pakkahuoneenkatu 8 specialises in
student and budget travel. Hours are from
10 am to 6 pm Monday to Friday, and from
10 am to 2 pm Saturday.

Bookshop Akateeminen Kirjakauppa at
Kirkkokatu 29 has a good and varied selection of English-language paperbacks.

Internet Resources & Library The public
library is at the kauppatori. It has four Internet terminals and a reading room with foreign
newspapers, including the *International
Herald Tribune*. Hours are from 10 am to 8
pm Monday to Friday, and from 10 am to 3
pm Saturday. The main Web site for Oulu is
www.ouka.fi/oulu_ee.html.

Left Luggage The train station has a left-
luggage counter, and both the train and
bus stations have 24-hour lockers that cost
10 mk.

Medical Services The pharmacy at
Kirkkokatu 11 is open daily from 9 am to 9
pm. The regional hospital is just north of the
centre on Kasarmintie.

Emergency For general emergencies call
☎ 112, for police call ☎ 10022 and for a
doctor, dial ☎ 10023.

Kauppatori

At the market square look for the squat
Toripolliisi statue, a humorous representation of the local police. A number of shops
– in quaint wooden storehouses – ring the
square. These sell woven pine baskets,
carved wooden cups and other typical
Finnish souvenirs.

Oulu Cathedral

The imposing, yellow, 19th century cathedral has Finland's oldest portrait (dating
from 1611) in its vestry. A much older

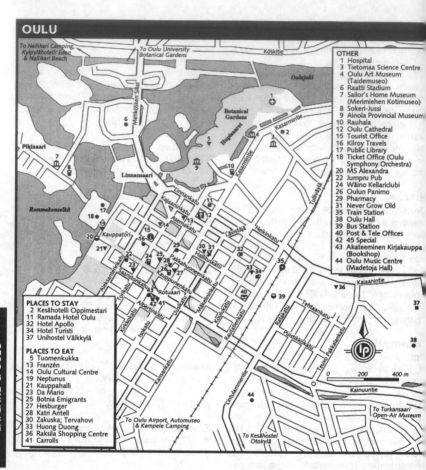

OULU

PLACES TO STAY
2 Kesähotelli Oppimestari
11 Ramada Hotel Oulu
32 Hotel Apollo
34 Hotel Turisti
37 Unihostel Välkkylä

PLACES TO EAT
5 Tuomenkukka
13 Franzén
14 Oulu Cultural Centre
19 Neptunus
21 Kauppahalli
23 Da Mario
25 Botnia Emigrants
27 Hesburger
28 Katri Antell
30 Zakuska; Tervahovi
33 Huong Duong
36 Raksila Shopping Centre
41 Carrolls

OTHER
1 Hospital
3 Tietomaa Science Centre
4 Oulu Art Museum
  (Taidemuseo)
6 Raatti Stadium
7 Sailor's Home Museum
  (Merimiehen Kotimuseo)
8 Sokeri-Jussi
9 Ainola Provincial Museum
10 Rauhala
12 Oulu Cathedral
15 Tourist Office
16 Kilroy Travels
17 Public Library
18 Ticket Office (Oulu
  Symphony Orchestra)
20 MS Alexandra
22 Jumpru Pub
24 Wäino Kellariclubi
26 Oulun Panimo
29 Pharmacy
31 Never Grow Old
35 Train Station
38 Oulu Hall
39 Bus Station
40 Post & Tele Offices
42 45 Special
43 Akateeminen Kirjakauppa
  (Bookshop)
44 Oulu Music Centre
  (Madetoja Hall)

church, built in 1777, stood here until the great fire of 1822. This version was designed by the German architect CL Engel. Hours are from 10 am to 8 pm daily from June to late August, or from noon to 1 pm daily at other times.

Tietomaa Science Centre

The mammoth Tietomaa Science Centre, in an old factory building, is Scandinavia's oldest and largest science museum; at any given time it's mobbed with hundreds of school children bused in from all ove[r] Finland. Sadly, many of the exhibits are i[n] Finnish only (as is the Omnimax film). Stil[l] between the UFO exhibit, hologram hal[l] junior science centre and the new 'world [of] sport' there's still plenty to gawk at. Admi[s]sion is a hefty 60 mk (children, students an[d] seniors 50 mk). Tietomaa is open from 10 a[m] to 8 pm daily in July and until 6 pm daily i[n] May, June and August. During the rest of th[e] year, hours are from 10 am to 4 pm on week[days] days and from 10 am to 6 pm on weekend[s]

Oulu Art Museum (Taidemuseo)

The Oulu Art Museum at Kasarmintie 7 is adjacent to Tietomaa. It has intriguing temporary exhibitions of both international and Finnish contemporary art, as well as a good permanent collection. It's open from 11 am to 6 pm Tuesday to Sunday (to 8 pm Wednesday). Admission is 15 mk; free on Friday.

Sailor's Home Museum (Merimiehen Kotimuseo)

The small home museum, on Pikisaari island at Pikisaarentie 6, formerly belonged to a local sailor. It is the oldest house in Oulu, built in 1737 and was transferred here from the town centre in 1983. It's open from 10 am to 6 pm from Monday to Thursday, 11 am to 5 pm Saturday and Sunday from early June to late August. It's open from 10 am to 4 pm from Monday to Thursday, 11 am to 5 pm Saturday and Sunday from mid to late May and September. Admission is 5 mk.

Ainola Provincial Museum

The provincial museum, near Ainola Park on Hupisaaret island, has displays dealing with everything from old Finnish coins to Sami culture – but unfortunately does not provide English translations (most Finnish museums do). It's open daily, year-round, and charges 10 mk admission.

Turkansaari Open-Air Museum

The excellent open-air folk museum on Turkansaari island, 13km south-east of the city, can be reached bus No 3 or 4. Originally the island was a trading post for Russians and Swedes; many old buildings remain. In summer there are all kinds of things you won't find back home – like tar-burning and log-rolling demonstrations – and plenty of folk music and dancing. Entry is 10 mk. The museum is open from 11 am to 8 pm daily from June to late August, and to 5 pm daily from early to mid-September.

Oulu University Botanical Gardens

The Botanical Gardens, in Linnanmaa north of the centre, are pleasantly landscaped with thousands of exotic plants – including unbelievably hardy 5m-tall cacti. A pair of greenhouses, named Romeo and Juliet, house tropical species. Entry is 10 mk. The greenhouses are closed Monday but the rest of the park is open daily year-round.

Car Museum (Automuseo)

The Automuseo's collection includes more than 50 old vehicles, ranging from a 1910 German Vomag to Cold War East German cars. Most of the cars and motorcycles here are privately owned. Hours are from 9 am to 6 pm daily from June to late September, and from 9 am to 4 pm Sunday to Friday at other times. Admission is 25 mk. The museum is on the Oulu-Kempele road, 5km south of Oulu.

Cycling

Oulu and the surrounding region has an extensive network of scenic bicycle paths, routinely praised as the best local cycling routes in Finland. Many of the paths are along the river or over bridges to the nearby islands.

The tourist office and train station rent bikes for about 30 mk per day, and a free route map is available from the tourist office. Nallikari Camping also rents bikes, sometimes at better rates.

Organised Tours

The 'Potnapekka' – a tourist trolley – travels around Oulu's pedestrian streets and bike paths in summer, from Rotuarri pedestrian street to Hupisaaret island or Nallikari beach. The fare is 16 mk (25 mk to both Hupisaaret and Nallikari); departures are from Rotuarri every hour on the hour, daily from mid-June to mid-August.

Cruises From May to September the MS *Alexandra* (☎ 881 1755) cruises the Oulu archipelago, with daily departures from the kauppatori. Cost is 50 mk.

Special Events

Oulu hosts two unusual winter events, both the largest of their kind anywhere in the world. The Oulu Tar Ski Race, held in early March, is a 70km race (40km for women) that is entering its second century. The Ice-Angling Marathon is a 48 hour contest held in early April (when the ice is still quite thick) and draws more than 400 participants.

The biggest summer event is Tar-Burning Week, a festival that takes place in late June, around midsummer.

Places to Stay

Camping Camp or rent a cabin at *Nallikari Camping (☎ 554 1541 or 377 911, Hietasaari)*, on Hietasaari island, 5km north-west of the city centre. To get there, take bus No 5, the 'Eden' bus. The busy, well established camping ground is open year-round, although they're inclined to think you crazy if you want to camp here anytime but summer! Camp sites cost 65 to 80 mk, cabins 130 to 700 mk. Nearby is the good Nallikari beach.

Another option is *Kempele Camping (☎ 515 455, Sohjanantie 67)* in the suburb of Kempele, about 14km south of Oulu. Sites cost 65 mk, cabins 120 to 420 mk. Kempele is open from June to late September.

Hostels The HI-affiliated *Unihostel Välkkylä (☎ 313 6311, fax 313 6754, unihostel@oyy.fi, Kajaanintie 36)*, east of the town centre, is open from June to late August. Beds in this student dormitory cost 70 to 100 mk; many rooms are equipped with kitchenettes. Facilities include sauna and laundry.

Also affiliated with HI, *Kesähostel Otokylä (☎ 530 8413, fax 530 8327, kristiinas@oyy.fi, Haapanatie 2)* is a student apartment building located 3km south-east from the train station. It is open to travellers from mid-May to mid-August, with beds from 70 mk and more

expensive single/double rooms. The kitchen, sauna and laundry facilities are yours to use.

Hotels Across the street from the Tietomaa Science Centre, *Kesähotelli Oppimestari (☎ 884 8527, fax 884 8529, Nahkatehtaankatu 3)* is a summer hotel open from June to early August. All rooms are non-smoking and equipped with kitchenettes; rates are 150/220 mk for singles/doubles.

Hotel Turisti (☎ 375 233, Rautatienkatu 9) is a suprisingly nice place just steps from the train station. It has rooms for 255/320 mk on weekends and in summer, 275/350 mk at other times.

Also close to the train station is *Hotel Apollo (☎/fax 374 344, Asemakatu 31-33)*, a standard hotel. It has rooms from 275/330 mk in summer and 300/360 mk at other times. The hotel's karaoke bar stays open until 4 am nightly.

The *Ramada Hotel Oulu (☎ 883 9111, fax 883 9100, Kirkkokatu 3)* is the most modern hotel in Oulu, with a good location overlooking the cathedral. There are 154 rooms, some of which have their own sauna. Prices start at 720/865 mk, or 400/460 mk on weekends and in summer.

Kylpylähotelli Eden (☎ 550 4100, fax 554 4103, Nallikari) is a deluxe spa hotel on Hietasaari island, near Nallikari Camping and the beach. Rooms start at 495/598 mk, although discounts are available for longer stays. All prices include unlimited use of saunas, water slides and lushly landscaped indoor pools.

Places to Eat

Oulu is the most cosmopolitan city in western Finland, and offers a good variety of restaurants in all price ranges. For grillis and fast food restaurants, try Rotuaari (the pedestrian street) or the blocks surrounding the train station.

Oulu specialities include *rieska* (flat bread), *leipäjuusto* (cheese bread), and *lohikeitto* (salmon soup). These can be found at the *kauppatori* or the adjacent *kauppahalli* (indoor market).

Finnish & International A nice place for lunch is the *Oulu Cultural Centre* (Oulun Kultuurikeskus), across the street from the tourist office. It has good meals from 10.30 am to 2 pm weekdays, ranging in price from 20 to 38 mk.

Near the train station, *Huong Duong* is a small Vietnamese place with lunch for 32 mk; there are Chinese, Indian and Turkish eateries nearby.

Botnia Emigrants on Rotuaari offers a 32 mk meal with potato, salad and your choice of grilled sausage (the house speciality). *Zakuska (Hallituskatu 13)* is a popular place for fine Russian cuisine.

At the kauppatori, *Neptunus* (☎ 372 572) is an old sailing ship, now a restaurant. Be warned: a full meal may be costly.

The finest place to dine in Oulu is *Franzén (Kirkkokatu 2)*. The building dates back to 1829 and has a German-style beer cellar. Main courses are from 85 mk.

Cafés *Katri Antell (Kirkkokatu 17)* has been an Oulu institution for a very long time; the first Katri Antell was founded in 1880. Come for its freshly baked pastries and cakes. *Tuomenkukka* is a pleasant café in a greenhouse at Ainola Park on Hupisaaret island.

Fast Food For good, cheap pizza, *Da Mario (Torikatu 24)* is a winner. A small pie costs 20 mk, a large one 40 mk. *Carrolls* on Isokatu makes a tasty 15 mk 'club burger', and two blocks north you'll find a *Hesburger*.

Self-Catering There are three enormous *supermarkets* at the Raksila shopping centre, near the bus and train stations.

Entertainment

Oulu – perhaps more than any other city in Finland – is a place where people insist on drinking their cold beer outside, in the sun, as soon as the snow melts. Wall-to-wall beer terraces flourish in summer on Rotuaari, the pedestrian section of Kirkkokatu, where you are serenaded by street musicians.

Bars The patio at *Jumpru Pub (Kauppurienkatu 6)* is a perennial favourite, and the central location can't be beaten. *Oulun Panimo* brews its own beer and is located not far from Rotuaari.

Never Grow Old (Hallituskatu 13) is a reggae pub with occasional live music. Also here is *Tervahovi*, locally famous as the 'king of pubs'. It's next door to Zakuska. On Pikisaari island, *Sokeri-Jussi* (Sugar John) is a big, old, timbered place with icy beers and outdoor tables that have good views of the centre. This is also a café and handicrafts shop. *Rauhala (Mannenkatu 1)* is the student pub, usually hopping from 2 pm. There's outdoor seating whenever weather permits, and occasional live music.

Clubs *Wäino Kellariclubi* is a basement-level club on Torikatu, great for live rock and very popular. *45 Special* on Saaristonkatu is another good choice for live music and dancing.

Oulu's hotels also attract large crowds of locals for their lively nightlife.

Classical Music The Oulu Symphony Orchestra holds concerts at Madetoja Hall in the *Oulu Music Centre*, Lintulammentie 1-3, on most Thursdays. The ticket office (☎ 314 7200) is at Kaarlenväylä 2.

Spectator Sports

Sporting events – including ice hockey, football and Finnish baseball – take place at Raatti Stadium and Oulu Hall. Contact the tourist office for information.

Getting There & Away

Air Oulu airport is one of the busiest in Finland. Finnair has many daily direct flights from Helsinki and all other major Finnish cities, and from Stockholm, Copenhagen and Oslo.

Bus The bus station is near the train station, and express buses connect with Oulu from all main centres. To reach nearby villages, catch a local Koskilinjat bus from the town centre.

Train The train station is just east of the centre. Six to 10 trains a day run from Helsinki to Oulu, the fastest trains covering the 680km in a little over six hours. There are also trains via Kajaani.

Car & Motorcycle Oulu is on road No 8, the West Coast road, 635km north of Turku. To reach Lapland take road No 4 north from Oulu; Rovaniemi is 215km away.

Getting Around

To/From the Airport The airport is 15km south of the centre. Arriving flights are met by a Finnair bus to Oulu (20 mk). From the bus or train station you can catch local bus No 19 to the airport (16 mk). The trip takes about 30 minutes.

Bus There is a good network of local buses. Each ride costs about 8 mk, and route maps are displayed at bus stops.

Bicycle The main roads north and south from Oulu are oversized motorways (freeways) which are off-limits to cyclists – fortunately there are many minor roads and bikeways. Pick up a bike route map at the Oulu tourist office.

AROUND OULU

The area around Oulu was a sea bed after the Ice Age and until a few thousand years ago. These days, it is relatively fertile farmland, which is still rising a centimetre every year.

Hailuoto Island
• pop 970   ☎ 08

Hailuoto is the opposite of Atlantis – it rose from the sea about 2000 years ago. This flat island is 200 sq km in size, and growing. Its population, mainly fishers, has been isolated for centuries. These days Hailuoto's main appeal is its quaint, sleepy fishing villages, as traffic is effectively regulated by ferries. Artists come here to seek inspiration, vacationers to bask on sandy beaches. Grey lichen, used for reindeer food on the mainland, is the main produce of Hailuoto.

Most of the island can be explored only on foot.

Orientation & Information The island is 30km long and has just one main road. Hailuoto village has shops and a bank. The tourist information office (☎ 810 1133) at the ferry harbour distributes free maps.

Things to See & Do The open-air **Kniivilä Museum**, in Hailuoto village, has a collection of old houses. It's open daily in June and July and charges 5 mk entry. **Marjaniemi** is the westernmost point of Hailuoto, with a lighthouse and a cluster of old fisherfolk's houses. Nearby is a short *luontopolku* (nature trail). There are good swimming **beaches** at Marjaniemi and at Pöllä harbour.

Places to Stay & Eat *Ranta-Sumppu Camping* (☎ 810 0690 or 810 0791), open year-round, is at Marjaniemi, 30km west of the ferry pier. There are 17 cottages for rent, and camping is possible too. Ranta-Sumppu offers buffet lunches.

Ailasto (☎ 810 0384, fax 810 0698) is the first place along the road from the ferry pier. Run by a Polish man who plays the keyboard on weekends, it has modern cabins at 300 mk per day. Rather expensive meals are available.

Saaren Leipä, a few kilometres west of Hailuoto village, sells fresh bread. There is a *café* at the ferry pier.

Getting There & Away Bus No 18 from Oulu crosses the 7km strait from the mainland on a free *lossi* (ferry) and continues across Hailuoto island to its westernmost point, Marjaniemi. There are two or three buses daily. If you are coming from Oulu by car, take road No 816.

Haukipudas
• pop 14,600   ☎ 08

Haukipudas is 20km north of Oulu at a scenic spot along the Kiiminkijoki river. The buttercup-coloured **church** is one of the most notable 'picture churches' in Finland, with superb naive frescoes on the walls and a

AROUND OULU

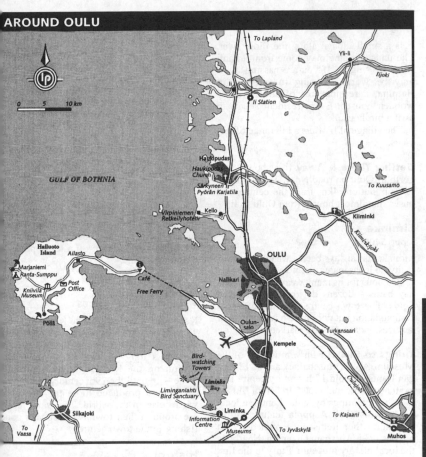

0   5   10 km

To Lapland

Yli-Ii

Iijoki

Ii Station

Haukipudas
Haukipudas
Church

Särkyneen
Pyörän Karjatila

To Kuusamo

GULF OF BOTHNIA

Virpiniemen
Retkeilyhotelli   Kello

Kiiminki

Kiiminkijoki

Hailuoto
Island   Ailasto

OULU

Marjaniemi
Ranta-Sumppu

Café

Post
Office

Kniivilä
Museum

Free Ferry

Nallikari

Pöllä

Oulun-
salo

Turkansaari

Oulujoki

Kempele

Bird-
watching
Towers

Liminka
Bay

Liminganlahti
Bird Sanctuary

Siikajoki

Liminka

Information
Centre
Museums

To Kajaani

*To
Vaasa*

To Jyväskylä

Muhos

small, wooden *vaivaisukko* (pauper statue)
outside. It's open year-round.

Places to Stay & Eat *Virpiniemen
Retkeilyhotelli* (☎ *561 4200, fax 561 4224,
virpiniemi@mail.suomi.net, Hiitomajantie
27),* at the seashore near Kello village, is
5km from the main road and 23km from
Oulu. It is an HI-affiliated Finnhostel that is
open year-round. Beds cost from 65 to 120
mk per person, and there is a kitchen and
sauna.

Särkyneen Pyörän Karjatila is next to
the church in Haukipudas village. It is a
150-year-old cowshed, now wonderfully
transformed into a cosy restaurant serving
'country-style' gourmet Finnish food from
45 mk.

Getting There & Away Haukipudas lies
on road No 847 north from Oulu, but can
also be reached by the main road No 4.
Buses run almost hourly from Oulu to
Haukipudas.

Ii
☎ 08

Ii is a small village along the Iijoki river. The unusual name may come from a Sami word for 'night'. If you are passing by, it may be worth stopping to see the **Iin Hamina**, a seaside area of attractive old wooden houses. Every resident seems to own a birdhouse.

The village of Ii offers a full range of services.

Getting There & Away Ii is about 35km north of Oulu on road No 4. Trains stop at Ii train station, 4km from the centre, and buses run almost hourly from Oulu to Ii.

Liminka
• pop 5400   ☎ 08

Liminka has always been a wealthy municipality, so it has many attractive old buildings. It is famous for its many weathered, wooden hay barns – dozens dot the flat, ploughed fields. The town centre does not offer accommodation but does have a wide range of services, including supermarkets.

Things to See The three museums of the Museum Area (Museoalue) are at Limingan Ranta, the old 17th century centre that is 500m off the main road. In **Lampi Museo** there are paintings by Vilho Lampi, a local artist. **Muistokoti Aappola** features furniture and other items once owned by an opera singer, Abraham Ojanperä. Nearby is the **local history museum**. Entry to the first two museums is 10 mk (valid for both); the third is free. All are open from noon to 6 pm daily from June to August.

Getting There & Away Liminka lies along road No 8. Several daily Raahe-bound buses make the 30km trip from Oulu to Liminka.

Liminganlahti Bird Sanctuary
☎ 08

The bird sanctuary at Liminka Bay (Liminganlahti) attracts more avian species than any other similar place in Finland. The wide bay is protected and funded by the World Wide Fund for Nature (WWF).

The 'great bird migration' is best seen in May, August and September. Several rare species of birds nest here during summer months, and up to 70 species of birds can be seen in a single summer day. The sanctuary *opastuskeskus* (information centre) is 600m off the road, with a guide in attendance from 9 am to 5 pm daily from May to August. You may borrow a telescope to use at any of four birdwatching towers – the nearest is just 400m away.

Getting There & Away The sanctuary lies several kilometres west of Liminka on road No 813. Raahe-bound buses stop at the Liminganlahti turn-off after stopping at Liminka village.

KAJAANI
• pop 37,000   ☎ 08

Kajaani is the centre of the Kainuu region. There's not much to see in the town itself, and the little that is here is chiefly related to Kajaani's long position as an important station on the Kainuu tar transportation route – up until the 19th century this region of Finland produced more tar than any where else in the world. That said, locals are proud of their town, which boasts good fishing in the town centre.

History

In 1651 Count Per Brahe founded the town of Kajaani. Soon after, King Karl IX had a castle built on an island in the Kajaaninjoki. Kajaani became a vital regional stronghold. Russians attacked in 1716, and destroyed the castle after five weeks of fighting.

Kajaani has been home to some colourful personalities. Elias Lönnrot, creator of Finland's national epic, the *Kalevala*, stayed here for a period in the 19th century, using Kajaani as a base for his travels. The long reigning president Urho Kekkonen lived here as a student.

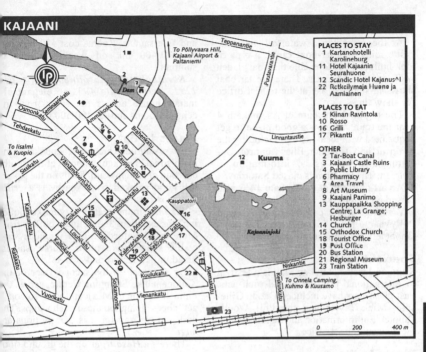

KAJAANI

To Pöllyvaara Hill, Kajaani Airport & Paltaniemi

Teppanantie

Putaanrantie

Linnantaustie

Kuurna

Kauppatori

Kajaaninjoki

Niskantie

To Onnela Camping, Kuhmo & Kuusamo

To Iisalmi & Kuopio

To Iisalmi & Kuopio

Osmonkatu Seminaarinkatu
Tehdaskatu
Sissikatu
Väinämöisenkatu
Pohjolankatu
Ämmäkoskenk
Brahenkatu
Kauppakatu
Linnankatu
Kirkkokatu
Sammonkatu
Kalliokatu
Lönnrotinkatu
Koivukoskenkatu
Kalevankatu
Urho Kekkosen katu
Kauppakatu
Asemakatu
Keskuskatu
Koulukatu
Vienankatu
Soikankatu
Vuorikatu

0   200   400 m

PLACES TO STAY
1 Kartanohotelli Karolineburg
11 Hotel Kajaanin Seurahuone
12 Scandic Hotel Kajanus^l
22 Retkeilymaja Huone ja Aamiainen

PLACES TO EAT
5 Kiinan Ravintola
10 Rosso
16 Grilli
17 Pikantti

OTHER
2 Tar-Boat Canal
3 Kajaani Castle Ruins
4 Public Library
6 Pharmacy
7 Area Travel
8 Art Museum
9 Kajaani Panimo
13 Kauppapaikka Shopping Centre; La Grange; Hesburger
14 Church
15 Orthodox Church
18 Tourist Office
19 Post Office
20 Bus Station
21 Regional Museum
23 Train Station

Information

Tourist Office The tourist office Kajaani Info (☎ 615 5555) at Pohjolankatu 16 gives information, arranges hotel reservations and sells fishing permits. The office is open in summer from 9 am to 6 pm weekdays, and to 1 pm Saturday. In winter the hours are from 9 am to 5 pm Monday to Friday

Post The post office is at Sammonkatu 13. It's open from 8.30 am to 8 pm Monday to Friday.

Internet Resources & Library The public library at Kauppakatu 35 has an Internet terminal. Library hours are from 10 am to 8 pm Monday to Friday, and to 3 pm Saturday.

Travel Agency Area Travel (☎ 632730) at Pohjolankatu 33 is the local American

Express affiliate. Hours are from 8.30 am to 5 pm Monday to Friday.

Medical & Emergency Services For a general emergency call ☎ 112, for police call ☎ 10022 and for a doctor dial ☎ 10023.

The Raatihuoneen Pharmacy on Kauppakatu is open from 8.30 am to 10 pm Monday to Saturday and from 10 am to 10 pm Sunday.

Things to See & Do

In the centre, the beautiful wooden **church** from 1896 is a rare example of neogothic architecture. It's typically Karelian, with lots of ornate wooden trim. The church is open daily in summer. Nearby is an **Orthodox church,** also open daily in summer.

Across the Kajaaninjoki from the town centre is **Kajaani Castle**, built in the 17th century and thoroughly damaged by war, time and some more recent mischief. It's not much to see, and admission is free.

At the Ämmäkoski waterfall, near the castle ruins, is a **tar-boat canal**, a type of lock built in 1846 to enable the boats laden with tar barrels to pass. There are tar boat shows in summer; ask at the tourist office for show times.

The **regional museum** at Asemakatu 4 near the train station is a good place to get acquainted with local history, including the *Kalevala* and its author, Elias Lönnrot. Unfortunately, there is no information in English. The museum is closed Saturday.

An **art museum** at Linnankatu 14 is also closed on Saturday.

Walking tracks can be found around Pöllyvaara Hill, just above the Kartanohotelli Karolineburg.

Special Events

Kainuun Jazzkevät in late May is a festival of international jazz, blues and rock acts. Past guest stars have included Dizzie Gillespie, Mick Taylor and the Phil Woods Quintet. For information and tickets contact the Kajaani tourist office.

Places to Stay

Camping *Onnela Camping* (☎ 622 703, *Onnelantie)*, east of the train station on Niskantie, is the best value in Kajaani. It has cabins from 145 to 270 mk. Camping is 80 to 90 mk. The place rents boats, canoes and bikes.

Hostel *Retkeilymaja Huone ja Aamiainen* (☎/fax 622 254, *Pohjolankatu 4)*, near the train station, is a guesthouse associated with HI. It's not the newest or tidiest place, and there are no amenities. Singles/doubles are 145/260 mk, breakfast and linen included.

Hotels In the town centre, *Hotel Kajaanin Seurahuone* (☎ 623 076, fax 613 4495, *Kauppakatu 11)*, has rooms from 415/540 mk on weekdays and 295/395 mk on weekends. All singles and doubles are 395 mk in summer.

Across the river, *Scandic Hotel Kajanus* (☎ 61641, fax 616 4505, *Koskikatu 3)* is

one of the largest and best hotels in North Finland, with 235 rooms, five restaurant and five saunas. Rooms cost 470/590 mk or 320/400 mk on weekends and in summer.

Kartanohotelli Karolineburg (☎ 61. 1291, *Karoliinantie 4)* is an elegant ol manor house across the river from th centre. Rooms start at 400/500 mk.

Places to Eat

Most restaurants are on Kauppakatu, th main street. The kauppatori is at the south east end of Kauppakatu. Stalls on the squar sell good smoked fish. Nearby is a *grill* good for cheap eats.

Pikantti, in the nearby Citymarket build ing, has excellent 35 mk lunch buffets from Monday to Saturday. This includes veg etable soup and a main course, salads bread, milk, dessert and coffee.

La Grange, on the second floor of th Kauppapaikka Shopping Centre, serves th Finnish version of Mexican food – so you' get 'cheese icing' on those nacho chips. Th best you can say for it is that portions ar *huge*.

There's a *Hesburger* on the ground floo of the Kauppapaikka Shopping Centre.

Rosso (Kauppakatu 21) offers a 50 mk lunch. Pizzas, pastas and steaks are on offe for dinner.

At the north end of Kauppakatu, adjacen to the pharmacy, *Kiinan Ravintola* provide good Chinese food and a nice atmospher (open Sunday).

Entertainment

Kaajani Panimo, on Kauppakatu, adjacen to the Rosso restaurant, is a popula brewery pub.

Getting There & Away

Air Finnair has daily flights from Helsink to Kajaani. The airport is 8km north-west o town; take bus No 4 (16 mk).

Bus Kajaani is the major travel hub in th Kainuu district. There are frequent depar tures for Kuhmo and other towns in th region during the week, but few departure on weekends. The local bus service is useful if you want to visit Paltaniemi.

Train Kajaani is on the main Helsinki-Oulu line. There are four daily trains from Helsinki, via Kouvola and Kuopio; the fastest train takes less than seven hours. The night train from Helsinki takes approximately 10 hours.

Car & Motorcycle Kaajani is 567km north of Helsinki on road No 5 that runs between Helsinki and Lapland. Kuusamo is about 250km farther north.

AROUND KAJAANI
Paltaniemi
The village of Paltaniemi is considered a suburb of Kajaani, although it has its own distinctive history. The first church was built here in 1599. In the centuries that followed, Paltaniemi became the regional centre for the Lutheran Church. You'll see some of the most exciting church paintings in Finland here.

The old wooden church was built in 1726, and its bell tower dates from 1776. The church is known for its wonderful old murals and ceiling paintings (some were altered and repainted in 1940). The Hell scene has been partly covered, apparently to avoid disturbing the locals. The church is open from 10 am to 6 pm daily in summer. An information tape in English is available on request.

Keisarintalli, an old wooden stable, was used as a boarding house for Tsar Alexander I when he toured Finland in 1819. This simple building was actually the best available for the exalted visitor. Ask at the church to be shown around.

The **Eino Leino House** (Eino Leino Talo) was built in 1978 to commemorate the centenary of the birth of Finland's famous poet Eino Leino, who was born in Paltaniemi. There is a café. The house and café are open from 11 am to 6 pm daily from mid-June to late July, and admission is free.

Getting There & Away Take local bus No 4 (the airport bus) from Kajaani to Pal-taniemi. There are hourly departures on weekdays, less often on weekends.

KUHMO
- **pop 12,500** ☎ **08**

The lively wilderness centre of Kuhmo is known for its annual chamber music festival, and for its Kalevala Village theme park. Kuhmo is also a natural base for those who are planning to hike along the UKK trekking route.

Technically, Kuhmo, with an area of 5458 sq km, is the largest city in Finland. Of course, there could hardly be an area more remote than the 'suburbs' of Kuhmo, along the Russian border. The town itself, with 7500 of the area's population, is small but unusually pleasant.

Information
Tourist Offices The Kuhmo tourist office (☎ 655 6382, fax 655 6384) is at Kainuuntie 126, just south of the town centre. It's open from 8 am to 6 pm Monday to Friday, and from 9 am to 4 pm Saturday from June to late August. During other times of year, it's open from 8 am to 5 pm Monday to Friday. The office stocks good maps and walking guides to the region.

Kainuu Nature Centre (☎ 877 6380, kaapalinna@metsa.fi), near the Kalevala theme park, is a national park information centre run by the Forest and Park Service (Metsähallitus).

Post The post office on Kainuuntie is open from 9 am to 8 pm Monday to Friday.

Internet Resources & Library The public library at Pajakkakatu 2 charges 20 mk per hour to use the Internet terminal. Library hours are from 10 am to 7 pm Monday to Friday (from 2 pm Thursday).

Medical & Emergency Services For a general emergency call ☎ 112, for police call ☎ 10022 and for a doctor dial ☎ 10023.

The Kuhmo health care centre is on Kirkkotie.

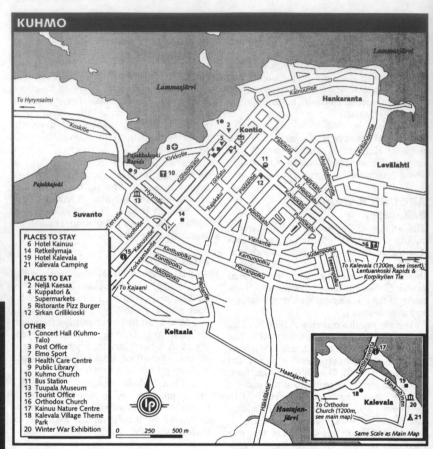

KUHMO

PLACES TO STAY
6 Hotel Kainuu
14 Retkeilymaja
19 Hotel Kalevala
21 Kalevala Camping

PLACES TO EAT
2 Neljä Kaesaa
4 Kuppatori &
    Supermarkets
5 Ristorante Pizz Burger
12 Sirkan Grillikioski

OTHER
1 Concert Hall (Kuhmo-
    Talo)
3 Post Office
7 Elmo Sport
8 Health Care Centre
9 Public Library
10 Kuhmo Church
11 Bus Station
13 Tuupala Museum
15 Tourist Office
16 Orthodox Church
17 Kainuu Nature Centre
18 Kalevala Village Theme
    Park
20 Winter War Exhibition

0   250   500 m

Same Scale as Main Map

Kalevala Village Theme Park

The Kalevala Village theme park, 3km from the centre, is the main sight in Kuhmo. It was named after the Finnish national epic, the *Kalevala* (see the boxed text 'The Kalevala' in the Facts About the Country chapter). There are Karelian exhibitions and artisan displays, and costumed employees demonstrating tar-making, woodcarving, fishing and so on. Tickets are 60 mk adult, 30 mk child, and include a guided tour. The park is open from 9.30 am to 6 pm daily

from June to late August. The adjacent **Winter War Exhibition** displays artefacts found in the Kuhmo wilderness. It is open from 9 am to 6 pm daily from May to late September. Admission is 20 mk.

Tuupala Museum

This charming Karelian farmhouse, at Tervatie 1, has been, in its past lives, a general store, pharmacy, inn, post office and home to the town's police chief. It's now a museum of local history. Hours are from

10 am to 4 pm Tuesday to Sunday, from June to late August. Admission is 10 mk.

Kuhmo Church
The striking 1816 wooden church in the town centre is a venue for concerts during the chamber music festival (see under Special Events). The church is open from 10 am to 6 pm daily in summer. At those times admission is free.

Orthodox Church
The Orthodox Church is a kilometre from the centre, on the road to the Kalevala Village theme park. It contains several 18th century icons that were painted in the Valamo Monastery before it was annexed by the Soviet Union, plus a 300-year-old Madonna icon. The church is open on request only; inquire at the tourist office.

White-Water Rafting
White-water rafting trips to Lentuankoski rapids, 15km north of Kuhmo, take place on weekends in June and August and daily during July, with a minimum of two persons. Cost is 50 mk per person for two or three people, 40 mk per person for four or more. Book through the Kuhmo tourist office.

Fishing
Fishing for perch and pike is popular at Pajakkakoski rapids near the town centre and at Lentuankoski rapids north of town. See Fishing in the Activities chapter for information about fishing permits and seasons, or inquire at the Kainuu Nature Centre.

Cycling
Rent bicycles at Elmo Sport, Kainuuntie 88, for 60 mk per day or 250 mk per week.

Special Events
The Kuhmo Chamber Music Festival, held in mid-July to August each year, attracts top musicians from around the world. More than 100 musicians participate each year. Most of the concerts are held at Kuhmo-Talo, a spacious, modern concert hall.

Tickets are from 20 to 85 mk; most cost 65 mk. There are also a few free concerts every day. For advance bookings contact the Kuhmo tourist office or the Kuhmo Chamber Music Festival (☎ 652 0936, fax 652 1961, marja.kahkonen@kajak.fi), Torikatu 39, 88900 Kuhmo.

Places to Stay
Camping *Kalevala Camping* (☎ 655 6382), near the Kalevala Village theme park, has camp sites for 65 mk and cabins for 150 to 370 mk. You can rent rowing boats and canoes here.

Hostel *Retkeilymaja* (☎ 655 6245), in the Piilolan school building, is an HI-affiliated hostel that is only open during the month of July. Beds are from 70 mk, and there is a kitchen and sauna.

Hotels *Hotel Kainuu* (☎ 655 1711, fax 655 1715, Kainuuntie 84) is the best place to stay in the centre. Singles/doubles start at 240/340 mk.

Hotel Kalevala (☎ 655 4100, fax 655 4200, Väinämöinen 9), near the theme park, is an upscale option. Modern rooms cost 450/600 mk (375/510 mk during low season). This place handles most rental services, including canoes.

Places to Eat
The small *kauppatori* is busy in summer, daily till late afternoon. Look for local specialities like karjalanpiirakka pies. Several *supermarkets* are right on the square.

Cheap snacks are served at *Sirkan Grillikioski*, near the bus terminal.

Ristorante Pizz Burger on Torikatu is an excellent, and reasonably priced, Italian restaurant. The 37 mk weekday lunch special is very generous.

If you're looking for a nice café, try the nearby *Neljä Kaesaa*, which offers a 30 mk lunch.

Getting There & Away
Air A minibus runs from Kajaani airport to the town of Kuhmo after the arrival of each

flight, and there is also a regular service the other way. The fare is approximately 100 mk per person.

Bus There are 12 daily buses from Kajaani, and a few buses from Nurmes and Oulu. Trains arriving in Kajaani connect with buses to Kuhmo.

Car & Motorcycle Kuhmo is on road No 76, 102km east of Kajaani.

AROUND KUHMO
Korpikylien Tie
Recommended for vehicles and cyclists alike, Korpikylien tie is a circular route east of Kuhmo that travels past WWII battle-fields, desolate farmhouses and real wilderness. It is possible to combine hitch-hiking or trekking along the route with travel on the twice-weekly bus that runs through Saunajärvi and Korkea. Pick up a map and route information at the Kuhmo tourist office.

UKK TREKKING ROUTE
Pockets of the now-rare Finnish wilderness still exist – in pristine condition – along the eastern border of Finland. They are best seen and experienced on a trek along the Urho K Kekkonen (UKK) route. This 240km trail is the nation's longest and greatest trekking route. It was named after President Urho K Kekkonen, and it's been in development for decades. New shelters and boardwalks are constantly being con-structed along this route.

The trail starts at the Koli Hill in North Karelia and continues along the western side of Lake Pielinen, ending at Iso-Syöte Hill far to the north of Kuhmo.

Two of the finest sections of the UKK route are the Kuhmo to Hiidenportti leg and the Kuhmo to Lentiira leg. The trek east from Kuhmo to Lentiira village via Iso-Palonen park takes at least four days and offers superb scenery.

The trail is well maintained in the Kuhmo area, with clear markings, and *laavu* (simple shelters) are spaced every 10 to 20km. Each laavu is near water and has an established campfire place, firewood and a pit toilet. Carry a sleeping bag and *plenty* of mosquito repellent to take advantage of this free open-air accommodation.

Pick up route maps at the Kuhmo tourist office or the Kainuu Nature Centre, also in Kuhmo.

HOSSA
☎ 08

Hossa, dubbed the 'fisher's paradise', is one of the most carefully maintained fishing areas in Finland. Trekking is also excellent, and some of the paths take you to beautiful ridges between lakes.

To visit Hossa you will need to plan in advance where to stay and where to purchase fishing permits. See Fishing in the Activities chapter for more information on permits.

Information
The Hossa information centre (☎ 732 361) provides everything for a successful stay. It rents cottages, boats, hiking gear and fishing equipment; sells fishing permits and hiking maps; and has a café/restaurant and lakeside sauna. In winter the centre rents cross-country skis.

Things to See
On the steep cliffs at Somero, in the north-west corner of the Hossa preserve, is **Värikallio** (Colour Rock). Its rock paintings, estimated to be 4000 years old, are the most northern ones in Finland. You can only reach the site via a marked hiking trail.

Activities
Hossa offers 100km of marked **hiking trails** in summer and 70km of ready cross-country ski tracks in winter. Some of the hiking trails are designed for people in wheelchairs.

Those who are interested in exploring by **canoe** can chose to paddle from Julma Ölkky or Iijärvi to Hossa. Each route is 10km, and longer trips are possible.

For those keen on **fishing**, there are des-ignated fly-fishing and spear-fishing areas within Hossa, designated fishing areas for children and the disabled, as well as special waters for fishing trout and salmon, pike and perch and rainbow trout. In winter, ice-fishing for salmon is popular.

Places to Stay & Eat

Adjacent to the Hossa information centre is *Karhunkaina-lon Leirintäalue*, a camping ground with sites for 70 mk.

On the road south from the information centre you have three choices of accommodation. *Hossan Lomakeskus (☎ 732 322)* is a large hotel with double rooms for 350 mk, and many kinds of cottages at the waterfront. Buffet lunch is available. At *Erä-Hossa (☎ 732 310)* you can rent cottages from 175 mk (the best cottages have a TV, sauna and microwave oven). Canoe rentals are available. *Lomamökit Paasovaara (☎ 732 319)* has cottages from 200 mk. There are meals for 45 mk, and a sauna. You can rent a bicycle here.

The Hossa information centre handles bookings for several rustic cottages scattered around Hossa. These are available to rent by the day or by the week. Rates are from 280 mk per day from late February to late September, and from 230 mk at other times.

There are five wilderness huts in Hossa that can be used free of charge. These sleep from three to seven people. Remember that the first person to arrive should be the first one to leave. All huts are suitable for staying overnight in winter. In addition to huts, there are several laavu in Hossa.

Getting There & Away

The best way to reach Hossa is by car, and motor vehicles are allowed within the Hossa area. There are daily post buses to Hossa from Kuusamo. You can reach Hossa from Kajaani by changing buses at Ämmänsaari; these buses run only on weekdays.

KUUSAMO

• pop 11,000   ☎ 08

Kuusamo is a frontier town about 200km north-east of Oulu. It's similar in feel to the towns of Lapland. There is little to see in Kuusamo itself, but the town serves as an

excellent base for planning and launching treks in the Kuusamo area. There are good services, including shops with trekking supplies.

History

A Lutheran parish for over 300 years, Kuusamo was incorporated as a municipality in 1868. By 1900, its population had grown to 10,000, and it had close relations with nearby Russia. During WWII, the village was a command centre for German troops, who also supervised the construction of the 'Death Railway' that operated for 242 days. When the Soviet army marched into Kuusamo on 15 September 1944, the Germans burned the town and blew up the railway. The Soviets retreated, after occupying Kuusamo for about two months, and the inhabitants of Kuusamo returned to their shattered town. A large number of refugees from the Soviet-annexed Salla region were settled around Kuusamo just after WWII.

Information

Tourist Office The Kuusamo tourist office (☎ 850 2910, fax 850 2901, ktassu@kuusamo.fi), Torangintaival 2, is in the Karhuntassu (Bear's Paw) Tourist Centre on road No 5 (the main highway) 2km southwest of the town centre. Hours are from 9 am to 7 pm Monday to Friday in summer, and from 9 am to 5 pm Monday to Friday at other times. The office has very good handouts, including *Kuusamo – Arctic Adventure* in winter and *Kuusamo – Green Adventure* in summer, which are full of useful information. A Forest and Park Service office (☎ 852 3241) is also here, with information on nearby trekking routes and national parks.

Post The post office is in the town centre on Ouluntie. It's open from 9 am to 8 pm daily.

Internet Resources & Library The public library is opposite the bus terminal, at Kaiterantie 22. It has 1:20,000 maps of

LAPLAND & OULU

the Kuusamo area and there is an Internet terminal. Hours are from noon to 8 pm Monday, Wednesday and Thursday; from 10 am to 8 pm Tuesday; from 10 am to 2 pm Friday and from 10 am to 3 pm Saturday.

Useful tourist orienated Web sites for Kuusamo are www.kuusamo.fi/ and www.travel.fi/kuusamo/.

Travel Agency Matka-Ruka (☎ 852 1395, fax 852 2015, travel.services@matkaruka.com) at Kitkantie 15 is a regular travel agency that also arranges reservations at any of over 600 accommodation units scattered around Kuusamo, and rounds up individual travellers for organised tours (see the Organised Tours section that follows). See also www.matkaruka.com/ on the Web.

Medical Services There's a pharmacy on Vanttajantie, across from the post office. Hours are from 8.30 am to 9 am Monday to Friday, and from 8.30 am to 7 pm Saturday. The town health care centre is on Vanttajantie opposite the pharmacy.

Emergency For a general emergency call ☎ 112, for police call ☎ 10022 and for a doctor dial ☎ 10023.

Things to See

About 500m south-east of the town centre on Kitronintie is the local **open-air museum**, with a cluster of old, grey buildings. It's open from noon to 6 pm daily mid-June to mid-August, and from 9 am to 3 pm Monday to Friday mid- to late August. Admission is free.

The **water tower** on Joukamontie has an observation platform with a good view over Kuusamo, and a café. The tower is open from noon to 8 pm in summer.

Kuusamotalo at Kaarlo Hännisentie 2 is a concert hall.

Organised Tours

There are a dozen or more independent tour operators based in Kuusamo, offering activities as diverse as ice climbing, river

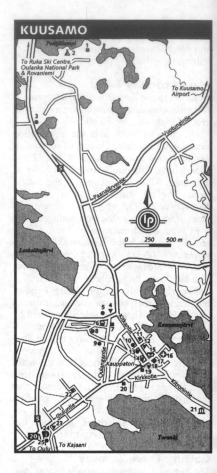

rafting, mountain biking, ice fishing, snowshoe hiking and more.

The largest such company is Ruka Palvelu Oy (☎ 860 8600, fax 860 8601). It offers regular weekly programs during the summer and winter high seasons: river rafting, fishing, canoeing and climbing from June to September; and dog sledding, ice fishing, snowmobiling and snowshoeing from November to March. Tours are priced from 350 mk per person.

Most organised tours only take place with two or more participants; if you are a

KUUSAMO

PLACES TO STAY
1   Kuusamon Tropiikki Spa
2   Rantatropiikki Camping
7   Kuusamon Kansanopisto
19   Hotel Martina
20   Sokos Hotel Kuusamo

PLACES TO EAT
4   Lunch Bar Ali-Baba
11   Ampan Pizza Bar
12   Rolls; Kauppakulma Shopping Centre
18   Grilli
22   Baari Martai
23   Supermarkets

OTHER
3   Kuusamon Uistin
5   Kuusamotalo Concert Hall
6   Bus Station
8   Public Library
9   Water Tower & Café
10   Matka-Ruka Travel Agency
13   Bjarmia Ceramics Factory
14   Jalopeura Pub
15   Post Office
16   Health Care Centre
17   Pharmacy
21   Open-Air Museum
24   Karhuntassu Tourist Centre; Kuusamo Tourist Office; Forest and Park Service; Kuukkeli Café
25   White Studio Ceramics

solo traveller, contact Matka-Ruka (see under Travel Agency) as they will ring around the various tour operators for you.

Places to Stay

Camping *Rantatropiikki Camping (☎ 859 6404, fax 852 1901, mypa.kuusamo@kt.inet.fi, Kylpyläntie)* is a camping ground 5km north of the centre. It is associated with the neighbouring spa. Camp sites cost 50 mk and there are cottages.

Hostel *Kuusamon Kansanopisto (☎ 852 2132, fax 852 1134, Kitkantie 35)* is an HI-affiliated hostel conveniently located across the street from the bus terminal. It has beds from 60 to 115 mk and is open year-round (closed Christmas week). There is a kitchen and a satellite TV in the common room. Sauna and laundry facilities are on the premises.

Hotels *Hotel Martina (☎ 852 2051, fax 852 2054, Ouluntie 3)*, on the kauppatori, has 32 rooms for one to four people. Singles/doubles cost 290/320 mk.

Sokos Hotel Kuusamo (☎ 85920, fax 852 1263, Kirkkotie 23) near the centre is a concrete box-like structure topped by a glowing *kota* (Lappish hut). There are 182 rooms, starting at 650/810 mk.

Some 5km north of Kuusamo on Kylpyläntie, *Kuusamon Tropiikki Spa (☎ 85960, fax 852 1909, mypa.kuusamo@kt.inet.fi)* is a modern hotel and spa (the spa is a plastic tropical wonderland with a 45m water slide). Rooms are from 550/650 mk, including use of the spa. Nonguests may use the spa for a modest fee.

Places to Eat

Kitkantie, the main road, has the most options – but for the best darn chow in Finland, veer off the beaten track to *Baari Martai*. The tiny, family-run lunch spot is on Airotie; look for the 'Koillismaan Lasi Ky' sign. A hearty, home-cooked lunch costs 35 mk.

Ampan Pizza Bar (Kitkantie 18) is popular for its good-tasting, reasonably priced pizzas.

Lunch Bar Ali-Baba (Kaarlo Hännisentie 2) is near the bus station, with inexpensive lunches available until 5 pm. It's closed on Saturday.

Rolls, in the Kauppakulma shopping centre on Kitkantie, serves fast-food sandwiches and burgers under 30 mk.

The *grilli* at the kauppatori is open past midnight. The market itself is busy until 3 pm most days. Karhuntassu Tourist Centre houses *Kuukkeli*, a café.

Adjacent to the tourist office are several giant *supermarkets* where you can stock up on trekking supplies.

Entertainment

The most interesting nightlife in Kuusamo is at the *Sokos Hotel* (see Places to Stay). *Jalopeura (Kitkantie 1)* is a very central pub.

LAPLAND & OULU

Shopping

There are some good buys in Kuusamo. Bjarmia is a ceramics factory at Vienantie 1, right in the centre. Another studio that makes ceramics is the White Studio, adjacent to the tourist office. The artist is from Britain. North of the centre on the main road (No 5), Kuusamon Uistin sells lures and sheath knives from its factory. Some of these products are exported throughout the world under the brand name Kuusamo. In the centre, Kesport Intersport sells trekking gear.

Getting There & Away

Air Finnair flies daily from Helsinki to Kuusamo airport, which is 7km to north-east of the town centre.

Bus Buses run daily from Kajaani, Oulu and Rovaniemi. There are frequent services to the ski centre at Ruka.

Car & Motorcycle Kuusamo is on road No 5, about 800km north of Helsinki. Hertz (☎ 0800-112233) at the airport is open 24 hours.

KARHUNKIERROS TREKKING ROUTE & OULANKA NATIONAL PARK
☎ 08

The 80km Karhunkierros (Bear's Ring), one of the oldest and best-established trekking routes in Finland, offers the most varied and breathtaking scenery in Finland. It's very popular during the *ruska* (autumn) period.

Because the loop runs through some isolated areas within Oulanka National Park, getting there will require some strategic planning. There are four possible starting points; the best section of the trail runs from the Ristikallio starting point to Juuma. At Juuma there's a short but demanding marked loop trail, the 9km Little Bear's Ring.

Information

The Oulanka visitor centre (☎ 863453) at Kiutaköngäs rapids in the middle of Oulanka National Park is accessible by car or by bus. The centre has nature exhibits and a slide show, and sells trekking supplies, maps and fishing licences. The centre also has a café.

At the northern end of the park on the Kuusamo-Salla road is the Hautajärvi visitor centre (☎ 016-839651, fax 016-839657), in Hautajärvi village, with identical services. Both centres are open from mid-February to late October; hours are from 10 am to 8 pm daily in summer, shorter hours at other times.

The 1:40,000 *Rukatunturi-Oulanka* map is useful for treks of any length. It costs 50 mk and is sold at both of the park's visitor centres and at the Kuusamo tourist office.

Trekking

The track is well marked and can be walked in light shoes on dry summer days. Prior to mid-June the ground is too soggy to make hiking enjoyable.

Day 1 – Start your trek at the parking area near Ristikallio. After 15 minutes you will reach the national park border. You can stop at a campsite at Aventojoki or proceed further to Ristikallio, which offers some breathtaking scenery. Proceed less than one hour farther to reach Puikkokämppä hut at a small lake. Continue another kilometre past the lake to reach Taivalköngäs waterfall (near the wilderness hut of the same name), with two sets of rapids and three suspension bridges.

Northern extension – If you really enjoy hiking, begin your trek farther north at the Hautajärvi visitor centre – this adds an extra 22km to the hike. The landscape is unimpressive until the path reaches the Savinajoki river. The deep Oulanka Canyon is a highlight of this part of the trek. A wilderness hut, Savilampi kämppä, is at the Oulanka riverfront near Lake Savilampi, 18km south of Hautajärvi. The distance from Lake Savilampi to Taivalköngäs – where you'll join the Ristikallio trail – is 4km.

Day 2 – The first leg is an 8km trek from Taivalköngäs through some ordinary scenery although there are a few beautiful lakes. After 4.2km, you can camp at Lake Runsulampi; there's dry wood available. About 4km farther east, you can stay overnight at Oulanka Camping, or continue to the Oulanka visitor centre. The Kiutaköngäs rapids, just 800m

KARHUNKIERROS TREK & OULANKA NATIONAL PARK

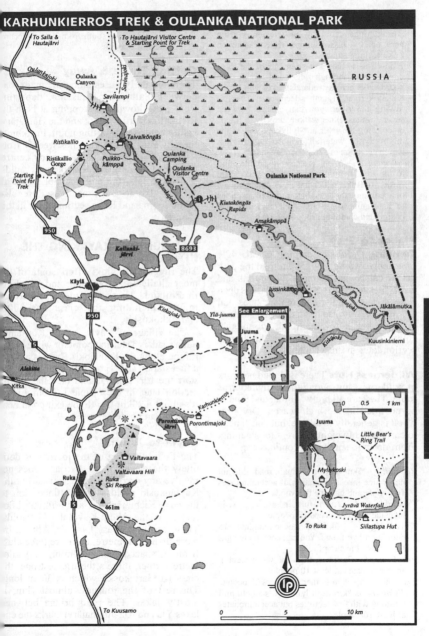

To Salla & Hautajärvi

To Hautajärvi Visitor Centre & Starting Point for Trek

RUSSIA

Oulankajoki

Oulanka Canyon

Savilampi

Savinajoki

Taivalköngäs

Ristikallio

Ristikallio Gorge

Puikko-kämppä

Oulanka Camping

Oulanka Visitor Centre

Oulankajoki

Starting Point for Trek

Oulanka National Park

Kiutaköngäs Rapids

Ansakämppä

950

8693

Kallunki-järvi

Käylä

Jussinkämppä

Oulankajoki

Jäkälämutka

Kitkajoki

Ylä-juuma

See Enlargement

Juuma

Kitkajoki

Kuusinkiniemi

950

5

Alakitka

Kitka

Karhunkierros

Porontimo-järvi

Porontimajoki

Valtavaara

Valtavaara Hill

Ruka Ski Resort

Ruka

5

461m

LAPLAND & OULU

Enlargement

0   0.5   1 km

Juuma

Little Bear's Ring Trail

Myllykoski

Jyrävä Waterfall

To Ruka

Siilastupa Hut

To Kuusamo

0   5   10 km

from the visitor centre, are noted for their rugged cliffs nearby. It's possible to reach Ansakämppä cabin by early evening from here, or even Jussinkämppä wilderness hut on Lake Kulmakkajärvi.

Day 3 – This is the most strenuous of the three days. A hike through ridges and forests (and boardwalks across wetlands) takes you to the Kitkajoki river, in another deep gorge. After following the river, you can choose between several routes, either walking directly to Juuma or crossing the river at Myllykoski to see the mighty Jyrävä waterfall (3km from Juuma) that has an elevation of 12m. There's a hut at Jyrävä.

Ruka extension – Juuma is a convenient end point to the trek. It is also possible to walk 23km further to Ruka, which has an excellent choice of accommodation and better road connections to Kuusamo. There are wilderness huts and designated camping grounds en route.

Places to Stay

Camping *Oulanka Camping (☎ 863 429, Liikasenvaarantie 139)*, 500m from the park visitor centre, has cottages for 200 mk and camp sites for 55 to 65 mk. The place is open June to late August and rents canoes and rowing boats. It also has a café and sauna.

There are a few camping grounds in Juuma; see Places to Stay in the Juuma section later in this chapter.

Wilderness Huts There is a good network of wilderness huts along the Karhunkierros route. They are all pretty similar and tend to be crowded in the high season. Dry firewood is generally available, but you'll need to carry a lightweight mattress for sleeping. From north to south, your options are:

Ristikallio – 5km east of the main road, this hut has a nice lakeside location. It accommodates 10 people and has dry firewood.

Puikkokämppä – 2.5km further east, is a basic lakeside hut that sleeps 10 people.

Taivalköngäs – 1.3km east, accommodates 15 people on two floors. You can cook on the gas stove or at the campfire.

Ansakämppä – 7km east from the visitor centre, accommodates at least 10 people.

Jussinkämppä – 9km farther on, sleeps 20 people.

Myllykoski – is 2km from Juuma. It's an old mill building with few facilities but accommodates at least 10 people.

Siilastupa – 4km from Juuma just opposite th Jyrävä waterfall, sleeps 12 people.

Porontimajoki – 8km south from Juuma, accom modates four people.

Getting There & Away

There are daily buses along the main roa between Salla and Kuusamo, departin from either town and stopping at both th Ristikallio starting point and the Hautajärv visitor centre and starting point. In summe there is a taxibus three times weekly fror Kuusamo to the Oulanka visitor centre Oulanka Camping and Kiutaköngäs rapids In winter, take the daily school bus. Ca ☎ 0200-4089 for bus timetables. Refer als to the Juuma and Ruka sections later in thi chapter.

CANOEING & KAYAKING THE KITKAJOKI

The rugged Kitkajoki offers some of th most challenging canoeing and kayakin in Finland. There are plenty of trick rapids, including the class IV, 900r Aallokkokoski.

The village of Käylä, on the Kuusamo Salla road, is a starting point for white-wate rafting along the Kitkajoki. There is a shop a fuel station and a post office. You can als start the trip from Juuma (see the Juum section later in the chapter). From Juum it's about a 20km trip to the exit point nea the Russian border.

Käylä to Juuma

The first 14km leg of the journey is defi nitely the easier of the two and does nc involve any carrying at all. You start at th Käylänkoski rapids, and continue 3km t the easy Kiehtäjänniva, and a further kilo metre to the Vähä-Käylänkoski rapids These are both class I rapids. After a bi more than a kilometre, there are three clas II rapids spaced every 400m or so. A kilo metre farther, there's the trickiest one, th class III Harjakoski, which is 300m long The rest of the journey, almost 7km, i mostly lakes. The road bridge betwee lakes Ylä and Ala-Juumajärvi marks the en

f the trip. It is a kilometre to Juuma from
ne bridge.

uuma to the Russian Border

'his 20km journey is the most dangerous
iver route in Finland. You should be an
xpert paddler, and you *must* carry your
anoe at least once – around the 12m, class
VI Jyrävä waterfall. Do inspect the tricky
nes before you let go and ask for local
dvice in case the water level is un-
avourable.

The thrill starts just 300m after Juuma,
vith the class II Niskakoski. From here on,
here is only a kilometre of quiet water.
Myllykoski, with a water-mill, is a tricky
lass IV waterfall. Right after Myllykoski,
he 900m Aallokkokoski rapids mean quick
•addling for quite some time. The Jyrävä
vaterfall comes right after this long section.
'ull aside before Jyrävä, and carry your
anoe. You might want to carry it from Myl-
ykoski to well beyond the Jyrävä waterfall,
kipping the Aallokkokoski rapids.

After Jyrävä things cool down consider-
bly, although there are some class III
apids. After about 6km, there is a wilder-
 less hut, the Päähkänäkallio. When you
neet the Oulankajoki, 7km downriver from
he hut, paddle upriver to Jäkälämutka or
lownriver to Kuusinkiniemi, 100m from
he Russian border. At either spot you can
ccess a four-wheel-drive forest road that
vill take you back to civilisation. You must
rrange return transport from this point in
dvance, as traffic is nonexistent.

ANOEING & KAYAKING THE OULANKAJOKI

iqually impressive, and demanding, among
he great Kuusamo river routes, the Oulanka-
oki gives you a chance to see mighty
anyons from a canoe or kayak. You *must*
arry your canoe at least four times – past
•arts of the Oulanka Canyon, and waterfalls
t Taivalköngäs and Kiutaköngäs. Study a
iver map before starting out.

The first leg, an 18km trip, starts from
oad No 5, north of Ristikallio. The first
'km or so is relatively calm paddling, until

you reach the impressive Oulanka Canyon.
The safe section extends for about a kilo-
metre, after which you should pull aside and
carry your canoe past the dangerous rapids.
You can overnight at Savilampi hut (see
Trekking in the Karhunkierros Trekking
Route & Oulanka National Park section).

Some 3km after Savilampi are the
Taivalköngäs rapids. You'll need to carry
your canoe, and there's a hut here, too. The
next 6km are quiet, until you reach Kiutaköngäs rapids, where you'll again need to
carry your canoe. The park visitor centre
and a camping ground are near here.

The second leg of the journey, a full
20km long, starts on the other side of Kiutaköngäs waterfall. You pass through 500m
of quiet waters, then there's another waterfall, and it's carrying-time again!

On the final leg, the river becomes
smooth and there is little to worry about as
far as rapids go. This leg is suitable for families with children.

JUUMA
☎ 08

The village of Juuma is the most popular
base for treks along the Karhunkierros
route. It's a convenient place to stock up
on supplies for the entire Karhunkierros
route.

Trekking

If you have only a little time for trekking,
you can take the 9km Little Bear's Ring, a
loop trail, to Myllykoski rapids and
Jyrävänjärvi lake. The trail is short but demanding, as it crosses varying terrain. On
the trail at Jyrävä is the Siilastupa wilderness hut; see Places to Stay in the
Karhunkierros Trekking Route & Oulanka
National Park section.

White-Water Rafting

Kitkan Safarit (☎/fax 853 458), at Juumantie 134, will arrange white-water
rafting along the Kitkajoki (see the earlier
Canoeing & Kayaking the Kitkajoki
section).

Places to Stay & Eat

There are plenty of accommodation choices in Juuma from June to August, and some places stay open throughout September. Cottages may be rented year-round; contact the Kuusamo tourist office or Matka-Ruka travel agency in Kuusamo for assistance.

The most convenient place to stay is *Lomakylä Retkietappi (☎ 863 218, Juumantie 134)*, right on the Karhunkierros trail. Open from June to late September, it has cottages at 130 to 350 mk, or you can camp for 50 mk per day. The café serves snacks and meals. The place also has a sauna, and rents rowing boats and bicycles.

The nearby *Jyrävä Camping (☎ 863 236, Juumantie 129B)*, open June to late August, rents cottages and has similar services.

Juuman Leirintä (☎ 863 212, Riekamontie 1), open mid-May to late September, has a sauna and café-grilli. Cabins cost 120 to 300 mk per day. Camp sites are 50 mk.

Getting There & Away

In summer, the post bus makes the 50km trip from Kuusamo to Juuma on weekday afternoons, returning to Kuusamo the following morning. There are two departures daily from mid-August to late May.

RUKA
☎ 08

Ruka is one of the most popular winter sports centres in Finland, and you'll see *Ruka!* bumper stickers on cars all over the country. Ruka is also a protected nature area, with abundant wildlife.

Prices and demand for accommodation keep Ruka somewhat off-limits for budget travellers in winter, but in summer it is a fine place to start or finish the Karhunkierros trek because there are good bus connections from Kuusamo.

Information

The Kuusamo tourist office provides information on Ruka activities and accommodation. To reach the ski resort directly, contact Rukakeskus Oy (☎ 858 1231, fax 868 1292), 93825 Rukatunturi.

A helpful tourist booklet, *Ruka!*, is published in Finnish and English.

The Ruka post office is near the main road, 3km from the town centre.

Tour operators in Ruka include Ruka palvelu Oy (☎ 860 8600, fax 860 8601) in the Safaritalo building. It arranges fishing tours, canoe safaris, white-water rafting expeditions and guided treks.

For a general emergency call ☎ 112, for police call ☎ 10022 and for a doctor dial ☎ 10023.

Skiing

There are 28 downhill ski slopes and 1 lifts on Ruka hill. The vertical drop is 201m and the longest run is 1300m – not bad averages at all for Finland, where hills are small and slope gently. Ruka also boasts cross-country trails totalling 250km. There are special areas for snowboarders.

The ski season runs from early November to mid-May, depending on snowfalls. During holiday periods such as Christmas and Easter it seems that almost the entire population of Finland can be seen on Ruka's slopes.

A ride up on the ski lift costs 15 mk, or you can buy a day pass for 120 mk (high season 130 mk). For children, one run is 1 mk and a day pass is 80 mk.

Alpine skis, including poles and boots, rent for 95 mk per day, children 70 mk per day. Ski goggles are an additional 25 mk. Snowboards (boots included) rent for 13 mk per day, and cross-country skis are 8 mk per day.

Ski lessons are available at Ruka for adults or children.

Tobogganning

A monster toboggan slope is open in summer for speed lovers – each ride is approximately 20 mk.

Places to Stay

Ruka is a very busy winter sports centre and at that time it may be difficult to find bed, especially at reasonable prices. Book accommodation in advance, or stay in Kuusamo.

Viipus Camping (☎ 868 1213, Viipuksenie) is at lake Viipusjärvi, several kilometres north of Ruka. It's open from June to mid-September and has camping sites and cabins. There's a shop, a sauna and boats for hire.

For *cottage rentals* in Ruka, contact the Kuusamo tourist office or the Matka-Ruka travel agency in Kuusamo.

The largest hotel in Ruka is *Hotel Rantasipi Ruka (☎ 85910, fax 868 1135)*, right at the foot of the ski slopes. Singles/doubles are from 620/730 mk.

Places to Eat

There are a few *cafés* in Ruka's main square, plus *Hillside Hamburger*. *Pizzeria Montagna Di Ruka* serves Italian-style pizzas. Nearby, *Riipisen Riistakauppa* specialises in expensive dishes of wild boar and bear, and is popular with Finnish celebrities in winter. Next door, *Riipisen Kahvila* is a nice café.

Getting There & Away

Ruka is 30km north of Kuusamo on main road No 5, and there is enough traffic to hitchhike. Most regular bus services to Kuusamo continue further north to Ruka. During ski season (early November to early May) a skibus shuttles between Kuusamo and Ruka, stopping at all of the big hotels. The one-way fare is 20 mk per adult, 10 mk per child.

AROUND RUKA

Valtavaara

Valtavaara hill is adjacent to the Ruka ski slope. If you have any interest in birds, this is the best place in the region: Some 100 species of birds nest here, and an annual birdwatching competition is held in the area in June. In this competition – called 'Ponauskilpailu', from the Swedish *poeng*, meaning 'point' – you score a point for every bird species you spot.

PUDASJÄRVI

pop 11,000   ☎ 08

Pudasjärvi is not the most interesting village in Finland, but it is the largest spot of civil-isation along the main Oulu-Kuusamo road. The travel agency Pudasjärven Matkailu Oy (see the Iso-Syote & Pikku-Syote section that follows) furnishes tourist information for the region

Things to See

The town's **open-air museum** can be found just off the Pudasjärvi to Ranua road, 7km from the village of Pudasjärvi. The museum is open Tuesday to Friday and Sunday from late June to mid-August.

The Pudasjärvi **church** is close to the museum. Built in 1781, it has a cemetery with an unusually long fence built of horizontally laid logs and covered by a roof. The fence and roof were built this way to keep wolves from digging up the dead bodies.

Places to Stay & Eat

Pudas-Maja (☎ 823 220, Sähkötie 3) is an HI-affiliated hostel close to the main Oulu-Kuusamo road. It's open from June to late September and charges 70 to 130 mk per bed depending on room size (many rooms have their own shower). There is a kitchen and sauna, and breakfast costs 30 mk.

In the village proper, *Texas* serves cheap weekday lunch specials.

Getting There & Away

Pudasjärvi is on the main Oulu-Kuusamo road, and several buses a day make the 1½ hour trip from Oulu.

ISO-SYÖTE & PIKKU-SYÖTE

☎ 08

Just two decades ago, Syöte, the southern-most fell in Finland, was covered by virgin forest. Not any more. Syöte's twin peaks, the Iso-Syöte and the Pikku-Syöte ('Big Syöte' and 'Small Syöte', respectively) are now dotted with ski lifts, ski tracks, hotels and restaurants.

In addition to its winter sports facilities, the Syöte area offers the visitor access to the protected government recreational area to the north and south-west of the Iso-Syöte. This area has walking tracks and a network of wilderness huts.

Information

Pudasjärven Matkailu Oy (☎ 823 400, fax 823 421) at Varsitie 7 in Pudasjärvi is a travel agency that provides tourist information and assistance for the Syöte region.

Skiing

At the Iso-Syöte, there are 21 downhill slopes and 11 lifts. The vertical drop is 192m and the longest run is 1200m. There are some 110km of cross-country trails, all clearly marked. You can rent skiing equipment and purchase lift passes at Romekievari station.

Trekking

Very few trekkers take advantage of the excellent walking tracks and wilderness huts around Syöte. See Places to Stay for a description of the area's wilderness huts.

Most trekkers use the Ahmatupa hut as a base, and do a loop around the northern part of the trekking area.

Another route, indicated by yellow markings on trees, makes a loop around Iso-Syöte hill. Additionally, the UKK route crosses through Syöte; see the UKK Trekking Route section earlier in this chapter.

Fishing

There are three fishing areas around Syöte, and the Forest and Park Service stocks all of them. Along the Pärjänjoki and Livojoki rivers, fishing is allowed from June to mid-September. In lakes Hanhilampi, Kellarilampi and Lauttalampi, near the Iso-Syöte, you can fish at any time except May. See the Activities chapter for information about fishing permits.

Places to Stay

Practically all accommodation in the Syöte region can and should be arranged by Pudasjärven Matkailu Oy (see the Information section). If you plan to stay, you can choose either a daily or a weekly rate.

Hotel Isosyöte (☎ 820 6111, fax 822 90(juha.kuukasjarvi@hotelli-isosyote.inet.fi at the Iso-Syöte ski centre has singles doubles from 370/540 in high season 340/480 at other times.

Some of the most luxurious *kelo* (pine) lo₁ cabins on top of Syöte Hill have microwav₁ ovens and TVs. In the spring high seasoı (the weeks surrounding Easter), these cabin₁ cost from 500 mk per night, or from 3000 ml per week (900 to 1350 mk per week iı summer). They accommodate six people.

For cheaper accommodation consider th₁ hostel in Pudasjärvi (see the Pudasjärv₁ section).

Wilderness Huts There are three huts an₁ several kota or laavu shelters around th₁ Syöte area. All these facilities can be use₁ free of charge.

The *Ahmatupa* wilderness hut is a goo₁ 'base camp' that sleeps at least six peopl₁ It has gas, comfortable mattresses and ₁ stove. During the winter high season, ther₁ is a café here, open till 4 pm. Just 50m awa₁ is *Ahmakota*, which gives shelter when th₁ hut is fully occupied.

Outside the 'official' trekking area, ther₁ is the lakeside *Toraslampi* hut, and th₁ *Romesuvanto* hut near the Pärjänjoki i₁ popular with fishers.

Places to Eat

Bring food supplies with you in summer, a₁ many places are shuttered once the sl₁ season winds down. Restaurants around th₁ downhill slopes are busy in winter, an₁ there are grillis and a few grocery stores i₁ the village of Syötekylä.

Getting There & Away

There is a bus service from Oulu to Syö₁ (140km trip north-east to Oulu) eac₁ weekday afternoon. The bus back to Oul₁ departs each weekday morning. The tri₁ takes about 2½ hours and costs about 65 ml

Language

FINNISH

The Finnish language, such a distinct national icon, sets Finland apart from its Western European neighbours. Finnish is a Uralic language closely related to Estonian; it has common origins with Samoyed and languages spoken in the Volga basin of Russia. The most widely spoken of the Finno-Ugric languages is Hungarian, but its similarities with Finnish are few. Finnish is not a Scandinavian language, nor is it related to Indo-European languages. There are, however, many words on loan from Baltic, Slavic and Germanic languages, and many words are derived from English. Linguists have also recognised some similarities between Finnish and Korean grammar.

Finnish is spoken by some six million people in Finland, Sweden, Norway and Russian Karelia. The country is known as *Suomi*, and the language as *suomi*. Finnish is not an easy language to learn. There are 15 cases for nouns, and at least 160 conjugations and personal forms for verbs. There are no articles (a, the) and no genders, but the word 'no' also conjugates. Many readers have written to us about their problems with the Finnish language. One particular reader found a clothes store named 'Farkku Piste' (Jeans Point) to be especially amusing. Fortunately, staff at most tourist offices and hotels will be fluent English speakers; bus drivers and staff at guesthouses, hostels and restaurants may not be – though they'll often dash off to fetch a neighbour, co-worker or bystander who can help! Finns who speak Finnish to a foreigner usually do so extremely clearly and 'according to the book'. Mistakes made by visitors are kindly tolerated, and even your most bumbling attempts will be warmly appreciated. A final note: in Finnish, ä is pronounced as in 'bat', and ö is pronounced 'er', as in 'her'. These letters are the last two in the Finnish alphabet. Lonely Planet publishes a *Scandinavian Phrasebook*, which is a handy pocket-sized introduction to Finnish, Swedish and other languages of the region.

Greetings & Civilities

Hello.	*Hei.*
Goodbye.	*Näkemiin.*
Good morning.	*Huomenta.*
Good evening.	*Iltaa.*
Thank you (very much).	*Kiitos (paljon).*
You're welcome.	*Ole hyvä.*
Yes.	*Kyllä.*
No.	*Ei.*
Maybe.	*Ehkä.*
Excuse me.	*Anteeksi.*
I'm sorry. (forgive me)	*Olen pahoillani (anna anteeksi).*
How are you?	*Mitä kuuluu?*
I'm fine, thanks.	*Kiitos hyvää.*

Essentials

Please write it down.	*Voitko kirjoittaa sen.*
Please show me (on the map).	*Näytä minulle (kartalta).*
I understand.	*Ymmärrän.*
I don't understand.	*En ymmärrä.*
Does anyone speak English?	*Puhuuko kukaan englantia?*
Where are you from?	*Mistä olet kotoisin?*
I'm from ...	*Olen ... -sta*
Age?/How old are you?	*Ikä?/Kuinka vanha olet?*
I'm ... years old.	*Olen ... -vuotias.*

Surname	*Sukunimi*
Given names	*Etunimet*
Date of birth	*Syntymäaika*
Place of birth	*Syntymäpaikka*
Nationality	*Kansallisuus*
Male/Female	*Mies/Nainen*
Passport	*Passi*

Small Talk

What's your name?	*Mikä sinun nimi on?*
My name is ...	*Minun nimeni on ...*

371

I'm a tourist/ student.	*Olen turisti/ opiskelija.*
Are you married?	*Oletko naimisissa?*
Do you like ...?	*Pidätkö ...?*
I like it very much.	*Pidän siitä paljon.*
I don't like ...	*En pidä ...*
May I?	*Saanko?*
How do you say ... (in Finnish)?	*Miten sanotaan ... (suomeksi)?*

Signs

Sisään	Entrance
Ulos	Exit
Avoinna	Open
Suljettu	Closed
Kielletty	Prohibited
WC	Toilets

Getting Around

I want to go to ...	*Haluan mennä ...*
How long does the trip take?	*Kauanko matka kestää?*
Do I need to change?	*Täytyykö minun vaihtaa?*
Where does ... leave from?	*Mistä ... lähtee?*
What time does ... leave/arrive?	*Mihin aikaan lähtee/ saapuu ...?*
it	*se*
the bus/tram	*bussi/raitiovaunu*
the train	*juna*
the boat/ferry	*vene/lautta*
the airplane	*lentokone*
The train is ...	*Juna on ...*
delayed	*myöhässä*
cancelled	*peruutettu*
left-luggage locker	*säilytyslokero*
one-way	*yhdensuuntainen*
platform	*laituri*
return (ticket)	*menopaluu (lippu)*
station	*asema*
ticket	*lippu*
ticket office	*lipputoimisto*
timetable	*aikataulu*
I'd like to hire a ...	*Haluaisin vuokrata ...*
bicycle	*polkupyörän*
car	*auton*
canoe	*kanootin*
rowing boat	*soutuveneen*
guide	*oppaan*

Directions

How do I get to ...?	*Miten pääsen ...?*
Where is ...?	*Missä on ...?*
What ... is this?	*Mikä ... tämä on?*

street/road	*katu/tie*
street number	*kadunnumero*
district	*kaupunginosa*
town	*kaupunki*
Is it near?	*Onko se lähellä?*
Is it far?	*Onko se kaukana?*
(Go) straight ahead.	*(Kulje) suoraan eteenpäin.*
(Turn) left.	*(Käänny) vasempaan.*
(Turn) right.	*(Käänny) oikeaan.*
at the traffic lights	*liikennevaloissa*
at the next/second/ third corner	*seuraavassa/toisessa/ kolmannessa risteyksessä*
here/there	*täällä/siellä*
up/down	*ylös/alas*
behind/opposite	*takana/vastapäätä*
north/south	*pohjoinen/etelä*
east/west	*itä/länsi*

Accommodation

I'm looking for ...	*Etsin ...*
the youth hostel	*retkeilymajaa*
the campground	*leirintäaluetta*
a hotel	*hotellia*
a guesthouse	*matkustajakotia*
the manager	*johtajaa*
What's the address?	*Mikä on osoite?*
Do you have a ...?	*Onko teillä ...?*
bed	*sänkyä*
cheap room	*halpaa huonetta*
single room	*yhden hengen huonetta*
double room	*kahden hengen huonetta*
for one night	*yhdeksi yöksi*

for two nights	*kahdeksi yöksi*
How much is it ...?	*Paljonko ...?*
per night	*on yöltä*
per person	*on henkilöltä*
Does it include	*Sisältyykö hintaan*
breakfast/sheets?	*aamiainen/lakanat?*
Can I see the	*Voinko nähdä*
room?	*huoneen?*
Where is the toilet?	*Missä on vessa?*
I'm/we're	*Olen/olemme*
leaving now.	*lähdössä nyt.*
Do you have ...?	*Onko teillä ...?*
a clean sheet	*puhtaat lakanat*
hot water	*kuumaa vettä*
a key	*avain*
a shower	*suihku*
sauna	*sauna*

Around Town

Where is the/a ...?	*Missä on ...?*
airport	*lentoasema*
bank	*pankki*
bus station	*linja-autoasema*
town centre	*keskusta*
embassy	*suurlähetystö*
entrance	*sisäänkäynti*
exit	*uloskäynti*
hospital	*sairaala*
market	*tori*
police	*poliisi*
post office	*posti*
public toilet	*yleinen käymälä*
restaurant	*ravintola*
telephone office	*Tele-toimisto*
tourist office	*matkailutoimisto*
I want to make a	*Haluaisin soittaa*
telephone call.	*puhelimella.*
I'd like to change ...	*Haluaisin vaihtaa ...*
some money	*rahaa*
travellers cheques	*matkashekkejä*

Food

I'm hungry/thirsty.	*Minulla on nälkä/jano.*
breakfast	*aamiainen*
lunch	*lounas*
buffet	*seisova pöytä*
dinner	*päivällinen*

café	*kahvila*
food stall	*grilli*
grocery store	*ruokakauppa*
market	*tori*
restaurant	*ravintola*
I'd like some ...	*Haluaisin ...*
I don't eat ...	*En syö ...*

Shopping

I'm looking for ...	*Etsin ...*
the chemist	*kemikaalikauppaa*
clothing	*vaatteita*
souvenirs	*matkamuistoja*
How much is it?	*Mitä se maksaa?*
I'd like to buy it.	*Haluan ostaa sen.*
It's too expensive	*Se on liian kallis*
for me.	*minulle.*
Can I look at it?	*Voinko katsoa sitä?*
I'm just looking.	*Minä vain katselen.*
Do you have ...?	*Onko ...?*
another colour	*muuta väriä*
another size	*muuta kokoa*
big/bigger	*iso/isompi*
small/smaller	*pieni/pienempi*
more/less	*enemmän/vähemmän*
cheap/cheaper	*halpa/halvempi*

Time & Dates

When?	*Milloin?*
today	*tänään*
tonight	*tänä iltana*
tomorrow	*huomenna*
yesterday	*eilen*
all day	*koko päivän*
every day	*joka päivä*
Monday	*maanantai*
Tuesday	*tiistai*
Wednesday	*keskiviikko*
Thursday	*torstai*
Friday	*perjantai*
Saturday	*lauantai*
Sunday	*sunnuntai*
January	*tammikuu*
February	*helmikuu*

LANGUAGE

Emergencies & Health

Help!	Apua!
Go away!	Mene pois!
Call a doctor!	Kutsu lääkäri!
Call the police!	Kutsu poliisi!
I'm allergic to ...	Olen allerginen ...
penicillin	penisilliinille
antibiotics	antibiooteille

March	maaliskuu
April	huhtikuu
May	toukokuu
June	kesäkuu
July	heinäkuu
August	elokuu
September	syyskuu
October	lokakuu
November	marraskuu
December	joulukuu

What time is it?	Mitä kello on?
It's ... o'clock	Kello on ...
in the morning	aamulla
in the evening	illalla
1.15	vartin yli yksi
1.30	puoli kaksi
1.45	varttia vaille kaksi

Numbers

1/2	puoli
1	yksi
2	kaksi
3	kolme
4	neljä
5	viisi
6	kuusi
7	seitsemän
8	kahdeksan
9	yhdeksän
10	kymmenen
11	yksitoista
12	kaksitoista
100	sata
1000	tuhat

one million	miljoona

SWEDISH

Swedish is one of the Scandinavian languages belonging to the Indo-European language family. It was separated from its original Germanic ancestor some 3000 years ago. *Finlandssvenska*, or 'Finland's Swedish', is very similar to the language spoken in Sweden, but local dialects have many Finnish words, so if you have learned Swedish in Sweden, you'll have some more learning to do! *Kiva*, or 'nice' is probably the most common Finnish word among Swedish speakers. The dialect used in Åland is closest to the Swedish of mainland Sweden. In Helsinki, an archaic, almost awkward form of Swedish is used as one of the two official languages of administration, and many of the city's Swedish speakers use an incomprehensible mix of Swedish and Finnish in conversation. People in farming and fishing communities in the Åland and Turunmaa archipelagos and in the small Swedish communities of the west and south coasts have their own unique dialects.

Greetings & Civilities

Hello.	Hej.
Goodbye.	Hej då.
Good morning.	God morgon.
Good evening.	God kväll.
Thank you	Tack
(very much).	(så mycket).
You're welcome.	För all del.
Yes.	Ja.
No.	Nej.
Maybe.	Kanske.
Excuse me.	Ursäkta.
I'm sorry.	Förlåt mig.
(forgive me)	
How are you?	Hur mår du?
I'm fine, thanks.	Jag mår bra, tack.

Essentials

Please write it down.	Var va, skriv ner det.
Please show me (on the map).	Var vänlig, visa mig (på kartan).
I understand.	Jag förstår.
I don't understand.	Jag förstår inte.

Does anyone speak English?	*Talar någon engelska?*
Where are you from?	*Varifrån är du?*
I'm from ...	*Jag är från ...*
How old are you?	*Hur gammal är du?*
I'm ... years old.	*Jag är ... år gammal.*
Help!	*Hjälp!*
Go away!	*Gå härifrån!*

Small Talk

What's your name?	*Vad heter du?*
My name is ...	*Jag heter ...*
I'm a tourist/ student.	*Jag är en turist/ student.*
Are you married?	*Är du gift?*
Do you like ...?	*Tycker du om ...?*
I like it very much.	*Jag tycker om det mycket.*
I don't like ...	*Jag tycker inte om ...*
May I?	*Får jag?*
How do you say ... (in Swedish)?	*Hur säger man ... (på svenska)?*

Getting Around

I want to walk to ...	*Jag vill gå till ...*
I want to drive to ...	*Jag vill åka till ...*
What time does ... leave/arrive?	*När avgår/anländer ...?*
Where does ... leave from?	*Varifran avgår ...?*
it	*den/det*
the bus/tram	*bussen/spårvagnen*
the train	*tåget*
the boat/ferry	*båten/färjan*
the airplane	*flygplanet*
How long does the trip take?	*Hur länge tar resan?*
Do I need to change?	*Måste jag byta?*
left-luggage locker	*förvaringsboxar*
one-way (ticket)	*enkel (biljett)*
return (ticket)	*retur (biljett)*
platform	*plattform/perrong*
station	*station*
ticket office	*biljettbyrån*
timetable	*tidtabell*

Signs

Ingång	Entrance
Utgång	Exit
Öppet	Open
Stängt	Closed
Förbjudet	Prohibited
WC	Toilets

I'd like to hire a ...	*Jag ville hyra en ...*
bicycle	*cykel*
car	*bil*
canoe	*kanot*
guide	*guide*

Directions

How do I get to ...?	*Hur kan jag åka till ..?*
Where is ...?	*Var är ...?*
Is it near/far?	*Är det nära/långt bort.*
What ... is this?	*Vilken ... är detta?*
street/road	*gata/väg*
street number	*gatunummer*
suburb	*stadsdel*
town	*stad*
(Go) straight ahead.	*(Gå) rakt fram.*
(Turn) left.	*(Vänd) till vänster.*
(Turn) right.	*(Vänd) till höger.*
at the traffic lights	*vid trafikljus*
at the next/second/ third corner	*vid nästa/andra/ tredje*
here/there	*här/där*
up/down	*upp/ned*
behind/opposite	*bakom/mitt emot*
north	*norr*
south	*syd*
east	*öst*
west	*väst*
northern/southern	*norra/södra*

Accommodation

I'm looking for ...	*Jag letar efter ...*
the youth hostel	*vandrarhemmet*
the campground	*campingplatsen*
a hotel	*ett hotell*
a guesthouse	*ett resandehem/ gästhem*
the manager	*direktör*

What's the address? *Vad är adresset?*

Do you have a ... *Finns det ...?*
available?
  bed   *en säng*
  cheap room   *ett billigt rum*
  single room   *ett rum for en*
  double room   *ett rum for två*

for one night   *för en natt*
for two nights   *för två nätter*

How much is it ...? *Vad kostar det ...?*
  per night   *per natt*
  per person   *per person*

Does it include   *Ingår priset frukost/*
  breakfast/sheets? *lakan?*
Can I see the room? *Får jag se ett rum?*
It's very dirty/   *Det är mycket orent/*
  expensive.   *dyrt.*
Where is the toilet? *Var är toaletten?*
I'm/we're leaving *Jag är/vi är på väg nu.*
  now.

Do you have ...?   *Har ni ...?*
hot water   *varmt vatten*
a key   *nyckeln*
a shower   *dusch*
sauna   *bastu*

Around Town

Where is the ...? *Var finns ...?*
  town centre   *centrum*
  entrance/exit   *ingång/utgång*
  hospital   *sjukhuset*
  market   *torget*
  police   *polis*
  post office   *postbyrån*
  public toilet   *toaletten*
  restaurant   *restaurang*
  telephone office *Tele-byrån*

I want to make a *Jag ville använda*
  telephone call. *telefon.*

I'd like to change ... *Jag ville växla lite ...*
  some money   *pengar*
  travellers cheques *resande-sheckar*

Food

I'm hungry/thirsty. *Jag är hungrig/törstig*
breakfast   *frukost*
lunch   *lunch*
buffet   *smörgårsbord*
dinner   *middag*

café   *kaffestuga*
food stall   *grill* or *gatukök*
grocery store   *butik*
market   *torg*
restaurant   *restaurang*

I'd like some ... *Jag ville gärna ha*
               lite ...
I don't eat ... *Jag äter inte ...*

beef   *biff*
beer   *öl*
bread   *bröd*
bread roll   *sämla*
cabbage   *kål*
carrot   *morot*
cheese   *ost*
chicken   *kyckling*
coffee   *kaffe*
drinking water   *drycksvatten*
egg   *ägg*
fish   *fisk*
ham   *skinka*
herring   *sill*
meat   *kött*
milk   *mjölk*
minced meat   *köttfärsk*
mushroom   *svamp*
oats   *havre*
omelette   *omelett*
onion   *lök*
open sandwich   *smörgås*
pea   *ärt*
pepper   *peppar*
pie   *paj*
pork   *svinkött*
porridge   *gröt*
potato   *potatis*
reindeer (meat) *ren (kött)*
rice   *ris*
rye   *råg*
salad   *salad*
salmon   *lax*

salt	*salt*
sauce	*sås*
sausage	*korv*
soup	*soppa*
steak	*biff*
stew	*låda*
sugar	*socker*
tea	*te*
vegetable	*grönsak*
vegetarian	*vegetarisk*
water	*vatten*

Shopping

How much is it?	*Vad kostar det?*
I'd like to buy it.	*Jag ville gärna köpa den.*
It's too expensive for me.	*Den är för dyr för mig.*
Can I look at it?	*Får jag se den?*
I'm just looking.	*Jag bara tittar.*
big/bigger	*stor/större*
small/smaller	*liten/mindre*
more/less	*mer/färre*
cheap/cheaper	*hillig/billigare*

Time & Dates

When?	*När?*
today	*idag*
tonight	*på kvällen*
tomorrow	*i morgon*
day after tomorrow	*övermorgon*
yesterday	*igår*
all day/every day	*hela dagen/varje dag*
Monday	*måndag*
Tuesday	*tisdag*
Wednesday	*onsdag*
Thursday	*torsdag*
Friday	*fridag*
Saturday	*lördag*
Sunday	*söndag*

What time is it?	*Vad är klockan?*
It's ... o'clock.	*Klockan är ...*
in the morning	*morgon bitti*
this morning	*i morse*
in the evening	*på kvällen*
1.15	*kvart över ett*
1.30	*halv två*
1.45	*kvart i två*

Numbers

1/2	*halv*
1	*ett* or *en*
2	*två*
3	*tre*
4	*fyra*
5	*fem*
6	*sex*
7	*sju*
8	*åtta*
9	*nio*
10	*tio*
11	*elva*
12	*tolv*
13	*tretton*
14	*fjorton*
15	*femton*
16	*sexton*
17	*sjutton*
18	*aderton*
19	*nitton*
20	*tjugo*
21	*tjugoen*
30	*trettio*
40	*fyrtio*
50	*femtio*
100	*hundra*
1000	*tusen*
one million	*miljon*

Glossary

You may encounter some of the following terms and abbreviations during your travels in Finland. See also the Language chapter and the Food section in the Facts for the Visitor chapter.

aapa – open bog
Ahvenanmaa – Åland
aitta – small wooden storage shed in a traditional farmhouse, used for accommodating guests
ala- – lower, in place names, as opposed to yli-, or upper
ämpäri – bucket
apteeki – pharmacy
asema – station

baari – simple restaurant serving light lager and some snacks (also called *kapakka)*
bruk – early ironworks precinct (Swedish)

erämaa – wilderness (also called *kaira* or *korpi*)
etelä – south

feresi – traditional Karelian dress for women, formerly worn daily but now worn only on festival days

grilli – stand or kiosk selling cheap hamburgers, grilled sausages and other greasy, good snacks

halla – typically a night frost in early summer that often destroys crops or berries
hämärä – twilight
hankikanto – springtime snow-cover solid enough to walk on
harju – ridge or esker, formed during the Ice Age
havupuu – evergreen tree
heinä – hay
hiidenkirnu – literally 'devil's churn'; a round-shaped well formed by water and small rocks and the dramatic force of moving ice during the late years of the Ice Age
hilla – highly appreciated orange Arctic cloudberry, which grows on marshlands (also *lakka* or *suomuurain*)
honka – pine

ilmavoimat – Air Force
itä(inen) – east

jää – ice
jääkausi – Ice Age; prehistoric period, some 10,000 years ago, when all of Finland was covered by a thick ice layer
jäätie – ice road; a road across a lake in winter
jäkälä – lichen
järvi – lake
joiku – sung lyric poem, *yoik* among Samis
jokamiehenoikeus – right of public access
joki – river
joulu – Christmas
joulupukki – Santa Claus
juhannus – see *Midsummer*
juoksuhauta – wartime trench

kaamos – twilight time, the period of darkness over the Arctic Circle when the sun doesn't rise at all
kahvila – café
kahvio – cafeteria, usually simpler than a *kahvila*
kaira – see *erämaa*
kala – fish
Kalevala – the national epic of Finland; *Kalevala* combines poetry, runes and folk tales with biblical themes, such as creation and the fight between good and evil
kalmisto – old graveyard, especially pre-Medieval or Orthodox
kämppä – wilderness hut, cabin
kansallispuisto – national park
kantele – traditional Karelian string instrument, similar to a harp (also *kannel*)
kapakka – see baari
katu – street

378

kauppa – shop
kauppahalli – indoor market
kauppatori – market square
kaupunki – town or city
kaura – oats
kelirikko – season of bad roads after the snow has melted
kelo – dead, standing, barkless tree, usually pine
kioski – small stand that sells sweets, newspapers and food items
kirjakauppa – bookshop
kirkonkylä – any village that has a church
kisat – games
kokko – bonfire, lit during Midsummer festivals
köngäs – rapids, waterfall
korpi – see *erämaa*
korsu – log bunker used as accommodation by soldiers during WWII
koski – rapids
kota – traditional Lappish hut, resembling a tepee or wigwam (from the Finnish *koti*)
kotimaa – 'home country'
koulu – school
kruunu – crown, krone (Scandinavian currency)
kuksa – Lappish cup, carved from the burl of a birch tree
kunta – commune or municipality, the smallest administrative unit in Finland
kuntopolku – 'fitness path'; jogging track in summer, skiing track in winter
kuusi – spruce
kylä – village

laakso – valley
lääni – province
laavu – permanent or temporary open-air shelter used by trekkers
lahti – bay
laituri – pier
lakka – cloudberry
lama – recession
lampi – pond, small lake
länsi – west
lappalainen – a Sami person
Lappi – Lapland
lappilainen – Laplander, either Finn or Sami

lehtipuu – deciduous tree
lestadiolaisuus – a strict Lutheran sect in north Finland
liiteri – shelter for firewood
linja-autoasema – bus station
lintu – bird
lohi – salmon
lossi – a small ferry for travel across a strait
luontopolku – nature trail
luppokota – see *kota*

maa – country, earth, land
maakunta – a traditional region, with tribal or cultural rather than administrative ties as opposed to a *lääni*
mäki – hill
mänty – pine tree, the most common of Finnish trees
majoitus – accommodation
makuupussi – sleeping bag
marja – berry
markka – Finnish unit of currency (plural *markkaa*, abbreviation *mk*)
Matkahuolto – bus station (name of the national bus line of Finland)
matkakoti – guesthouse, inn (also called *matkustajakoti*)
metsä – forest
Midsummer – (or *juhannus*) the longest day of the year, celebrated at the end of June on Friday evening and Saturday
mökki – cottage
mono – skiing shoe (plural *monot*)
muikku – vendace, a typical lake fish
mummonmökki – literally, 'grandma's cottage'
museo – museum
mustikka – blueberry

nähtävyys – tourist attraction
niemi – cape
nuoska – wet snow
nuotio – campfire

ohra – barley
öljy – oil
opas – guide (person) or guidebook
opastuskeskus – information centre, usually of a national park
opiskelija – student

Oy – abbreviation for Osakeyhtiö, often seen after company names (the equivalent of Limited in English); in Swedish it's Ab, short for Aktiebolag

pää – head, end
paja – workshop
pakkanen – below-freezing weather
pelto – cultivated field
petäjä – pine
peura – deer
pihlaja – rowan (tree)
pikkujoulu – 'Little Christmas', an informal party arranged by companies or schools
pirtti – small room in a traditional Finnish farmhouse
pitäjä – see *kunta*
pitkospuu – boardwalk constructed over wetlands or swamps
pitopöytä – large buffet table
pohjoinen – north
polku – path
polttopuu – firewood
poro – reindeer
poroerotus – reindeer roundup, held annually in designated places around Lapland
poronhoitoalue – reindeer herding area
poronkusema – Lappish (slightly vulgar) unit of distance: how far a reindeer walks before relieving itself
Praasniekka – also *Prazniek*; Orthodox religious festival that sometimes includes a *ristisaatto* to a lake, where a sermon takes place
pubi – pub serving strong alcohol and very little food
puisto – park
pulkka – boat sledge
puro – stream
puu – tree, wood
puukko – sheath knife

rakovalkea – log fire
ranta – shore
räntä – wet snow (snowing)
rauhoitettu – protected
ravintola – restaurant which also serves as a bar
reppu – backpack
retkeilymaja – hostel

retki – excursion
revontulet – Northern lights, literally 'fires of the fox'
riista – game
rinkka – rucksack
ristinsaatto – an annual Orthodox festival to commemorate a regional saint, involving a procession of the cross
roskakori – rubbish bin
rotko – gorge
routa – ground frost, causes *kelirikko*
ruis – rye
runo – poem
Ruotsi – Sweden
rupla – rouble (Russian)
ruska – period in autumn (fall) when leaves turn red and yellow
ruukki – early ironworks precinct (see also *bruk*)

sää – weather (also *säätila*)
saari – island
sääski – mosquito (in Lapland)
sähkö – electricity
Saksa – Germany
salmi – strait
salo – backwoods, wilderness
sauva – skiing stocks
savotta – logging site
savusauna – traditional Finnish smoke sauna with no chimney, just a small outlet for smoke
seita – holy idol or shrine in Lapland
selkä – lake
sieni – mushroom
sora – gravel
sota – war
sotilasalue – military area
SRM – Suomen Retkeilymajajärjesto, or Youth Hostel Association of Finland
suo – swamp, bog, marsh
suomalainen – Finnish, Finn
Suomi – Finland
suomu – gill

taajama – modern village centre, or any densely populated area
taisteluhauta – trench
taival – track, trail
takka – fireplace (inside a house)

talo – house or building
tanssilava – dance floor or stage
Tapaninpäivä – Boxing Day
teltta – tent
tervas – old pine tree stump with a high tar content and a distinctive smell; it burns well, so Finnish trekkers use it to light fires, even in wet weather (also *tervaskanto*)
tie – road
tori – market square
tsasouna – small prayer hall used by the Orthodox faith all over Finland (also *tšasouna*)
tukki – log
tulva – flood
tunturi – fell, a hill in Lapland
tuohi – birch bark
tupa – the largest room of the main building in a traditional farm
turve – peat

uimahalli – indoor pool
uistin – lure (in fishing)

uitto – log floating

vaara – danger, or wooded hill (typical in North Karelia)
vaellus – trek (verb *vaeltaa*)
vaivaisukko – a pauper statue outside many of the old wooden churches used as a receptacle for church donations
valaistu latu – illuminated skiing track
valtio – state, or government
vandrarhem – hostel (Swedish)
vehnä – wheat
Venäjä – Russia
vero – tax
vesi – water, sometimes lake
vilja – grain
virasto – state or local government office building
vuori – mountain
vyöhyke – zone

yliopisto – university
yö – night

Appendix – Alternative Place Names

The following municipalities may bear Finnish and/or Swedish names on maps and street signs:

Finnish	Swedish
Ahvenanmaa	Åland
Espoo	Esbo
Häme	Tavastland
Hämeenlinna	Tavastehus
Hamina	Fredrikshamn
Hanko	Hangö
Helsinki	Helsingfors
Hiittinen	Hitis
Houtskari	Houtskär
Inkoo	Ingå
Järvenpää	Träskända
Jepua	Jeppo
Karjaa	Karis
Kaskinen	Kaskö
Kauniainen	Grankulla
Kemiö	Kimito
Kirkkonummi	Kyrkslätt
Kokkola	Karleby
Korppoo	Korpo
Kristiinan-kaupunki	Kristinestad
Kruunupyy	Kronoby
Kustavi	Gustavs
Lapinjärvi	Lappträsk
Lappeenranta	Villmanstrand
Lapväärtti	Lappfjärd
Linnamäki	Borgbacken
Lohja	Lojo
Loviisa	Lovisa
Luoto	Larsmo
Maalahti	Malax
Maarianhamina	Mariehamn
Maksamaa	Maxmo
Mustasaari	Korsholm
Mustio	Svartå
Myrskylä	Mörskom
Naantali	Nådendal
Närpiö	Närpes
Nauvo	Nagu
Oravainen	Oravais
Pännäinen	Bennäs
Parainen	Pargas
Pernaja	Pernå
Pietarsaari	Jakobstad
Pinjainen	Billnäs
Pohja	Pojo
Pohjanmaa	Österbotten
Pori	Björneborg
Porvoo	Borgå
Pyhtää	Pyttis
Raasepori	Raseborg
Raippaluoto	Replot
Rauma	Raumo
Ruotsinpyhtää	Strömfors
Särkisalo	Finby
Siipyy	Sideby
Sipoo	Sibbo
Siuntio	Sjundeå
Sulva	Solf
Taalintehdas	Dalsbruk
Tammisaari	Ekenäs
Tampere	Tammerfors
Tenhola	Tenala
Tiukka	Tjöck
Turku	Åbo
Uusikarlepyy	Nykarleby
Uusikaupunki	Nystad
Uusimaa	Nyland
Vaasa	Vasa
Vantaa	Vanda
Vöyri	Vörå

The following islands and municipalities in Åland have no Finnish name:

Brändö, Eckerö, Finström, Föglö, Geta, Hammarland, Jomala, Kumlinge, Kökar, Lemland, Lumparland, Saltvik, Sottunga, Sund, Vardo

The following towns/islands in south-west Finland have no Finnish name:

Västanfjärd, Dragsfjärd, Liljendal, Korsnäs, Iniö

Acknowledgments

THANKS

Many thanks to the travellers who used the last edition and wrote to us with helpful hints, useful advice and interesting anecdotes:

Lynn Ackeroyd, Kelyn Bacon, Michael Baker, Patricia Bayens, Marcus Bednarek, Keith Blackshear, Mario Fernandez Cano, Penelope Curtis, Martijn Dalhuijsen, Kathleen O Dana, Shannon DeVaney, Chris Featherman, Jaakko Halmet, Kauko Hamalainen, Erik Heegaard, Guy Edward Helander, H G Holm, Ondrej Hradil, Miiinas Hujala, Ahmet Incesu, Kristine Johnson, Juha, Kenneth Kidd, Christine Kwong, Aino Laakso, Giavi Lara, Luis Manendez-Arias, Kathy & Michael McClean, James J McEldowney, Bill McKenney, Angel Montoro Martos, Alexander Morris, Suzanne Nuttal, Steve Page, Brian Payne, Sheridan Pettiford, Chris Phillips, Anthea Pitt, Minna Puustinen, R Ruitenberg, Virve Sammalkorpi, Steven Smith, C R Stephenson, Peter J Storey, Samantha Telleri, Zoltan Torok, Witold & Lore Tulasiewicz, E & H Verbeek-Graind'orge, Varpu Weyner, Jean Willyams, Matilda Wrede

LONELY PLANET

Phrasebooks

Lonely Planet phrasebooks are packed with essential words and phrases to help travellers communicate with the locals. With colour tabs for quick reference, an extensive vocabulary and use of script, these handy pocket-sized language guides cover day-to-day travel situations.

- handy pocket-sized books
- easy to understand Pronunciation chapter
- clear & comprehensive Grammar chapter
- romanisation alongside script to allow ease of pronunciation
- script throughout so users can point to phrases for every situation
- full of cultural information and tips for the traveller

'...vital for a real DIY spirit and attitude in language learning'
— *Backpacker*

'the phrasebooks have good cultural backgrounders and offer solid advice for challenging situations in remote locations'
— *San Francisco Examiner*

Arabic (Egyptian) • Arabic (Moroccan) • Australian *(Australian English, Aboriginal and Torres Strait languages)* • Baltic States *(Estonian, Latvian, Lithuanian)* • Bengali • Brazilian • Burmese • Cantonese • Central Asia • Central Europe *(Czech, French, German, Hungarian, Italian, Slovak)* • Eastern Europe *(Bulgarian, Czech, Hungarian, Polish, Romanian, Slovak)* • Ethiopian (Amharic) • Fijian • French • German • Greek • Hill Tribes • Hindi/Urdu • Indonesian • Italian • Japanese • Korean • Lao • Latin American Spanish • Malay • Mandarin • Mediterranean Europe *(Albanian, Croatian, Greek, Italian, Macedonian, Maltese, Serbian, Slovene)* • Mongolian • Nepali • Papua New Guinea • Pilipino (Tagalog) • Quechua • Russian • Scandinavian Europe *(Danish, Finnish, Icelandic, Norwegian, Swedish)* • South-East Asia *(Burmese, Indonesian, Khmer, Lao, Malay, Tagalog Pilipino, Thai, Vietnamese)* • Spanish (Castilian) *(also includes Catalan, Galician and Basque)* • Sri Lanka • Swahili • Thai • Tibetan • Turkish • Ukrainian • USA *(US English, Vernacular, Native American languages, Hawaiian)* • Vietnamese • Western Europe *(Basque, Catalan, Dutch, French, German, Greek, Irish)*

Lonely Planet Journeys

JOURNEYS is a unique collection of travel writing – published by the company that understands travel better than anyone else. It is a series for anyone who has ever experienced – or dreamed of – the magical moment when they encountered a strange culture or saw a place for the first time. They are tales to read while you're planning a trip, while you're on the road or while you're in an armchair in front of a fire.

These outstanding titles explore our planet through the eyes of a diverse group of international writers. JOURNEYS books catch the spirit of a place, illuminate a culture, recount a crazy adventure or introduce a fascinating way of life. They always entertain, and always enrich the experience of travel.

MALI BLUES
Traveling to an African Beat
Lieve Joris (translated by Sam Garrett)

Drought, rebel uprisings, ethnic conflict: these are the predominant images of West Africa. But as Lieve Joris travels in Senegal, Mauritania and Mali, she meets survivors, fascinating individuals charting new ways of living between tradition and modernity. With her remarkable gift for drawing out people's stories, Joris brilliantly captures the rhythms of a world that refuses to give in.

THE GATES OF DAMASCUS
Lieve Joris (translated by Sam Garrett)

This best-selling book is a beautifully drawn portrait of day-to-day life in modern Syria. Through her intimate contact with local people, Lieve Joris draws us into the fascinating world that lies behind the gates of Damascus. Hala's husband is a political prisoner, jailed for his opposition to the Assad regime; through the author's friendship with Hala we see how Syrian politics impacts on the lives of ordinary people.

THE OLIVE GROVE
Travels in Greece
Katherine Kizilos

Katherine Kizilos travels to fabled islands, troubled border zones and her family's village deep in the mountains. She vividly evokes breathtaking landscapes, generous people and passionate politics, capturing the complexities of a country she loves.

'beautifully captures the real tensions of Greece' – *Sunday Times*

KINGDOM OF THE FILM STARS
Journey into Jordan
Annie Caulfield

Kingdom of the Film Stars is a travel book and a love story. With honesty and humour, Annie Caulfield writes of travelling in Jordan and falling in love with a Bedouin with film-star looks.

She offers fascinating insights into the country – from the tent life of traditional women to the hustle of downtown Amman – and unpicks tight-woven western myths about the Arab world.

LONELY PLANET

Lonely Planet Travel Atlases

Lonely Planet has long been famous for the number and quality of its guidebook maps. Now we've gone one step further and produced a handy companion series: Lonely Planet travel atlases – maps of a country produced in book form.

Unlike other maps, which look good but lead travellers astray, our travel atlases have been researched on the road by Lonely Planet's experienced team of writers. All details are carefully checked to ensure the atlas corresponds with the equivalent Lonely Planet guidebook.

- full-colour throughout
- maps researched and checked by Lonely Planet authors
- place names correspond with Lonely Planet guidebooks
- no confusing spelling differences
- legend and travelling information in English, French, German, Japanese and Spanish
- size: 230 x 160 mm

Available now: Chile & Easter Island • Egypt • India & Bangladesh • Israel & the Palestinian Territories • Jordan, Syria & Lebanon • Kenya • Laos • Portugal • South Africa, Lesotho & Swaziland • Thailand • Turkey • Vietnam • Zimbabwe, Botswana & Namibia

Lonely Planet TV Series & Videos

Lonely Planet travel guides have been brought to life on television screens around the world. Like our guides, the programs are based on the joy of independent travel, and look honestly at some of the most exciting, picturesque and frustrating places in the world. Each show is presented by one of three travellers from Australia, England or the USA and combines an innovative mixture of video, Super-8 film, atmospheric soundscapes and original music.

Videos of each episode – containing additional footage not shown on television – are available from good book and video shops, but the availability of individual videos varies with regional screening schedules.

Video destinations include: Alaska • American Rockies • Australia – The South-East • Baja California & the Copper Canyon • Brazil • Central Asia • Chile & Easter Island • Corsica, Sicily & Sardinia – The Mediterranean Islands • East Africa (Tanzania & Zanzibar) • Ecuador & the Galapagos Islands • Greenland & Iceland • Indonesia • Israel & the Sinai Desert • Jamaica • Japan • La Ruta Maya • Morocco • New York • North India • Pacific Islands (Fiji, Solomon Islands & Vanuatu) • South India • South West China • Turkey • Vietnam • West Africa • Zimbabwe, Botswana & Namibia

The Lonely Planet TV series is produced by: Pilot Productions
The Old Studio
18 Middle Row
London W10 5AT, UK

Lonely Planet On-line
www.lonelyplanet.com *or* **AOL keyword: lp**

Whether you've just begun planning your next trip, or you're chasing down specific info on currency regulations or visa requirements, check out Lonely Planet On-line for up-to-the minute travel information.

As well as mini guides to more than 250 destinations, you'll find maps, photos, travel news, health and visa updates, travel advisories, and discussion of the ecological and political issues you need to be aware of as you travel. You'll also find timely upgrades to popular guidebooks which you can print out and stick in the back of your book.

There's also an on-line travellers' forum where you can share your experience of life on the road, meet travel companions and ask other travellers for their recommendations and advice.

And of course we have a complete and up-to-date list of all Lonely Planet travel products including travel guides, diving and snorkeling guides, phrasebooks, atlases, travel literature and videos, and a simple on-line ordering facility if you can't find the book you want elsewhere.

Lonely Planet Diving & Snorkeling Guides

Known for indispensible guidebooks to destinations all over the world, Lonely Planet's Pisces Books are the most popular series of diving and snorkeling titles available.

There are three series: **Diving & Snorkeling Guides**, **Shipwreck Diving** series and **Dive Into History**. Full colour throughout, the **Diving & Snorkeling Guides** combine quality photographs with detailed descriptions of the best dive sites for each location, giving divers a glimpse of what they can expect both on land and in water. The **Dive Into History** series is perfect for the adventure diver or armchair traveller. The **Shipwreck Diving** series provides all the details for exploring the most interesting wrecks in the Atlantic and Pacific oceans. The list also includes underwater nature and technical guides.

LONELY PLANET

Guides by Region

Lonely Planet is known worldwide for publishing practical, reliable and no-nonsense travel information in our guides and on our Web site. The Lonely Planet list covers just about every accessible part of the world. Currently there are nine series: travel guides, shoestring guides, walking guides, city guides, phrasebooks, audio packs, travel atlases, diving and snorkeling guides and travel literature.

AFRICA Africa – the South • Africa on a shoestring • Arabic (Egyptian) phrasebook • Arabic (Moroccan) phrasebook • Cairo • Cape Town • Central Africa • East Africa • Egypt • Egypt travel atlas • Ethiopian (Amharic) phrasebook • The Gambia & Senegal • Kenya • Kenya travel atlas • Malawi, Mozambique & Zambia • Morocco • North Africa • South Africa, Lesotho & Swaziland • South Africa, Lesotho & Swaziland travel atlas • Swahili phrasebook • Trekking in East Africa • Tunisia • West Africa • Zimbabwe, Botswana & Namibia • Zimbabwe, Botswana & Namibia travel atlas
Travel Literature: The Rainbird: A Central African Journey • Songs to an African Sunset: A Zimbabwean Story • Mali Blues: Traveling to an African Beat

AUSTRALIA & THE PACIFIC Australia • Australian phrasebook • Bushwalking in Australia • Bushwalking in Papua New Guinea • Fiji • Fijian phrasebook • Islands of Australia's Great Barrier Reef • Melbourne • Micronesia • New Caledonia • New South Wales & the ACT • New Zealand • Northern Territory • Outback Australia • Papua New Guinea • Papua New Guinea (Pidgin) phrasebook • Queensland • Rarotonga & the Cook Islands • Samoa • Solomon Islands • South Australia • Sydney • Tahiti & French Polynesia • Tasmania • Tonga • Tramping in New Zealand • Vanuatu • Victoria • Western Australia
Travel Literature: Islands in the Clouds • Sean & David's Long Drive

CENTRAL AMERICA & THE CARIBBEAN Bahamas and Turks & Caicos • Bermuda • Central America on a shoestring • Costa Rica • Cuba • Eastern Caribbean • Guatemala, Belize & Yucatán: La Ruta Maya • Jamaica • Mexico • Mexico City • Panama
Travel Literature: Green Dreams: Travels in Central America

EUROPE Amsterdam • Andalucía • Austria • Baltic States phrasebook • Berlin • Britain • Central Europe • Central Europe phrasebook • Czech & Slovak Republics • Denmark • Dublin • Eastern Europe • Eastern Europe phrasebook • Edinburgh • Estonia, Latvia & Lithuania • Europe • Finland • France • French phrasebook • Germany • German phrasebook • Greece • Greek phrasebook • Hungary • Iceland, Greenland & the Faroe Islands • Ireland • Italian phrasebook • Italy • Lisbon • London • Mediterranean Europe • Mediterranean Europe phrasebook • Paris • Poland • Portugal • Portugal travel atlas • Prague • Romania & Moldova • Russia, Ukraine & Belarus • Russian phrasebook • Scandinavian & Baltic Europe • Scandinavian Europe phrasebook • Scotland • Slovenia • Spain • Spanish phrasebook • St Petersburg • Switzerland • Trekking in Spain • Ukrainian phrasebook • Vienna • Walking in Britain • Walking in Italy • Walking in Switzerland • Western Europe • Western Europe phrasebook
Travel Literature: The Olive Grove: Travels in Greece

INDIAN SUBCONTINENT Bangladesh • Bengali phrasebook • Bhutan • Delhi • Goa • Hindi/Urdu phrasebook • India • India & Bangladesh travel atlas • Indian Himalaya • Karakoram Highway • Nepal • Nepali phrasebook • Pakistan • Rajasthan • South India • Sri Lanka • Sri Lanka phrasebook • Trekking in the Indian Himalaya • Trekking in the Karakoram & Hindukush • Trekking in the Nepal Himalaya
Travel Literature: In Rajasthan • Shopping for Buddhas

FREE Lonely Planet Newsletters

We love hearing from you and think you'd like to hear from us.

Planet Talk

Our FREE quarterly printed newsletter is full of tips from travellers and anecdotes from Lonely Planet guidebook authors. Every issue is packed with up-to-date travel news and advice, and includes:

- a postcard from Lonely Planet co-founder Tony Wheeler
- a swag of mail from travellers
- a look at life on the road through the eyes of a Lonely Planet author
- topical health advice
- prizes for the best travel yarn
- news about forthcoming Lonely Planet events
- a complete list of Lonely Planet books and other titles

To join our mailing list, residents of the UK, Europe and Africa can email us at go@lonelyplanet.co.uk; residents of North and South America can email us at info@lonelyplanet.com; the rest of the world can email us at talk2us@lonelyplanet.com.au, or contact any Lonely Planet office.

Comet

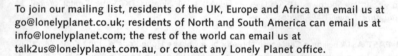

Our FREE monthly email newsletter brings you all the latest travel news, features, interviews, competitions, destination ideas, travellers' tips & tales, Q&As, raging debates and related links. Find out what's new on the Lonely Planet Web site and which books are about to hit the shelves.

Subscribe from your desktop: www.lonelyplanet.com/comet

Index

Text

Bold indicates maps.
Italics indicates boxed text.

Bold indicates maps.
Italics indicates boxed text.

Boxed Text

MAP LEGEND

BOUNDARIES

........................International
........................State
........................Disputed

HYDROGRAPHY

........................Coastline
........................River, Creek
........................Lake
........................Intermittent Lake
........................Salt Lake
........................Canal
........................Spring, Rapids
........................Waterfalls

ROUTES & TRANSPORT

........................Freeway
........................Highway
........................Major Road
........................Minor Road
........................Unsealed Road
........................City Highway
........................City Road
........................City Street, Lane

........................Pedestrian Mall
........................Tunnel
........................Train Route & Station
........................Metro & Station
........................Tramway
........................Cable Car or Chairlift
........................Walking Track
........................Ferry Route

AREA FEATURES

........................Building
........................Park, Gardens
........................Cemetery

........................Glacier
........................Pedestrian Mall
........................Urban Area

MAP SYMBOLS

✪ CAPITAL	National Capital	✈	Airport	←	One Way Street
◉ CAPITAL	State Capital		Ancient or City Wall	)(	Pass
● CITY	City	⁙	Archaeological Site	★	Police Station
● Town	Town	⊖	Bank	✉	Post Office
● Village	Village	🅿	Beach	⌂	Shelter
○	Point of Interest	⚇	Border Crossing	◈	Shopping Centre
		✕	Castle or Fort		Ski field
▪	Place to Stay	⌒	Cave	🏛	Stately Home
⚐	Camping Ground	✚	Church	▭	Swimming Pool
⊞	Caravan Park		Cliff or Escarpment	◙	Synagogue
⌂	Hut or Chalet	◐	Embassy	☎	Telephone
		⊕	Hospital	▣	Temple
▼	Place to Eat	❋	Lookout	❶	Tourist Information
⛾	Pub or Bar	▲	Mountain or Hill	◒	Transport
		🏛	Museum	🐾	Zoo

Note: not all symbols displayed above appear in this book

LONELY PLANET OFFICES

Australia
PO Box 617, Hawthorn 3122, Victoria
tel: (03) 9819 1877 fax: (03) 9819 6459
e-mail: talk2us@lonelyplanet.com.au

USA
150 Linden St, Oakland, CA 94607
tel: (510) 893 8555 TOLL FREE: 800 275-8555
fax: (510) 893 8572
e-mail: info@lonelyplanet.com

UK
10a Spring Place, London, NW5 3BH
tel: (0171) 428 4800 fax: (0170) 428 4828
e-mail: go@lonelyplanet.co.uk

France
1 rue du Dahomey, 75011 Paris
tel: 01 55 25 33 00 fax: 01 55 25 33 01
e-mail: bip@lonelyplanet.fr

World Wide Web: www.lonelyplanet.com *or* AOL keyword: lp
Lonely Planet Images: lpi@lonelyplanet.com.au

Lonely Planet's eKno

cheap calls, easy messaging and email

When you're out of sight, not out of mind.

you need eKno

If you're on the move and your family wants to reach you with an important message . . . Or you're crossing a border and want to make a booking for a hotel in the next town . . . Or you want to arrange a rendezvous with someone you met biking in Vietnam . . . Or you want to leave a message for a friend living in London . . .

so get eKno

eKno is a global communications service for travellers. eKno gives you cheap long distance calls plus eKno voice and email message services. eKno lets your friends and relatives leave you easily retrieved eKno messages – no matter where you are – and gives you an easy way to keep in eKno contact with other travellers. eKno is easy to use and doesn't cost the earth.

You tap into eKno with your private number. This number, plus a PIN, gives you access to your eKno message bank and a world of cheap international eKno calls.

www.ekno.lonelyplanet.com

COMMUNICATION CARD

www.ekno.lonelyplanet.com

COMMUNICATION CARD

www.ekno.lonelyplanet.com

COMMUNICATION CARD

www.ekno.lonelyplanet.com

Lonely Planet's eKno

Join Now
Tear out an eKno card, contact us online, or with a toll free call – and you're eKoff.

Join Online
The easiest way to join is online at
www.ekno.lonelyplanet.com
for all the info on eKno.
It is the best place for the most up to date information and any current joining offers.

Join by phone
To join from:

Australia	1 800 674 100
US	1 800 707 0031
Canada	1 800 294 3676
UK	0800 376 1704
New Zealand	0800 11 44 84
Germany	0 800 000 7138
International	+1 213 927 0101

Once you've joined, to use eKno always dial the access number for the country you're in.

Access Numbers

Australia	1 800 11 44 78
US	1 800 706 1333
Canada	1 800 808 5773
UK	0 800 376 1705
New Zealand	0 800 11 44 78
Germany	0 800 000 7139
International	+1 213 927 0100

New countries are being added all the time. To join from another country and for further information, visit the eKno website at *www.ekno.lonelyplanet.com*.
If the country you are in is not listed here or on the website, you can dial the international numbers listed above to join or access the service.

Toll free calls are provided where possible.

Details correct as at 5 May 1999

Where Did eKno Come From?

eKno – it's Lonely Planet for one number. *Ek* means one from Karachi to Kathmandu, from Delhi to Dhaka, and *no* is short for number.

We travel. Actually we travel quite a bit. And although we've used a heap of phonecards, we could never find one that really hit the spot. So we decided to make one. We joined with eKorp.com, an innovative communications company, to bring you a phonecard with the lot – budget calls from a stack of countries, voice messages you can pick up all over the world and even reply to, a way to keep in touch with other travellers and your own web mail address – and all from one number.
With eKno, you can ring home and home can ring you.

Now there are even more reasons to stay in touch.